INDIAN ECONOMY AND TRADE

INDIAN ECONOMY AND TRADE

P. Arunachalam

SERIALS PUBLICATIONS
NEW DELHI (INDIA)

First Published - 2011

ISBN: 978-81-8387-486-1

Published by

SERIALS PUBLICATIONS
4830/24, Prahlad Street, Ansari Road
Darya Ganj, New Delhi-110002 (India)
Phone : 23245225 Fax : 91-11-23272135
E-mail: serials@sify.com

Contents

Preface

The present volume a compendium of twenty subject oriented articles by research scholars and other subject experts. The articles have been widely acclaimed of research quality and worth research worthy. These articles have already presented in several seminars etc The authors of these articles are holding responsible position in teaching institution of national and international repute. The subject covered in these articles on economics and trade and their allied subjects. In addition to articles on economics and trade there are two-three articles which cover global problem of terrorism and its effects on nation's commerce and industry, imports, exports, indigenous production, employment, retrenchment and other monetary matters concerning the economy of the country.

F, Maria Albert, G. Paramasivan and J Sacratees have presented an interesting article on degradation of medicinal plants in India. Medicinal Plants play an important part in the traditional system of medicine in India like Ayurvedic, Unani system of medicine. More recently these have been widely used at international forum and western populace is also showing interest in these medicines plant and plant root based medicines. The article is most informative in the context of patent position of plants and trees used for Ayurvedic medicines at international patent authorities. Medicinal constitute an important natural wealth of the country. Medicinal plants, herbs, spices and herbal remedies are known to Ayurveda in India. According to WHO 80% of the world population rely upon such traditional plant based systems of medicine to provide them with the primary health care. Provides all information about medicinal plants in India. The article will create more awareness about the medicinal plants amongst all and enhance the use of medicine prepared by medicinal plants.

N Jamaluddin, Associated Professor in Commerce in URumu Dhanalakshi College Trichy, details the Economic Crisis and its effect on trade in European Countries Against its parts. But the global economic crisis had made clear that Europe remains less than the sum of its parts. The crisis has presented the European Union with its greatest Challenge, but even many committed Europeanist believe that the alliance is falling the domestic politics, disagree sharply about what to do combat the slump. They argue about whether the European Central Bank should worry more about the deep recession or future inflation. And they have rushed to protect jobs in their home markets at the expense of those in other member countries. The article brings forth the complicate problem in simple explanatory language. Assessment is made that Europe suffer more than EU Countries. Imports fell even more sharply than exports-by 56 per cent in April compared with April, 2008. Oil

Imports have been lower by 58 per cent. WTO has estimated a contraction in global trade by as much as 9 percent this year. Very interesting facts and figures have been quoted in the article.

Duraipandi Mavoothu in his article 'Implications of Right to Education Act 2009 on Future Technical Education.' The article critically examines the Act-2009 in the context of Technical education in the country. IT presents main features of Right to Education Act. It compares China's introduction of Compulsory Education Act in 1986 and shows that enrolment in primary schools and middle schools across China reached 98 percent. India's initiatives also are noteworthy like setting of Kendriya Vidyalaya (2500), Opening the door to Foreign Universities, Setting up a high power National Commission for Higher Education and Research (NCHER)m which will subsume all the national level higher education bodies like UGC, AICTE, MCI etc. Explains Technical Education and evaluates current status of Technical education in India. The article examines implications of Right to Education on challenges in future technical education. The author also presents some conclusive suggestions on the Right to Education Act, keeping in view the China's experience of Compulsory Education.

In yet another article Mr. N Jamaluddin, examines 'Global Crisis what needs to be done? Some Practical

Difficulties on worrisome decline in world Trade' deeply. Falling demand, constraints on finance in the US and Europe blamed for crisis in the Global Trade has been a principal casualty of the ongoing economic crisis. The World Trade Organization estimates trade to contract by 9 percent this year. Collapsing global demand severe curtailment of trade finance by banks and other leaders have been the main factors responsible. Together they have created constraints to export growth, especially in may development countries, obviously developed countries have been affected equally if not to a greater degree. The financial crisis that morphed into an economic crisis started in the US which still remains the epicenter of the crisis. Global Economic recovery is dependent to a large extent on how soon the US Economy stabilizes. The fall in demand and investment in the US and Europe is a principal reason for the major setback in world trade.

The article examine the very serious subject under heads like All Round Fall in Exports, Brazil the Government's timid response, Burma the crisis was already there, Cambodia the two sides of the grain of rice, Canada Opportunity lost, Chile an economy in recession, Cyprus women out of Jobs, El Salvador change course, Immediately, WTO Agenda, Looming Protectionism, implications of financial growth, threat for ecology, cites various international conventions on ecological status.

T Sridhar, Associate Professor, brings forth a very important topic Disinvestment in India: Recent developments. The article deals the topic with political angle and for point of view of economy.

PN Raghunathan, Professor cum Director Management Studies Jawahar Lal Institute of Technology, Coimbatore discusses burning topic of the day and a topic of interest to each and every one and a political topic of the day, 'Role of Black Money in Swiss Banks and its Impact on Indian Economy' India's black.

Money economy is ranked fifth highest at $ 22bn a year, coming in behind Russia, Medico Saudi Arabia and China. Personal account deposits in the bank, which have been misappropriated, are to the tune of $1500 billion in foreign reserve, an amount 13 times larger that the country's foreign debt. Black money possession and use is only concentrated in a thin slab of 3% of the Indian Public. The articles reveals many interesting facts and figures for the awareness of the public and rolls back its effect on t he Indian economy.

The articles deals with the basic roots of the black money like, its Nature, Constituent activities of Black Money, Sources of Black Money, Causes of Black Money, Role of Black Money in Swiss Bank, Black Money in India. Black Money in India accounts for 20% of GDP. Black Money generated every year must be around 400,000 crores, or $ 80 billion. It further discusses impact of black money, effects of black money on Indian Economy, black money and inflation, closes the article after fully explaining advantages and disadvantages.

GS Nalini in her article 'Anti-money Laundering-The New Mantra to Become an Economic Superpower country' is very comprehensive and informative article on the subject. Money Laundering refers to the conversion or Laundering of the money which is illegally obtained, so as to make it iappear to originate from a legitimate source. Money laundering is being employed by launderers worldwide to conceal criminal activity associated with it such as drug trafficking, terrorism and extortion. As per an estimate of the IMF the aggressive size of Money Laundering in the world could be somewhat between two to five percent of the world Gross Domestic Product (GDP). Money laundering is a serious, highly sophisticated and global criminal activity. The objective of the study is to know the process of conversion of black money into white money, causes of money laundering, also analysis the economic impact of money laundering in India, and enumerate various ways to combat money laundering. Starting with the Process of Money laundering, details causes of increase in money laundering, money laundering-the Indian Scenario, details the legal acts to combat the problems of money laundering. The study boldly confess that money laundering has harmful effect and threat to banking system in the whole world. It threatens national governments and international relations between them through corruption of officers and legal systems.

Money laundering serves as an important mode to terrorism financing. It also threatens the local merchants, economic stability. Also tarnishes country's reputation. The article further details the Role of Banks in Anti-money Laundering. It is a very informative article.

Terrorism-an Unwanted Weapon, is an article where terrorism, which is world wide evil find here a full definitions as per noted legal and political, and social personalities in the world. Covers types of terrorist activities, commonest terrorists attacks, Bombings, systematic genocide and spontaneous massacres, Random murders and Wounding, political purges, destruction or damage of structures and resources, hijacking, kidnapping or siege-and hostage situation, extortion and drug trafficking, disruption of information and communication networks, etc. It further discusses causes of terrorism in details, psychology of terrorism, Terrorist doctrines, foreign sponsorship. Concludes with certain suggestion to combat the terrorism.

The other important articles are : Economic Impact of Terrorism on Indian Economy, Self-Help Groups in the Upliftment of Tsunami Vic tims in Kanyakumari District (Tamil Nadu), Expenditure pattern of village Panchayat in Tamil Naud during Pre-Post Liberalization Period., Economic Development and Public Sector Banks, Affordable Housing Schemes—Business Models, Economic Impact of Terrorism in India, impact of Black Money in Swiss Bank Accounts of Indian Economy, A study of Corporate Hospitals in Hyderabad, impact of terrorism on Indian Economy, impacts of watershed development programs: experiences and evidences from Thoothukudi Tamil Nadu, prospects of retail pharma's in India.

All the above noted articles contains treatment for point of view of Indian Economy and various factors making effect and impact on Indian Economy and are full of latest information, facts and figures. Therefore Can easily by used by students and scholars alike for their respective studies. Since the variety and treatment of these articles is different in each and every article, hence new information for awareness and use.

Degradation of Medicinal Plants in India

F. Maria Albert, G. Paramasivan** & J. Sacratees****

INTRODUCTION

THE United Nations has declared 2010 as the Year of Biodiversity to encourage nations to conserve their plant and animal species. The Convention on Biological Diversity (CBD) was signed more than a decade ago, but species continue to disappear worldwide at a rapid rate. Local communities who have used medicinal plants for generations say that these species are becoming hard to find. They say climate change is a factor. A medicinal plant is any plant which, in one or more of its organs, contains substance that can be used for therapeutic purpose or which is a precursor for synthesis of useful drugs. The plants that possess therapeutic properties or exert beneficial pharmacological effects on the animal body are generally designated as 'Medicinal plants'. Although there are no apparent morphological characteristics in the medicinal plants growing with them. Yet they possess some special qualities that make them medicinally important. It has now been established that the plants which naturally synthesis and accumulate some secondary metabolites, like alkaloids, glycosides, tannins, volatiles oils and contain minerals and vitamins, possess medicinal properties.

Medicinal plants constitute an important natural wealth of a country. They play a significant role in providing primary health care services to rural people. They serve as therapeutic agents as well as important raw materials for the manufacture of traditional and modern medicine. Substantial amount of foreign exchange can be earned can by exporting medicinal plants to other countries. In this way indigenous medicinal plants play significant role of an economy of a country. Medicinal plants, herbs, spices and herbal remedies are known to Ayurveda in India since long times. The value of medicinal plants is being lost due to lack of awareness and deforestation. As a result many valuable

* Ph. D., Research Scholar, ** ICSSR Ph.D., Research Fellow, *** Assistant in Economics, Department of Economics, Manonmaniam Sundaranar University, Tirunelveli, -12, Tamilnadu, (*paramasivan_g66@yahoo.co.in*)

herbs are becoming rare and the information's of these precious resources are getting lost.

Human beings have been utilizing plants for basic preventive and curative health care since time immemorial. Recent estimates suggest that over 9,000 plants have known medicinal applications in various cultures and countries, and this is without having conducted comprehensive research amongst several indigenous and other communities (Farnsworth and Soejarto 1991). Medicinal plants are used at the household level by women taking care of their families, at the village level by medicine men or tribal shamans, and by the practitioners of classical traditional systems of medicine such as Ayurveda, Chinese medicine, or the Japanese Kampo system. According to the World Health Organization, over 80% of the world's population, or 4.3 billion people, rely upon such traditional plant-based systems of medicine to provide them with primary health care (Bannerman *et. al.* 1983).

Allopathic medicine too owes a tremendous debt to medicinal plants: one in four prescriptions filled in a country like the United States are either a synthesized form of or derived from plant materials (Srivastava, *et. al.* 1995). Even from the earliest trade data available, it is clear that the global market for medicinal plants has always been very large. According to the International Trade Centre, as far back as 1967, the total value of imports of starting materials of plant origin for the pharmaceutical and cosmetics industry was of the order of USD 52.9 million. From this amount, the total values grew to USD 71.2 million in 1971, and then showed a steady annual growth rate of approximately 5-7% through to the mid-1980s (Atisso 1983). To give an example of the extent of trade volumes even at that time, according to one report commissioned by the World Wide Fund for Nature, the total import in 1980 of "vegetable materials used in pharmacy" by the European Economic Community was 80,738 tons (Lewington 1992). India was the largest supplier by far, with 10,055 tons of plants and 14 tons of vegetable alkaloids and their derivatives.

However, it is only during the last decade that the real significance of the medicinal plants sector has begun to be realized. Interest in natural materials by the dominant economic powers had waned from the late 1960s to the early 1980s as new possibilities in biotechnology and the synthesization of drugs beckoned. But by the mid-1980s, there was a renewed interest in natural materials and approaches to health care, coupled with recognition that technology alone could not solve the pressing health care needs of the world's population (Tempesta and King 1994). This new drive for natural and plant-based medicines made itself felt in the market from the mid-1980s onwards. As Table 1 illustrates, growth in the market in various regions is now on average 3 to 4 times the average growth rates of the national economies in the same regions. Some of these phenomenal rates, in some cases nearly 20%, imply that the market is now doubling in size every 4-5 years.

The participation of various companies in the market also attests to its new strength and importance. By 1990, some 223 major companies worldwide (of which about half were in the United States) were reportedly screening plants for new leads; the figure had been zero in 1980 (Aryal 1993). Also in 1990, more than 2000 companies in Europe alone were marketing herbal medicinals, with 30% having a turnover in excess of $20 million- expenditure in the United States on "unconventional, alternative, or unorthodox" therapies reached $13.7 billion dollars during the same year (Tewari 1996).

Table 1
Natural Medicines Market: Regional Growth Rates 1991-98 (in %)

Region	*1991-92*	*1993-98*
EU	5	8
Rest of Europe	8	12
SE Asia	12	12
Japan	15	15
South Asia	15	15

MEDICINAL PLANTS AND INDIA

India's natural forests are home to about 8,000 medicinal plants that form the primary source of healthcare for 60-80% of the population, particularly the rural poor. In 2005 the UNDP and the Government of India implemented a programme across nine states to integrate conservation strategies for medicinal plants and traditional knowledge into existing policies and programmes. A Rapid Threat Assessment of 316 plants was prepared and species were divided into groups according to the degrees of threat as per the World Conservation Union criteria. This was achieved through a Conservation Assessment and Management Prioritisation Workshop organized in the respective states. In addition, a network of Medicinal Plants Conservation Areas was taken up in Madhya Pradesh, West Bengal, Orissa and Rajasthan as a means of in-situ conservation programme. Some state-level seed centres have also been established to supply genetically viable seeds and planting material for various stakeholder groups. Gender participation and inter-ministerial convergence and coordination were significant highlights of the project.

Medicinal plants which constitute a segment of the flora provide raw material for use in all the indigenous systems of medicine in India namely Ayurveda, Unani, Siddha and Tibetan Medicine. According to the World Health Organization (WHO), 80% of the population in developing countries relies on traditional medicine, mostly in the form of plant drugs for their health care needs. Additionally, modern medicines contain plant derivatives to the extent of about 25%. On account of the fact that the derivatives of medicinal plants are non-narcotic having no side effects, the demand for these plants is on the increase in both developing and developed countries. There are estimated to be around 25000 effective plant based formulations available in Indian medicine. Over 1.5m practitioners of the Indian system of medicine in the oral and codified streams use medicinal plants in preventive, promotional and curative applications. It is estimated that there are over 7800 medicinal drug manufacturing units in India, which consume about 2000 tonnes of herbs annually (Singh 2001). According to Exim Bank, the international market for medicinal plant related trade is to the tune of US$ 60 billion having a growth rate of 7% per annum. The annual export of medicinal plants from India is valued at Rs. 1200 million.

India is one of the richest reservoirs of biological diversity in the world. It is home to a great variety of ethno-medicinally important plant species, and is ranked 6th (sixth) among 12 mega diversity countries of the world. However, several factors are putting India's medicinal plants at risk of extinction: the increasing demand for herbal raw-material & products, the reliance of pharmaceutical companies on plants for drugs, the encroachment of civilization into plant habitat (including timber and mining operations, shopping malls and housing developments), and the innate sensitivity or rareness of certain species. The total number of flowering plant species although only 17,000, the intraspecific variability found in them make it one of the highest in the world. Out of 17,000 plants, the classic systems of medicines like Ayurveda, Siddha and Unani make use of only about 2000 plants in various formulations.

However, a survey conducted by the All India Coordinated Research Project on Ethnobiology (AICRPE) during the last decade recorded over 8000 species of wild plants used by the tribals and other traditional communities in India for treating various health problems. 30% of medicinal preparations are derived from roots, 14% bark, 16% whole plants, 5% flowers, 10% fruits, 6% leaves, 7% seeds, 3% wood, 4% rhizomes 6% stems and only less than 20% of the species used are cultivated. The forests have been the source of invaluable medicinal plants since the time man realized the preventive and curative properties of plants and started using them for human heath care. But today forest degradation processes adversely affect the resource base of medicinal plants. The problems are compounded by market-demand driven harvesting without any concern for representation and conservation. In the process essential regenerative components of a plant like roots, tubers, fruits, seeds, flowers and bark are indiscriminately collected, leading to degradation and depletion and even extinction of particular species. Due to this ruthless exploitation, many important medicinal plants species are becoming rare and some of them are critically endangered.

The global context briefly sketched above suggests several tremendous opportunities for India, a country unrivaled in terms of diversity of medical systems and practices, in addition to being a major storehouse of biological diversity, with 2 of the 14 megabiodiversity areas of the world located within its borders. The global market would appear to be more receptive than ever to the mounting of a concentrated Indian effort at supplying it with medical materials and know-how. Such an effort would also appear to be increasingly remunerative for the country. India is of course already an active participant in the global medicinal plants market having been for some time the world's largest supplier of raw materials (though an insignificant supplier of finished products) (Patnaik 1994). Of the 74 species accounted for in one of the studies mentioned above, India was known to be exporting 22 and importing 8 (Handa 1992), while the German study quoted earlier, which is now underway, has found India to be Germany's largest trading partner by far (Lange 1996). Moreover, medicinal plants are one of the most important components of the non-wood forest products sector which supplies over 80% of India's net forest annual export earnings (FAO 1995, Jain 1996).

Despite these promising indications, however, it is unclear whether India is truly exploiting her comparative advantage in the medicinal plants sector and tapping the full potential of an expanding consumer base. In addition, several concerns arise in relation to the current consequences of participation in the market, with regard to the sustainability and equitability of prevailing practices in the sector.

Table 2
Important Medicinal Plants in Demand

Aonla	*Chandan*	*Kalmegh*	*Satavari*
Aswahagandha	Chirata	Katki	Shankapushpi
Ashoka	Giloe	Kokum	Safed Musli
Atis	Guggal	Kerth	Senna
Baiberang	Indian Barbery	Liqorice	
Bael	Isabgol	Long Pepper	
Brahmi	Jatamansi	Madhunashini	

Source: National Medicinal Plants Board, New Delhi.

An institutional mechanism needs to be put in place to systematically assess and enlist the decline and loss of medicinal plant species and to monitor and assess threat to wild populations of prioritised species. 'Promote the protection of ecosystems, natural habitats and the maintenance of viable populations of species in natural surroundings.' The MoEF, however, has no long-term programme, strategy or dedicated funding for monitoring viable populations and undertaking assessment of medicinal plants. On a relatively small scale, some efforts have been undertaken by NGOs using IUCN Red List Categories and Criteria. According to such studies, 335 wild medicinal plants of India have been identified as being under various categories of threat of extinction ranging from Near Threatened, Vulnerable, Endangered to Critically Endangered. Eighty-four of these species of conservation concern have been recorded in high volume trade.

There is a need to put in place a long-term systematic threat assessment programme for important biota, including medicinal plants, which can be anchored in a network of institutions who are have the competence to study different groups of plants.

THREATS TO MEDICINAL PLANTS

The following sections discuss the threats and issues related to medicinal plants, but such threats exist in other parts of Northern Areas as well. Due to the following threats, about 30% of the total reported medicinal plants species are endangered, vulnerable or threatened. The number of threatened medicinal plants has risen to 33 out of which 5 are endangered, 18 are vulnerable and 10 are rare (Shinwari *et al.*, 2000).

Over-exploitation

Over harvesting is common for the more valuable plants such as kurth, Ephedra, Artimesia, sea buckthorn, and Berberis species. Increasing population and enhanced awareness about very few side effects of medicinal plants also encourage their over harvesting.

Lack of Proper Management

Due to uncontrolled collection of medicinal plants in the absence of proper management systems, the locals usually collect these plants prematurely using improper techniques like uprooting of plants, collection of wrong part of the plant etc. that result in poor quality of plant material.

Free Grazing & Agriculture

Free grazing of livestock is another threat to the viability of medicinal plant production in the region. Uncontrolled grazing is leading to degradation of pastures containing numerous medicinal herbs and shrubs. Also, expanding agriculture is also contributing to the elimination of many medicinal plants. Due to limited cultivable land there is rapid encroachment of forests and pastures. Conversion of this natural land cover to agricultural land and livestock grazing areas is leading to degradation of natural flora including medicinal plants.

Lack of Incentives

Poverty, limited cultivable land and lack of alternatives coupled with the need for longer term investment and difficult marketing discourage the locals from medicinal plant cultivation. Moreover, due to difficult access and absence of primary processing units the transportation cost of medicinal plants is high, leaving little profit margin for the growers (Rasool, 1998).

Loss of Knowledge

With the introduction of modern allopathic medicine the traditional local knowledge about medicinal plants is being lost rapidly in the main towns of the region while in the hamlets and villages it is usually confined to the aged people and herding segments of communities.

Lack of Awareness

Medicinal plants are gathered from the wild by collectors through the tribals, forest dwellers and other local people. The collected material is passed on to the traders in towns and cities. Each one of the major traders has one or more traditional drug manufacturers and private pharmacies as their customers for purchasing raw plant material. Generally, as the price paid to the gatherers is very low, the gatherers often mine the plants excessively to generate more income. Greed to earn more, coupled with the ignorance of the collector about plant biology and selective harvesting leads to the whole plant being destroyed.

Inefficiency of Handling

The collected materials are mostly dumped with the traders, who with their limited knowledge sort out the saleable ingredients in a crude manner, resulting in contamination with other materials leading to poor quality. Many of the medicinal plants are sensitive to climatic conditions, requiring proper drying and storage under specific temperature and humidity. This aspect is largely neglected by the collectors, growers and traders leading to deterioration and rejection of the produce particularly for the international market.

Transparency and Accountability

In the absence of any regulatory mechanism, the trade of medicinal plants is very secretive. Stakeholders like collectors, contractors, traders, wholesale dealers and companies involved in collection and processing of medicinal plants do not understand nor trust each other. Similarly in the absence of a proper management system, neither the collector nor the contractor who extract medicinal plant products from the wild will have any responsibility of replenishing the natural resources through re-planting. For this purpose, the role of local non-political voluntary organizations becomes significant and allows them to participate in collection and maintenance of natural resources.

Forest Fires

Forest fires are another cause of the destruction of trees, vegetation, thick layer of humus and animals. The two major causes of forest fire are:

Intentional fire: The forest is often set on fire by the villagers during the summer season to get a good growth of grass following the rains. The fire burns the debris that is lying on the forest floor and hence the grass is able to grow well in the rainy season. Sometimes it spreads and destroys vast tracts of valuable trees. The forest is also set a fire by the forest department to clear it of dry vegetation in order to avoid the risk of a huge fire. Firing is done from top to bottom by cutting fire-lines at regular intervals to control the fire. Villagers also set fire to pine leaves falling on the surface as they inhibit the undergrowth.

Accidental fire: Fire is also caused by man's carelessness. Unextinguished campfires of trekkers and picnickers, forest labourers throwing away burning cigarettes, bidis and matchsticks, villagers burning the unwanted material on their fields during summer, throwing away of torches used by travellers to see their way in the forest at night, and acid applied to increase the yield of resin. This acid may be spilled on the dry needles of a pine forest, thereby leading to forest fires.

The flow of air in the hills is upwards, which is responsible for huge fires, and a fire may go beyond control if it spreads from the bottom of a hill. It is easily controlled if it is from top to bottom. Too much dryness also helps in spreading fires.

There are several traditional methods of controlling fires: by beating the branches of trees on the fire, by throwing soil and water on it, and by cutting a fire-line to prevent its further spread. Removal of leaf litter by the villagers to spread under their cattle and for use as fuel is responsible for soil erosion, disturbances in the hydrological cycle in the hill areas and of organic manure in the soil. But at the same time too much accumulation of dry leaf litter increases the risk of forest fires.

Tourism

The Himalayan region is considered to be abundantly suited for tourism since it offers all kinds of attractions to tourists. A paradise for anglers and a challenge to hikers. The lush green valleys, emerald meadows, vast icefields have now started showing abrasion due to increasing human activity. Tourism brings a large number of people together, which leads to marked changes that are detrimental to the ecosystem as a whole. Tourism is found in the form of pilgrim tourism and for pleasure and adventure. To accommodate the large tourist influx, hundreds of new buildings are being constructed every year. The tourist activity has to be in consonance with the principles of conservation of nature and with the protection of associated resources.

SWOT ANALYSIS OF COLLECTION AND CULTIVATION

Medicinal plants have an immense potential in domestic and export market in India in general and Karnataka in particular. The soil and climatic conditions in Karnataka are highly suitable for cultivation of medicinal plants. The forests of Western Ghats and the deciduous forests of Deccan plateau are rich in medicinal plant biodiversity, suitable for managed collection. A SWOT analysis to examine the suitability of the region for collection and cultivation of medicinal plants revealed the following:

Strengths

- Existence of deep cultural and historical roots of traditional Indian medicine and the knowledge of the properties and therapeutic use of plants.
- Positive policy of state and union Governments for development of medicinal and aromatic plants.
- Availability of vast forest resources in the Western Ghats, hilly areas and man made forests, with rich sources of medicinal plants.
- Well informed farmers, scientific, trading and processing community, willing to share responsibilities.
- Availability of research and development support from UAS, CIMAP, IIHR, Biotech centre, FRHLT and many more private and public sector organizations and NGOs.

Weaknesses

- Over-exploitation of natural resources from their wild habitats.
- Inadequate information on international demand and supply.
- Inadequate research on sustainable harvest, collection, processing and value addition.
- Lack of infrastructure facilities for collection, drying, storage and processing.
- Lack of management planning.

Opportunities

- The international market for herbal products is growing at an annual growth rate of 7%.
- A growing market demand for high quality products certified for sustainable, environment-friendly collection and production.
- Consumer preference and concerns for organically grown products is increasing.
- Large stretches of virgin dry lands suitable for organic cultivation of medicinal plants.

Threats

- Depletion of natural resources at an alarming rate.
- Development of extra legal market mechanisms.
- High fluctuations in the international market price.
- Vagaries of nature like droughts, floods and forest fires.

CONCLUSION

From the ongoing review it may be concluded that a large land area of the world especially India and other developing countries is occupied by degraded land. In developing countries due to high population rate the cultivated land is under high pressure for more and more food production. India has very good wealth of medicinal plants since past but due to increasing population some important medicinal plant species have lost their diversity and shifting towards extinction. There is great demand of Indian medicinal plant in world market. Therefore to save the important medicinal plants they may be cultivated at degraded land of the country, as different medicinal plants also reclaim the degraded soil clear from the review. Thus plantation of herbal plants at degraded land will help to save the diversity of these herbal plants and simultaneously will help to minimize the pressure on crop lands and reclaim the degraded land of the country. The special significance of medicinal plants in conservation relates to the values that they hold for people. These values concern the contributions that medicinal plants can make to healthcare, financial income, cultural identity and livelihood security. It is believed that these contributions can sometimes be sufficiently great that a focus on medicinal plants has the potential to achieve much more, in terms of conservation and sustainable development, than just conservation of populations of the medicinal plants themselves, or sustainable production of materials for medicines.

It would be useful to investigate the geographical relationship between the overall value of medicinal plants to people and the distribution of plant diversity. It is suspected that medicinal plants often achieve their highest relative values in societies found in places richest in plant diversity. If this association is found to hold, then projects at many centres of plant diversity aimed at general biological conservation could often usefully have a focus on medicinal plants. Conservationists need to identify the conditions at field sites that are most favourable for releasing the potential offered by medicinal plants to achieve conservation and sustainable development. It is suggested that the contributions that medicinal plants can make are maximised if local people:

- feel that they receive significant health benefits from locally growing medicinal plants;
- receive an appreciable income from the sale of locally growing medicinal plants; ascribe special cultural significance to medicinal plants; and
- believe that there is reasonable chance that these benefits will persist in the future.

The current over-exploitation and soil compaction due to trampling seems to limit the ability of some species to propagate. Therefore, there is immediate need to conserve these important species for sustainable uses for the future. Efforts should be taken to start sustainable cultivation and harvesting programs. Therefore it is the need of hour to create mass awareness among people of rural areas about conservation of the degraded medicinal plants. An institutional network for assessment of threatened medicinal plant species and

their recovery, through well designed participatory species recovery interventions involving scientists, foresters and local communities must be established.

Reference

Anonymous (2001), The Key Role of Forestry Sector in Conserving India's Medicinal Plants. Technical Report, Foundation for Revitalization of Local Health Traditions, Bangalore.

Arora RK. (1997), Ethnobotany and its Role in the Conservation & Use of Plants: Genetic Resources in India. *Ethnobotany*, 9, 6–15.

Banerjee, D. K. (1977), Observations on Ethnobotany of Araku Valley, Visakhapatnam District, Andhra Pradesh. *J. Sci. Club.*, 33, 14-21.

Bhat, H. R. (2000), Medicinal Plants of Devarayanadurga Forests. Deputy Conservator of Forests, Government of Karnataka.

Chandola S, Singh SK (2003), Status and Scope of Medicinal Plants in Bhagirathi Valley of Garhwal, Uttaranchal-Conservation Strategy. *Indian Forester*, 126, 950–963.

Hamilton, A. (1995), The People and Plants Initiative. In: Martin, G.J. (Ed.). Ethnobotany A Methods Manual. WWF International Chapman & Hall, London, pp. X-XI.

Jain, S. K. (1981), Glimpses of Indian Ethnobotany. Oxford & IBH Publishing Co., New Delhi.

Jain, S. K. (1991), Dictionary of Indian Folk Medicine and Ethnobotany. Deep Publication, New Delhi.

Jarvie, J. & Perumal, B. (1994), Ethnobotanical Uses and Loss of Knowledge Concerning Forest Trees Among Some Iban in Sarawak. Tropics, 3, 155-162.

Kumar, V. and Asija (2000), Biodiversity Conservation in: Biodiversity-Principles and Conservation. Agrobiosis (India), Jodhpur

Marshall, N. T. (1998), Searching for a Cure: Conservation of Medicinal Wildlife Resources in East and Southern Africa. TRAFFIC- International, Cambridge.

Mehrotra, S. & Mehrotra, B. N. (2005), Role of Traditional and Folk Lore Herbals in the Development of New Drugs. Ethnobot., 17, 104-111.

Mishra R. (1946), A Study in the Ecology of Low Laying Lands. *Indian Ecology*, 1, 1–27.

Mishra R. (1946), An Ecological Study of the Vegetation of Banaras Hindu Univesity Grounds. *Journal of Indian Botanical Society*, 25, 39–59.

Mishra R. (1945), Botanical Chart of the Banaras Hindu University Grounds: *Journal of Banaras Hindu University*, pp. 49–72.

Mishra R. (1944), The Vegetation of the Raj Ghat Ravines: *Journal of Indian Botanical Society*, pp. 113–121.

Negi, C. S., Sunil. N., Lokesh. D., Rao. K. S. & Maikhuri R. K. (2002), Ethnomedicinal Plant Uses in a Small Tribal Community in a Part of Central Himalaya, *India. J. Hum. Ecol.*, 14(1): 23-31.

Parrota, J. A. (2001), Healing Plants of Peninsular India. CABI, New York.

Posey D A, Dutfield G. (1996), Beyond Intellectual Property: Toward Traditional Resource Rights for Indigenous Peoples and Local Communities, Canada: International Development Research Centre. p. 303.

Rama Rao, N & Henry, A. N. (1996), The Ethnobotany of Eastern Ghats in Andhra Pradesh, India. B.S.I., New Delhi.

Rao, B.T., Lakshmi, B.B. & Rao, L. M. (2001), Medico-Ethnology and Conservation of Medicinal Plants of Paderu Forest Division–Visakhapatnam, *Ecol. Env. & Cons.*, 7(2): 117-131.

Rao, B.T., Lakshmi, B.B., Rao, L.M., Ramaneshwari, K. & Hymavathi, V. (2000), Medicinal Plants of Paderu Forest Division in the Eastern Ghats of Visakhapatnam. *Asian J. Micr. Biotech.*

Shanley, P. & Luz, L. (2003), The Impacts of Forest Degradation on Medicinal Plant Use and Implication for Health Care in Eastern Amazonia. Bioscience, 53 (6), 573-584.

Singh M. *PhD Thesis (unpubl).* Banares Hindu University, Varanasi; 1993. Ecological Studies of Some Medicinal Plants of Indian, p. 175.

Singh, H. P. (2001), National Perspective on Development of Medicinal and Aromatic Plants. Technical Report, Agri. Watch.

Sinha R. K. (1996), *Ethnobotany the Renaissance of Traditional Herbal Medicines.* INA, Sri Publishers, Jaipur, p. 242.

Toledo, V. M. (1995), New Paradigms for a New Ethnobotany; Reflections on the Case of Mexico. In: Schultes, R.E. and Von Reis, S. (eds.) Ethnobotany: Evolution of a Discipline. Chapman and Hall, London. pp. 75-88.

Verma A. (1999), *Field Survey of Naturally Occurring Medicinal Plants of Banaras Hindu University Campus; PhD thesis (unpubl), submitted to the Banaras Hindu University, Varanasi.* p. 262.

Economic Crisis and Its Effect on Trade in European Countries Against Its Parts

*N. Jamaluddin**

INTRODUCTION

THE European Union is an extraordinary experiment in shared sovereignty, creating a zone of peace that now stretches from Britain to the Balkans. The union of 27 countries is the world's most formidable economic bloc, incorporating 491 million people in an integrated market that produces nearly a third more than the United States.

But the global economic crisis had made clear that Europe remains less than the sum of its parts.

The crisis has presented the European Union with its greatest challenge, but even many committed Europeanist believe that the alliance is falling the domestic politics, disagree sharply about what to do combat the slump. They have feuded over hoe much to stimulate the economy. They argue about whether the European central bank should worry more about the deep recession or future inflation. And they have rushed to protect jobs in their home markets at the expense of those in other member countries.

The latest European parliamentary elections on Sunday drove home the point. Only 43 per cent of Europeans voted – a record low turnout, despite the financial crisis and compulsory voting in some countries. Far-right parties opposed to the European Union and to immigrants from poor member countries, recorded gains, as did the greens. Those who did vote weighed in largely on national issues.

With American leadership undercut by divisive foreign wars and the U.S. economic model of market freedom and Europe matters. The "European model" of significant government involvement in the economy; close supervision of finance, industry and labour; and generous state –run pensions and health care is being praised in some circles as a freshly viable alternative to Anglo-American-style capitalism.

* Associate Professor in Commerce, Urumu Dhanalakshmi College, Trichy-19

EUROPE SUFFERS MORE

But although the subprime mortgage crisis began in the U.S., Europe is arguably suffering more the international monetary fund estimates that European banks hold more bad assets that American ones and have written down much less. Budget deficits are rising, and unemployment, especially among the young, is already its highest in 10 years.

With the response hobbled by a fractious European Union, many economists now expect the downturn to last longer here than across the Atlantic.

"We are in a moment of a very severe crisis" said Joschka Fischer, a Green Party politician and former German foreign minister. "we have a traumatic lack of leadership, we are caught right in the middle by the flood."

The central tension in the union has always been between national priorities and collective interests. Ceding national rights and powers -over currency, trade, customs duties- has never been simple, even in good times. In bad times, like the current downturn, national politics trump the common interest. Leaders move to protect their own industries, workers and voters at the expense of those elsewhere. Workers still seethe at the sacrifices they feel they make on behalf of integration.

At the Goodyear Dunlop tire factory in Amiens, in northern France, Thierry Fagot, 36, is losing the job ha has held for 13 years. He sees competition within the alliance as part of the reason.

"I feel like I was fooled; I mean, we created Europe to protect us, and for a long time it worked," he said, explaining that Europe provided a market for the factory's tires and established safety rules. "Now, with the competition of Eastern countries, I feel like Europe created this situation where we're losing our jobs to another EU country. How can this be for the greater good?"

The European Union is not about to collapse amid such antagonisms. But some of the continent's most devoted advocates are scaling down their ambitions. Few speak any longer of a Europe that is a significant political or military counterweight to the United States.

Fischer, the green Party politician, is a committed European who bemoans "the post-89 generation's" indifference to the ideals of a European density, and the retreat, under the pressure of the crisis, to nationalist goals and rhetoric.

TRANSNATIONAL CRISIS

"Crisis are always moments of truth because they relentlessly expose both the strengths and weakness of all the players involved", said Fischer, criticizing in particular the narrow, national vision of the German government

He said the European central bank, which sets a major borrowing rate for the 16 nations that use the euro as a common currency, has done well. But the European commission, the union's main executive body, "played a zero role in the present crisis, and this was a transnational crisis, so the role of the commission should have been just the opposite."

Instead, European leaders are concentrating on passing the long-delayed Lisbon treaty, to create a European president and foreign minister and simplify decision -making. But the treaty has little to say about economic matters.

The strains are evident in the way counties have worked to bail out their own banks and rescue national factories of global automobile companies, when a broader European policy would be more logical. But they are also visible in the inability to agree on a policy toward Afghanistan or on a joint energy policy to reduce European dependence on Russian natural gas.

Germany and France together are the traditional motor of the European union, but relations between them are cold, with the French president, Nicholas Sarkozy, and German chancellor, Angela Merkel, putting national interests first, whether the issue is social benefits or saving jobs in the faltering car industry.

DIVISIONS EVIDENT

Divisions are also evident between northern Europe and southern Europe with more fiscally responsible countries like Germany only reluctantly promising to help floundering economies like those of Spain and Greece. Solidarity, meant to be the great principle of the European Union, is fraying as well on east - west lines, with the countries that use the euro reluctant to jeopardize the currency's stability by rescuing members outside the so-called euro zone, like Bulgaria and Romania.

Few want to consider what happens to Ukraine, a nonmember, where many European banks, especially German and Australian ones, are heavily invested.

And the promise of a Europe "without borders" has been undermined by a reaction in hard times against immigrants from around the region who are seen as competing for jobs.

Before the European parliamentary elections, Mr. Sarkozy and Ms Merkel issued a joint letter. "We want a strong Europe that protects us, we reject a bureaucratic Europe that mechanically applies nitpicking rules," they wrote.

But they disagree sharply on the role of public spending and the European central bank. Mr. Sarkozy favors more stimulus and giving the central bank the flexibility to buy bonds or public sector loans top help revive lending. Ms Merkel, in contrast, has attacked rising budget deficits and criticized the central bank for reducing interest rates too much and risking future inflation.

They agree, however, on protecting jobs in their home markets. While Mr. Sarkozy has been criticized for providing billions to protect French car companies, Ms Merkel, with a national election in September, has just brokered an expensive deal for Opel, the European branch of general motors, almost, almost entirely based on saving German jobs.

The former French president Valery Giscard d'Estaing said that since the French rejected a European constitution he helped to draft in 2005, national leaders had dominated those who favour a stronger union.

"It's retrograde," he said in an interview. "In a short –term crisis, you crisis, you may have national intervention to protect people, but it's not a policy, it's just a reaction," he said, putting the single market at risk. "the trend must be to see the European market as a whole."

In Calais, France, the Schaeffler chain Drive System factory, German-owned, makes parts for Opel. A third of the workers were laid off a month ago including Dany Valcke, 53. he was a foreman, but now, as he says, "time is all I've got," and he doubts he will ever find another factory job.

"Europe is a good thing; it allows our countries to have a stronger voice in the world, and it brought peace," Valcke said. "but economically, it's not so good. Many have lost their jobs to European countries where the work force is cheaper. They are part of Europe, but if you want Europe, you can't have these two competing systems."

The European union "didn't try hard enough to help its people through the crisis. It probably doesn't even have the power for this," he said. Then he asked, a bit plaintively: "sometimes I wonder what it's for, if not for this? I find the U.S. government response to the crisis much more appropriate."

In Romania, on the other side of the union, the workers are suffering, too. But they take some comfort in being part of a larger, richer bloc than their old, soviet one, and in general blame local leaders for their problems.

Cristina Lincu, 32, went to find work in Spain in 2001. now she is back home, with her husband and baby son. The crisis hit their small Madrid grocery prices in Romania, so they came back and bought land for a house. In a way, she gained from the crisis, Lincu said, but she is concerned about her fellow Romanians in Spain. There, "the vast majority of immigrant workers were doing low-paid or not very dignified jobs, but now even Spaniards want those jobs," she said.

As for the future, opinions are divided, but few predict that the European experiment is over. The Lisbon Treaty is expected to pass eventually, strengthening the union's powers. And today's leaders, however divided, may learn to grapple with economic challenges collectively, even as they learned to avoid the military conflicts of an earlier age.

"It will be tough, we'll have setbacks, history will beast us up we'll have painful years, nut I think crisis creates leaders, the right leaders,", said Fischer the German Green party politician. "I'm not pessimistic."

AMERICANS ARE NOW SPENDING FEWER DOLLARS

For the first time since World War II, Americans are spending fewer dollars than they spent s year earlier.

That reluctance – or inability – to spend has led to the sharpest rise in the savings rate on this country since the government began calculating the statistic in the 1950s.

HOME OWNERSHIP

People's attitudes toward credit and home ownership are undergoing a fundamental shift," said David A. Rosenberg, the chief economist and strategist of Gluskin Sheff, a money management firm based in Toronto.

Rosenberg said he expected that the savings rate, which rose to a 14-year high of 5.7 per cent of disposable income in April, would continue to grow until it surpassed the record high of 14.6 per cent, set in May 1975, when the country had just emerged from a severe recession and Americans were pessimistic about the country's economic outlook.

Trends can be found in both personal consumption spending and savings rates using three month moving averages, to smooth out gyrations.

Over the three month period, the savings rate averaged 4.8 per cent.

Until this cycle, the smallest year-over-year rise in consumption spending was a 1.8 per cent increase in the 12 months through April 1961, a period that also ended shortly after a recession concluded. But the year-over-year figures have been down in every month of 2009.

UNEMPLOYMENT

A collapse of income has not caused this decline in spending. While government figures show that wages are down because of rising levels of unemployment, that has been more than offset by lower collections and by a sharp increase in government transfer payment as the economic stimulus measures take effect.

The figures on spending are in nominal dollars, not adjusted for inflation. Real consumer spending, adjusted for inflation, fell for brief periods during recessions in the mid-1970s and the early 1980s. But in neither case did the decline last as long, or go as deep, as the current one.

The sharpest falloff in consumer spending in the current cycle was in the purchase of durable goods like vehicles and furniture. That decline seems to have stabilized. Spending on nondurable goods like food and clothing is also down for the first time since the 1940s, and is continuing to fall.

Consumer spending on service is still rising, Albert at the lowest level in memory. A large part of that increase reflects rising payments for medical services, which have continued to take more money even as the recession deepens.

At its worst, late last year, spending on durable goods was down 12.6 per cent, year-over-year. That decline, while the largest in more than 50 years, was not nearly as great as the decline in production that took place as the financial crisis cut off credit for trade financing.

"The demand numbers never fell like the production inventory and trade numbers," said Robert Barbera, the chief economist of ITG, a research firm. "you can have a rebound for all these numbers," he added, even if demand does not recover.

Exports from countries like China do appear to be picking up, a fact that has encouraged speculation that the global recession may almost be over, if it has not already ended. But it remains to be seen whether demand will rise.

If American consumers remain cautious, as Rosenberg forecasts, a real recovery may depend on an increase in demand from places other than the United States.

CONCERNS ON THE TRADE FRONT

India's trade performance continues to disappoint. For the seventh month in a row, exports declined in April, and the drop was by as much as 33.2 per cent compared with trhe previous year. India has fared worse than many other asian countries such as China and south Korea. It is quite misleading to say that the share of exports need not be a major cause for worry in the larger context of growth and employment. The fact is that most of the export-oriented industries such as textiles, and gems and jewellery are labour intensive and there are reports of large scale retrenchment in these sectors. A fail in exports is reflected in the underperformance of the manufacturing sector over the past several months, as the monthly industrial production figures show Rs.51 to the dollar- has not mitigated the woes of exporters. Although when stated in rupee terms the decline in exports at 16.4 per cent does not appear to be large, the fact is that the rupee depreciation can only partially sustain the viability of exports. Besides, the rupee has more recently reversed course and has appreciated against the dollar, Coping with a highly fluctuating exchange rate has been a challenge even to the largest companies engaged in international trade, information technology, and other services that generate income and expenditure streams in multiple currencies. Many of India's exporters are from the medium - and small – scale sectors.

CONCLUSIONS

Imports fell even more sharply than exports – by 56 per cent in April compared with April 2008. Oil imports have been lower by 58 per cent, thanks to lower demand and reduced oil prices. The fall in import demand reflects the downturn in several sectors of the economy. The narrowing of the merchandise trade deficit from $8.7 billion is therefore not an unmixed blessing, although it does ease the pressure on the current account. It is too much to expect striking improvement in export performance until the major export destinations – the Unites States, the European Union, and Japan _ start climbing out of the deep recession into which their economies have sunk. The WTO has estimated a contraction in global trade by as much as 9 per cent this year. A major reduction in global demand and a severe curtailment of trade finance have been principal factors.

Reference

J. R. Nadkarni (2008), International Trade Past, Present & Future, Tata Mc-Graw Hill Publications, 2nd Edition, New Delhi

Paul Switcher (2008), Anatonomy of European Trade- World Bank Meet- Paris.

Report of IMF (2008-09), Chapter 4, Section 2 , IMF Publications, Washington D.C.

IBRD Report on Prospects and Retrospect's of World Trade in the Globalized Era.

Mid Term Appraisal of ADB (Asian Development Bank)-2008.

European Continients Trade Look-Pioneer - Report 22nd' June 2009.

Guardian Report on Western European Countries, April 2009- New Jersy, USA.

Implications of Right to Education Act 2009 on Future Technical Education

*Duraipandi Mavoothu**

INTRODUCTION

THE Right to Education Act 2009(RTE) is the gateway to India's development. After the enactment of Right to Information Act 2005, the next breakthrough act was RTE. It makes the education the fundamental rights of the children in the age group of 6-14 years and from class 1 to 8. China introduced the Compulsory Education Act in 1986 which is similar to India's RTE 2009. Because of that act, today china started reaping the benefits. In 2008, the enrollment in primary schools and middle schools across the China reached 98%. China gives very much importance to vocational and technical education. It gives free access to secondary vocational education since 2009. China produces much more engineers, doctors, scientists, and other professionals than India. They have many world-class universities. Mathematically, China is at least 2.5 decades ahead of India in education. After the introduction of the RTE, the Union HRD Minister Kapil Sibal announced three major initiatives. They are:

1. Setting up of 2500 Kendriya Vidyalayas,
2. Opening the door for foreign universities, and
3. Setting up a high-power National Commission for Higher Education and Research (NCHER), which will subsume all the national level higher education bodies like UGC, AICTE, BCI, MCI, etc.

In the light of the above developments, it is pertinent to analyse what are the implications of that on future technical education in India.

THE MAIN FEATURES OF RIGHT TO EDUCATION ACT 2009

The following are the salient features of the Right to Education Act 2009:

- Free and compulsory education to all children of India in the 6 to 14 age group;

* Reader, School of Management Studies, Cochin University of Sc. & Tech., Kochi.

- No child shall be held back, expelled, or required to pass a board examination until completion of elementary education;
- A child who completes elementary education shall be awarded a certificate;
- Calls for a fixed student-teacher ratio;
- Will apply to all of India except Jammu and Kashmir;
- Provides for 25 per cent reservation for economically disadvantaged communities in admission to Class One in all private schools;
- Mandates improvement in quality of education;
- School teachers will need adequate professional degree within five years or else will lose job;
- School infrastructure (where there is problem) to be improved in three years, else recognition cancelled; and
- Financial burden will be shared between state and central government.

WHAT IS TECHNICAL EDUCATION?

Technical education creates 'specific human capital' (Becker, 1964)[1] and is not portable across one's life and from job to job. Technical education is to imbibe specific job-relevant skills that can make the employee more readily suitable for a given job and would make him/her thus more productive[2]. Technology is commonly defined as a discipline or body of knowledge and the application of this knowledge combined with resources to produce outcomes in response to human desires and needs. Technology education draws its content from four universal domains: (1) sciences, (2) humanities, (3) technologies, and (4) formal knowledge. The sciences and humanities domains contain all recorded knowledge of the sciences and humanities. The technologies domain likewise contains all recorded knowledge related to the types of technology. The formal knowledge domain consists of language, linguistics, mathematics, and logic[3].

COMPULSORY EDUCATION AND TECHNICAL EDUCATION:CHINA'S EXPERIENCE

China introduced the Compulsory Education Act in 1986. As China consolidated the momentum of its rapid economic gains and drives more openly into the market environment, the quality of human resources was considered as an important determinant of the country's competitiveness. However, there is very narrow access to higher education, particularly among the poor. The students who exit from education system create an oversupply of labour with senior secondary schooling, thereby affecting their wages and eventually dampening returns on investment[4]. A comparison between India and China in promoting high quality technical education shows that China has developed the technical education sector much more rapidly than India. China has produced more than 5,000 Ph.D. holders per year compared to India's

1,000. China has also successfully implemented the concept of scalability (Pai,2009)[5]. Overall, China has encashed its Compulsory Education Act 1986 to promote its vocational and technical education.

THE CURRENT STATUS OF TECHNICAL EDUCATION IN INDIA

Since 1947, when independence was achieved, India has been one of the few developing countries to invest extensively in both Science and Technical education. India's first IIT was started in 1950 at Kharagpur. India's technical education landscape was initially dominated by the Indian Institutes of Technology (IIT), which had good faculty and facilities and the Indian Institute of Science (IISc) which had a good three-year Bachelor of Science diploma/ degree programme in engineering. However, the growth of IITs and IISc, in terms of both scalability and accountability, seemed to have gradually declined beginning in the late 1960's. In fact, no IIT or IISc was again put in place until 1995, which clearly indicates a failure on the part of the Indian government. A large number of private engineering colleges with poor facilities and unqualified faculty thus came about after 1970; constituting nearly 75 per cent of the total intake of engineering students. These colleges now number approximately 1,100 compared to the seven IITs and one IISc, causing the IT industries, et al, to deem only about 20 per cent of first degree holders employable. Thus, technical education developed a distorted image; graduating over 2,30,000 Bachelor's degree students, 20,000 Master's degree students, and 1,000 Ph.D. degree students in 2006. By contrast, according to a December 2008 report from the Indian Institute of Technology in Bombay, IITs and IISc graduate only 1 per cent of this number at the Bachelor's level, 4 per cent at the Master's level, and 40 per cent at the Ph.D. level. For a mere 3,000 seats in IITs there are close to 3,00,000 applicants. Experience has shown that at least 10-15 per cent of those applicants are of IIT quality and comparable to the students at major public universities in the U.S. A direct consequence of this was an enormous, but unfortunate growth of coaching institutes where many students enrolled for two years prior to taking the IIT entrance exam. The fact that a large number of non-IIT students turn out to be equally competent and innovative was largely ignored until about a decade ago[6].

Table 1
India's Higher Education Institutions [Branch-wise share (in %)]

Branch	*Percentage*
Arts, Science & Commerce	56
Medical	10
Engg., Technical & Architecture	07
Teacher Training	08
Polytechnics	06
Others	13
Total	100%

Source: The Financial Express (Online), Dec. 26, 2009]

The above table shows that the Indian higher education is dominated by the general education. The vocational and technical educations are given a backseat driving.

Implications of RTE on Opportunities in Future Technical Education. If the RTE is delivered effectively, efficiently and equitably, then there will be a lot of opportunities in India in the field of technical education in future. It is said that in the Twenty First Century, 'a nation's ability to convert knowledge into wealth and social good through the process of innovation is going to determine its future'7. For that a strong foundation of technical education is a must. The following are the implications of RTE on opportunities in future technical education:

Quality Technical Education: As there will more aspirants every year, there will be growth in the supply of quality professional higher education (Kumaraswamy, 2008)[8].

- *Internal Efficiency:* Availability of more aspirants and seats leads to generating maximum output at minimum cost.
- *Opportunities for Faculty Positions:* There will be a lot of opportunities for faculty positions in technical institutes.
- *Competition:* The quality of the IITs and IIMs remain largely untested currently since there is no meaningful competition. If the Harvards, Kellogs, MITs and the Stanfords are freely allowed to set up shop in India, the strength and quality of the institutions may get validated or competition may force them to improve their quality. In that case, there may even be an influx of foreign students seeking seats, which will help commercial expansion of our technical education.
- *Demographic Dividend:* India's demographic and economic conditions appear remarkably conducive to future technical educational development. The working age population in US, UK, Japan and some Western European countries are decreasing, while the same is increasing in India and Brazil. This will lead to shifts in jobs, skills and talent globally. A report by PricewaterhouseCoopers says that mature economies are increasingly aware that they will be unable to withstand the pressure from emerging economies by competing head on with their human capital potential[9]. India has a lot of opportunities in human capital development. Of the BRIC countries, India is projected to stay the youngest with its working-age population estimated to rise to 70% of the total demographic by 2030 - the largest in the world[10]. To tap this opportunity India must go for a strategic investment in human capital. It reinforces the justification for further investments and policy changes in technical education.
- *Business Opportunity:* Educating and training India will be a huge business and social opportunity[11]. Venugopal Dhoot, the Chairman of

Videocon Group, says that the deregulation of higher education will result in creation of annual revenues of close to $100-billion and generate job opportunities for 20 million people in the field of education alone. Jeremy Williams, Chief Academic Officer, Knowledge *Universe Education*, estimates that India needs 2 million new teachers today and will be short 18 million teachers by 2015[12].

The English Advantage: English, as a subject, is taught up to under graduation in India. The entire technical education is in English. English is the language of business in India and the large English-speaking workforce is a benefit to investors and employers. Investment in learning English language as such a great business opportunity[13]. Gauri Kartini Shastry demonstrated that Indian districts where it is easier to learn English benefited more from globalization: they experienced greater growth in information technology jobs[14].

IMPLICATIONS OF RTE ON CHALLENGES IN FUTURE TECHNICAL EDUCATION

The following are the implications of RTE on challenges in future technical education:

1. *Scalability in Public Institutions:* The government-run technical institutes are always lagging in scalability. The IISc(Bengaluru) discontinued the diploma/degree courses in the engineering disciplines between the 1960's and 1980's and the concept of scalability (i.e. having a large student intake and a higher student to faculty ratio as is obtainable in reputed pubic universities in the U.S) was never addressed. A large number of private engineering colleges with poor facilities and unqualified faculty thus came about after 1970; constituting nearly 75 per cent of the total intake of engineering students. These colleges now number approximately 1,100 compared to the seven IITs and one IISc, causing the IT industries, et al., to deem only about 20 per cent of first degree holders employable[15].
2. *Intermediation:* The coaching classes for the entrance tests to get admissions in premier technical institutes like IITs, IIMs, NIFTs, NIDs, IIFTs, etc. will become still more commercial as there will be more aspirants for each seat and every one will try to increase the chances of getting the admission. More resources will go to the intermediary product (coaching classes) than to the final products (technical programmes).
3. *Exorbitant Fee:* There will be hectic fee even in the government-run technical institutes to augment the revenue and to grow on their own.
4. *Shortage of Faculty:* Whether the technical institutes can attract the young scholars to come to teaching at the frugal rate at which they pay the faculty?

5. *Private Actors:* Technical education in the private sphere is largely a mediocre commercial activity that needs radical reforms[16]. In India there is an artificial shortage of good institutions. The IITs and IIMs are so selective and there are a large number of people wanting to get educated. But then India does not have a tradition of not-for-profit organisations setting up universities or colleges. Except, of course, those set up by the church and other such organisations. Supply would follow demand and here in India the public universities do not have the resources or the seats to meet the public demand. That is why private universities have come up[17]. Today, the government retains art subjects, and the private encash on the engineering and technological courses[18].
6. *Low Rate of Return:* The future output from the technical institutes may be far more than the labour market demands. So, the social rate of return to technical education investments may be below the returns to investment in alternative forms of capital. This may cast doubt whether further public expenditures in this sub-sector are justifiable.
7. *Alternate Financing:* Scholarships and student loans that eventually would help reduce the differences in rates of return. But, given the present experience with these types of alternate financing is not encouraging.
8. *Personal Cost of Education:* In her book entitled *Academic Capitalism*, Professor Sheila Slaughter discusses the ascendance of a corporate regime in higher education, which has focussed on using universities and knowledge as instruments of power and control, both within America and across the globe. Personal cost of education has risen with the decline of state support for universities. Racial, class, gender and regional inequalities have deepened[19]. The increasing number of aspirants will lead to self-financing technical institutes. That will increase the personal cost of technical education. It is already evident in India. Human capital investment in all countries is focusing on significant labour-market gains for the individuals, such as higher post-tax earnings, higher participation in the labour market and improved employment probability[20].
9. *Technical Education to the Disadvantaged:* Providing quality technical education and training to the disadvantaged children is going to be the big challenge[21].
10. *Imperfect Information:* There is a problem of imperfect information. People may not know which skills to invest in, or who provides the best education and other instruction. So, the students and the parents will have the 'herd mentality'[22]. It is already happening in India.

SUGGESTIONS

The following are the suggestions/strategies to mitigate and reckon with the potential challenges in future technical education in the light f RTE:

1. *The IIT Model:* The IIT model of success needs to be replicated on a far larger scale (Narayana Murthy, 2009)[23]. In fact, no IIT or IISc was again put in place until 1995, which clearly indicates a failure on the part of the Indian government[24]. While replicating these models, the issue of scalability must be addressed. Several reports regarding technical education or the AICTE guide lines state a figure of 15:1 as the desired student to faculty ratio. While this figure is perhaps the norm in Ivy League schools in the U.S., it is not so in reputed public universities such as Berkeley, Illinois where the ratio is more than 20:1. These are primarily research universities with huge undergraduate enrollments where postgraduate students are involved in various aspects of faculty assistance. Tier I institutions in India must adapt this model and concentrate more on research. Enrollment into the existing IITs can be doubled within a year or so if incremental investments in infrastructure are made. In terms of hostel space, room sharing should be considered except for Ph.D. scholars, as is common in non-IIT schools and was the prevalent model before 1947 as well. One can make efficient use of classroom space during the daytime, run labs during both mornings and afternoons, and admit students in both semesters. Thus, more than 20,000 quality IIT undergraduate students can be generated in a four year time frame while some of the Tier II institutions can be upgraded to IIT status with no difference in undergraduate quality[25].
2. *Increase the 'Available Seats to Aspirant' Ratio:* The 'available seats to aspirant' ratio will have to go up for bringing down the coaching class fees and the tension level of the aspirants and the parents.
3. *Avoid Intermediation:* It is necessary to channelise the huge amounts spent by society on intermediary coaching classes for financing the actual end-education (Kumaraswamy, 2008)[26].
4. *Balancing Between General and Technical Educations:* Both general and technical educations contribute to economic growth. So, a balance has to be struck between size of general education and technical education. As compared to industrially mature economies such as Korea, Germany, Japan and the UK, where at least 70% of workers between 15-29 years have formal vocational skills, the corresponding proportion for India is a dismal 2%[27].
5. *Public-Private Partnership (PPP):* Utilise the private sector's efficiency in running technical institutes and raise resources by unlocking the government's brand value. The PPP can be opened only to public limited companies, which have greater financial reporting requirements than other entities like trust, societies and private companies. We need entities that are subject to adequate disclosure requirements and internal governance processes. There are listed public limited companies like NIIT in the education sector. It is believed that government is very

serious about PPP in educational sector. In India the PPP model has proved to be successful in sectors like telecom, power, roads and ports[28].

6. *Decentralisation:* Involve local bodies in setting up and running the technical institutes. For example, in China, the municipal governments-supported universities became more popular than the provincial universities for the vocational programmes, especially in short-cycle courses[29].
7. *Short-cycle Courses:* Universities and Colleges must give equal importance to both short-cycle courses and 4 or 5-year academic programmes.
8. *Socialistic Programmes:* Provide incentives for socialistic programmes such as reservations, creating facilities in remote centres and so on to meet the demand of technical institutions.
9. *Resource Prioritisation:* It would be prudent to target governmental resources to those fields of study where the demand in labour market is high[30].
10. *Nationalisation of Admission Tests:* Nationalise the admission tests to technical courses as a National Testing Service on the lines of GMAT and mandate all the technical institutes to partner this initiative.

CONCLUSION

India needs the best intellect available for government, business, military, or any aspect of society to strive for global excellence (Narayana Murthy, 2009)[31], and this can be achieved only by making use of the opportunities thrown out by the RTE in the field of technical education in future. Looking ahead, the future of technical education in India can be bright if certain decisions can boldly be taken for India to emerge as a leader in research and development as similar route taken by China several years ago[32]. Though the industrial revolution was initiated in England, subsquently England lost the economic power to German, France and USA due to the fact that it did not focus on the vocational and technical education. And the general education dominated over the technical education in England. That's a great lesson for India now; and so let us see that India does not do the same mistake that of England.

Notes & Reference

1. Becker, G. S. (1964), '*Human Capital*', National Bureau of Economic Research, New York.
2. Tilak, J.G.B. (2002), '*Vocational Education and Training in Asia*'. In Keeves, J.P. and Watanabe, R., 'The Handbook on Educational Research in the Asia Pacific Region', Kluwer Academic Publishers.
3. *http://education.stateuniversity.com/pages/2536/Vocational-Technical-Education.html"*>Vocational and Technical Education - Current Trends, Preparation of Teachers, International Context-HISTORY OF</a> [Accessed on 12 March 2010].

4. Hossain, S.I., '*Making an Equitable and Efficient Education: The Chinese Experience*'. Available at: http://www-wds.worldbank.org/external/default/WDSContentServer/WDSP/IB/2000/02/24/000009265_3971104185041/additional/116516322_20041117170042.pdf [Accessed on 12 March 2010]
5. Pai, M.A. (2009), '*Higher Technical Education in India at the Crossroads*'. Available at: *http://casi.ssc.upenn.edu/iit/pai [Accessed on 12 March 2010]*
6. [5]
7. Singh, V. P. '*Education: A Fundamental Right in India*'. Available at: *http://www.legalserviceindia.com/articles/edu_pes.htm [Accessed on 12 March 2010]*
8. Kumaraswamy, V. (2008), "Correcting Distortions in Higher Education Market", *The Hindu Business Line*, May 16.
9. *www.pwchk.com/webmedia/doc/633077569676719728_hra_keytrends_mar06.pdf* [Accessed on December 16, 2009]
10. *www.investmentcommission.in/human_capital.htm* [Accessed on 06 January 2010].
11. Mavoothu, D. (2010), '*Global Trends in Human Capital Development: Implications for India*', Paper Presented in a 2-day International Conference on 'Investment in Human Capital' organized by P.G. and Research Department of Economics, Loyola College, Chennai, India, February 8-9, 2010.
12. Karen Henke (2009), '*India's Human Capital and Educational Technology*', Available at: *http://www.longtaillearners.com/2009/08/indias-human-capital-and-educational-technology/* [Accessed on 06 January 2010]
13. [11]
14. Gauri Kartini Shastry (2008), '*Human Capital Response to Globalization: Education and Information Technology in India*'. Available at SSRN: *http://ssrn.com/abstract=1334684 [Accessed on 06 January 2010]*
15. [5]
16. Raj Kumar, C. (2008), '*India Needs Global Universities*', *The Hindu*, 23 May 2008, p.11.
17. *The Hindu*, 01 September 2009, p.3 (Educationplus), Kochi.
18. [11]
19. Krishna Kumar (2009), '*Are Indians Really a Challenge?*', *The Hindu*, 19 August 2009.
20. [11]
21. [11]
22. [11]
23. Narayana Murthy, N.R. (2009), '*Securing India's Science Future*', The Hindu, November 13, 2009, p.8.
24. [5]
25. [5]
26. [8]
27. Palit, A. (2009), '*Let's Get Technical*', *The Financial Express*, Dec. 26, 2009. Available at: *http://www.financialexpress.com/printer/news/559176/* [Accessed on 12 March 2010]
28. [11]
29. [4]
30. [4]
31. [23]
32. [5].

Global Crisis What Needs to be Done? Some Pratical Difficulties on Worrisome Decline in World Trade

N. Jamaluddin

INTRODUCTION

Falling demand, constraints on finance in the U.S. and Europe blamed for crisis in the Global trade has been a principal casually of the ongoing economic crisis. The world Trade organization estimates trade to contract by 9 per cent this year. Collapsing global demand and severe curtailment of trade finance by banks and other leaders have been the main factors responsible.

Together they have created constraints to export growth, especially in many development countries., obviously developed countries have been affected equally if not to a greater degree.

FINANCIAL SCIENCE

The financial crisis that morphed into an economic crisis started in the U.S. which still remains the epicenter if the crisis. Global economic recovery is dependent to a large extent on how soon the U.S. economy stabilizes. The fall in demand and investment in the U.S and Europe is a principal reason for the major setback in world trade.

ALL ROUND FALL IN EXPORTS

Exports from the U.S. are down 30 per cent and imports 34 per cent in the first quarter of the year compared to the previous three months. Japan, heavily dependent on the U.S. market, saw its exports plunge 45.5 per cent in March this year on year basis. Consequently its economy, the second largest in the world, contracted by 15.2 per cent, its worst ever performance since 1955. exports from China and Brazil fell by 20 per cent in the first quarter compared with a year ago. Countries more closely linked to the U.S., Mexico for instance through the NAFTA, have fared even worse. Its exports fell by 29 per cent

* Associate Professor in Commerce, Urumu Dhanalakshmi College, Trichy-19.

while its economy declined 21.5 per cent, more than three times the rate of contraction in the U.S.

India too is witnessing sizable contraction in its exports, especially in dollar terms. Compounding the exporters' woes have been the exchange rate movements. They have been thoroughly unpredictable. A sharp depreciation of the rupee taking it beyond 51 to the dollar has been followed more recently by an unanticipated appreciation. The dollar is now trading between 46 to 47.

The crisis in trade, though originating from the financial and economic crises, has not probably received the same degree of attention from policy makers the way those crises have. Nevertheless following the G-20 summit in London and thereafter, trade related issues have been brought back to centre stage as it were.

The current financial and economic crisis is throwing millions of people into poverty, especially the most vulnerable in the developing world. This is happening amidst the ongoing food, water, energy, ecosystem, and climate crises. Together, these crises are undermining the efforts to achieve the Millennium Development Goals and setting back development progress of the past few decades.

The financial and economic crisis requires a collective response from the international community. Leading economies should continue and further strengthen the coordination of their stimulus programmes to revive global economic growth. Apart from addressing urgent needs in such areas as social safety nets, health, and education, programmes should lay a solid foundation for shared growth and sustainable development. Furthermore, the international community should ensure that developing countries have not only the fiscal space to launch their own stimulus programmes but also access to international markets for a rapid resumption of trade.

Central to the new economic foundation are new growth poles that can potentially contribute to economic recovery, decent job creation, and reduced threats of food, water, energy, ecosystem and climate crises, which have disproportionate impacts on the poor. Investing stimulus funds in such sectors as energy efficient technologies, renewable energy, public transport, sustainable agriculture, environmentally friendly tourism, and the sustainable management of natural resources including ecosystems and biodiversity, reflects the conviction that a green economy can create dynamic new industries, quality jobs, and income growth while mitigating and adapting to climate change and arresting biodiversity decline.

Such investments should be scaled up significantly in all countries and be supported by national and international policy instruments and incentives such as updating building codes and enforcement of internationally agreed environmentally friendly shipping regulations. It is also essential to have green investments at the community level to reduce vulnerability and strengthen resilience. Major events such as the climate negotiations in Copenhagen in December 2009 and the 2010 High Level Meeting of the United Nations General Assembly on Biodiversity are opportunities for urging the expansion of green investments.

To be able to scale up such investments, many developing countries will require financial support. It is imperative, therefore, that the world's leaders resolve to deliver on commitments, including those made by G8 and G20 leaders, to support developing countries, especially the most vulnerable, in coping with the effects of the current crisis. This includes augmented balance-of-payments support, trade finance, lending by the multilateral banks, and concessional finance for the poorest countries.

Fiscal reforms can shift the burden of taxation from jobs, income and savings to the overuse of resources, resource depletion and environmental degradation, thereby encouraging green investments. Carbon pricing can advance these aims. There is also a need for phasing out perverse subsidies that encourage excessive use of fossil fuel based production inputs in agriculture and fishing sectors. Both carbon pricing and the reform of perverse subsidies, however, must be accompanied by measures to protect the access by the poor to food security and energy. The revenues saved by phasing out such subsidies could be reallocated towards the development of green job skills, the provision of clean, affordable energy alternatives for the poor, and support to other green sectors with broad economic benefits.

Trade needs to be revived and trade policies need to support both development and the transfer of environmentally sound technologies. These include technologies to make clean energy affordable to developing countries as well as to support climate change mitigation and adaptation including ecosystem-based adaptation. It is important to avoid any measures that could result in new protectionism, including measures in stimulus packages. Early conclusion of the Doha Round trade negotiations can facilitate a green recovery, in particular the negotiations on environmental goods and services, fisheries subsidies, and reforming agriculture rules that would be conducive to fostering food security for all. The Aid for Trade mandate should be fulfilled. Reliable finance should be provided to small and medium-sized enterprises for investment in green businesses.

The shift towards a green economy requires education for sustainable development including training in new job skills and newly required health systems. All stakeholders must double efforts to provide training on a range of skills for decent and remunerative jobs protected by adequate health care. A particular focus should be given to the poor, vulnerable groups including women, youth, and to small and medium sized enterprises and farms. These green jobs training programmes can be integrated into both formal and informal education schemes. Similarly, green jobs related health issues should be taken into account by formal health systems. These efforts will assist developing countries in leapfrogging to a greener and inclusive economic development path. Skill transfer and the sharing of experience in labour health protection is an area ripe for international – both North-South, South-South, and triangular—cooperation.

Capacity of national and local governments should be strengthened to facilitate the transfer of knowledge and technology, including by exploring and using intellectual property related mechanisms for the benefit of developing countries. The various parts of the United Nations System through the United Nations Development Group should coordinate their efforts to formulate guidance to UN Country Teams on mainstreaming green economic principles into the United Nations Development Assistance Framework and the Regional Coordination Mechanism. National development agencies could be encouraged to do the same. Significant additional financial and technical assistance should be mobilised to support the efforts of Member States to shift their economies towards a green path. To be efficient and coherent, an integrated approach should be adopted when pursuing a green economy. Green investments in transport, renewable energy, tourism and long-term investment in agriculture, for example, should aim to generate environmental and health co-benefits and to expand agriculture and food production.

To ensure that short-term emergency actions do not undermine the longer-term sustainability of interventions, stimulus plans should avoid lock-in to business-as-usual patterns of consumption and production. In addition, a sound monitoring and accounting system is essential. There is a need for a rapid standardization and operationalisation of the System of Environmental-Economic Accounting and additional systems that adequately capture the social and environmental dimensions of economic transformations.

The solidarity of the international community is being tested. Let this economic recovery be the turning point for an ambitious and effective international response to the multiple crises facing humanity. The most representative testing case is when governments meet to seal the deal on climate change in Copenhagen in December 2009. Let Copenhagen be the turning point for ushering in a global green economy.

- The Basel Convention on the Control of Transboundary Movements of Hazardous Wastes and their Disposal (BASEL CONVENTION)
- The Convention on International Trade in Endangered Species of Wild Fauna and Flora (CITES)
- International Labour Organization (ILO)
- International Maritime Organization (IMO)
- United Nations Environment Programme (UNEP)
- United Nations Educational, Scientific and Cultural Organization (UNESCO)

- United Nations (UN)
- UNITED NATIONS Economic Commission for Europe (UNECE)
- UNITED NATIONS Economic and Social Commission for Asia and the Pacific (ESCAP)
- United Nations Framework Convention on Climate Change (UNFCCC)
- United Nations Human Settlements Programme (UN-HABITAT)
- United Nations Industrial Development Organization (UNIDO)
- World Bank Group
- World Intellectual Property Organization (WIPO)
- World Meteorological Organization (WMO)
- World Trade Organization (WTO)
- United Nations World Tourism Organization (UNWTO)

The increase in the cost of a barrel of oil, the development of agro-fuels and international speculation affected Benin through a general increase in the price of basic goods. For example, the price of corn – the most widely consumed product – increased by 220%. Low farm productivity and growing demand led to the over-consumption of locally produced foodstuffs and caused difficulties regarding distribution of these products to consumers' homes. The Government reduced taxes and, through the Office Nationale pour la Sécurité Alimentaire (National Office for Food Security) created buffer stocks – temporary stocks to be used as reserves – that ameliorated the effects of the crisis to some extent, but above all enriched middlemen, who continued to sell at high prices and make large profits at the expense of consumers and the State. The poorer and more vulnerable consumers still have great difficulty in obtaining food and receive few real benefits from the subsidies.

Civil society has carried out awareness-raising campaigns in various inhabited areas regarding the degradation of the mangrove swamps which reduces the productivity of lagoons considerably and threatens this ecosystem. It has also collaborated both as a partner and in liaison with the Government in promoting the means to combat the crisis, the green revolution and food for schools.

BRAZIL THE GOVERNMENT'S TIMID RESPONSE

Although the domestic banking system was not exposed to the kind of speculative investments that hit the financial systems in the United States, Europe and part of Asia, Brazil is paying the price of being integrated into the international economy. In the last quarter of 2008, the GDP fell 3.6% in comparison with the previous quarter. Every sector of the economy contracted, manufacturing being hit the worst, falling more than 7%. In the short term, a still more somber scenario is likely to unfold, with increasing unemployment and social disruption. In case the Government rises to the challenge, Brazil still has a chance of attenuating these risks, but until now the monetary policy has been incompetent and the Federal Government's spending policy has been extremely timid.

As important as it is to stop the economic decline in the short-term, it is even more important to prepare for the future and reset the path of the world economy. Green investments are the next frontier of investment and innovation, promoting environmentally sustainable growth strategies that increase the efficiency in the generation and use of energy. New regulatory and supervisory strategies are to be defined by focusing on how to make financial systems work in the promotion of development and the distribution of income and wealth. The current crisis offers a clear opportunity to attain the effective democratization of international institutions, a chance that cannot be missed.

BURMA THE CRISIS WAS ALREADY THERE

Burma has long been suffering an internal domestic financial crisis. Inflation in basic commodity prices, including food and fuel, led to widespread protests as individuals could no longer afford them and the price increases translated into job losses. The market for consumer or small business credit is functionally non-existent. At its heart, the development of a free market economy in Burma is a myth, and the rights to develop industries within the country are reserved for the ruling junta, their families, and their cronies. The global financial crisis has further worsened the country's economy. The fishing, mining, garment, food processing and advertisement industries, for instance, have all suffered. Burmese living abroad are also financially distressed and thus unable to send as much money back to their families as they had before.

CAMBODIA THE TWO SIDES OF THE GRAIN OF RICE

The price of food and oil skyrocketed in the first semester of 2008 and began dropping slowly in the second semester of the year. The sudden increase in the global price of rice, which has reached 100%, has made some rice surplus traders a handsome profit, but it has seriously affected the food security of 31% of the population (up to 4 million people).

The most vulnerable are those peasants living in the Tonle Sap region, who went into debt just to make ends meet. They had to resort to selling their productive assets, or take their children out of school to help with household income generating activities. The Government has responded with a USD 40 million programme to provide food aid to vulnerable people around the Tonle Sap region.

CANADA OPPORTUNITY LOST

As the recession continues to deepen, reports of job losses in Canada become more frequent and more devastating. The Budget 2009 saw an opportunity for the Federal Government to lessen the blow of the recession by focusing on

Canada's most vulnerable citizens. But, instead of using Government stimulus funds to get a number of things on a better track such as social and gender equality, the reduction of climate change and the improvement of public infrastructure (including soft infrastructure such as heath care and child care), the Government chose to address the crisis by consistently underplaying both the severity and potential duration of the downturn, and treating the stimulus as something that could just get the economy back to normal. Jobs that are being created by Government investments are in male dominated industries, while women are over-represented in part-time and precarious work and are often the first to be laid off. Civil society organizations are concerned that, as Canada focuses on reversing the economic downturn, environmental and sustainability standards will drop.

CHILE AN ECONOMY IN RECESSION

The fall in the international price of commodities has been felt acutely, as the country's economic and trade structure is heavily dependent on the export of a limited range of primary products with low added value. The fall in the price of copper affects the rate of exchange, the terms of trade, the balance of payments and general economic activity. By 2009, in step with similar worldwide tendencies, the Chilean economy entered a recession. The fall in pension fund resources, which are invested in Chilean and foreign financial assets, has affected financial markets, causing a considerable reduction in the population's retirement savings, amounting towards the end of 2008 to a loss of USD 27,000 million, more than 26% of the total resources.

CYPRUS WOMEN OUT OF JOBS

It is gradually occurring that taxes, the State's largest revenue source, are poised to fall dramatically as a result of the shrinking market. This will minimize the Government's flexibility to stimulate public investments and programmes in order to alleviate the negative effects of the crisis. Furthermore, there is persistent low productivity in the public sector, which will reduce the Government's ability to respond promptly and effectively to the rapidly escalating economic crisis. Unavoidably, Cyprus will also have to deal with unemployment, which is expected to rise from 3.9% in 2008 to 4.5% in 2009. Tourism, an industry that employs mainly women, is expected to experience a continued decline in revenues, probably resulting in a large percentage of women losing their jobs.

EL SALVADOR CHANGE COURSE, IMMEDIATELY

The privatization programmes implemented in recent years have resulted in the failure to invest in agricultural production for food security, instead of concentrating on importing basic grains, while trade liberalization policies have led to inflation and decreased purchasing power, thereby weakening the country's capacity to face the worldwide crisis. The national economy, which is intimately dependent on trade with the United States, began to suffer when exports, tourism and family remittances began to drop at the end of 2008. It is estimated that remittances will fall 3% in 2009 and 2010. El Salvador should change course and strengthen the foundations for a sustainable development model that reconstructs agricultural and industrial productive capacity and generates social welfare.

ERITREA BETWEEN HUNGER AND OPPRESSION

Reports from different sources indicate progress in certain areas of the MDGs, such as reducing infant mortality and maternal morbidity. However, the extremely repressive political climate in Eritrea and the impossibility of obtaining reliable data make it difficult to accept these accounts at face value. The reality is that due to the Government's failed economic policies, the national and local economies both had reached a breaking point long before the global financial crisis manifested itself in late 2008, as is evident from the country's miserable ranking on numerous independent reports (which are dismissed as enemy propaganda). To address the economic crisis, and begin to tackle the deep poverty suffered in the country, Eritrea needs to embark on an immediate transition to a democratic system of governance with the support of the international community. Meanwhile, humanitarian aid monitored by independent international NGOs appears to offer the most effective emergency plan to ensure the survival of the poorest members of the population, who are suffering not only from the economic crisis but also from severe political repression.

GERMANY THE UGLY FACE OF DEREGULATION IS BEING REVEALED

It is already clear that the financial crisis will have a major impact on the social welfare of several million Germans. Unemployment is on the rise and the ugly face of deregulation is being revealed. Non-standard employment relationships are the first to go: the number of temporary workers dismissed in recent months, up to and including January 2009, is estimated at around 120,000. The number of jobless might climb, from the current 3.4 million, to almost 4 million before the end of 2009. The real surge, however, has occurred in relation to the category of short-time workers: in February, more than 16,900 companies applied to put 700,000 workers on short time for economic reasons: 648,800 more than the previous year. The austerity policies being carried out in the social sector will continue unabated in the wake of the massive bank bailout, thus possibly setting the course for a further dismantling of the welfare state and for an increase in widespread poverty.

WTO AGENDA

WTO Director general Pascal Lamy in a recent to the organization's General Council has emphasized the following.

1. Trade should be kept open and protectionist measures eschewed. The WTO has asked G-20 countries to strongly support the WTO monitoring mechanism of trade related measures.
2. Try and keep trade open by concluding the tDoha round, the most ambitious multilateral trade deal ever. Although considerable pregress has been achieved after more than eight years of tortuous negotiations, an agreement remains elusive. At a time of a global crisis the differences are likely to be sharper making the task of the negotiators that much more difficult.
3. The WTO, Assian development Bank and other multilateral organization have been stressing the aid for trade agenda. That will enable the poorest countries to invest and improve in productive capacity and participate in the global trading system.
4. Finally, unfreezing trade finance. According to reliable estimates, trade finance fundes some 90 per cent of the global merchandise trade worth $16 trillion. The G-20 countries have earmarked $250 billion towards trade finance over the next two years but that may be too small an amount in the present circumstances.

LOOMING PROTECTIONISM

Two other developments have aggravated the downturn in global trade. Protectionism has emerged as a major threat to trade liberalization not only for now but over the foreseeable future. Voters in many countries have come out against outsourcing and other vehicles of globalization. Political leaders find it convenient to blame other countries for loss of jobs.

Recent developments in the U.S. and other developed countries show how protectionism can creep in through some subtle and not so subtle means.

The proposal to extend the tax net to cover certain activities of U.S. based multinationals out side the country is one such development. A stricter visa regime in the U.S. may discriminate against Indian IT companies. Restrictions have been placed on imports in many countries. In India, the ban on export of food crops is only now being lifted.

Again, many developed countries including the U.K., Switzerland and the Netherlands will ensure that banks recently baled out with tax payers' money confine their lending to domestic borrowers. Instances such as these are bound to multiply if as expected employment levels fall in those countries. Unfortunately an economic recovery will not lift protectionism automatically.

The crisis in world trade has been magnified by the far flung nature of multinational companies and their operations. Raw materials sourced from one country are converted into intermediate goods in another country.

Finished products emerge in third country. Truly globalized industries such as the deeply troubled automobile industry source their requirements from different countries. The pain in one country is automatically transmitted across the globe.

IMPLICATIONS OF UNBRIDLED FINANCIAL GROWTH

In 1972, the study 'the Limits to Grow' by the club of Rome gave the wake up call that there are clear limits to global economic growth. The authors, with the use of computer modeling, drew some ominous conclusions. Within a time span of less than 100 years, the world would run out of the nonrenewable resources like oil, leading to a collapse of the economic system, which can be avoided only by an immediate limit on population and pollution as well as a 'cessation of economic growth'.

There were, of course, others who counter argued that man's ingenuity, aided by science and technology, would make good the depletion of resources and the damage caused to the environment. However, international opinion turned out to be on the side of caution as underscored by the United Nations Conference on the Human Environment, which met at Stockholm in June 1972.

The reasoning, in simple terms, ran like this. The pre-agriculture economy, which was based on subsistence and barter, was resources - friendly. Later, agricultural economy prospered on a combination of labour and seemingly endless economy brought in physical capital (inventions of machinery and tools) as well as financial capital (money, banking, joint stock companies etc) and modern economy added organization (capital markets, exchange markets multinationals etc).

All through these changes, which occurred over several millennia, man assumed that land and its resources were inexhaustible, notwithstanding the damages caused by wars, revolutions, population growth and the unprecedented post-war prosperity.

THREAT FOR ECOLOGY

The study, the limits to growth and the Stockholm conference, exposed not only the possibility of resources depletion but also the looming crisis for human environment and ecology. It took 20 more years for the world to fully realize the threat facing mankind and get into action.

The Rio conference of 2002, popularly known as Earth summit, brought the international community together to institute action on various fronts such as combating climate change, conservation of biodiversity, energy, etc. ironically, around the same tome that the world was woken up to the possibility of limits to economic growth, the global financial growth was unshaked from its traditional, time-tested moorings. The oil crises of the 1970s and their aftermath brought to end financial growth, both economies, all in the name of market efficacy.

As countries the world over switched to the floating exchange rates after decades of fixed rates, the foreign exchange market began to grow by leaps and bounds. In the United States alone, forex transactions leaped from 10.7 per cent of the GDP in 1970 to 195.3 per cent within a decade.

Similarly, between 1980 and 2008, the size of the world stock markets is estimated to have swelled from about$3 trillion to over $35 trillion, most of which are said to be speculative nature. The world derivatives market again is estimated at about $480 trillion face or nominal value, 12 times the size of the entire world economy.

WHITHER REAL GROWTH

This kind of financial leveraging appears to have reached incredible levels in the current global meltdown. According to the latest McKinsey report, the current debt levels amount to more than three tomes the GDP in the United States and Europe, where historically they have been around 150 to 200 per cent.

The implications of unbridled financial growth can only be awesome. The world is being run out on dept, which is untenable, 'Can swelling be muscle? Can debt be money?" goes an ancient tribal proverb. Instead of being a catalyst or the sinews has become an end in itself.

The consequences of financial growth running far ahead of real growth are already blatant. Income differentials have been skewed both within and across nations, not only widening the chasm between the haves and have notes but also leading to a colossal waste in the name of consumerism.

The real economy based on agriculture, manufacturing and services has been undermined and neglected. The unprecedented surge in money and capital and their free flow across economies have globalised money laundering fuelling terrorism and many other anti social activities.

A Core Agenda for Disinvestments in India – Recent Developments

*T. Sridhar**

INTRODUCTION

If reports are anything to go by, the public sector disinvestments programme is up and running . Not a day passes without some news pertaining to public sector sale.

The budget and the Economic survey that preceded it have vetted the appetite for a programme that had come to a halt during the tenure of the first UPA government. The budget underplayed what the government would do during the current year. Only Rs. 1120 crore is expected through the sale of public sector enterprises.

FINANCIAL SCENE

Finance Minister Pranab Mukherjee in his budget speech, however, laid down the contours, as it were, for the revival of the disinvestments programme.

BLUEPRINT INDICATED

In his speech Mr. Mukherjee talked of divesting PSE shares with the main objective of widespread shareholder participation (the wealth of the nation should at least partly rest with the people) the government would retain at least 51 per cent equity in the PSEs, government banks and insurance companies would remain in the public sector and the government would provide all support including capital infusion, he had said.

A few days before the budget, the Economic Survey had made a visionary statement The suggested objectives included.

1. Revitalise the disinvestments programme to generate atleast Rs. 25000 crore a year.

* Associate Professor in Economics, National College, Trichy-1, Tamilnadu

2. Complete the process of selling 5-10 per cent equity in previously identified non Navratnas.
3. List all unlisted public sector enterprises and sell a minimum of 10 per cent of their equity to the public.
4. Auction all loss making PSEs that cannot be revived.
5. For those in which net worth is zero, allow negative bidding in the form of debt write off.

FM'S REALISTIC STAND

It is evident that while the survey has a medium-term programme in mind where it would be possible to under take disinvestments routinely, the Finance Minister is much more guarded and, though criticized for not being bold enough, is realistic.

Public sector disinvestments is the art of the possible. There is no point in setting ambitious targets in the budget when there is very little chance of executing the plan without raking up controversies. A disinvestments programme is controversial to begin with (this applies to most other countries too). The success of the programme ought to be viewed over the medium term.

For public policy, the process of disinvestments us much more important than any particular transaction. Neither should the achievement of specific targets including budgetary ones have anything budgetary ones have anything more than short-term significance. The occurrence of several fortuitous circumstances makes for the success or failure of particular PSE sale. Stock markets, for instance have been fickle, to say the least and can never be taken for granted.

LACK OF CONTINUITY

Unfortunately political compulsions have prevented successive governments from ensuring continuity in the disinvestments exercise. It may be argued that a political consensus is difficult to arrive at but it should be possible to separate the really controversial aspects from the core agenda.

The previous UPA government downgraded the programme and the commission appointed by the NDA government. It also abolished the ministry. The motivations were largely political.

While restarting the programme the present government does not have access to the wealth of information and precedents that a continuously run programme would have generated. Also, disinvestments takes a long time to be successfully completed. The disinvestments Commission in one of its Key recommendations wanted PSEs to be corporatised before their shares were offered to the public. One lesson that all governments have learnt is that programmes like these yield sub-optimal results if they are turned on and off at will.

Political does decide the outcomes of disinvestment policies. With a determined ideological opposition it was not possible for the previous government to achieve anything of consequence. Even so, it should have been possible to work out a core agenda that would meet with acceptance from as many political parties as possible acoss the political spectrum.

Such an agenda should include a clear understanding of what the disinvestments programme can do. For instance.

A clear understanding that disinvestments of the day will not lead to privatization. The Finance Minister has categorically said that the government will keep control by holding on to at least a 51 per cent stake. Banks and insurance companies now in the government fold will remain so. A commitment on those lines and the government's resolve to maintain it is necessary for the programme to get started at this juncture. It is not that privatization or strategic sale has no place in the disinvestments scheme. It is simple that they will not be acceptable.

Arriving at correct valuations in public sector sale programmes has been the most controversial. Thee is a need for universally acceptable methods to value a PSE but they remain accounting concepts unable to satisfy critics. In any case, a step by step disinvestments programme may not fetch the same price as a big bang privatization would, incidentally even when PSEs start listing and offer their shares to the public it does not follow that the government will collect the proceeds. It is only when the government unloads its stake that it can lay claim to the proceeds. A PSE can make a fresh issue but the sale proceeds would not go to the government.

CONCLUSION

It is too much to hope but there is at least a case for the better informed among political leaders to reach a consensus over the pricing. With stock markets being erratic the price that a particular tranche of a PSE sale gets ay be vastly different from what it gets when made at different stages or by comparable entities at the same time. Unfortunately politicians out of power will invariably find fault with valuations especially those fixed by the markets.

Reference

Daniels, Les (1998), Superman: The Complete History (1st ed.). Titan Books. p. 11. ISBN 1-85286-988-7.

Bartels, L. M. (2008), Unequal Democracy: The Political Economy of the New Gilded Age. Princeton, NJ: Princeton University Press

Henderson, David R. (1998), "The Rich—and Poor—Are Getting Richer". Hoover Digest.

Kenworthy, L. (1999), "Do Social-Welfare Policies Reduce Poverty? A Cross-National Assessment" Social Forces 77(3), 1119–1139.

Bradley, D., E. Huber, S. Moller, F. Nielsen, and J. D. Stephens (2003), "Determinants of Relative Poverty in Advanced Capitalist Democracies", *American Sociological Review,* 68(1), 22–51.

Richardson, Benjamin J. (2008), Socially Responsible Investment Law: Regulating the Unseen Polluters (Oxford University Press, 2008).

Harrington, Cynthia (2003), "Socially Responsible Investing." Journal of Accountancy. January 2003, 1-11

Dimensions of Indian Economy – Some Myths and Realities

T. Sridhar[*]

INTRODUCTION

Any setback in agriculture may be offset by industry, services. The Outlook for the economy in 2009-10 has got clouded by the erratic behaviour of the monsoon. Himachal Pradesh, Punjab, Haryana and Western Uttar Pradesh had deficient rainfall till the middle of July. Drought conditions prevail in all the districts of Assam while several districts in West Bengal and Madhya Pradesh had deficit rainfall. However, copious rainfall is expected in August and even in September.

There may not thus be a significant decline in the output of food and cash crops in the 2009- 10 agricultural season. In some quarters it is feared that overall production may drop by 10 per cent, mainly in rice as Punjab and Haryana are large producers of the fine cereal. Procurement operations have been successful with over 50 per cent purchased at the enhanced minimum support price. With satisfactory procurement in other regions as well the aggregate quantity acquired out of the 2008-09 crops has set a new record. This has been helped by a record output of rice at 99.15 million tones and wheat at 80.58 million tones.

HOPES ON FARM FRONT

It is now anticipated that there may not be a setback in 2009-10 though experts are more cautious and expect a decline in total output by more than 10 per cent to 220 million tones. The rice content will be significantly lower but will be offset to some extent by higher yields of coarse cereals and pulses. Latest reports show vigorous rainfall in some parts of Madhya Pradesh and Gujarat while meteorological experts forecast bountiful rainfall in August and even in September. The actual outcome may not thus be as disappointing as feared in some quarters.

[*] Associate Professor in Economics, National College, Trichy-1, Tamilnadu

Consumers will not however be affected much thanks to the record corp of 233.88 million tones in 2008-09 and two good yields earlier. With larger crops of fine cereals procurement of wheat has been gratifying at 25 million tones and rice at 32 million tones so far in the marketing season ending in September.

HUGE BUFFER STOCKS

Even allowing for a larger off take through fair price shops and under various welfare programes buffer stocks are still around 56 million tones.

These stood at 36.16 million tones in July 2008 – the peak was 63 million tones in July 2002. The off take of around 36 million tones in 2009-10 can be easily met even if procurement out of current season's crops does not exceed 35 million tones. In 2006-07 when the output was 217.3 million tones the quantity of rice and wheat procured was 34.31 million tones.

Any rise in prices in the open market later this year due to speculative activity can be countered through sales of food grains from buffer stocks. It will of course be necessary to import pulse on a larger scale if they can be secured advantageously from neighbouring countries. Even now some pulse are unduly expensive while there has been an inexplicable rise in prices of some pulses are unduly expensive while there has been an inexplicable rise in prices of some varieties of rice. A clear picture will emerge after September when it will also be possible to assess the rabi prospects precisely.

LESS DEPRESSING EXPORTS

He experience on the foreign trade front may be different this year. Details for April –May of course have not been encouraging though the Union Minister of Commerce and Industry has observed signs of improvement. Tangible benefits may also be derived by importers, if the rupee tends to appreciate against the greenback henceforth with a larger net forex inflow.

The bridging of the trade gap in 2008-09 could not have been managed but for the large foreign exchange reserves. The current account deficit increased to $29.82 billion in 2007-08 even with a rise in invisible receipts by nearly $ 15 billion.

This was because the trade gap was higher by $27.78 billion. It was necessary to draw down reserves to the extent of $20.08 billion as net additions to assets on capital account were only $9.74 billion.

Developments in the industrial sector have of course been heartening. Industrial output rose by 1.2 per cent in April and 2.7 per cent in May with better performance of all industries other than export segments.

The rise in general index for April – May was 1.9 per cent while a negative trend was noted under this head since last October and the rise for the whole year was only 3.4 per cent against 8.5 per cent . The uptrend this year has been in evidence in June as well.

The growth in GDP may not thus be adversely affected by any likely setback in the agriculture sector, as the services sector too has been functioning profitably and growth in exports of software and other services may be impressive. The GDP is thus likely to rise by 7-7.5 per cent and by 8-9 per cent in 2010-11 and subsequent years. The developments in the external sector have recently been favourable and the efforts to increase two way trade with many important countries may yield tangible results.

ACTIVE BOURSES

The stock markets have therefore been quite active in recent weeks. There are indications of large inflows of FII funds and reserves accretions may be sizable in the coming months with a steady rise also in the value of the Indian currency, though at a slower pace than in 2007-08.

The borrowing programmes in 2008-09 could be put through than as to the surplus resources in various pockets. Banks could increase their deposits in the twelve months ended July 3 by Rs. 724678 crore against Rs. 585449 crore.

However, expansion of back credit was less pronounced at Rs. 393148 crore Fresh investments were therefore higher by as much as Rs. 319728 crore .

This performance cannot be repeated in 2009-10 as there is an ambitious programme of expanding agricultural credit. There may also be a keen demand for funds from industry and trade. It may thus be necessary for the Finance Ministry to raise resources even in forex terms for avoiding the emergence of unduly stringent conditions in the money market.

CONCLUSION

Since the borrowing programme of the State and the Central Government may not have smooth sailing the objective should be to provide then necessary incentives for entrepreneurs in the private sector and also for ensuring faster additions to forex reserves by FII and other foreign interest.

Reference

Datt, Ruddar & Sundharam, K.P.M. (2005), "2". Indian Economy, S. Chand. pp. 15–16, ISBN 81-219-0298-3.

Sankaran, S (1994), "3". Indian Economy: Problems, Policies and Development. Margham Publications. p. 50. ISBN.

Kumar, Dharma (Ed.), "1". The Cambridge Economic History of India (Volume 2). pp. 32–35

Kumar, Dharma (Ed.) (1982), The Cambridge Economic History of India (Volume 2) c. 1757-c. 1970. Penguin Books.

Bharadwaj, Krishna (1991), "Regional Differentiation in India", In Sathyamurthy, T.V. (ed.). Industry & Agriculture in India Since Independence. Oxford University Press. pp. 189–199. ISBN 0-19-564394-1.

Datt, Ruddar & Sundharam, K.P.M.. "50". *Indian Economy*. pp. 847–850.

Datt, Ruddar & Sundharam, K.P.M.. "50". *Indian Economy*. pp. 850–851.

Kelegama, Saman and Parikh, Kirit (2000), *Political Economy of Growth and Reforms in South Asia*

Sam Staley (2006), "The Rise and Fall of Indian Socialism: Why India Embraced Economic Reform".

Role of Black Money in Swiss Bank and Its Impact on Indian Economy

P. N. Raghunathan[*]

INTRODUCTION

Definition

"The sum total of transaction deliberately kept out of the books of accounts by household and business in the economy"

As some economist put it, "Black money is nothing but any transaction which is conducted without regard to taxation, regulation or law of trade." Here are some breath-taking facts about the Indian black market:

1. India's black money economy is ranked fifth highest at \$22bn-\$27bn a year, coming in behind Russia (\$32bn- \$38bn), Mexico (\$41bn-\$46bn), Saudi Arabia (\$54bn-\$55bn) and China (\$233bn-\$289bn).
2. The black economy is currently estimated to be 50% of India's gross domestic produce (GDP).
3. Personal account deposits in the bank, which have been misappropriated, are to the tune of \$1,500 billion in foreign reserve, an amount 13 times larger than the country's foreign debt.
4. Black money possession and use is only concentrated in a thin slab of 3% of the Indian public.

In another word Black money may be defined as the money that is generated by activities that are kept secret in the sense that these are not reported to the authorities. As such this money is also not accounted to the fiscal authorities i.e., taxes are not paid on this money. Contrasted to this is the white money that is shown in relevant accounts and tax paid, if due. Parallel economy connotes the functioning of an unsanctioned sector in the economy whose

* Professor cum Director, Department of Management Studies, Jawaharlal Institute of Technology, Kaliyapuram, Coimbatore-641 105, (*E-mail: pnragu@yahoo.com*)

objectives run parallel, rather in contradiction with the aroused social objectives. This is variously termed as 'black economy', 'unaccounted economy', 'illegal economy', 'subterranean economy', or 'unsanctioned economy'.

Black money runs the black market and generates taxable income that taxpayers do not report in order to evade taxes to the Income Tax Department of India. It is the heart and soul of the underground economy and often called No. 2 money.

It exists in many countries: In rich nations like Belgium, Italy, and Spain; in poor nations like Haiti and Nepal; in developing nations like Indonesia, the Philippines, and Thailand.

History

The period 1946-61 was one of the intense creativity. A black or parallel economy emerged both in the wake of the Second World War and the expansion of the economic activity in the post-independence period. Incentives were provided through the taxation laws to promote savings and investment; this made the tax laws more complex. Then, there was the need for larger revenues to finance the plans of economic development. Thorough investigations were, therefore, conducted into the structure of taxation not only with a view to widen the base of income tax but also to look for new taxes and to prevent tax evasion and avoidance. The Income-tax administration came under heavy strain due to the increase in the volume and complexity of its work.

NATURE

There are two powerful ethical props for a different view than the one the court has taken.

1. It is a plain fact that many high-earning persons evade income tax by ruthlessly exploiting the loopholes in the laws. Black money is the outcome of this practice. And neither the income tax department has mounted an effective campaign to hunt out these tax cheats, nor has the court, any court, felt provoked to order a comprehensive crackdown.
2. The widespread ruse of doling out big money to top executives and others by describing it as reimbursement.

Constituent Activities of Black Economy

1. Legal activities that are not reported to the tax authorities and the income which goes untaxed and unreported. For instance: it is not illegal to clean someone\\\'s house, to feed people or to drive them. It is, however, illegal to hide the income generated by these activities and not to pay tax on it. In most countries of the world, this is a criminal offence, punishable by years in prison.
2. Illegal activities, which needless to say, are also not reported to the state (and, therefore, not taxed). The money generated by these activities is

largely held in foreign exchange outside the banking system or smuggled abroad (even through the local banking system).

Sources of Black Money

A parallel or a black market is an illegal structure that is created in response to government intervention, which produces excess supply or demand for a product. When the price of foreign currency is set below the market-clearing rate, an excess demand is usually generated for acquiring foreign currency. The government has the choice of either devaluating the currency, or maintaining strict controls over exchange, such as setting quotas on the purchase of foreign exchange. Such currency controls are designed by governments in order to limit the use of foreign exchange in transactions. This parallel economy, or black market, emerges through the manipulation of the economic forces of supply and demand for both currency and commodities. A black market also emerges when trade and industry create an artificial situation of scarcity or glut, and in the process amass high returns on their investments by profiteering. As a result of profiteering activity, the black market generates unreported income and wealth, which escape detection by official statistics. Much of the strength of the black market can be attributed to the resale of officially allocated foreign exchange holdings and to the incentive to under invoice and smuggle exports. He argues that an increase in the black market rate, given the official exchange rate, creates an incentive for residents abroad to channel their remittances through the black market. This raises their private receipts in terms of home currency and deprives the central bank of this foreign exchange. Economists studying black market activity in developing countries advocate that it is best to keep the black market premium rate as low as possible. By influencing the determinants of the black market exchange rate, developing counties can keep the black market premium rate low and increase their official foreign exchange currency holdings.

There are several factors responsible for the emergence - of black money. It would be relevant to discuss those factors so that a correct understanding about the genesis, growth and expansion of black money can be made. The principal factors are:

(i) *Beginning of the evil:* The beginning of this evil can be traced to the Second World War. During this period supplies of industrial goods from the traditional suppliers of the West were cut off. This resulted in severe shortages in many vital lines. The British Government indulged in large inflationary finance for war efforts. This led to price escalation. Taxes too were raised sharply on higher incomes and excess profits. In these circumstances many indulged in black marketing. And at the same time, they evaded taxes. Huge profits were made in respect of goods that were in short supply. This created a psychology of making money out of shortages and not out of production/expansion of sales. These circumstances and the psychology formed the backdrop of what followed subsequently.

(ii) *Controls and licensing system:* The system of controls, permits, quotas and licenses which are associated with misdistributions of the commodities in short supply results in the generation of black money. The Wanchoo Committee explaining this factor as a source of black money observed, "In spite of the vigilance exercised by the Government, controls and regulations came to be used by the unscrupulous for amassing money for themselves. Since considerable discretionary powers lay in the hands of those who administered controls~ this provided them with a scope for corruption - 'speed money' for turning a blind eye to the violation of controls. All this gave rise to trading in permits, quotas and licenses, malpractices in distribution and in the process; it generated sizeable sums of black money."

Price and distribution controls have in the past led to the generation of black money on a significant scale. Any price control without any adequate machinery of distribution and speedy arrangement for increasing supplies is potentially a source of black money generation.

Rent control leads to *"pugree system"* and is, therefore, another source of black money. Similarly, the system of licenses requires large number of inspectors for completing various formalities and thus good amount of hush money has to be paid. Where controls are not implementable, they have led to harassment and black money generation.

(iii) *Tax structure:* High tax rates and defective tax structure have also been responsible for the existence of black money to a large extent. Take for instance direct taxation. Till recently the tax on income and on wealth was very high to invite evasion. The marginal rate of income tax was as high as 75 per cent. And when it was combined with the tax on wealth, it was still higher. For example, for a person with net wealth of Rs. 12 lakh, the combined tax rate came to 95 per cent. And for a person with a net wealth exceeding Rs. 18 lakhs, the marginal tax rate exceeded cent per cent. This was the situation in respect of personal taxation until a decade ago. The corporate tax rate too was very high. In these circumstances the temptation /gain from tax evasion was substantial.

Even in the case of indirect taxes the situation is no better. In fact worse, as the revenue from these taxes constitute a big proportion of all the tax revenues. For example, in the case of government, revenue from customs and central excise duties has been as much as 80 per cent of the total revenue. Hence even a small fraction of the evaded tax runs into crores of black money. According to the National Institute of Public Finance Policy the excise evasion is rampant in such sectors as copper, cotton fabrics and plastics. It is also suggested by the Institute that the tax-evasion through the underestimation of production and sales is most pronounced in manufacturing, trade, hotels and restaurants.

(iv) *Donation to political parties:* Ever since the Government decided to ban donations to political parties in 1968, it prompted businessmen to fund political parties, especially the ruling party, with the help of black money. Ostensibly, this decision was taken to reduce the influence of big business on the electoral process, but in practice what happened was precisely the opposite. Businessmen everywhere have by now learnt that they should pay a certain charge out of the black money to the coffers of political parties and then be sure that the political leaders will only bark but not bite. Big business, in the process, has been able to tame the political leadership. This is evidenced by the relaxation of various controls, permitting business houses to enter areas reserved for the public sector, putting a large number of banned items on the Open General License list etc.

The political instability witnessed in the country in -various states has resulted in widespread horse-trading of the MLAs at the state levels and MPs at the Central level. In this process of buying political support, black money plays a crucial role. Consequently the determination of the ruling political party to curb black money has become very weak. As a consequence, businessmen feel they have an unfettered license to spin black money, pay a small part to the political parties as donations and then enjoy the rest the way they like. Unless the link between black money and political power is broken, there is no hope of controlling the generation of black money or its link with crime.

(v) *Ineffective enforcement of tax laws:* Whereas the Government has an armory of tax laws pertaining to income tax, sales tax, stamp duties, excise duty etc., their enforcement is very weak due to widespread corruption in these departments. The high rates of these taxes induce businessmen to avoid recording of these transactions. This evasion largely goes unchecked and thus sets in a chain reaction for the generation of black money at the wholesale, retail as well as production levels.

(vi) *Generation of black money in the public sector:* Every successive five-year plan is planned for a larger size of investment in the public sector. The projects undertaken by the public sector have to be monitored by the bureaucrats in Government departments and public sector undertakings. Tenders are invited for the various works and these tenders are awarded by the bureaucracy in consultation with the political bosses.

Thus, a symbiotic relationship develops between the contractors, bureaucracy and the politicians and by a large number of devices costs 'are artificially escalated and black money is generated by underhand deals. Instability of the political system has given a further momentum to this process. Since the ministers are not sure of their tenure and in a majority of cases, the tenure is very short, the principle 'Make hey while the sun shines' is adopted by most of them. The larger numbers of scandals that are unearthed by the Opposition only support the contention that huge investment in the public sector is a big potential source for black money generation. In this process, bureaucrats act as brokers for political leaders and thus the nexus between business, bureaucracy and politicians promotes the generation of black money.

(vii) *Ceiling on depreciation and other business expenses:* Government has imposed restriction. It has also circumscribed expenses on advertisement, entertainment, guest houses, and payment of perquisites to directors. The purpose of these restrictions is to protect the shareholders and consumers from the unscrupulous action of businessmen. But businessmen feel that these restrictions are unjustified. They take the maximum advantage of these provisions but do not like to part with the remaining part of by various clandestine devices; they convert it into black money and use it either for conspicuous production to satisfy the wants of the rich and elite sections of society.

OTHER SOURCES OF BLACK MONEY:

1. Evasion of taxation in various forms
   (a) Personal income
   (b) Corporate tax
2. Real estate transaction
3. Excise duty evasion
4. Customs duty evasion (import)
5. Evasion of sales tax
6. Smuggling
7. From exports
8. From public expenditure
9. From private corporate investors
10. Film industry.
11. Professional income.
12. Construction (both private and public)
13. Selling of licenses and permits
14. *Others:* gambling, bribes, high level corruption, financial transaction, HAWALA, prizing, coaching classes etc..

WHAT DO THE PEOPLE DO WITH BLACK MONEY?

Black money owners try to get rid of their bad money rapidly in many ways: by purchasing real estate, jewelry, gold, automobiles, paintings, expensive clothes and accessories, and so on; by parking it in overseas banks; by traveling abroad; by giving it to politicians for election. They cannot afford to hide money because tax collectors may confiscate it. They purchase products or services so fast that sometimes prices of things they buy remain artificially high.

Causes of Black Economy

1. High rates of taxation
2. Corruption business practice
3. Stringent controls and regulations in income tax proceedings
4. Political corruption
5. Bureaucratic corruption
6. Prohibited trade like liqure, illegal drugs etc.,
7. Manipulation of Public expenditure
8. Political funding as development funds for the party and donations
9. Increasing inflation
10. Deficiency of taxation system (based on party charisma and attract vote bank)
11. Inadequacy of power to the tax authorities
12. Ineffective enforcement of tax law
13. Lack of publicity of persons of black money.
14. Black markets
15. Demonstration effect.

ROLE OF BLACK MONEY IN SWISS BANK

This is so shocking... If black money deposits was an Olympics event. India would have won a gold medal hands down. The second best Russia has 4 times lesser deposit. U.S. is not even there in the counting in top five! India has more money in Swiss banks than all the other countries combined!

Recently, due to international pressure, the Swiss government agreed to disclose the names of the account holders only if the respective governments formally asked for it. India is not a poor country by seeking the following details one can come to know the reality. With personal account deposit bank of $1,500 billion in foreign reserve which have been misappropriated, an amount 13 times larger than the country's foreign debt. Just read the following details and note how these dishonest industrialists, scandalous politicians, corrupt officers, cricketers, film actors, illegal trade and protected wildlife operators, to name just a few, sucked this country's wealth and prosperity. This may be the picture of deposits in Swiss banks only. DISHONEST INDUSTRIALISTS, scandalous politicians and corrupt IAS, IRS, IPS officers have deposited in foreign banks in their illegal personal accounts a sum of about $1500 billion, which have been misappropriated by them. This amount is about 13 times larger than the country's foreign debt. With this amount 45 crore poor people can get Rs. 1,00,000 each. This huge amount has been appropriated from the people of India by exploiting and betraying them. Once this huge amount of black money and property comes back to India, the entire foreign debt can be repaid in 24 hours. After paying the entire foreign debt, we will have surplus amount, almost 12 times larger than the foreign debt. If this surplus amount is invested in earning interest, the amount of interest will be more than the annual budget of the Central government. So even if all the taxes are abolished, then also the Central government will be able to maintain the country very comfortably. Some 80,000 people travel to Switzerland every year, of which 25,000 travel very frequently. 'Obviously, these people won't be tourists. They must be travelling there for some other reason,' believes an official involved in tracking illegal money.. And, clearly, he isn't referring to the commerce ministry bureaucrats who've been flitting in and out of Geneva ever since the World Trade Organisation (WTO) negotiations went into a tailspin! Black money in Swiss banks - Swiss Banking Association report, 2006 details bank deposits in the territory of Switzerland by nationals of following countries:

Top Five

INDIA	$1,456 BILLION
RUSSIA	$470 BILLION
U.K.	$390 BILLION
UKRAINE	$100 BILLION
CHINA	$96 BILLION

BLACK MONEY IN INDIA

It is said that black money in India accounts for 20% of GDP. If this is true, then black money generated every year must be around Rs 400,000 crore or $ 80 billion. This is a huge amount, more than the entire budget of the government at the Centre. We have a government that spends about Rs. 350,000 crore a year, most of it on itself, and asks for accounts of every paisa. On the other side, we have black money worth Rs. 400,000 crore every year, which is just guesswork, and there are no accounts. This money goes into property, which is why real estate prices are so high, and of course five-star hotels. If the government could have all this money, or even a small fraction, there would be no need for revenue or fiscal deficits, and no need for huge borrowings to make two ends meet.

How big is $ 100 billion? It is bigger than you think. It is worth Rs. 500,000 crore, which makes it bigger than the central budget. It is more than twice our annual exports. It is equivalent to 30 times what Enron is supposed to have invested on its Dabhol project. It is more than what the US government is expected to pay those who have suffered from the September 11th smash. And, if you must know, it is a fifth of our annual GDP, which is itself a big figure.

Here are some estimates: Social Scientist wrote in its issue of August 1972 that according to Wanchoo Committee nearly Rs. 1400 crore were unreported in 1968-69 to evade tax and as a result of this evasion, tax revenue of Rs. 470 crore were lost for that year. In the Illustrated Weekly of India of October 25, 1981, Nani Palkhiwala, a former ambassador to the United States, cited an estimate that each year Indian economy generated nearly Rs. 12,000 crore of black money. The National Institute of Public Finance and Policy ranged it to be between Rs. 31,584 crore and Rs. 36,786 crore during 1983-84. As recent as year 2008, Indian newspapers reported that Rs. 70,00,000 crore are in Switzerland banks – it couldn't be all black. No one knows the accuracy of any of these statistics, but they are mind-boggling and show that black money is growing. Also, the estimates of the underground economy as a percentage of GDP vary considerably.

Poonam Gupta and Sanjeev Gupta wrote in Economic and Political Weekly of January 16, 1982 that for the year 1967-68 the black economy "constituted 9.5 per cent of the official GNP... however, by 1978-79 the amount had jumped to nearly half of the official GNP." Since then some economists have estimated that unreported economy grew from 20 per cent of GDP in 1980s to 40 per cent in mid 1990s. Again, no one knows the accuracy of any of these statistics, but they show that the underground economy is booming.

In 2006, the most recent Global Financial Integrity study, developing countries lost an estimated $858.6 billion (about Rs. 43 lakh crore) to $1.06 trillion (abot Rs. 51 lakh crore) in illicit financial outflows. Even at the lower end of the range of estimates, the volume of illicit financial flows coming out of developing countries increased at a compound rate of 18.2 per cent over the five-year period analysed for the study. On average, for the five-year period of this study, Asia accounts for approximately 50 per cent of overall illicit financial flows from all developing countries.

This report shows that the average amount stashed away from India annually during 2002-06 is $27.3 billion (about 136,466 crore). It means that during the five-year period the amount stashed away is 27.3x5=136.5 billion (about 692,328 crore). It is not that all these amounts went to Swiss banks. It has gone to different tax and secret shelters. The share of Swiss banks in dirty money being a third of the global aggregate, some $45 billion out of the 136.5 billion stashed away from India would have been hoarded in these years in Swiss banks.

The important point is that this is only for five years. More amounts were stashed away during the Nehruvian regime. So the loot for 55 years will be several times higher. In fact, in those days the rupee commanded a better value per dollar. So fewer rupee could get more dollars. So the estimation that the Indian money stashed away may be of the order of $1.4 trillion (about Rs. 71 lakh crore).

IMPACT OF BLACK MONEY

The circulation of black money has adversely affected the Indian economy in several ways. It would be of interest to study the impact of black money on the Indian economic and social system.

(i) It leads to the misdirection of precious national resources.

A part of black money is kept in a form that contributes nil/Little to productive activities.

(ii) It has enormously worsened the income-distribution, and has thereby undermined the fabric of the fixed income salary class finds itself ever be the lower rung of the income-ladder. They pay taxes. Quite a number among them, though not the corrupt activities of getting bribes/ commissions, etc. But in general they are not able to catch up with the people in business, or in professions, or many of those employed. Many in these categories make black activities. Many high placed official and honest employees earn much less than an average small shopkeeper in big cities like Bombay and Delhi.

(iii) The existence of a big-sized unreported segment of the economy is a- big handicap in making a correct analysis and formulation of right policies for it. For example it is not possible to calculate accurately the vital indicators of progress like saving-income ratio, sectorial composition of national income, etc. Nor is it possible to monitor the developments in the economy with precision. Much of these estimates/ monitoring of the economy are bound to be guesswork. No wonder the government's policies cannot be firm in their perception and deal weak data base.

(iv) Black money results in transfer of funds from India to foreign countries through clandestine channels. Such transfers are made possible by violations exchange regulations through the device of under - invoicing of exports and over-invoicing of imports thus finds itself in a paradoxical situation,' where capital and more particularly foreign exchange resources are scarce, (the country) becomes a de facto lender of aid and capital to economically advanced and wealthier nations, with the concealed outflow of funds." The situation has worsened further over the years.

(v) Black money requires for its protection, proliferation and expansion of a service organisation composed of musclemen, touts and brokers to combat the forces of law and order on the one hand and on the other hand, there are income t ax advisers, or chartered accountants in the pay of black money operators. Then there are contact men, better known as liaison officers who negotiate favors from top bureaucracy and political bosses through bribes of black money. This has developed a new black money culture in the business world.

(vi) Last but not the least; black money has corrupted our political system in a most vicious manner. At various levels, MLAs, MPs, Ministers, party functionaries openly and shamelessly go on collecting funds.

EFFECTS OF BLACK MONEY ON INDIAN ECONOMY

- Affects public revenues,
- Degenerates the investable surplus,
- Delimits the national productivity,
- Drains the balance of payments,
- Distorts equity and equality concepts of economic distribution.

HAWALA SCAM – Financing Illegal Trade: What makes the illegal market prosper is the large amount of black money that is easily accessible to traders. Thus money can be transferred to any country of the world through the illegal money market. The existence of a massive black economy consisting of both domestic and foreign currency makes such trade possible. Illegal trade is financed either by high value precious metals like gold and silver or by liquid money through a network of unauthorised moneylenders. In the former case gold is smuggled physically and then converted into the desired currency. However gold smuggling is risky and a preferred mode is through the illegal money market. The uniqueness of this system is that there is no physical transfer of currency. This mechanism referred to as the hawala in India, the hundi in Bangladesh and the chit fund in Sri Lanka operates on the same principles.

BLACK MONEY AND INFLATION

Black money is harming our national economy and we have achieved an economic growth rate of five per cent per annum whereas the economy should have grown at the rate of eight per cent in order to make up for the rising population pressures and infrastructural development requirements. Black money is the chief inhibiting factor in the process of national economic development.

The menace of black money has also increased the rich poor divide. The poor families are unable to afford even the square meals whereas the rich and the neo-rich are enjoying the luxuries of life. The Indian society has become poorer. Only the few sections of the society, which account for fifteen per cent of the total population, have been able to enjoy the highest standards of living in this subcontinent. Therefore, the real poverty has increased and not decreased over a period of fifty years. The black money menace started during the seventies and it is now at its peak and the masses have suffered due to rising prices, inflation in business, poor exports and industrial recession. The rich few, however, have not felt the heat and continue to lead luxurious lives at the cost of their poor countrymen. It has connotation for which you have to exercise care and caution by utilizing your brain for converting a portion of black money or the entire money by converting into white money on a piece meal basis. In this form, you will be able to avoid the rigors of economic measures including taxation.

Black money could be curbed only through the strict efforts of the state and this is for the benefit of the masses as well. We should disclose our real incomes and must pay taxes regularly. We should avoid unhealthy means of making money. The nation must get out of the evil net of black money. Only the honest Indians could save the nation.

Even after 40 years of independence, our country is faced with poverty and numerous economic ills. Even though socialistic pattern of society has been accepted in the constitution, our country is far away from socialism and her economy is in the grip of private enterprises. In fact, India has unlicensed economy which has given birth to corruption, inflation and black money. The concept of mixed economy has been harmful to both private and public enterprises. It has jeopardized our economy and hit the common man below the belt. The poor man has been becoming poorer and rich richer just because of the economic ills like inflation and black money. Black money which runs a parallel currency in wealth which is made overnight in violation of the rules and provisions stipulated by the state and a collusion with the state officials does not go unchecked. This kind of money is earned setting aside all human and moral values.

ADVANTAGES

The black economy has many more important functions:

- The black economy is a cash economy.
- It is liquid and fast.
- It increases the velocity of money.
- It injects much needed foreign exchange into the economy and inadvertently increases the effective money supply and the resulting money aggregates.
- It fosters economic activity and employs people.
- It encourages labour mobility and international trade. Black economy, in short, is very positive. With the exception of illegal activities, it does everything that the official economy does and, usually, more efficiently.

The black economy is especially important in times of economic hardships. Countries in transition are a private case of emerging economies, which are a private case of developing countries that are called (in less politically correct times) \\\"Third World Countries\\\". They suffer from all manner of acute economic illnesses. They lose their export markets, they are technologically backward, their unemployment skyrockets, their plant and machinery are dilapidated, their infrastructure decrepit and dysfunctional, they are lethally illiquid, they become immoral societies (obligations not honoured, crime flourishes), their trade deficits and budget deficits balloon and they are conditioned to be dependent on handouts and dictates from various international financial institutions and donor countries.

It enhances exports (and competitiveness through imports), it encourages technology transfers, it employs people, it invests in legitimate businesses (or is practiced by them), it adds to the wealth of the nation (black marketers are big spenders, good consumers and build real estate), it injects liquidity to an otherwise dehydrated market.

DISADVANTAGES

Hence, what is morally wrong with the black economy? The answer, in brief: It is exploitative. Other parts of the economy, which are not hidden (though would have liked to be), are penalized for their visibility. They pay taxes. Workers in a factory owned by the state or in the government service cannot avoid paying taxes.

The money that the state collects from them is invested, for instance, in infrastructure (roads, phones, electricity) or used to pay for public services (education, defense, policing). The operators of the black economy enjoy these services without paying for them, without bearing the costs and worse: while others bear the costs. This encourages them, in theory to use these resources less efficiently.

And all this might be true in a highly efficient, almost ideal market economy. The emphasis is on the word \\\"market\\\". Unfortunately, we all live in societies, which are regulated by bureaucracies that are controlled (in theory, rarely in practice) by politicians. These elites have a tendency to misuse and to abuse resources and to allocate them in an inefficient manner.

SUGGESTIONS

All citizens should be obliged to file annual, personal tax returns (universal tax returns, like in the USA). This way, discrepancies between personal tax returns and other information can lead to investigations and discoveries of tax evasion and criminal activities.

All citizens should be obliged to file bi-annual declarations of personal wealth and assets (including real estate, vehicles, movables, inventory of business owned or controlled by the individual, financial assets, income from all sources, shares in companies, etc.).

Tax laws should permit wide publicity through media regarding persons found guilty of tax evasion.

Social conscience needs to be aroused amongst people against tax evasion, for attaching social stigma for tax evaders and to work as sentinels for identifying black marketers and tax dodgers.

The most important measure for checking evasion is to establish credibility of the government regarding its own integrity before exhorting persons to pay their taxes correctly.

Disentitling tax evaders / defaulters to avail of the facility of payment of taxes in the installments and getting credit facilities from banks.

Streamlining procedure for speedy determination of tax disputes. Special courts for this need to be set up.

Paying special attention towards training for detection of tax frauds, evasion and black money generation, including deputation of IT officers to other countries for training to tackle cross border tax evasion.

Providing adequate security to tax officials, conducting search and surveys.

Improving morale of the tax department officials by providing them adequate infrastructure and other facilities, by recognition of their merit and giving them the place that they deserve in the overall government set up.

- Government expenditures need fresh audits and all wasteful expenses to be curtailed.
- Our Existing Systems are back dated and needs more amendments.
- Tax slabs to be simplified and user friendly.
- Anti Corruption laws needs a fresh look & strict implementations.
- All transactions are to be brought under e-transactions.
- Political leaders and parties contributions & expenditures need a close watch and accountability.
- All funds incoming & outgoing to NGO's, Religious trusts to be tightened and transparent.
- Every one of us should have the guts to say no to bribery and come forward to account our income & expenses as well as pay taxes.
- Tax structures are to be simplified and uniform taxes to be implemented.
- No transactions to be allowed & invoice or a bill is a must for all the services, purchases.
- Identifications cards details and pan card numbers to be mentioned in all transactions.
- Any person who indulges in corruption, black marketing and unlawful activities should be booked & brought to judicial notice.

- Defaulters & big borrowers list to be announced periodically so that they can be prevented to cheat banks & financial institutions in the long run.
- Integrity in Public and private life is the most essential to weed out corrupt practices.
- All loopholes in Laws to be plugged and efficient implementations of Tax collections to be improved.
- All commodities to be brought under taxes right from the source of its production, distributions and at its consumer end with strict, simplified VAT.
- Concessions & rebates to Corporates, MNC's are to be strictly watched so as to avoid misuse these privileges.
- Many times Large corporate companies evades Excise duty by declaring wrong information as export use and divert it to domestic market.
- All pending disputes need a faster recovery irrespective of corporates or big MNC's influences, political pressures.
- Investments in overseas details are to be sought by the Government and sources of investments to be checked and taxed accordingly.
- Public Distribution systems to be transparent.

CONCLUSION

The government will get more money in its treasury than ever before by adopting a simple way of collecting income tax and by eliminating the income tax department. In the absence of a very simple and fair tax method, black money will continue to balloon, befog and baffle bureaucrats, bleach businesses' balance sheets and income statements, and buttress the underground economy.

References

www.Google.com

India's*Black Economy* Monday, The writer is at the Centre for Economic Studies & Planning, Jawaharlal Nehru University, Delhi, Feb 14, 2005 at 0000 hrs IST

http://www.dailytimes.com.pk/, 9-5-2008_pg4_19

Deepak, *Black Money (Parallel Economy).*

Kumar Kush Prasad, The Economist Magazine, World Politics, Business, Finance & More. Interpret the World Economist.com

Vasant G. Gandhi, What to Do About Black Money?

Sivaharimani, Black Money.

Saraswathi (2009), Reasons and Problems of Black Money, 11 Jan. 2009 have developed number of methods for the purpose of "Structuring" and "Laundering" currency in the process of converting it from "dirty" to "clean" funds. The major risk to a bank is in the potential for complicity and violation of Acts if such funds are channeled through that Bank.

In India, we have certain statutes, as given below that incorporate measures which attempt to address the problems of Money Laundering:

The Income Tax Act, 1961 The Indian Penal Code and Code of Criminal Procedure, 1973 The Conservation of Foreign Exchange and Prevention of Smuggling Activities Act, 1974; The Narcotic Drugs and Psychotropic Substances Act, 1985 The Benami Transactions (Prohibition) Act, 1988 The Prevention of Illicit Traffic in Narcotic Drugs and Psychotropic Substances Act, 1988.

In November, 2002, Parliament approved the long-pending legislation to prevent the offence of Money Laundering. The President gave its assent to the Bill in January, 2003. The Bill was originally passed in December 1999 by the Lok Sabha and sent to the Rajya Sabha. The Upper House approved the Bill in July 2002 with amendments suggested by the Select Committee.

The Act allows for confiscation of property derived from or involved in Money Laundering. Co-operative banks, non-banking financial companies, chit funds and housing financial institutions come under its ambit. The Act also makes it mandatory for banking companies, financial institutions and intermediaries to maintain a record of all transactions of a prescribed value and to furnish information whenever sought within a prescribed time period. Thus, these entities are required to maintain the record of the transactions for 10 years. The minimum threshold limit for certain categories of offences under the Indian Penal Code and other legislations has been fixed at Rs. 30 lakh in the Bill. This limit is further likely to be reduced to Rs. 10 lakh.

The below table shows that Indians have more money in Swiss banks than the sum of all others. Here are the top five countries: Indian industrialists, politicians and officers have deposited their illegal money there, which is about 13 times larger than the country's foreign debt. With this amount 45 crore poor people can get Rs. 1,00,000 each.

Amount of Black Money in Swiss Bank

Countries	*Amount*
India	$1,891 Billion
Russia	$610 Billion
China	$213 Billion
UK	$210 Billion
Ukraine	$140 Billion
Rest of the world	$300 Billion

Source: Swiss Banking Association Report 2008.

According to the estimates, Indian black money in Swiss banks amount to a sum of about 1,891 billion U.S. dollars. Once this huge amount of black money comes back to India, the entire foreign debt can be repaid in 24 hours. And, after that the country will have surplus amount, almost 12 times larger than the foreign debt. Government of India should take proper measures to bring the black money back to our nation and utilize it for our national development. If this surplus amount is invested in earning interest, the amount of interest will be more than the annual budget of the Central government. So even if all the taxes are abolished, then also the Central government will be able to maintain the country very comfortably.

On 20th February, 2009 the American President Mr. Barack Obama has exerted immense pressure on USB Bank to disclose the details of deposits by tax evading Americans in this Bank. He has taken this step even at the risk to his life. On the other hand, our political leaders have not taken any action despite lapse of 6 long months. The Opposition Parties are also not interested.

Because most of the amount is owned by politicians and it is every Indian's money. This money is the result of our sweat and blood. The wealth generated and earned after putting in lots of mental and physical efforts by Indian people must be brought back to our country. If tax avoidance is the reason for the flight of funds, it will be difficult for the union government to lay its hands on the entire deposits of Indians in tax havens. By putting this issue in G20, IMF, Egmont Group and global agenda may resolve this problem. The money if utilized for Infrastructure development can boost our economy many fold and we will be an economic super power.

HARMFUL EFFECTS OF MONEY LAUNDERING:

Money Laundering threatens national governments and international relations between them through corruption of officials and legal systems. It undermines free enterprise and threatens financial stability by crowding out the private sector, because legitimate businesses cannot compete with the lower prices for goods and services that businesses using laundered funds can offer. The economy, society, and ultimately the security of countries used as Money Laundering platforms are all imperiled. There are few specific challenges which are posed by Money Laundering activities throughout the world.

Terrorism

Terrorism is an evil which affects each and everybody. Now and then we can find terrorist attacks being made by terrorists. These attacks definitely cannot be done without the help of money. Money Laundering serves as an important mode of terrorism financing. Terrorists use a wide variety of methods to move money within and between organisations, including the financial sector, the physical movement of cash by couriers, and the movement of goods through

"Money Laundering is perfectly describes what takes place – illegal or dirty money is put through a cycle of transactions or washed, so that it comes out the other end as legal or cleans money. In other words, the source of illegally obtained funds is obscured through a succession of transfers and deals in order that those same funds can eventually be made to appear as legitimate income." **—Robinson**

OBJECTIVES OF THE STUDY

The following are the main objectives of this study:

- To know the process of conversion of black money into white money.
- To study the various causes of money laundering.
- To analyse the economic impact of money laundering in India.
- To enumerate various ways to combat money laundering.

MONEY LAUNDERING PROCESS

Money Laundering is not a single act but is in fact a process that is accomplished in three basic steps as enumerated below:

1. *Placement*: "Placement" refers to the physical disposal of bulk cash proceeds derived from illegal activity. This is the first step of the Money Laundering process and the ultimate aim of this phase is to remove the cash from the location of acquisition so as to avoid detection from the authorities. This is achieved by investing criminal money into the legal financial system by opening up a bank account in the name of unknown individuals or organizations and depositing the money in that account.
2. *Layering:* "Layering" refers to the separation of illicit proceeds from their source by creating complex layers of financial transactions. Layering conceals the audit trail and provides anonymity. This is achieved by moving money to offshore bank accounts in the name of shell companies (fake companies), purchasing high value commodities like diamonds and transferring the same to different jurisdictions. Now, Electronic Funds Transfer (EFT) has become boon for such layering exercise. Different techniques like correspondent baking, loan at low or no interest rates, money exchange offices, back-to-back loans, fictitious sales and Purchases, trust offices, and recently the special purpose vehicles are utilized for the purpose of laundering the money.
3. *Integration*: "Integration" refers to the reinjection of the laundered proceeds back into the economy in such a way that they re-enter the financial system as normal business funds. The launderers normally accomplish this by setting up unknown institutions in nations where secrecy is guaranteed. New forms of business give a platform for integration exercise. Now a person can start a business with just a webpage and convert his illegal money to legal by showing profits from the webpage. There are other ways like capital market investments,

real estate acquisition, the catering industry, the gold market, and the diamond market etc. Money Laundering at its simplest, is the act of making money that comes from "Source A" look like it comes from "Source B".

CAUSES OF INCREASE IN MONEY LAUNDERING

There are various causes for increase in Money Laundering and the few of them can be enlisted as follows which is popularly known as 'Features of an Ideal Financial Haven':

- No deals for sharing tax information with other countries.
- Availability of instant corporations.
- Corporate secrecy laws - as the corporate law of certain countries enables launderers to hide behind shell companies.
- Excellent electronic communication.
- Tight bank secrecy laws (E.g. Swiss bank).
- A Government that is relatively invulnerable to outside pressures.
- A high degree of economic dependence on the financial services sector.
- Increase in sophistication and employment of professional people for doing the task.

MONEY LAUNDERING: THE INDIAN SCENARIO

Money Laundering is the process by which large amounts of illegally obtained money is given the appearance of having originated from a legitimate source. Thus, we can say Money Laundering is the introduction of illegally gained assets into the legal financial system with the aim of covering up its true origin. Therefore, we can say that the major objectives of Money Laundering activities are:

(a) Concealing the true ownership of illegally-obtained money and

(b) Placement, layering and integration of such funds.

The concept of Money Laundering can be traced back to the "Hawala" transactions well known in India for long time now. Hawala mechanism facilitates the conversion of money from black to white. "Hawala" is an Arabic word meaning the transfer of money between two persons using a third person. The Hawala mechanism usually does not leave any paper trail and thus is a nightmare for the investigative agencies. The profits generated from Hawala transactions are covertly invested in real estate, films etc. so as to launder them.

A few years back it was thought of only petty crime, but with the changed circumstances, especially after September 11, 2001 terrorist attack on World Trade Centre, Money Laundering is considered as a very serious crime. Worldwide special Acts have been passed to check such activities. The criminals

Anti-money Laundering – The New Mantra to Become an Economic Super Power Country

G.S. Nalini[*]

INTRODUCTION

MONEY Laundering refers to the conversion or "Laundering" of money which is illegally obtained, so as to make it appear to originate from a legitimate source. Money Laundering is being employed by launderers worldwide to conceal criminal activity associated with it such as drug trafficking, terrorism and extortion. As per an estimate of the International Monetary Fund (IMF), the aggregate size of Money Laundering in the world could be somewhere between two and five per cent of the worlds Gross Domestic Product (GDP). Money Laundering can also be associated with significant distortions to a country's imports and exports. On the import side, criminal elements often use illicit proceeds to purchase imported luxury goods, either with laundered funds or as part of the process of laundering such funds. Such imports do not generate domestic economic activity or employment, and in some cases can artificially depress domestic prices, thus reducing the profitability of domestic enterprises.

Money Laundering is a serious, highly sophisticated and global criminal activity. It is the practice of engaging in financial transactions to conceal the identity, source, or destination of illegally gained money. Money Laundering typically involves transferring money through several countries in order to obscure its origins. In recent years, especially since the events of September 11, 2001, worldwide efforts to combat Money Laundering and the financing of terrorism have assumed heightened importance. Money Laundering and the financing of terrorism are global problems that not only threaten security, but also compromise the stability, transparency, and efficiency of financial systems, thus undermining economic prosperity.

[*] Lecturer in Commerce Department, Govindammal Aditanar College for Women, Tiruchendur-628 215, Tuticorin District, Tamilnadu, India.

the trade system. Charities and alternative remittance systems have also been used to disguise terrorist movement of funds.

Threat to Banking System

Across the world, banks have become a major target of Money Laundering operations and financial crime because they provide a variety of services and instruments that can be used to conceal the source of money. Launderers generally use this channel in two stages to disguise the origin of the funds first, when they place their ill gotten money into financial system to legitimize the funds and introduce these funds in the financial system and second, once these funds have entered the banking system, through a series of transactions, they distance the funds from illegal source. The banks and financial institutions through whom the 'dirt money' is laundered become unwitting victims of this crime.

- Financial institutions that accept illegal funds cannot rely on those funds as a stable deposit base. Large amounts of laundered funds are likely to be suddenly wired out to other financial markets as part of the laundering process, threatening the institution's liquidity and solvency. A financial institution's reputation and integrity can be irrevocably harmed if involved in Money Laundering.
- Currencies and interest rates can be distorted by money launderers' investment practices, based as they are upon factors other than market returns.

Threat to Local Merchants

Local merchants and businesses may find that they cannot compete with front companies organized to launder and conceal illicit funds. Many such front companies offer their services and goods at below-market rates and even at a loss. Because their primary objective is the laundering of money, they do not need to compete in the marketplace and make a profit for their owners.

Threat to Economic Stability

Money Laundering may also distort some economic sectors and create instability in their markets. Money launderers may channel funds to sectors or areas where funds are unlikely to be discovered whether or not investment is needed or real returns are offered. The often sudden departure of investments from those sectors may impair the industries involved.

The infiltration and sometimes saturation of dirty money into legitimate financial sectors and national accounts can threaten economic and political stability. An IMF working paper concludes that Money Laundering impacts financial behaviour and macro-economic performance in a variety of ways including policy mistakes due to measurement errors in national account statistics, volatility in exchange and interest rates due to unanticipated cross border transfer of funds, the threat of monetary instability due to unsound asset structures, effects on tax collection and public expenditure allocation due to misreporting of income and many more such ways.

Tarnishing the Country's Reputation

Money Laundering and terrorist financing do nothing for the reputation of the host country. The loss of investor confidence that follow revelations of large-scale involvement in such activities can sharply diminish opportunities for growth. Once a country's reputation is tarnished, it takes years to repair.

BANKS ROLE IN ANTI-MONEY LAUNDERING

The following lists provide examples of potentially suspicious activities that should raise red flags for further investigation to determine whether the transactions or activities reflect illicit activities rather than legitimate business activities and whether a SAR (Suspicious Activity Reporting) should be filed. Some of the suspicious activities which the banks can keep an eye on are listed as follows.

Activity Inconsistent with the Customer's Business

- A customer opens several accounts for the type of business he purportedly is conducting and frequently transfers funds among those accounts.
- A customer's corporate account has deposits or withdrawals primarily in cash rather than cheque.
- The customer engages in unusual activity in cash purchases of traveler's cheques, money orders, or cashier's cheques.
- A corporate customer who frequently makes large cash deposits and maintains high balances, but does not use other banking services.
- A retail business has dramatically different patterns of cash deposits from similar businesses in the same general location.
- A retail business routinely makes numerous deposits of cheques, but rarely makes cash withdrawals for daily operations.
- Unusual transfer of funds among related accounts or accounts that involve the same principal or related principals.
- A business owner, who has only one store, who makes several deposits the same day using different bank branches.
- A customer frequently makes large dollar transactions without an explanation as to how they will be used in the business, or the purchases allegedly are for a business that generally does not deal in large amounts of cash.

other than that for which they were originally scheduled is known as hijacking. So, hijacking maybe defined as the infiltration with hidden arms of a plane or even a ship. There are several possible aims:

- The extortion of political concessions.
- The extortion of money for private or political ends.
- The search for asylum abroad.
- A desire for publicity. Hijacking May also is the result of a deranged mind.
- However, in most cases, these acts are politically motivated.

Hijacking has become of late, the burning issue of the day, as were the Barbary pirates in the 18th century. The Barbary predators were not motivated by ideological passion. They led to fervent national movement. They were for all their violence and threats, entrepreneurs playing the game of snatching and selling from men.

These acts of terrorism not only case suffering to large number of innocent individuals, they also affect society of the state as a whole. Moreover, modern terrorism with sophisticated technological means at it is disposal and the future possibility of access to biological and nuclear weapons, present a clear danger to the very existence of civilization itself.

Experience has shown that unilateral measures are inadequate to cope with the problem effectively. Since the nature of the threat transcends national boundaries, it must be properly dealt with in the international as well as in the national level.

COMMONEST TERRORIST ATTACKS

- Bombing
- Attacks by Grenade, Mortars, Missile, Sniping, Shooting, Arson & Sabotage
- Kidnapping
- Hijacking
- Siege & Hostage Taking
- Bombing is the single most favored terrorist attack.

BOMBINGS

(a) Roadside

(b) Letter

(c) Car

(d) Time-fuse

(e) Pressure

(f) Suicide

SYSTEMATIC GENOCIDE & SPONTANEOUS MASSACRES

Genocide

(a) Deliberate planned murder of large groups of people.

(b) Usually for social or ethnic reasons.

SPONTANEOUS MASSACRE (USUALLY IN WARTIME)

Examples of Spontaneous Massacres

(a) Holocaust of WW II

(b) Cambodia between 1975 and 1978

(c) Since 1991 in Bosnia

(d) Since 1994 in Rwanda

(e) In 1939 the NKVD (KGB) at Katyn Wood near Simulensk, Russia murdered over 4000 Polish Officer POWs. The executions carried out by the NKVD were blamed on the Nazis as a war in 1941 and did not come to light until 1991.

RANDOM MURDER & WOUNDING

(a) All deaths caused by terrorism are murder.

(b) Civilian personnel are often targeted by terrorist's results in the death or wounding of innocent men, women and children in an effort to create terror and force the general population.

(c) Terrorist attack seemingly occurs at random and without warning ads to terror in the general population.

(d) If large amount of civilians are killed over a period of time this may serve to create counter terrorist feeling in the population that previously supported them.

(e) Terrorists may issue warnings to lesson civilian casualties.

POLITICAL PURGES

1. When a government internationally targets dissidents.
   (a) Detention for unspecified periods.
   (b) Confinement of mentally healthy individuals in mental health facilities.
   (c) Release from confinement is not common.
   (d) Death from malnutrition and untreated medical conditions while detained.
   (e) Execution style murders.

- Asia/Pacific group on money laundering (1998), "Money Laundering *methods and Proceeds of Crime Typologies Workshop*", Wellington, New Zealand.
- World Bank Institute, "*Anti-Money Laundering Literature Search -Control & Investigation*", *http://www.worldbank.org/wbi/governance.*

Gaurav (2009), "*Indian Black Money in Swiss Bank: Myth and Reality*", *Bangalore.*

Byrne, John J. (2000), "Know Your Customer: What Happened and What Happens Next?" *Journal of Money Laundering Control,* Vol 3. No. 4.

B. Raman (2009), *Suspected Indian Money in Foreign Bank Accounts*", South Asia Group Analysis, Paper No. 3169, *http://www.emeraldinsight.com/10.1108/13685200410809878*

Controller of the Currency Administrator of National Banks (2000), "*Bank Secrecy Act / Anti Money-Laundering* ".

J. Sadakkadulla (2008), "*Anti Money Laundering and KYC: Indian Banks' Role*".

Kathleen M. Beans (2003), "Controlling Money Laundering Risks at Community Banks", *RMA Journal.*

Terrorism – An Unwanted Weapon

Leela Bhaskar[*]

HISTORICALLY, the word "terrorism" was first used to describe the politics by which the French revolutionary government maintained itself in power, particularly during the "Region of Terror" from 1793 to 1794. In the nineteenth centaury the word also came to be used for the activities of groups seeking to overthrow governments by disrupting the prevailing habits of obedience among the citizens of a state. But political terrorism first began intruding on the public consciousness during 1960s when the first notable case was the abduction and subsequent killing of the United States Ambassador to Guatemala.

Eduardo Jimenez Arechaga, a noted international lawyer, has defined terrorism as acts, which in themselves maybe classical forms of crime murder, arson, the use of explosives but which differ from classical criminal acts because they are executed "with the deliberate Intention of causing pain and disorder and terror within an organized society, in order to destroy social discipline, paralyze the forces of reaction of a society, and increase the misery and suffering of the community.

Brain Jenkins of the Rand Corporation maintains that the primary goal of terrorism is to instill fear via the threat of violence. It is violence for effect. The victim maybe totally unrelated to the terrorists. Terrorism is aimed at the people watching.

Regardless of the national origin, the terrorist is required to subordinate himself totally to the group to which he belongs. He must cease being an individual and become the living embodiment of the ideology he espouses. This means among other things, having no use for acts of violence that is not ideologically motivated.

International civil aviation is threatened by acts of terrorism ranging from bomb threats against aircraft in flight, attacks on airline offices or airport installations, the seizure of aircraft and their diversion to a destination

* Reader in Economics, The Ethiraj College for Women.

Avoiding the Record Keeping Requirement

- A customer is reluctant to provide the information needed to file the mandatory report, to have the report filed, or to proceed with a transaction after being informed that the report must be filed.
- A customer is reluctant to furnish identification when purchasing negotiable instruments in recordable amounts.
- Unusually large deposits of U.S. food stamps (often used as currency in exchange for narcotics).
- A customer tries to force a bank employee into not filing any required record keeping or reporting forms.

Fund (Wire) Transfers

- Wire transfer activity, which is inconsistent with the customer's business.
- Periodic wire transfers from a personal account(s) to bank secrecy haven countries.
- Large incoming wire transfers on behalf of a foreign client with little or no explicit reason.
- Frequent or large volume of wire transfers to and from offshore banking centers.
- Deposits of funds into several accounts, usually in amounts of less than $3000, which are consolidated subsequently into one master account and transferred, often outside of the country.

Insufficient/Suspicious Information by Customer

- The customer's financial statements differ from those of similar businesses.
- A customer makes frequent or large transactions and has no record of past or present employment experience.
- The discovery that a customer's home/business phone is disconnected.
- The customer's background is at variance with his or her business activities.
- Unusual or suspicious identification documents that the financial institution cannot readily verify.

Bank Employee Activities

- Lavish lifestyle cannot be supported by an employee's salary.
- Absence of conformity with recognized systems and controls, particularly in private banking.
- Reluctance to take a vacation.

Bank-to-Bank Transactions

- Significant changes in currency shipment patterns between correspondent banks.

- Increase in large amounts of cash without a corresponding increase in the filing of mandatory currency transaction reports.
- Deposits with a Federal Reserve Bank or its branches are disproportionate to the previous historical volume or volumes of similarly sized depository institutions.
- Significant turnover in large denomination bills that would appear uncharacteristic given the bank's location.
- Inability to track the true account holder of correspondent or concentration account transactions.
- The rapid increase in the size and frequency of cash deposits with no corresponding increase in non cash deposits.

Other Suspicious Customer Activities

- A large loan is suddenly paid down with no reasonable explanation of the source of funds.
- A customer insists on meeting bank personnel at a location other than their place of business.
- Money orders deposited by mail, which are numbered sequentially or have unusual symbols or stamps on them.

CONCLUSION

Money Laundering has been called the world's third largest industry, and is associated with all manner of crime. Combating Money Laundering is a dynamic process because the criminals who launder money are continuously seeking new ways to achieve their illegal ends. The degree of organization displayed in Money Laundering is a major cause for concern of banks and bank supervisors. Banks and other financial institutions can protect themselves against Money Laundering by implementing an effective KYC Policy, checking the source of funds, monitoring the conduct of accounts, and by learning to recognize suspicious transactions. Employees of banks are also being trained to recognize suspicious transactions. Anti-Money Laundering should not be only the responsibility of the Government, but also the private players. Private sector actors, banks and non-banks will need to take more responsibility to eliminate practices that encourage crime, undermine financial systems, and damage their own institutions. Let's join together to fight against Money Laundering and make our nation as an economic Super Power Country.

References

Sandhya Singh (2008), "*Money Laundering in Banking Sector*", Lecturer in MBA, SRMSCET, Bareilly.

Vijay Kumar Singh, "*Controlling Money Laundering in India–Problems and Perspectives*", Assistant Professor of Law, Hidayatullah National Law University, Raipur, Chhattisgarh.

DESTRUCTION OR DAMAGE OF STRUCTURES AND RESOURCES

(a) Any target is acceptable to terrorists.

(b) The more valuable the property the greater the attraction to the terrorist the publicity will be correspondingly higher.

(c) The destruction of significant landmarks and structures is preferred.

HIJACKING, KIDNAPPING OR SIEGE – AND HOSTAGE SITUATIONS

(a) Popular in the 1960s & 1970s has declined in recent years.

(b) Little chance of successfully escape by the terrorists and leaves many witnesses.

(c) Success of counter – terrorist groups.

(d) Selected buildings can be occupied by protesters who then threaten to destroy the property if forcible ejected.

(e) Stockholm syndrome.

RACKETEERING, EXTORTION, DRUG TRAFFICKING, ETC.

(a) Usually to obtain funding for future operations.

(b) May use extortion to gather funds from families in another country to protect family members in the country of organ.

(c) Payment of protection money to protect business in areas where the terrorist group is active.

(d) Produce narcotics for export

(e) May force women into prostitution around military bases in order to gain funds and information.

DESTRUCTION OR DISRUPTION OF INFORMATION & COMMUNICATION NETWORKS

(a) Target water or electrical supply to demonstrate vulnerability of government.

(b) May involve computer hoaxes, hackers or introduced computer viruses

(c) Target large government branches

POISONING OF CONSUMER FOOD PRODUCTS

(a) Potent but uncommon form of terrorism

(b) Intentionally introduce contaminants into food supply or consumers products.

(c) Economic costs as well as public health issue

(d) Can be used to cause the financial collapse of commercial enterprise.

BRAINWASHING & PSYCHOLOGICAL WARFARE

(a) Used to get POWs to make statements against their government.

(b) Keep long-term prisoners disoriented and easier to interrogate.

(c) Used in Korean and Vietnam War against American POWs.

THREATS &HOAXES OF TERRORIST ACTIONS

(a) A terrorist group may

(b) make a threat, of which they ate capable of carrying out, however with no intention to do so the hoax has the effect of tying up security

(c) Heightens feelings of panic in the public. In achieving widespread fear the terrorist is as successful as actually carrying out the attack without any of the logistical costs.

(d) Some terrorists groups have codeword known only to the group and security forces to authenticate the terrorist group and not a hoax or copycat.

TYPES OF TERRORIST ATTACKS SUMMARY

- Bombings
- Genocide & spontaneous massacres
- Random murder & wounding
- Deliberate murder, wounding or mutilation
- Forced suicide of victim
- Depopulation or ethnic cleansing
- Political purges
- Destruction or damage of structures and resources
- Hijacking , kidnapping or siege-and hostage situations
- Racketeering, extortion, drug trafficking, etc
- Destruction/disruption of communication networks
- Poisoning of consumer food products
- Brainwashing & psychological warfare
- Threats & hoaxes of terrorist actions

INTERNATIONAL TERRORISM

During the last few decades the ruthless deeds of terrorists have cast a long shadow over many countries. Terrorism has found its niche in the political scene across the globe and international terrorism, though comparatively less than that of domestic variety has run out of control despite increased government efforts to combat it.

Terrorism still remains a perpetual source of public and government concern. A sequence of bombings in the World Trade Centre, New York and Bombay baffled the police and military network.

Terrorism is not a new phenomenon, "in one form or another it pervades recorded history. Yet, each time it reappears, still very complex, it looms as a new menace". A number of attempts have been made to define terrorism but while defining terrorist each state keeps certain issues in mind in terms of its sociologist background, historical experience and sense basic value system.

CAUSES OF TERRORISMS

The planning of an act of violence involves so many different interests that there is no telling where it will lead to or what the final result will be. The process may start with one man or a group, fired by the political beliefs that it is a good necessary one. It cannot be achieved through argument ane the conventional means of persuasion. The opposition is too powerful and too entrenched. So a short cut is called for. The zealot, often neurotic and self-observed, never pauses to reflect that perhaps his aim is unreasonable and unacceptable to a majority. The aim could also be the release of fellow terrorists, or it could be specific demands for funds or other concession or just to terrorize so that the people are reminded that a neglected cause exists. Such acts besides stretching that government resources allows the sponsoring agencies also to keep the terrorist squads trim and trained propaganda mileage is an added advantage because then it can be claimed that the terrorist leader looks after followers. The victims and their families presenting a picture of sorrow and grief back home are also likely to weaken the official stand on the issue. Thus act as a point scored by the terrorists towards whatever cause they have.

But, primarily terrorism is the strategy of the weak. It is the first reason of the correct and the last resort of the man whose beliefs cannot stand the light of reasoned examination. The essence of terrorism is to sow dear, to make heroes out of murders and thereby to convince opponents that the terrorists' cause is right and the authorities are wrong. What keeps the terrorists on the job relentlessly is one hope that eventually the public will get fed up and tired of endless news about killings bombings and finally may come to believe that the nation is faced with an insoluble problem.

The former is conducted by unconventional means but with real military alms and targets; whereas terrorism is indiscriminate in both. It is planned for public effect, not for military objectives. Brains Jenkins, research analyst in terrorism at the Rand Corporation and advisor to the U.S. State Department on political conspiracy and violence says," Terrorism is theater; it is aimed at the people watching, not at the actual victims, often enough innocent by-standers, airline passengers etc do stand to lose life and limb simply because they happen to be there when the terrorists were in the actual process of their theatrical display. What the terrorists really do is to apply the well tried techniques-the gangster and blackmailer to political situations. In the process he dresses it up and packages it as a splendidly contemporary piece of ideological finery.

Among the terrorist bands hardly any recruits come from the grass root level. It is normally the fancy gunslingers like "Carlos", who hit the headlines. The public image built by Illych Ramirez Carlos alone has lead to any number of money spinning books and novels with him as the main character.

PSYCHOLOGY OF TERRORISM

Terrorism like many other crimes of insanity is infectious. It perpetuates itself. It causes itself to happen. One incidence causes two more, which cause more and more incidents. Carlos Marigheilla, Fidel Castro's associate codified the aims of terrorists and the method to achieve them in his mini-manual for whom Guerrillas published in 1969. He said that terrorists must use revolutionary violence to identify with a popular cause and so gain a popular base. This leaves the government with no alternative except to intensify repression thus playing into the hands of terrorists.

A well-known psychologist has said that terrorism can only be prevented by a state, prepared to risk the lives of innocent by-standers, including women and children in order to prove opinion and almost certain destruction of men and materials in the hands of terrorists, more often than not, make the governments relent. Some well-known terrorist leaders claim that violence was not simply a means of ending an injustice, but also improving element in itself, "violence is cleansing force, it makes him fearless and restores his self-respect"

TERRORIST DOCTRINES

Nuclear war doctrines are in essence, terrorism practiced by an industrial State, legitimated by the people of the industrial world. Under the nuclear doctrines entire population and nation are held hostages to threat of mass annihilation. They constitute repudiation of the "Hague Convention" and a crime against humanity under Nuremberg Laws. Yet the people of industrial nations have been conditioned to accept these terrorist doctrines as legitimate strategy for their security.

Terrorism is ultimately derived from that ability of a small member being in a position to cause injury or death to its victims in a spectacular manner have a demonstration effect and then use it to achieve their objectives. Currently, hijacking of aircrafts and holding of hostages are two most favored forms of aircraft terrorism.

FOREIGN SPONSORSHIP

Modern weapons are expensive and till such time the leader has acquired adequate standing to draw volunteers and funds, he will almost always prone to development of terrorist activities. It is in the interest of not so friendly neighbors to generate a state of instability in the border areas so that they could exploit the situation if and when direct conflict occurs with the legitimate government.

The Strong State has Become Stronger and Even More Repressive

Three major causes of rise in terrorism, state terrorism, in other words as being the soil out of which both phenomenon, right now are growing and of course reinforce each other. Common theme: increased asymmetry between ruler and the ruled.

There is an Increase in Structural Violence

Let us only look at two types:.depriving people of land and depriving people of soil. The former is what happened to Palestinians in west Asia and to Africans driven out by the whites in southern part of Africa. In both cases, the victims become non-citizens in their own hands. The latter is what happens when rich land owners, transnational corporations and others buy up soil and deprive people of basic production factor for subsistence.

There is an Increase in Direct Violence

Torture is reported to be more widespread today than even before; it is not only our perception of the phenomenon that has expanded due to the excellent documentation by amnesty international and other organization.

There is an Increase in the Threat of Direct Violence

The ultimate direct violence at the disposal of the state is the weapons of mass destruction, atomic, biological, chemical, and radiological and now, coming laser and particle beams.

India's Counter – Terrorism Set-up Consists of the Following

The state police and its intelligence set-up: Under India's federal constitution, the responsibility for policing and maintenance of law and order is that of the individual states. The central government in new Delhi can only give them advice, financial help, training and other assistance to strengthen their professional capabilities and share with them the intelligence collected by it. The responsibility for follow-up action lies with the state police.

Physical Security Agencies

These include the central industrial security force, responsible for physical security at airports and sensitive establishments; the national security guards, a specially trained intervention force to terminate terrorist situations such as hijacking, hostage taking, etc; and the special protection group, responsible for the security of the prime minister and former prime ministers.

Paramilitary Forces

These include the central reserve police; force and the border security force, which assist the police in counter-terrorism operation which called upon to do so.

The Army

Their assistance is sought as a last resort when the police and paramilitary forces are not able to cope with a terrorist situation. But in view of Pakistan's large-scale infiltration in Jammu and Kashmir and the presence and activities of a large number of Pakistani mercenaries, many of them ex-servicemen, the army has a more active, permanent and leadership role in counter-terrorism operations here. What India is facing in J&K is not just terrorism, but a proxy war being war being waged by the Pakistani army through its jihadi surrogates.

In Recent Months, There have been Two Additions to the Counter-terrorism Setup

A counter-terrorism division in the ministry of external affairs, expected to be patterned after the counter-terrorism division of the US state department. It will be responsible for coordinating the diplomatic aspects of counter-terrorism, such as briefing other countries on Pakistan's sponsorship of terrorism against India, processing requests for extradition and mutual legal assistance, servicing the work of various joint working group's on counter-terrorism which groups on counter-terrorism which India has set up with a number of countries, etc.,

Studies on terrorism emphasize that terrorism is a product of many factors, which contribute to an environment propitious for terrorism. The most critical factors identified at the global level are:

- Socio-economic and political tensions and injustices in modern industrial societies.
- Deep-rooted ethic, ideology and religious divisions.
- Unresponsive or insensitive governments.
- Ineffective security forces.
- Access to global audience through news media.

Any terrorist movement is a product of despair and frustration caused partly by the failure of its leaders to mobilize mass support for a conventional and peaceful mode of agitation but largely because of the failure of the state to evolve democratic methods of resolving people's problems. It's product of distortions and development.

Various strategies-both at the domestic level and at the international level can be effectively used to fight terrorism:

- Measures to root out the causes of terrorism, if possible.
- Steps to prevent acts of terrorism as far as practicable.
- Measures to tackle existing terrorist's threats to the best of one's ability
- Post-incident measures for restoring normalcy and taking curative/ preventive steps against recurrence of such acts.

What is it like to be a terrorist and why should anyone want to be one? It is easy to dismiss terrorists as mad fanatics but in fact they need to level headed to cope with long periods of meticulous planning in between bouts of violent activity. It is fascinating to gain some insight into the mindset of terrorists. And what about those unfortunate enough to be victims of terrorism? Being bombed or held hostage by 6terrorists is the stuff of nightmares, but the legacy of dread after the ordeal can be even worse.

Psychological profiles of terrorists are completely different from popular perceptions or media portrayals. When the news of an outrage breaks there is a tendency to describe the terrorists as being mentally unbalanced, having broken the rules-but not necessarily those followed by most of the population. The terrorists will usually have a relatively normal psychological profile. There is no common personality that is unique to those who commit acts of political violence; the violence occurs because people have chosen that path for a variety of reasons. Most terrorism involves long periods of inaction interspersed with short bouts of activity. The terrorist needs to be able to be patient during the long and dull planning stages of preparation for an attack. It is doubtful whether such inactivity would appeal to, or satisfy the needs of a psychopathic personality. Terrorists are committed individuals prepared to carry out often-horrific acts, accepting that such deeds may have severe consequences for them personally. They perform violent actions because they believe in their cause. Terrorists may be unpleasant and they maybe scared, but they are rarely cowards. If they were, it is likely that they would have become terrorists in the first place.

People become terrorists for very different reasons:

- Nationalism is the strongest motivation to take up terrorism.
- Sense of belonging-individuals who have problems adjusting to society, or who have overwhelming need to belong, may find sanctuary in terrorism.
- Importance of group network - there are many different layers to terrorist organizations. The majority are involved in setting up the network that enables such acts to be committed.

In assessing the mindset of the terrorists, then, two factors stand out. The first is, terrorists usually have a very strong motivation and the strength of this motivation is the principal key to while they are prepared to kill and maim. The second is that terrorists usually operate in close-knit groups that reinforce their motivation and encourage certain tendencies, particularly the ones that enable individual terrorists to escape the intense guilt that they might otherwise feel for the consequence of their action.

Various conventions and codes of conduct exist for combating terrorism at the international level. International cooperation is a must to achieve the desired results in the field of counter measures. There is an immediate requirement of having an unambiguous and well-defined legal framework to deal with international terrorism. Cooperation is also very essential in the field of intelligence gathering. Major nations must rise above their vested interests and look at this menace as the problem of humanity. Terrorism needs to be precisely defined. Then the law should be made fool proof, that no nation can circumvent it.

The credibility of the intelligence system should be of high order. The respond beyond passive defense and to consider means of active prevention, pre-emption and retaliation, a consensus should be reacted in the countries affected by terrorism. The aim should be to prevent and deter impending future attacks. Borders vulnerable to terrorist actions should be sealed and inter-state movements regulated. Governance should ensure action to prevent illegal import of arms to the country by clandestine groups. Diplomatic channels should be exploited to prevent the inflow of weapons. Employment opportunities need to be enhanced. This would effectively stop the availability of young people to join the rank of terrorists. Sound protective measures can be in the form of increased security, protection for affected leaders or officials, increase in check points, enhancement in dog squads and bomb detection teams, more buffer zones.

Various suggestions to combat terrorism have been offered.

- Firm action by the government against terrorists and should not play "politics with terrorism."
- Dealing with terrorism and take appropriate action in all cases of failure.
- Police and army personnel evolved in tackling terrorism should be honest in their acts. They should also be better equipped in terms of their armaments.
- The need for educating the citizens so as to give them confidence and building up resistance against possible acts of terrorism by organizing debates in schools and colleges, local clubs and other social organization.
- Media to create awareness among the public. Both the print and electronic media should be firmly advised to show more responsibilities in not making heroes of terrorists.

It is unlikely that terrorism will be eradicated in the foreseeable future because the causes of political violence – ethnic rivalries, ideological conflicts, and state repression – are unlikely to disappear. Perhaps the best that can be hoped for is that terrorism will be contained and reduced to a level the politicians and the people they represent will find "acceptable". Such containment will not, however, address the causes of terrorism. Prolonged negotiation, sustained in the face of terrorist attacks, by thoughtful representatives of the parties involved may offer a better solution in the long term.

Terrorism is a menace that particularly targets democratic societies which have to fashion a global and comprehensive response to tackle it."

References

Aditya Bakshi (2004), Terror on the High Seas.

Ajay Lele (2004), Bio - Weapons.

M.G. Chitkara and Giridhari Sharma (2004), In'ernational Terrorism.

Deepak Rao and Seema Rao (2004), Terrorism.

K. R. Gupta (2004), Global Terror.

Lakshmi Krishnamurthi, Responding to Terrorism.

A. S. Narang Pramila Srinivasan, Terrorism - The Global Perspective.

Ramesh Chandra (2003), Global Terrorism.

L. R. Reddy (2002), Bio-Terrorism.

Verinder Grover, (2002), International Encyclopedia of Terrorism.

R. Thandanvan, Terrorism Challenges and Remedies.

Economic Impact of Terrorism on Indian Economy

*J. M. Arul Kamaraj** & *J. Arul Suresh**

INTRODUCTION

World in recent past, has witnessed several economies burning with disaster & crisis. Today every nation faces some or the other economic, social or communal unrest. Further, globalization has enabled the impact of these tremors to be felt even at remotest part of the world. India till FY 2008 had seen a steady growth with its GDP shining as high as 9.3%. Subsequently, the economy was hit with US Sub Prime Crisis, Satyam scandal & the Mumbai 26/11 Terrorist attacks. Many believe that terrorism can't hamper ones economic activity as it only destroy a small fraction of the stock of capital of a country. However, a broader look at the geo-political & economical scenario can easily erode this misconception. India has been facing the terrorism threat as long as since 1970. Terrorism in India is primarily attributable to Islamic, Naxalite and various other radical movements. At least 232 of the country's 608 districts were afflicted, at differing intensities, by terrorism. Over a period of time terrorism has severely affected Indian economy.

INDIAN ECONOMY

The economy of India is the twelth largest economy in the world by market exchange rates and the fourth largest by purchasing power parity (PPP) basis. India was under social democratic-based policies from 1947 to 1991. The economy was characterised by extensive regulation, protectionism, and public ownership, leading to pervasive corruption and slow growth. Since 1991, continuing economic liberalisation has moved the economy towards a market based system. A revival of economic reforms and better economic policy in 2000s accelerated India's economic growth rate. By 2008, India had established itself as the world's second-fastest growing major economy. However, the year 2009 saw a significant slowdown in India's official GDP growth rate to 6.1% as

* Lecturer, Department of Social Work, Loyola College, Chennai-34.

well as the return of a large projected fiscal deficit of 10.3% of GDP which would be among the highest in the world

EVILS OF SOCIETY

Evils of society are people who do not respect human values, create nuisance and terror. Is there a special kind of race where these people came from?. Evils will always be created by society, as we know no body will born with this type of qualities. Lets take a simple scenario, there is guy on the street he has no proper guidance, he don't have enough money to live and he don't have any idea of what to do. One corrupted politician approached him and offered him money to create terror against his opponents, with no other choice this guy accepted the offer and now he will become evil against society. There are many people in the society who is lack of guidance and encouragement, politicians gather these people and create terror on us to gain their power. Now the entire society is controlling by these evils. We need to contribute some of our efforts to break this kind of chain in our society. We can't blame these people because they don't have other choices to opt for survival. We need to encourage people who are in desperate need of help for basic eminities. Ofcourse there are some educated professionals who committed crimes as we all know but we need to work against these things. We are creating loop holes in our society , there are no evils in the society we are creating them unknowingly.

GLOBAL FINANCIAL MELTDOWN AND INDIAN ECONOMY

As a result of the global financial meltdown, India's economy had already started to contract prior to the November 29th attacks. GDP growth rates had already fallen from 7.9% in the first quarter of the current financial year to 7.6% in the second quarter. Moreover, the overall growth rate for the first half of the current year showed regressing figures (7.8%) when compared to the previous year (9.3%). Fear had already spread in the city of Mumbai; fears of losing one's job or home. Thus, the terrorists attacks of Mumbai arrived at a time when fear was already an epidemic in the city.

A s a result of the economic crisis, the mood of business in India has turned highly pessimistic. Citibank estimates that GDP growth will be 6.8% in 2008-2009 and 5.5% in the next fiscal year. Goldman Sachs and Merrill Lynch expect 2009-2010 growth to be 5.8%, Nomura believes it will be 5.3% and First Global puts it at an alarmingly low of 3.5%.

In October 2009, exports fell down by 12.1%. It is highly unlikely—likely or unlikely? just making sure that the $200 billion target for 2008-2009 will be missed. The ABN AMRO Purchasing Managers' Index, an early indicator of the mood of manufacturing, is at its lowest since it was set up in April 2005, indicating that manufacturers are bearish. Taking one specific sector as an example; vehicle sales ware estimated to slide by 25.5% in the last three months of the calendar year and by more than 34% in January-March 2009. Moreover, the Real estate market is also suffering, and the Bombay Stock Exchange (BSE) Sensex has been hovering around 9,000, a far cry from the 21,000 it had crossed in January.

Looking on the brighter side of things, Inflation, fell to 8.40% for the week ending on November 22, from almost 13% in August. This allowed the Reserve Bank of India (RBI) the benefit of focusing on boosting growth rather than fighting inflation. RBI governor D. Subbarao, announced a 1% cut in the lending rate, effective December 8, where the rate at which the RBI lends money to banks now stands at 6.5% The government has, meanwhile, cut the controlled price of petrol and other petro-products due to the fall in inflation. Furthermore, the Indian central government has also been announcing ingredients of a stimulus package to help boost the economy. On that day, when terrorists still held hostages just a few blocks away, the Bombay Stock Exchange resumed its activity. The markets flared up in patriotic defiance, with the benchmark Sensex index closing up 66 points on a day when most expected it to drop. However, with GDP growth slowing to 7.6% and foreign institutional investors withdrawing more than $13 billion from its equity markets, India's economy has already yielded defeat, leaving its Sensex at less than half where it stood a year ago.

With all this loss that India incurred, it will take a while for things to go back to the way they used to. For three days after the incident, trains have run empty, schools and offices have remained closed, and Bombay's residents, heeding a call from the government, have stayed indoors. On the next Friday afternoon, when some of the fear started to fade away and considerable public activity was witnessed, a false alarm about more armed gunmen at train stations sent back the city's residents into quivering fear. Despite all these happenings, it is highly unlikely that the world is going to miss participating in an economy growing between 7 to 8% annualy.

IMMEDIATE IMPACT OF TERRORISM

The immediate impact of terrorism is ; destruction of property, loss of life, and loss of money, but the greatest loss of them all is uncertainty and fear, which impacts economic activity. Hospitality and transportation tourism sectors are amongst the first areas to feel the pain. Gross earnings from foreign tourists are currently around 1% of GDP. Hence, an affected tourism sector will impact the overall economy. Furthermore, holiday destinations such as Goa, are feeling the pinch even more because of intelligence reports suggesting that they could be future targets for terrorists. Hotel occupancy has gone down 25% and rates plunged in western India. Civil aviation is another sector in the dumps. But it was already troubled prior to the attacks.

Overall damage to India's economy is indeed significant. Analysts have already started giving initial estimates that suggest the loss in business due to the attacks to be about $100 billion, arising from crucial institutions, such as the stock exchanges, commodities and money markets, and business and commercial establishments which remained closed. Furthermore, the foreign exchange front got hit by $20 billion. Even though the terrorist attacks were devastating to the city and its people, it is just a matter of time before the situation worsens, as harsher consequences are expected on the long run. While the short-term impact is easy to predict, what happens down the line remains impossible to assess.

TOURISM – GLOBAL IMPLICATIONS

India's Ministry of Tourism released numbers showing a 2.1% drop in tourists when comparing November 2007 to November 2008. This comes on the heels of a 15% to 20% annual growth rate in number of tourists for the past three years. Tourists no longer feel it safe to tour in India after the deadliest attacks one after the other. The biggest example is Mumbai's 26/11 terror attacks. The attacks came at a time when India's economic had already begun to slow down due to global recession. Exports & Imports were down. Inflation rose to almost 13%. Mumbai brings in 40% of foreign trade, 60% of customs duty collections, 40% of income tax collections, 20% of central excise collections and $10 billion in corporate taxes. The Mumbai terror attack has been the most dramatic in a long series of terror events in India. It involved foreign hostages and places where business leaders, executives and foreigners frequented. It has therefore been a much more potent media drama than any of the previous terror events. This grabbed worldwide attention and there is certainly a negative impact on India's risk and security perception. It has dent foreign investors' views of India. This has lead to a drop in investments too.

IMPACT ON INDUSTRIES

The immediate impact of terrorism is the loss of life, destruction of property and loss of man-sdays. Terrorist , cleanliness and warm hospitality. It also re-instills a sense of responsibility towards tourists and re-enforces the confidence of foreign tourist towards India as a preferred holiday destination. Despite the slowdown and the recent incidents, global companies are expected to continue to exhibit their confidence in India. Foreign investors need to put their money somewhere and India still looks very attractive.

IMPACT OF TERRORIST ATTACK AT MUMBAI ON INDIAN ECONOMY

According to Economists, the already damaged Indian economy due to the global financial crisis will be further affected by the recent terrorist attacks in the city of Mumbai, however, the impact of the attacks on the economy is expected to be short lived. Even though Mumbai suffers from a considerable poor population sectarianism, it has managed to transform itself from a city known for textiles and kitschy, to a powerful financial capital that serves as a gateway for India to the rest of the world. Mumbai's economy, which contributes as much as 5% of India's $1 trillion GDP and nearly a third of its direct taxes, stands as a beacon of India's success in integrating itself in the global economy. In the recent past, this has made the city a more attractive target for terrorists that desire to shed India's success. In 2003, 60 people were killed by car bombs, and in 1992 and 1993, Hindu-Muslim riots claimed another 1,000. In July 2006, 187 people were killed as coordinated bombs ripped through commuter trains in the crowded city. Throughout all the obstacles that Mumbai has faced, it has still managed to become a prominent capital of Asian finance that rivals Hong Kong and Tokyo. Its stock exchange is among the world's busiest, its banking community is the envy of South Asia, and its restaurants and nightlife are comparable to those of any global cultural capital.

MAJOR HINDRANCE FOR INDIAN ECONOMIC GROWTH

Short-Term Impact

Loss of Human Capital

The human costs have been horrendous. Estimates are in past 5 years 4000+ were killed in terrorist attacks. This puts India next to Iraq both in terror deaths and terror incidents. The recent 26/11 Mumbai attacks itself left 257-300 dead and 700 injured which includes several high profile individuals such as Shri Ashok Kapur, chairman of Yes Bank who was killed in attack.

INVESTOR BEHAVIOR

Frequent attacks on commercial & government institutions shatter the confidence of the investors causing heavy investment drainage. One example of the same is the terrorist attack in Indian Parliament in 2001, which internationally provoked insecurity & discouraged the investors (FII's & FDI's), obstructing the economic growth. A heavy impact of this can be observed at the stock market that keep diving down post any major terrorist event.

SHORT TERM FINANCIAL LOSS

In short term the obstacles like loss suffered due to the diversion of business away from the city to other locations, lost earnings of public due to disability and trauma among survivors etc. Drains out the productivity levels & impact the respective economy adversely. Post 26/11 the Taj & Trident Hotels incurred heavy loss as operations were halted for 3-4 months. After 26/11 Mumbai attack Pak cricket team had to cancel its Mumbai tour due to which BCCI has incurred a loss to the tune of INR 120 crore. Another such incident was Post Ex-PM Indira Gandhi's assassination 1984 riots which hit the economy severely especially the Agriculture & Transport industry that lost hundreds of crores.

RETRENCHMENT EFFECT ON SPECIFIC INDUSTRIES

The Jaipur serial blasts, J&K Terrorism & Mumbai 26/11 attacks did have immediate and concentrated impacts on a number of industries: most notably, airlines, aerospace, travel, tourism, insurance, lodging, restaurants, recreation and related activities. Gross earnings from foreign tourists are currently around 1% of GDP. Post 26/11 terrorist attack estimates suggest that nationally hotels have seen about 60% booking cancellations. Hotel occupancy in western India is down some 25% and rates have plunged. These industries suffered concentrated economic and job losses. Of course, regions or localities with heavy concentrations of these industries suffered disproportionately as well.

LONG-TERM IMPACT

Political Instability

The assassinations of 2 Ex-PM of India, Mrs. Indira Gandhi, Mr. Rajeev Gandhi already had jolted Indian politics & economy at large. India had lost 2 of its strongest pillars which otherwise would have taken Indian politics, Business & industry at unimaginable heights. Recently speaking the siege of South Mumbai has taken toll as home minister Shivraj Patil, Chief minister Vilasrao Deshmukh & Home minister R.R. Patil had to resign. This further unstabilized the Indian industry from a long-term perspective. The Political instability at times have also let to erosion of FII's & FDI's.

GLOBAL IMPLICATIONS

India, post Kargil war then Attack on Parliament now 26/11 has lost millions of business as the trade link between the two countries are frozen during such period. Agri-Exporters in bordering states have taken heavy burns. This has resulted in unemployment in these regions, which in turn again triggers riots. 26/11 Attack involved foreign hostages and places where business leaders, executives and foreigners frequented. This will lead to a drop in investments.

LONG TERM FINANCIAL LOSS

The direct economic damage done by terrorist attacks: buildings and infrastructure destroyed, productive lives ended. The structural damages post 26/11 attacks was amounting to total of INR 500 crores, which subsequently took its toll on the insurance industry. Another form of longer-term costs security involves the opportunity cost of spending additional money to fight terrorism. Currently India ranks on 9th position in the world for highest military expenditure (2009-10), which amount to sum total of USD 32,700,000,000. Further, a variety of new spending on security occurred after this incident. As all this happens, economic resources will be directed to shoring up security and diverted away from more productive private sector activity.

RUSSIA, INDIA, AND CHINA IN COMBATING TERRORISM

Russia, India and China, a grouping known by the acronym RIC, today agreed to cooperate in the fight against terrorism emanating from Pakistan and Afghanistan. The meeting between the three countries was aimed at providing stability to the region. The three countries also agreed to give an impetus to the trilateral relations in areas like health, agriculture, disaster mitigation, climate change and mitigating the impact of the global slowdown.

India's External Affairs Minister S M Krishna, Russian Foreign Minister Sergei Lavrov and Chinese Foreign Minister Yang Jei Chi held an meeting in Bangalore on 27th October 2009 to chart the path forward.The ministers said they had agreed on the need for trilateral dialogue in areas like global economic governance architecture, climate change, trade policy and development cooperation which would contribute to global peace and prosperity.

They reviewed the progress made during the eight rounds of the trilateral dialogues. The three leaders discussed the situation in the region, paying attention to the terrorism emanating from Pakistan and Afghanistan. After the meeting, the leaders told reporters that the discussions were "productive". They claimed that they had identified new areas of cooperation. "The cooperation between the three countries in their fight against terrorism and transnational crimes will provide stability to the region," a joint statement noted.

CONCLUSION

To conclude with, lets not forget that the enemies of our nation have vowed to "bleed India through thousand cuts". Even if terrorism represents a small fraction of the overall economic risk in India, it may have a large impact on the allocation of productive capital across the country. In any part of the world terrorism is unwanted as it not only kills the human life but also the infrastructure, industry ultimately shackling its overall growth.

References

Alamgir, Jalal (2008), India's Open Economy Policy, Routledge, London.

Clutterbuck, Richard (1994), 'Terrorism in an Unstable World, Routledge, New York.

Economic Survey, Government of India, 2008 -2009.

Kumar, Dharma (1982), The Cambridge Economic History of India (Volume 2), Penguin Books.

Lakshmana Rao, V. (1994), Essays on Indian Economy, Ashish Publishing House, New Delhi.

Laqueur, Walter (1987), The Age of Terrorism, George Weidenfield and Nicolson Ltd: London.

Merkl, Peter H. (1986), Political Violence and Terror: Motif and Motivations University of California Press: Berkeley and Los Angeles.

Report on Currency and Finance of RBI, 2009.

Rao, N.P. (1982), 'Terrorism-Violence and Human Destruction - Causes Effects and Control Measures, Anmol Publishers, New Delhi.

Roy, Tirthankar (2000), The Economic History of India, Oxford University Press.

Sankaran, S. (1994), Indian Economy: Problems, Policies and Development, Margham Publications.

http://www.asiaecon.org/special_articles/read_sp/12094

http://timesofindia.indiatimes.com/news/india/800-terror-cells-active-in-country /articleshow/3356589.cms

Self Help Groups in the Upliftment of Tsunami Victims in Kanyakumari District

P. Balamirtham & I. Uma Devi***

INTRODUCTION

Self Help Group (SHG) is a group of individuals voluntarily formed with 10 to 20 members having similar identity, heritage, caste, or occupation for a common cause. The members mutually contribute to the common fund on a regular basis and lend the same to its members for meeting productive needs. In case of need, the group may borrow funds from banks and financial institutions and lend the same to the members. The members of Self Help Groups individually and as a group jointly promote industrial ventures. The profit earned from the group activity is shared by its members equally.

The role of Self Help Groups in the upliftment of families in suffering is much appreciable. The families in financial difficulties find SHGs as a boon in amlieorating their financial problems. Similarly SHG's formed in areas which are in crisis have assisted much to the upliftment of poor who are affected by such crisis. It is especially true in underdeveloped countries like India, where more than 50 per cent of the people live below poverty.

One of such memorable occassions which took place in Kanyakumari district during the last tsunami is still in the memory of many. The present paper examines the role of SHG's in the upliftment of victims of tsunami in Kanyakumari district.

METHODOLOGY

The data collected from 100 sample respondents through an interview schedule from a randomly selected Self Help Groups functioning in the tsunami hit area have been the base for the present study study. All the respondents have been

* Project Investigator (UGC Major), Reader, P.G. Dept of Economics, Vivekananda College, Agasteeswaram, Kanyakumari District-629701

* Project Fellow, Vivekananda College, Agasteeswaram, Kanyakumari District.

living in the tsunami hit area and directly affected by tsunami. The impacting variables and their role have been assessed through Garrets ranking method. Similarly for evaluating the problems faced by the members of SHG's in the tsunami hit area Garrets ranking scores have been employed. Secondary data collected from District Rural Development Agency, Nagercoil, Kottar Social Service Society, Nagercoil and other published sources have been used.

TSUNAMI

The volcanic erruptions on the deep sea in the Indian ocean on 26th December 2004 produced tsunami waves which devasted the shores of Indonesia, Srilanka, India, Thailand and many other surrounding countries.

The rare earthquake took place in the Indian Ocean on the Western coast of Northern Samutra at a magnitude of 9.0 on the Richter Scale struck at 6.58 A.M and led a sequence of 15 quakes across Andaman and Nicobar islands. On that day the waves in the sea raised upto 15 meters height.

The tsunami the sea swallowed 2,29,866 lives and caused 10 billion$ worth damages at the global level. Tsunami affected Indian shores badly Tamilnadu is the state which directly faced the worst consequences of tsunami. Tamilnadu fishermen community is the worst hit one. There were 1000 fishermen killed in the tidal wave. Further it damaged 2000 mechanised boats and above 20000 catamarans. Apart from boats, fishermen lost their implements such as nets and household properties worth several lakhs of rupees. Several thousands of huts belonging to the fishermen were completely washed away. The total loss estimated in Tamilnadu, Andra Pradesh, Kerala and Pondicherry was Rs. 5322.05 crores. In Tamilnadu alone the money value of loss was estimated at Rs. 2730.70 crores.

In a few hours many affluent fishermen were ripped off their wealth. Heavy damages were caused to the west coastal road from Kanyakumari to Kodimunai and the bridge connecting Mela Manakudi and Keela Manakudi villages was completely washed away leaving only the pillars. It shows that tsunami made an irrepairable loss in Kanyakumari District.

SHG's AND THEIR ROLE

SHG's formed exclusively with women members have made remarkable achievement in the uplift of tsunami affected victims. During and after tsunami SHG's function well in the tsunami hit area in Kanyakumari district

There are 13356 SHG's functioning in Kanyakumari district.In these SHG's nearly 216185 women enrolled as members. After tsunami for, assisting the tsunami hit people SHG's were formed in large number in the tsunami hit area in Kanyakumari district. The Government, rendered support by all means to SHG's. The details of new SHGs formed in the Tsunami hit area in Kanyakumari District are presented in Table 1.

Table 1
Self Help Groups in Tsunami Hit Area in Kanyakumari District

Panchayats	*No. of SHGs*	*Percentage*
Kanyakumari	361	18.65
Reethapuram	104	5.37
Manavalakurichi	125	6.45
Kallukoottam	223	11.52
Ganapathypuram	205	10.59
Mandaikadu	152	7.85
Pallapallam	143	7.39
Puthalam	152	7.85
Anjugramam	67	3.46
Kollencode	403	20.82
Total	1935	100

Source: NABARD, Nagercoil.

Table 1 shows that SHGs have been formed in large number in different panchayats in the tsunami hit area in Kanyakumari District. As the maximum of 403 SHGs were formed in Kollencode town Panchayat followed by Kanyakumari Panchayat with 361 SHGs and Kallukottam with 223 SHGs. Only 63 SHG's were formed in the tsunami hit area Anjugrammam Panchayat. The main reason for the slow growth of SHGs in Anjugramam Panchayat is that there is low awareness about SHG's in Anjugramam Panchayat about SHG's. further, the NGO activity is also very poor in the Panchayat.

ASSISTANCE THROUGH REVOLVING FUND

Revolving fund is the loan amount sanctioned by the Government of Tamilnadu to the SHGs for sanctioning loan to its members. A sum of Rs. 45000 is sanctioned to SHG's as revolving fund. In the total loan amount Rs. 15000 is sanctioned as subsidy. The loan amount excluding subsidy is to be repaid to the Government by the SHG's. Once after repaying the loan, if needed the SHG's can again borrow revolving fund again from the Government The details of revolving fund sanctioned to SHG's in the tsunami hit area in Kanyakumari district are presented in the Table 2.

It is clear from Table 2 that a total sum of Rs.262.70 lakhs has been sactioned as revolving fund in the tsunami hit area. The maximum amount of Rs.48.50 lakhs was sanctioned for various SHG's functioning in Ganapathipuram Panchayat followed by Kollencode and Palapallam Panchayats.SHG's in Manavalakurichi Panchayat are granted a minimum amount of revolving fund. It shows the slow functioning of SHG's in Manavalakurichi town Panchayat.

TRAINING PROGRAMMES CONDUCTED

Women in the Tsunami hit area have developed their family and set aside their losses made by tsunami not alone by joining in the SHG, but also

Table 2
Revolving Fund for SHG's in the Tsunami hit area

Panchayats	*Revolving fund sanctioned (Rs.in lakhs)*	*Percentage*
Kanyakumari	29.70	11.3
Reethapuram	15.30	5.82
Manavalakurichi	12.10	4.60
Kallukoottam	14.90	5.67
Ganapathypuram	48.50	18.46
Mandaikadu	19.80	7.53
Pallapallam	31.40	11.95
Puthalam	27.90	10.62
Anjugramam	16.30	6.20
Kollencode	46.80	17.81
Total	262.70	100

Source: NABARD, Nagercoil

undergoing various training programmes conducted by various agencies. The NGO's sponsoring SHG's with the support of the Government of Tamilnadu conducts two types of orientation programmes to the members of SHG's. They are:

(i) Basic Orientation training

(ii) Skill training

Both of the training programmes imparted by the NGO's guided the members of SHGs to start industrial activities. Further the programmes instill confidence in the minds of tsunami hit women which makes them to be bolder to face the challenges. The details of the basic orientation training programmes and skill development programmes conducted in the tsunami hit area to the SHG members are presented in Table 3.

Table 3 makes it clear that through the basic orientation training programmes conducted to SHG's in the Tsunami hit area as the high 210 groups have benefited in Kanyakumari Panchayat, followed by Ganapathipuram Panchayat with 185 groups. Similarly through the skill training programmes the 95 SHG's in Reethapuram panchayat and 94 SHG's in Manavalakurichi have benefitted as the maximum.

IMPACT OF SHGS ON THEIR MEMBERS AFTER TSUNAMI

The SHGs formed in the tsunami hit area provided monetary and non monetary assistances to its members . The assistances extended include The findings are presented in table 4 infusing self confidence with women, encouraging thrift habit, creating self employment, creating co-operative spirit, upliftment of the area, improving leadership quality, and for relieving from the clutches of the money lenders. The assistances extended include.

Table 3
Training Programmes Conducted to Members of SHG's in the Tsunami hit Area

Panchayat	*Total no of SHGs in the panchayat*	*Basic Orientation training*		*Skill Training*	
		No. of SHG's Undergone training	*Expenditure Rs. (lakhs)*	*No. of SHG's Undergone training*	*SHG's Expenditure Rs (lakhs)*
Kanyakumari	361	210 (17.76)	4.43 (17.84)	40 (8.65)	0.80 (8.65)
Reethapuram	104	54 (4.56)	1.12 (4.51)	95 (20.56)	1.90 (20.56)
Manavalakurichi	125	58 (4.90)	1.23 (4.95)	94 (20.34)	1.88 (20.34)
Kallukuttam	223	106 (8.96)	2.20 (8.86)	36 (7.79)	0.72 (7.79)
Ganapathipuram	205	185 (15.65)	3.88 (15.63)	32 (6.92)	0.64 (6.92)
Mandaikadu	152	94 (7.95)	1.96 (7.89)	22 (4.76)	0.44 (4.76)
Pallapallam	143	120 (10.15)	2.53 (10.19)	43 (9.30)	0.86 (9.30)
Puthalam	152	134 (11.33)	2.81 (11.32)	50 (10.82)	1.00 (10.82)
Anjugramam	67	57 (4.82)	1.22 (4.96)	50 (10.82)	1.00 (10.82)
Kollencodu	403	164 (13.87)	3.44 (13.85)	0	0.00
Total	1935	1182 (100)	24.82 (100)	462 (100)	9.24 (100)

Source: NABARD, Nagercoil.

The ranks awarded by sample respondents with respect to the above seven variables are further analysed through Garrets ranking technique. The findings are presented in Table 4.

Table 4
Impact of Self Help Groups on Members

Impacting Variable	*Size of Impact (Ranks as assigned by the respondents)*							
	I	*II*	*III*	*IV*	*V*	*VI*	*VII*	*Total*
Infuse self confidence	21	22	9	15	21	12	0	100
Encouraging thrift habit	34	20	10	24	9	3	0	100
Creating self employment	12	10	30	15	3	10	20	100
Creating co-operative sprite	8	13	15	11	18	21	14	100
Uplift of the area	2	12	11	14	15	20	26	100
Improving leadership quality	7	8	5	9	9	27	35	100
Relieving from the clutchesof the money	16	15	20	12	25	7	5	100

Source: Primary data.

It is obviously from clear the Table 4 that women in the tsunami hit area have been assisted by SHG's in large scale. "Infusing self confidence" is considered foremost to be the important one by 21 respondents and no one has mentioned it as the least one. 34 respondents have reported that encouraging thrift habit is another important impacting variable and no one has considered it as the least. 20 and 14 respondents have considered creating self employment and creating co- operative sprits as an important impacting variable respectively and some they as important one by 12 and 8 respondents respectively. Most of the respondents have mentioned upliftment of the area (26) and improving leadership quality (35) are less important impact but the same has been considered as best by 2 and 7 respondents respectively. Relieving from the clutches of the money lenders is another important impacting variable considered as the which is one foremost by 16 respondents and 5 respondents mentioned the same as the least important one.

The data collected from the randomly selected 100 sample respondents with regard to seven impacts are analyse 4d through Garrets Ranking technique. The findings are presented is Table 5.

Table 5
Impact of SHG's on Members

Impacting Variable	*Means/score*	*Rank*
Infuse self confidence	56.21	2
Encouraging thrift habit	62.02	1
Creating self employment	49.32	4
Creating co-operative spirit	46.38	5
Uplift of the area	41.19	6
Improving leadership quality	38.32	7
Relieving from the clutches of the money	53.56	3

Source: Primary data.

As is evident from table 5 that the members of SHG's have been much benefitted through SHG's in respect of the variables, encouraging thrift habit 62.02 mean scores followed by infusing confidence (56.21) and 'relieving from the clutches of money lenders (53.56)in the order of priority.

PROBLEMS OF THE SHG'S

The SHG's functioning in the tsunami hit area suffer from many problems. Some of important the deficiencies pointed out by the sample respondents are lack of strong leadership,financial deficit, misuse of group money by leaders , Lack of education among the members, non awareness of government scheme and non- repayment of the loan amount by the members. While some of the problems listed above are acute, a few are lighter. On the basis of the ranks assigned by the sample respondents the problems are analyzed through Garrets ranking technique. The findings are presented in Table 6.

Table 6
Problems Faced by Members of Self Help Groups

Problems	*Rank*							
	I	*II*	*III*	*IV*	*V*	*VI*	*VII*	*Total*
Lack of strong leadership	32	20	9	24	9	4	2	100
Financial deficit	21	20	10	15	21	11	2	100
Misuse of group money by leaders	7	8	5	9	9	26	36	100
Lack of education in member	8	13	15	11	18	17	18	100
Non awareness of government scheme	18	15	20	12	25	7	3	100
Members don't repay the loan amount	12	14	30	15	3	15	11	100
Other problems	2	10	11	14	15	20	28	100

Source : Primary data.

The table clearly reveals that members of SHG's in tsunami hit area in Kanyakumari district have been facing many problems after tsunami. One of the important problems is lack of strong leadership 32 respondents have ranked it as the first and foremost problem. 20 respondents have considered it as the second important problem. Financial deficit is another problem faced by the members of SHG's. 21 respondents have reported this problem as the important one and only 2 members have considered it as the least problem. Another problem which is faced by SHG's is the misuse of group money by leader. But this problem is not considered acute. Hence 36 members have assigned least score to this variable. Only 7 members have mentioned it as the most important problem. Lack of education is also a problem faced by SHG members. 8 members have reported it as a primary problem and 18 members have mentioned it as a least one. Non awareness of government schemes and members not repaying the loan amount are also the problems to be counted. 18 and 12 members have mentions the above problems as the important one respectively. In the same way 3 and 11 respondents have revealed them as least important one. Apart from this there are few other problems that are inevitably mentioned by the respondent. But they are not significant. It shows that inspite of the several assistances provided for the upliftment of members, it has several criticisms.

The ranks awarded by the sample respondents with respect to seven variables are further analysed through Garrets ranking technique. The findings are presented in Table 7.

Table 7 shows that absence of strong leadership is the most important problem facesd by the members of 8 SHG's in the tsunami hit area. Hence the variable has the heighest mean score of 60.65. The other variables with which the SHG's suffer in order are financial deficit (55.56), awareness of Government scheme (54.70) and non repayment of loan (51.73).

Table 7
Problems of SHG's in Tsunami Hit Area

Problems	*Means/ score*	*Rank*
Lack of strong leadership	60.65	1
Financial deficit	55.56	2
Misuse of group money by leaders	36.09	7
Lack of education in member	45.86	5
Non awareness of government scheme	54.70	3
Members don't repay the loan amount	51.73	4
Other problems	40.31	6

Source: Primary data.

CONCLUSION

In the upliftment of women affected by tsunami in Kanyakumari district SHGs have done yeomen service. SHGs have been so active after tsunami in Kanyakumari District.The active role played by SHGs in assisting the members SHG's in the tsunami hit area has wiped the hard tears of those who have been wounded by tsunami. It is possible for the SHGs only through the co-operation of the Government and NGOs who have sponsored such SHGs. Among the different assistances extended by SHGs a few alone have much impacted on women than the other assistances. Inspite of these hard facts, there are hue and cry in some corners as to the pains and problems as they are experiencing in availing assistances from SHG's. A much more concentrated effort on the part of the SHG's will remove such hardship.

References

Janine Rodgers (2001), "Women and Service Sector Employment", The Global Context. *The Indian Journal of Labour Economics,* Vol. 44, No. 2, April June, p. 24.

Jeyaraman Ajay Salty Senthil Kumar and Selvaraj (2004), "Role of Self Help Groups in Fisher Women Development", *Penisular Economist,* Vol. XII, No. 2, 196. 200

Misra, P. K. (2002), Empowerment of Rural Youth Through Self help Groups and Co-operative *Tamil Nadu Journal of Co-operation,* pp. 53 59.

Jayakumar, Bandula, TRO and Tsunami South Asia Intelligence Review, Vol. 13, No. 3, March 28, New Delhi, *www.satp.org*.

La, John (2004), "Forced Remittances in Canadas Tamil Enchaves Peace Review, Vol. 16, No. 3, September, pp. 379–85.

Expenditure Pattern of Village Panchayat in Tamilnadu During Pre and Post-liberalisation Period

R. Balasubbiramani *

INTRODUCTION

PUBLIC expenditure refers to the expenditure incurred by the Central, State and Local Governments to satisfy collective social wants. The advantages of Public expenditure were not fully appreciated by the traditional economists. They considered market mechanism as a better method whereby the working of the economy could be guided and the allocation of resources could be decided. But today due to the continuous expansion of state activities and other public bodies the volume of public expenditure has been increasing in almost all countries of the world. As the scope of the functions of the Government was restricted in the past there was no need for theory of public expenditure. In the present century the development of the functions of the state in social matter and public utilities has increased public expenditure in a large degree. Accordingly the importance of public expenditure has also increased.

STATEMENT OF THE PROBLEM

In the above pages we have discussed the evolution of the Panchayat Raj Institution in India and in Tamil Nadu. We have seen that prior to 1992, the Panchayat Local bodies had no constitutional status. They depended on the state government for functioning and financial support. The functions and roles of all the local bodies varied among state. After the 73rd constitutional amendment local bodies are given constitutional status and it changed the role of them. Further, State Finance Commission is assigned the role of assigning the share in taxes to local bodies and grants-in-aid.

So, a major impact with finance of the rural and urban local bodies and correspondingly function of them also changed. So it is necessary to know

* Faculty of Economics, Department of Management Studies, Sree Amman Arts And Science College, Chittode, Erode-638102, Tamilnadu, (*E-mail- econbalu@yahoo.com*)

how the new arrangements have strengthened finances of Panchayats under the heads like own source income, share in taxes, own source and grants-in-aid have changed before and after the adoption of new Act in 1994. Like revenue mobilisation how pattern of expenditure has undergone any change has to be studied need a study so as to assess and understand the impact of new acts. As we implemented the new act in 1996 in Tamil Nadu, a comprehensive analysis of sample village finance five year for before 1996 and five year after 1996 would be in order.

OBJECTIVES OF THE STUDY

On the light of the above problem following objectives were framed:

1. To study the patten of expenditure and untrend among the different village panchayats within a panchayat union, and
2. To study the disparities before and after the implementation of 73rd amendment.

METHODOLOGY

To achieve the above objectives an empirical enquiry was necessary. So ten year period was chosen in such a way to have 5 years before and 5 years after the implementation of new act in 1996 and to collect and analyse the finance of the village panchayat. The ten year was ranging between 1991 to 2001. However, for an individual researcher, due to time and resource constraints, the area of coverage had to be restricted. So it was decided to confine the study area to one Rural Panchayat Union which includes twenty six village panchayats. One union was chosen as it has all the necessary characteristics for undertaking a study of this kind.

For this study Tiruchengode Panchayat Union was selected as it is the native place of the researcher and is the head quarters of Namakkal District, in Tamil Nadu. This Panchayat Union with 26 Panchayats incorporates three kinds of village panchayats. Out of 26 panchayats, six panchayats are predominated by agricultural activities with good irrigation. Seven village Panchayats are dominated by small and industria activities and thirteen village panchayats are having dryland cultivation and less industrial activities in Namakkal District, Tamil Nadu.

Apart from the primary data collected from the annual accounts & Registers, Administrative Report of Tiruchengode Union Panchayat and consolidated administrative Reports of the Tiruchengode Union Panchayat were also scrutinised by visiting frequently the office of Tiruchengode Union panchayat as well as village panchayats. The researcher collected details and information by personal interviews with officials and ex-councillors of the Union Panchayat. Simple statistical tools were used to analyse the data to draw conclusions. Also trend line were computed with the principle of least squares.

SCOPE OF THE STUDY

India is an agricultural economy and vast majority of our population are living in rural areas. With the advent of planning it was realized that an earnest efforts could be made to tone up the economic life of the people to rise their standard of living. A very few literature available on the rural local bodies confined themselves to problem village panchayats and pointout that they have to undertake more and more responsibilities. There is no corresponding increase in their financial resources. This may be due to low level income and as such they contribute little in the direction of social change. Some studies strongly advocated for the establishment of Panchayat Raj Financial Corporation and establishing village panchayat on solid financial base. The current study is an attempt to understand the finances of Tiruchengoide Union Panchayat as a sample study. It analyse the revenue and expenditure as well as the overall financial position of sample Panchayats. The findings of the study may through a broad position of the finances of Panchayats and need not be reflecting the exact situation of entire Tamil Nadu due to variation between different Panchayats in different districts.

TREND AND PATTERN OF EXPENDITURE

The major items of expenditures considered for analyses are: salaries, electric charges, revenue expenditure, capital expenses, advances and deposits and other items. Out of 26 village Panchayats about 11 villages incurred between 20 per cent to 30 per cent of total expenditures on salary account. The remaining 15 village Panchayats incurred less than 20 per cent of total expenditure but more than 10 per cent of total expenditure in on salaries of their employees. On the whole Tiruchengode Union Panchayats incurred an average of 21 per cent of its expenditure on salary during the years 1991-2001.

EXPENDITURE ON POWER SUPPLY

Maintenance of streetlight and water supply involve expenditure on power. Next to expenses on salary power bill is another important expense for village Panchayats. Which includes for paying streetlight and for the supply of drinking water bills etc. under this account, 15 villages incurred expenses ranging between 20 per cent to 30 per cent their of total expenditure. Seven village Panchayats incurred expenses between 31 per cent to 40 per cent of total expenditures on power. The remaining four village Panchayats spent less than 20 per cent of total expenditure on power bill. In average around one fourth of the among spent on power bill. In average around one fourth of the amount spent on power bill in all the 26 village Panchayats. Maintenance of water supply and streetlight is considered to be one of the basic services a local body is expected to render to the public. Hence this expense is necessary.

REVENUE EXPENDITURE

The revenue expenditure covers maintenance of radio, TV, library, sanitation public health and maintenance of road and bridges etc. Only one village Panchayats (viz., 26) incurred 42 per cent of their expenditure on revenue expenditure for maintaining social infrastructure facilities. About 3 village Panchayats spent amount ranging between 31 per cent and 40 per cent of their total expenditures. Out of their total expenditures, around 21 per cent to 30 per cent was incurred on revenue expenditure by 12 village panchayats. The remaining 10 village Panchayats incurred expenses from 10 per cent to 20 per cent of their total expenditure.

During the 1991-92 to 2000-2001, the expenditure made for buying hand pumps, street lamps, TV and Radio was about 22 per cent of their total expenditures of 26 village Panchayats.

CAPITAL EXPENDITURE

Capital expenditure includes the new installation of hand pumps, laying roads and construction of bridge otherwise called as social infrastructure for the village Panchayats for their development purposes. Further, implementations of social infrastructure facilities provide employment opportunities to the community of the village or neighbourhood village Panchayats. Under capital expenditure about 11 village Panchayats incurred expenses between 11 per cent to 20 per cent of their total expenditures. About 9 village Panchayats spent between 21 per cent and 30 per cent of their total expenditure on capital expenditures. The remaining 6 village Panchayats incurred expenses less than equal to 10 per cent of their total expenditures. Average expenditure incurred by sample Panchayats on capital items constituted about 17 per cent of the total expenditure during the study period (1991-92 to 2000-2001).

ADVANCES AND DEPOSITS

In one of the foregoing paragraphs, role of advances and deposits in Panchyats finance was explained. About 22 village Panchayats incurred less than or equal to 10 per cent to total expenditure on adcvances and deposits. Only 3 village Panchayats incurred expenses ranging between 11 per cent to 20 per cent of their total expenditures. On this item, only one village (viz., Devanankuruchi) Panchayats did not incur any expenditure on advances and deposits to total expenditures. The mean percentage share of advances and deposits to total expenditure was around 5 per cent only for all 26 village Panchayats during the period 1991-92 to 2000-2001.

OTHER EXPENDITURES

The expenses incurred in all village panchayats are with the motive of promoting the welfare of the people. Except one village Panchayats (viz, Sirumolasi) all other village Panchayats incurred around 4 per cent of their total expenditures on other expenditures. Altrnately mean expenditure incurred by a sample Panchayats under other expenditures constituted about 4 per cent of the total expenditure.

HEADWISE AVERAGE EXPENDITURE DURING PRE (1991-1996) AND POST (1997-2001) IMPLEMENTATION OF 73RD AMENDMENT IN 1996

In addition to the pattern and trend of public expenditure, an attempt was made to study the difference between the share of distribution of amount of expenditure on different categories between the pre and post reform period of 73rd Amendment, which was implemented in Tamil Nadu in 1996-97. In other words an attempt was made to find was there any marked difference in the pattern or type of expenditure in Panchayats after the implementation of New Panchayat Act in 1996 and the implementation of popularly elected body rule. The period of our study was divided in to two consisting of two five years each and have 1991–1996 as prior to new act and the period between 1997 and 2001 as post to new act.

On the whole Tiruchengode Union Panchayats incurred an average of 21 per cent of its expenditure on salary during the years 1991-2001.

Maintenance of streetlight and water supply involves expenditure in power. Next to expenses on salary, power bill is another important expense for village Panchayats, which includes paying for street light, for the supply of drinking water etc. Under this account, 15 villages incurred expenses ranging between 20 per cent to 30 per cent their of total expenditure. Seven village Panchayats incurred expenses between 31 per cent to 40 per cent of total expenditures. The remaining four village Panchayats spent less than 20 per cent of total expenditure on power bill. In average around one fourth of the amount spent on power bill in the 26 village Panchayats.

Maintenance of water supply and streetlight is considered to be one of the basic services a local body is expected to render to the public. Hence this expense is necessary.

The revenue expenditure covers maintenance of radio, TV and library, sanitation public health and maintenance of road and bridges etc. Only one village Panchayats (viz., Animoor) incurred 42 per cent of their expenditure on revenue expenditure for maintaining social infrastructure facilities. About 3 village Panchayats spent amount ranging between 31 per cent to 40 per cent of their total expenditures. Next to this out of their total expenditures, around 21 per cent to 30 per cent incurred on revenue expenditure by 12 village Panchayats. The remaining 10 village Panchayats incurred expenses from 10 per cent of their total expenditures.

During the 1991-92 to 2000-2001, the expenditure made for buying hand pumps, street lamps, TV and Radio was about 22 per cent their total expenditures of 26 village Panchayats.

Capital expenditure includes the new installation of hand pumps, laying roads and construction of bridge otherwise called as social infrastructure for the village Panchayats for their development purposes. Further, implementations of social infrastructure facilities provide employment opportunities to the community of the village or neighbourhood village Panchayats. Under capital expenditure about 11 village Panchayats incurred expenses between 11 per cent and 20 per cent of their total expenditures. About 9 village Panchayats spent between 21 per cent and 30 per cent of their total expenditure on capital expenditures. The remaining 6 village Panchayats incurred expenses less than equal to 10 per cent of their total expenditures.

Average expenditure incurred by sample Panchayats on capital items constituted about 17 per cent of the total expenditure during the study period (1991-92 to 2000-2001).

About 22 village Panchayats incurred less than or equal to 10 per cent to total expenditure on advances and deposits. Only 3 village incurred expenses ranging between 11 per cent to 20 per cent of their total expenditures. On this item, only one village (viz., Devanankuruchi) Panchayats did not incur any expenditure on advances and deposits to total expenditures. The mean percentage share of advances and deposits to total expenditure was around 5 per cent only for all 26 village Panchayats during the period 1991-92 to 2000-2001.

The expenses incurred in all village Panchayats are with the motive of promoting the welfare of the people. Except one village Panchayats (viz, Sirumolasi) all other village Panchayats incurred around 4 per cent of their total expenditures on other expenditures.

Alternately mean expenditure incurred by a sample Panchayats under other expenditures constituted about 4 per cent of the total expenditure.

The mean percentage share of all the Panchayats on salary during the period 1991-1996 was 17.69 per cent. There were 14 Panchayats out of 26 incurred lesser proportions than the mean of all the sample Panchayats. So about 55 per cent had spent lesser average amount on salaries in Panchayats than the mean proportion of expenditure during the first period.

If we compare with the mean proportion or as percentage share of expenses on different heads between the two period of time (prior to implementation of new Panchayat Act) and after the implementation of Act in 1996-97) we find that in average for all the 26 Panchayats during 1996-2001 about 24.76 per cent of expenditure was incurred on salaries of Panchayats employees which is about 7 per cent higher than the previous five year period.

In about half of the Panchayats average expenditures on salaries of employees was less proportionate than the mean proportion for the entire Panchayats union. So during both the period proportion of salary paid varied between Pancheyats. However in average during the post new act period (1996-2001) average salary was higher than the previous period. Perhaps this might have been due to the fact that all government employees' salaries were raised around 1998-99.

Similarly on streetlight and water pump in 11 Panchayats spent lesser than the mean proportion of expenditure for the 26 Panchayats.

In the same way during the second half period around 15 Panchayats incurred expenses on power supply maintenance lesser than the union average of 28.69 per cent of the total expenditure.

In similar lines on revenue expenditures and capital as well as other expenses we find that around in half of the Panchayats both during the first and second half individual Panchayats spent less than the Panchayats union mean proportion of total expenses under each of the above heads.

One important aspect one can note here is when we compare the proportion of mean expenditure on salaries, power supply or street light and water supply maintenance, revenue expenditure and other expenses were higher during the second half of our study period or after the implementation of new act than the first half of the period.

Whereas in the case of mean expenditure on capital items during the period after the implementation of new act was lesser than the first half. Perhaps the role assigned to Panchayats in maintaining capital items have been modified after 1996-97 and therefore correspondingly the Panchayats average expenditure on those items has declined.

PER CAPITA EXPENDITURE UNDER VARIOUS HEADS

In the foregoing pages we have discussed the pattern of expenditures incurred by our sample 26 Panchayats in the union in two different ways. One for the entire 10-year period and the other by dividing the 10 year period into two period as prior to new Panchayats act and post new act. In all those analyses we have used the proportion of expenses on different heads out of the total expenditures. Those analyses have given only in relative terms. To understand how far the actual mean expenses in rupee terms under each head was incurred for the union as such for the entire 10 years and how many Panchayats incurred less than or more than the mean expenditure.

ANNUAL CHANGE IN PUBLIC EXPENDITURE

Those data reveal the fact that there is no uniform change in the public expenditure of the sample Panchayats. Further, some Panchayats have registered negative growth in public expenditure for some years over the previous year while others have registered positive growth. Some Panchayats have registered negative growth for more than one year. For the year 1992-93, we find out of 26 sample Panchayats, 21 Panchayats have registered negative growth in public expenditure. In other words, each of them has spent lesser amount in 1992-93 than for the year 1991-92. Similar trend prevailed for the year 1994-95 with 13 Panchayats and 1995-96 with 15 Panchayats registering negative growth. Likewise, in 1999-2000 and 2000-2001 also in 9 and 14 Panchayats respectively total expenditure fell over the previous year.

If we analyse these changes by considering the new Act in 1996, we can try to analyse the impact of constitutional amendment and the emergence of State Finance Commission and its effect on finances of Panchayats. When the annual change in public expenditure of sample Panchayats are considered from that angle we find that after 1996-97 fewer Panchayats registered negative growth in public expenditure than prior to 1995-96.

OVERALL GROWTH OF EXPENDITURE

It indicates that other than the Panchayat Pirithi, all other Panchayats have registered a positive growth with varying rate of growth ranging from less than 43 per cent of the first year to nine times that much as the first year. So, over years, Panchayats expenditures have grown without any uniform change. It is common knowledge that there is no end for local bodies and in general for governments to serve the people. Such service to the people will lead to public expenditure. Here the fluctuations in public expenditure of Panchayats reveals the fact that there were fluctuations in the services provided by Panchayats also.

CONCLUSION

One of the objectives of this study was to find out the impact of amended provisions of the local bodies act of 1994 and implemented in Tamil Nadu since 1996 as well as the consequences of the recommendations of the State Finance Commission on the finances of our sample Panchayats. But our study has revealed that all these changes have not influenced the finances substantially. This is evident from the fact that we did not find much variation in the volume of revenue mobilised , expenditure incurred and overall finances of the Panchayats between the first half and the last half of the period of study. In other words we did not find much difference in the finances of our sample Panchayats prior to and after the implementation of new acts of the constitution in 1996. Perhaps this may be due to the time frame of five years after 1996 we have chosen is not sufficient to capture the changes initiated by the Government and many changes have been brought into operation in 1999-2000. To realise the full impact of finance commission's recommendations it may take another three or four years. So our modest effort to understand the impact of new act on the finances has revealed that the time required to make such study needs some more years of operation of the amended provisions of the constitution.

References

Tamilnadu Panchayat Act 1958 and 1994.

Report of the State Finance Commission for local bodies, Government of Tamilnadu, 1994, November-1996.

Panchayat Raj institutions in India, Government of India, Ministry of Rural development New Delhi 1991.

Tiruchengode Union Panchayat annual reports in Tamil Nadu.

Ecomomic Development and Public Sector Banks

*R. Balasubbiramani**

INTRODUCTION

In 1990s the world witnessed the collapse of Marxism, the end of cold war and a new wave of political freedom and human right across the globe. Most of the countries including India have brought above a paradigm shift in economy from the controlled economy to liberalized market economy.While acknowledging the limit to open economy, Mr. Manmohan Singh the then finance minister provided a promising thrust for open economy through our developmental programs. Social justice parameters will be the main index to measure the movement of open economy of our country. He articulated the need to move away from the notion of economic structure to dynamic pattern, to changes with all most priority to the process of social economic developmental process of the economy. According to him, living an independent yet inter-dependent world shaped by high-tech, communication and capitalism compelled us to go before globalization that is required in all areas of the life and ideologies. Therefore, he suggested Liberalization, Privatization and Globalization (LPG) is a paradigm shift in our conceptual framework, perception, attitude and developmentally approach. Therefore, globalization is a process that can be perceived in the growth of international trade, satisfaction of international labour market, financial flows, transactional co-operations of multinational enterprises. Proliferations of tourism and reforms of politics to achieve the objectives of operation of universal standard. The nature and terms of Mr. Manmohan Singh's approach to Indian LPG has changed his promises of globalization in the Indian contest. With this background let us go for our study LPG in the public sector banking and economic development.

PRIVATISATION OF PUBLIC SECTOR BANKS

Privatisation of public sector banks is an integral part of the agenda that was taken up to accomplish financial sector reforms adopted by the dictates of India at the dictates of IMF,World Bank and WTO.

* Faculty of Economics, Department of Management Studies, Sree Amman Arts And Science College, Chittode, Erode-638102, Tamilnadu, (*E-mail- econbalu@yahoo.com*)

The first set of 14 private banks was nationalized in 1969. During these 35 years the banking landscape had undergone a dramatic change. There had been a spectacular growth in the banking system in all parameters. The total number of bank branches during these years jumped over eight-fold-from 8262 to 69071. The growth had been phenomenal in rural India where the number of branches went up from 1833 to 32,227. The total deposits of all commercial banks shot up by all most 332 times and their advances soared 240,50 times. It shows the èffect of the nationalization of banks on the expansion of banking industry in all parameters.

Nationalisation of banks has not only had its impact on the expansion but also acted as the largest stimulant to the growth of the Indian economy in various ways. Target lending to the agriculture sector has made funds easily available in this sector resulting to huge production of agricultural good. Lending to small scale and cottage industries has not only helped the growth in the industrial production but also has generated considerable employment in rural sector. On the other hand, new private banks do not have any presence in rural India and naturally do not have any responsibility or commitment towards the majority population of the country who live in the rural areas.

But this social responsibility of the public sector banks are sought to be pruned out through the route of privatization where the public will have no say on the affairs of those banks.

Different strategies, suitable to the particular and prevailing situation are adopted to accomplish the privatization goal. At the time of nationalization of private banks, the capital invested by those private owners were returned to them by the Government of India contributing its investment in the capital structure of those banks and thereby all those banks were brought wholly under the State sector. In June 1994, the Act was amended providing for disinvestments of Government's share of bank's capital upto 49 per cent. With this one after another public bank started selling the Government's share of capital to the private individuals and groups. Another strategy that has been adopted to reduce the government's control is to return the Government is remaining investment in the public sector banks. In the meantime, in December 2000 Government has brought a Bill in the Parliament providing for privatization of its capital upto 67 per cent and to retain only 33 per cent in its hands. Due to serious agitation by bank employees and officers and opposition by the public, the Bill has been referred to the Standing Committee of Finance. Just before assuming the office of prime ministership Dr. Manmohan Singh announced in public that the public sector character of the nationalized banks would be retained. But, within the few months another strategy was adopted. This time it is through the process of merger and acquisition by which such an outside as well as inside systemic pleasure will be mounted on the public sector bank that their ownership,. governance, activities etc. will virtually be in the hands of private capital.

THE MERGER AND ACQUISITIONS OF PUBLIC SECTOR BANKS

In the banking scenario of India till now only one Public Sector Bank (PSB) (New Bank of India) was merged with another PSB (Punjab National Bank) in 1993. However, that merge was not all market driven rather it was to rescue the former for safeguarding the interest of the deposits. But, what Narasimhan Committee Report (1991) suggested for merger and acquisitions of PSB was generated from Central Government's adoption of new economic policy as per the dictate of the IMF and the World Bank. This Committee recommended broad pattern of the structure of the banking system which that stated inter alia that there should be 3 to 4 large banks (SBI) which would become international in character. The Committee was of the view that the said system should be market driven and based on profitability considerations and brought about through a process of mergers and acquisition. Despite these recommendations there was no move for any such merger of PSB till 2003.

It was only when Finance Minister Mr. P. Chidambaram gave a call for consolidation of Public Sector Banks in the annual general meeting of IBA on August 28, 2004, the heads of the PSBs started discussing-which bank would global up which another bank. Finance Minister's view was that through merger and acquisitions Indian banking industry would achieve world class status which was further emphasized by Mr. Pritiviraj Chavan, Minister of State in the PMO. He stated that the PSBs would be given full managerial autonomy to build a world class banking system. Some banks would also be permitted to operate in the international banking market. This was in line with the guidelines of WTO when the banking sector would have to be opened up, he stated. He further said that only banks that become Basic III capital requirement compliant as prescribed by the Bank for international settlements would be allowed to enter global banking market. He pointed that the large banks would only be able to ensure that they were not burdened by stressed asset and therefore he emphasized that bank management would be given freedom on the merger proposal. Government has also decided to give freedom to banks tap the capital market to encourage the banks to reduce its government holding as below as 51 per cent.

It appears as if the Indian public sector banks completed all their tasks in the country and now they should go abroad. But is India over banked? Against a total population of 1.1 billion there are only about 250 million bank accounts and if the multiple accounts are excluded the number will drastically come down. So there are enormous opportunities for the Indian banks going to boom if in the growing economy millions of people get jobs and will need bank accounts.

The Chief Executive Officers of Union Bank and Bank of India decided to marge these two banks in the last week of December 2004. The merger decision was to be finalized but due to the opposition by all workmen and officers of Union Bank against the merger, the decision could not be finalized.

Mr. R.K. Hegde, Executive Director of Union Bank was planning the inorganic growth in line with the trend in the Indian banking system to consolidate. He viewed that through merger and acquisition country's bank would achieve size and scale comparable to that of global banks. While the total capital of City Group of the US is $67 billion, the total capital of State Bank group only $ 6.7 billion, the total capital of all other public sector banks in India will come around only $13 billion. So attaining to comparable size even by Union Bank and Bank of India combine for competition is a mere propaganda but not the reality.

A study for the ILO on mergers and acquisitions in the financial sector has examined several of the arguments and claims by proponents of M & A and has said that it has resulted in few banks loss of employment and diminishing access to services for consumers. The report also brings out that there has been considerable skepticism among small business about claims that they would benefit and point to studies that show that larger financial institution tend to charge more and higher fees than their smaller counterparts and that there is an inverse relationship between sizes of financial institutions and their loan portfolios to smaller business. In terms of consumers, they lose personal services and the cost of the service also has increased.

Through merger it is sought to reduce the operating cost of the banks because reduction in operating cost is a key fact to adhere to new capital adequacy ratio under Basie II norms, in order to reduce the operating costs branches will be closed down, non and less remunerative services of social obligation will be drastically curtailed, use of sophisticated and newer technology will pay attention to the creamy layer of the customer and by all these means banking services will be out of reach of the ordinary customers-' class, banking will emerge in place of mass banking in the merged entity profit will be main consideration and naturally credit deposit ratio will come down in the backward regions leading to aggravate the regional imbalance.

National Association of Software Service Companies Study shows that a merger results in savings of 54 per cent of its investment for technology in terms of the hardware being used in one unit of the merged entity. This will save huge expenditure enabling the new entity to go for newer and more sophisticated forms of technology resulting to large number of job sharinkage and the existing work done will compelled to exit the banks in a big way through various means.

LATIN AMERICAN EXPERIENCE

Over the 1990s many Latin American economics opened their domestic financial sector including banking to foreign direct investment to an unprecedented extent. Whereas the FDI entered these strategic sectors of the economics with what was made out as a missionary agenda of strengthening the capital base of ailing and failing domestic banks and infusing international best practices and technology, the experience during the short time of foreign bank presence in Latin America has vindicated every apprehension on its role. The Latin American Experience showed that the expensive domination by the foreign banks has given rise to conditions of: (a) stalled overall growth in credit with domestic banks also reducing loan exposure (b) far greater financial instability during episodes of shock to the domestic economy and (c) uncertainty and slow economic growth due to foreign banks acting as conduits for transmission of contagion and strategic decisions from parent banks on to developing markets. These consequences are but an expression of the loss of economic sovereignty that comes hand in hand with the excessive reliance on foreign investment.

Despite the dismal experience of Latin American economies staring in the face, emerging market economics continue to believe in the virtues of foreign investment in banking and therefore liberalize the financial sector and encourage foreign investment in the sector. Among the latest to this line are some of the major Asian economics-South Korea, Japan, India-which had till the 1990s highly protected and segmented banking regime with a strong emphasis on social and development banking. The question before us is -do we turn a blind-eye to history and allow Asia to go the Latin America way.

Except Chile where concentration of banking asset has accompanied gains in efficiency of intermediation, in all other countries the situation has worsened with consolidation. Finally, a very revoking flash from the study of bank-level.

The argument the Indian banks need to grow in order to compete with the "big boys" on the global stage is misplaced because however big they grow as a result of mergers, they are never going to be able to compete with them on their terrain (Table 1). Anybody can guess how the much talked about merger of BOI and Union Bank of India with a combined asset of 32 billion dollar can ever put up a challenge to the Indian giant SBI having an asset worth of 91 billion dollar, leave about facing MNC banks with many fold asset base. And, the question of how well they are able to cope with foreign banks on Indian soil is an issue relating to regulatory approaches and policy structures that protect Indian banking. This regulation and protection is necessary not because of some vague xenophobic fears but simply because banking is far too important a tool for social and economic development.

A report commissioned by the G 10 group of industrialized nations, released on 25 January 2001 warned that banking failures in Japan might be repeated elsewhere following the recent wave of consolidation in the financial services industry. The report showed that in 13 countries, studied, there was a high level of M & A activity involved banking firms, accounting for 60 pr cent of all financial mergers and 70 per cent of their value. The report revealed that recent M & A activity had provided only 'weak' evidence of increased efficiency and called on regulators to be alert to the possible harmful effects on competition. The report concluded that the creation of ever larger and more complex banks

Table 1
The Number of Banks in Latin American Countries

	1996-2003		*Change*	*% Change*
Argentian	117	80	-37	-32
Brazil	253	177	-76	-30
Chile	31	25	-6	-18
Columbia	39	27	-12	-31
Costa Rica	30	21	-9	-29
Mexico	40	32	-9	-21
Peru	22	15	-7	-32
El Salvador	18	13	-5	-28

Source: Banking FDI in Latin America.

Table 2
Top 10 Banks by Asset Size (in billion $) As on 31.05.04

International Banks	*Asset Size*	*Indian Banks*	*Asset Size*
Mizuho Financial Group	1285	State Bank of India	91
Citi Group	1264	ICICI	28
UBS	1121	PNB	23
Credit Agricole	1105	Canara Bank	22
HSBC Holding	1034	BOB	19
Deutsche Bank	1015	BOI	19
BNP Paribas	989	Central Bank of India	14
Mitsubishi Tokyo Financial	975	Union Bank of India	13
Sumitomo Mistsui Financial	950	IOB	11
Royal Bank Scotland	806	Syndicate Bank	10

Source: CMIE.

and financial conglomerates "increased the possibility that the 'work out' or wind down... would be difficult and could be disorderly". The report also noted that the creation of more complex institutions had made it more difficult to assess their financial health, and contributes to the systemic instability of the global financial system.

MERGER AND ACQUISITION OF PUBLIC SECTOR BANKS

Financial sector reform prepared by the Narashimam Committee, ever since the finance minister of the Govt. of India spoke about the need of "consolidation" of public sector banks (PSB) through merger and acquisition/ amalgamation in order to grow "in scale and muscle" so that they can compete "effectively with world class banks", the issue has come to the centre stage of policy discussion within the banking industry. Encouraged by the finance minister's blessing to the move, protagonists of new economic policy have started singing the virtues of "Consolidation" deliberately ignoring the dangerous implication of such a move at this critical juncture of socio-economic development of the country. Experience gathered from countries those who have religiously financial sector reform as desired by World Bank/IMF/WTO and moreover the study conducted by non less than an organization like ILO, say different story that the consolidation of banks resulted in closure of branches in massive scale leading to huge surplus in manpower which later were thrown out of jobs. Apart from huge job loss accumulation of wealth in few hands resulted in creating social and cultural strife as the interest of small traders and poorer section and completely overlooked.

ILO REPORT REVEALS FAILURE OF TWO-THIRDS OF FINANCIAL MERGERS

A new ILO report released in Geneva, on February 5, 2001, revealed that "two-thirds of M & As fail to achieve their objectives", despite the often massive job losses and organizational restructuring they entail. The report the employment impact of mergers and acquisitions in the banking and financial services sector attributes much of this to the disregard for the human resources fall-out of redundancies, which can seriously undermine operational capabilities and morale. A study by KPMG referred to in the report finds that M & A deals are 26 per cent more likely to be successful if they paid satisfactory attention to cultural issues. The report quotes conservative estimates that at least 130,000 finance jobs have disappeared in Western Europe as a result of M & As during the 1990s and predicts that approximately 300,000 more banking jobs will disappear between 1999 and 2002 as the result of merger-led consolidation. The report also suggests that job losses associated with mergers mostly affect operational areas such as branch networks and lower hierarchical levels, which are often predominately feminine. The resulting impacts are gender differentiated and may be arresting or even reversing progress in affirmative programmes.

The notion that big is intrinsically better in the business world is increasingly being brought question. At best, forced growth through M & As is a high risk strategy-jeopardising shareholder value and even long term survival. Yet even where mergers 'succeed' in conventional terms-by driving up unaccounted for by the new 'super-corporations' that is paid by shareholders, employees, the environment, competition, intellectual property, corporate governance, transparency, regulation and even national economic sovereignty. As the KPMG study quoted at the beginning of these briefing show, even the conventional figures for mergers don't add up. When we begin to look beyond shareholder value it becomes clear that mergers consistently impoverish us all. It is time for full cost merger accounting allowing decisions to be made on the basis of the real world, rather than the power hungry ambitions of large corporations.

WITH SO MUCH POTENTIAL GAIN, WHO PAYS THE PRICE

Shareholders: There was a time when corporations provided not only jobs in the communities in which they located, but also contributed to local infrastructure and essential services through taxation. Nearly 60 per cent of U.S. controlled corporations and 74 per cent of foreign firms, doing business in the U.S., paid no federal taxes in 1991, the last year figures were available. Driven by the dynamics of globalization the state not only allows large corporations lucrative tax breaks, but also on occasions directly subsidise their operations with public funds.

Employees: As wages are driven downwards, communities compete with one another for scare employment. By undercutting one another, they effectively absorb more of the production costs of the worlds most powerful and profitable companies. When companies merge inevitable restructuring of the newly merged entity results in job losses in the quest for ever greater economies, and ever higher profits. A recent ILO study of the financial services sector concluded that not only do mergers result in job losses-the neglect of human factors is "a frequent cause of failure".

A 1999 KMPG study showed that 53 per cent mergers actually destroy shareholder value, and a further 30 per cent bring no measurable benefit. The number of mergers and acquisitions increased by 43 per cent a year between 1995 and 1999. Developed countries and their transnational corporations hold 97 per cent of patents worldwide.

CONCLUSION

- Gradualism over foreign equity in foreign banks is to be observed, as the RBI Governor explained, financial integration should be approached continuously in a country-specific context.
- Banks consolidation will be the only theoretical gains if the main argument in favour of growing in size through the merger and acquisition route for public sector banks is to take on competition globally.
- The objective of Globalisation in the Indian context will succeed only if it includes the rural economy in the big picture.
- A clear case for consolidation among India's larger public sector banks is yet to be made. These banks have been improving their performance consequent to deregulation, banks to an enhanced commercial orientation, greater autonomy and injection of market discipline. They need to focus now on human resource development issues, risk management and technological upgradation. A preoccupation with mergers at this stage is not only distraction, it could derail the steady improvement in performance in the banking system over the past decade.
- The role of public sector bank in priority sector is to continue for more period until the objectives of rural development is not obtained.

- The ILO in study, done in 2000, painted a grim picture of massive job loss of talent through increased mergers with anxiety and stress for those that were not sacked. The merger will produce the most concentrated banking market in the industrialized world.

References

Narasimhan Committee Report-1991.

Banking FDI in Latin America.

World Bank Report-2006.

CMIE.

Economic Development Merger of Public Sector Banks. (Tanuj Kumar Bisoyee).

Relevance of Affordable Housing Schemes by Real Estate Players in India in the Emerging Scenario: A Study with Focus on Sustianable Business Models

*Manoj P. K.**

INTRODUCTION: HOUSING PROBLEM IN INDIA AND ITS COMPOSITION

HOUSING is one of the most primary human needs. Housing problem in India is very acute, particularly among the poor and other marginalized categories, in spite of the appreciable growth in institutional finance to housing in the ongoing reforms era. This is because, majority of the shelter-less population is beyond the reach of the formal institutional mechanism for housing finance. In fact, as per the 11th Five Year Plan (2007-2012) estimates [1], as of 2007 viz. the end of the 10th Five Year Plan (2002-07), the total urban housing shortage in India has been 24.71 Million units. Furthermore, of this 24.71 Million units as high as 99.84 per cent belongs to EWS (Economically Weaker Section) and LIG (Low Income Group) categories. The balance 0.16 per cent alone relates to MIG (Middle Income Group) and HIG (High Income Group) put together. That is, 21.78 Million for EWS (88.14 per cent), 2.89 Million for LIG (11.70 per cent) and the balance 0.04 Million for MIG and HIG together (0.16 per cent) [2]. Thus, urban housing shortage is virtually a problem of EWS and LIG categories in India – those to whom the formal housing finance system is inaccessible and often unaffordable too. Besides the huge urban housing shortage as above, there is a sizeable rural housing shortage of 7 Million (2007) also.[3] For the ongoing 11th Plan (2007-2012), the total urban housing shortage alone (including the backlog 24.71 Million as of 2007) is 26.53 Million units.

STATEMENT OF THE RESEARCH PROBLEM AND THE OBJECTIVES OF THE STUDY

'Housing for All' has been widely accepted as an imperative for balanced housing development (and hence national economic development also, because

* Faculty (Techno-Management), Dept. of Applied Economics, Cochin University Science and Technology Kochi, Kerala–682 022, (*E-mail: manoj_p_k2004@yahoo.co.in*)

of the vast forward and backward linkages of housing industry with over 250 ancillary industries, and also its high employment generation potential) for a developing nation like in India and that too in an economy that is adversely affected by the global financial slowdown. National Urban Housing and Habitat Policy 2007 (NUHHP) has officially recognized 'Affordable Housing for All' as its goal [4]. Besides, NUHHP seeks to promote, inter alia, sustainable development of habitat with a view to ensuring equitable supply of land, shelter and services at affordable prices to all sections of society. Given the magnitude of the housing shortage and budgetary constraints of the Government, public sector efforts alone are not adequate to face the above challenge. Rather, a 'multi-stake holders' approach involving the other stakeholders like Private Sector, the Cooperative Sector, the Industrial Sector, Services/Institutional Sector, is very much essential [5]. Models like PPP (Public Private Partnership) are becoming growingly significant in this context.

Statement of the Research Problem

Huge urban housing shortage being a reality in India and so also the weakness of the formal institutional housing finance system in addressing the housing needs of the poor and other marginalized sections, and after all the need for balanced and equitable housing development for faster economic development of the nation, it may be stated that urgent policy initiatives are required to promote affordable housing initiatives. Because of the budgetary constraints of the Government, affordable housing initiatives of the Private sector (like, residential real estate developers) need to be promoted, the Government's role being primarily that of a 'Facilitator' rather than a 'Regulator'.

Though there is no universally accepted definition of 'Affordable housing', in India it is generally 'perceived to be related to low and lower-middle income households and relates to the affordability of the cost of purchase of the house rather than the rentals' [6]. Besides, 'affordable housing' is used in India in the context of urban housing [7]. (Hence, rural housing is not studied in detail in this paper).

Affordable housing (budget housing) is yet to pick up considerable momentum in India, in spite of the huge untapped market for low priced housing units and also reasonably favourable Governmental policies and regulatory environment including various fiscal concessions and incentives for housing. There are growing instances of real estate developers fast changing their business models in favour of affordable housing. But, after a boom in the early 2000s, the housing market is only slowly picking up since FY 2006 [8]. Thus, detailed and systematic analysis is required to delve into such issues as (i) the real relevance of promotion of affordable housing in India, given the peculiar housing situation existing in the country, (ii) sustainable business models for affordable housing for real estate developers to mitigate the urban housing problem in India, the one which is more acute than the rural housing problem. Pragmatic policies based on the above analysis could foster balanced and equitable economic development, apart from just 'Housing for All'. Thus, the research problem for this paper may be spelt out as follows: '*Examining the significance of affordable (budget) housing projects of real estate developers in India for mitigating the urban housing problem in the country and also to suggest sustainable business models for such 'budget housing' initiatives.*

Objectives of the Study

(i) To make an overall study of the housing situation in India, the problem of housing shortage and the significance of housing to the national economic development;

(ii) To make a detailed study of the urban housing problem in India, its nature, broad trend and patterns, including the major international experiences in this regard;

(iii) To study the case of affordable housing and its relevance in the current scenario.

(iv) To suggest sustainable business models for promotion of affordable (budget) housing market in India, considering relevant national and international developments in this regard and also preliminary empirical studies of real estate developers offering affordable housing products.

REVIEW OF RELEVANT LITERATURE

Mathur, G C (1980)[9] in his article entitled 'Housing the Poor', has analysed the underlying reasons for the housing shortage and the very slow pace of housing development in India. He has observed that to improve the housing conditions of the poor, it is essential to have a realistic approach keeping in view the scarce resources that are available for investment in this sector. Accordingly, the most effective strategy for housing the poor is to go for self-help to the possible extent, construction of houses in stages, provision of essential services, community facilities and public utilities. The vital significance of low cost houses for the rural and urban poor has been specially highlighted by the author.

Cherunilam, Francis and Heggade, Oddeyar D (1987)[10] in their book 'Housing in India' have covered the aspects of housing situation in India and have made a critical review of the governmental initiatives in alleviating the chronic problem of housing shortage in India. They have observed the poor housing conditions in India and have pointed out the underlying reasons for slow progress in housing development in India. Further, the authors have attempted to analyze the importance of housing in the economy, various dimensions of housing problem, slums, housing through the various Plan periods, rural housing, co-operative housing, and social housing schemes.

Buckley, Robert M. (1996) [11] in his book 'Housing Finance in Developing Countries' has examined in detail the housing policy in developing countries, at a time when their systems have started facing unprecedented changes; particularly because of the wide-spread economic liberalisation the world over, and also in the backdrop of the failure of many centrally planned economies. His analysis focuses on the implications for housing finance based on its historic developments in view of the current most turbulent nature of the global financial system. He points out the utmost significance of the role played by non-budgetary Government policies on the provision of housing.

Nair, Tara S. (1999) [12] in her commentary 'Housing: The Missing Concerns' has pointed out that the unfortunate part of Indian housing scenario is the financial imprudence of the political leaderships in the country which has taken the dream of a shelter further away from the poor. She has argued that the real gainers of the budgetary sops offered by the government are the urban middle class, middle-income housing projects and housing finance institutions; not the poor who really need housing finance. She has pointed out that only about ten per cent of the total housing finance requirement is met by the formal system, and over three-fourth of the total is met from informal sources.

Manoj (2004) [13] in his paper 'Dynamics of Housing Finance in India' has systematically traced the growth and development of the housing finance system in India. The significance of housing to the economy and prospects of housing finance industry in India are explained. The risk factors and challenges to housing finance in India along with the respective remedial measures have been described. It has also been suggested that an active mortgage backed securitization (MBS) market can further strengthen the housing finance system, and that models like housing microfinance, SHG financing (like, 'Grameen bank' model of Bangladesh) should pick up in India also.

National Urban Housing and Habitat Policy 2007 (NUHHP) [14], is the Official policy on urban housing and habitat of the Ministry of Housing and Urban Poverty Alleviation, Govt. of India. It gives an elaborate account of the current status of urban housing in India, housing shortage, the role of various governmental agencies in housing development etc. The policy intends to promote sustainable habitat in the country and delineates specific areas of action and an action plan towards achieving 'Housing for All' – its ultimate goal.

Report of the 11th Five Year Plan (2007-2012) Working Group on Urban Housing with Focus on Slums [15] Ministry of Housing and Urban Poverty Alleviation, Govt. of India has given the estimates of the housing shortage as at the end of the 10th Plan, and projections over the 11th Plan period including the level of investment expected.

Manoj (2009) [16] in his book (Edited), "Emerging Technologies and Financing Models for Affordable Housing in India" gives a detailed picture of the various technologies for affordable housing that are picking up in India and elsewhere in the world and also the various financing models for low cost housing. These technologies include gypsum load bearing walls, straw-bale construction etc. while the financing models include microfinance and the like.

Research Gap

It may be noticed that while there has been many macro level research studies in the area of housing development and housing finance, almost all of them underlining the vital significance of housing development in a developing nation like India, the studies relating to emerging paradigms like 'Affordable Housing' are very rare. Hence the present study seeks to bridge the above research gap by making a study of the relevance of affordable housing in India, including suggestion of business models for the same.

METHODOLOGY OF THE STUDY

The study is based on extensive analysis of the available secondary data regarding the affordable housing projects of major real estate players, who are members of the industry association viz. CREDAI (Confederation of Real Estate Developers' Association of India). This is supported by field survey data, from interviews with principal officers of the eight selected CREDAI members (that is, those having specialized affordable housing schemes and having their operations in Central part of Kerala, Trichur and Ernakulam Districts), and for the above convenience sampling has been adopted.

SIGNIFICANCE AND RELEVANCE FOR HOUSING DEVELOPMENT IN INDIA

Housing investments have got tremendous potential for contributing towards economic growth of an economy. The major reasons pointed out by (Manoj) (2003)[17] in this regard are briefly discussed below:

Promotion of GDP Growth

Housing and infrastructure can drive the economy significantly by creating additional demand and hence raising the spending capacity of people through a series of series of linkage effects - both forward and backward. Investment in houses improves the income of people having lower income ie. those who have relatively higher Marginal Propensity to Consume (MPC). High MPC results in demand for the consumption of goods which in turn results in higher GDP.

Creation of Employment

Housing is one of the top employment generators for the economy. An international study revealed that construction of each new single-family house needs 1591 man-hours of labour equivalent to 0.869 year of full time labour. Further, a survey in India undertaken by National Building Organization (NBO) revealed that 2 million housing units per year will lead to creation of an additional 10 million man years of indirect employment.

Linkage Effects

Housing has got linkages - both forward and backward - with over 250 industries including such core industries like cement, steel, timber, ceramics, tiles etc. Thus, small initiative in housing can propel multiplier effects in the whole economy through the generation of further demand. NBO has observed that Re.1 increase in expenditure on housing sector increases GDP by 0.78 due to multiplier effect.

Best Option to Kick-Start a Recession Hit Economy

Apart from the benefits as discussed above, housing is supposed to be the most preferred investment avenue in a recession-hit economy, since it can trigger investment in other sectors as detailed above and hence kick-start the economy. (It may be pointed out here that the above fact was all the more relevant in the Indian economy during the late 1990s, viz. FY 1996 to FY 2000, when there was an industrial slump while housing finance sector was quite active particularly with the entry of commercial banks).

Regarding the significance of affordable housing, it may further be pointed out that since India is now facing an industrial recession as part of the global financial crisis, boosting housing development particularly through inclusive models (like, promotion of affordable housing units, housing microfinance etc.) seems to be the best way to kick-start the economy and revive it fast. In short, all the points as discussed above are more relevant at present than ever before.

Given the special characteristics of housing investments as noted in the earlier paragraph, the utmost significance of housing for a developing nation like India for its rapid economic development need not be overemphasized. So also is the relevance of the present study which seeks to identify strategies to further promote affordable housing in India. As already noted in the last paragraph, all the benefits of housing investments have got added significance in the ongoing recession era. The following facts further underscore the relevance of the study.

As per the 11th Five Year Plan (2007-2012) estimates [18], as of 2007 the total urban housing shortage in India has been 24.71 Million units of which as high as 99.84 per cent belongs to EWS and LIG categories. Thus, the housing problem of the 99.84% per cent of the urban shelter-less population (EWS and LIG) still persists and is by and large unsolved. Furthermore, there has been a moderation in housing finance growth in the recent past, since FY 2006 (RBI, 2009a) [19]. In short, in the ongoing scenario when 'like all emerging economies, India too has been impacted by the crisis and by much more than what was expected earlier' (RBI, 2009b)[20], there is vital significance for promotion of affordable housing for equitable and balanced housing development of the nation and hence its faster economic development.

HOUSING SCENARIO IN INDIA AND THE INSTITUTIONAL SYSTEM FOR HOUSING FINANCE

In spite of the fact that investment in housing is an important driver of economic development of any nation, in India housing finance remained as an activity that failed to occupy the key position that it deserved during the early days of planned development. Only during the late seventies there was any organized attempt to set up an institutional mechanism for the purpose of providing housing finance to the needy sections of the society. It was only in 1977 that HDFC (Housing Development Finance Corporation) – the pioneer development institution for housing finance in India the private sector - was set up, though a fully owned government company HUDCO (Housing and Urban Development Corporation) was set up way back in 1970 to undertake housing and urban development programmes. Furthermore, it was after one more decade (1988, to be specific) that a formal housing finance system emerged in India with the formation of National Housing Bank (NHB) in 1988. At that time nearly 80 per cent of the housing stock in the country was financed from informal sources (RBI, 2009)[3].

When NHB was formed in 1988 as a fully owned subsidiary of the RBI with a mandate 'to operate as a principal agency to promote housing finance institutions both at local and regional levels and to provide financial and other supports to such institutions and for matters connected therewith or incidental thereto' there were about 400 housing finance companies (HFCs) in India, functioning as NBFCs (Non Banking Finance Companies) regulated by the RBI. These companies included many small ones with restricted or localized activities and also those engaged in construction/development but offering housing credit as well. The only exception in this regard has been HDFC – the pioneer HFC in India and also the largest among the HFCs in India ever since its inception in 1977. At present (December 2009), there are 43 HFCs registered with the NHB of which 20 have the permission to provide housing finance and also to accept public deposits, while the remaining 23 have permission only to provide housing finance. Housing sector has been given priority status by the successive Union Governments and is accordingly entitled to substantial allocations in the various Plans, apart from a large number of fiscal and monetary incentives.

There has been an appreciable growth rate in housing finance by institutional intermediaries in housing finance in India, in the post reforms era. Among these agencies, commercial banks (CBs) and housing finance companies (HFCs) alone are the prominent ones. The third agency viz. ACHFs (Apex co-operative housing federations), actually the most inclusive of the three which caters to the credit needs of the common man, is becoming insignificant year after year. Roughly nearly two-third of the current market is owned by CBs and the balance over one-third by the HFCs (Table 1). In spite of the appreciable growth of institutional finance to housing in India, the housing shortage is still on the rise, particularly since the 2000s. As of FY 2007 (viz. the end of the Xth Plan, 2002-07), the total urban housing shortage itself in India was 24.71 million units. (Besides, there is another 7 million units towards the rural housing shortage) (RBI, 2009) [3]. (Table 2).

Table 1
Housing Loan Disbursements by various Institutional Agencies

(Rupees in Crores)

Agency	*FY: 2001*	*FY:2002*	*FY:2003*	*FY:2004*	*FY:2005*	*FY 2006*	*FY 2007*	*FY: 2008*
CBs	5553.11	8566.41	23553.70	32816.39	50398.00	58623.00	69859.00	78242.00#
HFCs	12637.85	14614.44	17832.01	20862.23	26000.00	30109.00	40141.00	46164.00
ACHFs	867.72	677.58	641.48	623.08	421.10	520.00	550.00@	550.00@
Total	19058.68	23858.43	42026.86	54301.70	76819.10	89252.00	110550.00	124956.00
Growth	–	25.18 %	76.15 %	29.21 %	41.47 %	16.18 %	23.86 %	13.03 %

Source: (1) *Report on Trend & Progress of Housing in India* for 2001-2006, NHB, New Delhi.
(2) *Report on Trend and Progress of Banking in India* for 2007-2008, RBI, New Delhi.
(3) *India's Financial Sector: an Assessment*, RBI, Report of CFSA (Committee on Financial Sector Assessment), March 2009.

Notes: @ Exact figures of co-operative housing disbursals are not available from the RBI/ NABARD/NHB sources. Thus, 550 Crores is taken as an estimate for the last two years. However, its presence or absence is not likely to have any significant impact in the overall scenario, as it is very small. The estimate itself is an optimistic one, going by its constantly declining trend.

\# Estimated at 12% above FY 2007 figures, 12% being the estimated growth rate during FY 2008.

Another notable fact is that the housing shortage almost entirely (over 99 per cent) relates to the poor sections of the population (low income group and economically weaker sections).

Table 2
Housing Stock and Shortage, 1991-2007 (Million Nos.)

	Housing Stock (Nos in Million)				
Year	*Pucca*	*Semi-Pucca*	*Kutcha*	*Total*	*Housing Shortage*
1991	29.80	06.20	03.20	40.70	08.23
1997	40.07	06.64	03.35	50.08	07.57
1998	42.13	06.72	03.37	51.85	07.36
1999	44.28	06.80	03.40	53.67	07.18
2000	46.55	06.83	03.42	55.56	06.93
2002	41.17	08.08	02.74	55.80	10.56
2007	47.49	09.16	02.18	66.30	24.71

Source: *Annual Report 2006-'07*, Ministry of Housing & Urban Poverty Alleviation, Govt. of India; in *The Economic Times dt. 13.08.2007*, Chennai Ed.

Thus, the problem of housing shortage is still acute in India, and this fact points to the need for alternate models for inclusive housing development in India – one that offers affordable houses to the masses. In fact the housing shortage grew almost 4 times during the period FY 1991– 2007. In this regard, it is noteworthy to state that the mortgage to GDP ratio in India stands at an abysmal level of 7.40% (as of 2008) (RBI, 2009) [3] which is one of the lowest among the world nations – whether developed or developing. Thus, though India's position has improved significantly from 3.4% (2001) to 7.40% (2008), its current status is nowhere when compared with other nations.

HOUSING THE URBAN POOR: AN OVERVIEW OF THE CROSS-COUNTRY EXPERIENCES

In this section let us examine the cross-country experiences in respect of housing the urban poor. As already noted, fast growing pace of urbanization is the main reason behind the alarming growth in urban housing poverty and in most of the developing countries that have gone for economic deregulation in the recent past, the problem persists. However, some of the economies have been successful in tackling the housing problem reasonably well.

Urbanization, *Slum Formation and Remedies for the Urban Housing Problem*

Worldwide, because of the rapid pace of urbanization, slum formation is an ever growing problem. Table 3 shows the fast pace of urbanization that is going on the world over. By 2030 about 60 per cent of the global population is expected to be in urban areas.

Table 3
Global Trend in Urbanization: 1970–2030

Particulars	*1970*	*2000*	*2030*
Urban Population (%)	37%	47%	60%
Rural Population (%)	63%	53%	40%
Total Population (%)	100%	100%	100%

Source: UN–Habitat, *Global Urban Observatory 2005.*

The worst part of urbanization is the formation of slums – places where people have to live in a highly congested and unhealthy surroundings devoid of the basic amenities of life like clean water, sanitation facilities etc. Slums adversely affect the personal and socio-economic wellbeing of the dwellers and also hinder the economic development of the nation as a whole. Globally, nearly 1 billion people live in slums. Further, it is estimated that nearly 60 per cent of the urban population typically live in the slums whereas the remaining live in non-slum areas. However, just 05 per cent of the urban land is occupied by the urban slum-dwellers while the remaining 95 per cent goes to the privileged rest who accounts for 40 per cent of the population. Table 4 shows the global trends in slum formation and urban growth.

Table 4
Global Trends in Slum and Urban Growth Rates (in Percentages)

Particulars	*Regions*	*Urban Growth*	*Slum Growth*
Urban Growth Significantly higher than Slum Growth	Latin America and the Caribbean	02.21	01.28
	Northern Africa	02.48	-00.15
	Eastern Asia	03.39	02.28
	South-Eastern Asia	03.82	01.34
Urban and Slum Growth Similar	Western Asia	02.96	02.71
	Southern Asia	02.89	02.20
	Sub-Saharan Africa	04.58	04.53
Developed World		00.75	00.72
World		02.24	02.22

Source: Adapted from, UN-Habitat, *Global Urban Observatory 2005.*

It may be observed from Table 4 that, in general, slum formation takes place almost at the same pace as the urbanization. For the world as a whole as well as for the developed nations this is the trend. For certain regions urban growth is faster than that of slum formation. The UN-Habitat estimates that in order to ensure that the shelter-less people do not end up in slums, at the global level we need a new city of with one million population every week for the next 20 years. Further, in India, with a huge housing gap of nearly 25 million units, it is estimated that it requires 5,00,000 units every year for the next 20 years. Moreover, it is well recognized that markets will not meet the housing needs of the poor people. Regulatory regimes for housing for the poor, like the Urban Land Ceiling Regulation Act (ULCRA) in India have also been found to be not effective because of poor governance. However, housing schemes through subsidy and incentives for the private sector have been seen to be effective in many countries. Some of these experiences are given in next section.

ALLEVIATION OF URBAN HOUSING POVERTY: CROSS COUNTRY EXPERIENCES

In China, the housing market was liberalized only during the late nineties. For people living in sub-standard living conditions (slums), a 'one-time' equity grants based on the market value of their existing housing are given to enable them to access mortgage instruments. Land leases are auctioned to developers to supply housing on a home ownership basis. Developers are provided incentives in the form of tax reductions or tax exemptions. Accordingly, China could develop more than 20 million housing units during the last five years.

Chile has pioneered in the up-front capital subsidy programme in 1977. This programme has eliminated all slums from Chilean cities. Here, on the supply side, social housing is built by the private sector. On the demand side, subsidies are given to poor families to increase effective demand for the private 'social' housing. Chile has set aside 05.8 % of its national budget for providing such subsidies.

In South Africa (along with Singapore, Cuba and Sweden) has got one of the best success stories in providing housing for the poor called social housing. Here minimum standards for housing and services have been laid out by the Government. A viable market for low-cost housing has been established through subsidy programme. This has been made possible through establishing partnership with housing institutions, communities, the private sector and NGOs. Accordingly, 1.4 million houses with secure tenure have been constructed in the last ten years for the poorest of the poor.

In Thailand, "The Baan Mankong" (meaning "Secure housing" in Thai) Program has channeled government funds through the Community Organizations Development Institute. Thai Government has earmarked a budget of about US$ 470 million for the infrastructure subsidy and housing loan interest subsidy. This works out to US$ 1650 per family. Accordingly, Thailand puts its existing slum communities (and their community networks) at the center of a process of developing long-term, comprehensive solutions to problems of land and housing.

Apart from the four global success stories (viz. China, Chile, Thailand and South Africa) in respect of urban housing poverty alleviation as discussed above, other glaring examples (that followed more or less similar pattern of participatory or partnership form of development) include Brazil, Egypt, Mexico, and Tunisia. In all these countries, the respective central government has been in the 'driving seat' in the implementation of inclusive policies for housing, land reforms and regularization.

Some low-income or middle-income countries like Colombia, El Salvador, Philippines, Indonesia, Myanmar and Sri Lanka, have managed to prevent slum formation by anticipating and planning for growing urban populations by investing in low-cost and affordable housing.

In view of the above success stories, it appears that slums are a reflection not of market failure but of societal failure. The poor must have access to housing in homes they can afford. Since market forces will never provide housing that the poor can afford, and further market forces will never have the ability to do so until these masses cease being poor, it is up to government to take the initiative. The government can stimulate the creation of sustainable and affordable housing for the poor through the involvement of private sector. Reform measures in (i) the land (grant of land security to poor, reduced government interventions in land market), (ii) finance (down marketing housing finance, fiscal incentives to the private sector developers, micro-finance institutions), (iii) capital subsidies targeted subsidies in various forms (like, up-front subsidies to the poor, or through savings institutions, or to the developers). One of the key requisites for such initiatives to be successful is that of ensuring a governance system that is open, transparent and is able to implement the 'rule of the law' in its true letter and spirit.

AFFORDABLE HOUSING IN INDIA: RELEVANCE IN THE CURRENT SCENARIO (SINCE 2007)

In the ongoing scenario in India, there has been added significance for promotion of affordable housing in India. The main reasons for the above situation include both (i) Demand side factors, and (ii) Supply side factors.

Considering the supply side factors, it may be noted that the housing demand in India (estimated to be 24.71 Million as of 2007) (See Table 2) is primarily that of the EWS and LIG segments (as high as 99.4 per cent) and housing problem of the MIG and HIG segments are virtually nil (just 0.6 per cent) (Table 5).

Table 5
Composition of Housing Shortage in India

Category	*Housing Shortage (Millions)*	*Percentage*
EWS (Economically Weaker Sections)	21.78	88.14
LIG (Low Income Group)	02.89	11.70
Sub-Total (EWS+LIG)	24.67	99.84
Middle & High Income Groups (MIG+HIG)	00.04	00.16
Grand Total	24.71	100.00

Source: *Annual Report 2006-'07*, Ministry of Housing & Urban Poverty Alleviation, Govt. of India; in *The Economic Times dt. 13.08.2007*, Chennai Ed.]

Regarding the supply side factors, it may be pointed out that the traditional role played by real estate players in the ongoing era (since 2007) is quite different from what it was about 15 years back (at the commencement of reforms process in 1992). Table VI is self explanatory in this regard.

Table 6
Changed Status of Real Estate Players in the Ongoing Era (Since 2007)

During 1992 – Initial years of Reforms	*Since 2007 and afterwards*
Unorganised sector, controlled by Development authorities	Organised sector, with high level of Private sector participation
Traditional construction techniques - Funding from unorganized sector - Loans on a Quarterly basis/ distant intervals	Moderm construction techniques - Funds from organized sector - Loans are availed at frequent intervals at a few days' notice

Source: Compiled by the Author from various sources, like policy statements, reports.

Because of the above reasons, affordable housing has become a business model for many an established player in the market, and many others are planning to enter into the market. However, there are problems faced by this market segment. Empirical studies point to the rising costs as one of the worst problems, hence pointing to the need for more Governmental supports like subsidies. Next session discusses these issues in detail.

AFFORDABLE HOUSING SCHEMES: SOME PRELIMINARY FINDINGS FROM KERALA

A preliminary (pilot) study has been conducted in Kerala state, by choosing a eight real estate developers located in the central Kerala (having housing projects in Ernakulam and Trichur cities – two of the total five Municipal Corporations in the state of Kerala). All these Developers are having membership in the CREDAI – Kerala unit (formerly, Kerala Builders' Forum, KBF) and are having 'Affordable (Budget) Housing' as a major business segment. Major observations from the above study are as follows:

- Besides the 08 Developers having 'Affordable Housing' projects presently in Kerala, many other players have plans to initiate such projects in the near future.
- Those developers having affordable housing projects are starting more such projects in different destinations, particularly in the Tier – III cities and such other suburban locations for the upper middle income group.
- Typically affordable housing units are in the range of 20 to 25 lakhs for independent houses ('villas') and 12.5 to 18 lakhs for flats and apartments.
- Developers with affordable housing projects have generally responded that they are increasingly into this segment because of the general slump in the market which has affected the prospects of the premium housing segment and the growing demand from upper middle income customers (particularly salaried class) who can afford only the budget homes.
- While there is considerable demand from the lower middle income and low income segments for budget housing units (typically at 15-20 lakhs range) developers often find it difficult to limit their cost structure to suit the price range of customers.
- The recent hike in the interest rate of housing loans by banks and housing finance companies (HFCs) and also the lowering pay packets of software professions in view of the general slump in the industry have resulted in slower credit off-take.
- One of the worst problems faced by the Developers while providing low priced (budget) housing units is that of constant cost escalation in raw materials, like cement, sand, steel etc. also rise in labour costs. Some materials like sand are not available also. Land cost continues to be the most critical component as always.
- In states like Kerala, the taxes are significantly on the higher side, so also the transaction costs.
- All developers demand more policy support from the Government in the form of subsidies and other incentives, because of the rising costs of the inputs.

SUSTAINABLE MODELS FOR AFFORDABLE HOUSING IN INDIA: SOME SUGGESTIONS

In view of the growing costs of the developers on the one hand, and the need for promotion of affordable housing from a national economic perspective, it is imperative that Government should, (i) ensure larger participation by the private sector in housing development, (ii) provide better incentives to the private parties to attract the private sector. In the Indian context, a PPP (Public Private Partnership) models seems to be quite good and one such typical model is shown in Figure 1 below.

As per this model, the central government has to take the lead role - the role of an enabler or facilitator. The government provides fiscal concessions (tax rebates, exemptions, tax holidays etc.) for builders and developers for constructing affordable houses in notified urban or semi-urban areas with clear specifications regarding the minimum quality, size etc. as well as the maximum cost of construction. Apart from fiscal concessions as above, easier clearance of necessary permissions and sanctions (like, transfer of title, building permits etc.) may also be offered to them so that it is practically possible to construct such houses. NGOs, community organizations, Self Help Groups (SHGs) and such other organizations having adequate track record in social service that come forward to construct budget houses, after obtaining prior Governmental approval. Government support may be (i) through financial assistance, and

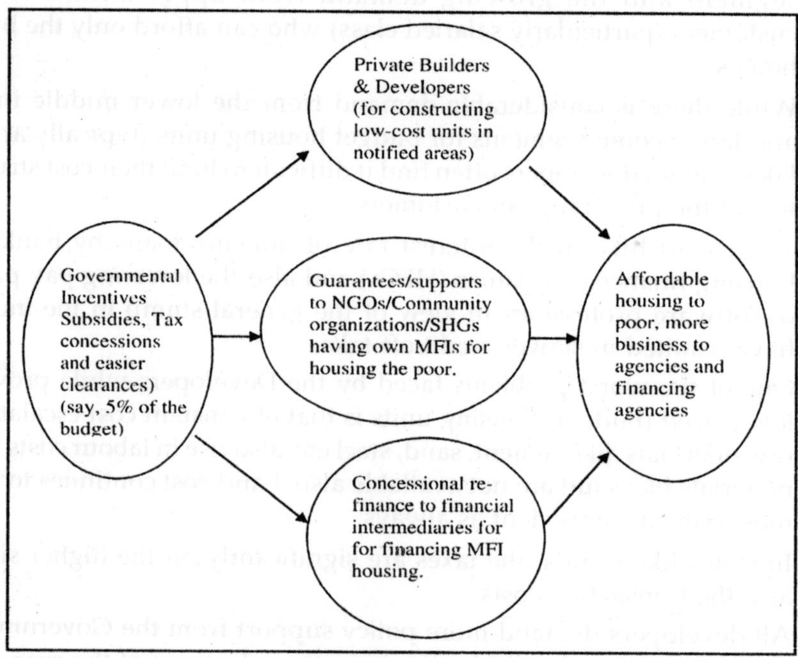

Figure 1: A PPP Model for Affordable Housing in India

(ii) by providing guarantee for the housing loans availed by the beneficiaries through such intermediaries. Besides, financial intermediaries be provided refinance at concessional rates for onward lending (as housing loans) to the beneficiaries.

CONCLUDING REMARKS

Given the vast market potential for the affordable housing segment in India in the ongoing scenario and also the tremendous capability of housing to contribute towards the national economic development, the role of the Government as a facilitator for housing development through time tested models like PPP need not be over emphasized. The success stories in other developing nations should be an eye-opener for India too, and it is high time that Central Government should move in the above direction by providing incentives to attract the private sector into the field of housing development.

References

Report of the 11th Five Year Plan (2007-2012), Working Group on Urban Housing with Focus on Slums, Government of India, Ministry of Housing and Urban Poverty Alleviation, New Delhi, p.31.

Ibid., p. 33.

Reserve Bank of India (RBI), Committee on Financial Sector Assessment (CFSA), *India's Financial Sector: an Assessment,* March 2009, p. 192.

Preamble, *National Urban Housing and Habitat Policy 2007*, Government of India, Ministry of Housing and Urban Poverty Alleviation, p. 1.

Ibid., p. 1.

CRISIL, *Background Paper*, National Conference on 'Affordable Housing for All', 02 June 2007, p.3.

National Housing Bank (NHB), Govt. of India, "Urban Housing", *Official Website of NHB viz. www.nhb.org.in.*

Reserve Bank of India (RBI), Committee on Financial Sector Assessment (CFSA), *India's Financial Sector: an Assessment,* March 2009, p.192.

Mathur, G.C. (1980), "Housing the Poor", *Yojana*, Vol. XXIII, No. 24, Jan. 01.

Cherunilam, Francis and Heggade, Odeyar D. (1987), *Housing in India,* Himalaya Publishing House, New Delhi.

Buckley, Robert M. (1996), *Housing Finance in Developing Countries*, Macmillan Press, London.

Nair, Tara S. (1999), "Housing: The Missing Concerns", Commentary, *Economic and Political Weekly*, Vol. XXXIV, No. 28, July 10, p. 1871.

P. K, Manoj (2004), "Dynamics of Housing Finance in India", *Bank Quest*, Vol. 75, No. 3, Sept.

NUHHP (National Urban Housing and Habitat Policy 2007), Ministry of Housing and Urban Poverty Alleviation, Govt. of India, New Delhi.

Report of the 11th Five Year Plan (2007-2012), Working Group on Urban Housing with Focus on Slums", Ministry of Housing and Urban Poverty Alleviation, Govt. of India, New Delhi.

P. K, Manoj (Ed.) (2009), "Emerging Technologies and Financing Models for Affordable Housing in India", Directorate of Public Relations and Publications, CUSAT, April.

Manoj P K (2004), "Dynamics of Housing Finance in India", *Bank Quest,* IIBF, Mumbai, Vol. 75, No. 3, Sept.

Report of the 11th Five Year Plan (2007-2012), Working Group on Urban Housing with Focus on Slums, Government of India, Ministry of Housing and Urban Poverty Alleviation, New Delhi, p. 31.

Reserve Bank of India (RBI), Committee on Financial Sector Assessment (CFSA), *India's Financial Sector: an Assessment,* March 2009, p. 196.

RBI, *Annual Policy Statement 2009-10,* April 21, 2009, p. 2.

Economic Impact of Terrorism in India

B. Gangabai[*] *& D. Kumar*[**]

INTRODUCTION

CURRENTLY, the biggest challenge that the human civilization faces is that of 'Terrorism'. Terrorism is not just a phenomenon, but also a multifaceted and multi-dimensional concept, since the beginning of recorded human history. However, it is still hard to be defined. Terrorism can be defined in many ways. It can be described as a tactic or a strategy; a heinous crime or a holy duty; a justified reaction to oppression or hegemony and an inexcusable abomination.

Secessionism, ethno-nationalism, demand for equality and equal distribution of resources, religious fundamentalism, antipathy to foreign rule/ domination/hegemony are some of its forms, as well as its driving forces. However, one thing has been common to all the terrorist activities, i.e., the political motives that always backed all sort of terrorist activities. The Encyclopedia of Britannica describes terrorism as *"the systematic use of terror or unpredictable violence against governments, publics, or individuals, to attain a political objective". The FBI further describes it as either being "domestic or international terrorism; domestic terrorism being the illegal or threatened use of violence within a country or without foreign direction in furtherance of political or social objectives; and international terrorism being violent acts dangerous to human life that are a violation of the criminal laws of the United-States, or any state"*.

OBJECTIVE OF THIS PAPER

The objective of this paper is to identify the economic impact of terrorism in India. On this basis the paper is as follows. The first part of the paper is found out what are terrorism and its definition. The second part analyzes the terrorism in India and what are the things motivate all terrorist acts. In the third part this paper elucidate the economic impact of terrorism in India.

* PhD. Research Scholar, Jamal Mohamed College, Trichy.

** Reader in Economics, Jamal Mohamed College,Trichy.

All terrorist activities happen in violation of national/international order, law and morality for purposes of intimidation, coercion or ransom. Unmanaged globalization, poverty, and unequal distribution of resources are some of the chief factors that led to the emergence of terrorism in recent times.

Terrorism is a global problem and various terrorist organizations (of different forms and size) are operating throughout the world from east to west and north to south. It is worth noting here that no country, not even the USA that is the only superpower in the world, can fight it unilaterally. Nations find themselves highly incapable of fighting this grave problem, which is haunting all of us. Keeping in view the gravity, importance and severity of the problem, the United Nations have also passed an internationally accepted resolution on terrorism, known as the 'United Nations Security Council Resolution- 1373' in 2001. Currently, the United States, India, Britain, Russia, Spain, Afghanistan, Iraq and many other South East Asian and West Asian countries are the biggest targets of terrorism.

Beginning with several attacks in the 20th century, terrorism took a more gruesome form in the 21st century with less frequent, but more destructive assaults. It includes various kinds of threats in the form of assassinations, kidnappings, hijackings, bomb scares and bombings, and cyber attacks (computer-based), it may also involve the use of chemical, biological, nuclear and radiological weapons in order to carry out its activities. Inclusion of more modern methods, as well as its expansion add to the danger and lead to an advanced level of difficulty in handling the task.

The United States Department of Defense defines terrorism as "the calculated use of unlawful violence or threat of unlawful violence to inculcate fear; intended to coerce or to intimidate governments or societies in the pursuit of goals that are generally political, religious, or ideological." Within this definition, there are three key elements—violence, fear, and intimidation—and each element produce terror in its victims. The FBI uses this: "Terrorism is the unlawful use of force and violence against persons or property to intimidate or coerce a government, the civilian population, or any segment thereof, in furtherance of political or social objectives." The U.S. Department of State defines "terrorism" to be "premeditated politically-motivated violence perpetrated against non-combatant targets by sub-national groups or clandestine agents, usually intended to influence an audience.

There are three perspectives of terrorism: the terrorist's, the victim's, and the general publics. The phrase "one man's terrorist is another man's freedom fighter" is a view terrorists themselves would accept. Terrorists do not see themselves as evil. They believe they are legitimate combatants, fighting for what they believe in, by whatever means possible. A victim of a terrorist act sees the terrorist as a criminal with no regard for human life. The general public's view is the unstable. The terrorists take great pains to foster a "Robin Hood" image in hope of swaying the general public's point of view toward their cause.

This sympathetic view of terrorism has become an integral part of their psychological warfare and needs to be countered vigorously.

NATIONALISM ON THE RISE

Nationalism intensified during the early 20th century throughout the world. It became an especially powerful force in the subject peoples of various colonial empires. Although dissent and resistance were common in many colonial possessions, and sometimes resulted in open warfare, nationalist identities became a focal point for these actions.

Gradually, as nations became closely tied to concepts of race and ethnicity, international political developments began to support such concepts. Members of ethnic groups saw opportunities to realize nationalist ambitions. Several of these groups chose terror as a method to conduct their struggle and make their situation known to world powers they hoped would be sympathetic. In Europe, both the Irish and the Macedonians had existing terrorist campaigns as part of their ongoing struggle for independence, but had to initiate bloody uprisings to further their cause. The Irish were partially successful, the Macedonians failed. Whose states had been absorbed by others or had ceased to exist as separate nations.

DAMAGED LEGITIMACY

The "total war" practices of all combatants of WWII provided further justification for the "everybody does it" view of the use of terror and violations of the law of war. The desensitization of people and communities to violence that started in World War I accelerated during World War II. The intensity of the conflict between starkly opposed ideologies led to excesses on the part of all participants. New weapons and strategies that targeted the enemies' civilian population to destroy their economic capacity for conflict exposed virtually every civilian to the hazards of combatants. The major powers' support of partisan and resistance organizations using terrorist tactics was viewed as an acceptance of their legitimacy. It seemed that civilians had become legitimate targets, despite any rules forbidding it.

COLD WAR DEVELOPMENTS

The bi-polar world of the Cold War changed perception of conflicts the world over. Relatively minor confrontations took on significance as arenas where the superpowers could compete without risking escalation to full nuclear war. Warfare between the East and the West took place on the peripheries, and was limited in scope to prevent escalation. During the immediate postwar period, terrorism was more of a tactical choice by leaders of nationalist insurgencies and revolutions. Successful campaigns for independence from colonial rule occurred throughout the world, and many employed terrorism as a supporting tactic. When terrorism was used, it was used within the framework of larger movements, and coordinated with political, social, and military action. Even when terrorism came to dominate the other aspects of a nationalist struggle, such as the Palestinian campaign against Israel, it was (and is) combined with other activities.

Throughout the Cold War, the Soviet Union provided direct and indirect assistance to revolutionary movements around the world. Many anti-colonial movements found the revolutionary extremism of communism attractive. Leaders of these "wars of national liberation" saw the advantage of free weapons and training. They also realized that the assistance and patronage of the Eastern Bloc meant increased international legitimacy. Many of these organizations and individuals utilized terrorism in support of their political and military objectives. The policy of the Soviet Union to support revolutionary struggles everywhere, and to export revolution to non-communist countries, provided extremists willing to employ violence and terror as the means to realize their ambitions.

THE INTERNATIONALIZATION OF TERROR

The age of modern terrorism might be said to have begun in 1968 when the Popular Front for the Liberation of Palestine (PFLP) hijacked an El Al airliner en route from Tel Aviv to Rome. While hijackings of airliners had occurred before, this was the first time that the nationality of the carrier (Israeli) and its symbolic value was a specific operational aim. Also a first was the deliberate use of the passengers as hostages for demands made publicly against the Israeli government. The combination of these unique events, added to the international scope of the operation, gained significant media attention. The founder of PFLP, Dr. George Habash observed that the level of coverage was tremendously greater than battles with Israeli soldiers in their previous area of operations. "At least the world is talking about us now."

Another aspect of this internationalization is the cooperation between extremist organizations in conducting terrorist operations. Cooperative training between Palestinian groups and European radicals started as early as 1970, and joint operations between the PFLP and the Japanese Red Army (JRA) began in 1974. Since then international terrorist cooperation in training, operations, and support has continued to grow, and continues to this day. Motives range from the ideological, such as the 1980s alliance of the Western European Marxist-oriented groups, to financial, as when the IRA exported its expertise in bomb making as far a field as Colombia.

CURRENT STATE OF TERRORISM

The largest act of international terrorism occurred on September 11, 2001 in a set of coordinated attacks on the United States of America where Islamic terrorists hijacked civilian airliners and used them to attack the World Trade Center towers in New York City and the Pentagon in Washington, DC. Other major terrorist attacks have also occurred in New Delhi (Indian Parliament attacked); Bali car bomb attack; London subway bombings; Madrid train bombings and the most recent attacks in Mumbai (hotels, train station and a Jewish outreach center). The operational and strategic epicenter of Islamic terrorism is now mostly cent red in Pakistan and Afghanistan.

TERRORISM IN INDIA

The recent terror attack in Mumbai was something first of its kind given the scale of devastation and casualties. As a nation we went through a trauma that perhaps no Indian can ever come out of. It left the entire nation reeling in desolation and deep grief. There was anger amongst people and each and everyone joined hand to fight against terror.

Terrorism is the acts of unlawful violence and war. It feeds off the personal suffering by luring governments into actions that abandon hard-earned freedoms of modern civilization.

TWO THINGS MOTIVATE ALL TERRORIST ACTS

- *Social and political injustice:* People choose terrorism when they are trying to right what they perceive to be a social or political or historical wrong—when they have been stripped of their land or rights, or denied these.
- *The belief that violence or its threat will be effective, and usher in change. Another way of saying this is:* The belief that violent means justify the ends. Many terrorists in history said sincerely that they chose violence after long deliberation, because they felt they had no choice.

Every soul under the sun wishes peace to take root, for peace nurtures an enabling environment that makes human progress possible. Though terrorism has now become a buzzword used mostly for political motives, yet terrorism gnaws an enabling environment. It ought to be discouraged.

More importantly, India's terrorism problem is largely specific to Kashmir. There is a difference between terrorists and freedom fighters and one should not equate them. India must muster International support in this issue and put pressure on Pakistan to stop supporting these terrorists. India habitually points fingers at Pakistan, which are the hotbed and the epicenter of terrorism all around the world. But merely pointing fingers will not help matters. For a small country like Pakistan to be able to infiltrate groups of Indians and recruit them to the terrorist's cause indicates failures of the intelligence on the other hand. We have to look into this fact. There is no co-ordination between the central intelligence agencies and the states. Each points a finger at others each time a bomb blast takes place. The flaws of the criminal justice system match this, which is rudimentary by the standards of mature democracies. Whether it is the Bombay bomb blasts of 1992 or the Gujarat riots in 2002, justice takes many years to deliver. Justice has neither been done, nor seen to be done. India needs to be tough but not reactionary to the causes of terrorism.

THE ECONOMIC IMPACT OF TERRORISM

Terrorism has had a very bad impact on the economy of the world, as it turned out to be effective in hampering all sorts of economic movement. By means of infusing suspicions, it blocked all the new economic initiatives that help in boosting the economy of a nation/s.

It should be noted here that the country not only suffered in terms of net economic loss, but on other fronts as well. The recent Mumbai Terror attacks (India) show similar trends. During the 60 hours of mayhem spread by the terrorists, business witnessed a disruption, thereby bringing a loss of about Rs. 4000 crore to Mumbai, according to D S Rawat, Secretary, and ASSOCHAM. Many other sectors, such as Tourism and Aviation, which were already facing the heat of the global slowdown, were badly hit. To be more specific, the Tourism sector that was already witnessing a 20% slowdown due to the global crunch, and the recent terror attacks have made matters worse by forecasting a further decline of 10% - 15% for in-bound tourism this season. A 30% decline has been lately observed in the sale of Mumbai-bound air tickets, thereby forcing Kingfisher, Air India and Jet Airways to reschedule or combine flights.

IMPACT ON INDUSTRIES

That's the macro picture. A sectoral analysis sheds more light on the possible damage to different industries. "Terrorism's economic impact has normally been short lived," says a report titled, *Economic Impact of Terrorism,* by securities firm Anand Rathi Financial Services. "The immediate impact of terrorism is the loss of life, destruction of property and loss of man-days. Terrorist acts also cause uncertainty, which impacts economic activity. Tourism is one of the first areas to be hit, with hospitality and transportation feeling the pain the most. Gross earnings from foreign tourists are currently around 1% of GDP. A marked slowdown in tourism activity will have a perceptible impact on not only the hospitality and transportation sectors, but also on the overall economy.

"The impact on the earnings side (through lower room occupancy, depressed room rental, lower passenger traffic or lower air fares) may eventually reverse once the situation normalizes. On the expenditure side, though, the impact of higher costs from increased preventive arrangements and higher insurance premiums is likely to be more permanent." An important subset of tourism — medical tourism — is also likely to slow in the short term.

"Hospitality and tourism are two sectors that will certainly take a direct hit," says Chakrabarti of ISB. "This will be a gut reaction to the event and, if nothing else happens, then things will soon get back to normal." According to Rangar, "Estimates suggest that nationally hotels have seen about 60% booking cancellations." Holiday destinations such as Goa are feeling the pinch even more because of intelligence reports that they could be future targets for terrorists. Hotel occupancy in western India is down some 25% and rates have plunged. Civil aviation is another sector in the dumps. But it was already troubled before the attacks.

Rangar believes the overall damage to India's economy could be significant. "Analysts have already started giving initial estimates that suggest the loss in business due to the attacks would be about $100 billion, arising from crucial institutions, such as the stock exchanges, commodities and money markets, and business and commercial establishments which remained closed," he notes. "There is also a hit of $20 billion on the foreign exchange front. But though the numbers are alarming, it is just a matter of time before the city and its people rise to face the situation."

Exports, already down, could be further hit as foreign buyers put off visits. "International clients prefer to stay at five star hotels such as the Taj and the Oberoi," says Ganesh Kumar Singh, president of the Federation of Indian Export Organizations. They now see a risk staying at any five star hotels. The U.S. commercial nuclear mission has put off its India trip, as have delegations from several other countries.

The perception of increased risk in India could also impact the IT industry, which depends on client visits to seal deals. But the larger firms in the IT industry have already spread their risk; they have back-up operations in other countries such as China. The effect there will be only temporary. Some analysts, however, believe that the business process outsourcing (BPO) industry may not be so lucky. "Oil & gas and other large operations are vulnerable to attack," says the Anand Rathi report. Beefing up security will add to their costs. But these are strategic industrial assets for the country as a whole, and part of the expenditure is likely to be borne by the government.

POLITICAL FALLOUT

On the political front, the siege of South Mumbai has already taken its toll. Union home minister Shivraj Patil — responsible for the nation's security — has resigned. Former finance minister P. Chidambaram has taken over that job. Prime Minister Singh has taken charge of the finance portfolio. But the finance ministry, in today's global crisis and domestic slowdown, is a fulltime job. Some observers believe that Singh may not be able to do justice to it, given his other responsibilities.

In the state of Maharashtra, too, of which Mumbai is the capital, heads have rolled. Chief minister Vilasrao Deshmukh has been forced to resign. The last straw was his going to visit the ruined Taj with a filmmaker who specializes in disaster movies in tow. The press dubbed it "terror tourism" and the Congress leadership in Delhi sacked Deshmukh. The state deputy chief minister and home minister R.R. Patil, who belongs to Nationalist Congress Party, a partner of the Congress party, told a press conference "small incidents like this [the Mumbai terror attacks] do happen in big cities". He, too, had to step down after a public outcry.

GLOBAL IMPLICATIONS

Political implications are also apparent at the international level. One of the terrorists' targets was Nariman House, a Jewish center, and as a consequence, India and Israel are moving closer. India has also moved closer to the U.S., which sent Secretary of State Condoleezza Rice to visit the subcontinent. After visiting both India and Pakistan in an effort to avert armed confrontation – which many in India called for, especially since the media labeled the terrorist attacks as "India's 9/11" – Rice urged Pakistan to cooperate with India in nabbing the terrorists. "At such times of crisis, the positive aspect is that not only do we see all the political forces internally standing up as a single force to face the situation, but internationally as well there is solidarity in the fight against terrorism," says Bundeep Singh Rangar, chairman of the Delhi-based Indus View, a research and advisory firm. Chakrabarti of ISB adds: "I don't see a serious international fallout. There will be some diplomatic efforts at trying to pinpoint Pakistan and some pressure will build up on Pakistan. There has been talk in Washington about reacting to the Mumbai event as a multi-country initiative rather than treating it as just an India-Pakistan affair. But the problem, ironically, is that Pakistan now has an elected government and they can't come out looking like they are giving in to India's demands even if they believe that India's demands are right. For decades, public opinion in Pakistan towards India has been negative. The perception of public approval of terrorist activities targeted at India must change before politicians can change. The Mumbai incident by itself will have only a temporary impact. But if the talk of a military solution between India and Pakistan aggravates then that can have a worse effect on capital flows than the terror attack."

GLOOM AND DOOM

The attacks came at a time when India's economy had already begun to slow as a result of the global recession. The widespread fear and anxiety have added to the gloom.

The mood of business has turned highly bearish. Citibank estimates that GDP growth will be 6.8% in 2008-09 and 5.5% in the next fiscal year. Goldman Sachs and Merrill Lynch expect 2009-10 growth to be 5.8%, Nomura believes it will be 5.3% and First Global puts it at a bottom-of-the-barrel 3.5%.

Exports are down. In October, they fell 12.1%. The $200 billion target for 2008-09 will most likely be missed. Manufacturers are pessimistic. The ABN AMRO Purchasing Managers' Index, an early indicator of the mood of manufacturing, is at its lowest since it was set up in April 2005. To take one specific sector, the Society for Indian Automobile Manufacturers estimates that vehicle sales could slide 25.5% in the last three months of the calendar year and more than 34% in January-March 2009. Real estate is also in the dumps. The Bombay Stock Exchange (BSE) Sensex has meanwhile been hovering around 9,000, a far cry from the 21,000 it had crossed in January.

INDIA'S EXTERNAL COUNTER-TERRORISM POLICIES

India has been the victim of Pakistan-sponsored terrorism since the 1950s. In those years, Pakistan's ISI had supported the insurgent/terrorist groups in India's northeast region and provided them sanctuaries, training, arms and ammunition in the Chittagong Hill Tracts of the then East Pakistan. India's anxiety to stop this played an important role in its assistance to the people of East Pakistan to liberate them selves.

Since 1980, the ISI has been providing sanctuaries, training, arms and ammunition in Pakistan to religious terrorist groups operating in Punjab, J&K and other parts of India. It is also infiltrating the mercenaries of the Pakistani pan-Islamic jihad organizations into India to promote cross-border terrorism.

India has taken up this issue with the US since 1992 and wants Pakistan declared a State sponsor of international terrorism under US laws and has punitive action taken against it. In 1993, the Clinton administration placed Pakistan on a watch list of suspected State sponsors of international terrorism for six months and forced Nawaz Sharif who was then in power, to sack Lieutenant General Javed Nasir, then ISI's director-general, and other senior officers. This did not have any effect on the use of terrorism by the ISI.

Since 9/11, Pakistan's military-intelligence establishment has been collaborating with the US in taking action against Al Qaeda elements posing a threat to US nationals and interests. But it has not taken any action against cross-border terrorism directed against India and to destroy terrorist infrastructure in PoK and the Northern Areas.

After the attack by terrorists belonging to LET and JEM on the Indian Parliament in December 2001, India mobilized and deployed its Army on the border in response to public pressure for action against the terrorist infrastructure in Pakistani territory. In response to appeals from the US, UK and other friendly governments, India refrained from action against Pakistan. Under US pressure, Pakistan banned LET and JEM, but not HUJI and HUM, and arrested some of their leaders and cadres. They have since been released.

US officials themselves admit Pakistan has not implemented its assurances to the US that it would put a stop to cross-border terrorism in J&K. Despite this, the US is reluctant to act against Pakistan because of its cooperation in assisting the US in neutralizing Al Qaeda elements that have taken shelter in Pakistan.

India has made it clear that there will be no question of any talks with Pakistan on the normalization of bilateral relations till it stops cross-border terrorism, winds up the terrorist infrastructure in its territory and gives up the use of terrorism as a weapon against India.

TRENDS OF TERRORISM

Terrorism is a global crime. It has become the predominant geopolitical theme. The affairs of the world are influenced in important areas by the terrorist agenda. The thinking of policy makers and law enforcers is shaped increasingly by the need to respond appropriately to the threat of terrorism. Terrorism represents a challenge not just to the bases of civilized society, but also to the very foundations of the world order. Terrorism activities threaten fundamental nations' law and order, human rights and it is the enemy of mankind. Terrorism, in one form or another, has been around for a long time, and there is no realistic prospect of its becoming extinct in the foreseeable future. All of those concerned with the effective combat of terrorism must be prepared for the long haul. There is no simple solution to terrorism.

Terrorism is fuelled by various factors. These include the openness of free societies, the easy access to technologies by means of violence and a radical and global ideology of hatred. Conflicts in some countries particularly in the Middle East have inevitably formed a global issue and solidarity among terrorists. This global issue has become a unifying factor to share the sufferings and establish a sense of togetherness based on religious brotherhood among the believers to resist against the oppressor.

The threats we face from terrorism are constantly changing in all sorts of ways. Just when progress is being made against a terrorist group, splintering often occurs, and hardliners break away and form splinter groups committed to the campaign of violence. It is feared that weapons of mass destruction previously controlled by governments can now be purchased on the black market. It is said that not only the weapons but also the scientists with the knowledge of how to make them are available if the price is right. And finance may be the key. Terrorists, like more conventional criminals, need access to adequate funds in order to finance their activities. Weapons, communication systems and transport all come at a price, as does training.

Terrorism seeks power through violence, and money is a means to achieve that. Terrorism needs access to international payment systems in order to finance and sustain its campaigns. Terrorists, like organized criminals, make active use of credit card fraud and check fraud. This is why vigorous identification checks regime must be exercised on potential customers by credit card companies. The loopholes are in the area of money laundering legislation that must be closed.

Terrorism has, in fact, become a global phenomenon with increasing and rather well identifiable links between different terrorist group and organization. They use each other's areas for recruitment and training, exchange of illegal weapons, engage in joint planning and ventures and also provide administrative and other logistic support. This type of terrorist activities show a new dimension due to circumstances characterized by the advancement of science, technology and diverse social, economic, political and historical reasons conditioning it.

The development of computer science, satellite and mobile links have also affected the modernization of terrorist activities. This further facilitated by support of states/governments unfavorable to each other. An element of international terrorism comes into the picture when specific persons of the nation are designed as targets by the members of another group outside that nation. It is, therefore, described as warfare without territory. It is warfare without neutrals and with few or no by standards. Another form of global terrorism is sponsored terrorism, which is operated from safe areas in another country, which are out of reach of the counter insurgency forces of the targeted country.

There cannot be any single cause of terrorism. Causes of terrorism may range from socio-economic and political conditions to theories based on the personality and environment of the terrorist. Terrorism is motivated by a variety of inner drives ranging from financial gains to revenge, from fundamentalism to deprivation, political frustration, regional disparities, marginalization of sub-national groups, extremism, despair, injustice, discrimination, resentment against the existing regime, feeling of insignificance, intervention into personal freedom, weak government, separatism and oppression, inequality etc.

Terrorism produces harmful effects in several ways. The consequences of terrorism can be disastrous for all countries, both rich and poor, and their people. The normal social life gets totally disturbed and a large number of innocent lives go in vein. Fear and terror haunt everybody and the productivity of people is miserably stalled. Everything may come to a halt and the dream of leading a life of happiness and peace is shattered. Economic and social development of the society cease to uncertainly. Almost all become paralyzed amid terrorist incidents.

Terrorism breaks down the social, economic political and legal structures of the affected countries and the entire process of development stops. Socio-cultural mosaic goes to rack and ruin, and the economy of the country suddenly becomes a shamble. The rule of law and human rights crumble and people suffer terribly. For developing countries, terrorism is fatal to their development planning because they can hardly withstand the violent assaults of terrorism; their longing for a better and brighter future goes up in smoke. Moreover, terrorism not only weakens the established political authority but also brings about political instability. In that situation the maintenance of the rule of law and human rights become almost impossible.

Terrorism idealizes violence, does away with morality, distorts politics, promotes totalitarianism, subverts progress, destroys the apparatus of freedom in democratic societies. In fact, it destroys the will of a civilized society to defend itself. It appears that everything the mankind strives for collapses like a house of cards. As a matter of fact, terrorism is war against civilization.

Today, terrorism poses a great threat not just to human life, human rights, dignity and democratic values but to very existence of a civilized life. If the present trend continues, human civilization itself will be a casualty.

SUGGESTIONS FOR STEMMING THE GROWTH OF TRANSNATIONAL CRIME

The answer seems to be intensifying law enforcement, more vigilance along borders, depriving the criminals of their profits, assisting poor countries with their efforts at strict law enforcement by way of providing training to their law enforcement officers, providing necessary technology, harmonizing laws, sharing information, concluding international agreements to facilitate co-operation and co-ordination in law enforcement and more importantly, political will and commitment.

Profits generated by organized crime far exceed those that legitimate business enterprises could make. The incentive for organized crime, whether local or transnational, is profit. If organized crime syndicates can be deprived of their profits, they will cease their activities - altogether. It will therefore be worthwhile to examine and explore the ways and means of depriving them of their profits. The most effective way to do this is confiscation of the proceeds of such illegal activity by judicial means or with sufficient safeguards, by administrative means.

The international community responded to the phenomenal growth of transnational organized crime by signing in the year 2000, the UN Convention against Transnational Organized Crime. By the end of 72 hours 124 countries have signed the Convention. This is an indication of the enormity of the problem transnational crime poses to the world.

The most significant step in the direction of the prevention of transnational organized crime is the adoption of the UN Convention against Transnational Organized Crime. It has obligated states to act despite constraints of bank secrecy and also to extend co-operation in confiscating and seizing of assets obtained through corruption and transferred to different jurisdictions.

The following four protocols add muscle to the convention, namely,

i. Protocol to Prevent, Suppress and Punish Trafficking in Persons, specially Women and Children.

ii. Protocol against the Smuggling of Migrants

iii. Protocol against trafficking in Firearms and

iv. Protocol against Corruption

Combating terrorism at regional level is becoming effective and popular. The external support is often found in every operation of terrorist acts in any part of the world whether in the context of inter-connection between a group and its rival group, a group and its enemy state, or a state and its unfriendly state. It is here that regional cooperation can be an effective instrument for the suppression to terrorism. In Europe, besides their individual national legal and institutional measures, a historic convention known as the "European Convention on the Suppression of Terrorism, 1977" was signed and ratified. "South Asia Countries also recognized the importance of combating terrorism at regional level and consequently, signed a Convention titled the "Convention on Suppression of Terrorism, 1987" and ratified it.

Similarly, in view of the complexity and problems of terrorism some bilateral and multilateral agreements between groups of countries have also been concluded. And many countries have extradition treaties between them.

At the international level, response and cooperation against international terrorism has been invoked many a time, and a variety of measures and counter-measures have been designed for checking the menace of terrorism. Concerned by the increase of terrorist acts, the United Nations General Assembly in 1972 established a 35-member ad hoc Committee on International Terrorism, and in 1977 asked it to study the underlying causes of terrorism and recommend ways to combat terrorism. In 1979, the Assembly stressed the importance of International cooperation for dealing with the acts of international terrorism. Adopting the report of the Committee, it condemned all acts of international terrorism that endangered or took human lives or jeopardized fundamental freedoms.

In 1994, the General Assembly adopted a Declaration on Measures to Eliminate international Terrorism, which condemned all acts and practices of terrorism as criminal and unjustifiable, wherever and whomever they were committed. States were urged to take measures at the national and international levels to eliminate international terrorism.

Important international Conventions on terrorism are the Convention on Offences and Certain Other Acts Committed on Board Aircraft (Tokyo, 1963), the Convention for the Suppression of Unlawful Seizure of Aircraft (The Hague, 1970); the Convention for the Suppression of Unlawful Act against the Safety of Civil Aviation (Montreal, 1971); the Convention on the Prevention and Punishment of Crimes against Internationally Protected Persons, including diplomatic Agents (New York, 1973); the Convention on the Physical Protection of Nuclear Material (Vienna, 1980); the Protocol for the Suppression of Unlawful Acts of Violence at Airports Serving International Civil Aviation (Montreal, 1988); the Convention for the Suppression of Unlawful Acts against the Safety of Fixed Platforms located on the Continental Shelf (Rome, 1988) and the Convention on the Marking of Plastic Explosives for the Purpose of Detection (Montreal, 1991).

The UN General Assembly also adopted the Convention against the Taking of Hostages in 1979 and the Convention on the Safety of United Nations and Associated Personnel in 1994, and International Convention for the Suppression of Terrorist Bombings in 1997.'

Despite all these Conventions adopted and ratified, declarations made, and resolutions passed against international terrorism within the UN system outside, terrorism has become a ubiquitous phenomenon in the contemporary international affairs, and continues to grow. Every state is supposed to refrain from organizing, instigating assisting or participating in acts of civil strife on terrorist acts in another state or involved in organized activities within its territory directed towards the commission of such acts as well as prosecuting and punishing the perpetrators of terrorist acts. A concerted action has to be initiated and sustained by all States whether they are affected or not in collaboration and co-operation with each other with strong determination and will to root out terrorism altogether from the world.

Of course, mutual agreement at the international, and regional levels have consolidated and strengthened co-operation between the countries in the fight against terrorism. Hard line policies against terrorism adopted by some countries have achieved success in this regard. But, it seems that combating of terrorist activities in a significant proportion will be possible only if terrorism is condemned and fought universally, unequivocally and effectively, by all the countries in the world.

CONCLUSION

Terrorism has no respect for national boundaries, and the problem-taking place in any part of the world today will sure enough to become the problem of all tomorrow. Terrorism is a monster like Frankenstein's creation that is too horrible and dangerous. It is even a threat to those countries that create or promote it. Therefore, terrorism is a phenomenon which must be condemned, fought, resisted, controlled and, eventually, eliminated at all levels-national, regional and international. Conditions necessary for wiping out terrorism must, accordingly, be cultivated and strengthened nationally, regionally and internationally, and unilaterally, bilaterally or multilaterally.

Terrorist acts confronted by a state cannot be eliminated by the affected States alone because of the international linkage of the terrorist groups. It is, therefore, clear that all the nations must form a common front to fight terrorism. If the much needed spirit of international cooperation in the required degree is not properly established, the world would become a dangerous place to live. It is for this reason that one nation's peace and security will be determined by the success of all nations' response to any kind of terrorism particularly for international terrorism.

Fighting with terrorism should not only be the duty of government and role of civilians, and civil society is equally significant. Firstly, strong movement is required against all fundamentalist ideologies. Secondly, unity in diversity should be encouraged at all possible levels. This is the third point that no Indian citizen should feel insecure just for belonging to any religion, caste, or sect. The spirit of secularism and unity in diversity must be championed by all and sundry. Lastly, we must also be attentive and be more alert and should never hesitate in informing the police of any suspicion.

Reference

Arun Jaitely (2002), Terrorism and India, Lalit Doshi Memorial Lecture.

Aravind Shukla (2009), Impact of Terrorism on Social, Economic and Legal Structure of the Countries, Obstacle to Global Peace.

Alan B. Krueger (2007), Understanding Terrorism, November 3.

Bhaskar Dasgupta (2005), The Economic Impact of Terrorism, November 18.

Hari K. Sharma (2008), Terrorist Attacks will Further Weaken a Slowing Indian Economy, December 11.

Mrudula E. (2007), Terrorism- Global Economic Impact, Icfai University Press.

Nayan Chanda (2008), Terrorism Halt India's Global Rise?

Impact of Block Money in Swiss Bank Accounts of Indian Economy

G. H. Nagaraj *

THE subject remains fuzzy with fantastic guesstimates put out on the amount of money kept with banks in overseas tax havens. Recently, R.Vaidyanathan, a professor of finance at the IIM-Bangalore, who has been researching the subject, claimed that billions of dollars of deposits belonging to India remain unclaimed with Swiss banks because their original depositors might have died without leaving a will or even a clue as to the existence of such depositors.

There is a possibility that these sums can never be repatriated to India as banks have their own rules for dealing with deposits that are unclaimed for long. According to Dr.Vaidyanathan, the problem of salting away the money abroad is all pervasive today. Swiss banking has become synonymous with secrecy but there are many other banking centres around the world which actively encourage offshore banking and have strict secrecy laws. According to the Organisation for Economic co-operation and Development (OECD), there are currently 20 odd such centres that lure overseas investors to deposit money by promising, among others, a high degree of banking secrecy.

The G-20 (The Group of Twenty) countries recently agreed that these centres must be forced to share information and adopt internationally acceptable codes of conduct. The idea is not to impede tax and criminal investigations under the pretext of secret banking laws. But relying on tax havens to, pull down the veil of 'secrecy has had mixed results. Some countries have co-operated to a greater degree than others. Recent reports indicate that some leading countries would go slow with their efforts to 'name and shame' off-shore centres whose governments do not co-operate.

The issue of bringing back to the country ' money allegedly stashed away by Indians in Swiss banks and certain other centres has once again become

* Faculty, Dept. of Pol. Science, And Public Administration, Maharaja's College, University of Mysore, Mysore-570005.

topical. Just before the general elections, senior BJP leader LK. Advani released the findings of a taskforce on the subject appointed by him.

The taskforce's report was comprehensive. While the furious and mostly political debate that followed the report did not earn any mileage for the BJP in the elections, it did rekindle the existing debate on a subject that has been part of the Indian middleclass psyche for as long as one can remember. Public perceptions have remained strong of domestic money being stashed away illegally in Switzerland and a number of other countries that have strict banking secrecy laws. Among the alleged perpetrators are politicians, bureaucrats, criminals as well as businessmen engaged in mispricing of goods and services involved in otherwise genuine trade transactions.

India has done well to initiate a dialogue with Swiss authorities. The Finance Minister has said that every effort will be made to bring back the money deposited illegally abroad. But there are practical difficulties.

One, the size of the alleged money transfers. Estimates have varied between Rs. 30 lakh crore and Rs. 70 lakh crore. According to Dr.Vaidyanathan, over the 60 years since Independence, the country could have lost as much as $ 1.5 trillion. The wide range of figures quoted is an indication of how difficult the task is going to be.

Two, even granting that funds from India would have found a safe haven in Switzerland and other places, it is not clear whether all of them are the outcome of illegal transactions. For instance, of the several account holders in tax havens, there will be a significant number of non-resident Indians who may not even be assesses under Indian tax laws.

Three, contrary to the hype generated, it is not as though ail banking transactions in tax havens are tainted. In fact, Switzerland has a high banking tradition going back to several decades. Most offshore centres too have strict bank licensing laws. This ensures that only branches of leading banks are opened there. Many off-shore centres are actively promoted by their national governments. Besides, it is not an offence in many countries for off-shore banks to canvas deposits from residents. Until fairly recently secrecy in banking was a virtue. Today even outside tax havens the business of banking is conducted with secrecy. Four, tax avoidance by individuals and companies might be the single important factor driving business to those centres. In India, for more than four decades after Independence, personal tax rates used to be high. There was also scarcity of foreign exchange. It was rationed. Many individuals who managed to keep money abroad not oniy avoided taxes but also had ready access to foreign exchange.

High taxes to blame: Five, if tax avoidance is the reason for the flight of funds, it will be difficult for the Indian government to lay its hands on the entire deposits of Indians in tax havens. If indeed the Swiss authorities lift the veil of secrecy and give Indian tax authorities account particulars of Indians, the government cannot confiscate the entire money any more than it can in a similar domestic situation. There will sure be fines and punishments for transgressing Indian foreign exchange laws. But a sweeping assertion that all ihe money kept by Indians abroad belongs to India is unwarranted.

Six, there is money laundering by the narcotics Irade and terrorists and is obviously more serious. It does merit a crackdown using all possible measures.

The hype over the amount of money kept abroad seems to suggest that it will be child's play for the Union Government to lay its hands on the funds provided, of course, that it is willing to act. The Swiss authorities have indicated that they may be willing to share information on particular accounts if concrete leads are provided. A list of suspects prepared on the basis of perceptions alone will not do: Yet tax evasion is a threat to public finance.

Technology, especially the super efficient ways of transferring money in seconds across the globe, has complicated the picture and made individual governments' tasks that much more difficult.

A recent deal between the U. S. and Switzerland allows American authorities access to 4,450 secret accounts maintained by Americans in the Swiss banking giant UBS.

This is considered path breaking: other centres and even Switzerland may be more willing to share information. But it must be remembered thai the outcome in the U.S. came after UBS was caught offering to help Americans hide their money. The bank agreed to pay $ 780 million fine and restitution. The message for India is to concentrate on specifics and join international efforts at reducing the role of tax havens.

Inflation is a global phenomenon in present day times. The concept of inflationary gap is very useful concept in economic analysis. The inflationary gap not only measures statically the pressure of inflation in the economy; it also highlights the nature and the extent of anti-inflationary measures, both fiscal and monetary and others which the government can adopt to cure the economy of the malady of inflation. It is of great practical significance. Inflation is defined as the relative increase in prices at a given point of time, over the price level during the corresponding period of the previous year. In case prices at a point of time are higher than the prices during the corresponding period of previous year there is said to be an occurrence of 'inflation' -the opposite of deflation. Monetarists believe that inflation is caused by increase in demand. The main factors which cause an increase in the size of demand are;

Increase in public expenditure Increase in private expenditure Reduction in taxation Repayment of past internal debts Rapid growth of population Black money Deficit financing Cheap money policy Increase in consumer spending.

The existence of huge amount of black money in the economy is also responsible for increase in demand, people spend such unaccounted or unearthed or easy money extravagantly on buildings, marriages, luxurious items, private expenditure, consumption expenditure as well as investment expenditure is an important cause of the emergence of excess demand in the economy; there by creating demand for commodities that leads to inflationary tendency.

Much of the corruption starts with politicians and then bureaucrats get involved in the process. If the political set-up is permitted, then it will have a profound impact on the bureaucracy. The central Vigilance commission had identified nearly 127 modes of corruption. The important are Misappropriation of public money or stores Incurring pecuniary obligations of persons with whom the public servants have official dealing Showing favours to contractors and firms Borrowing money from contractors/firms with whom one has official dealings Claiming false TA, HRA, etc. Possession of disproportionate assets; Acquiring immovable property, etc., without prior permission/intimation; Causing loss to government by negligence or otherwise; Abuse of official position/powers; Acceptance of illegal gratification in recruitments, postings, transfers, promotions etc; Acceptance of gifts; Under assessment of income tax, estate duty etc. for pecuniary gain; Misuse of imported and allotted quotas by various firms with connivance of public servants. Acceptance of sub-standard stores/ works.

The central Bureau of Investigation (CBI) charge-sheeted against many civil servants for involving in corruption and multicrore scams, the most important popular scams investigated by the CBI are Mahesh Prasad, Beck Julius, K. Arumugam, and Phool Chand Singh, top bureaucrats of Bihar cadre, accused in the fodder scam conspiracy case, registered on April 27, 1996, by the CBI involved in fraudulent withdrawals of Rs. 37 crore during 1994-95 from the Chaibasa treasury using fake bills from suppliers and fake supply orders. The CBI chargesheeted Neera Yadav for allotting land worth crores of rupees at a throwaway price, and a high-powered commission is also investigating the allegations. In a secret ballot of the Uttar Pradesh IAS association, Neera Yadav was named one of the three most corrupt officers in the state.

Another top bureaucrat of U.P. cadre Akhand Pratap Singh was punctured by various scams like the pipeline scam and medicine scam: CBI raided of Akhand's 17 properties in Lucknow, Delhi.

Hariyana and Uttaranchal on March 21, 2005 revealed 13 Indian and Imported cars, Rs. 36 lakh in cash, Rs. 38 lakh in cash, Rs. 38 lakh in banks, Indira Vikas Patra worth Rs. 8 lakh and Jewellery worth Rs. 17 lakh. Akhand, whose name also features in the IAS association's list of notoriety, had assets worth Rs. 100 crore.

Ravi Shankar Srivastava, sevior IAS officer accused in 2004 by the Rajasthan Anti-corruption Bureau for taking bribe as a member of the State Revenue Board, and possessing cash and property worth nearly Rs. 3 crore.

CBI chargesheeted against Subhash Sharma, Anand Mohan Sharan and Vijay Risbud in 2004 for criminal conspiracy, bribe and corruption. The case was registered on March 26, 2003. The CBI accused the threee officers of showing under favour to DLF Universal limited, New Delhi, and demanding Rs. 1.10 crore.

Gautam Goswami top civil servant of Bihar cadre accused in 2005 of illegally diverting Rs. 17 crore meant for relief to victims of 2004 floods. He resigned from IAS, 2005, to join a private organization. But the centre has not accepted his resignation. The article quoted only few popular scams that are created huge black money in the economy by means of corruption in India corruption happens every where and it is practicing by the lower level to top level bureaucrats of Government Departments. A common man is a sufferer of the malpractice and corruption in India.

The article quoted only few popular scams that have created huge black money in the economy by means of corruption. But in India corruption happens every where and it is practicing by the lower level to top level bureaucrats of Govt Departments. A common man is a sufferer of the malpractice and corruption in India.

It needs hardly be said that inflation has for-reaching social and political consequences for society. Inflation with black money of bureaucrats is socially unjust and inequitable for society, because it produces a deep impact on the distribution of income and wealth in favour of bureaucratic classes and sections who are already affluent and well-off. This creates a sense of grievance and heart-burning in those sections of society which are adversely affected by inflation.

CONCLUSION

To check and control an inflationary boom, RBI has been taken on the monetary front like, Increased rediscount rate, sale of Government Securities in the open market, Higher Reserve Requirements, consumer credit control Higher margin requirements etc. The Government has been taken on the fiscal front like, Government expenditure, taxation, public borrowings, debt management, overvaluation and other measures.

In addition to above measures the Govt. must set up strong hold institutions and agencies to remove corruption. In India corrupts are treated as an honest in process of accountability. A general assessment, working of the Lokayuktas shows that a number of complaints are generally increasing year after years. However, there is no uniform law in the country on the subject. To conclude. "The institution of lokpal is to still-born while that of Lokayuktas in states are ineffective. But strengthening of Lokayuktas and Lokpal is a sure way to avoid black money in the economy by way of corruption.

References

Fadhia B.L. Kuldeep Fadia, Public Administration - Administrative Theories and Concepts.

Sethi. M.L. (2006), "Money, Banking, International Trade and Public Finance". Lakshimi Narain Agrawal. Publication, Agra.

Preeti Dilip Pohekar (2007), "Urge of Lokpal to Arrest Corruption in India". *Southern Economist*, Volume 45, pp. 33-37, Jan. 15.

Debashish Mukerji, Ajay Uprety, Vittal. N. (2005), "The Decline and Fall of the IAS: *The Week*, pp. 45-55, June 5.

"Service Quality in Private Health Care Organisations"– A Study of Corporate Hospitals in Hyderabad

*P.G. Ramanujam**

INTRODUCTION

QUALITY is the new buzzword with International Standards Organisations (ISO) certifications being chased by an increasing number of organisations. In developed countries quality as an issue has been in the forefront for management of various types of institutions. Various systems and methodologies have been developed to study different dimensions of quality. The entry of multinationals, the opening of Indian economy and the increased purchasing power and consciousness in the middle class consumer have been some of the factors which have raised quality awareness in our country. Quality has indeed emerged as the managerial imperative of the new millennium. So far, quality has been understood only as a concept dealing with manufacturing products. Manufacturing companies have been adopting various quality control measures like statistical quality control, quality designs for manufacturing and the six-sigma approach for eliminating defects in various stages of manufacturing. Presently, the service industries are also enforcing quality in their business operations. Concepts of quality of life (QOL), quality enhancement, quality assurance, quality level and total quality management are currently having significant impact on human services like health and education. Quality is therefore gaining new dimensions in the present scenario.

There is no generic definition of quality and one can find quality defined as excellence (Garvin, 1984); value (Cronin and Taylor, 1992); confirmation to specifications (Garvin, 1988); and meeting customers' expectations (Parasuraman, Zeithaml and Berry, 1985; Gronross, 1990). The Oxford English Dictionary defines quality as a noun meaning "degree of excellence". The Bureau of Indian Standards defines quality as the totality of features and

* Professor & HOD, School of Management Studies, Swarnandhra College of Engineering & Technology, Seetharampuram–534280, W.G. Dt., A.P., (*E-mail: puppalagramanujam@yahoo.co.in*)

characteristics of a product or service that bear on its ability to satisfy stated or implied needs. There are different aspects and dimensions of quality. Quality is what the customer says it is. It is not what the provider says it is. Quality is measured by the extent of the satisfaction of the customer. Quality may be recognized by the customers in terms of prompt delivery or lack of error in services. Quality can be summed up as the fitness of a product or service for its intended purpose or use which should conform to customers' requirements or needs. Therefore, quality is an ongoing process where the customer is a key determinant.

Maintaining good relations with the customer is essential in the wake of liberalization and globalization. One of the important aspects to serve the customer better is to understand the customer. Quality has come to be recognized as a strategic tool for attaining operational efficiency and improved business performance (Babakus and Boller, 1992). This is true for both the goods and service sectors. However, the problem with management of service quality in service firms is that quality is not easily identifiable and measurable due to inherent characteristics of service which make them different from goods. With increasing competition in the service industry, delivery of quality in services has become a priority for the service marketers. This is because service quality offers one of the major ways of achieving success. Service quality is considered as a measure of how well the service delivered matches customer's expectations or providing a better service than what the customer expects. It is the delivery of excellent or superior service relative to customer expectations. Establishing service quality may be one of the major ways of differentiation, particularly in cases of service organizations such as the hospitals where majority of them offer nearly identical services to the customers. The features which constitute the base for measuring service quality vary from industry to industry. The conceptualization and measurement of service quality has been one of the most debated topics in services marketing literature.

LITERATURE REVIEW

A survey of literature on the subject reveals that the issue of service quality has received considerable attention among the marketing scholars. A number of studies have been conducted on this important subject. Among the several research studies undertaken in the variable of service quality, some of the important ones include studies on importance of customers' perception of quality (Teas, 1993); the strategic benefits of service quality (Andrian, 1995); tangible aspects of service quality (Carman, 1990); assessing the effects of quality on customer satisfaction (Cronin and Michael, 2000); and measuring service quality (Cronin and Taylor, 1992). The results of these studies reveal that service quality has a significant impact on satisfaction and behavioral intentions. The transactional aspects along with human aspects of the personnel like expertise, friendliness, reliability, service value etc. affect the service quality and relationship quality which in turn has a significant influence on the customer satisfaction and future interaction with the organization.

Consistent delivery of superior quality service is the strategy that is increasingly being offered as a key to service providers to position themselves more effectively in the market place (Brown, Stephen and Teresa, 1989). Lehtinen and Laitamaki, 1985 present a holistic view on how to measure, monitor and operationalise customer perceptions of service quality in health care organizations. John, 1989 argues that there are four dimensions of health care service quality: the curing dimension, the caring dimension, the access dimension and the physical environment dimension. Reidenbach and Sandifer Smallwood, 1990 developed an instrument based on the original ten dimension questionnaire developed by (Parasuraman et al., 1985). Though initial efforts in defining and measuring service quality emanated largely from the goods sector, a solid foundation for research work in the area was laid down in the mid- eighties by Parasuraman, Zeithaml and Berry (1985, 1988, 1994). Researchers have found that customers do not perceive quality as a uni-dimensional concept. Customers' assessment of quality includes perceptions of multiple factors (Parasuraman, Zeithaml and Berry, 1993). Customers consider five dimensions in their assessment of service quality (Parasuraman, Zeithaml and Berry, 1988). The service organisations measure quality in terms of customer expectations of the service with the performance of specific service provider for each of the five quality dimensions.

One major contribution of Parasuraman, Zeithaml and Berry was to provide a terse definition of service quality. They defined service quality as the gap between the customers' perceptions and expectations of service performance. Based on this conceptualization and operationalization, they proposed a service quality measurement scale called SERVQUAL. The SERVQUAL instrument identifies service quality from the customer's perspective. Based on the Gaps Model and the work done by Fitzsimmons and Fitzsimmons (1990), they have identified five dimensions with which consumers judge service quality. The SERVQUAL scale constitutes an important landmark in the service quality literature and has been extensively applied in different service settings. It is basically a multiple-item scale used for measuring the five dimensions of service quality, each dimension containing multiple items that measure the fundamental attributes of service. Thus, SERVQUAL is a diagnostic tool that uncovers an organisations major strengths and weaknesses in the area of service quality. SERVQUAL can also be used for comparing service firms to identify the criteria for superior service quality.

SERVICE QUALITY

Service quality is the delivery of excellent or superior service relative to customer expectations. It is a focused evaluation that reflects the customers' perception of the specific dimensions of service. Sometimes, as in the case of a pure service, service quality may be the most critical determinant of customer satisfaction. Providing quality service would mean the art of identifying customers' needs and excel in them. The service organisations measure quality in terms of customer expectations of the service with the performance of specific service provider for each of the five quality dimensions. These dimensions represent how customers organize information about service quality in their minds. On the basis of an exploratory and quantitative research, these five dimensions were found relevant for services such as banking, insurance, health care, repair and maintenance, securities brokerage and others. In most cases, customers will use all of the five dimensions to determine service quality perceptions (Parasuraman, Zeithaml and Berry, 1994).

DIMENSIONS OF SERVICE QUALITY

The five dimensions of service quality are reliability, responsiveness, assurance, empathy and tangibles. This can be seen from Figure 1.

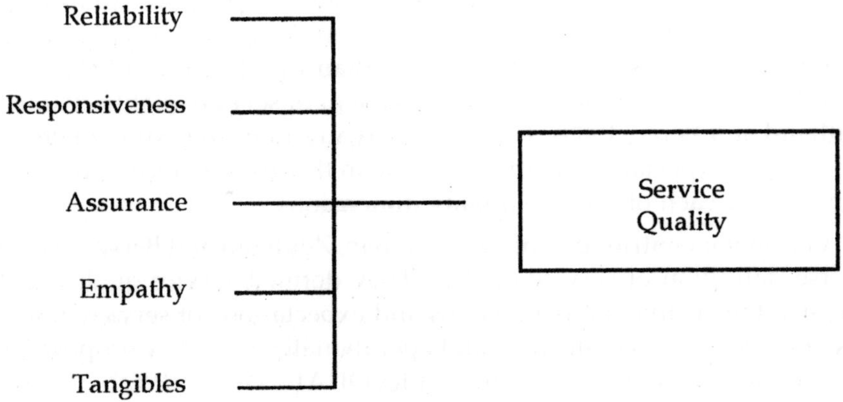

Figure 1: Dimensions of Service Quality

Reliability : The ability to perform the promised service dependably and accurately.

Responsiveness : The willingness to help customers and to provide prompt service.

Assurance : The knowledge, and courtesy of employees as well as their ability to inspire trust and confidence.

Empathy : The provision of caring, individualised attention to customers.

Tangibles : The appearance of physical facilities, equipment, personnel and communication materials.

In today's customer driven market, it is being felt increasingly that it is the quality that will ultimately decide the value of the services. The concept of service quality in the context of health care services offered by hospitals would focus on the technical quality as well as the functional quality. The technical quality of goods or services can be improved with the help of new generation of sophisticated technologies whereas the functional quality of human resources can be improved by strong emphasis on behavioural areas such as attitudes, service-mindedness, accessibility, inter-personnel relations, appearance and commitment. Quality depends upon the level of excellence of the medical, nursing, paramedical, managerial, front line and supportive services given to the patients.

With increasing awareness among consumers about their rights, the patient, as consumer of health services, expect and demand quality healthcare. In the light of these developments, healthcare providers need to have a closer look at the perception of their patients and try to provide medical and health services to meet their expectations. The expectation of the public for quality medical care is very high especially of the middle class. There is a growing pressure on health care providers and professionals to maintain and improve the quality of healthcare with emphasis on cost effectiveness.

Employees communicate the real spirit of the hospital. They are indeed, its living and breathing extensions. The manner in which they perform the duties assigned to them, what they say and do, how they say and do it and the degree of cordiality and cooperation that exists among them make for the efficient and smooth functioning of the hospital. It is their professional excellence, personal-touch-in-service, humanitarian approach, ethical values that play a significant role in the satisfaction of patients. Some of the staff, particularly at the lower level, do not understand the meaning, relevance and content of patient relations. They should be made to understand that the patient is their customer, who has come to them in pain and suffering and hence, should be accorded hospitality of a high order.

Many of the hospital personnel come in direct contact with the patients. They face hostility from ailing patients and their anxiety stricken attendants. Patients, who are suffering, need all the sympathy, empathy and unstinted support they can get. Hence, the hospital personnel should put in all their efforts into relieving the pain and anxiety of the patients and help them resolve their problems, however, trivial they may seem. Their services are important, since their activities contribute directly to the patients' comfort and peace of mind. The house- keeping, nursing, food and beverage staff, and for that matter, staff in any department should always be polite and accommodating and should not lose their temper under any circumstances. The staff should be constantly reminded that the hospital is judged by their work, conduct and behaviour towards patients. The performance and response of customer-contact employees heavily influence customers' perceptions of service quality.

THE INDIAN HEALTH SCENARIO

In a country like India, the problem of health is an enormous one, where majority of poor is outside the effective medical network. The government facilities are marked by poorly managed services, sub-optimal utilization of existing services, poor plans, incompetent administration, ill equipped hospitals, poorly trained and motivated manpower. Due to a rapid increase in the overhead expenses in the health care services of the government sector, very little money is available for medicine and equipment. As a result, most of the government hospitals, particularly at the state government level are unable to acquire any new technology. The government hospitals have failed to equip poor to become customers in basic medical services nor have they provided them free effective medical services.

While the largest variety of health disorders are treated at the government hospitals, their service conditions are relatively poor. Cases of medical negligence and deficient services are on the increase. The public is complaining more and more about low standards of medical practice, long waiting times, inapt diagnosis and blatant errors of medical judgment. Further the more competent doctors tend to get snatched by private hospitals. Alternatively the government employed doctors have their own practice or offer consultancy to big hospitals. Treatment for those who can afford will shift to private hospitals while the common man will still have to depend on government hospitals.

GROWTH OF PRIVATE HEALTHCARE

In the Indian environment where majority of the government hospitals are found in a deplorable condition, charitable trusts, voluntary agencies, private hospitals and corporate sector have come ahead to carry forward the task of making available to the society the best possible health services. Curtailed health budgets, high costs of administering public hospitals and falling standards in primary health care have prompted state governments to pitch for private sponsorship of health care and even support private ventures. In view of the limited financial resources available with the public exchequer, the private sector has to play a dominant role in the years to come.

During the last two decades, the government spending on health care is overtaken by private spending. In 1987, the government share on health care funding was 1.6% out of a total of 4.3% of GDP. By 2005 the governments share declined to 1.3% while the private sector share increased to 4.7%. The added thrust on privatization is quite evident in the policy prescriptions regarding secondary and tertiary care. Eventually the government will focus on primary health care leaving the secondary and tertiary levels of health care to the private sector.

The demand pattern for health care has changed considerably in the last two decades. On the suppliers' side, private hospitals are investing huge amount of capital to meet the growing demand for hospital services. Many hospitals have become complex organisations with specialty and super specialty departments. From customers' side, they are demanding high quality services at reasonable price. The changing attitude of the people at large is being amply demonstrated by the fact that while there is a government hospital just the next door and providing almost free medical attendance; people are shelling out huge chunks of money and going to the private and corporate hospitals. This demonstrates that people don't mind paying more for a better and more reliable health service. The health care customer is changing qualitatively. The rising literacy rate, higher levels of income and increasing awareness through deeper penetration of media, has brought the Indian consumer closer to demand quality health care. With nuclear families on the rise, the bread earner of the family and indeed, every member of the family now have access to regular health check-ups. All these factors have not only contributed to the growth of health care sector in India but also for quality health care services.

NEED AND IMPORTANCE OF THE STUDY

One of the yardsticks to measure the success of any service organisation is the quantum of satisfaction it will produce in the public. This is very much true with the hospital where the quality of treatment to a large extent can be measured from the level of patient satisfaction. It is only during the last two or three decades that a different view of health care services has come into vogue, and slowly recognition of the finer elements of patient care such as medico-social services, patient care relations, patient guidance counseling etc., has been introduced into hospital activities. Unlike in the earlier days when hospitals were judged by the medical services they provided, they are now judged on the quality of service they give, i.e. personalized services rendered by courteous, caring and friendly staff. Hospitals will do even better if they could possibly combine high tech with a high touch. Thus, the human factor is very essential in a hospital, unlike in other organisations, since a hospital involves care of the physical, clinical and also the psychological aspects of patients.

The health care sector has become very competitive and is changing rapidly. The rise of the patient as a consumer, the introduction of innovative technologies and a new breed of entrepreneurial managers are all factors behind the scenes of this industrial metamorphosis. Today, the survivors in the health care sector will be those who provide best quality services to the customers through time honored managerial decisions and application of sound marketing policies. In spite of the substantial growth and notable achievements of the health care services during the last two decades, it is not free from problems. Inefficient organization, poor strategic planning and lack of quality consciousness are important reasons that contributed for the plight. There is therefore, the need for a comprehensive study to analyse the service quality perceptions of the customers of hospitals in health care sector.

Consumer opinion yield valuable information about the functioning of healthcare system which should be taken into account while assessing the quality of hospital services. The prime function of the hospital is patient care and to know the quality of hospital services, it becomes imperative to know what impressions the patients carry about the hospital, where they come for treatment. Hence, to assess the quality of services in the hospitals there is a need to measure the perceptions of the customers regarding the quality and delivery of services and their overall satisfaction which can be used as a feedback to enhance the quality of the services. The literature review suggests a study for the existence of research gap in service quality of healthcare sector in India. In spite of a large number of qualitative research papers, there remains a dearth of empirical studies examining the important dimensions determining the service quality of healthcare organizations, especially the hospitals. To fill this gap, a service quality perception study has been undertaken in three private corporate hospitals in Hyderabad. The study of service quality perceptions from the patient' viewpoint provide a basic feedback to the hospitals in the light of their patient oriented and patient centric efforts in attracting and satisfying the patients.

SCOPE OF THE STUDY

Hyderabad has been selected for the study because it is the capital of Andhra Pradesh and is the biggest city in terms of business development, industrial and population growth. Coming to the health care services, while many cities have witnessed growth of public and private health organizations, Hyderabad has witnessed an unprecedented growth. Infact, it has been described as a 'medi-city' since it has the largest number of corporate hospitals compared to many other cities in India. Patients come to these hospitals for quality treatment from all over the state, different parts of the country and some patients also come from abroad. While the number of hospitals in the state other than Hyderabad is very less and confined to a few cities and towns, corporate hospitals in the capital city are going up day by day. Therefore, in view of these positive factors, the leading hospitals of the private sector in Hyderabad are chosen for the study to get the required information and obtain necessary insights.

OBJECTIVES OF THE STUDY

The main purpose of the study is to examine how well the corporate hospitals in the private sector in Hyderabad are meeting the customers' expectations on the service quality dimensions.

Keeping this in view the following specific objectives have been set for the study.

1. To throw light on health care scenario in India and review some of the studies on service quality.

2. To determine the actual level of service quality scores in the three private corporate hospitals in Hyderabad with respect to the five dimensions of service quality.
3. To make an analysis of the degree of service quality across the corporate hospitals.
4. To offer suitable suggestions on how to improve the level of service quality in the private health organizations.

METHODOLOGY AND SAMPLING

To pursue the above mentioned objectives, an exhaustive study of health care services is undertaken. The data required for the present study is collected from primary as well as secondary sources. The primary data is collected mainly through questionnaires, discussions and observations.

Since the present study covers various aspects relating to quality of health care services, a sample of three corporate hospitals in Hyderabad from the private sector are chosen for the study. As the number of hospitals in the city is increasing, it is not possible to cover all the hospitals for the study. Hence, a sample of three hospitals each from both public and private sectors known for their distinct and commendable health care service has been chosen for the study. The three private corporate hospitals are Apollo Hospital, Yashoda Hospital and CDR Hospital.

The specific reasons for choosing these hospitals are:

1. The hospitals are the earliest corporate hospitals to be set up in the city as well as the state both in the public and private sectors.
2. The hospitals have made very huge investments in the health care sector.
3. The hospitals employed substantial workforce in their organisations.
4. The hospitals have 30-50 specialist departments, offering multi-speciality and super-speciality health services.
5. The hospitals have a large customer base.

The data are collected through the administration of structured questionnaires for the customers of the three corporate hospitals. Since the universe was large and infinite, and administering the questionnaire to the customers on a random basis is difficult, probability sampling methods such as stratified sampling or systematic sampling could not be followed. Therefore, convenience sampling is adopted for the study. However, necessary care is taken in the study to cover customers from different socio- economic backgrounds. From the three hospitals, a sample of 300 patients was randomly selected with 100 patients from each of the sample hospital. The details of the sample hospitals and sample size can be observed from Table 1.

Table 1
Sample Hospitals and Size

Private Corporate Hospitals	*Sample Size*
Apollo Hospital	100
Yashoda Hospital	100
Cdr Hospital	100
Total	3000

Apart from the tabular analysis, percentages and averages, scaling techniques are employed in the present study. The patients' perception regarding the five dimensions of service quality is measured on a five-point Likert scale using SERVQUAL. The secondary data has been collected from magazines and brochures of the sample hospitals, books relating to service sector, health sector and quality management, journals, newspapers and websites.

THE RESEARCH INSTRUMENT

In the present study, a comparative study of public and private health organizations is made to analyze the customers' perceptions of service quality in the hospitals using SERVQUAL consisting of 25 aspects that measure customer perceptions regarding the five service quality dimensions on a five-point Likert scale. The study is based on primary data obtained through a well-designed questionnaire. The respondent is asked to respond to each of the aspects in terms of five points. The five points (i) strongly agree (ii) agree (iii) neither agree nor disagree (iv) disagree and (v) strongly disagree constitute the scale.

The customer evaluates each of the 25 service quality aspects in terms of his satisfaction and indicates his agreement or disagreement with each aspect in the scale. The Likert scaling technique assigns a scale value to each of the five responses. The responses to various aspects are scored in such a way that a response indicative of the most favorable attitude is given the highest score of 5 and that with the most unfavorable attitude is given the lowest score of 1. In that way all the items are scored ranging from 5 for strongly agree to 1 for strongly disagree. The permissible range of mean for each aspect would be from 1 to 5. The possible range of service quality, therefore, would be 25 to125.

The total respondents selected for the study is 300, out of which 100 patients are selected from each of the three private sector health organizations. The total minimum score for each aspect for each hospital would be 100 [i.e. 100 respondents x 1 (minimum score). The maximum score for each aspect for each hospital would be 500 (i.e. 100 x 5). Therefore, the possible range of service quality score for each hospital would be from 100 to 500 and for the three hospitals together would be from 300 to 1500. The scores assigned for each individual response will enable to quantify the response directly. The degree to which each attribute is present has been evaluated with the help of these scores.

QUESTIONNAIRE DESIGN

The questionnaire consists of 25 service quality aspects, of which 5 aspects each pertained to service quality dimensions of responsiveness, assurance and empathy, 6 aspects to reliability dimension and 4 aspects to tangibles.

Reliability: The ability of the hospital employees to perform the promised service dependably and accurately.

1. The hospital provides services as promised.
2. The hospital shows great concern in solving problems or complaints.
3. The hospital provides the service in a right manner for the first time.
4. The hospital provides services at the time scheduled.
5. The diagnosis made by the hospital is always accurate.
6. The hospital maintains error-free records of the customers.

Responsiveness: The willingness and readiness of the hospital staff to help customers and to provide prompt service.

7. The paramedical staff keep the customers informed about the time when services will be provided.
8. The employees give prompt services.
9. The employees are always willing to listen and help you.
10. The employees show readiness to respond to your request.
11. The employees inform you of any changes in advance.

Assurance: The knowledge and courtesy of the hospital employees as well as their ability to inspire trust and confidence.

12. The employees have the knowledge to solve your problems.
13. The employees are always friendly and courteous to you.
14. The employees connect you with the correct individual.
15. The employees instill hope and confidence in the customers.
16. The customers feel safe and confident in the hands of the employees.

Empathy: The behaviour, attitude and approach of the hospital staff in the provision of caring, individualised attention to customers.

17. The hospital staff pays special attention to individual customers.
18. The employees understand the specific needs of the customers.
19. The employees have the customers' best interest at heart.
20. The staff is caring the customers wholeheartedly.
21. The employees remember the patients and their previous problems.

Tangibles: The appearance of physical facilities, equipment, personnel and communication materials in the hospital.

22. The hospital has sophisticated and modern equipment.
23. Waiting room and consultation rooms are visually appealing.
24. The procedures in the hospital are all computerized.
25. The physical facilities in the hospital are visually appealing.

ANALYSIS OF DATA

In order to have a better understanding of the service quality in hospitals a comparative analysis of the three corporate hospitals has be made in the present study.

Table 2 shows the total score and the mean score for each of the three corporate hospitals respectively against all the 25 aspects of the five dimensions of service quality. Successively service quality regarding each dimension reliability, responsiveness, ássurance, empathy and tangibles is arrived for each hospital.

Table 3 reveals the service quality scores for each of the three hospitals and also the average score for the five dimensions of service quality. The cumulative service quality score for each hospital is computed and compared for further analysis.

The analysis of service quality standards in the study has been done at two levels:

(1) Studying the mean score of each hospital and their scores against each service quality dimension (Tables 2) and

(2) Analyzing the weighted average score for each of the 5 dimensions of service quality for each hospital (Table 3).

The study on quality on hospital services achieves three important objectives. First, it consolidates multiple service quality conceptualizations into a single measuring frame work. Secondly, it probes into the customer's perceptions of service quality in the private corporate hospitals in Hyderabad and thirdly, the study measures the service quality in the hospitals with regard to the five dimensions. A more in-depth, comprehensive study on a larger sample can provide generalized conclusions.

Mean scores of the corporate three hospitals regarding the five dimensions of service quality are displayed in Table 2. An analysis of the data revealed that all the three hospitals are providing satisfactory service regarding all the service quality dimensions. Apollo Hospital has witnessed highest service quality score of 3.77, very closely followed by Yashoda (3.76) and CDR Hospital (3.63). All the three private hospitals have performed much above the average score (>3.0). The study revealed that all the three hospitals are perceived by the patients to perform excellent service quality on the tangibles dimension, very well regarding assurance, satisfactorily with regard to reliability and responsiveness and moderately on the empathy dimension.

Reliability: The ability to perform the promised service dependably and accurately.

As can be seen from the table, all the three corporate hospitals have performed well on reliability dimension with mean scores greater than the average score (> 3.0). However, compared to Yashoda (3.74) and CDR Hospitals (3.55), the patients are more satisfied with Apollo (3.77).

Table 2
Nature of Service Quality in Corporate Hospitals

Item no.	*Apollo* Total Score	*Apollo* Mean Score	*Yashoda* Total Score	*Yashoda* Mean Score	*CDR* Total Score	*CDR* Mean Score	Average Mean	Total Score
1	394	3.94	395	3.95+	361	3.61#	3.87	1150
2	368	3.68	375	3.75+	331	3.31#	3.62	1074
3	380	3.80	373	3.73#	392	3.92+	3.81	1145
4	373	3.73	384	3.84+	357	3.57#	3.73	1114
5	382	3.82+	372	3.72	368	3.68#	3.76	1122
6	362	3.62+	348	3.48	323	3.23#	3.49	1033
Reliability	377	3.77+	374	3.74	355	3.55#	3.71	1106
7	375	3.75	374	3.74#	380	3.80+	3.76	1129
8	377	3.77	395	3.95+	364	3.64#	3.80	1136
9	376	3.76#	385	3.85+	378	3.78	3.80	1139
10	370	3.70	384	3.84+	353	3.53#	3.71	1107
11	326	3.26	345	3.45+	318	3.18#	3.31	989
Responsiveness	364	3.64	376	3.76+	358	3.58#	3.67	1098
12	372	3.72#	379	3.79	382	3.82+	3.77	1133
13	393	3.93#	393	3.93#	411	4.11+	3.97	1197
14	395	3.95+	376	3.76	355	3.55#	3.79	1126
15	368	3.68	370	3.70+	360	3.60#	3.67	1098
16	368	3.68+	367	3.67	337	3.37#	3.61	1072
Assurance	379	3.79+	376	3.76	369	3.69#	3.76	1124
17	377	3.77+	375	3.75	348	3.48+	3.70	1100
18	366	3.66	376	3.76+	362	3.62#	3.69	1104
19	353	3.53	366	3.66+	341	3.41#	3.53	1060
20	366	3.66	367	3.67+	365	3.65#	3.66	1098
21	339	3.39	353	3.53+	332	3.32#	3.43	1024
Empathy	360	3.60	366	3.66+	349	3.49#	3.60	1075
22	429	4.29+	411	4.11	407	4.07#	4.18	1247
23	384	3.84	387	3.87+	353	3.53#	3.79	1124
24	414	4.14+	388	3.88#	388	3.88#	3.99	1190
25	390	3.90+	385	3.85#	388	3.88	3.89	1163
Tangibles	404	4.04+	392	3.92	384	3.84#	3.96	1180
Service Quality	377	3.77+	376	3.76	363	3.63+	3.74	1116

Note: + indicates highest score; # indicates lowest score.

Apollo Hospitals has been rated highest on the reliability dimension. The patients expressed their satisfaction regarding the accuracy of the diagnosis (3.82) and maintenance of error free records (3.62). Regarding other aspects they were moderately satisfied with Apollo. With respect to Yashoda, the patients are satisfied with the hospital about providing services as promised (3.95), providing services at the time scheduled (3.84) and showing great concern in solving customer problems and complaints (3.75). However, the hospital needs to improve with regard to providing the service in the right manner for the first time. CDR Hospital has been rated lowest in almost all aspects of reliability and if the hospital does not show improvement it will surely have a negative impression in the long run. Though patients expressed satisfaction with regard to providing the service in a right manner for the first time they are unhappy with regard to all the other aspects of reliability dimension.

Responsiveness: The willingness to help customers and to provide prompt service.

Table 2 shows that all the three corporate hospitals performed well on responsiveness dimension. Among the three hospitals, the patients expressed more satisfaction with Yashoda (3.76), followed by Apollo (3.64) and CDR Hospitals (3.58).

An analysis of the data reveals that Apollo Hospital has been rated moderate by the patients regarding responsiveness dimension. Yashoda Hospital fared well with regard to responsiveness dimension. Patients of Yashoda are found to be happy with regard to employees giving prompt services (3.95), their willingness to listen and help them (3.85), showing readiness to respond to their request (3.84) and informing them of any changes in advance (3.45). However, some of the patients felt that they were not being informed about the time when the services will be provided. Coming to CDR, a considerable size of the patients felt that the hospital needs to provide satisfactory service with regard to employees providing prompt services, showing readiness to respond to their request and informing the customers of any changes in advance. The customers are satisfied only with regard to informing them about the time when services will be provided (3.80). The hospital needs improvement with regard to other aspects of responsiveness.

Assurance: The knowledge, and courtesy of employees as well as their ability to inspire trust and confidence.

Table 2 observes that all the three corporate hospitals have fared well on assurance dimension. Among the three private hospitals Apollo Hospital (3.79) has been perceived to provide superior service quality compared to Yashoda (3.76) and CDR (3.69).

Regarding Apollo, the patients felt that the employees connected them with the correct individual (3.95) and they felt safe and confident in the hands of the employees. However, the patients are not fully satisfied with the knowledge of the employees to solve their problems. The patients are of the opinion that the service quality of Yashoda regarding assurance was moderate. They felt that the employees in Yashoda Hospital instilled hope and confidence in them. With regard to CDR Hospital, a mixed response was observed from the patients. Though the patients are satisfied with the friendly and courteous nature of the employees towards them (4.11) and the knowledge of the employees to solve their problems (3.82), they are of the opinion that the other aspects need to be improved. The patients hoped that the employees of CDR instill hope and confidence in them for their speed recovery and make them feel safe and confident in their hands.

Empathy: The provision of caring, individualised attention to customers.

Table 3 reveals that compared to the other dimensions of service quality the corporate hospitals are providing low quality service to the patients regarding empathy. Among the three hospitals, Yashoda (3.66) is perceived to provide better service followed by Apollo (3.60) and CDR (3.49).

The patients of Yashoda are found to be satisfied with the employees because they were caring them wholeheartedly (3.67) and having customer's best interest at heart (3.66). They are also of the opinion that the employees understood their specific needs (3.76) and remembered them and their previous problems (3.53). The customers are moderately satisfied with the special attention given by staff to individual customers. Apollo has been rated moderate with regard to empathy. The customers are satisfied with the special attention given to individual customers by the staff (3.77) in Apollo. CDR Hospital is observed to be least performing as it has been perceived by the patients to provide lowest service quality among the three private hospitals in all the five aspects of empathy and this will surely bother the hospital in the long run. The customers are not satisfied and the hospital needs to improve with regard to all aspects of empathy dimension.

Tangibles: The appearance of physical facilities, equipment, personnel and communication materials

As can be observed from Table 3 all the three corporate hospitals have excelled in delivering superior services to the customers on the tangible dimension compared to the other dimensions of service quality. Apollo Hospital has the highest mean score of 4.04 followed by Yashoda (3.92) and CDR (3.84). Apollo Hospital which is showing its lead among the three private hospitals fared very well on the tangibles dimension. Its customers are highly satisfied with the sophisticated and modern equipment (4.29), the computerization procedures (4.14) and physical facilities available in the hospital (3.90). They are moderately satisfied with the waiting room and consultation rooms. Regarding Yashoda, the customers are mainly satisfied with the sophisticated and modern equipment (4.11) and the waiting room and the consultation rooms (3.89). However, they felt that the physical facilities in the hospital should be more appealing. CDR Hospital is rated lowest among the three corporate hospitals. The customers felt that CDR needs to improve with regard to its equipment and appearance of the waiting room and consultation rooms.

Table 3 provides an overall picture of the service quality in private corporate hospitals. In the overall analysis the data revealed that among the three corporate hospitals, Apollo Hospital is perceived by the patients to deliver

Table 3
Service Quality In Private Corporate Hospitals – The Overall Picture

Quality Dimension	*No of Items*	*Min and Max Scores*	*Expected Mean Score*	*Actual Score*			*Average Score*
				Apollo	*Yashoda*	*CDR*	
Reliability	6	6-30	18	22.59	22.47	21.3	22.12
Responsiveness	5	5-25	15	18.20	18.83	17.9	18.31
Assurance	5	5-25	15	18.95	18.80	18.45	18.73
Empathy	5	5-25	15	18.01	18.03	17.48	17.84
Tangibles	4	4-20	12	16.16	15.71	15.36	15.74
Service Quality	25	25-125	75	93.91	93.84	90.49	92.74

superior service quality with a mean score of 3.77 (Table 2) and cumulative service quality score of 93.91 (Table 3) which is much above the expected mean score of 75.0. Hence, Apollo has emerged as the leading provider of service quality with highest scores against three of the five service quality dimensions. Apollo is perceived by the patients to be best on reliability (22.59), assurance (18.95) and tangibles (16.16) dimension of service quality. Table 3 shows that the cumulative mean score of reliability (22.59) assurance (18.95) and tangibles (16.16) for Apollo is highest among the three hospitals and above the expected mean scores of 18, 15 and 12 respectively. Even in the other 2 dimensions it is rated to be moderate. Yashoda Hospital is rated second with a mean score of 3.76 (Table 3) and total cumulative service quality score of 93.84 (Table 3). The study also observes that there is not much difference in the scores between Apollo and Yashoda Hospitals. Yashoda has done well on responsiveness (18.83) and empathy (18.03). Even with regard to the other three dimensions it is given a moderate score. CDR Hospital is rated the lowest among the three private hospitals in the study. Even though the cumulative score (90.49) in table 3 is above the expected mean score of 75, compared to other two private hospitals it is low. CDR has been perceived by the patients as delivering lowest service quality among the three private hospitals in all the 5 service quality dimensions. CDR could not reach the patients expectations mainly on the empathy, reliability and responsiveness dimensions of service quality.

An analysis of table 3 revealed that the corporate hospitals in the private sector in Hyderabad are perceived by the customers to deliver quality service to the customers with a cumulative score of 92.74 which is much above the expected mean score of 75. The corporate hospitals have showed their strength and superiority in providing quality service to the customers on the tangibles dimension. As perceived by the customers they have displayed their superiority on the tangibles and assurance dimension. The hospitals are perceived to be good on the reliability and responsiveness dimensions and moderate on the empathy dimension of service quality. Empathy, which is perceived to deliver lowest service quality among the five dimensions, needs to be concentrated.

It is evident from the study that the corporate hospitals need to concentrate on areas where the patients expressed some deficiencies with regard to the five dimensions of service quality. To improve on the responsiveness, assurance and empathy dimensions, the hospitals need to provide adequate and periodic training for hospital staff in behavioural science to make them more patient-oriented with personalised services, humanitarian approach and ethical values which would build confidence in the patients' for their speedy recovery and play a significant role in satisfaction of patients. The doctors and physicians should be involved in continuous learning to further improve their knowledge to provide competent services to the patients.

Regarding reliability, the hospitals should adopt quality control measures and TQM techniques for improving laboratory work to get accurate results in minimum possible time. In order to reduce the dissatisfaction of the patients with regard to solving their problems and complaints, the hospitals need to develop an easy and formal effective complaint handling system which would be accessible and useful to the patients and contribute to the welfare of the hospital. Service quality regarding tangibles should be further improved by taking all steps to provide a clean, peaceful, and hopeful environment to the patients through good looking buildings, visually appealing physical facilities, superior diagnostic facilities, sophisticated and modern equipment which play a big role in making the visit and stay of the patients and attendants more meaningful, comfortable and convenient in the hospital environment.

CONCLUSIONS

Human factor is very essential in a hospital, unlike in other organizations, since the hospital involves care of the physical, clinical and also the psychological aspects of patients. It is the professional excellence, personal-touch- in- service, humanitarian approach and ethical values of the hospital personnel that play a significant role in the satisfaction of patients. Hence, hospitals will do even better if they combine high tech with a high touch. Results of the study reveal that patients define health care quality in terms of the five dimensions of reliability, responsiveness, assurance, empathy and tangibles. SERVQUAL has been found to be a consistent and reliable instrument to measure service quality in health care sector. The results of the study pinpoint the areas for attention by the public and private hospitals to improve upon health care service quality.

The study reveals that the corporate hospitals in Hyderabad, to a large extent are providing quality services to the customers. In fact, with regard to tangibles, the hospitals are performing extremely well. On the assurance aspect of health care service that is most critical to the patients, the hospitals have excelled in delivering quality service to their customers. In dimensions such as reliability and responsiveness the hospitals are performing satisfactorily. However, the major matter of concern for the corporate hospitals is the empathy dimension which has been perceived by the patients as 'moderate' in delivering service quality. Corporate hospitals need to concentrate more on the empathy dimension. Timely, professional, caring and competent service is what the patients expect from the heath care organizations. Although the corporate hospitals in Hyderabad are providing satisfactory services in most of these areas, improvements are still needed to meet patients' expectations. The study clearly indicates there is scope for service quality improvement by corporate hospitals in Hyderabad, especially on empathy and then on responsiveness and reliability dimensions.

References

Andrian, P. (1995), "The Essence of Services Marketing", Prentice Hall of India, New Delhi, pp. 224-226.

Babakus E. and Boller G. W. (1992), "An Empirical Assessment of the Servqual Scale", *Journal of Business Research,* Vol. 24 (3) pp. 253-268.

Bhattacharyya D. K. (2005), "Research Methodology", Methods and Techniques, Viswas Prakashan, New Delhi.

Brown, Stephen W. and Teresa A. Swartz (1989), "A Gap Analysis of Professional Service Quality", *Journal of Marketing,* 53, April, pp. 98.

Carman J. (1990), "Consumer Perceptions of Service Quality: An Assessment of SERVQUAL Dimensions", *Journal of Retailing,* Vol. 66, Spring, pp. 33-55

Christian Groonos (1984), "Strategic Management and Marketing in the Service Sector - A Service Quality Model and its Marketing Implications", *European Journal of Marketing,* 18 (4), pp.36-44

Cronin, J. Joseph and Steven A. Taylor (1992), "Measuring Service Quality - A Re-examination and Extensions", *Journal of Marketing,* 56, July, pp. 55-68

Cronin Joseph. J and Michael K Brandy (2000), "Assessing the Effects of Quality, Value and Customer Satisfaction on Consumer Behavioral Intentions in Service Environments". *Journal of Retailing,* Vol. 76 (2), pp.193-28

Crosby Lawrence A. (1991), "Building and Maintaining Quality in the Service Relationship", in Brown, Stephen W., *et al.* (eds.), Service Quality: Multi-disciplinary and Multi National Perspectives, Lexington, Lexington Books, pp. 269-88.

Fitzsimmons, J. A., and Fitzsimmons. M. J. (1990), Service Management: Operations, Strategy, and Information Technology, (3rd Ed.) Boston, McGraw-Hill, pp. 43-67.

Garvin, D. (1984), "What Does Product Really Mean?" *Sloan Management Review,* 26, pp. 25-43.

Garvin, D. (1988), "Managing Quality–The Strategic and Competitive Edge", Free Press, New York.

Gupta, S. P. (2005), "Statistical Methods", Sultan Chand and Sons Publishers, New Delhi.

John, Joby (1989), 'Perceived Quality in Health Care Service Consumption: What are the Structural Dimensions?', Developments In Marketing Services, 12, Jon M. Hawes and John Thanopoulos (eds.), Orlando, FL, Academy of Marketing Science, pp. 518-521

Lehtinen, J. R. and Jukka, M. L. (1985), 'Applications of Service Quality and Services Marketing in Healthcare Organizations', Building Marketing Effectiveness in HealthCare, Academy for Health Sciences Marketing, D. Terry Paul (ed.), pp. 45-48.

Newman, Karin and Alan Cowling (1996), "Service Quality in Retail Banking: The Experience of Two British Clearing Banks", *International Journal of Bank Marketing,* Vol. 14, No. 6, 1996, pp. 3-11

Parasuraman A., Valarie A. Zeithaml, and Leonard L. Berry (1985), "A Conceptual Model of Service Quality and its Implications for Future Research", *Journal of Marketing,* Vol. 49, Fall, 1985, pp. 41-50

Parasuraman A., Valarie A. Zeithmal and Leonard L. Berry (1988), "SERVQUAL: A Multiple Item Scale for Measuring Consumer Perceptions of Service Quality", *Journal of Retailing,* 64, Spring, pp. 12-40

Parasuraman A., Valarie A. Zeithmal and Leonard L. Berry (1993), "Strategic Positioning on the Dimensions of Service Quality", *Advances in Services Marketing and Management,* Vol. 2, ed. Greenwich, CT JAI Press, pp. 207-228

Parasuram A., Valarie A. Zeithaml and Leonard L. Berry (1994), "Reassessment of Expectations as a Comparison Standard in Measuring Service Quality: Implications for Further Research", *Journal of Marketing,* Vol. 58, Jan. pp. 111-124

Reidenbach, E. and Sandifer, S. B. (1990), 'Exploring Perceptions of Hospital Operations by a Modified SERVQUAL Approach', *Journal of Health Care Marketing,* 10:4.

Teas, Kenneth R. (1993), "Expectations, Performance Evaluation and Consumer's Perceptions of Quality", *Journal of Marketing,* 57, October, pp. 18-34.

Impact of Terrorism on Indian Economy

*C. Sathya Kumar**

INTRODUCTION

The Indian economy is one of the fastest growing in the world and India is predicated to become a superpower in the coming years and has covered a long ground since it was liberalized in 1991. India's economy has been one of the starts of global economics in recent years, growing 9.2% in 2007 and 9.6% in 2006. Growth had been supported by markets reforms, huge inflows of FDI, rising foreign exchange reserves, both in IT and real estate boom, and a flourishing capital market. It is not new and it is unfortunate that we are facing hostilities from our neighboring countries since intention to destabilize our country and our economy.

INDIAN ECONOMY - AN OVERVIEW

The economy of India is the fourth largest in the world, with a GDP of $3.63 trillion at purchasing power parity (PPP), and is the tenth largest in the world with a $69. Growth in the Indian economy has steadily increased since 1979, averaging 5.7% per year in the 23 year growth record. Indian economy has posted an excellent average GDP growth of 6.8% since 1994 India, the fastest growing free market democracy in the world, registered a growth rate of 8.2 per cent in Financial Year 2004. India has emerged the global leader in software and business process outsourcing services, raking in revenue of US$ 12.5 billion in the year that ended March 2004. Agriculture has fall to drop because of bad monsoon in 2005. There is a paramount need to bring more area under irrigation. Export revenue from the sector are expected to grow from $8 billion in 2003 to $ 46 billion in 2007. India's foreign exchange reserves are over US$ 102 billion and exceed the forex reserves of USA, France, Russia and Germany. This has strengthened the Rupee and boosted investor confidence greatly. A strong BOP position in recent years has resulted in a steady accumulation of

* Faculty, Research Centre in Commerce, Scott Christian College (Autonomous), Nagercoil-629 003, K. K. Dist (T.N), (*E-mail: c.sathyakumar@yahoo.com.*)

foreign exchange reserves. The level of foreign exchange services crossed the US $100 billion mark on Dec. 19, 2003 and was $ 142.13 billion on March 18, 2005. Reserve money growth had doubled to 18.3% in 2003 - 04 from 9.2 in 2002-03, driven century by the increase in the net foreign exchange assets of the RBI. Reserve money growth declined to 6.4% in the current year to January 28, 2005. During the current financial year 2004-05 board money stock (M3) (up to December 10, 2004) increased by 7.4 per cent (exclusive of conversion of non-banking entity into banking entity 7.3 per cent). Economics the current and various studies conducted across the globe envisage India and China to rule the world in the 21st century.

SECTORS OF INDIAN ECONOMY

There are three major sectors of Indian Economy.

Agriculture

Agriculture and allied sectors like forestry, logging and fishing accounts for 25% of the GDP. It employs almost 58% of the total work force. It is the largest economic sector and plays a significant role in the overall socio-economic development of India. Due to steady improvement in irrigation, technology and modern agricultural practices, the yield per unit area of all crops has increased tremendously.

Industry

Index of industrial production which measures the overall industrial growth rate was 10.1% in October 2004 as compared to 6.2% in October 2003. The largest sector here holds the textile industry. Automobile sector has also demonstrated the inherent strength of Indian labor an capital. The three main sub sectors of industry ; Mining & quarrying, manufacturing and electricity, gas & water supply recorded growths of 5%, 8.8% and 7.1% respectively.

Services

The service sector is the fastest growing sector. It has the largest share in the GDP accounting for about 48% in 2000. Business services, communication services, financial services, community services, hotels and restaurants and trade services are among the fastest growing sectors.

RECENT GROWTH TRENDS IN INDIAN ECONOMY

India's Economy has grown by more than 9% for three years running and has seen a decade of 7%+ growth. This has reduced poverty by 10% but with 60% of India's 1.1 billion population living off agriculture and with droughts and floods increasing poverty alleviation is still a major challenge. Today, India has the fourth largest economy in terms of purchasing power parity (PPP) behind only the USA, China, and Japan. It is slated to overtake Japan and becomes the third major economic power in the next ten years. India is also one of the markets in the world which offers high prospects for growth and earning potential in practically all areas of business. Indian economic growth has been among the fastest in the world in the recent years.

Indian Economy grew at an annual average growth of 7.6 per cent during the Tenth plan and has set a target of 9 per cent for the Eleventh five year plan. One of the landmark structural changes achieved by Indian economy is that today services sector contributes more than 50% of India's GDP, which is a general characteristic of any developed economy. For the financial year 2006-07, the share of services, industry, and agriculture in India's GDP was 55.1 per cent, 26.4 per cent, and 18.5 per cent respectively.

The structural transformation that has adopted by the national government in recent times has reduced growth constraints and contributed greatly to the overall growth and prosperity of the country however there are still major issues around federal Vs state bureaucracy, corruption and tariffs that require addressing. India's public debt is 58% of GDP according to the CIA world fact book, and this represents another challenge.

During this period of stable growth the performance of the Indian service sector has been particularly significant. The growth rate service sector was 11.18% in 2007 and now contributes 53% of GDP. The industrial sector grew 10.63% in the same period and now 29% of GDP. Agriculture occupies 17% of the Indian economy.

Investor sentiment in India has improved significantly in the first quarter of 2009, according to a survey conducted by Dutch financial service firm ING. With foreign assets growing by more than 100 per cent annually in recent years, Indian multinational enterprises (MNEs) have become significant investors in global business markets and India is rapidly staking a claim to being a true global business power, according to a survey by the Indian school of Business and the Vale Columbia center on Sustainable International investment.

The per capita income in real terms (at 1999-2000 prices) during 2008-09 is likely to attain a level of U$$ 528 as compared to Quick Estimate for the year 2007-08 of US $ 500. The growth rate in per capita income is estimated at 5.6 per cent during 2008-09, as against the previous year's estimate of 7.6 per cent.

TERRORISM

Terrorism has been detailed as the intentional use of or threat to use violence against civilians or against targets in order to attain political aims. Between 1968 to 2004 the world has witnessed 16730 incidents in 149 countries. The basic objectives of terrorism have remained largely unchanged over the more sophisticated and, at times devastating tactics. Thus along with the increasingly global scope of terrorism, has raised important questions about its economic impacts in countries around the world. A number of terrorist groups make damaging their targets economies a priority. Such groups may seek to physically destroy productive assets as well as redirect resources away from productive uses. The evidence for the success of such attacks is mixed.

TERRORISM AND INDIA

Cross-border terrorism-blamed for most of India's recent attacks are not the only threat to India's internal security. It also faces an armed Maoist insurgency that affects vast swaths of territory across 16 of its 28 states, and that Prime Minister Manmohan Singh called the country's "single biggest challenge to internal security. "In addition, several militant and insurgent outfits are active in the country's northeast. Meanwhile, the disputed territory of Kashmir remains a tinderbox of conflict six decades after independence. The Times of India's terror report-India's economy has grown by more than 80% a year, among the fastest rates in the world. The country's benchmark Sensex stock index actually rose in the days following the blasts, its growth unchecked by the disaster. The fundamentals of the economy are strong, and there is a high degree of resilience," says Viren Mehtam Mumbai based partner at the financial services arm of accounting Gaint Ernst & Young.

Many believe that terrorism can't hamper ones economic activity as it only destroy a small fraction of the stock of capital of a country. India has been facing the terrorism threat as long as since 1970. At least 232 of the country's 608 districts were affected, at different intensities, by terrorism. Over that it had been major hindrance for Indian economic growth. Security experts do not share this optimism. Ajai Sahni, executive director of the Institute for Conflict Management, points out that India has invested dangerously little in its internal security apparatus. "India is one of the most under-policed states in the world, "he says, "the U.N. norm is for 222 police personnel for every collapsed, so that those targeting cities are able to use rural bases without fear.

Since Microsoft became the first big foreign company to set up shop in Hyderabad in 1988, the southern Indian city has emerged as an IT hub to rival the outsourcing mecca of Bangalore. Home to more than 200 IT multinationals today, its success has earned it the nickname Cyberabad. 'But it has earned the attention of terrorists as well. On staturday, Hyderabad was targeted for the second time in four second time in four months as tow bombs filled with metal pallets detonated in crowded areas of the city, leaving at leat 42 people dead and more than 60 wounded.

That may be a tall order, given that terror attacks are becoming more audacious. The key economic hubs of Mumbai, Bangalore and Coimbatore have all been attacked in recent years, resulting in the deaths of hundreds of people. Since 2004, The Times of India reported Monday, India has lost more lives to terrorism than any country other than Iraq.

In fact, the high-risk, high-return nature of India's economy is part of the reason many foreign investors are here in the first place. "Investors have come in and stayed after factoring in the security problem," says Soumitra Choudhury, economic advisor at ICRA, an associate of Moody's Investors Service." I don't thick small-scale attacks will affect growth in the long run". Security experts do not share this optimism. Ajai Sahni, executive director of the Institute for Conflict Management, points out that India has invested dangerously little in its internal security apparatus.

The security situation might well prevent the benefits of India's economic beem from reaching its less developed parts. Retired Brigadier B.K. Ponwar, who heads the Counter-Insurgency and Jungle Welfare College in the eastern state of Chhattisgarh, points out those vast areas of the country are unable to attract investment due to various security threats. "Chattisgarh has a wealth of mineral resources, but who wants to go there?" he asks. "The tea and oil industries in the northeast are barely limping along. "Even in its wealthiest cities, India's poor can still bear the cost of its security lapses. "It is usually the poor who get killed in terrorist incidents, and the value of their lives is marginal, "says Sahni. "That is why there is no effect on politics, economy or governance."

The assassinations of 2 Ex-PM of India, Mrs. Indira Gandhi. Mr. Rajeev Gandhi already had jolted Indian politics & economy at large. India had lost 2 of its strongest pillars which otherwise would have taken Indian politics. Business & Industry at unimaginable heights. Recently speaking the siege of South Mumbai has taken toll as home minister Shivraj Patil, Chief Minister Vilasrao Deshmukh A& Home minister R.R. Patil had to resign. This further unstabilized the Indian industry from along-term perspective. The political instability at times have also let to erosion of FII's & FDI's.

It is not new and it is unfortunate that we as a country are facing hostilities from our neighboring countries since intention to destabilize our country. China the Big Brother supports Pakistan in their Endeavour to divide with Nepal, terrorists use Nepal as easy entry and exist points. Our borders with Pakistan and Bangladesh are porous and not fully sealed. We face trouble on the North-East side with China claiming Arunachal Pradesh. These countries hobnob with these terrorists and have helped them to establish their bases from where they can carry out their evil acts.

IMPACTS OF TERRORISM ON ECONOMIC ACTIVITY

Most research on various types of conflicts and their economic effects tend to focus on conventional forms of war and, to a much lesser extend, on terrorism. The recent literature investigating the economics of terrorism can be divided broadly into two groups; studies analyzing the economic impacts resulting from terrorist attacks. An increasing number of terrorist incidents may indicate increased political instability in a country.

IMPACT OF TERRORISM ON INVESTMENTS

Terrorist incidents have an immediate and direct economic impact on a nation's capital stock-both physical and human.

DETERRING FOREIGN DIRECT INVESTMENT

Abadie and Gardeazabal (2005) examine the impact of terrorism on foreign direct investment (FDI) which, they hypothesize, may be greater than its impact on economic growth.

DEPRESSING STOCK MARKET VALUATION

Chen and Siems (2004) measure the impact of terrorism on equity indices using an event study metrology. Abnormal returns (deviations of post –event index values) and cumulative abnormal returns are the dependent variables and the number of military and terrorist actions is the events. Cumulative abnormal returns on he Dow Jones Industrial Average equity index, the author find that of the eight terrorist incidents studied, just two – the Sept. 11 attacks and the 1985 bonding of an Air India jetliner – were followed by statistically significant negative abnormal returns on the day of the attacks.

ON TRADE AND TOURISM INDUSTRY

More terrorist attacks at airlines, airports, transportation and utilities is related to lower real GDP per capita growth and capital formation to GDP.

SHORT-TERM IMPACT

Loss of Human Capital

The human costs have been horrendous. Estimates are in past 5 years 4000+ were killed in terrorist attacks. This puts India next to Iraq both in terror deaths and terror incidents. The recent 26/11 Mumbai attacks itself left 257-300 dead and 700 injured which includes several high profile individuals such as Shri Ashok Kapur, Chairman of Yes Bank who was killed in attack.

INVESTOR BEHAVIOR

Frequent attacks on commercial & government institutions shatter the confidence of the investors causing heavy investment drainage. One example of the same is the terrorist attack in Indian Parliament in 2001, which internationally provoked insecurity & discouraged the investors (FII's & FDI's), obstructing the economic growth. A heavy impact of this can be observed at the stock market that keep diving down post any major terrorist event.

SHORT TERM FINANCIAL LOSS

In short term the obstacles like loss suffered due to the diversion of business away from the city to other locations, lost earnings of public due to disability and trauma among survivors etc. drains out the productivity levels & impact the respective economy adversely. Post 26/11 the Taj & Trident Hotels incurred heavy loss as operations were halted for 3-4 months. After 26/11 Mumbai attack Pak cricket team had to cancel its Mumbai tour due to which BCCI has incurred a loss to the tune of INR 120 crore. Another such incident was Post Ex-PM Indira Gandhi's assassination 1984 riots which hit the economy severely especially the Agriculture & Transport industry that lost hundreds of crores.

RETRENCHMENT EFFECT ON SPECIFIC INDUSTRIES

The Jaipur serial blasts, J&K Terrorism & Mumbai 26/11 attacks did have immediate and concentrated impacts on a number of industries: most notably, airlines, aerospace, travel, tourism, insurance, lodging, restaurants, recreation and related activities. Gross earnings from foreign tourists are currently around 1% of GDP. Post 26/11 terrorist attack estimates suggest that nationally hotels have seen about 60% booking cancellations. Hotel occupancy in western India is down some 25% and rates have plunged. These industries suffered concentrated economic and job losses. Of course, regions or localities with heavy concentrations of these industries suffered disproportionately as well.

LONG-TERM IMPACT

Political Instability

The assassinations of 2 Ex-PM of India, Mrs. Indira Gandhi, Mr. Rajeev Gandhi already had jolted Indian politics & economy at large. India had lost 2 of its strongest pillars which otherwise would have taken Indian politics, Business & industry at unimaginable heights. Recently speaking the siege of South Mumbai has taken toll as home minister Shivraj Patil, Chief Minister Vilasrao Deshmukh & Home minister R.R. Patil had to resign. This further unstabilized the Indian industry from a long-term perspective. The Political instability at times have also let to erosion of FII's & FDI's.

Global Implications

India, post Kargil war then Attack on Parliament now 26/11 has lost millions of business as the trade link between the two countries are frozen during such period. Agri-Exporters in bordering states have taken heavy burns. This has resulted in unemployment in these regions, which in turn again triggers riots. 26/11 Attack involved foreign hostages and places where business leaders, executives and foreigners frequented. This will lead to a drop in investments.

Long Term Financial Loss

The direct economic damage done by terrorist attacks: buildings and infrastructure destroyed, productive lives ended. The structural damages post 26/11 attacks was amounting to total of INR 500 crores, which subsequently took its toll on the insurance industry. Another form of longer-term costs security involves the opportunity cost of spending additional money to fight terrorism. Currently India ranks on 9th position in the world for highest military expenditure (2009-10), which amount to sum total of USD 32,700,000,000. Further, a variety of new spending on security occurred after this incident. As all this happens, economic resources will be directed to shoring up security and diverted away from more productive private sector activity.

CONCLUSION

To conclude with, lets not forget that the enemies of our nation have vowed to "bleed India through thousand cuts". Even if terrorism represents a small fraction of the overall economic risk in India, it may have a large impact on the allocation of productive capital across the country. In any part of the world terrorism is unwanted, as it not only kills the human life but also the infrastructure, industry ultimately shacking its overall growth.

References

Abadie, Alberto and Javier Gardeazabal (2005), "Terrorism and the World Economy", Working Paper Harvard Kennedy School of Government, *http://ksghome.harvard.edu/~aabadie/twe.pdf.*

Barro, Robert (1991), "Economic Growth in a Cross-section of Countries", *Quarterly Journal of Economics,* Vol. 106, pp. 407–443.

Becker, Gary and Kevin Murphy (2001), "Prosperity Will Rise Out of the Ashes", *Wall Street Journal,* Oct. 29.

Blomberg, S. Brock, Gregory Hess and Akila Weerapana (2004), "Economic Conditions and Terrorism", *European Journal of Political Economy,* Vol. 20, pp. 463-478.

Blomberg, S. Brock, Gregory Hess and Akila Weerapana (2004), "An Economic Model of Terrorism", *Conflict Management and Peace Science,* Vol. 21, pp. 17-28.

Chen, Andrew and Thomas Siems (2004), "The Effects of Terrorism on Global Capital Markets", *European Journal of Political Economy,* Vol. 20, pp. 349-366.

Drakos, Konstantinos and Ali M. Kutan (2003), "Regional Effects of Terrorism on Tourism in Three Mediterranean Countries", *Journal of Conflict Resolution,* Vol. 47, pp. 621-641.

Eldor, Rafi and Rafi Melnick (2004), "Financial Markets and Terrorism, "*European Journal of Political Economy,* Vol. 20, pp. 367-386.

Fighel, Yoni and Yoram Kehati (2002), "Analysis of Recent Al-Qaida Documents, Part 1: Mending the Hearts of the Believers", International Counter- Terrorism Working Paper. Available from *http://www.ict.org.il/articles/articledet.cfm?articleid=453.*

Fleischer, A., Buccola, S. (2002), "War, Terror, and the Terrorism Market in Israel", *Applied Economics,* Vol. 34(11), pp. 1335-43.

Gupta, Sanjeev, benedict Clements, Rina Bhattacharya and Shamit Chakravarti (2004), "Fiscal Consequences of Armed Conflict and Terrorism in Low and Middle-Income Countries", European *Journal of Political Economy,* Vol. 20(2), pp. 403-421.

International Monetary Fund (2001), "How Has September 11 Influenced the Global Economy", World Economic Outlook, International Monetary Fund, Washington, D.C.

Johnston, R. Barry and Oana M. Nedelescu (2005), "The Impact of Terrorism of Financial Markets", IMF Working Paper No. WP/05/06, International Monetary Fund.

Nitsch, Volker and Dieter Schumacher (2004), "Terrorism and International Trade: An Empirical Investigation", *European Journal of Political Economy*, Vol. 20, pp. 423-433.

Tavares, Jose (2003), "The Open Society Assesses Its Enemies: Shocks, Diasters, and Terrorist Attacks", Prepared for the Canegie -Rochester Conference on Public Policy, Nov. 21-22, 2003.

World Bank (2003), "Twenty-seven Months - Intifada, Closures, and Palestinian Economic Crisis: An Assessment", World Bank Report No.26314, World Bank.

World Bank (2002), "Fifteen Months–Intifada, Closures, and Palestinian Economic Crisis: An Assessment", World Bank Report No.24931, World Bank.

Impacts of Watershed Development Programmes: Experiences and Evidences From Thoothukudi, Tamil Nadu

J. Edison, G. Paramasivan** & J. Sacratees****

INTRODUCTION

India is one of the major agricultural countries with more than 70% of the population depending on it. Indian agriculture is dependent on monsoon which is not uniform over the years. Nearly three fourths of the cultivable land in India is dependent on monsoon, which is contributing nearly 42% of the total production from agriculture. About 60% net sown area in India is rain-fed, supporting 87% pulses and coarse cereals, 77% oil seeds, 66% cotton as cash crop and 50% cereals. The entire 67.7 m ha forests, grasslands, 80% mangoes and apples, all dry land and temperate fruits, 67% livestock and 40% human beings are distributed in the unirrigated agro-ecologies. During 1985-95, rain-fed regions witnessed higher agricultural growth rate of 4.01% compared to 2.90% in the irrigated areas. However, during the post-1995 liberalization, the growth in rain-fed agriculture1 decelerated to almost zero, as against that of the irrigated region to 2.07%. The productivity of any crop mainly depends on two natural resources- land and water in addition to management practices. Therefore the conservation, up gradation and utilization of these two natural resources on scientific principles is essential for the sustainability of rain fed agriculture. The watershed concept for development of rain fed agriculture is gaining importance over the years and it amply demonstrated that watershed developmental tools are very effective in meeting the objectives and mission. In the words of eminent economist, C. H. Hanumantha Rao "Watershed development has been conceived basically as a strategy for protecting the livelihoods of the people inhabiting the fragile ecosystems experiencing soil erosion and moisture stress". Watershed Development Programme aims at

* Ph.D. Research Scholar, **ICSSR Ph.D., ***Research Fellow, and Assistant Professor, Department of Economics, Manonmaniam Sundaranar University, Tirunelveli, -12, TamilNadu

creating a scenario where the Government acts as a facilitator and the people at the grass root level become the real executioner of the programme.

Rainfed agriculture in India's semi-arid tropics is characterized by low productivity, degraded natural resources, and widespread poverty. Most of the hundreds of millions of people living in the Indian semi-arid tropics depend on agriculture and natural resource management for their livelihoods, so development planners are eager to implement productive, environmentally sustainable land and water management systems. Watershed development projects are designed to harmonize the use of water, soil, forest, and pasture resources in a way that conserves these resources while raising agricultural productivity, both by conserving moisture in the ground and increasing irrigation through tank and aquifer-based water harvesting. Watershed projects have become widespread in rainfed areas in recent years, with a current annual budget from all sources that exceeds US$500 million (Farrington, Turton, and James 1999). The Indian Planning Commission's Working Group on Natural Resources Management has noted that, in spite of spending about Rs. 192,510 million (US$ 4500 million) for watershed development in the rain-fed region of India, the results are 'invisible', and the treated areas have reverted to their 'original status'. Clearly, the development processes require a thorough examination.

The literature on watershed development in India is growing rapidly, but most of it is confined to qualitative descriptions of success stories. Some of these contain excellent insights into the social processes that contribute to successful watershed development, but there is little frank discussion of less successful projects. The few quantitative studies available tend to be based on a small number of heavily supervised projects, with no information about long-term effects. Benefits after the first year or two were typically assumed, and, not surprisingly, cost-benefit findings were almost always favorable. At the same time, the vast majority of projects were never evaluated, and there were good reasons to suspect that most of them had little impact (Kerr and Sanghi 1992).

WATERSHED DEVELOPMENT PROGRAMMES

In our country, developmental activities are charted out through Five-year plans. The IX Five year plan is formulated with four dimensions viz., Improvement of quality of life, Generation of productive employment, Regional balance, and Self-reliance. Theses dimensions are reflected by programmes developed on watershed basis. In addition it also supports agriculture and rural development, food security, empowerment of women, gender equity, environmental sustainability and encouraging people's representative bodies.

The Union Ministry of Agriculture (MOA), Ministry of Rural Development (MORD), and Ministry of Environment and Forests (MOEF) along with their respective departments in the States, are the three main government ministries in charge of watershed development programmes in the country. Each programme focuses on different aspects and activities within the ministry's development criteria. The MOA has worked in watershed development since the 1960s and mainly deals with issues, including erosion-prone agricultural lands, optimizing production in rain-fed areas and reclaiming degraded lands. The Department of Agriculture and Cooperation and the Department of Agricultural Research and Education of the MOA are involved in all aspects of watershed development. They are supported by two autonomous bodies; the Indian Council of Agricultural Research, and the National Institute for Agricultural Extension and Management. The MOA is currently implementing several schemes/programmes, including the National Watershed Development Project for Rain-fed Areas, Soil and Water Conservation in the Catchments of River Valley Projects (RVPs) and Flood Prone Rivers, Watershed Development Project in Shifting Cultivation Areas, Reclamation of Alkali Soil, Watershed Development Fund and Externally Aided Projects (EAPs). The MORD has been implementing watershed development projects only since the late 1980s. It deals with nonforest wastelands and poverty alleviation programmes having components of soil and water conservation. Watershed programmes implemented by MORD include the Drought Prone Areas Programme, Desert Development Programme, Integrated Wastelands Development Programme, and EAPs. Since 1989, the MOEF has been implementing the National Afforestation and Eco-development Project, with the intention of promoting afforestation and development of degraded forests within an integrated watershed approach. Up to the X Plan (2002–07), nearly 51 mha has been developed on watershed basis. The MORD accounted for 63% of the 'treated' area, spending nearly 50% of the total funds and the MOA 'developed' the remaining 37% of the area, but used slightly more than 50% of the total funds. The MOEF and Planning Commission had only limited involvement.

THE OBJECTIVES OF WATERSHED DEVELOPMENT PROJECTS

- Developing wastelands/degraded lands, drought -prone and desert areas on watershed basis, keeping in view the capability of land, site-conditions and local needs.
- Promoting the overall economic development and improving the socio-economic condition of the resource poor and disadvantaged sections inhabiting the programme areas.
- Mitigating the adverse effects of extreme climatic conditions such as drought and desertification on crops, human and livestock population for their overall improvement.
- Restoring ecological balance by harnessing, conserving and developing natural resources i.e. land, water, vegetative cover.

- Encouraging village community for: Sustained community action for the operation and maintenance of assets created and further development of the potential of the natural resources in the watershed.
- Simple, easy and affordable technological solutions and institutional arrangements that make use of, and build upon, local technical knowledge and available materials.
- Employment generation, poverty alleviation, community empowerment and development of human and other economic resources of the village.

NATIONAL WATERSHED DEVELOPMENT PROGRAMME

The Department of Land Resources in the Ministry of Rural Development is administering three area-based watershed programmes for development of wastelands/degraded lands namely Drought Prone Areas Programmes (DPAP), Desert Development Programme (DDP) and Integrated Wastelands Development Programme (IWDP) to check the diminishing productivity of wasteland and loss of natural resources. The DPAP was launched in 1973-74 to tackle the special problems faced by those areas that are constantly afflicted by drought conditions. Presently, 972 blocks of 195 districts in 16 States are covered under the Programme. DDP was launched in 1977-78 to mitigate the adverse effects of desertification. Presently, 235 blocks of 40 districts in 7 States are covered under the Programme. IWDP has been under implementation since 1989-90. The projects under the IWDP are generally sanctioned in areas that are not covered under DDP or DPAP. Since 1 April 1995, these three programmes are being implemented on the basis of Common Guidelines for Watershed Development. Details of projects sanctioned and funds released from 1995-96 to 2007-2008 are as under:

Table 1
Details of Projects Sanctioned and Funds Released

(Since 1995-96 to 2007-2008)

Name of Scheme	*No. of project sanctioned*	*Area covered (in lakh ha.)*	*Total funds released by Centre (Rs. in crores)*
DPAP	27439	130.20	2837.81
DDP	15746	78.73	2103.23
IWDP	1877	107.0	2797.56
Grand Total	45062	322.93	7738.60

The projects under DPAP and DDP are sanctioned for 500 ha each while the IWDP projects cover an area of 5000-6000 ha. The cost norms for all the three schemes have been revised to Rs. 6000 sper ha. Under DPAP and DDP, it is shared between the Centre and the States in ratio of 75:25. In case of IWDP, the cost sharing between the Centre and State Governments is in the ratio of 11:1. Funds are released in seven installments, six installments at the rate of 15 per cent and the last installment at the rate of 10 per cent. The first installment is released along with the initial sanction-order and subsequent installments on receipt of utilization for 50 per cent of the available funds as well as the following documents:

- Quarterly Progress Reports
- Utilisation Certificates
- The Audited Statement of Accounts for the previous years and
- Evidence of satisfactory completion of institutional arrangements.

Projects are implemented by District Rural Development Agencies/Zilla Parishads (DRDAs/ZPs) through Project Implementing Agencies (PIAs). PIAs could be a Line Department (of the State Government), Panchayati Raj Institutions or a reputed NGO. One PIA normally handles 10-12 watershed projects covering an area of about 5000-6000 hectares. The PIA is required to maintain a technical team of 4 experts called Watershed Development Team (WDT) and individual projects (500 hectares) are planned and executed by the local people living in the watershed area called the Watershed Association (WA) through an elected body called Watershed Committee (WC).

The Department of Land Resources has brought out a new initiative called Hariyali with an objective of empowering PRIs both financially and administratively in implementation of Watershed Development Programmes. Under this initiative, all ongoing area development programmes namely, Integrated Wastelands Development Programme (IWDP), Drought Prone Areas Programme (DPAP) and Desert Development Programme (DDP) are to be implemented through the PRIs. New projects under the aforesaid area development programmes are being implemented in accordance with the guidelines for Hariyali from 1 April 2003. Projects sanctioned prior to this date shall continue to be implemented as per the Watershed Development Guidelines of 2001.

In the new arrangement, Gram Panchayats shall implement projects under overall supervision and guidance of Project Implementation Agencies (PIAs). An intermediate panchayat may be the PIA for all the projects sanctioned to a particular Block/Taluka. In case, these Panchayats are not adequately empowered, then the Zilla Panchayat can either act as PIA itself or may appoint a suitable Line Department like Agriculture, Forestry/Social Forestry, Soil Conservation, etc., or an Agency of the State Government/University/Institute as PIA. Failing these options, the ZP/DRDA may consider appointing a reputed Non-Government Organization (NGO) in the district with adequate experience and expertise in the implementation of watershed projects or related area development works as the PIA after thoroughly examining their credentials.

The Project Implementing Agency (PIA) will provide necessary technical guidance to the Gram Panchayat for preparation of development plans for the watershed through Participatory Rural Appraisal (PRA) exercise, undertake community organisation and training for the village communities, supervise watershed development activities, inspect and authenticate project accounts.

WATERSHED DEVELOPMENT AND NABARD

Watershed Development Fund in Tamil Nadu has been created to treat 100 watershed projects at a cost of Rs. 60 Crores with the assistance of National Bank for Agriculture and Rural Development (NABARD). The scheme has been in operation since 2004-05 and the duration of the scheme is six years. Under Restructured National Watershed Development Project for Rainfed Areas (RNWDPRA) for XI Five Year Plan period (2007-2012), it is proposed to take up 500 watersheds in 22 districts, where the area has less than 30% assured means of irrigation in arable lands and having slopes less than 8%. The pattern of assistance is in the ratio of 90:10 for the Centre and State respectively. The minimum area for a watershed is 500 Ha.

Table 2
Physical / Financial Achievement Under NWDPRA

Year	*Financial (Rs. In Lakhs)*			*Physical (in Ha.)*	
	Allocation	*Release*	*Expenditure*	*Target*	*Achievement*
2002-03	1,407.067	1,407.067	1,407.067	31,268	31,268
2003-04	1,525.000	1,525.000	1,525.000	33,888	33,888
2004-05	2,089.063	2,089.063	2,089.063	46,227	46,424
2005-06	1,990.160	1,990.160	1,990.160	44,227	44,227
2006-07	3,738.700	3,738.700	3,738.700	83,082	83,082
2007-08	2,391.300*	2,391.300	2,391.300	29,227	29,227
Total	13,141.290	13,141.290	13,141.290	2,68,116	2,68,116

Source: XI Fiver Year Plan

*Rs. 10.76 crores allotted for undertaking preparatory works under XI Fiver Year Plan–(2007-2008)

DROUGHT PRONE AREA PROGRAMME (DPAP)

To combat the above-mentioned problems and to feed the teeming population along with hunger for land for non-agricultural purposes, essential for nation's development, watershed approach is the correct tool. The Watershed approach encompasses the following.....

- Utilization of land in accordance with land capability
- Water resources development.
- Soil and water conservation measures
- Promotion of alternate land use systems and
- Socio-economic development of watershed population.

In the earlier five-year plans more focus was made on high yielding varieties, fertilizer usage in order to stabilize and step up the food production especially in the irrigated parts of the country. After the introduction of high yielding, short duration, fertilizer responsive varieties, green revolution was happened. But during that period not much emphasis was given to the dry land/rain fed areas, which frequently hit by vagaries of monsoonic rains. By realizing the fragile natural resources base in dry lands especially food, fodder and fuel, the DPAP was launched in the year 1973-74. This programme will concentrate on the areas, which are frequently affected by severe drought situations due to erratic, uneven distribution of monsoonic rainfall. By considering the DPAP programme was launched with an objective to minimize the adverse effects of drought condition on cultivation of crops, production of livestock, the soil productivity of dry land tracts and enriching the water resources and establishment of soil and water conservation structures. It also aims to promote economic development of the village community. It generates employment to the rural poor and encourages other allied income generating activities in the project areas. Finally it emphasis ultimately on the empowerment of socio-economic conditions of the poor and disadvantaged section in the village. This in turn restores the ecological balance through simple, feasible technological measures that are cost effective and energy efficient in a sustainable manner. This paper briefly explains about the DPAP project and its location, land use pattern, and economic features of the Thoothukudi district and the surveyed watershed areas.

LOCATION

Thoothukudi (Tamil: தூத்துக்குடி) district is located at the Southern tip of the Indian sub continent at 8°19′ to 9°20′ latitude an 77°40′ to 78°10′ longitude. Thoothukudi is situated in the extreme south-eastern corner of Tamil Nadu state and bounded on the north by the districts of Tirunelveli, Virudhunagar and Ramanathapuram, on the east and south-east by Gulf of Mannar and on the west and south-west by the district of Tirunelveli. Tuticorin is traditionally known for its pearl fishery and shipbuilding. Thoothukudi became the centre of the Indian independence movement in the early 20th century. The story of our country freedom struggle cannot be complete without mentioning the supreme sacrifices of the illustrious sons of the district like with such leaders as the Maveeran Sundaralinga Kudumbanar, Tyagi Vadivu , Thalapathy Venni Kalady, the people's poet Subramania Bharathi, born at Ettayapuram of this district was also the proud sons of the soil, Veerapandi Kattabomman who waged a war against the British, and V.O. Chidambaram Pillai. In 1906, the freedom fighter V. O. Chidambaram Pillai, with the help of Bal Gangadhar Tilak, launched the first Swadeshi ship S.S. Gaelia from this port town in British India. Tuticorin, one of the oldest sea ports in the world, was the seaport of the Pandyan kingdom after Korkai near Palayakayal and later was taken over by the Portuguese in 1548, captured by the Dutch in 1658, and ceded to the British in 1825. The lighthouse built in 1842 marked the beginning of the history of Thoothukudi harbour development. Tuticorin was established as a Municipality in 1866 with Roche Victoria as its first chairman. It attained the status of Corporation on August 5 2008 after 142 years.

It is the Seventh largest city in Tamil Nadu. It is the Tenth largest City in Tamilnadu after Chennai, Madurai, Coimbatore, Trichy, Salem, Erode, Tirunelveli, Vellore & Tirupur. It is a Seaport which serves Southern Tamil Nadu including the inland cities of Coimbatore, Erode, Madurai and Tirunelveli. It is one of the major seaports in India with its history dating back to the 6th century. The area of the district is 4621 Sq.k.m. and the population is 1572273. The district has three revenue divisions, eight taluks, twelve blocks, two municipalities, twenty town panchayats and 468 revenue villages. Seven assembly constituencies are in this district. The No. of panchayat in the district is 408. The administrative headquarters is an urban agglomeration and also one of the taluk headquarters within the district. This is the district headquarters. The DPAP blocks are Vilathikulam, Pudur, Kovilpatti, Kayathar, Sattankulam, Udangudi, Ottapidaram and Thoothukudi covering 5 taluks except SriVaikundam and Tiruchendur.

Agriculture is the main occupation on which 70% of the people depend. But the recent boom in the industrial sector has put the district prominently in the country's industrial map. Major industries such as SPIC, Chemical Industries, Heavy Water Plant and Thermal Plant are located here and Thermal Power Plant promises hope for a bright future. Hundreds of ancillary units have also sprung up. Textile units and match industries crowd the Kovilpatti belt. The fast growing Thoothukudi Port in the changing economic scenario has added pep to the development of the district. During this year 1533 vessels entered this port and cargo to the tune of 1.87 crore tones are handled. Exports of certain raw materials and finished products are shipped to for about twenty foreign countries. Thoothukudi port has been issued the prestigious ISO 9002 certificate for the port operation and services and had joined the select group of World ports by becoming the first Indian major port to get such certificate. The climate is hot and dry. The district has a coastal line of 135Kms. And territorial waters covering thousands of hectares. The city is also famous for the production of salt. The district particularly in and around Tuticorin is the major salt producer in the state and contributes 30% of the total salt production of Tamil Nadu. It is also called "Pearl City" in view of the pearl fishing being conducted periodically.

AREA AND POPULATION

The following Table 3, shows that the area, blocks wise populating and literates in Thoothukudi District.

Table 3
Area, Blocks wise Population and Literates in Thoothukudi District

		Population			Literates		
Block	*Area (Hec)*	*Persons*	*Male*	*Female*	*Persons*	*Male*	*Female*
Thoothukudi	366	405363	203368	201995	309707	163647	146060
Srivaikuntam	244	112440	54799	57641	83477	43237	40240
Karunkulam	349	79443	38673	40770	52326	28571	23755
Tiruchendur	136	118862	56591	62271	90438	44522	45916
Udangudi	197	72415	33454	38961	56591	26469	30122
Alwarthirunagari	213	116877	55669	61208	87966	43723	44243
Sattankulam	276	80396	36151	44245	60165	27585	32580
Ottapidaram	738	114759	56989	57770	76555	42328	34227
Kovilpatti	419	204641	100524	104117	144358	78438	65920
Kayatar	570	103713	50236	53477	62207	35059	27148
Vilathikulam	623	91560	44936	46624	60252	33238	27014
Pudur	490	71804	35433	36371	47364	27051	20313
Total	4621	1572273	766823	805450	1131406	593868	537538

Source: Thoothukudi Census 2001.

The total population of this district as per 2001 census is around fifteen lakhs. The density of population per Sq.km is 338 as against the 478 for the State. The sex ratio is 1049 females for every 1000 males. The percentage of literacy is 63. Fifty nine per cent of the people live in the rural areas. The district has SC population of 2.5 lakhs which constitutes17% of the total population. Tamil is the main language spoken here, whilst English is also widely used. As per the 2001 census, the total population of the district was 15, 72,273. Hindus form the majority of the population (78.58%), followed by Christians (16.71%), Muslims (4.63%) and others (0.08%).

IRRIGATION

There are no big reservoirs in this district. In Ottapidaram taluk there is one small reservoir at Eppodumvendran village. However Papanasam and Manimuthar Dams which are located in the Tirunelveli district under Tamirabarani system are the main sources of irrigation. Besides Tamirabarani River, there is a river named as "Vaipar" in Vilathikulam Taluk and a river named as "Karumeni" which traverses through Sathankulam and Tiruchendur Taluks. The different sources of irrigation are channels, tanks and wells which covers 40130 hectares in the district. Out of this, 16705 hectares were covered by well. The Table 4, explain the sources of water supply.

Table 4
Sources of Water Supply Year: 2006-2007

Name of the District	*Canals (Nos.)*	*Length (Km.)*	*Wells used for irrigation purpose only*	*Tube Wells*	*Wells used for Domestic Purposey*	*Reservoirs*	*Tanks (Nos.)*
Thoothukudi	4	78.04	24156	661	14354	Nil	634

Source: Directorate of Economics and Statistics, Chennai-6.

LANDS UTILIZED PATTERN

The total geographical area of Thoothukudi district extends over 4, 59,054 ha. which is 3.53 per cent of total TamilNadu state area. Net cultivable area is 1, 59,453 ha. which is 34.74 per cent of total area of district. Cultivable waste and other fallow lands spread over 71,286 ha. Constituting 15.52 per cent of total geographical area in the district. Land utilization pattern in Thoothukudi district is given in Table 5.

Table 5
Lands utilized Pattern in Thoothukudi

Category	*Area in hectares*	*Percentage*
Geographical area	4,59,054	100%
Forest	11.002	2.4%
Barren uncultivable Land	19.944	4.3%
Non-agricultural Land	68.573	15%
Cultivable waste Land	20.154	4.4%
Permanent pastures and othergrazing Land	5.052	1.1%
Net area sown	1,88,296	42.0%

Source: Department of Statistics, Thoothukudi-2001.

The above table shows that the lands utilized pattern in Thoothukudi district. The net area sown is 42.0% which indicates the predominance of agriculture in the district. The area under cultivable waste is only 4.4% which can be reclaimed for cultivation.

Among the 13 watersheds, the net area sown is more in Athanoor watershed of Ottapidaram block (941.6 ha.) followed by Sillankulam watershed in the same block (908.8 ha.). The least is observed in Komaneri watershed of Sattankulam block (225.2 ha.) The cultivable waste and other fallows is observed more in Mudivaittanendal watershed of Thoothukudi block followed by Komaneri in Sattakulam and Kadalaiyur watershed in Kovilpatti block. The forest area and permanent pastureland is not available in all the surveyed watersheds. Further, it is noticed that the miscellaneous tree crops area are more in Kumarasakkanapuram watershed (387.2 ha). in Vilathikulam block block followed by Keelakarantahi watershed (350.4 ha.) in Pudur block.

PRODUCTION OF PRINCIPAL CROPS

Paddy is mainly cultivated in Srivaikundam, Sattankulam and Tiruchendur taluks. Cumbu, Cholam, Kuthiraivali and other Pulses are raised in the dry tracts of Kovilpatti, Vilathikulam, Ottapidaram and Thoothukudi taluks. Cotton is being cultivated mainly in Kovilpatti, Ottapidaram and Thoothukudi taluks. Groundnut cultivation is mainly undertaken in Kovilpatti, Tiruchendur and Sattankulam taluks. Groundnut cake is being used as manure and cattle feed. With 35% share, the district is the top producer of Cumbu in Tamil Nadu. Palmyrah trees are grown mostly in Tiruchendur, Srivaikundam, Sattankulam and Vilathikulam taluks. Jaggery is produced from palmyrah juice; the production of jaggery is the main occupation of the people of Tiruchendur and Sattankulam taluks. Banana and other vegetables are raised in Srivaikundam and Tiruchendur taluks. Greens are the cultivated in Pudukottai, which bridges Thoothukudi and Tirunelveli.The road going towards kulayankarisal from Thiruchendur has banana farms on one side and a salt farm on the other; each farm needs a different type of water. Thoothukudi is the largest exporter of bananas in Tamilnadu.

Table 6
Area and Production of Principal Crops

Total Cultivated Area	1,97,413 Hec	
Net Area Sown	1,88,296 Hec	
Area Sown more than once	9,117 Hec	
Area, Production of Principal Crops	*Area (hec.) in '000'*	*Production (Tonnes)*
Rice	21721	96920
Millets and Other Cereals	–	52184
Pulses	–	23,365
Sugarcane (Gur)	98	11,610
Groundnut	2,762	5,450
Gingely	3,352	1,270
Cotton (BL) (in Lints)	17,450	13,900
Important Agri. Crops	Paddy, Chillies, Banana and Cumbu	
Important Non-Agri. Crops	Chenna, Cotton	
Agricultural Land Holdings		
Holdings	2,24,102	
Area	2, 83,916.76 (Hec.)	
Average size of Holdings	1, 2 (Hec.)	

Source: Department of Statistics, Thoothukudi-2001.

Out of the total area of 450954 hectares, 169689 hectares are brought under the cultivation of different crops which is nearly 40% of total area of the district. The important food crops in the district are paddy, cholam, cumbu, ragi, varagu, samai and commercial crops are banana,cotton chilly, sugarcane and groundnut. The major crops cultivated in surveyed watershed are maize, cumbu and cholam, among the millets, groundnut, gingelly and sunflower in oil seeds, all types of pulses (black gram, green gram, cowpea, and red gram), cotton, chillies, turmeric and tuber crops as commercial crops and jasmine, rose and chrysanthemum are also grown. Whereas, in Sattankulam and Udangudi block watersheds palmyrah, coconut, acacia, neem are the predominant perennial crops. Only in limited area, some pulses and millets are cultivated. Since the rainfall is unimodel only one rain fed crop is raised in a year. The vegetables like chillies, bhendi, annual moringa and some fruit trees are also raised with protective irrigation facilities. The multi various cropping pattern in these watershed areas are due to the presence of red, black, clay loam, sandy and laterite soil types.

DPAP PROJECT

Drought Prone Area Programme (DPAP) on watershed basis was launched by the Ministry of Rural Development, Government of India, along with other two departmental programmes namely, Integrated Wastelands Development Project (IWDP) and Desert Development Programme (DDP) with effect from 01.04.1995. The guidelines and objectives of these programmes are clearly spelt out. DPAP is under implementation in 947 blocks of 164 districts in 13 states. The DPAP V batch watersheds were implemented in 34 watersheds spreading over 17, 278 have in eight blocks of Thoothukudi district. The details of the watersheds with code and treated area are furnished in Table 7.

Table 7
Particulars of V Batch Watersheds in Thoothukudi District

Name of the Block	*Name of the Watershed*	*Watershed Code*	*Treated area (ha.)*
Thoothukudi	Kattalankulam	Gal A(5)	510
Kootudankadu	Gal b	505	
Mudivaittanendal	Gal b	525	
Kovilpatty	Avalnatham	4A1 C4b4	520
Kadaliyur	4A1 C3b5	520	
Katturamanpatti	4A1 C4a5	520	
Erachi	4A1 C3b4	520	
Villiseri	4AB4a1	520	
Kayathar	Kalangaraipatty	4A1B4a11	520
Karadikulam	4A1B4a12	520	
Koppampatty	4A1B4a12	520	
Cholapuram	4A1C2B1	520	
Thirumalapuram	4A1B2b4	520	
Pudur	Kilakaranthai	4A1C3C9	500
Senkottai	4A1C3C5	500	
Melakalloorani	4A1D1d14	500	
Mavilodi	4A1D1C1	500	
Inam vadamalapuram	4A1D1C4	500	
Vilathikulam	Marthandampatti	4A1C3a9	500
Manthikulam	4A1C3a10	500	
Virusampatty	4A1C3a4	500	
Kumarasakkanapuram	4A1D1d2	500	
Arungulam	4A1c3a14	500	
Ottapidaram	Oonamakulam	4A1C1b123	505.7
Silankulam	4A1C3a14	505	
Athanoor	4A1C1b12	503.3	
Parivallikottai	4A1C1b10	505	
P. Duraisamypuram	4A1C1b17	502	
Sattankulam	Komaneri	4A1a3C2	494.1
Pidaneri	4A1a3C2	501.2	
Puthantharuvai	4A1a3a2	510.5	
Udangudi	Chettiapathu	4A1B1C16c	504.0
Manadu Thandupathu	4A1a3b3	502.1	
Paramankurichi	4A1a3b4	505.1	

Source: Report of DPAP Project.

The various developmental activities of DPAP fall under three broad categories viz. Land resources development through soil and water conservation measures, development of water resources through in-situ moisture conservation and harvesting of rainwater with proper utilization of existing irrigation sources and finally increasing vegetative cover by means of agro forestry, silvi pasture or by establishment of fodder grasses fodder legume crops and other alternate land use systems.

THE MAJOR OBJECTIVES OF THE DPAP PROJECT

Promoting economic development of the farming community by optimal and effective utilization of natural resources namely the land, water and vegetative cover in micro watersheds of around 500ha.

- Generation of employment and development of human and economic resource base with special emphasis on improving the economic and social status of the poor and disadvantaged sections in the area.
- Promoting savings and investments of money by forming Self Help Group's and helping them in income generating activities.
- Restoration of ecological balance in a watershed through community action for operation and maintenance of various assets created. Further development of exploring potential natural resources by the use of simple, feasible and affordable technological solutions and institutional arrangements.
- Distribution of benefits from land and water resources, equitably and improving bio-mass production and
- Creating greater access to income generating opportunities, which focus on human resource development.

THE EXPENDITURE

The particulars of component wise expenditure details of V batch DPAP watersheds are furnished in Table 8.

Table 8

Component Wise Expenditure Details Watersheds in Thoothukudi District

Particulars	*Allocation (L.Rs.)*	*Funds released (L.Rs.)*	*Expenditure (L.Rs)*	*Balance (L.Rs.)*
Community organization	34.00	34.00	11.24	22.76
Training	34.00	34.00	10.27	23.47
EPA	27.20	27.20	24.91	2.29
Works	516.80	162.00	196.11	-34.11
Adminstration	68.00	48.80	45.47	3.33
Total	680.00	306.00	288.30	17.70

Source: Report of DPAP Project

Among the different components the expenditure for Entry Point Activity (EPA) was utilized as per the norms. The expenditure on community organization and training should be spent at an early date by providing training and exposure visits to the watershed beneficiaries for effective functioning of the various organisations in the watersheds, before carrying out the activities. Major components of works in DPAP involves EPA, Soil and Water Conservation works (SWC), Water Resources Development and Management (WRD), Afforestation and Plantations, Crop demonstration, Formation of Community Organizations (CO) and Organizations of Trainings. Amongst the different components, major expenditure has been utilized on WRD followed by SWC (summer ploughing). since, the project is in the II year of implementation, the expenditure on crop demonstrations, fruit plantations and tree afforestation will be executed based on the location, soil types and farmers preference in the ensuring years.

LIMITATIONS OF WATERSHED DEVELOPMENT PROJECTS

There are a number of schemes aiming at development of degraded lands being implemented by the different Ministries and even different Departments in the same Ministry. Most of the schemes have their own guidelines and field officers get confused. In some cases, one particular Department/officer deals with similar type of activities through different guidelines.

1. District Rural Development Agencies are over burdened with a number of schemes and hardly find any time to monitor and supervise the project implementation.
2. Relationship of Watershed Committees with Panchayats and exact role and responsibility of Panchayats remain unspecified giving rise to confusion.
3. The guidelines deal with a number of programmes like DPAP, DDP, IWDP and EAS. Funding mechanism, Monitoring and Evaluation and functioning of project widely differ leading to confusion at the level of DRDA and Project Implementing Agencies.
4. Frequent changes of district officials and preference of a particular Department by the DRDA for execution of land based schemes at times result in improper implementation of the projects under the Scheme.
5. There is no involvement of senior State Government Officials and officers of the line departments. The programme is viewed by them as exclusive programme of DRDA only and not that of the concerned Department. This attitude is perhaps due to that reason that the PIAs/ Watershed Committees receive the funds directly from DRDA.
6. The wage rates in and among the States vary considerably and ceiling of Rs. 4000 per ha is not adequate.

7. People's participation does not come very easily universally. The Watershed Committees at times become pressure groups patronised by local politicians/influential persons.
8. The selection of watersheds is not done as per guidelines in most of the cases and actual treatable areas are left behind. Delineation of watershed area remains quite vague and the coverage of area by treatment remains unspecified.
9. The States are not willing to share the project cost and aspire for I 00 per cent grant-in aid.

STRENGTHS OF WATERSHED DEVELOPMENT PROJECTS

People at the grassroots level are actually involved in the finalisation of the action plan and implementation of the same.

1. They are not only associated in carrying out physical activities but also financial operations like payment of wages to the labourers and management of the Watershed Fund as well as Watershed Development Fund.
2. The villagers are also required to contribute @ 5 per cent to I 0 per cent of the funds utilised on their land in form of wages, raw material or cash ensuring better participation and actual involvement in the project.
3. Creation of Watershed Development Fund provides effective mechanism for the post project sustenance.
4. The provision for nominating suitable number of women to Watershed Committees takes care of gender issues to some extent.
5. Induction of Panchayat members also associates Panchayati Raj Institutions in implementation of the project. Registration of Watershed Committees in the appropriate Act of the State concerned, provides for effective measures to ensure accountability.
6. Engagement of a local person as the Secretary to the Watershed Committee provides an element of transparency as he is the key person in operating Watershed Development Fund and the funds of Watershed Committees.
7. As the user group consists of only those persons who are holding the lands in respect of watersheds, it eliminates entrance of unwanted/unconcerned elements in the Watershed Committees to a great extent. Creation of Watershed Development Fund effective mechanism for the post project sustenance. Dovetailing of other schemes and provision of revolving fund takes care of the landless persons.
8. The guidelines also seek participation of the landless persons through constitution of self-help groups and associating its members in the Watershed Committee. Provision of revolving fund further helps in mitigating the problems of the rural poor.

CONCLUSION

Watershed programme is a demand driven participatory approach is gradually institutionalized. This kind of innovative project was started implementation after 1998 through large scale adoption of common guidelines issued by Ministry of Agriculture and Ministry of Rural Development, Government of India Since it is a complete shift from conventional programmes implemented so far by Government agencies people involved in the pragrammes had experienced a new paradigm. Still they could not able to come out of the conventional type of project implementation, it needs some more time to understood fully about this participatory, stake holders approach. In this juncture, the Mid-term evaluation conducted in 13 watersheds of 8 different blocks in Thoothukudi district found that officials, Watershed Development Team did their level best to make the programme participatory. But due to some field level constraints, it was not made cent per cent. Still it needs lot of orientation on the part of Project Implementing Agency (PIA) (Watershed Development Teamand User Groups (UGs) to prepare the people for the post project activity for the sustainability of the watershed programme.

There is an urgent need for action research on the grassroots of watershed management. Many of the academic respondents commented that there has been so little comprehensive research on the watershed development that the whole debate over how they function is being steered by anecdotal information. There is therefore a serious knowledge gap on the process of local politicisation and local understanding of the watershed development system. NGOs involved in natural resource management activities, whether this is watershed, wasteland, water or forest based, have been relatively slow in forging working alliances with Gram Panchayats. Many NGOs work with watershed development simply because they cannot avoid doing so, but have no active program or ideology of support.

Reference

Bharat R. Sharma and Christopher A. Scott, (2005), Watershed Management Challenges: Introduction and Overview, Malhotra Publishing House, New Delhi, p. 1.

Deborah Bossio, Andrew Noble, Jules Pretty (2005), Frits Penning de Vries and David Molden, Linking Land, Soil and Water Management, Malhotra Publishing House, New Delhi, p. 22.

Farrington J., C. Turton, and A.J. James, (Ed.), (1999), Particpatory Watershed Development: Challenges for the Twenty-first Century, New Delhi: Oxford University Press.

Hanumantha, Rao, C. H. (2000), Watershed Development in India: Recent Experiences and Emerging Issues. *Economic and Political Weekly*, XXXV(45): 3943-3947.

Hayami, Y., V. Ruttan (1984), Induced Innovation Model of Agricultural Development, in Agricultural Development in the Third World, ed. C. Eicher and J. Staatz. Baltimore, Md., USA: Johns Hopkins University Press.

India, Ministry of Agriculture (1991), WARASA: National Watershed Development Project for Rainfed Areas (NWDPRA) Guidelines, 2nd Ed. New Delhi: Ministry of Agriculture.

India, Ministry of Rural Development (1994), Guidelines for Watershed Development, New Delhi.

MORD, Report, Ministry of Rural Development, New Delhi, 2000.

National Commission on Farmers, Ministry of Agriculture, New Delhi, 2006.

National Portal Content Management Team, Reviewed on: 31-03-2009.

NCF, Report, National Commission on Farmers, Ministry of Agriculture, New Delhi, 2006.

NRAA, Report, National Rain-fed Area Authority, Ministry of Agriculture, New Delhi, 2008.

Panchayati Raj and Natural Resources Management, Report, 2000.

Planning Commission, Report of the Working Group on Natural Resources Management: Eleventh Five Year Plan (2007-2012), Planning Commission, Government of India, New Delhi, 2007.

Samra J. S., and K. D. Sharma (2009), Watershed Development: How to Make 'Invisible' Impacts 'Visible'? *Current Science*, Vol. 96, No. 2, 25 January.

Sharma, R. (2002), Report, Ministry of Rural Development, New Delhi.

Sikka, Alok, K. (2002), Participatory Watershed Management for Land and Water Care: Planning, Impact Evaluation, Sustainability and Future. In: Watershed Management: Issues and Policies for 21st Century. Associated Publishing Company, PO Box no. 2679, New Delhi, India. pp. 128-135.

Suhas P. Wani and Y. S. Ramakrishna, (2005), Sustainable Management of Rainwater Through Integrated Watershed Approach for Improved Rural Livelihoods, Malhotra Publishing House, New Delhi, p. 3.

APPENDIX - 1

Table 1
Land Utilization Statement of the Surveyed Watersheds (Area in Hectares)

	Name of the block /watershed												
Particulars	*1*	*2*	*3*	*4*	*5*	*6*	*7*	*8*	*9*	*10*	*11*	*12*	*13*
Forest	–	–	–	–	–	–	–	–	–	–	–	–	–
Barren and uncultivable land	212.5	–	54.7	–	–	–	–	–	–	` 59.0	–	–	2.1
Land put to non agricultural use	12.0	115.3	–	161.8	186.6	118.5	172.0	196.8	30.7	154.8	88.7	152.1	31.6
Cultivable waste	243.6	1.8	–	–	4.8	0.8	10.2	0.4	0.3	–	–	5.6	137.4
Permanent pastures	–	–	–	–	–	–	–	–	–	–	–	–	–
Miscellaneous tree crops	–	–	– –	–	2.2	350.4	50.1	387.2	220.6	–	–	0.4	77.1
Current fallows	513.8	202.1	180.1	272.1	984.3	198.9	510.08	106.7	109.4	97.0	283.3	17.7	33.8
Other fallow	667.8	85.5	1.2	–	–	–	–	–	–	–	18.7	97.2	194.8
Net area sown	281.2	504.8	858.0	233.2	345.7	336.4	354.8	661.1	423.5	941.6	908.8	225.2	494.2
Total geographical area	1930.9	909.5	1094.4	667.1	1523.6	1005.0	1097.9	1352.2	784.5	1252.4	1299.5	498.2	971.0

Source: DRDA/DPAP, Thoothukudi

1. Thoothukudy - Mudivaittanendal
2. Kovilpatty - Kadalaiyur
3. Kovilpatti - Villiseri
4. Kayathar - Kalangaraipatty
5. Kayathar - Koppampatty
6. Pudur - Kilakaranthai
7. Pudur - Senkottai
8. Vilathikulam - Kumarasakkanapuram
9. Vilathikulam - Virusampatty
10. Ottapidaram - Athanoor
11. Ottapidaram - Sillankulam
12. Sattakulam - Komaneri
13. Udangudi - Chettaipathu

Table 2
Time Series Data for Rainfall by Seasons

	South West Monsoon		*North East Monsoon*		*Winter Season*		*Hot Weather Season*		*Total*		
Year	*Normal*	*Actual*	*Normal*	*Actual*	*Normal*	*Actual*	*Normal*	*Actual*	*Normal*	*Actual*	*% Deviation (+ or–or =) from*
1997-1998	59.9	30.2	429.4	659.5	62.0	10.0	110.9	94.3	662.2	794.0	+119.90
1998-1999	59.9	152.4	429.4	525.6	62.0	69.1	110.9	17.5	662.2	764.7	+115.48
1999-2000	59.9	40.2	429.4	297.0	62.0	127.0	110.9	55.5	662.2	519.7	-21.5
2000-2001	59.9	127.9	429.4	312.8	62.0	52.3	110.9	127.0	662.2	520.0	-6.4
2001-2002	59.9	57.8	429.4	286.52	62.0	27.4	110.9	141.5	662.2	513.4	-22.4
2002-2003	70.1	27.7	426.0	359.0	42.6	59.9	116.1	112.4	654.8	557.0	-14.9
2003-2004	86.8	48.1	410.1	319.5	46.6	47.1	112.2	108.6	665.7	517.9	-21.0
2004-2005	86.8	151.1	410.1	551.4	46.6	61.5	112.2	171.1	665.7	935.10	+42.6
2005-2006	86.8	48.4	410.1	453.6	46.6	36.1	112.2	139.9	665.7	678.0	+3.4
2006-2007	86.8	62.0	410.1	670.6	46.6	40.2	112.2	64.4	665.7	837.2	+27.7

Source: Directorate of Economics and Statistics, Chennai.

PROSPECTS OF RETAIL PHARMA'S IN INDIA

*N. Sulaiman** *& V. Balakrishnan***

INTRODUCTION

Retailing is one of the pillars of the economy in India and accounts for 35% of GDP. The retail industry is divided into organized and unorganized sectors. Over 12 million outlets operate in the country and only 4% of them being larger than 500 sq ft (46 m^2) in size. Organized retailing refers to trading activities undertaken by licensed retailers, that is, those who are registered for sales tax, income tax, etc.

These also include the corporate-backed hypermarkets and retail chains, and also the privately owned large retail businesses. Unorganized retailing, on the other hand, refers to the traditional formats of low-cost retailing, for example, the local Kirana shops, owner manned general stores, pann/beedi shops, convenience stores, hand cart and pavement vendors, and pharma retailing.

Rs. 20,000 Crore Indian drug industry is facing many challenges. It has enormous responsibilities as the health situation in the country is in bad shape. For instance, over 20 million women and 80 per cent of children suffer from anemia. Thousands of flood-affected people suffer from leptospirosis. Their plight worse due to non-availability of related drugs.

The market in India is highly fragmented, as there are more than 10,000 licensed firms with a total annual turnover of Rs 540 billion. Out of this, Only 300 companies are in the organized sector. In many small-scale units, including outsourcing companies, the workers are not paid adequately. Naturally, the employees tend to migrate to better-paying companies after gaining experience of a year or two.

---

* Asst. Professor cum Liaison Officer, Annamalai University Study Centre, Mysore-570001-Karnataka.

** Professor in Management, DDE Annamalai University, Annamalai Nagar- 608002-Tamilnadu.

HISTORY OF PHARMACY

Pharmacy is the health profession that links the health sciences with the chemical sciences and it is charged with ensuring the safe and effective use of pharmaceutical drugs. The word derives from the Greek word pharmakon, meaning "drug" or "medicine" (the earliest form of the word is the Mycenaean Greek pa-ma-ko, attested in Linear B syllabic script).

The scope of pharmacy practice includes more traditional roles such as compounding and dispensing medications, and it also includes more modern services related to health care, including clinical services, reviewing medications for safety and efficacy, and providing drug information. Pharmacists, therefore, are the experts on drug therapy and are the primary health professionals who optimize medication use to provide patients with positive health outcomes.

An establishment in which pharmacy (in the first sense) is practiced is called a pharmacy, chemist's or (in the United States) drug store. US drug stores commonly sell not only medicines, but also miscellaneous items such as candy (sweets), cosmetics, and magazines, as well as light refreshments or groceries.

The word pharmacy is derived from its root word pharma which was a term used since the 15th–17th centuries. In addition to pharma responsibilities, the pharma offered general medical advice and a range of services that are now performed solely by other specialist practitioners, such as surgery and midwifery. The pharma (as it was referred to) often operated through a retail shop which, in addition to ingredients for medicines, sold tobacco and patent medicines. The pharmas also used many other herbs not listed. In its investigation of herbal and chemical ingredients, the work of the pharma may be regarded as a precursor of the modern sciences of chemistry and pharmacology, prior to the formulation of the scientific method.

RETAIL INDUSTRY IN INDIA

Indian apparel retailers are increasing their brand presence overseas, particularly in developed markets. While most have identified a gap in countries in West Asia and Africa, some majors are also looking at the US and Europe. Arvind Brands, Madura Garments, Spykar Lifestyle and Royal Classic Polo are busy chalking out foreign expansion plans through the distribution route and standalone stores as well. Another denim wear brand, Spykar, which is now moving towards becoming a casual wear lifestyle brand, has launched its store in Melbourne recently. It plans to open three stores in London by 2008-end.

The low-intensity entry of the diversified Mahindra Group into retail is unique because it plans to focus on lifestyle products. The Mahindra group is the fourth large Indian business group to enter the business of retail after Reliance Industries Ltd, the Aditya Birla Group, and Bharti Enterprises Ltd. The other three groups are focusing either on perishables and groceries, or a range of products, or both. Like these pharmaceutical companies like, cipla, Rambaxcy, Dr. Reddy laboratory, Novarodisk and also mitigating their efforts for retail bussiness. But there the problem in india is Self medication, spurious drugs circulation. Awareness is lacking among consumers towards identifying batch and expiry dates. Espicially rurel India is enormously and extensively suffering due to lack of awareness and education. Hence there imperative need to control and promote fair practices of retail pharma in India and stopping the operation of unauthorized drug outlet and checking the practices of unqualified personnel in selling is need of the howz. This study aims at emphasizing on evolving appropriate policy matters, and implementation of the same .The role of Government is rather crucial and drug companies co-operation in this regard is still in the infancy in India. This cruk of the issue as far as retail pharma is concerned.

GOVT. INITIATIVE

Government is planning to setup a central Drugs Authority [CDA] to regulate pharmaceutical and cosmetic sector in the country. Ministry of health and family welfare has reported that there is a proposal to setup a Central Drugs Authority of India to provide technical vision and policy direction for the pharmaceutical and cosmetics sectors and their regulation in the country. Chemicals and fertilizers Minister said, the issue would be examined in the light of the upcoming decision on the Proposed National pharmaceutical policy, 2006. Due to this, Cabinet has also considered to draft national pharmaceutical policy. Pricing policy is not uniform among drug companies. Sometimes if the profit margin is exorbitantly high enough and it became beyond the reach of common man. Moreover the chemical components needed for using the ailment is not well established and checked by regulating bodies. This leads to formulation of uniform guidelines for checking the contents and efficacy.

SIGNIFICANT CHANGES

The number of local pharma multinationals increased to 12 in 2004-08. The new entrants are Dr.Reddy's laboratories, wockhardt, Nicholas Piramal, Sun pharmaceuticals, Unichem, Torrent Pharmaceuticals, Cadila Health care, Lupin and Cadila Pharma. The drug sector had only one Indian multinational, Ran Baxy Laboratories, till 2004.

While Ranbaxy is the largest in terms of geographical presence and number of global subsidies (25 Countries). Dr. Reddy's ranks second with presence in ten countries. The third and fourth positions are Sun pharmaceuticals (eight countries) and wockhard (seven countries).

In the couple of issue back, we dabbled upon the importance and growing presence of Mergers and Acquisitions shaping the global pharmaceutical industry. Big ticket acquisitions have spread their tentacles far and wide, bringing players and markets closer and to same extent, consolidating the otherwise hugely fragmented industry. While the war for assets has been heating up, valuations have been skyrocketing (through lately some plateauing of premiums has been witnessed). This, however, has not be a major hindering factor. Corporate globally are all happy (and amply) justifying with expensive valuations. If anything, the pace of buy-outs has jumped many folders.

PATENT POSITION

Though patents play a crucial role in many industries, its relevance and importance in pharmaceuticals in paramount. At times, patent expiry on key products can have a significant impact on earnings of a company. At $12.9bn, 'Lipitor' (Atorvastation) for example, accounts for almost 30% of Pfizer. Inc's global pharmaceutical sales of $45bn. When the product faces patent expiration a few years down the line, it is estimated that it could wipe of almost 25% of Pfizer's current net earnings. Mergers during an impending patent expiry help to spread/diversify revenues over a larger base, thereby reducing the blow of sinking sales post patent expiry, some merger and acquisition concluded in the backdrop of patent expiry include Astra's Merger with Zeneca in 1998 (Patent on Losec and Zestril expires), pharmacia's merger with Upjohn in 1995 ('Halcion and Xanax patent expires') and Sanofi's merger with Aventis ('Ambien' and 'Eloxatin' patent expires).

DEVELOPMENT PIPELINES

In the LPG era/Research and Development is essence of pharmaceutical industry. The avenues of discovering new drugs, that offer signification benefits over a known compound, are getting fewer. Drug development costs, on the otherhand are skyrocketing. Making pipeline expansion extremely expensive. Generally, product pipelines the world over are drying up. Weak pipelines- which represent probable future in market drugs are an indication of treacherous times that lay ahead. Weak pipeline suggest that over a period of time, revenues will inevitably diminish. Merger and Acquisition offer a lease of life for pipeline starved corporate. On the other hard, merging entities can also work with the added advantage of a larger Research & Development team and streamlining overlapping drug candidates.

RESEARCH AND DEVELOPMENT COSTS

Pharmaceutical companies are following the practice of shared loyalty. Global companies locate their Research and development in a different location around the world. They invest on product innovation around 50%.When success comes benefits shared when failure takes place risk is also distrilinked among them.

A logical extension of the above point is rising R&D costs. As development costs rise (estimated $800 mn to put a drug into market), mergers offer a means to attain this high critical mass. A larger revenue base also bloats the risk taking capability of companies involved in research, marking sure that a strong and sustainable income stream feeds Research and Development costs.

MARKETING MASS

Drug marketing has become a key cost center in the pharmaceutical space. Sales force sizes for ethical drugs are growing rapidly on the one hand, while an increasing presence of OTC products in making way for heavy advertising spends. Mergers and consolidation can help streamline sales and marketing efforts. They can offer to cut costs (reducing merged sales forces team). While increasing revenues and product portfolios. Strategic marketing presence is also a key rationale in many Merger and Acquisition deals. For example, companies with little or no presence in a particular market may look to buy-out a local company with an established sales team.

These reflect some of the major agenda in driving pharmaceutical consolidation. But whatever the reason, successful integration (of products, process and people) of the too organizations is the key to delivery.

INDIA'S ENTRY IN THE CONSOLIDATION CHART ON FOUR PARAMETERS

Indian Companies Shopping Overseas

This includes (a) Generic companies as targets, which has received the maximum attention from our 'me too' boys. Moving on from the small sized acquisitions earlier on, the true big ticket trend started from Matrix Lab's acquisition of Belgium-based Docpharma in June 2005. This was followed by Dr. Reddy,s takeover of Betapharm in Feb. 2006 and Ran baxy's acquision of Romania based Terapia.

(b) CRAMS (Contract Research and manufacturing Services) Companies as targets. India's inherent advantage of low cost manufacturing and technical capabilities puts it at the forefront in grabbing a large chunk of the outsourcing pie, and access to overseas plants/technologies of dedicated contract manufactures to Big Pharma perceived to give a fillip to this sun rise industry. These assets bring along a reputed clientele and an established presence. Shasun's acquisition of Rhodia's CRAMS division and Nicholas Piramal's acquisition of Pfizer's Morpeth facility address opportunities in this space.

Indian Companies Shopping India

The space has seen relatively low action, with sellers largely comprising of MNCs looking to dispose off local assets (Glen Mark's asset-buyout of GSK's Ankleshwar unit in 2002); or buyers vying for specific brands/technologies (Wockhart's acquisition of Dumex for brands farex and protinex; and Matrix's takeover con-cord Biotech, marking its entry into stations and immunosuppresants).

Indian Companies Shopping for an R&D Pipeline

Forming a miniscule portion of India's participation in global consolidation, these are restricted to accessing technology/early stage of pipeline for small start-ups. Biocon's acquisition of Nobex in 2006 is a case in point.

Foreign Companies Shopping in India

The story of overseas buy-outs Indian assets has not taken off too well, with just one big-ticket acquisition (Matrix labs by the Vs-based Mylan) till date. This was followed by Actavis acquisition of chennai based Grandix. Low cost manufacturing is the key driver for Merger and Acquisition in this Space. However, the promoter- Controlled structure of most Indian Pharma's is keeping the pace slow.

The pace of consolidation is expected to continue. Skyrocketing valuations witnessed over the last two years are, however, likely to cool off as degree of rationale and some tight purse strings in a check on galloping premiums.

SUGGESTIONS AND RECOMMENDATIONS

The frame of new policy world now consist of five main elements.

Public–Private partnership to help families, drugs provided at concessional prices to government-run hospitals, the government, on its part, would promote competition to certain prices, the chemical Ministry would move from cost-based to a price monitoring system and The Ministry Would setup a 14-member committee including 11 members from the industry to work on the interim order of the supreme court.

CONCLUSION

The new pharma policy is likely to call for a central mechanism to oversee R&D Projects in the country. It will also propose a revised eligibility criteria for Research and Development benefits offered by the government. Priority may be given to maintenance of central database on grants, implementation and outcome of the ongoing Research and Development efforts for better focus and avoiding duplication and unfair practices of pharmaceutical retailing in India.

References

Monica Joshi (2007), Pricing Power Back, *Dalal Street,* Vol. XXII, No. 3, Jan. 22 to Feb-04, pp. 26.

Monica Joshi (2007), Pop the M&A Pill Part I, *Dalal Street,* Vol. XXII, No. 5, Feb-19 to March 07, pp. 18.

Monica Joshi (2007), Pop the M&A Pill-Part II, *Dalal Street,* Vol. XXII, No. 08 April 12-15, pp. 24.

Monica Joshi (2007), Pop the M&A Pill-Part III, *Dalal Street,* Vol. XXII, No. 9 April 16-29, pp. 23

Monica Joshi (2007), Health India-Part I, *Dalal Street,* Vol. XXII, No. 10 April' 30–May 13' 07, pp. 24.

Monica Joshi (2007), Battle of the Bidders, *Dalal Street,* Vol. XXII, No. 12 May 28-June 10, pp. 20.

Satya Sundaram I (2007), "Building the Pharmaceutical Brands", Facts for You. March 2007, pp. 7 to 11.

Index

Predominance of Spices and Plantation Crops

The implications of WTA on Kerala's agricultural sector assumes significance due to the high trade intensity of Kerala's cash crops. While more than 80% of the gross cropped area is under spices, coffee, tea, rubber, cashew, arecanut and coconut, Kerala has a decisive share in the export and import of these commodities at the national level. Kerala occupies a unique position in respect of area, production and export of a number of traded crops such as coffee, pepper, cardamom, turmeric, rubber, cashew, ginger, tea, arecanut and coconut. The state contributes 92% of the national output of pepper and rubber, 76% of the cardamom, 45% of the coconut, 20 to 22% of coffee, 14% of cashew, 13% of ginger and 6 to 7% of the tea (see Table 1).

The state has a unique position in the production of four plantation crops, viz tea, coffee, cardamom and rubber. The state accounts for 42% of the area and 43% of the production of these four crops. The total area under these crops is 6.41 lakh hectares which constitute approximately 30% of the net cropped area in the state.

Export Intensity of Kerala's Products

The traded crops contribute nearly three-fifth of the value of agricultural output in the state. Certain agricultural products of the state show high degree of trade intensity. Kerala's export share is as high as 95% for cashew shell liquid, 94% for pepper, 92% for rubber, 83% for spices oil, 67% for cashew kernal, 74% for cardamom, 46% for ginger, 22% for turmeric, 27% for curry powder and 16% for vanilla. (See Table 2).

The aggregate earnings from the agricultural exports from Kerala including coir and marine products is nearly Rs 5000 crores which accounts for approximately 30% of Kerala's agricultural SDP. The implications of WTA on Kerala's agriculture need to be examined in this context.

Since Kerala's agricultural sector is highly trade intensive and the state is emerging fast as a consumerist state, WTA is likely to have tremendous implications for the state. On the one hand it will promote higher export if there is price competitiveness for Kerala's products. On the other hand, this

Table 1

Production of Major Crops in Kerala and their Percentage Share in India's Production (Qty: MT).

	Pepper		*Cardamom*		*Tea*		*Coffee*		*Natural Rubber*		*Coconut**		*Cashewnut*		*Ginger*	
Year	*Qty*	%	*Qty*	%	*Qty*	%	*Qty*	%	*Qty*	%	*Qty*	%	*Qty*	%	*Qty*	%
1995-96	68568	94.96	5380	68.1	64802	8.52	45000	20.19	474555	93.62	5155	39.80	82760	2.57	46455	22.13
1996-97	56546	91.83	4550	68.68	69319	8.81	47320	23.08	512756	93.33	5276	40.40	68963	16.51	46371	19.94
1997-98	46040	80.77	5290	66.96	65225	7.8	50659	22.19	541935	92.82	5210	40.97	56885	13.23	43617	17.30
1998-99	68510	91.35	4990	69.6	58726	6.87	49886	18.82	559099	92.41	5132	40.94	51336	14.26	39362	13.93
1999-00	47543	80.58	6585	70.58	61955	7.40	60470	20.71	572820	92.05	5680	46.83	65547	14.25	41344	14.36
2000-01	60929	95.65	7580	72.33	69132	8.15	70550	23.42	579866	91.98	5536	43.66	66178	12.73	42699	13.43
2001-02	58240	93.33	8383	73.76	66090	7.8	66690	22.19	580350	91.91	5479	42.27	65867	14.64	40181	14.51
2002-03	57358	93.94	8680	72.82	55348	6.54	63322	23.01	594917	91.61	5709	45.54	66087	14.37	32412	10.68
2003-04	69015	92.31	8875	76.64	57553	6.77	68900	25.47	655135	92.06	5876	48.25	65655	13.97	32972	8.28
2004-05	68362	92.03	8616	75.48	49508	5.96	54300	19.71	690768	92.14	5727	44.63	63701	13.85	30567	13.29

* Coconut production in million nuts.

Table 2

Export of Major Crops from Kerala and their Per cent Share in India's Production (Qty:MT).

	Pepper		*Cardamom*		*Tea*		*Coffee*		*Natural Rubber*	*Cashew kernel*		*Ginger*	
Year	*Qty*	%	*Qty*	%	*Qty*	%	*Qty*	%	*Qty*	*Qty*	%	*Qty*	%
1995-96	24419	92.69	233	10.2	NA	NA	360	0.21	1130	33275	47.00	2860	15.47
1996-97	46264	96.6	53	3.14	75666	47.29	503	0.28	1598	38546	56.00	4905	16.49
1997-98	34380	95.75	NA	-	79829	39.78	2163	1.21	1415	39441	52.00	4240	15
1998-99	34864	100	475	25.01	101466	48.23	10087	4.76	1840	43665	57.00	1441	16.6
1999-00	42100	100	550	35.48	77342	40.94	10010	4.09	5989	50022	51.67	1560	17.78
2000-01	18639	85.38	825	53.39	94839	46.58	5374	2.18	13356	49874	55.04	2752	43.77
2001-02	21448	93.75	630	61.11	96155	50.61	3685	1.73	6995	54717	55.72	2560	39.6
2002-03	15094	69.85	475	69.66	103544	56.15	3103	1.5	55311	66859	64.2	2415	28.54
2003-04	15710	94.07	435	57.46	86794	47.40	3195	1.37	75905	68119	67.56	2089	44.48
2004-05	13358	94.4	387	59.54	86589	42.07	1808	0.85	46150	79950	63.12	2518	19.37

would lead of rise in imports due to high degree of consumerism partly influenced by external remittances and substantial remittances from rest of India. The WTA trade regime provides both opportunities as well as threat to Kerala's agriculture. While it enhances the export potential for Kerala's agricultural products, it also can be a source of threat to Kerala's agriculture due to heavy imports of edible oil, pepper, rubber, coconut products etc in the absence of adequate safeguards.

Enhanced Export Opportunities for Kerala's Products

The WTA is aimed at making international trade free and fair by enhancing market access to the products of the members. The liberalisation of world trade if happens would benefit Kerala's agricultural products by enhancing their export opportunities.

Greater Potential for Traditional Items

The unexploited potential for enhancing the exports of traditional items such as pepper, cardamom, ginger, turmeric, cashew kernals, cashew shell liquid, coir products and marine products can be fully exploited. The export potential of these items has not been adequately exploited due to the absence of adequate infrastructural and policy support on the one hand and lack of product development, value addition and market promotion on the other.

The establishment of an Agri-Export Zone in horticulture covering 9 southern districts would go a long way in enhancing the export of horticultural products from Kerala.

High Potential for Nutraceutical Components

The world nutraceutical industry is projected to grow to $ 3 trillion by 2010 as per the World Bank projection. This rapidly growing segment is alternatively termed as Functional Foods, Nutraceuticals, Dietary supplements, Designer Foods, Medicinal foods, Vita foods, Therapeutic foods etc. The first Nutraceutical Summit in India organised by EXIM BANK in October 2003 had projected good prospect for India to tap the ever growing world market. Since Kerala is rich in tropical fruits (like pineapple and banana), nuts and spices, there is great potential in providing value added ingredients and components to the rapidly expanding nutraceutical industry in the world.

High Potential for Cosmaceutical and Oleo-chemical Products

Since the cosmetics and personal care products industry are projected to grow at 10% annually in Asia and Pacific region and slightly more in advanced countries, there is tremendous potential for export of natural products like herbal extracts, coconut ingredients, turmeric and medicinal plants. Many new products with pharmaceutical properties are made out of coconut oil with properties such as skin penetration, wringle removal, moisturising, anti-arthritis and anti-inflammation. If appropriate product innovations are made, Indian coconut oil can find new applications with greater value addition (Coronacion p 16). The booming market for organic cosmeceutical products and rising spending on personal care products and toiletries in Europe, US and Asia-Pacific regions provide excellent opportunities for Indian coconut industry to capitalise. Along with the extremely good opportunities for coconut oil in oleo-chemical industry, new applications for turmeric, medicinal herbs extracts are also increasing the demand for these products. The establishment of an Agri-Export Zone in Medicinal Plants in Kerala covering 9 districts is a right step which could promote the availability of medicinal plants for conversion into value added products for export.

Rising Demand for Organic Products

The world market for organic agricultural products is projected to grow from $ 26 billion (1% of world retail market for agricultural products) in 2002 to around $ 140 billion by 2010. The US, EU and Japan alone will have a market of $ 102 billion in the year 2010. Since Kerala has a number of natural advantages like tropical coastal climate, low fertiliser consumption and pockets free of fertilisers and chemicals, the state is ideally suited for the production of a range of organic agricultural products like fruits, vegetables, tea, cardamom, rubber, cashew and spices. There is good potential for latex produced through organic farming which is needed for the production of condoms for fighting HYV and AIDS.

Food Ingredients for Industrial Uses

Food ingredients for industrial use consist of a diverse range of product groups such as vegetable oils and fats, dried fruits and edible nuts, spices and herbs, natural gums and resins, essential oils, and oleoresins, dried vegetables, natural colours and flavours, honey, seeds and vegetable saps and extracts. These ingredients are consumed in maximum quantity in global packaged food industry. The estimated turnover of the global packaged food industry in 2002 was $1400 billion which is expected to grow by 12-15% annually. (EXIM BANK 2003 (2)). The packaged food industry comprises mainly of three sectors, viz, bakery products, chilled food and dairy products which account for 50% of the industry in 2004. Since Kerala has strength in fruits, nuts, spices and herbs, oils and oleoresins, there is high potential for export of these value added products and food ingredients.

Export of Fruits and Fruit Products

Pineapple continues to dominate international trade in tropical fruits. In 2000, pineapple accounted for 46% of world exports followed by mangoes at 24%. The export value of tropical fruits in 2000 was $2.1 billion of which 37% was accounted by processed tropical foods. US, EU, Japan, Canada & China continue to be the largest importers of tropical fruits. Kerala has very high potential for enhancing the export of fresh as well as processed pineapple products. The world pineapple export in 2000 was 8.68 lakh tonnes compared to 4.40 lakh tones of mango shipments (EXIM BANK 2002). Since health departments of UK and USA have recommended to consume 100 kg. of fruits per capita per year compared to the present level of 50-52 kgs, there is extremely good export potential for tropical fruits. (EXIM BANK 2003 (2)).

Banana and plantain are the other two products which also are in good demand in EU and in gulf countries. Kerala has natural advantages in certain varieties which have good export potential. The growing market for pineapple can be effectively exploited as part of the efforts of the Agri Export Zone which has commenced operations in Kerala.

Floricultural & Herbal Products

Other products which have potential for large exports are floriculture and cut flowers, organic vegetables, processed meat products, medicinal plants and health supplements. The implementation of the recommendation of the WTO (Prof.M.S.Swaminathan) Commission to declare the Western Ghat area from Silent Valley to Wynad as a bio-valley would provide tremendous opportunity for herbal exports. It needs to be noted that India accounts for only $100 million out of the $ 60 billion world trade in medicinal and aromatic plants, while Chine accounts for 40% (GoK 2004 p. 56). The establishment of a AEZ for medicinal plants covering 9 districts in Kerala is expected to promote large scale export of medicinal plants and herbal extracts to the rapidly expanding global market.

Adverse impacts

The new trade regime under WTA is also likely to create certain adverse impacts on Kerala's agricultural sector.

Higher Price Volatility

The decade, 1995 to 2005 has shown greater price volatility for Kerala's products as domestic prices were more sensitive to variations in international prices. The following table shows the pattern of price movement for major agricultural products in Kerala. (Table 3).

The period 1999-2001 witnessed unprecedented crash in domestic commodity prices which ranged from 40-60% during this period.

Enhanced Import of Spices and Plantation Products

As a consequences of the removal of quantitative restrictions and reduction in import duties, there was enhanced import of pepper, cardamom, coconut products and rubber products into

Table 3
Prices of Major Agricultural Commodities in Kerala (Rs/Kg).

Year	Arecanut (Rs/100 Nos)	Black Pepper	Cashew nut	Coconut with husk (Rs/100 Nos)	Ginger	Paddy	Rubber	Tapioca	Turmeric
1995-96	39	69	29	360	52	5	46	3	22
1996-97	43	88	27	480	41	6	47	3	27
1997-98	44	174	28	443	47	6	36	3	36
1998-99	65	181	35	453	56	6	30	3	59
1999-00	75	205	36	476	64	7	31	4	45
2000-01	42	125	23	281	49	6	30	3	33
2001-02	33	69	25	341	31	6	32	3	27
2002-03	32	77	27	473	34	6	39	4	34
2003-04	35	68	28	584	69	7	50	4	41
2004-05	40	60	35	635	73	7	52	4	41
2005-06	43	60	29	495	-	6	67	4	38
Range of values	32-75	60-205	23-36	281-635	31-73	5-7	30-67	3-4	22-59
S.D	13.38	54.75	4.27	102.20	14.18	0.60	11.76	0.52	11.82
C.V	29.98	51.22	14.58	22.39	27.48	9.75	28.13	15.12	33.41

India. These were partly the outcome of the above mentioned factors and partly due to the proliferation of Free Trade Agreements with Srilanka, Thaliland, SAARC countries and negotiations for FTAs with ASEAN, EU and BIMSTEC.

Adverse Impact on Terms of Trade

The parity index is employed to examine the relative impact of input and output prices on agricultural sector. If the ratio of prices received by the farms to the prices paid by the farmers is equal to 100 (or unity) then the farmers are neither gainers or loosers due to relative changes in prices of outputs and inputs. If input prices have increased faster than output prices, the terms of trade is seen to be adverse to the agricultural sector. Table 4 shows that terms of trade has been adverse to agriculture during the period 1995 to 2004. The parity index had declined from 82 to 48 from 1999 to 2001 which recovered partly to 59 in 2004. Hence, it is evident that terms of trade has emerged more adversely to agriculture since 1999.

Decline in Competitiveness

Another consequence of the WTA was the decline in the degree of competitiveness of major products of Kerala's interest. The following table shows that the Nominal Protection Coefficient (NPC) has gone up for majority of crops exhibiting decline in cost competitiveness (See Table 5). NPC is the ratio of domestic price to international price and if the ratio exceeds one it reflects lack of competitiveness. Considering the cost of landing and logistics an NPC of 1.1 to 1.15 is considered to be the threshold value for considering competitiveness. Since NPC has been higher than 1.15 for cardamom, coffee and ginger, these products lacked competitiveness. However competitiveness has improved for rubber and turmeric.

Promotional Measures Required

If the export potential created by the post WTA environment is to be effectively exploited, the Centre and State Governments will have to initiate appropriate pro-active promotional measures to enhance market access for Kerala's products.

Table 4

Indices of Parity-prices Received and Prices Paid by Farmers from 1995–2004 (Base: 1952-53 = 100)

Year	*Price received by farmers*	*Growth rate*	*Farm Cultivation Cost*	*Growth rate*	*Domestic Expenditure*	*Growth rate*	*Prices Paid by Farms*	*Growth rate*	*Parity Index on Col. 2&8*
1995	1802	–	3312	–	1641	–	2331	–	77
1996	2079	15.37	3928	18.60	1810	10.30	2666	14.37	78
1997	2486	19.58	4571	16.37	1979	9.34	3007	12.79	83
1998	2447	-1.57	4895	7.09	2107	6.47	3212	6.82	76
1999	2907	18.80	5556	13.50	2246	6.60	3532	9.96	82
2000	2492	-14.28	6173	11.11	2384	6.14	3836	8.61	66
2001	1927	-22.67	6584	6.66	2489	4.40	4048	5.53	48
2002	1999	3.74	6684	1.52	2542	2.13	4122	1.83	49
2003	2454	22.76	7056	5.57	2615	2.87	4295	4.20	57
2004	2651	8.03	7360	4.31	2705	3.44	4459	3.82	59
Annual averag egrowth rate		5.50		9.40		5.70		7.50	

Economic Review for different years.

Table 5
Estimation of Nominal Protection Coefficient (NPC) for Major Crops

Year	*Pepper*	*Cardamom*	*Rubber*	*Turmeric*	*Coffee*	*Ginger*
1996-97	1.08	2.20	1.73	3.77	1.59	2.91
1997-98	1.06	2.31	0.79	3.14	1.80	3.81
1998-99	1.05	2.45	0.63	0.76	1.50	4.78
1999-00	1.25	3.31	0.44	2.16	1.35	2.08
2000-01	1.68	3.76	0.72	1.14	1.24	2.55
2001-02	1.10	2.45	0.30	2.46	1.21	2.83
2002-03	1.07	2.38	0.37	1.66	1.92	2.91
2003-04	1.34	2.44	0.45	1.27	1.79	4.16
2004-05	1.34	2.18	0.61	0.76	1.79	2.34
2005-06	1.37	2.25	0.75	0.77	1.64	2.10

Source: estimated from export-import value given in http://dgft.delhi.nic.in/.

The following measures are to be urgently initiated for this purpose.

(1) Provide international market intelligence and information on trade opportunities.

(2) Aggressive trade promotion measures.

(3) Strategy to improve cost competitiveness of Kerala's products through appropriate support measures.

(4) Reduction of cost of production through measures to enhance productivity, reducing yield gap and better resource use.

(5) Enhancing cost competitiveness by means of cost sharing through scaling up of production through groups/cluster farming and providing common facilities.

(6) Aggressive product diversification and value addition are to be initiated.

(7) Greater co-ordination and linkage between different agencies and departments involved in different stages of agricultural development such as technology development and technology transfer, support services, value addition, marketing and exports for achieving synergy through the power of partnership.

(8) Innovative scaling up systems like contract farming (not corporate farming), cluster farming, SHGs of agricultural workers/women. These may be legalised as alternative farming systems qualifying for government support.

Safeguard measures needed

The adverse impact on Kerala's agriculture can be minimised by formulating appropriate safeguard measures

(1) Tariff rates to be pegged at appropriate levels to prevent unnecessary import of spices and other horticultural crops.

(2) Trade information and trade promotion measures have to be strengthened.

(3) Port of entry may be insisted on certain products like pepper, arecanut, rubber, ginger etc which will make import monitoring easy and more effective.

(4) Channelised imports from non-producer or third party sources to be prevented by evoking Rules of Origin (ROO)

(5) Strengthening vigilance to ensure that products imported as raw materials for the specific use of the processing and extracting industries are not released to the domestic market forcing the domestic prices to decline.

(6) Inclusion of pepper, cardamom, coconut, copra and coconut products, tea, coffee and rubber in the negetive list while signing Free Trade Agreements.

Conclusion

In the context of booming merchandise trade in the post-WTA period, a variety of promotional and regulatory policies and measures are to be formulated by the Centre and the State to equip the farming community to take advantage of the emerging trade opportunities as also to minimise the adverse impacts. The excellent trade potential for agricultural products of Kerala can be translated into physical achievements only if adequate support is provided in terms of market intelligence, policy support, excellent infrastructure and more than anything else the leadership and co-ordination at the highest level with effective participation of all stake holders. There is also urgency to identify the potential threats for formulating appropriate strategies and actions for safeguarding the genuine interests of the farming community. A holistic approach synergising the role of all departments, agencies and stakeholders involved in agricultural development and trade is the need of the hour.

Reference

Government of Kerala, *Economic Review* 02, 03, 04, 05, 06, State Planning Board.

Danilo M. Coronacion (2003), "Constraints and Opportunities on Marketing and Trading in Coconut Products in the Changing Global Scenario", in Vasu K.I. and P.K. Thampan (ed) (2003) *Coconut for Rural Prosperity Proceedings of the International Coconut Summit 2003* APCC, Jakartha, pp. 3-27.

EXIM BANK (2002), *Agri-Export Advantages,* Vol. I, Issue 4, July-Aug., p.10

EXIM BANK (2003(1)), *Agri-Export Advantages,* Vol. II, No. 6, November, p. 2.

EXIM BANK (2003(2)), *Agri-Export Advantages,* Vol. II, No. 2, March, pp. 4-5.

M. Mohandas (2007), *Impact of Free Trade Agreements and Preferential Trade Agreements on Kerala's Agriculture,* Study of Virtual University for Agriculture Trade (VUAT) for the UNCTAD.

GLOBALIZATION AND AGRARIAN DISTRESS IN KERALA

V. Mathew Kurian

Introduction

The farmers of Kerala are now in great distress. The distress has become so acute that some of the farmers have already committed suicide. The suicide rate also shows a growing trend. One could notice a close relationship between the policies pursued by the Government of India, obliging globalization and the agrarian distress of Kerala. So in this paper first we introduce the term 'globalization'. Then the transformation of Kerala's agrarian economy would be explored in the light of the process of globalization. It would be followed by a discussion on the emerging agrarian distress of Kerala in the neo-liberal globalization era. Finally, we plan to seek the redressel of the agrarian distress in Kerala.

Introducing Globalization

The term 'globalization' was coined only recently. It was first introduced into business literature by Theodore Levitt in an article published in Harvard Business Review.[1] Since then it has assumed wider currency. Now one cannot come across a 'social discourse' without the mention of globalization. However, there is no unanimously accepted definition of globalization. There are multiple views. Some consider it as the ushering in of a 'new global order'. To some others, it is imperialism under a new garb.

In this paper, we view globalization from three perspectives.[2]: (1) as a programme/project, (2) as an ideology and (3) as a process. As a programme, it is the creation of transnational corporations (TNCs). These business conglomerates want maximum freedom of operations all over the world. The following definition of 'globalization' by Percy Barnevik, president of ABB, an electronics transnational company reveals it. "I would define globalization as the freedom for my group to invest where and as long as it wishes, to produce what it wishes, by buying and selling wherever it wishes, and all the while putting up with as little labour laws and social convention constraints as possible"[3].

TNCs perceive the entire world economy as a single unit. They want the regional and national economies to be integrated with the world economy through neo-liberal programmes. 'Market' is being identified as the core vehicle for this integration. So globalization may be defined as 'marketization' on a global scale. Privatization and liberalization were prescribed to facilitate 'global marketization'.

Globalization also represents an ideology. In this sense, it bears 'neo-liberalism' which promotes a set of coherent beliefs, views and ideas legitimizing global capitalism. 'Neo-liberalism' is projected as the only one ideology that is legitimate, respectable and possible. The neo-liberal creed may be summed up in three beliefs: (1) belief in private property, (2) belief in market laws and (3) belief in free enterprise and free trade.

Globalization also may be considered as a 'process'. In this perspective, the world's economy has been subjected to a process of capitalist transformation for the last five hundred years. Global economy reached the new phase of 'globalization' through various stages of transition.

When we 'unmask'[4] globalization, the colonialism and imperialism of capitalism would be revealed to us. Appropriation and accumulation of 'economic surplus' by private capital constitute the essential ingredients of capitalism. The nature and methods of these have changed over time. When we trace the history of capitalism, broadly, we come across two phases: (a) colonialism and (b) neo-colonialism.

Under 'colonialism'[5], capitalism underwent tremendous changes. Based on these changes, the colonial history of capitalism may be distinguished into mercantile capitalism, competitive industrial capitalism and monopoly industrial capitalism.

In the post-second world war era, political colonialism was liquidated and the colonies became independent countries. These newly liberated countries were identified as the third world. Though the third world started enjoying political freedom, they failed to follow an independent economic policy. As they had to depend on western capital and technology for modernizing and developing the economy, that resulted in their subjugation to multi-national corporations and their allies like the IMF and World Bank. The emerging situation has been called 'neo-colonialism'[6]. Neo-colonialism implies economic colonialism. The idea is that even without direct metropolitan political support, MNCs could continue their economic exploitation in the newly liberated third world countries.

By the dawn of 1980s, the big MNCs became TNCs.[7] As their name indicates, in addition to extending into several countries, these mega enterprises stand beyond or above the nation state. Their financial and technological capacity defies borders and transcends state power. With increasingly numerous mergers, takeovers and alliances the concentration of wealth at the top reached such a degree that, for the first time in history, economic power succeeded in liberating itself from the national legal framework and from governmental control.

On the basis of technological transformation, neo-colonial era of capitalism is differentiated into industrial and post-industrial societies. The electronic revolution facilitated, the establishment of 'post-industrial society' and 'net work economy',[8] accelerating the pace of globalization. TNCs are now predominantly engaged in commodifying information technology and biotechnology and genetic engineering. They also earn huge profits in transacting speculative finance capital[9]. All these have become integral parts of globalization. General Agreement on Tariff and Trade (GATT), a forum to promote free trade in manufactured goods is being restructured into World Trade Organisation (WTO)[10], a full fledged institution with immense powers to monitor globalization. Third world countries like India were pressurised to join this ordeal of globalization. The political economy of Kerala played a remarkable role in all the phases of historiographic capitalist globalization. In the emerging new globalization Kerala's agriculture is facing a severe crisis and the farmers and farm workers are inflicted with severe distress.

Globalization and the Agrarian Economy of Kerala

We have already referred to the various phases of capitalist globalization. Kerala's agrarian economy responded to these external impositions. In this section we will discuss the agrarian transformation of Kerala as part and parcel of the process of globalization.

Merchant Capital of Europe and Kerala's Agrarian Economy

The first phase in the modern history of the agrarian economy of Kerala coincided with the 'mercantile capitalism' of the west, ranging the period roughly between sixteenth and eighteenth centuries. During this period, crops like pepper, ginger, cardamom and cinnamon were procured by European merchants from Kerala, of course, with the political and military patronage of the metropolis and sold it in different parts of the world and through 'triangular trade'[11] appropriated much of global surplus. The grip of merchant capital of Europe over Malabar Coast ranged the period of the Portugese, Dutch, French and a portion of British supremacy in the region.

Malabar as a source of precious spices like pepper was known all over the world even very early times. So traders from distant lands used to come to this part of India for trade in spices. The Portugese explorer Vasco da Gama arrived at

Calicut in 1498. When he along with other fellow Portugese citizens set foot on shore at Calicut, an Arab trader who understood their language, surprised at what he saw in no very courteous strain inquired, "what devil has brought you here?" They replied, our king has sent us to get pepper.[12]

The Portugese played a dual role in the agrarian economy of Kerala: one negative and the other positive. By displacing the Arabs from the Malabar Coast, they monopolized trade in spices. The Portugese extracted much of the region's agricultural 'surplus value' through 'unequal trade'[13] and direct plunder. The monopoly of spices trade in Europe netted them fabulous profits from 800 to 1000 per cent on the capital invested.[14]

On the positive side, the shifts in the world demand for spices of Kerala pressurized the Portugese to introduce some improvements in its mode of cultivation.[15] So they encouraged a much more systematic and scientific way of farming cash crops than the farmers of Malabar had hither to practiced. But it also led to a change in the economic balance between food crops and cash crops which still persists.[16]

The Portugese introduced in Kerala a number of new crops like cashew nuts, tobacco, tapioca, pineapple and papaya. They also initiated changes in the cultivation and management of coconuts. Coconut was not a major crop of Kerala prior to the arrival of the Portugese. For household and local use coconut was grown, but there was nothing like a cultivation for the purpose of trade. In 1503 the Portugese learnt the use of coir for ship making. From that time onwards coir became an important article of trade and more for coir than for copra, coconut cultivation became popular.

The trade in Malabar spices and other oriental goods enriched Portugal. Inspired by this unusual Portugese gain, other European countries also struggled to come to Malabar Coast for trade. The second European country to establish power in Malabar was Netherlands. The Dutch could finally drive out the Portugese from the coast of Malabar.

From the point of view of the agrarian history of Kerala, the Dutch should be remembered for their innovation of plantation type of agriculture in this region. They promoted a number of plantations in coconut and other crops and did much to improve the cultivation of these crops. The Dutch were the first to initiate commercialization of indigo cultivation in Malabar. But they could not remain longer in this region due to the rivalry of the British and the French. Ultimately, the British succeeded in driving out all other Europeans not only from Kerala but also from the rest of India. Finally India became a true colony of the British.

The Formation of Industrial Capitalism in Europe and the Agrarian Transformation of Kerala

As capitalism underwent structural transformation from mercantile to industrial capitalism and imperialism the composition of trade also got altered. During the mercantile phase spices and textiles were bought and sold as final commodities by the British. But as industrial capitalism emerged in Britain, Kerala was conditioned to provide raw materials for the emerging British industries and also to buy their manufactured goods. In the phase of monopoly capitalism, British industrial capital as well as finance capital penetrated into different parts of India, including Kerala.

We may discern two types of agrarian changes during the latter half of British colonialism and imperialism in Kerala. One is the introduction and commercialization of a number of new industrial crops like coffee, cocoa, cinchona, tea, oil palm and rubber. It is through the Kew garden of Great Britain that most of these new crops reached Kerala. The second type of change during the period of imperialism was due to migration of British capital into Kerala for starting a number of plantation enterprises. D.H. Buchanan correctly observes, "leadership in planting has been taken mainly by European, often with large joint stock companies registered in London.[17] In a study Uma Devi shows how the surrender of political supremacy of Travancore to British since the Treaty of 1805 (by which the Maharaja of Travancore agreed to accept the advice of British Government when offered) helped to accelerate cash crop cultivation in the state to cater to British economic interests[18].

The British fully tapped the virgin forest soil of Travancore, Cochin and Malabar by exploiting the cheap labour from these regions and Tamil Nadu.

Finally, the profitability of European owned plantations attracted indigenous capital to this line of agrarian activity. Most of the native plantation owners were formerly some how connected with the European planters. Members from the Syrian Christian community were the pioneering native planters[19].

With the popular emergence of plantation system of 'farm firms' economic dualism i.e., a 'modern' agrarian sub-sector co-existing with a 'traditional' sub-sector of agriculture, became a conspicuous feature of the agrarian economy of Kerala. A well organized, capital intensive and wage labour using plantation type of agriculture of crops like coffee, cardamom, *tea and rubber co-exited with* subsistence agriculture mainly for food like paddy, tapioca, banana, different types of plantains and vegetables.

Agrarian Economy of Kerala in the Neo-colonial Era

Post-second World War era witnessed neo-colonialism in the world. India won political freedom in 1947. But our economic dependence on multinational capital continued. The multinational corporations, which constituted the essence of neo-colonialism, found India as a very attractive place for profit maximization. The relatively cheap labour, and a potential 'internalised market' for consumer goods were factors favouring the inflow of multinational capital into India. Due to scarcity of capital and technological know-how, the Government of India welcomed Direct Private Foreign Investment for industrialization.

A large number of multinational corporations were manufacturers of agro-based commodities like tyre, chocolate, coffee, tea and many others. Kerala being more suited for the production of raw materials like rubber, companies requiring them were quite keen in raising these crops in the state.

As the Government of India followed a policy of import substitution and export promotion, it also took keen interest in raising and developing such crops like pepper, rubber, tea, *cashew, coconut,* cocoa, tea and vanilla in Kerala. The Government and multinational firms like Cadbury jointly worked in the introduction and promotion of crops like cocoa in Kerala.

New Globalization and the Agrarian Distress in Kerala

The Government of India started initiating a number of neo-liberal economic policies since the early 1980s. These policies were sharpened in the 1990s by the introduction of the so-called New Economic Policy. These policies had terrific consequences on the agrarian economy of Kerala.

Liberalization of foreign trade resulted in the sharp decline of commodity prices. Only rubber commands a relatively profitable price. As a result, agricultural income of many farmers has declined. But the cost of production of these crops only increased, mainly by the withdrawal of Government by the subsidies in inputs like chemical fertilizers. The cost on agricultural credit also went up by the change in monetary policy. The small farmers largely borrowed from the moneylenders and cooperative banks for meeting their agricultural and domestic requirements. The fall in agricultural incomes coupled with the rise in cost of cultivation and cost of living have made a large number of farmers heavily indebted. (See table in the Appendix). In order to overcome this crisis, farmers in Kerala are now committing suicide. In suicide rate Wayanad stands top in the state. More than 1500 farmers of Kerala have already ended their life in the last five years. During the previous six months 80 farmers committed suicide in Kerala.

Some Steps Taken to Solve the Agrarian Distress of Kerala

There were governmental as well as non-governmental initiatives in redressing the agrarian distress of the state. The people's campaign for the Ninth Five Year Plan accorded top most priority to agriculture and rural development. Some achievements could be attained in the promotion of vegetable cultivation, installation of agrarian infrastructure etc. Though the so-called Kerala Development Plan maintained the local institutions for planning, it failed to sustain the former spirit of people in the planning process and agrarian development.

The new government already initiated some programmes for the relief of farmers. The waiving of loans of the families of farmers who committed suicide and the slashing of the interest rate an agricultural loans are examples. The newly enacted Debt Relief Bill by the Kerala Assembly is a progressive step.

The Non-governmental organizations like the Indian Farmer's Association (INFAM) are also extending some services for the redressel of the agrarian distress of Kerala.

The Government of Kerala appointed a committee under the chairmanship of Dr. M.S Swaminathan to study the WTO issues on Kerala's agriculture.[21] In its Report the Commission gave a number of useful suggestions to solve the agrarian crisis of the state.

Some Suggestions for the Development of Kerala's Agriculture

The following are some of the suggestions to overcome the negative consequences of globalization in Kerala's agriculture:

A Two-Pronged strategy for Farm Households

Increased specialization in a few cash crops in Kerala has led to severe displacement of food crops and excessive food dependence on other states. One could notice the highest suicide rates in cash crop intensive areas. This can be minimised if farm households resort to relative food self sufficiency by allocating the productive resources of the family including labour prudentially. So there could be a balanced growth approach between food production and cash crop production.

Organic Farming for Sustainable Agricultural Development

Though the land input is relatively scarce, Kerala is blessed with other natural resources like water and sunshine for the sustainable development of agriculture. By popularizing such measures like watershed management,[22] and organic manuring, Kerala's agriculture can be promoted considerably. Under decentralized planning, local governments can organize such programmes.

Promotion of Countervailing Market Forces

The economic status of the farmers of Kerala is now largely governed by the trends of world market forces. The farmers have no power in price fixing. If farmers are properly organized through communitarian institutions like the cooperatives and the production of crops is coordinated with processing and marketing, there would be countervailing market power which would definitely empower the farmers.

Protection of Bio-diversity through the Appropriation of TRIPs

In bio-resources and the knowledge on its use value, Kerala is relatively rich. Now transnational agribusinesses like Cargil and Monsanto are taking keen interest in the state's agriculture and natural resources for patenting it. Now it is too late for the state to appropriate such opportunities for the benefits of the farmers. The patenting of 'Arogya Pacha' in favour of the Kani tribe of Kerala is a positive step in this direction.

Restoration of Subsidies

While the 'farm-firms[23]' of the first world are protected by various types of subsidies, why should Indian/Kerala farmers are denied of it. In a state like Kerala whose agriculture is exposed to the vagaries of the world market forces, require rational subsidization assistance and other government supports for stable development.

Conclusion

In this paper we put forwarded the thesis that Kerala's agriculture followed a pattern of dependent development according to the requirements of global capitalism. Under the new globalized capitalist regime the state's agriculture is facing a severe distress. However the state's agriculture has the potential to redress this crisis. By building up farmer friendly institutions, appropriate technological advancement and active patronage of the government at the state and central levels, the agrarian economy of Kerala can be developed substantially.

Notes and References

1. Theodore Levitt, "The Globalization of Markets", *Harvard Business Review*, (May-June 1, 1983) pp. 92-103. A similar expression to globalization, namely, 'global village' was first popularized by Marshall Mc Luhan, a Canadian philosopher in 1968 in his book, *War and Peace in the Global Village'*.
2. Bob Goutz-Waar and Julice de Santa (2002), "Globalization and Modernity" in Ninan Koshy, ed., *Globalization: Imperial Thrust of Modernity*, Mumbai: Vikas Adyayan Kendra.
3. Quoted in Jaceques B Gelinas (2003), *Juggernaut Politics-Understanding of Predatory Globalization*, London and New York: Zed Books, p. 3.
4. James Petras and Henry Veltmeyer (2001), *Globalization Unmasked-Imperialism in the 21st century*, Delhi: Madyam Books.
5. For a brief account of colonialism see V. Mathew Kurian, "Political Economy of Colonialism", *Mainstream*, Vol. XXXVI, No. 11, March 7, 1998, pp. 11-12.
6. Kwame N. Krumah (1965), Neo-colonialism: The Last State of Imperialism, London: Nelson.
7. See Samir Amin (1997), *Capitalism in the Age of Globalization*, Delhi: Madyam Books.
8. Darin Barney (2004), The Network Society, Malden: Polity.
9. Under Globalization, financial systems have been growing faster than their underlying economics. India is no exception to this trend. According to a recent study by the Mc Kinsey Global Institute the present financial stock of the world is $118 trillion and is likely to exceed $200 trillion by 2010. Indian contribution to it is only $900 billion which is1.37 times its nominal GDP. See Niranjan Rajdhyaksha, "the Age of Finance," *Business World*, 21st March, 2005, pp. 50-51.
10. See V. Mathew Kurian (2006), "New GATT and Third World: An Overview", *Mainstream*, Vol. XXXII, Nos 51 (November 5, 194) pp. 31-23 and "WTO Agreements and Agriculture: A Third World Perspective", *Mainstream* vol. XLV No. 1, December 23, pp. 91-95.

11. In 'triangular trade', the country which buys the products of another sells a portion of it to a third one and uses a part of the proceeds to buy their products, which is being sold to another country. In this process, the total 'surplus' appropriated would be much larger.
12. Quoted in K. P. Padmanabha Menon (1937), *History of Kerala*, Ernakulam: Cochin Government Press.
13. See Arighiri Emmanuel (1972), *Unequal Exchange–A study of Imperialism of Trade*, London: NLB.
14. A.I. Chicherov (1971), *India-Economic Development in the 16th – 18th centuries-outline History of Crafts and Trade*, Moscow: NAUKA Publishing House.
15. K. M. Panikker (1929), *Malabar and the Portugese*, Bombay: Taraporevala and Company, p. 1.
16. George Wood Cock (1967), *Kerala-A Portrait of the Malabar Coast*, London: Faber, p. 156.
17. D. H. Buchman (1934), *The Development of Capitalist Enterprise in India*, New York: Macmillan, p. 58.
18. Uma Devi (1989), *Plantation Economy of the Third World*, Bombay: Himalaya Publishing House.
19. Paul Erik Back (1997), *Plantation Production and Plantation Power*, Delhi: OUP, pp. 138-207.
20. See S. Mohankumar and P.K. Sharma (2006), "Analysis of Farmer Suicides in Kerala", *Economic and Political Weekly*, April 22.

    Jose George and P. Krishna Prasad, "Agrarian Distress and farmers' suicides in the Tribal District of Wayanad", *Social Scientist*.
21. *WTO and the Agrarian Problems of Kerala*, Thiruvananthapuram: Farm Information Bureau of Kerala, 2004.
22. For a detailed account on Water Harvesting *Refer Human Development Report*, 2006 of UNDP.
23. See Samir Amin, *The Liberal Virus*, Delhi: AAAKAR Books, 2005, p. 32.

Appendix-I

Annual Loss sustained by the State of Kerala due to the Price Fall of Major Plantation Crops during 2000-2001

Crop	*Production since 1995*	*Highest monthly Jan-01 (Rs/qt)*	*Price during (Rs.) (Rs/qt)*	*Differences*	*Loss (Rs in Crores)*
Coconut (in No.)	600 crores	693 (Rs/100 nuts)	200 (Rs/100 No)	493	2958
Rubber	572820	52 (Rs/kg)	27 (Rs/kg)	25	1432
Pepper	64,335	22,367 (Rs/qtl)	11,570	10,797	695
Arecanut	92,481	12,542 (Rs/qtl)	2551	9991	924
Coffee	61,150	9720 (Rs/qtl)	3370	6350	388
Tea	68,373	7747 (Rs/qtl)	5147	2600	178
Cardamom	5295	59,300 (Rs/qtl)	46,000	13,300	70

Note: The difference in market price shown above is based on the highest monthly price of the last five years and the price during January 2001.

Source: State Agricultural Prices Board, Government of Kerala

Appendix-II

Income, Expenditure and Indebtedness of Farmer Households–July 2002-June 2003

States (1)	Annual Cultivation Income (2)	Annual Total Income (3)	Annual Cultivation Expenditure (4)	Annual Consumption Expenditure (5)	(2)-(4) (6)	(3)-(5) (7)	Incidence of indebtedness (per cent) (8)	Extent of indebtedness (9)
AP	8916	19,608	12,085	28,632	-3169	-9024	82.0	23,965
Assam	21,504	37,932	3,370	32568	18,134	5364	18.1	813
Bihar	10,152	21,720	6809	29,508	3343	-7788	33.0	4476
Gujarat	13,968	32,208	11,456	37,524	2512	-5316	51.9	15526
Haryana	17,928	34,584	18,270	52,968	-342	-18384	53.1	26007
J & K	29112	65856	6342	49308	22770	16548	31.8	1903
Karnataka	15192	31392	10344	31296	4848	96	61.6	18135
Kerala	13440	48048	7793	51000	5647	-2952	64.4	33907
MP	11952	17160	8886	28068	3066	-10908	50.8	14218
Maharashtra	15156	29556	10793	32268	4363	-2712	54.8	16973
Orissa	4032	12744	3143	20364	889	-7620	47.8	5871
Punjab	33864	59520	25945	58080	7919	1440	65.4	41576
Rajastan	4308	17976	7668	39456	-3360	-21480	52.4	18,372
Tamil Nadu	7908	24864	8597	30072	-689	-5208	74.5	23963
Uttar Pradesh	10032	19596	9151	34788	881	-15192	40.3	7425
West Bengal	8844	24948	8429	32016	415	-7068	50.1	5237
All-India	11628	25380	8791	33240	2837	-7860	48.60	12585

Sources: NSSO (2005 and 2006 b) .

CROPPING PATTERN IN KERALA–SPATIAL INTER TEMPORAL ANALYSIS

K. P. Mani

Introduction

In India, just after green revolution gross area under cultivation remained at 1578 lakh hectares, of which the contributions of food crops and non food crops respectively being 78.78 per cent and 21.22 per cent. All the states except Kerala and Gujarath had reasonable area under food crops. But compared to these trends, the area under food crops substantially declined since 1985. In 1992-93, gross cropped area remained at 1854 lakh hectares, the shares of food crops and non food crops respectively being 67.24 per cent and 25.27 per cent. Though, the fall in the share of area under food crops is marginal compared to the shares in 1970-71, many states recorded significant reduction in area under food crops. The states among this category are, Andhra Pradesh, Gujarath, Haryana, Karnataka, Kerala, Orissa, Rajasthan and Tamil Nadu.

Agriculture Growth: Macro Perspectives

Conventional economics believed that the agriculture sector is the back bone of the Indian economy. To a great extent, this argument is valid also because even after significant structural changes in the Indian economy as a consequence of reforms, the sector contributes nearly 20 per cent of Gross Domestic Product, provides employment for 59 per cent of the population and liberally contributes towards foreign exchange earnings (2005). These reforms process and the resultant changes brought some rapid tilts in the behaviour and performance of the agricultural sector. One important consequence is the notable shifts in cropping pattern skewed in favour of cash crops. These trends are the result of two factors. Firstly, the shift in cropping pattern is a trend started by late 1980 at the national level and various reasons can be attributed for this. Secondly, reforms process compelled this shift because of the new strategy of export led growth. The cropping pattern in favour of cash crops necessitated substantial changes in the composition of inputs and also its distribution. In this context it is appropriate to examine the growth trends since reforms and examine its pattern and distribution.

The mid sixties which were marked by the beginning of the green revolution was something like a watershed in the growth of the Indian agriculture. During the pre revolution period, production of all crops recorded an impressive average growth rate of 3.13 per cent per annum. During the subsequent period, the growth rate remained subdued at 2.10 per cent. The rate of expansion of agricultural production was remarkably higher during the eighties. The production indices of food grains showed a steep rising trend through out the decade except for a downward movement during 1986-87 and 1987-88. More spectacular was the rising trend in the output of non food grains particularly during the second half of the decade. The production of all crops recorded a growth rate of 2.77 per cent during the first half of the eighties, and it accelerated to 3.92 per cent during the second half of the decade, compared with 2.10 per cent during 1964-65. During the nineties, however the growth rate of agricultural production slowed down considerably to 2.64 per cent and the growth rate of food grains decelerated to 1.63 per cent. Not only that the growth rate decelerated, the absolute production levels of food grains remained far below the plan targets also. Food grains output failed to keep pace with the population growth and consequently, the per capita availability of food grains which had reached a level of 510 grams per day in 1991 declined to an average level of 482 gram per day during the subsequent years and reached 464 gram per day in 2002. These broad trends in the growth rates of agricultural production are directly or indirectly linked to a series of related issues like input supply, markets, price policy, trade policy etc.

Kerala State: A Prelude

When India became free, three administrations ruled this region–two princely states, Travancore and Cochin, and Malabar which was under the direct administration of the British. One of the first steps taken by independent India was to amalgamate small states together so as to make them viable administrative units. Accordingly, Travancore and Cochin states were integrated to form the Travancore Cochin state on 1st July, 1949. However, Malabar remained as part of the Madras province. Under the state Reorganization Act of 1956, Travancore Cochin states and Malabar were united to form the state of Kerala on 1st November, 1956. The state represents only 1.18 per cent of the total area of India but 3.43 per cent of the total population of the country is in Kerala.

From Table 1 it is evident that the state income has made gradual growth over the years. The state income in current prices made 49.84 times increase over 1950 and 1999. During the same period, per capita income at current prices made only an increase of 32.76 times. Further between 1990-91 and 2003-04, state per capita income at current prices increased by 5.86 and 5.23 times respectively. These trends indicate that disproportionate population size compared to the share of the state in the total country area are the root causes of her many problems like low per capita income and huge unemployment. The severity of the problem of low per capita income will be crystal clear when we realize that the state is ranked 15th (2003) in terms of per capita income among the 28 states in India.

Table 1
Income Profile of Kerala State

Year	*State (current price) (Rs. crore)*	*State income (1980-81 prices) (Rs. crore)*	*Per capita income (current prices)*	*Per capita income (1980-81 price)*
1970-71	1255	1255	594	594
1980-81	3823	3823	1508	1508
1990-91	10668	4892	3718	1705
1994-95	28375	25335	9327	8327
1999-00	62557	27319-	1946	8617
2004-05*	89451	44054	27048	13321

Source: Govt. of Kerala Economic Review. *Refers to quick estimates and the base is 1993-94.

The Kerala state, despite its low per capita income, displays a set of unusually high development indicators such as adult literacy, life expectancy, infant mortality and birth rate. The Kerala model, especially the performance of its quality of life indicators has attracted wide spread attention. The state enjoys a high percentage of literacy equal to that in the USA. According to the 2001 census, male and female literacy are 94.20 per cent and 87.86 per cent respectively, compared to the All India figures of 75.85 per cent and 54.16 per cent. Life expectancy also stood above the All India level. Male life expectancy rate increased from 68 years in 1991 to 73.67 years in 2001, while female life expectancy improved from 52 years in 1961 to 75 in 2001. The improvement in health care is further reflected in the favourable infant mortality rate and birth rate. Infant mortality rate improved from 120 in 1961 to 22 in 1991 and 11 in 2001. (See Table 2).

Various hypotheses have been formulated for the conflicts in Kerala's development experience which can be sum up in the dual issues of relatively low per capita income and high performance in human development indicators. One hypothesis, which is traditional, is the backwardness in agriculture and industry sectors.

Table 2
Trends in Development Indicators of Kerala state

	India 1961	*Kerala 1961*	*India 1971*	*Kerala 1971*	*India 1981*	*Kerala 1981*	*India 1991*	*Kerala 1991*	*India 2001*	*Kerala 2001*
Literacy										
males	34	54	40	54	47	75	63	94	75.85	94.20
females	13	38	19	66	25	65	39	86	54.16	87.86
Birth rate (1000)	42	39	41	37	37	26	31	17	24.80	16.70
Infant mortality (1000)	165	120	129	61	114	39	58	22	60	11
Life expectancy (years)	42	46	46	61	57	65	59	68	65.10	73.67
Males	41	50	45	62	50	63		68	64.10	71.67
Females	44	52	49	64	51	67		71	65.80	75.00

Source: Government of Kerala Economic Review.

Significance of the Study

The reduction in area under food crops in Kerala from 40.43 per cent in 1970-71 to 18.74 per cent in 1992-93 and 16.52 in 2002-03, is a phenomenon happened very rarely in any country. The gravity of the problem is more severe when the state is 50 per cent short of food grains. The area index of food grains has lost considerably and continuously from 102.55 in 1976-79 to 58.38 in 1999-02, whereas the gain in the productivity was not adequate enough to make good this short fall. On the other hand, the index of area under non food crops increased from 100.52 in 1976-79 to 159 in 1999-02. It is also worthwhile noting that among the non food categories, the growth of area expansion index is tremendous in the case of coconut and rubber. Hence in this paper an attempt is made to examine the spatial and inter temporal shifts in cropping pattern in Kerala and the determinants causing this shift.

Methodology

The study is based on secondary data collected for the period 1975-76 to 2002-03. To reveal inter temporal shifts, the entire period was disaggregated to decennial data and compound growth rates were calculated with the support of exponential functions and kinked exponentials.

$Y = \infty \rho^{t}$, Log Y = log ∞ + t logρ, CGR = anti log (1-ρ) x 100, where Y = relevant variable

The motive factors were analysed theoretically using supply response models, because in agriculture, crop shift decisions and resultantly supply decisions are taken months before the actual products reach the market and prices are realised. The production decisions are therefore taken on the basis of expected prices. Accordingly,

Different models have been developed, the major being,

Cobweb Model

The commonly used proxy for expected price is the previous year's actual price,

$P_t = P_{t-1}$

Adaptive Expectations

This formulation too supposes that price expectation is based on past price or prices, but the agents are allowed to learn from mistakes so that expected price is given by,

$P_t = P_{t-1} + (P_t - P_{t-1})$

Nerlovian adjustment log model

Model I

$$A_t = b_0 + b_1 RP_{t-1} + b_2 RY_{t-1} + b_3 CV_{RP} + b_4 CV_{RY} + b_5 A_{t-1} + V_t$$

$$A_t = b_0 + b_1 RPR_{t-1} + b_2 CV_{RPR} + b_3 I_t + b_4 SSR_t + b_5 A_{t-1} + v_t$$

Where, At = the actual area planted and hectares under the crop concerned

RP_{t-1} = relative price in terms of competing crop

RY_{t-1} = relative yield in terms of competing crop

CV_{RP} CV_{RY} coefficient of variation of the preceding three years relative price and yield

RPR_{t-1} = relative gross profitability in terms of competing crop

CV_{RPR} = a measure of relative profitability risk

I_t = gross irrigated area under all crops

SSR_t = rainfall of sowing season for the concerned crop

ARIMA Process

The ARIMA process expectation also assumes that past price determines price expectations but past disturbances are taken into account as well. Here,

$$P_t = P_t - e_t = \Pi P_{t-1} + \Pi P_{t-2} + \Pi P_{t-3} + \ldots\ldots\ldots\ldots + \Pi P_{t-q} + \partial_{t-1} + \partial_{t-2} +$$

The Model and Estimation

The above mentioned models cannot be as such applied for the Kerala agriculture because of the weak data base. Hence, the following models were developed and estimated considering problems of data deficiency and quality

Area response model,

$$A_t = A_0 + a_1P_{t-1} + a_2R_t + a_3W_t + V_t \quad (1)$$

$$(A_t - A_{t-1}) = \partial\,(A_t - A_{t-1}) \quad (2)$$

Yield response model,

$$Y_t = a_0 + a_1\,P_{t-1} + a_2R_t + a_3\,W_t + V_t \quad (3)$$

$$(Y_t - Y_{t-1}) = \partial\,(Y_t - Y_{t-1}) \quad (4)$$

Where,

A_t = desired area in hectares under the crop in the year t

A_{t-1} = actual area in hectares under the crop in the year t

P_t = farm harvested price in the period t

R_t = price risk as measured by the standard deviation of price in the past 3

Years from the period t

W_t = pre sowing months average rainfall in the period t

W = average rainfall in the year t

Y_t = actual yield of crop in kgs in the year t

∂ = coefficient of adjustment

Trends in Land Utilization in Kerala

Any discussion on agricultural sector starts with examining the land utilization pattern and the profile of land holdings which are available from Tables 3. From Table 3 it is seen that since 1990, the gross cropped area made a notable decline from 302000 hectors to 2271000 hectors the rate of fall being 24.80 per cent. This is mainly due to the diversion of the farmers from agricultural operations to non agricultural operations mainly arguing that the agricultural operations are becoming uneconomic because of escalating input prices and increasing labour cost. Another notable feature is the significant shift in cropping pattern skewed towards cash crops.

Table 3
Trends in Land Utilization Kerala ('00 hector)

	1975-1976	*1980-1981*	*1985-1986*	*1990-1991*	*1995-1996*	*1997-1998*	*2004-2005*
Total geographical area	38855	38855	38855	38855	38855	38855	38855
Forest	10815	10815	10815	10815	10815	10815	10815
Net sown area	21892	21796	21910	22468	22690	22860	21727
Total cropped area	29813	28848	28666	30200	30660	22710	29424

Source: Economic Review Government of Kerala.

Discussion

Both geographically and climatically Kerala forms a distinct region, whose topography is dominated by the Western Ghats. Kerala is one of the states in India, where its land resources are put to more intensive use than any where else mainly because of the low per capita availability of land in the state. According to the current statistics (2005) out of the total geographical area of 3885 thousand hectare, one fourth was under forests and about 1.26 per cent was barren and uncultivable land. Another 8.28 per cent was put to non agricultural use. Kerala had a net sown area of 2239 thousand hectares in 2001-02 forming 57.63 per centof the total area. The area sown more than once was just 808 thousand hectares compared to 3123 hectors in 1952-53, the intensity of cropping being 1.36.

Out of the gross cropped area of 2349 thousand hectares in 1960-61, rice occupied 778.91 hectare, forming 33.15 per cent of the gross cropped area. But the share of gross cropped area under rice consistently came down to 28 per cent in 1980-81 and 15.45 per cent in 2002-03. In absolute terms, the area under rice declined from 778.91 thousand hectares in 1960-61 to 678.28 thousand hectares in 1980-81, the average annual fall being 0.68 per cent. Further between 1980-81 and 1999-00, the area under rice declined by 30.53 per cent, absolute fall during the 15 years period being 207.13 thousand hectares. The fall in cumulative area in 1995-96, compared to 1960-61 being 307.76 thousand hectors. The area divided for all food crops together was about 46 per cent in 1960-61 but it came down to just 16.52 per cent in 2002-03. The major reason is the domination of cash crops like coconut and rubber. In the year 1960-61, coconut constituted 21.31 per cent and rubber constituted 5.23 per cent of the gross cropped area. These shares marginally improved to 22.77 per cent and 8.24 per cent respectively by 1980-81. But since 1980-81, there is a tremendous leap. The area under coconut reached 982.10 in 1995-96, almost double the area in 1960-91. Similarly, area under rubber reached 449 thousand hectares in 1995-96, an increase of 3.68 times compared to 1960-61. While the area under rice declined by 336.55 thousand hectares between 1980-81 and 1999-00, area under coconut and rubber increased by 330.73 thousand and 211.23 thousand during the same period. These three crops constituted 60 per cent of the gross cropped area in 1960-61 and 62 per cent in 1999-00 and the trends clearly establish the claim that Kerala farmers are shifting the area under rice to coconut and rubber while the state is 50 per cent short of rice production compared to consumption requirements and when the state lacks linkages to absorb coconut and rubber. (see Table 4).

In the succeeding section an attempt is made to examine the inter district, intra district and inter temporal shifts in cropping pattern with reference to rice, coconut and rubber on production and yield.

Table 4
Gross Cropped Area Under Major Crops in Kerala (1960-61 to 1999-2005), (000ha)

Crops	*1960-1961*	*1970-1971*	*1980-1981*	*1990-1991*	*1999-2000*	*2004-2005*
Rice	778.91	874.93	678.28	559.45	348.20	289.97
	(61.20)	(57.67)	(55.38)	(52.40)	(50.34)	(49.62)
Coconut	500.76	719.14	651.37	870.02	1080.0	897.76
	(56.64)	(56.96)	(47.61)	(45.02)	(62.83)	(54.61)
Rubber	122.87	179.26	237.77	384.00	469.9	480.54
	(13.90)	(14.18)	(17.36)	(19.95)	(28.72)	(29.46)
Coffee	16.80	31.56	57.95	75.05	83.7	84.64
Tea	37.63	37.59	36.16	34.71	36.8	NA
Other Plantations	205.91	295.90	385.88	560.35	NA	NA

Figures in brackets corresponding to rice indicates the share of the area of rice in the total area under food crops and for other crops the figures in brackets indicate the percentage share to area under non food crops.

Source: Compiled from: Government of Kerala (1975), Agricultural Statistics in Kerala, The Bureau of Economics and statistics, Thiruvananthapuram. Government of Kerala, Economic Review (for various years) State Planning Board, Thiruvananthapuram. CMIE (1999) India's Agricultural Sector–A Compendium of Statistics Bombay, July.

Cropping Pattern: Inter District Analysis

Inter district analysis presented in Tables 7 and 9 clearly show that area under rice declined in all the districts between 1975-76 and 2002-03. Maximum fall occurred in Trichur district (64.28 thousand hectares), followed by Kozhikode, Malappuram and Palakkad districts. There is fall in Kannur and Alappuzha districts also, but it is due to the division of these districts respectively to Kasaragod and Pathanamthitta. All the districts together made a decline of 382.27 hectors during the time span. Decade wise, the fall is 242.97 thousand hectares between 1975-76-1985-86 and 139.30 between 1985-86 -1999-00. Hence, we may infer that the relative contribution of rice to the total cropped area consistently declined in all the districts in the state, the steep fall being in northern parts.

Table 5
Production of Major Crops in Kerala (1960-61 to 2004-05)

Crops	*1960-61*	*1970-1971*	*1980-1981*	*1990-1991*	1999-2000	2004-2005
Rice (000tons)	1067	1298	1271	2803	703	667
Coconut (mill nuts)	3220	3981	3008	4232	5479	5727
Rubber (000Tons)	23.	73.	140	307	580	690
Coffee (000tons)	7	12	23	35	66	54
Tea (000tons)	40	41	50	60	66	57

Source: *Compiled from:* Government of Kerala (1975), Agricultural Statistics in Kerala, The Bureau of Economics and statistics, Thiruvananthapuram. Government of Kerala, Economic Review (for various years) State Planning Board, Thiruvananthapuram. CMIE (1999) India's Agricultural Sector–A Compendium of Statistics Bombay, July.

Table 6
Productivity of Major Corps in Kerala 160-6- to 2004-05 (kg per hect)

Crops	*1960-1961*	*1970-1971*	*1980-1981*	*1990-1991*	*1999-2000*	*2004-2005*
Rice	1371	1484	1587	1943	2182	2301
Coconut (nuts)	6430	5536	4618	4864	6049	6379
Rubber	187	439	590	800	1222	1437
Coffee	442	398	406	475	786	642
Tea	1073	1103	1402	1827	1791	1502

Source: *Compiled from*: Government of Kerala (1975), Agricultural Statistics in Kerala, The Bureau of Economics and statistics, Thiruvananthapuram. Government of Kerala, Economic Review (for various years) State Planning Board, Thiruvananthapuram. CMIE (1999) India's Agricultural Sector–A Compendium of Statistics Bombay, July.

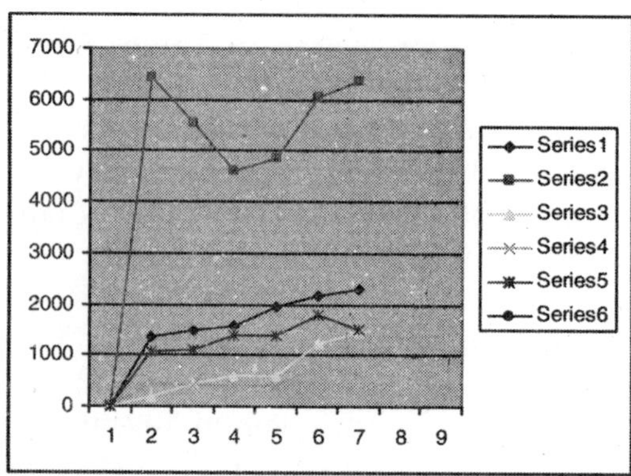

Series 1 Rice, 2 Coconut, 3 Rubber, 4 Coffee, 5 Tea, 6 others

CHART 1: Productivity Trends of Major Crops (1960-61 to 2004-05)

Naturally, this fall should be reflected in an increase of the area of other crops particularly coconut and rubber felt "Apriori". In the case of area under coconut, maximum increase is recorded in northern districts, particularly Malappuram (32.78 thousand hect) and Kozhikode (22.16 thousand hect) between 1975-76 and 2002-03. During the same period Trichur district and Palakkad district respectively recorded an increase of 23.89 thousand hectares and 26.70 thousand hectares. It is important to note that Kollam and Kottayam districts record a fall in the area under coconut. During the period 1975-76 to 199-00 the net increase in the area under coconut in the state is 102.06 thousand hectares, decade wise split being -50.37 thousand hectares and 152.43 thousand hectares. Compared to the fall in the area under rice between 1985-86 and 1999-00 (139.30 thousand hect) it is seen that the spread in area under coconut is higher than the spread in the case of staple food rice. Hence we may infer that, in the recent years, there is definitely a trend in favour of coconut plantations in Northern Kerala.

Kerala state contributed nearly 90 per cent of rubber production in the country. Inter district data reveal that since 1975-76, rubber plantations were extended to all the districts. It is also seen that over the last 25 years, area under rubber cumulatively increased by 169.13 thousand hectares.

In the succeeding paragraphs an attempt is made to examine the variations in production and yield with respect to rice, coconut and rubber at the inter district level during the period 1975-76 to 2002-03 (see also Tables 5 and 6). Rice production improved from 1067.53 thousand tonnes in 1960-61 to 1364.87 thousand tonnes in 1975-76. Since then it started to decline and the current production (2003) is 1187.2 thousand tonnes. The productivity being 1558kg/hect in 1975-76 and 2012kg/hect in 2002-03. The districts which recorded maximum in production are, Palakkad and Thrissur districts of which Palakkad district served as the "rice bowl" of Kerala immediately after the formation of the state in 1956.

The production of coconut increased from 3439 million nuts in 1975-76 to 5303 million nuts in 1999-00, respective yield being 4962 and 5890. Among the districts, net additions

Table 7

Quinquennial and Decennial Changes in the Area, Production and Yield of Rice in Kerala (1975-76 to 2002-03)

Districts	*(A) 75/76 85/86*	*(A) 85/86 90/91*	*(A) 90/91 95/96 -*	*(A) 95/96 02/03*	*(P) 75/76 85/86*	*(P) 85/86 90/91*	*(P) 90/91 95/96*	*(P) 95/96 02/03*	*(Y) 75/76 85/86*	*(Y) 85/86 90/91*	*(Y) 90/91- 95/96*	*(Y) 95/96 02/03*
TVM	-11.1	-4.67	-4.33	-4.22	-11.9	-8.7	-8.1	-7.2	244	-18	-27	-23
KLM	-18.2	-4.28	-5.23	-4.65	-20.8	-2.45	-11.5	-10.4	208	165	-61	-48
ALP	-40.2	-4.63	-5.81	-4.87	-28.9	-19.6	-32.4	-31.5	536	172	361	369
KOT	-12.2	-5.59	-1.25	-0.98	-17.9	-4.61	-6.61	-2.36	100	-567	-165	-89
IDU	-7.6	3.17	-0.38	-0.12	-9.3	-5.8	-0.85	-0.41	395	118	-10	-05
EKM	-14.2	-21.7	-3.06	-4.01	10.22	-40.1	-1.64	-0.24	345	-55	56	28
THR	-31.2	-21.1	-11.8	-10.5	-10.2	-22.6	-15.2	-11.4	313	150	89	74
PGT	-13.4	-15.1	-5.6	-2.8	-42.6	17.9	-11.1	-8.65	-98	322	10	8
MAP	-23.4	-13.5	-9.8	-4.5	-32.1	-12.2	-10	-8	15	134	128	121
KOZ	-37.3	-6.6	-8.6	-5.3	-43.2	8.1	-4.2	-2.1	14	36	17	21
KNR	-33.9	-31.0	-22.8	-20.1	33.5	-46.2	-6.5	-5.4	231	98	-143	-141

Area in 000 hectres production in 000 metric tonnes

TVM Thiruvanathapuram KLM Kollam ALP Alapuzha KOT Kottayam IDU Idukki EKM Ernakulam THR Thrissur PGT Palakkad MAP Malappuram KOZ Kozhikode KNR Kannur 3 districts are not covered in this study.

Source: (1) Government of Kerala (1975) Agricultural Statistics in Kerala, The Bureau of Economics and Statistics, Thiruvanathapuram.

(2) Government of Kerala, Economic Review (various years), State Planning Board, Thiruvanathapuram.

Table 8

Quinquennial and Decennial Changes in the Area, Production and Yield of Coconut in Kerala 1975-76 to 2002-03

Districts	*(A) 75/76 85/86*	*(A) 85/86 90/91*	*(A) 90/91 95/96 -*	*(A) 95/96 02/03*	*(P) 75/76 85/86*	*(P) 85/86 90/91*	*(P) 90/91 95/96*	*(P) 95/96 02/03*	*(Y) 75/76 85/86*	*(Y) 85/86 90/91*	*(Y) 90/91- 95/96*	*(Y) 95/96 02/03*
TVM	0.98	12.5	2.39	2.47	-.074	.099	.134	.135	-1.56	1.80	.65	.64
KLM	-29.3	9.10	1.21	1.34	-.141	.020	.033	0.187	1.32	.890	.674	.587
ALP	-24.1	17.9	-2.1	-1.8	.110	-	-	-	1.13	.272	-.077	-0.74
KOT	-0.91	-1.81	-5.68	-3.21	.100	.007	-	-	-1.72	1.24	.43	.41
IDU	6.11	2.72	1.51	1.24	-0.01	0.02	0.015	0.014	-2.85	1.56	0.798	0.478
EKM	8.90	6.63	-2.36	-1.54	.058	.019	.067	.047	-.515	1.26	.400	.487
THR	9.66	20.4	6.26	5.47	.048	.018	.122	.154	.173	.589	.087	.047
PGT	9.35	11.80	5.55	5.21	.024	.050	.051	.024	-.701	.600	.966	.687
MAP	-5.03	37.1	.812	.784	.047	.192	.147	-.147	-.213	.732	.888	.784
KOZ	14.0	10.5	-2.4	-2.57	-.067	.188	.170	.174	-.812	1.07	1.17	1.54
KNR	31.8	31.5	6.85	5.68	-.001	.040	.034	.035	-0.03	.044	.024	.014

Area in 000 hectares Production in 000 metric tonnes.

Source: (1) Government of Kerala (1975) Agricultural Statistics in Kerala, The Bureau of Economics and Statistics, Thiruvanathapuram.

(2) Government of Kerala, Economic Review (various years), State Planning Board, Thiruvanathapuram.

Table 9

Quinquennial and Decennial Changes in the Area, Production and Yield of Rubber in Kerala 1975-76 to 2002-03

Districts	*(A) 75/76 85/86*	*(A) 85/86 90/91*	*(A) 90/91 95/96-*	*(A) 95/96 02/03*	*(P) 75/76 85/86*	*(P) 85/86 90/91*	*(P) 90/91 95/96*	*(P) 95/96 02/03*	*(Y) 75/76 85/86*	*(Y) 85/86 90/91*	*(Y) 90/91- 95/96*	*(Y) 95/96 02/03*
TVM	100	4.01	3.51	3.57	3.53	7.03	9.92	8.54	-.180	.231	.290	.357
KLM	-6.4	4.54	2.33	2.98	-4.37	7.14	9.82	8.35	-.	.017	-.027	-.214
ALP	-.678	.114	.193	.198	.313	-.582	.833	.874	.226	-.202	.200	.201
KOT	28.37	79.37	-55.45	-10.2	16.11	32.71	30.37	28.65	-	.205	.243	.547
IDU	15.19	4.46	1.49	1.24	.054	11.02	9.90	8.97	-.139	.292	-.196	.214
EKM	17.71	12.38	3.64	3.57	7.12	18.16	20.62	18.74	-.082	.234	.327	.354
THR	1.27	.877	1.22	1.34	-11.1	3.02	4.68	2.47	-.203	.223	.293	2.96
PGT	7.73	4.38	4.62	5.47	3.33	5.38	7.88	6.54	-	.167	.201	.187
MAP	4.03	1.21	3.42	2.41	2.28	3.43	7.47	6.54	-	.123	.200	2.01
KOZ	-2.19	1.68	.844	.748	-1.47	4.16	5.35	4.57	-	.192	.263	265
KNR	-1.43	4.01	4.29	4.17	-.697	7.26	7.69	7.41	-	.208	.167	.147

A area in 000 hectares Production in 000 metric tonnes.

Source: (1) Government of Kerala (1975) Agricultural Statistics in Kerala, The Bureau of Economics and Statistics, Thiruvanathapuram.

(2) Government of Kerala, Economic Review (various years), State Planning Board, Thiruvanathapuram.

are the maximum in Kozhikode, Malappuram and Kannur districts followed by Thrissur, Palakkad, Ernakulam and Thiruvanathapuram districts. It is striking to observe that in Kollam district production came down.

Kerala has the virtual monopoly over production of rubber in the country. The state's rubber production increased by 3.14 times and yield 1.63 times over the last 20 years. In absolute terms, yield improved from 611kg/hect in 1975-76 to 1222 in 1999-00. Leaving home district Kottayam, the other districts made commendable performance of production of rubber are Ernakulam, Thrissur and Thiruvanathapuram. The good performance of production and yield is definitely due to the efforts taken by the Rubber Board. But the crucial question as raised earlier is whether the excess supplies of rubber in relation to consumption "within state" will able to find attract sufficient margins permanently. It is true that still there is wide gap between present production and consumption. But the relevant question is whether the gap will be filled by domestic rubber or imported rubber.

The above discussions validate our hypothesis that the cropping pattern of Kerala state has turned in favour of cash crops particularly coconut and rubber at the cost of area under rice, the staple food of the state.

Table 10
Gross Change in Area between 1975-2003 (000 hect)

Districts	*Rice*	*Coconut*	*Rubber*	*Gap*	*Gap after 2% for other crops*
Thiruvanathapuram	-20.11	15.86	17.62	-	-
Kollam	-27.77	-18.98	0.45	46.30	37.04
Alapuzha	-41.45	-8.35	-0.371	50.17	40.14
Kottayam	-19.12	-16.63	52.30	-	-
Idukki	-11.18	4.90	21.15	-	-
Ernakulam	38.99	13.17	33.73	-	-
Thrissur	64.28	23.89	11.26	12.63	10.10
Palakkad	34.21	26.70	16.74	-	-
Malappuram	46.80	32.78	8.67	5.35	4.28
Kozhikode	52.65	22.16	0.34	30.15	24.12
Kannur	67.16	6.38	6.87	53.91	43.12
Total	382.27	102.06	169.13		158.80

Computed from Tables 1, 2 and 3.

Determinants

Shifts in cropping pattern make take place due to different reasons. It may be due to price expectations, fears about a fall in price, impact of government strategies, variations in climatic factors and so on. Agricultural economists used to discuss this issue using various measurement tools. The popular methodology in order to discuss the determinants is called as supply response models, where the farmer decisions are discussed from two angles, area response and yield response. From Table 11, it is seen that the coefficient of determination ranged from 0.2950 and 0.9861 in the districts under study. The significance of R square values were indicative of the fact that the variables included in the area responses models were capable of explaining sizable proportion of the variation in the area. The coefficient of farm price was positive and significant in six districts, namely Thiuvanathapuram, Alappuzha, Ernakualam, Trichur, Kozhikode and Kannur. On the other hand the coefficient remained to be negative and insignificant in three districts. Also it is surprising to note that in Palakkad

Table 11
District wise Estimated Regression Coefficients of the Price Elasticities of Area of Rice

Dist.	*R square*	∞	*Coef* P_{t-1}	*Coef* A_{t-1}	*Coef* R_t	*Coef* W_t	*Elsas. SRE*	*Elsas. LRE*
Thiruva Nathapur	0.513**	0.823	0.031**	0.13	-0.04*	0.0007	0.516	0.593
Alapuzha	0.45	1.79	0.009***	0.249	-0.034**	0.0009*	0.33	0.44
Kollam	0.55	12.89	-0.007	0.67**	0.11*	0.006	-0.01	-0.04
Kottayam	0.61*	42.56	0.122	0.507**	-0.02	-0.009	0.011	0.02
Ernakulam	0.29	1.28	0.003*	0.038	-0.005	0.0001	0.17	0.17
Thrissur	0.74	0.68	0.003**	0.47	-0.005	-0.0001	0.16	0.31
Palakkad	0.98***	116.17	-0.07	0.85**	-0.02	-0.003	-0.03	-0.25
Malappuram	0.40	36.81	-0.11	0.51***	0.32	0.03	-0.16	0.33
Kozhikode	0.60	0.72	0.008***	0.27	0.03	0.0001	0.33	0.46
Kannur	0.52	0.33	0.12*	0.66**	0.23	0.04	0.28	0.84
Kerala	0.24	914.62	0.12	0.28	0.57	0.04	0.01	0.014

*significant at probability level 0.1
**significant at probability level 0.05
***significant at probability level 0.01

district, one of the major rice producing centres of the state, the coefficient seems to be negative and insignificant. Hence, we may infer that generally area under rice in Kerala is price responsive. The average rainfall was used as a proxy for computing the influence of weather on area allocation decisions. Its effect was found to be positive in seven districts out of ten, but the coefficient was found to be significant only in Alapuzha.

However, this inference supports our finding that the rice cultivation in Kerala is rainfed. In other words, we may conclude that the rainfall favourably influenced the area allocation decisions of the farmers. The risk factor which is represented by the standard deviation of price of immediately preceding three years was found to be negative in seven districts indicating farmers risk aversion behaviour. This may be one of the reasons for the claim by the farmers that rice cultivation is uneconomic in Kerala and hence they switch over to the cash crops.

Yield Response Analysis

From Table 12, it is seen that coefficient of determination was significant in Thiruvanathapuram, Alappuzha, Kollam, Trichur, Palakkad and Kozhikode. The farm harvest price was found to be significant only in two districts namely, Trichur and Kozhikode. Hence, we may infer that the price factor is not playing a significant role in deciding the yield. The inference is very relevant for Kerala because, the farmers are reluctant to improve yield by applying more inputs primarily due to the disproportionate growth of input prices compared to stagnant output price. The price risk factor was negative in many districts again reflecting the farmers risk aversion behaviour as revealed in the case of area response. Hence, we may infer that the situation of rice production in the state can be augmented only if some policy prescriptions are launched by the government to make the farmers risk bearers. The rainfall variable was found to have a positive impact on productivity levels in all districts except Ernakulam. Thus we may also suggest that the yield can be improved by adopting better technology involving adequate use of inputs such as fertilizers, HYV seeds.

Table 12
District wise Estimated Regression Coefficients of the Determinants and Price Elasticities of Yield of Rice

Dist.	*R square*	*∞*	*Coef* P_{t-1}	*Coef* A_{t-1}	*Coef* R_t	*Coef* W_t	*Elsas. SRE*	*Elsas. LRE*
Thiruva Nathapur	0.79**	0.38	0.03	0.62***	-0.04	0.11***	0.04	-
Alapuzha	0.36**	0.38	0.03	0.02	0.07	0.14***	0.02	0.11
Kollam	0.78***	0.81	0.18	0.62***	-0.43	0.03	0.08	0.03
Kottayam	0.86***	0.80	.0.01	0.86	0.01	0.01	-0.02	0.23
Ernakulam	0.29	0.53	0.04	0.21	0.02	0.01	0.05	0.06
Thrissur	0.75***	0.17	0.01	0.27	-0.02	-0.001*	0.35	0.49
Palakkad	0.67***	0.65	0.01	0.21	0.01	0.01	0.28	0.19
Malappuram	0.29	0.80	0.88	0.34*	0.04	0.001	0.27	0.42
Kozhikode	0.57**	0.61	0.01***	0.20	0.03	0.001	0.51	0.59
Kannur	0.14	0.79	0.003	0.21	0.014	0.0007	0.06	0.06
Kerala	0.56	0.64	0.006**	0.05	-0.02	0.004	0.36	0.38

*significant at probability level 0.1
**significant at probability level 0.05
***significant at probability level 0.01

Conclusion

Shifts in cropping pattern in favour of cash crops in majority of economies in recent years and the consequent reduction in area under food crops weakens the sustainability of food availability. The Indian economy characterised by low per capita income and large population would bring a rapid growth in the direct and derived demand for food grains. The reduction in area under food crops in Kerala from 40.43 per cent in 1970-71 to 18.74 per cent in 1992-93 and 16.52 in 2002-03, is a phenomenon occurred very rarely in any country. The study clearly established the claim that Kerala farmers are shifting the area under rice to coconut and rubber while the state is 50 per cent short of rice production compared to requirement. The study also revealed that, district wise, the crop shifts are more in Northern Kerala and the two crops towards which there is a significant shift are rubber and coconut displacing rice, in conformity with the state level trend. The farmers supply responses were also examined with the help of supply response models. Supply response estimates helped to identify the major factors deciding farmer responses, the major being, farm price, rainfall, risk at all levels and input prices. The situation of rice production in the state can be augmented only if policy prescriptions are launched by the government to make the farmers risk bearers. Yield can be improved by adopting better technology involving adequate, efficient, effective right type of inputs.

References

Grirappa and M. Vevekananda (1984), Agricultural Development in India, Ashish Publishing House, New Delhi.

Hazell PBR (1982), Instability in Indian Food Grain Production, Research Report 30, IFPRI Washington USA.

Hen Chandra Lal Das (1993), Agricultural Efficiency in India, Mittal Publishing House, New Delhi.

Ranaram Das Gupta (2000), Indian Agricultural Economy An Analysis, Concept Publishing Company New Delhi.

World Bank (1993,) Problems of Marketing and Input Supply, Selected Readings, UK.

Dantwala M. L. (1986), Strategy of Agricultural Development since Independence, Oxford and IBH New Delhi.

Deshmukh M. B. and Bhargave M. P. (1954), Capital Formation in Agriculture, *Indian Journal of Agricultural Economics*, Vol. 9, No 1.

Directorate of Economics and Statistics, Government of Kerala, Statistics for Planning Thiruvanathapuram.

Mani K. P. (1996), Some Reflections on Capital Formation in Indian Agriculture, *Indian Journal of Agricultural Economics*, Vol. 51, No. 4.

Mani K. P. (2003), An Appraisal of the Agricultural Input Supply System in Kerala, Kerala Agricultural University, funded by the Indian Council of Agricultural Research.

Mani K. P. (2004,) Capital Formation in Agriculture Role of Cooperatives in Kerala, Kerala Agricultural University, funded by the KRPLLD.

Ministry of Finance, Economic Division, Government of India, Economic Survey.

National Bank for Agriculture and Rural Development, Various Reports.

National Bank for Agriculture and Rural Development (1991), Institutional Finance for Agriculture, New Delhi.

Deepak Nayyar (1990), Indian Economy at the Cross Roads: Illusions and Realities, *Economic and Political Weekly*, Vol. 28, No. 15.

Hanumantha Rao (1994), Agriculture Growth, Rural Poverty and Environmental Degradation in India, Oxford University Press New Delhi.

Hanumantha Rao and Ashok Gulati (1994), Indian Agriculture Emerging Perspectives and Policy Issues, *Economic and Political Weekly*, December.

Rao G. V. K. (1992), Strategies for Agricultural Development in the Nineties, *Financing Agricululture*, Vol. 24, No. 1.

Nilakantha Rath (1989), Agricultural Growth and Investment in India, *Journal of Indian School of Political Economy*, Vol. 1, No. 1.

Reserve Bank of India (1997), Occasional papers, Vol. 18, No. 2 and 3.

State Planning Board, Government of Kerala (1997), Report of the Task Force on Agricultural Financing, Thiruvanathapuram.

State Planning Board, Government of Kerala Economic Review.

Swaminathan M. S. (1992), Agriculture for the 21st Centaury New Thinking Needed, *Financing Agriculture*, Vol. 24, No. 1.

World Bank (1991), India 1991 Country Economic Memorandum, Vol. 2, Agriculture Challenges and Opportunities, Washington DC USA.

AN EMPIRICAL VALIDITY OF MARKET INTEGRATION HYPOTHESIS WITH REFERENCE TO PEPPER MARKET IN KERALA

K. Sham Bhat & M. V. Kanakaraj

SECTION-I

Introduction

An efficient marketing system in agricultural sector is essential to keep the pace of agricultural growth. In ordinary parlance an agricultural market can be said to be efficient if there is a uniform price for an identical product prevailing in the entire market area. Agricultural marketing is a specialised activity which endeavours to establish equilibrium between production and consumption (Ghatage, 1958). However, it is the type of competition prevalent between the contracting parties that determine whether there will be a rise in revenue to the farmers, fall in consumer's price or rise in profit of middlemen or a combination of all these possibilities (Jasdanwalla, 1966).

Marketing efficiency is of great significance as it is the pivot to farmer's response to agricultural production and marketed surplus. In an efficient marketing system, producers are able to get remunerative prices to their products and consumers to get the product at affordable prices. Attainment of remunerative prices will tempt them to produce more; and this will lead to greater marketable surplus. Greater marketable surplus will help to generate capital formation and foreign exchange. Crop specialisation through the principle of comparative cost advantage is possible only in a competitive and efficient market. In other words, an efficient marketing system is the pre-condition to achieve food security.

The efficient marketing system depends on market mechanism. And the efficiency of market mechanism in turn depends on regional price integration. Uniformity of prices can be attained through the integration of national economy. The difference between prices at various location points should not be higher than warranted by reasonable calculation of transport and other costs (Gadgil, 1961).

For examining the efficiency of a marketing system, one must inevitably look at the degree to which village primary, secondary and terminal markets are related to each other (Lele, 1971). Thus the concept of market integration emerges in the picture. Whenever the actions of agents of one market affect the actions of agents of other markets, it is said to be a situation of integrated market. Markets are known to be interlinked when transaction in one influences the terms of exchange in other markets. According to Faminow and Benson (1990) integrated markets are those where prices are determined interdependently; which is assumed to mean that price change in one will be fully passed on the others. Monke and Petzel (1984) defined integrated markets as markets in which prices of differentiated products do not behave independently. Ravallion (1986) observes that equilibrium will have the property that, if trade takes place at all between any two regions, then price in the importing region equals price in the exporting region plus the unit transport cost incurred by moving between the two. Goodwin and Schroeder (1991) cautions that markets that are not integrated may convey inaccurate price information that might distort producer's marketing decision and contribute to inefficient product movements.

Thus, an interrelated or interdependent movement of prices between spatially separated markets can be said to be a situation of market integration. An integrated market system is synonymous with an efficient marketing system. Therefore, the concept of market integration percolates the basic principle of attainment of maximum utility with the most efficient utilisation of resources available in the marketing system.

Policy makers have argued that liberalisation is required to attain marketing efficiency and stabilised growth in agriculture. Agricultural scientists were of the opinion that if markets are not integrated, correct price signals will not be transmitted through the marketing channels and the farmer will not be able to specialise according to long term comparative advantage. Since market integration offers a clear picture of the process of transmission of prices, it is quite significant for the success of pricing policy and liberalisation programmes (Ghosh, 2000). Therefore, an integrated market is a pre-requisite for an effective implementation of policies such as economic reforms, liberalisation policies, agriculture or famine policies. Following the global view on liberalisation and of an economic crisis; Government of India has also announced a package of major economic policy reforms in 1991. Economic reforms have taken place in industrial, agricultural and financial sector. This may have a direct or indirect impact on market integration. The economic rationality behind these reforms is to strengthen market forces and to allow the free play of market forces.

On the above background, let us examine the earlier literature pertaining to the study area which will be immensely useful to identify the gap of the studies. For simplicity and clarity the earlier studies are classified into two. They are: (i) International Studies, and (ii) National Studies.

International Level Studies

Fafchamps (1972) examined reasons behind the wealthier farmers in growing cash crops. He argued that the correlation between individual and aggregate output is also likely to decrease with market integration, thereby reducing the price and revenue correlation. A glimpse of strong pleading for market integration can be obtained through–'food' market integration via reduced trade restriction, better roads and transportation, and/or government food shops can be a powerful tool to boost cash crop production and to increase responsiveness of small farmers to price incentives.

Hays and Mc Coy (1978) examined spatial and temporal aspects of marketing efficiency for the traditional marketing system for millet and sorghum in Northern part of Nigeria. Analysis of pricing efficiency of the marketing system was accomplished by examining movement between prices at fifteen selected locations in Nigeria's four Northern States during 1969-71. Spatial price relationship were analysed by examining inter-market price differentials in relation to transport and other transfer costs. Temporal price relationship were analysed by examining significance of storage costs as a factor in explaining seasonal price rises. The analysis revealed that positive price spreads is due to an erratic nature of supply, an inadequate dissemination of information on prices and supply in the various markets and lack of specialisation in trade by traders. Storage operations were considered to be the reason for intertemporal price increases. The author points out that lack of market integration among the fifteen urban locations studied resulted in spatial price differentials that in some cases exceeded transfer costs.

Harris (1979) in his detailed survey of studies revealed that correlation coefficient analysis fails to explain market integration due to secularly rising prices and it is caused by increased population growth and effective demand, widening range of crop varieties, trading relationship of a joint destination market, monopoly procurement at fixed prices, inflationary trend etc.

Lundahl and Petersson (1982) made an attempt to calculate correlation coefficient in the same manner as carried out by Blyn with Cumming's data for Haitian market for the period 1969-1974. Rice, grain, millet, grain corn, ground corn and red beans are the products chosen for the analysis. The average correlation coefficients for the raw series, after grouping and detrending were obtained. The average coefficients for each of the products are approximately in the same range as the one calculated by Blyn (1973). The lower correlation coefficient is cited probably for trade which is not uni-directional. The scholar argued that the specific nature of Haitian marketing system also nullifies the use of price series correlation for market integration.

Analysing market integration of international trade in cotton was the subject matter to Monke and Petzel (1984). The data for the estimation of the pair wise price relationship included twenty series of monthly prices. Monthly prices were averaged to produce annual series for the period 1962-79. The prices are deflated by the World Bank index of CIF prices to generate stable time series and reduce the possibility of spurious correlation. Thirteen international price series are included and the data are organised by staple length. Bivariate price regression and hedonic index estimation are the methods used to identify whether differentiated products are amenable to treatment as homogenous commodity. The analysis reveals that the international cotton market is integrated across the shorter staple lengths; and short, medium and long staple cotton may be treated as a homogeneous commodity. The authors were of the opinion that consumption rather than production adjustments are the constraints for price movements of exports of alternative countries.

Heytens (1986) employed Ravallion model to examine the validity of market integration hypothesis with reference to Gari (processed cassava) price and Yam prices. The results indicate that gari market comprised a fairly well integrated system after the first five years. Yam prices from a subset of eastern Nigerian cities result showed a dismal integration due to local seasonality. Besides, the author points out that as a matter of fact the Ravallion model gives a much broader range of results than earlier bivariate correlations.

Ravallion (1986) throws light on the inferential dangers in using bivariate correlation or regression coefficients as a measure of spatial market integration in agriculture. He suggests that the main dangers of the simple bivariate model can be avoided if the static bivariate model is extended into a dynamic model of spatial price differentials with the same data. By accepting short run dynamic adjustment process, Ravallion offers an approach to test long run market integration. The analysis was done by using data on the interregional price differentials for rice in Bangladesh during the turbulent post-independence period (1972-75). Ravallion posits an autoregressive distributed lag relationship between each local price of a commodity and an appropriate reference price level. The analysis revealed that market segmentation performs poorly as a restricted form of the general model for all districts and short run integration continues to be weak when long run integration is imposed.

Delgado (1986) developed a variance component method to test food grain market integration in Nigeria. The approach is to decompose the variance of food grain prices into components. The model was applied to eighteen months of weekly grain prices for twenty two villages in Northern Nigeria for the period August 1976 to March 1978. Empirical result revealed that markets are not well integrated during the harvest period.

Dahlgran and Blank (1992) investigated the integration of a system of discontinuous and continuous markets. For empirical test of integration, data from six western U.S. alfalfa markets from April 1, 1984 to March 29, 1987 were used. The analysis revealed that continuous markets are less integrated during discontinuous market operation and long run market integration differs by season.

Sorensen (1993) attempted to study the impact of product market integration on welfare of an economy. Usually there are welfare gains from integration either due to increasing returns to scale or to firms' or unions' loss of market power. The author's main purpose was to show that in an economy with centralised wage setting, integration of product market may give rise to lower welfare. The experiment was made with a general equilibrium model. It is shown that highly centralised as well as completely decentralised economies in general, have better employment performance than economies with a degree of centralisation in between. Utility function is applied to illustrate how integration of product market may give rise to a decline in welfare. The analysis concluded that the real wage is higher and employment, real income and profits are lower when product markets are integrated.

Kallfass' (1993) analysis revealed that the choice among spot market sales, long-term contracts and vertical integration depends on key factors such as specific physical assets, specific location, and difficulty in monitoring quality as suggested in theoretical analysis. Kallfass' findings do not confirm the hypothesis that greater vertical integration is necessarily cost saving. Hence, he argues that government policy should not distort competition between different distribution systems by favouring a particular type of co-ordination.

Zanias (1993) investigated the degree of spatial market integration in European community of agricultural product markets. Failure to observe a single price throughout the community could be attributed to one or more of the following: (i) lack of linkage by arbitrage between agricultural markets between member states, (ii) impediments to efficient arbitrage and (iii) imperfect competition in one or more of the markets. Zanias with the help of co-integration analysis investigated the impact of the above reasons to nullify the force of the law of one price in the European community agricultural product market. Law of one price is tested for four European community agricultural products which differ both in terms of product characteristics and policy framework namely, soft wheat, cow's milk, potatoes and pig carcasses. Test result reveals an existence of a single price in the soft wheat market; and it may be due to the operation of minimum intervention prices rather than the different markets being truly integrated in a spatial sense. Zanias observes that market integration fails in the European community milk markets due to non-tariff barriers to intra–community trade or imperfect competition. In the case of pig carcasses and potatoes, co integration is established in three out of six cases.

The intention of Gardner and Brooks (1994) was to examine the extent to which economic reforms in Russia constituted genuine price liberalisation, i.e., food prices that respond to supply and demand conditions. Both linear and non-linear equations were worked out to test market integration. Test result showed that for every commodity, the hypothesis that $\beta_1 = 1$ in all cites can be rejected at one per cent level of significance and hence there is little consistency across commodities in which city is most closely integrated with the Moscow price. The results of city market prices also indicated a similar trend. From OLS estimates strong evidences for lack of consistent relationship between the distance and income variable and the city price difference were also obtained. They have observed that the behaviour of these price series is dominated by oblast-level (formal or informal) regulation of enterprises and markets. Hence, there is a need for local political reform for effective market integration.

An empirical testing of spatial market integration of Philippines rice market was made by Silvapulle and Jayasuriya (1994). The analysis was based on the monthly average price of rice of five selected markets for the period January 1975 to December 1989. Johansen's multiple cointegration technique was employed to test market integration. The result of the Johansen's multiple co-integration technique indicates that Phillippines rice markets are generally well integrated in the long run with Manila as the central market.

Baharumushah and Habibullah (1994) made an attempt to determine whether prices of black and white pepper in a market are in parity with prices in a reference market. The co integration method developed by Engle and Granger (1987) was employed to analyse the long run relationship between prices in different markets. The period of observation spans from the first week of January 1986 to the last week of December 1991. The test results shows that regional pepper markets in Malaysia are spatially linked. The authors concluded that due to low transportation cost and risk, the degree of co integration is unaffected by distance and hence price changes are fully and immediately passed on to the other markets.

Carvalho, *et. al.* (1994) examined the agro-industrial vertical integration process in Brazil's sugar cane and alcohol sector in the period 1970-92. The analysis revealed that the Brazilian sugar sector already has vertical integration and it was due to well established relaxation of restriction, seasonality of the raw material, emphasis on profit, and administrative price practices.

Alexander and Wyeth (1994) employed Granger method of co integration and Johansen's maximum likelihood procedure to test market integration and employed data on monthly prices from January 1979 to December 1990. The method was illustrated with data on prices in different parts of the Indonesian market. The authors observed that the consumer price Index (CPI) is consistently co integrated with all the rice price series, which means an existence of apparent market integration. Besides, this analysis also revealed that supply sources are more important than demand sources in driving prices.

Zhao (1995) in an article seeks to draw general trends for the development of the integration of agricultural production, processing and marketing in China. He concluded that there is a high degree of integration of agricultural production, processing and marketing. Besides, he pointed out that integration of agricultural production, processing and marketing and the close links between agricultural production supply and sales result from the development of market economy.

Angulo and Gil (1996) analysed the impact of vertical integration on price transmission in the Spanish poultry sector by employing error correction model. Feed price, producer's price and consumer prices are considered for the analysis. Monthly data from January 1981 to December 1992 were considered for an empirical analysis. Angulo and Gil's computation of impulse response functions and decomposition of the forecast errors variance shows that producer and consumer prices immediately rise after shock. They further pointed out that these response endure is for approximately two years, indicating that poultry firm tend to price according to long term goals, thereby showing the price adjustment process.

Fafchamps and Gavian (1996) studied spatial integration of livestock market in Niger by using co-integration approach. The study shows that livestock markets are poorly integrated. Prices are seldom co-integrated, suggesting that large price differentials occasionally persist between adjacent areas for long periods of time. Parity bound approach indicates that one has to assume high transportation costs and large quality variation to reconcile the data with efficient spatial arbitrage. Besides, the analysis confirms descriptive studies that have emphasised regional segmentation in west-African livestock trade.

Bijman (1996) examined the link of biotechnology and vertical integration in the Dutch potato chain. In general studies on the impact of biotechnology have stated that development and introduction of technology may lead to vertical integration on the agrofood chain, making farmers more dependent on the input supply industries and the food industry. It is pointed out that even without biotechnology the agrofood sectors is experiencing structural changes leading towards more horizontal and vertical integration. Further, the analysis revealed that biotechnology will reinforce the trend only if consumers accept products made with the new technology.

Rozelle, *et. al.* (1997) examined the impact of liberalisation on rural market integration in China. The impact of market integration on pushing producers to more effectively utilise their comparative advantage was also analysed. Price and market liberalisation were taken as a way of raising the efficiency of China's food economy and to increase rural income. A unique and comprehensive set of data on provincial prices of major food commodities between 1988 and 1995 were considered for the analysis. The analysis revealed falling coefficients of variation for provincial rice and maize and it implies a sign of increasing integration. The number of pair of province that became integrated went up by more than four times for rice markets and more than doubled for maize markets during 1988-89 and 1991-93. This is an indication of an expanding geographic range of spatial market integration.

Increase in rank correlation coefficient results reveals that liberalisation policies appear to have been successful in encouraging farmers to move into crops in which they have a comparative advantage.

Baulch (1997) developed an alternative methodology known as parity bound model (PBM) to test Philippine rice market integration. The author argued that all the conventional tests such as price correlation, causality, error correction and co-integration rely on price data alone and fail to recognize the pivotal role played by transfer costs. Transfer costs comprising transportation, loading and unloading costs and traders' normal profit determine the parity bounds within which the prices of a homogeneous commodity in two geographically distinct markets can vary independently. Violations of the spatial arbitrage conditions indicate that there are impediments to trade between markets and to be viewed as evidence of a lack of market integration. The parity bound model developed in his article assesses the extent of market integration by distinguishing among three possible trades. They are: (i) the parity bound (spatial price differential, equals transfer cost), (ii) inside the parity bound (price differentials are less than transfer costs), and (iii) price differentials exceed transfer costs. To assess the statistical reliability of the parity bound model, a series of Monte Carlo experiments were performed. Three alternative trading scenarios for the spatial price equilibrium model integrated, partially integrated and independent markets are considered in the Monte Carlo simulations. The analysis revealed that the sum of the probabilities of trade (i) and (ii) are interpreted as the probability of market integration, of Philippine rice markets.

Munir, *et. al.* (1997) analysed market integration of Indonesian vegetable market. Vegetables like Chilli, shallot, potato and cabbage in nine consumer and three producer markets in Indonesia are considered for the analysis. The results revealed that none of the markets are segmented. Further, short run and long run market integration tests revealed that transportation and product perishability are the important factors in explaining the speed of price transmission.

Khedhiri (1999) empirically analysed agricultural market integration in Tunisia. Cointegration technique was employed to examine the objective. The empirical result shows that the degree of market integration is low for wholesale market, particularly for the storage products. Besides, the analysis revealed that the distance between markets and the volume of transaction can not explain the lack of linkage between the markets.

Ismet, *et. al.* (1999) evaluated the long run spatial price relationship in Indonesian rice markets and factors affecting the degree of market integration. Multivariate co-integration test was employed to verify market integration hypothesis with weekly price data for the period 1982-1993. Besides, they classified their evaluation into pre-self sufficiency and post-self sufficiency period. The co-integration tests revealed a smaller degree of market integration in Indonesian rice market. Further the analysis revealed that government intervention in terms of rice procurement significantly influenced market integration during the period of post-self sufficiency (1985-93).

Asche, *et. al* (1999) employed Johansen's multiple co-integration technique to test the law of one price and to evaluate the possibility of product aggregation. Their empirical investigation also include (a) a co-integration analysis of world Salmon export prices during 1986-1996, (b) an analysis of the dynamic relationship between the price series and (c) an error correction model which assess short run responsiveness of the prices to one another. For empirical analysis five species of salmon were considered. Since multivariate cointegration test indicates four cointegration vectors, (hence one common stochastic trend in the system) they concluded that there is one market for all Salmons. Parameter stability test indicates that the Salmon market is well integrated during the study period.

National Level Studies

Lele (1967) examined market integration of Sorghum prices in Western India. Five primary markets in Sholapur district and two terminal markets are selected for the analysis. The analysis is based on weekly wholesale prices for the period 1958 to 1963. The two hypotheses tested in this article are: (i) markets of agricultural commodities in underdeveloped countries are closely interrelated (ii) Price differences between markets do not tend to be greater than transport costs because of the competitive nature of wholesale trade. Correlation coefficient is used to test the degree of market integration. Lele obtained high correlation coefficient between prices and maintains that it support the hypothesis that agricultural markets are fairly competitive and that price movements in a single market are influenced by prices in other markets.

Lele (1971) made an extensive study of market integration of Indian grain markets. Comparable varieties price data for the year 1954-1965 of rice, wheat and Jowar in four major states such as West Bengal, Tamil Nadu, Punjab and Maharashtra were considered for the analysis. Correlation coefficient is used to test the hypothesis. The analysis revealed the following conclusions: (i) By and large collusion, either tacit or overt is uncommon in the Indian grain trade. High profits earned by few traders are not monopolistic returns but can be attributed to the large volume of operations resulting from their command of capital, (ii) Examination of regional price disparities suggests that grain markets are closely related to each other, (iii) The study of market integration suggests that a reasonably well organised competitive system of private trade exists in India, and (iv) Existence of price difference between regions are mainly due to lack of adequate transportation facilities and hindrance to perfect mobility imposed from outside the trade sector such as transport bottlenecks and official restrictions.

Blyn (1973) questions the validity of using correlation coefficients to test the presence of market integration. He maintains that even if markets are well integrated, correlation measures of their price series will not necessarily be high. Besides, he observes that time series correlation should be restricted to residuals remaining after the trend and seasonal components have been removed. An increase in population may affect all prices in a region, even if each market within the region was independent of others. Blyn reworked Cumming's eight year collection of monthly wheat prices in eight Punjab markets and Delhi by eliminating trend and seasonal influences. The analysis revealed that even if markets are well integrated, correlation coefficients may not be high because these markets are not simply supply centres but also centres of importance for local consumption.

Thakur (1974) examined pricing efficiency of the marketing system by analysing price trends, market integration and price spread in the marketing channel of Gujarat foodgrains. Weekly wholesale prices from 1965-1971 were used for the analysis. Correlation coefficient is used to test the degree of market integration. Test result revealed that the existing foodgrain marketing system in Gujarat on the whole is not efficient.

Naik and Arora (1986) attempted to identify the marketing channel and the marketing function performed by Indian arecanut producers and market intermediaries and assesses the pricing efficiency. Concurrent method is used to compute the price spread. Price series correlation was employed to measure market integration. The authors revealed that lower price spread and high degree of market integration between primary and Nagpur markets indicate higher efficiency in Nagpur channel than in Kanpur channel.

Patnaik (1988) examined the evidence of inter market integration with regard to the major produce in which the particular market is specialized and to find out the price signals between primary market depend upon the interest/activities of the major participants of the system. The study was carried out by the monthly price data of groundnut pod, kernel, oil and cake of selected six markets of Rayalseema region of Andhra Pradesh for the period 1963-81. The analysis revealed that market integrations is achieved by transmission of price signals with regard to pods.

From the data collected from a market survey, Palaskas and White (1993) tried to examine the dynamic relationship of market commodity prices of rice, potatoes and mustard in three locations of West Bengal. Co integration technique was employed to test the hypothesis of market integration. Test results reveal that the prices of rice, potato and oil of the peripheral market and the central market are co-integrated; but there is a lower degree of integration of paddy and rice prices.

Padmanabhan (1993) tried to evaluate the performance efficiency of the market for Jaggery in Tamil Nadu. He examined the cost price relationship in jaggery production and marketing, and also to analyze temporal variation in the price of jaggery. The degree of market integration was assessed by working correlation of prices between markets at vellore and in each of Madras city, Salem, Coimbatore, Madurai, Tirunelveli, Ernakulam and Kolhapur. The wholesale weekly prices for the period 1982-83 were considered for the analysis. High correlation coefficient was obtained between the markets. Hence, the analysis concluded that the market of Jaggery is well integrated.

Narasimham (1994) examined the integration of groundnut markets of Rayalseema region of Andhra Pradesh. The study covered a period of six years from 1973 to 1979 with daily price data. Narasimham have considered Bombay as terminal market and Hyderabad and Madras as regional markets. Koyck's distributed lag model was employed to examine the objective. The analysis revealed that the oil price integrates the groundnut markets vertically.

Nasurudeen and Subramanian (1995) examined the validity of (i) vertical integration of seed price to price of its oil and cake and (ii) horizontal integration of prices of different oils. Ten oil products were considered for the analysis of horizontal and vertical price integration. Koyck's distributed lag model was employed to test the integration of oil prices. Horizontal integration test results revealed that the price of groundnut oil influenced the prices of all other oils except castor oil. Castor oil price was influenced only by linseed oil price since they are substitutes. Vertical integration results revealed that there exist some imperfection in seed price formation. It is also inferred that the price of industrial oil influenced the price of edible oils but not vice versa. The researchers concluded that vertical integration in oilseed price was much quicker as compared to horizontal integration in oil prices.

An attempt is made to study the long run behavior of the farm prices of coconut in various markets of Kerala by Mathew, et. al. (1997). Average yearly farm price considered for the analysis is arrived by taking a simple average of monthly farm prices of 23 years data from 1970 to 1992 for 25centers in Kerala. The co-integration method developed by Engle and Granger is employed in the study to test the coconut market integration. The test result indicated that the farm price of coconut in various markets of Kerala were integrated of order one. After establishing the order of integration of each variable, pairwise co-integration were carried out with the farm price of Trichur market as the independent variable and the respective farm price in other markets as dependent variables. The study revealed that all the market except Calicut market was integrated with Trichur market.

Thakur (1998) made a detailed study of validity of market integration hypothesis of weekly wholesale prices of wheat market of Gujarat and apple in different terminal markets of India for the year 1985-86 to 1995-96. The analysis revealed that wheat and apple markets are integrated. Besides, the analysis cautioned that high degree of integration may come simply as a result of collusion on the part of traders.

Ghosh (2000) examined spatial integration of rice markets in India. The empirical analysis was carried out on the basis of data of monthly wholesale prices of rice for the period from March 1984 to April 1997. Price data relates to state-specific varieties of rice quoted in different market centres of four selected states viz. Bihar, Orissa, Uttar Pradesh and West Bengal. To examine whether intra-state and inter-state regional rice markets are integrated and linked together into a single economic market, the maximum likelihood (ML) method of co-integration developed by Johansen and extended by Johansen and Juselius was employed. To examine the univariate time-series properties of the data and for non-stationarity, Augmented Dickey Fuller test was conducted. The finding of one common stochastic trend for Uttar Pradesh implies that all the prices are pair-wise co-integrated. On the other hand, the presence of multiple common stochastic trends in Bihar, Orissa and West Bengal signifies that the prices are not pair wise co-integrated.

Basu and Dinda (2003) attempted to evaluate empirically spatial integration of potato market in Hooghly district of West Bengal. Bivariate price correlation as well as co-integration test and error-correction method developed by Engle-Granger has been used to show whether potato markets are integrated or not. The study is based on time series data on wholesale and retail prices of potato in the selected three important market centres namely, Champadanga, Tarakewshwar and Sheoraphully in the district of Hooghly for the period of January 1998 to December 2000. On the basis of high values of correlation coefficient, the analysis revealed that markets are strongly correlated and they are highly interdependent in price formation.

Pramod Kumar and Sharma (2003) tried to evaluate price integration and pricing efficiency to the state of Haryana. Johansen's multiple cointegration method was employed to test price integration. The integration tests were carried out with the monthly wholesale price of coarse paddy for four markets of Haryana. To know the impact of liberalisation the period was divided into pre-liberalisation (October 1978 to September 1989) and post - liberalisation period (October 1989 to September 2001). The multivariate cointegration tests results indicates the presence of three cointegrating vectors at one per cent level of significance for both pre and post–liberalisation periods. It implies that all the four paddy markets are cointegrated and hence exhibit a long run relationship. However, results of error correction model reveal a very weak association between these markets. The authors observed that this weak association is because of paucity of availability of information and lack of quicker dissemination of available information. But the adjustment process was found to be quicker in post-liberalisation period in comparison with pre-liberalisation period.

However, the above national and international studies pertaining to market integration hypothesis reveals the following gap in the literature: (i) Most of the studies pertaining to market integration hypothesis has given much emphasis on food-crops. Market integration analysis related to cash crops was almost neglected. (ii) At the national level, studies related to market integration of agricultural products are mainly related to states such as Maharashtra, Tamil Nadu, West Bengal, Punjab, Gujarat, Andhra Pradesh and Orissa. Here again it can be cited that food crop is the major item of analysis. However, an integrated study pertaining to Kerala economy with reference to cash crops are lacking. (iii) Some international studies have shown that liberalisation had a positive effect by reduced marketing margins and hence liberalisation and commercialization made market efficient. However, the studies examining the impact of economic liberalization on market integration are a rare phenomenon in the literature with special reference to Indian states. At national level no serious attempt is made to know the effect of liberalisation on marketing efficiency. In the era of government regulations, there is a chance to distort competition and hence efficiency. It is quite natural that with easing of regulations and restrictions there is greater chance for disseminations of market information which ultimately will lead to an efficient and competent market. (iv) On methodological front, majority of studies have used price series correlation to measure market integration. But correlation coefficient can not be taken as a reliable indicator of market integration, since common trends in time series analysis may make an upward bias of the results. It can also be maintained that a perfect monopoly or price fixing by a central authority can produce a coefficient of one as a perfectly competitive market. Therefore, it can be concluded that even though price series correlation indicates the nature of price movements among markets; it cannot be taken as a true indicator of market integration. To get rid of the problem from correlation, economists began to apply regression techniques. A regression has the benefit of adding time trend to the relationship. But in practice studies ignore the time series properties of price data and the results obtained may be biased and inconsistent. Therefore, the results of regression techniques is affected by econometric short coming as spurious regressions, non-stationarity in the data, inappropriate use of first difference etc. Hence, there is a scope for examining the hypothesis with the help of Johansen's multiple co-integration test, and (v) According to National Family Health Survey (2001) only 28 per cent of Indian agricultural area is covered under non-food crops; while the same is 76 per cent to the state of Kerala. Among Indian states, Kerala has more or less dominance over production of some major non-food crops. Pepper accounts 97 per cent, rubber 92 per cent, cashew 85 per cent, cardamon 70 per cent, ginger 60 per cent and coconut 43 per cent of Indian production (Kerala state Land use Board, 1997). Though Kerala had a near monopoly over pepper production and also fetches valuable foreign exchange, no serious attempt has so far made to know the validity of market integration of Kerala's pepper markets.

On the above background, the main objective of the study is to examine the validity of market integration hypothesis of pepper markets of Kerala. Besides, the study also tried to examine the impact of economic reform on market integration and transmission mechanism of prices between the selected pepper markets of Kerala. The rest of the article is as follows: Section-II presents the methodology of the study. Empirical results and discussions are presented in Section-III. Finally, concluding remarks were presented in Section-IV.

SECTION-II

Methodology

Four major pepper assembling markets of Kerala, namely Tellicherry, Kozhikode, Kochi and Alleppey were selected for the analysis. Monthly data of market prices of pepper product for April 1974 to March 2005 were collected for examining the objectives of our study. To examine the impact of economic reform on the validity of market integration hypothesis and transmission mechanism of prices between the selected markets, price series were divided into two. They are: (i) April 1974 to June 1991, and (ii) July 1991 to March 2005.

Validity of market integration hypothesis and transmission mechanism of prices will be examined with the help of Dickey-

Fuller test, Phillips-Perron test, Johansen's multiple co integration technique and Error Correction Models. It consists of three stages. They are (i) Data series has to be tested for stationarity, (ii) Verification of co integration between the markets, and (iii) Once the market is co integrated, error correction model should be estimated to identify transmission mechanism of prices between the markets.

In our study, Dickey-Fuller and Phillips–Perron tests were conducted to know the stationarity of data series and validity of market integration hypothesis pertaining to pepper product of Kerala. Johansen's multiple co integration technique was employed to verify the validity of co integration among the markets. After obtaining co integration, transmission mechanism of excess prices among the markets were tested with the help of error correction model and it is explained below.

Dickey-Fuller Test (DF)

To test whether the series Y_t is stationary, the test have been provided by Dickey and Fuller (1979, 1981) and it is presented below:

$$\Delta Y_t = \alpha_o + \rho\, Y_{t-1} + e_t$$

Test result reveals that Y_t is stationary if $\rho < 1$, non-stationary if $\rho = 1$, and non-stationary and explosive if $\rho > 1$. If 'ρ' is negative and statistically significant, the alternative hypothesis that Y_t is integrated of order I(1) is accepted. Dickey and Fuller derived critical values for the test from Monte Carlo experiments and is given as 'τ' statistics.

Phillips-Perron Test

Phillips and Perron (1988) developed a generalization of the Dickey-Fuller procedure that allows for fairly mild assumption concerning the distribution of errors and it can be concluded with the following regression equation.

$$Y_t = a_o{}^* + a_1{}^*\, Y_{t-1} + \mu_t \text{ and}$$

$$Y_t = \sim_o + \sim_1 y_t - 1 + \sim_2 (t - T/2) + \mu_t$$

Where T = number of observation and the disturbance term μ_t is such that E = 0, but there is no requirement that the disturbance term is serially uncorrelated or homogeneous. Instead of Dickey-Fuller assumption of independence and homogeneity, the Phillips-Perron test allows the disturbance term to be weakly dependent and heterogeneously distributed.

Phillips and Perron characterize the distribution and derive test statistics that can be used to test hypothesis about the coefficients a_i* and $\sim_i$ under the null hypothesis that the data are generated by $Y_t = Y_{t-1} + \mu_t$ If the coefficients are negative and statistically significant, the series is said to be stationary. The critical values of the Phillips-Perron statistics are precisely those given for the Dickey-Fuller test.

Multiple Co-integration Test

A recently popular approach to analyse co integrated system was developed by Johansen (1988, 1991). It extends the Engle-Granger procedure to a multivariate context where there may exist more than a single co integrating relationship among a set of 'n' variables (Sarker, 1993). Johansen proposed a maximum likelihood method for estimating long run equilibrium relationship or co integrating vector and derives likelihood ratio test for co integration in a Gaussian Vector Error Correction Model.

Following Johansen and Johansen and Juselius (1990), the model is explained on the following way. Given a vector of Y of 'n' potentially endogenous variables, the model of Y as an unrestricted vector auto regression with k lags of Y can be specified as

$$Y_t = aY_{t-1} + \ldots\ldots\ldots\ldots\ldots + a_k Y_{t-k} + u_t$$

$$\text{Where } u_t \sim IN(O, S) \tag{1}$$

And Y is (n x 1) and a_i is an (n x n) matrix of parameters.

In its reduced form with each variable in Y_t regressed only on lagged values of both itself and all other variables can be specified as

$$\Delta Y_t = C_1 \Delta Y_{t-1} + \ldots\ldots + C_{k-1} Y_{t-k+1} + \pi Y_{t-k} + u_t \tag{2}$$

Where $C_i = -(i - a_t - \ldots\ldots\ldots - a_i)$; $(i = 1, \ldots.\ k-1)$

And $\pi = -(I - a_i - \ldots\ldots - a_k)$

π Can be represented as

$\pi = \alpha\ \beta'$, where α is the speed of adjustment to disequilibrium, while β' is the matrix of long run coefficients in such a way that $\beta'\ Y_{t-k}$ in equation 2 represents upto (n-1) cointegration relationship in a multivariate model ensuring that Y_t converge in their long run steady state solutions.

Rewriting equation 2 as

$$\Delta Y_t + \alpha\ \beta' Y_{t-k} = C_1\ \Delta Y_{t-1} + \ldots\ldots + C_{k-1}\ \Delta Y_{t-k+1} + u_t \quad (3)$$

Enables correcting short run dynamics by regressing ΔY_{t-k} and Y_{t-k} separately on the right hand side of equation 3.

Thus the vector V_{ot} and V_{kt} are obtained from,

$$\Delta Y_t = X_1\ \Delta Y_{t-1} + \ldots\ldots + X_{k-1}\ \Delta Y_{t-k+1} + V_{ot} \quad (4)$$

$$Y_{t-k} = Z_1\ \Delta Y_{t-1} + \ldots\ldots + Z_{k-1}\ \Delta Y_{t-k+1} + V_{kt} \quad (5)$$

Equation 5 is used to form the residual (product moment) matrices as

$$R_{ij} = Z'\ \Sigma\ V_{it}\ V'_{jt}\ (1, J = O, k)$$

The null hypothesis that there are 'r' cointegrating vectors is tested by using two likelihood ratio tests called the trace test and the maximum eigen values. If H_1: is a special case of H_2: for r = p, then the likelihood ratio trace statistic is defined as

$$-2\mathrm{In}(Q;H_2/H_1) = -T\sum_{i=r+1}^{p}\mathrm{In}\left(1-\hat{\lambda}_i\right)$$

Similarly, the maximum eigen value statistic for testing $H_2(r)$ in $H_2\,(r+1)$ can be defined as:

$$-2\mathrm{In}(Q;r/r+1) = -T\,\mathrm{In}\left(1-\hat{\lambda}_{r+1}\right)$$

The asymptotic distribution of these likelihood ratio tests represent multi-variate version of the Dickey-Fuller distribution.

Thus, when there are 'n' price series and (n-1) potential co integrating relationship, it first test the null of zero co integrating relationship; if that is rejected, it then test the null that there is only one co integrating relationship and proceeds in stepwise way to test the null of higher number of such relationships upto (n-1). The test statistic is compared with the critical values which are generated through simulations and are reported in Johansen and Juselius (1990).

Johansen's method has several superiority over Engle-Granger's co integration method. Engle-Granger does not provide any procedure for testing multiple co integrating vectors when there are three or more variables. Again for conducting the test of integration in Engle-Granger method, it is necessary to identify the central (exogenous) and the peripheral (endogenous) markets. But Johansen's multiple co integration method treats all the variables as explicitly endogenous and takes care of the endogenous problem by providing an estimation that does not require arbitrary choice of variable for normalization. Further, since Johansen's test is carried out in a vector autoregressive model of reduced form, the problem of simultaneity can be avoided.

By examining the distributional properties of maximum likelihood estimates of co integrating vector, it is observed that the maximum likelihood estimator is super-consistent, symmetrically distributed and median unbiased– asymptotically and that an optimal theory of inference applies (Cheung and Lai, 1993). Johansen's approach also provides a very flexible format for investigating the properties of the estimates under various assumptions about the underlying data generating process (Sarker, 1993).

When variables are co integrated, the residuals from the equilibrium regression can be used to estimate the error correction model. With error correction model, price transmission in time series can be estimated. Error correction model employed to know price transmission among selected markets of the present study are presented below.

$$\Delta AL_t = \alpha_o + \beta_1 EC + \alpha_{11} AL_{t-1} + \alpha_{12} AL_{t-2} + \alpha_{21} KO_{t-1} + \alpha_{31} KZ_{t-1} + \alpha_{32} KZ_{t-2} + \alpha_{41} TL_{t-1} + \alpha_{42} TL_{t-2} + e_{1t} \quad (1)$$

$$\Delta KO_t = \alpha_o + \beta_2 EC + \alpha_{11} KO_{t-1} + \alpha_{12} KO_{t-2} + \alpha_{21} AL_{t-1} + \alpha_{22} AL_{t-2} + \alpha_{31} KZ_{t-1} + \alpha_{32} KZ_{t-2} + \alpha_{41} TL_{t-1} + \alpha_{42} TL_{t-2} + e_{2t} \quad (2)$$

$$\Delta KZ_t = \alpha_o + \beta_3 EC + \alpha_{11} KZ_{t-1} + \alpha_{12} KZ_{t-2} + \alpha_{21} AL_{t-1} + \alpha_{22} AL_{t-2} + \alpha_{31} KO_{t-1} + \alpha_{32} KO_{t-2} + \alpha_{41} TL_{t-1} + \alpha_{42} TL_{t-2} + e_{3t} \quad (3)$$

$$\Delta TL_t = \alpha_o + \beta_4 EC + \alpha_{11} TL_{t-1} + \alpha_{12} TL_{t-2} + \alpha_{21} AL_{t-1} + \alpha_{22} AL_{t-2} + \alpha_{31} KO_{t-1} + \alpha_{32} KO_{t-2} + \alpha_{41} KZ_{t-1} + \alpha_{42} KZ_{t-2} + e_{4t} \quad (2)$$

Where,

EC - Error correction term,

AL - Alleppey market price,

KO - Kochi market price,

KZ - Kozhikode market price, and

TL - Tellicherry market price.

If 'β_I' (i=1......4) has a negative sign and statistically significant, it can be inferred that there is an indirect strong long term price transmission mechanism across the selected markets of pepper product in Kerala. The values of 'α_i's depict the degree of influence of different market prices on dependent markets.

SECTION-III

Empirical Results and Discussion

Before examining an existence of co integration, it is necessary to determine the order of integration of the selected data series. Stationary tests were employed to identify whether the series have finite variance and a tendency to return to the mean. To check stationary of data series, unit root test has been employed. Both Dickey-Fuller and Phillips-Perron tests were conducted for the pooled, pre-reform and post-reform period. Further, the necessary tests were carried out on the log of monthly wholesale prices of the selected pepper markets of Kerala.

Dickey-Fuller and Phillips-Perron test (with and without trend) results for the monthly price series of the selected markets are presented in Table 1. Initially, tests have been conducted on the price series in levels, then on the first difference. Test results of price in levels of the selected markets with and without trend

Table 1
Results of Dickey-Fuller (DF) and Phillips-Perron (PP) Tests

	Sample: 1974.4 to 2003.3; Test Statistics at levels			
	without trend		*With trend*	
MarketPrice	*DF*	*PP*	*DF*	*PP*
(1)	*(2)*	*(3)*	*(4)*	*(5)*
Alleppey	-1.410	-4.543*	-2.285	-17.188*
Kochi	-1.237	-2.477	-1.652	-8.582*
Kozhikode	-1.256	-2.981**	-1.748	-12.943*
Tellicherry	-1.287	-3.308**	-1.793	-12.315*
	Test Statistics at First difference			
	Without trend		*With trend*	
Alleppey	-9.599*	-270.652*	-9.594*	-270.143*
Kochi	-8.765*	-362.782*	-8.771*	-362.187*
Kozhikode	-10.111*	-323.106*	-10.118*	-322.517*
Tellicherry	-10.169*	-292.86*	-10.173*	-292.322*
	Sample: 1974.4 to 1991.6; Test Statistics at levels			
	without trend		*with trend*	
Alleppey	-1.186	-3.619*	-1.596	-10.390*
Kochi	-1.086	-2.457	-1.492	-6.442*
Kozhikode	-1.156	-3.414**	-1.710	-11.789*
Tellicherry	-1.203	-3.902*	-1.663	-11.386*
	Test Statistics at First difference			
	Without trend		*With trend*	
Alleppey	-8.026*	-170.871*	-8.014*	-170.350*
Kochi	-9.648*	-225.771*	-9.630*	-225.33*
Kozhikode	-8.301*	-167.650*	-8.287*	-167.134*
Tellicherry	-8.243*	-169.210*	-8.230*	-168.696*
	Sample: 1991.7 to 2003.3; Test Statistics at Levels			
	Without trend		*With trend*	
Alleppey	-1.514	-4.817*	-1.218	-6.877*
Kochi	-1.421	-2.913**	-0.965	-2.733
Kozhikode	-1.375	-3.023**	-0.544	-2.989
Tellicherry	-1.407	-3.004**	-0.597	-2.92
	Test Statistics at First difference			
	Without trend		*With trend*	
Alleppey	-5.660*	-99.231*	-5.721*	-98.663*
Kochi	-7.510*	-152.449*	-7.620*	-152.423*
Kozhikode	-5.861*	-151.650*	-6.036*	-150.294*
Tellicherry	-6.061*	-119.882*	-6.259*	-118.993*

Note: *Shows significant at one per cent level and **shows significant at five per cent level.

revealed that Dickey-Fuller test does not reject the null hypothesis at least at five per cent level during pooled, pre-reform and post-reform periods. However, Phillips-Perron test has rejected unit root hypothesis in certain markets at least at 5 per cent level of significance. The null hypothesis was rejected (both Dickey-Fuller and Phillips-Perron tests) during pre-reform, post-reform and pooled periods at one per cent level in the case of first difference of price series of the selected pepper markets of Kerala. Hence, it can be concluded that price series of the selected pepper markets of Kerala were integrated of order one during pooled, pre-reform and post-reform periods. It implies that market integration hypothesis pertaining to the selected market prices of pepper product of Kerala were accepted during the period of our study.

The reason for the integrated nature of individual markets can be cited as follows. Alleppey market is the nearest assembling centre for all the southern districts of Kerala. As far as Kozhikode market is concerned, it is a major pepper producing district and the district is surrounded by highly productive pepper producing areas. Kochi market is an assembling centre and it is also a terminal market in which pepper products are exported to various countries. Finally, Tellicherry market has its own unique features that quality wise the products of Tellicherry market is internationally acclaimed and is labelled as "Tellicherry Garbled Extra Bold".

After confirming that the price series of the selected pepper markets of Kerala are integrated of order of one, the next procedure is to examine the rank of 'π' or the co integrating vectors. Generally, integrated markets must share a common trend and will have common integrating vector. For examining this issue, Johansen-Juselius method of multiple co integration test were conducted and its results were presented in Table 2. The likelihood ratio test results indicate the presence of three co integrating vectors at one per cent level of significance for the pooled period. It implies that all the four markets were in fact cointegrated and shares market information on changes in prices. Thus the empirical evidence suggests that all the selected pepper markets of Kerala do exhibit a long-run relationship during the pooled period of our analysis.

Table 2
Results of Johansen's Multiple Cointegration Test

Null hypothesis	*Eigen value*	*Likelihood ratio*	*Critical value (1 per cent)*	*Critical value (5 per cent)*
(1)	(2)	(3)	(4)	(5)
Sample: 1974.4 to 2003.3				
r = 0	0.218	178.879*	70.1	63.0
r ≤ 1	0.162	98.197*	48.5	42.4
r ≤ 2	0.106	40.475*	30.5	25.3
r ≤ 3	0.115	3.792	16.3	12.3
Sample: 1974.4 to 1991.6				
r = 0	0.871	422.480*	70.1	63.0
r ≤ 1	0.468	11.494	48.5	42.4
r ≤ 2	0.009	1.856	30.5	25.3
r ≤ 3	-2.10E-14	-4.239E-12	16.3	12.3
Sample: 1991.7 to 2003.3				
r = 0	0.841	286.599*	70.1	63.0
r ≤ 1	0.233	36.693	48.5	42.4
r ≤ 2	0.004	0.613	30.5	25.3
r ≤ 3	2.629E-14	3.578E-12	16.3	12.3

Note: *denotes rejection of the hypothesis at 1 per cent level.

But once data is subdivided into pre and post-reform periods, co integration results are not in parity with the pooled data results. Here the null hypothesis of zero co integrating vector has rejected. Proceeding further, the null hypothesis of one co integrating vector has accepted; which means that there is only one factor which integrates the markets. The number of co integrating vectors differs during pre and post-reform periods compared to pooled period. However, it implies that there is sharing of market information among the four markets during pooled, pre-reform and post-reform periods in the long run.

After examining the long-run association between the markets, the next stage is to identify the direct and indirect transmission mechanism of prices between the markets and it will be examined with the help of error correction models. To get an autocorrelation free error correction model, two months lag was considered. Besides, we restricted to the order of one to estimate the required Error Correction Model for simplicity, convenience and comparison between the periods of our study.

The results of the Vector Error Correction Model (VECM) for pooled, pre-reform and post-reform periods are presented in Tables 3, 4 and 5 respectively. It can be observed from the results of Table 3 that all the error correction coefficients except one are significant with the desired negative sign. It implies

Table 3
Results of Error Correction Model during Pooled Period

(1)	*Δ Alleppey* *(2)*	*Δ Kochi* *(3)*	*Δ Kozhikode* *(4)*	*Δ Tellicherry* *(5)*
ECM	-0.05	-0.003	-0.02 ***	-0.09
	(3.18)*	(0.17)	(1.64)	(6.21)*
Δ (Alleppey (-1))	0.26	0.28	0.29	0.37
	(3.18)*	(3.32)*	(3.56)*	(5.12)*
Δ (Alleppey (-2))	0.14	0.27	0.15	0.24
	(1.67) ***	(3.14)*	(1.81)***	(3.25)*
Δ (Kochi (-1))	-0.09	-0.21	0.42	-0.006
	(0.89)	(1.93)***	(4.05)*	(0.06)
Δ (Kochi (-2))	0.06	-0.05	0.08	0.04
	(0.66)	(0.55)	(0.92)	(0.51)
Δ (Kozhikode (-1))	-0.44	-0.20	-1.06	-0.48
	(4.93)*	(2.16)**	(12.05)*	(6.16)*
Δ (Kozhikode (-2))	-0.08	-0.04	-0.37	-0.21
	(0.94)	(0.54)	(4.46)*	(2.88)*
Δ (Tellicherry (-1))	0.44	0.17	0.58	0.20
	(3.24)*	(1.22)	(4.37)*	(1.75)***
Δ (Tellicherry (-2))	0.04	-0.07	0.27	0.07
	(0.42)	(0.61)	(2.43)**	(0.79)
Constant	14.07	17.90	17.52	15.06
	(0.31)	(0.39)	(0.40)	(0.39)
R^2	0.14	0.09	0.41	0.26
	0.12	0.06	0.39	0.24
$\bar{R}^2$	0.12	0.06	0.39	0.24
Log likelihood	-2798.91	-2806.85	-2789.42	-2751.55
AIC	16.28	16.32	16.22	16.00
SC	16.39	16.44	16.33	16.12

Note: Parentheses represent t-values
*significant at one per cent level,
**significant at five per cent level, and
*** significant at ten per cent level.

Table 4
Results of Error Correction Model during Pre-reform Period

(1)	*Δ Alleppey* (2)	*Δ Kochi* (3)	*Δ Kozhikode* (4)	*Δ Tellicherry* (5)
ECM	0.19	0.10	0.20	0.21
	(6.70)*	(3.57)*	(6.52)*	(7.25)*
Δ (Alleppey (-1))	-1.07	-0.26	-0.43	-0.38
	(5.42)*	(1.33)	(2.09)**	(1.91)***
Δ (Alleppey (-2))	-0.51	-0.11	-0.11	-0.09
	(2.78)*	(0.58)	(0.58)	(0.51)
Δ (Kochi (-1))	-0.22	-0.37	-0.16	-0.21
	(2.04)**	(3.27)*	(1.38)	(1.85)***
Δ (Kochi (-2))	0.11	-0.15	0.17	0.14
	(1.13)	(1.50)	(1.65)***	(1.37)
Δ (Kozhikode (-1))	-0.39	-0.06	-0.63	-0.34
	(1.65)***	(0.26)	(2.51)**	(1.42)
Δ (Kozhikode (-2))	-0.78	0.20	-1.10	-0.82
	(3.30)*	(0.86)	(4.39)*	(3.35)*
Δ (Tellicherry (-1))	1.61	0.34	1.14	0.85
	(5.34)*	(1.12)	(3.56)*	(2.75)*
Δ (Tellicherry (-2))	1.40	0.03	1.31	0.98
	(4.63)*	(0.10)	(4.07)*	(3.13)*
Constant	11.73	16.44	13.69	11.50
	(0.55)	(0.75)	(0.60)	(0.52)
R^2	0.39	0.14	0.37	0.37
$\bar{R}^2$	0.36	0.10	0.34	0.34
Log likelihood	-1450.26	-1454.76	-1462.68	-1456.83
AIC	14.31	14.36	14.43	14.38
SC	14.47	14.52	14.60	14.54

Note: Parentheses represent t-values
*significant at one per cent level,
**significant at five per cent level, and
*** significant at ten per cent level.

that there is strong indirect price transmission of pepper product from one market to the other during the pooled period. There is a direct transmission of pepper prices from Alleppey market to all the other markets. Kozhikode market pepper price is directly influenced by Kochi market pepper price. Kozhikode market pepper price of pepper also has a direct bearing on Alleppey, Kochi and Tellicherry market pepper prices. Again, Tellicherry market price of pepper is directly able to influence the Alleppey and Kozhikode market prices of pepper. Further,

Table 5
Results of Error Correction Model during Post-reform Period

(1)	*Δ Alleppey* *(2)*	*Δ Kochi* *(3)*	*Δ Kozhikode* *(4)*	*Δ Tellicherry* *(5)*
ECM	-0.04	0.01	0.03	-0.09
	(1.19)	(0.38)	(1.02)	(2.91)*
Δ (Alleppey (-1))	0.29	0.31	0.25	0.37
	(2.23)**	(2.33)**	(2.06)**	(3.30)*
Δ (Alleppey (-2))	0.13	0.26	0.10	0.23
	(1.01)	(1.90)	(0.78)	(1.96)**
Δ (Kochi (-1))	-0.03	-0.24	0.63	0.14
	(0.19)	(1.44)	(4.12)*	(1.00)
Δ (Kochi (-2))	0.05	-0.09	0.15	0.08
	(0.32)	(0.58)	(1.04)	(0.58)
Δ (Kozhikode (-1))	-0.44	-0.12	-0.89	-0.57
	(2.67)*	(0.73)	(5.66)*	(3.92)*
Δ (Kozhikode (-2))	-0.05	0.01	-0.27	-0.23
	(0.38)	(0.05)	(2.04)**	(1.91)***
Δ (Tellicherry (-1))	0.39	0.15	0.25	0.17
	(1.60)	(0.62)	(1.11)	(0.80)
Δ (Tellicherry (-2))	0.03	-0.07	0.12	0.07
	(0.19)	(0.39)	(0.67)	(0.44)
Constant	21.01	26.12	24.59	22.80
	(0.20)	(0.24)	(0.24)	(0.25)
R^2	0.14	0.11	0.44	0.24
$\bar{R}^2$	0.08	0.05	0.41	0.18
Log likelihood	-1199.01	-1201.89	-1191.98	-1179.86
AIC	17.14	17.19	17.04	16.87
SC	17.35	17.39	17.25	17.08

Note: Parentheses represent t-values
*significant at one per cent level,
**significant at five per cent level, and
*** significant at ten per cent level.

it can be concluded that Alleppey market is dominant among the selected markets of Kerala.

The results of Table 4 reveals that error correction coefficients of all the markets are highly significant with a positive sign; which means that the existence of indirect transmission mechanism of prices from one market to the other during pre-reform period is negligible. Here Alleppey market pepper price directly affects the pepper price of Kozhikode and Tellicherry markets. Pepper price of Kochi market is also able to influence pepper price of Alleppey and Tellicherry markets. In the pre-reform period, Kozhikode market pepper price has influenced only Alleppey market pepper price. Similarly there is a direct pepper price transmission from Tellicherry market to Alleppey and Kozhikode markets.

Table 5 results reveals that error correction coefficient of Tellicherry market are significant with negative sign and the remaining are positive and insignificant, which implies that indirect price transmission is stronger during post-reform period than pre-reform period. The influence of Alleppey and Kochi markets are similar to those in pooled period. In the case of Kozhikode market pepper price, there is a direct transmission of pepper prices to Alleppey and Tellicherry markets. But Tellicherry market pepper price is not able to influence directly the pepper price of any of the other markets. As in pooled period, Alleppey market turned out to be the dominant market during the post-reform period also.

Thus, the results indicate that price transmission between the selected markets of Kerala is comparatively stronger during post-reform period than the pre-reform period. In other words, through economic reforms and trade liberalization, there is greater dissemination of market information among markets; which ultimately lead to well integrated markets and thereby excess price in one pepper market has transmitted into the other. It can also be observed from Table 6 that Alleppey market is the dominant market followed by Kozhikode, Kochi and Tellicherry markets during our period of study.

Alleppey market is not a predominantly pepper producing market, but it is able to decide prices of other markets to a greater extent. The main reason is that Alleppey is the nearest assembling centre to all the southern districts of Kerala and it resulted to an edge over other markets. As far as Kozhikode market is concerned, it is one of the dominant pepper producing districts of Kerala. Besides, Wynad the second largest pepper producing district of Kerala is nearest to the Kozhikode market. These factors are responsible for pepper market of Alleppey to be dominant followed by Kozhikode market.

Table 6
Impact of Price of Pepper Across the Selected Markets (at one lag)

	Pooled period				*Pre-reform period*				*Post reform period*			
Independent ..... →	*Alleppey*	*Kochi*	*Kozhikode*	*Tellicherry*	*Alleppey*	*Kochi*	*Kozhikode*	*Tellicherry*	*Alleppey*	*Kochi*	*Kozhikode*	*Tellicherry*
↓*Dependent Market*												
Alleppey	-	×	√	√	-	√	√	√	-	×	√	×
Kochi	√	-	√	×	×	-	×	×	√	-	×	×
Kozhikode	√	√	-	√	√	×	-	√	√	√	-	×
Tellicherry	√	×	√	-	√	√	×	-	√	×	√	-

Note: √ shows significant price transmission.
× shows insignificant price transmission.

Lesser dominance of Tellicherry in comparison with Alleppey and Kozhikode markets is due to its unique features. Pepper products of Tellicherry market is superior in quality and is ranked as one of the best in international markets (George, 1989). Hence, it is not able to influence other variety of adjacent markets due to peculiar variety of pepper product.

Kochi market is the terminal market and it is not able to make a desired impact like the other selected markets of Kerala. This may be due to the fact that surrounding areas of Kochi market is not dominant in pepper production. Further, Kochi market is a place from where the pepper products of other assembling centres are procured and exported.

SECTION-IV

Concluding Remarks

Dickey-Fuller, Phillips-Perron, Johansen's multiple co integration and Error Correction Models were employed to examine the validity of market integration hypothesis and transmission mechanism of prices between the selected pepper markets of Kerala. The analysis revealed that all the selected pepper markets of Kerala are well integrated and exhibited a long-run relation between the markets during the period of our study. The error correction model result reveals that there is strong transmission mechanism of prices from one market to the other during pooled period. Further, transmission mechanism of prices across the markets is stronger during post-reform period than the pre-reform period. This may be due to the influence of recent economic reforms and liberalisation in dissemination of market information. The present study also revealed that Alleppey is the dominant market followed by Kozhikode, Kochi and Tellicherry markets. Alleppey market is dominant because it is the most accessible assembling centre to the southern districts of Kerala. Dominance of Kozhikode market is due to the fact that it is a highly pepper producing district surrounded by similarly productive areas. Kochi market is primarily exposed to international trade than domestic trade. Hence, it is not as dominant as Alleppey and Kozhikode markets. Tellicherry market is also not able to make much influence like other markets due to its unique quality of pepper.

References

Alexander, Carol and John Wyeth (1994), "Co-integration and Market Integration: An application to the Indonesian Rice Market", *Journal of Development Studies*, Vol. 30, No. 2, pp. 303-328.

Angulo, A. M and J. M. Gil. (1996), "Vertical Integration and Price Transmission in the Spanish Poultry Sector", *World Agricultural Economics and Rural Sociology Abstracts*, Vol. 38, No. 9, p. 709.

Asche, Frank, Helge Bremnes and Cathy R. Wessells (1999), "Product Aggregations, Market Integration and Relationship between Prices: An Application to World Salmon Markets", *American Journal of Agricultural Economics*, Vol. 81, No. 3, pp. 568-581.

Baharumshah, Ahmad Zubaidi and Muzafar Shah Habibullah (1994), "Price Efficiency in Pepper Markets in Malaysia: A Co-integration Analysis", *Indian Journal of Agricultural Economics*, Vol. 49, No. 2, pp. 205-215.

Basu, Jyotish Prakash and Soumyananda Dinda (2003), "Market Integration; An Application of Error Correction Model (ECM) to Potato Market in Hooghly District, West Bengal", *Indian Journal of Agricultural Economics*, Vol. 58, No. 4, pp. 742-751.

Baulch, Bob (1997), "Transfer Costs, Spatial Arbitrage and Testing for Food Market Integration", *American Journal of Agricultural Economics*, Vol. 79, No. 2, pp. 477-487.

Bijman, J.W. (1996), "Biotechnology and Vertical Integration in the Dutch Potato Chain in Economics of Innovation-The Case of Food Industry", *World Agricultural Economics and Rural Sociology Abstracts*, Vol. 38, No. 9, p. 709.

Blyn, George (1973), "Price Series Correlation as a Measure of Market Integration", *Indian Journal of Agricultural Economics*, Vol. 28, No. 2, pp. 56-59.

Carvalho, F.C. De; Marques S.A, Maia M.L and Yoshil R.J. (1994), "Study of Market Integration in Sugar-alcohol Agri-business in the State of Sao Paulo 1970-92. Brazil", *World Agricultural Economics and Rural Sociology Abstracts*, Vol. 36, No. 2, p. 129.

Cheung, Yin-Wong and Kon S. Lai (1993), "Finite Sample Sizes of Johansen's likelihood ratio tests for cointegration", *Oxford Bulletin of Economics and Statistics,* Vol. 55, No. 3, pp. 313-328.

Dahlgran, Roger. A and Steven C. Blank (1992), " Evaluating the Integration of Contiguous Discontinuous Markets", *American Journal of Agricultural Economics,* Vol. 74, No. 2, pp. 469-475.

Delgado, Christopher L. (1986), "A Variance Components Approach to Food Grain Market Integration in Northern Nigeria", *American Journal of Agricultural Economics,* November, pp. 970-979.

Dickey, David A. and Wayne A. Fuller (1979), "Distribution of the Estimators for Autoregressive Time Series with a Unit Root", *Journal of American Statistical Association,* Vol. 74, No. 366, pp. 427-431.

Dickey, David. A and Wayne A. Fuller (1981), "Likelihood Ratio Statistics for Autoregressive Time Series with a Unit Root", *Econometrica,* Vol. 49, No. 4, pp. 1057-1071.

Engle, R.F. and C.W.J. Granger (1987), "Cointegration and Error Correction, Representation, Estimation and Testing", *Econometrica,* Vol. 55, No. 2, pp. 251-276.

Fafchamps, M. and S. Gavian (1996), "The Spatial Integration of Livestock Markets in Niger", *Journal of African Economies,* Vol. 5, No. 3, pp. 366-405.

Fafchamps, Marcel (1972), "Cash Crop Production, Food Price Volatility and Rural Market Integration in the Third World", *American Journal of Agricultural Economics,* Vol. 74, No. 1, pp. 90-99.

Faminow, Merle D and Bruce L. Benson (1990), "Integration of Spatial Markets", *American Journal of Agricultural Economics,* Vol. 72, No. 1, pp. 49-62.

Gadgil, D. R. (1961), "Agricultural Price Policy–A Suitable Basis for Achieving Targets", *Yojana,* September.

George, C. K. (1989), *Spices of India–An Overview, Proceedings of the Workshop on Strategies for Export Development of Spices* (Ed), C. K. George, *et. al.*, Spices Board, Cochin, pp. 1-14.

Gardner, Bruce L. and Karen M. Brooks (1994), "Food Prices and Market Integration in Russia. 1992-93", *American Journal of Agricultural Economics,* Vol. 76, No. 3, pp. 641-646.

Ghatage, M.B. (1958), "Development Work of Agricultural Marketing–Its Scope and Method", *Agricultural Marketing,* Vol. 1, No. 1, p. 3.

Ghosh, Madhusudan (2000), "Co-integration Tests and Spatial Integration of Rice Markets in India", *Indian Journal of Agricultural Economics*, Vol. 55, No. 4, pp. 616-626.

Goodwin, Barry K. and Ted C. Schroeder (1991), "Co-integration Tests and Spatial Price Linkages in Regional Cattle Markets", *American Journal of Agricultural Economics*, Vol. 73, No. 2, pp. 452-464.

Harris, Barbara (1979), "There is Method in My Madness or Is It Vice Versa? Measuring Agricultural Market Performance", *Food Research Institute Studies*, Vol. XVII, No. 2, pp. 197-218.

Hays, H.M and J.H Mc Coy (1978), "Food Grain Marketing in Northern Nigeria; Spatial and Temporal Performance", *The Journal of Development Studies*, Vol. 14, No. 2, pp. 182-192.

Heytens, Paul J. (1986), "Testing market integration", *Food Research Institute Studies*, Vol. XX, No. 1, pp. 25-40.

Ismet, M. Barkley A.P. and Llewelyn R.V. (1999), "Government Intervention and Market Integration in Indonesian Rice Market", *World Agricultural Economics and Rural Sociology Abstracts*, Vol. 41, No. 3, p. 196.

Jasdanwalla, Z.Y. (1966), *Marketing Efficiency in Indian Agriculture*, Allied Publishers Private Limited, New Delhi.

Johansen, S. (1988), "Statistical Analysis of Co integrating Vectors", *Journal of Economic Dynamics and Control*, Vol. 12, pp. 231-254.

Johansen, S. (1991), "Estimation and Hypothesis Testing of Co-integrating Vectors in Gaussian Vector Autoregression Models", *Econometrica*, Vol. 59, pp. 1551-1580.

Johansen, S. and K. Juselius (1990), "Maximum Likelihood Estimation and Inference on Cointegration with Application to the Demand for Money", *Oxford Bulletin of Economics and Statistics*, Vol. 52, pp. 169-210.

Kallfass, H.H. (1993), "Cost Advantages Through Vertical Integration in the Agricultural Sector-Germany", *World Agricultural Economics and Rural Sociology Abstracts*, Vol. 35, No. 9, p. 751.

Kerala State Land Use Board, (1997), Land Resource Based Perspective Plan for 2020 A.D., Vikas Bhavan, Thiruvananthapuram.

Khedhiri, S. (1999), "Empirical Analysis of Agricultural Market Integration in Tunisia", *World Agricultural Economics and Rural Sociology Abstracts*, Vol. 41, No. 11, p. 869.

Lele, Uma J. (1967), "Market Integration: A Study of Sorghum Prices in Western India", *Journal of Farm Economics*, Vol. 49, No. 1, pp. 147-159.

Lele, Uma. J (1971), *Food Grain Marketing in India- Private Performance and Public Policy,* Cornell University Press, Ithaca and London.

Lundahl, Mats and Erling Petersson (1982), "Price Series Correlation and Market Integration: Some Further Evidence", *Indian Journal of Agricultural Economics*, Vol. 37, No. 2, pp. 184-190.

Mathew, M. Thomas, V. Venkitachalam and Sebastian (1997), "Long Run Relationship of Coconut Market in Kerala; A Co-integration", *Agricultural Situation in India*, pp. 777-780.

Monke, Eric and Todd Petzel (1984), "Market Integration: An Application to International Trade in Cotton", *American Journal of Agricultural Economics*, pp. 481-487.

Munir, A., Suresh Waran S., H. Selassie and J. C. Nyankore (1997), "Market Integration in Developing Countries–A Case Study of Selected Vegetables in Indonesian Market", *World Agricultural Economics and Rural Sociology Abstracts*, Vol. 39, No. 12, p. 946.

Naik, Gopal and V. P. S. Arora (1986), "Marketing Pattern and Pricing Efficiency in Indian Arecanut Market", *Indian Journal of Agricultural Economics*, Vol. 41, No. 2, pp. 172-182.

Narasimham, N. V. (1994), *A Model for Commodity Price System Analysis*, Himalaya Publishing House, Bombay.

Nasurudeen, P and S. R. Subramanian (1995), "Price Integration of Oil and Oilseeds", *Indian Journal of Agricultural Economics*, Vol. 50, No. 4, pp. 625-633.

National Family Health Survey (2001), (NFHS-2), India 1998-99–Kerala–International Institute for Population Sciences–Mumbai, India, December.

Padmanabhan, K. (1993), *Economic Analysis of Marketing*, Printwell, Jaipur, India.

Palaskas, Theodosios B. and Barbara Harriss White (1993). "Testing Market Integration: New Approaches with Case Material from the West Bengal Food Economy", *The Journal of Development Studies*, Vol. 30, No. 1, pp. 1-57.

Patnaik, K. Uma Shankar (1988), "A Changing Pattern in the Integration of Groundnut Markets", *Indian Journal of Agricultural Economics*, Vol. 43, No. 4, pp. 631-642.

Phillips, Peter and Pierre Perron (1988), "Testing for a Unit Root in Time Series Regression", *Biometrica*, Vol. 75, pp. 335-346.

Pramod Kumar and R. K. Sharma (2003), "Spatial Price Integration and Pricing Efficiency at the Farm Level: A Study of Paddy in Haryana", *Indian Journal of Agricultural Economics*, Vol. 58, No. 2, pp. 201-217.

Ravallion, Martin (1986), "Testing Market Integration", *American Journal of Agricultural Economics*, Vol. 68, No. 1, pp. 102-109.

Rozelle, Scott, Albert Park, Jikum Huang and Hehui Jin (1997), "Liberalisation and Rural Market Integration in China", *American Journal of Agricultural Economics*, Vol. 79, No. 2, pp. 635-642.

Sarker, Rakhal (1993), "A Maximum Likelihood Cointegration Analysis of Canadian Lumber Exports", *Canadian Journal of Agricultural Economics*, Vol. 41, No. 1, pp. 97-110.

Silvapulle, Param and Sisira Jayasuriya (1994), "Testing for Philippines Rice Market Integration: A Multiple Co-integration", *Journal of Agricultural Economics*, Vol. 45, No. 3, pp. 369-380.

Sorensen, Jan Rose (1993), "Integration of Product Markets and Lower Welfare in An Economy with Centralized Wage Setting", Scottish *Journal of Political Economy*, Vol. 40, No. 3, pp. 323-329.

Thakur, D. S. (1974), "Food Grain Marketing Efficiency: A Case Study of Gujarat", *Indian Journal of Agricultural Economics*, Vol. 29, No. 4, pp. 61-74.

Thakur, D. S. (1998), "Agricultural Marketing Efficiency: Agenda of 21st Century", *The Bihar Journal of Agricultural Marketing*, Vol. VI, No. 2, pp. 133-149.

Zanias, G. P. (1993), "Testing for Integration in European Community Agricultural Product Markets", *Journal of Agricultural Economics*, Vol. 44, No. 3, pp. 418-427.

Zhao, J.W. (1995), "The Development Trends of Integration of Agricultural Production, Processing and Marketing–Chinese Rural Economy", *World Agricultural Economics and Rural Sociology Abstracts*, Vol. 37, No. 2, p. 122.

PART–III

POPULATION, EMIGRATION AND CHILD LABOUR

7

POPULATION AGING

S. Irudaya Rajan & Sabu Aliyar

The sharp increase in numbers of older people and their proportion in relation to the working age population is a worldwide phenomenon, with vast economic and social implications. In India, the process is occurring much faster in the south, as compared to the northern States (Irudaya Rajan 2005). Among the South Indian States, Kerala is unique. As it is demographically ahead of the rest of the country and is in the final stages of the demographic transition (to low fertility and mortality), the ageing scenario of Kerala is much more prominent than in any other State in India (Zachariah and Irudaya Rajan 1997). For instance, a child born today in Kerala is expected to live over 71 years of age. (The female child is expected to live 76 years, six more than her male counterparts). The younger age group, on the other hand, is shrinking. Thus, on an average, a woman in Kerala ends up producing just 1.6 children, which is a below replacement level of fertility. The recently released 2001 census shows that Kerala has more than 10 per cent of its population comprising of elderly. We have to give more attention to ameliorating their conditions.

In Kerala, as in other parts of the country, families have customarily supported elderly persons. With Kerala having undergone the demographic transition, however, the number of caregivers in families has been on the decline. Reduction in family size, national and international job-seeking flows out-migration, and a high work participation rate of women, have contributed to an attenuation of resources for the care of the elderly. At the same time, the increasing presence of older persons in the State is making people of all ages more aware that we live in a diverse and multigenerational society. It is no longer possible to ignore ageing, regardless of whether one views it positively or negatively.

Even when families can support the older generation, they essentially have difficulty in doing so because people above sixty years today live much longer than those of former generations and require care and medical treatment for many more years. Many older persons in Kerala who have worked in the formal sector and who have participated in pension or other income security schemes will be able to economically support themselves in varying degrees during their post retirement years. However, most of them are not covered by any such schemes and earn their livelihood in the informal sector by working even at the age of 80 years. The majority of them are women. They have not been able, for one reason or another, to accumulate sufficient savings to ensure their well being in old age. It is vital that the social safety nets should be extended to cover all elderly persons.

Population Aging: Inter-state Analysis

As of 2001, India accommodates 77 million elderly people, a figure second only to the number of elderly in China. 29 million of India's elderly are above 70 years and 8 million are above 80. Uttar Pradesh led with the highest number of elderly (11 million) followed by Maharashtra (8.5 Million), West Bengal (5.7 million) and Tamil Nadu (5.5 Million). The smallest number of elderly is found in the union territory of Lakshadweep. In terms of the *proportion* of elderly in the population, the low fertility State of Kerala ranks number, with 10.5% of its population comprising of elderly in 2001. Punjab and Himachal occupy the second largest position in terms of percentage of elderly, followed by states of Tamil Nadu (8.9) and Maharashtra (8.7). Dadra Nagar Haveli registered the lowest proportion (4). The percentage of elderly in the 80 years and above category is highest in Himachal Pradesh (1.3 Per cent), followed by Kerala (1.2 Per cent).

India is one of the few countries in the world where males out number females. However, among the elderly, female life chances are higher. Thus, at any age, there are more widows than widowers. Moreover, according to the 2001 census, the sex ratio among Indian elderly of 60 years and above is 1028 females for 1000 males. The trend is in favor of males in the

Table 1
Elderly in India, 2001

		60+		*70+*		*80+*	
Rank	*India/states*	*Population*	*%*	*Population*	*%*	*Population*	*%*
	INDIA	76826245	7.5	29376651	2.9	8060098	0.8
01	Kerala	3338428	10.5	1402678	4.4	389332	1.2
02	Punjab	2200153	9.0	939859	3.9	299106	1.2
03	Himachal Pradesh	548890	9.0	245121	4.0	81152	1.3
04	Tamil Nadu	5545499	8.9	2097100	3.4	557029	0.9
05	Maharashtra	8464895	8.7	3094957	3.2	780039	0.8
06	Goa	112858	8.4	41928	3.1	10969	0.8
07	Pondicherry	81082	8.3	31939	3.3	8223	0.8
08	Orissa	3044221	8.3	1168791	3.2	293770	0.8
09	Uttaranchal	655726	7.7	258515	3.0	70331	0.8
10	Karnataka	4065985	7.7	1611495	3.0	457643	0.9
11	Andhra Pradesh	5798171	7.6	2082435	2.7	505185	0.7
12	Haryana	1590118	7.5	656182	3.1	184587	0.9
13	Tripura	232896	7.3	106606	3.3	35296	1.1
14	Chhattisgarh	1506393	7.2	534077	2.6	135486	0.7
15	West Bengal	5708014	7.1	2275599	2.8	670812	0.8
16	Madhya Pradesh	4292242	7.1	1609752	2.7	436919	0.7
17	Uttar Pradesh	11701369	7.0	4470314	2.7	1273057	0.8
18	Gujarat	3502295	6.9	1310502	2.6	374579	0.7
19	Rajasthan	3829791	6.8	1473636	2.6	394208	0.7
20	Manipur	145775	6.7	61569	2.8	17211	0.8
21	Jammu & Kashmir	678384	6.7	274603	2.7	82415	0.8
22	Bihar	5513117	6.6	2046843	2.5	566871	0.7
23	Lakshadweep	3732	6.2	1288	2.1	381	0.6
24	Jharkhand	1580601	5.9	553844	2.1	148144	0.5

Contd...

		60+		70+		80+	
Rank	India/states	Population	%	Population	%	Population	%
25	Assam	1562062	5.9	601856	2.3	169824	0.6
26	Mizoram	49066	5.5	20108	2.3	5313	0.6
27	Sikkim	29144	5.4	11018	2.0	2716	0.5
28	Delhi	720743	5.2	269146	1.9	70929	0.5
29	Daman & Diu	8045	5.1	2930	1.9	811	0.5
30	Chandigarh	44977	5.0	18170	2.0	5216	0.6
31	Andaman & Nicobar Islands	17478	4.9	6222	1.7	1676	0.5
32	Meghalaya	105870	4.6	39790	1.7	11258	0.5
33	Arunachal Pradesh	49967	4.6	18063	1.6	5655	0.5
34	Nagaland	90540	4.5	37709	1.9	13644	0.7
35	Dadra & Nagar Haveli	8818	4.0	2618	1.2	611	0.3

Source: Based on the 2001 census.

age group of 70 + years, but then, it becomes favourable to females in the population of 80 years and above. Kerala has recorded the highest sex ratio-1247 females per 1000 males. The situation improves further to 1319 among elderly of 70 + years, and 1472 among elderly of 80 years and above (Table 2).

Table 3 shows various indices of population ageing in India. Kerala has registered the highest median age (27.9 years), indicating its status as a forerunner of demographic transition, followed by Goa (27.6 years), Tamil Nadu (27 years) and Pondicherry (26.5 years).

The highest Index of ageing in the country is also reported for Kerala (40.2) followed by Goa (33.9), Tamil Nadu and Pondicherry. This is also true for median ageing and aged dependency ratio.

Aging In Kerala

According to the first census (1961 census) of Kerala state (Kerala state was formed as an independent State in 1956), the number of elderly aged 60 and above was just 10 lakhs. It increased to 26 lakh in 1991 (a 160 per cent increase). According to the latest 2001 Census, Kerala had 33 lakh elderly persons representing around 10.5 per cent of the total population. Their numbers are expected to increase to 57 lakhs in 2021 and 120

Table 2
Sex Ratio among Elderly, 2001 Census

	Sex Ratio (Females per 000 males)		
India/State	60+	70+	80+
India	1028	991	1051
Andaman and Nicobar Islands	766	827	932
Sikkim	772	734	752
Nagaland	780	786	765
Jammu and Kashmir	846	820	837
Bihar	882	827	811
Uttar Pradesh	886	821	830
Arunachal Pradesh	889	892	900
Chandigarh	891	887	953
Assam	949	876	923
Meghalaya	957	991	1050
Delhi	963	925	996
Punjab	971	865	922
Mizorzm	977	1019	1184
Lakshadweep	979	1024	1177
Manipur	986	988	1033
Haryana	991	863	884
Utharanchal	1002	952	984
Jharkhand	1005	945	891
Tamilnadu	1013	977	1040
Himachal Pradesh	1021	997	1027
Orissa	1022	958	892
West Bengal	1047	1032	1093
Tripura	1064	1105	1230
Rajasthan	1084	1108	1261
Madhya Pradesh	1084	1112	1240
Andhra Pradesh	1099	1051	1215
Karnataka	1111	1137	1258
Gujarat	1148	1239	1410
Maharastra	1150	1063	1218
Chhattisgarh	1181	1182	1175
Pondicherry	1222	1239	1249
Daman & Diu	1239	1370	1886
Kerala	1247	1319	1472
Goa	1260	1424	1553
Dadra & Nagar Haveli	1270	1381	1406

Table 3
Indices of Ageing, 2001 Census

State	*Median Age*	*Index of ageing*	*Age Dependency ratio*
Jammu and Kashmir	21.6	18.7	11.6
Himachal Pradesh	24.5	29.1	15.1
Punjab	24.2	28.8	15.2
Chandigarh	24.6	17.2	7.6
Uttaranchal	21.5	21.2	13.8
Haryana	21.8	20.9	13.3
Delhi	23.5	16.0	8.4
Rajasthan	20.1	16.9	12.8
Uttar Pradesh	19.6	17.2	13.6
Bihar	19.5	15.8	13.0
Sikkim	21.6	15.4	9.0
Arunachal Pradesh	19.8	11.3	8.3
Nagaland	20.0	12.4	7.7
Manipur	23.1	20.6	11.1
Mizoram	21.7	15.6	9.3
Tripura	23.3	21.6	12.3
Meghalaya	18.1	10.8	8.6
Assam	21.6	15.7	10.3
West Bengal	24.1	21.4	11.9
Jharkhand	20.6	14.7	10.8
Orissa	24.1	24.9	14.1
Chattisgarh	22.3	19.6	13.0
Madhya Pradesh	21.1	18.4	13.1
Gujarat	23.6	21.0	11.5
Daman and Diu	23.7	18.6	7.5
Dadra and Nagar Haveli	22.3	11.3	6.6
Maharashtra	24.4	27.2	14.8
Andhra Pradesh	24.4	23.7	12.6
Karnataka	24.3	24.1	12.7
Goa	27.6	33.9	12.5
Lakshadweep	23.0	18.0	10.3
Kerala	27.9	40.2	16.5
Tamil Nadu	27.0	33.0	13.9
Pondicherry	26.5	30.8	12.6
Andaman and Nicobar Islands	24.5	16.7	7.5
All India	22.7	21.1	13.1

lakhs in 2061 and the proportion is likely to reach 40 per cent in 2061. While the Kerala population is growing at less than one per cent, the growth of the elderly over the 1991-2001 decade was much faster, and the trend is likely to continue over next few decades. Over 1961-1991, the growth rate among the old old hovered around 3 per cent. It is expected to register a growth rate of around 4 per cent in the coming decades.

Table 4
Demographic Profile of Elderly, 1961-2061

	Number of Aged(millions)			*Percentage total*			*Growth Rate (per cent)*		
Year	*60+*	*70+*	*80+*	*60+*	*70+*	*80+*	*60+*	*70+*	*80+*
1961	0.99	0.36	0.09	5.1	1.9	0.4	-	-	-
1971	1.33	0.50	0.13	6.2	2.3	0.6	3.47	3.66	4.71
1981	1.91	0.71	0.19	7.5	2.8	0.7	4.38	4.35	4.88
1991	2.57	1.00	0.29	8.9	3.4	1.0	3.48	4.06	5.59
2001	3.33	1.40	0.39	10.5	4.4	1.2	2.94	3.99	3.45
2011	4.20	1.94	0.54	12.2	5.6	1.6	2.61	3.86	3.85
2021	5.75	2.46	0.76	16.0	6.8	2.1	3.69	2.68	4.07
2031	7.78	3.52	1.01	21.3	9.7	2.7	3.53	4.31	3.29
2041	9.88	4.86	1.48	27.8	13.7	4.2	2.70	3.81	4.65
2051	11.48	6.22	2.11	34.4	18.6	6.3	1.62	2.80	4.26
2061	11.95	7.18	2.76	39.6	23.8	9.1	0.41	1.54	3.08

Note: Compiled by the authors for the periods 1961-2001 using the Indian censuses. The figures for the years from 2001 to 2061 are extracted from the population projections done by the authors.

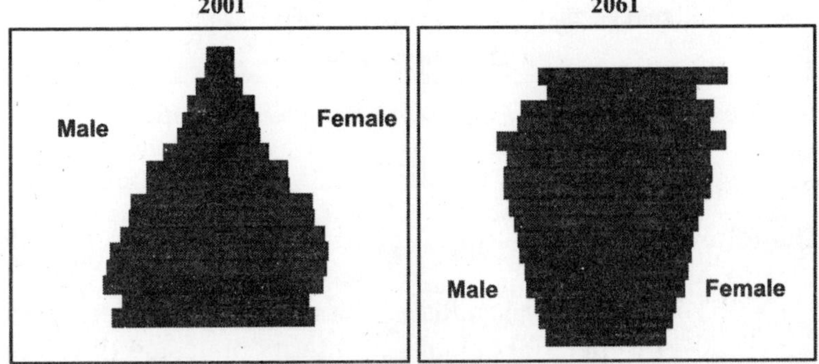

Figure 1: Age Pyramids for Kerala, 2001 and 2061

The number of the oldest old (aged 80 and above) in Kerala was just 290000 in 1991. It is expected to increase to 8 lakh in 2021 and further to 27 lakh by 2061.The growth rates among the oldest old is higher than the young old and old old in Kerala over the last 40 years and it is expected to slow down in the coming decades. The age pyramids for Kerala are presented (2001 and 2061) to indicate the speed of ageing in Kerala. Though the number of elderly in Kerala is much lower as compared to the populous states of India, Kerala leads with the highest proportion of elderly among Indian states and union territories, and has relatively more women as compared to male elderly than in any other State in India. Kerala has the highest female expectation of life at birth and the gender gap was around 6 years in 2000. At age 60, a Malayali woman is expected to live 21 years, as against 19 years in the case of their male counter parts.

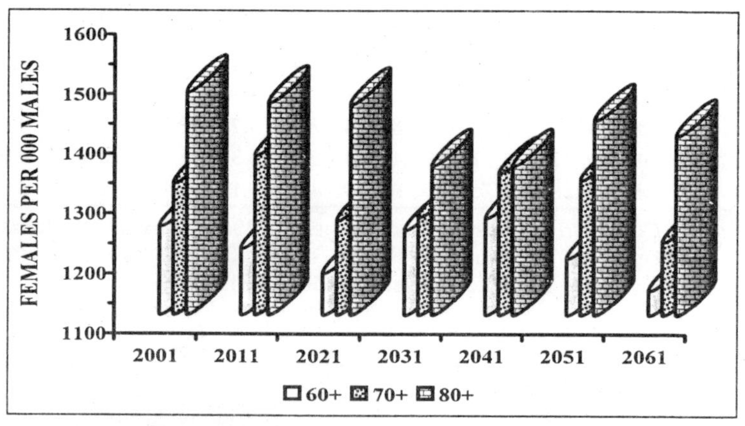

Figure 2: Sex Ratio among Elderly in Kerala 2001-2061

Dependency Ratios

The following ratios are presented for Kerala for the periods 1961 to 2061.

- *Young Dependency Ratio*: The number of persons aged 0-14 to per 100 persons of intermediate age (working age 15-59).

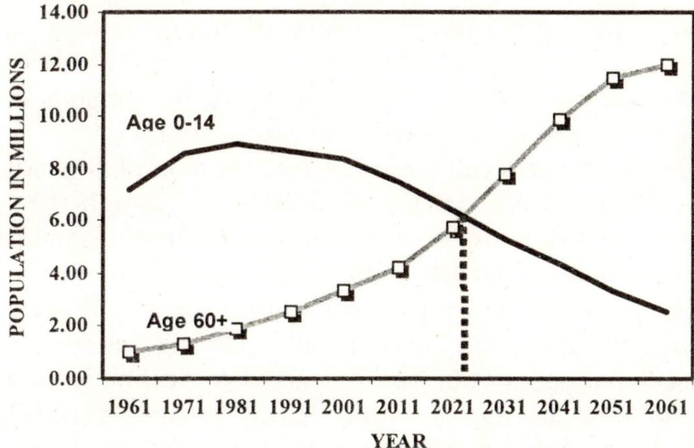

Figure 3: Expected Crossover Between and the Aged in Kerala

- *Aged Dependency Ratio*: The number of persons aged 60 years and above per 100 persons of working age (15-59)
- *Total Dependency Ratio*: The number of persons in the non-working age group (0-14 and 60+) to per 100 persons of working age (15-59)
- *Index of Ageing*: The proposition of the population aged sixty and above to the population aged 0-14. It is intended to measure the structure of dependency.
- *Index of children*: The population of aged 0-14 per 100 to population aged 60 years and above.
- *Index of parents to children*: The population aged 60-74 per 100 to population aged 40-44.
- *Index of oldest old to young old*: The population aged 80 years above per 100 to population aged 60-64.

The Young Dependency Ratio, 82.7 in 1961, declined to 75.2 in 1971, 61.5 in 1981 and 49.9 in 1991, whereas the aged dependency ratio increased from 11.3 in 1961 to 11.6 in 1971, further to 13.2 in 1981 and 14.4 in 1991 respectively. The increase of the aged dependency ratio was by 3 points whereas the decrease in the child dependency ratio was by 23 points. At the present juncture, households in Kerala have gained in terms of reduced burden of dependents, having to take care of fewer children without having too much strain of having to care for elderly persons. Currently, every 100 persons in the working age group take care of 17 old people.

The decline in fertility has reduced the overall dependency burden from 94.0 in 1961 to 64.3 in 1991. Though the aged dependency ratios are on the increase, the overall dependency ratio has shown a decline of 30 points during 1961-91.

The projected age dependency ratios for the period 2001-2061 are also shown in the same table. During this period, the young dependency ratios are expected to decline from 41 in 2001 to 16 in 2061. On the other hand, the aged dependency ratios are expected to increase from 17 in 2001 to 76 in 2061. The implications of these ratios for the future is that instead of every six working age persons there would be only two working persons in 2061 who will have to share the responsibility of taking care of at least one aged person. More over, the probability of this aged person being a woman, who is a widow, less skilled, less educated and not working, non-recipient of social security allowance, unhealthy without health insurance, is also much higher.

Table 5
Dependency Rations, Aging Index and Familiar Dependency Ratios for Kerala, 1961-2061

	Dependency ratio				*Familial dependency ratio*		
Year	*Young*	*Old*	*Total*	*index of aging*	*0-14/60+*	*60-74/40-44*	*80+/60-64*
1961	82.7	11.3	94.0	13.7	731	105	23
1971	75.2	11.6	86.9	15.5	647	107	26
1981	61.5	13.2	74.7	21.6	466	134	27
1991	49.9	14.4	64.3	28.9	370	136	33
2001	41.1	16.5	57.6	40.1	250	130	38
2011	32.8	18.4	51.2	56.1	178	123	42
2021	26.6	24.0	50.6	90.4	111	148	44
2031	22.8	33.3	56.1	146.2	68	194	45
2041	20.3	46.3	66.6	228.2	44	255	55
2051	18.1	61.9	80.0	342.7	29	332	78
2061	16.0	76.1	92.0	476.1	21	377	109

Note: All ratios refer to 100.

The index of ageing, nearly 14 in 1961, increased to 15 in 1971 and 29 in 1991. We can also see from the table that the increase between 1961 and 1971 was by only 2 points, whereas this increase was 6 points between 1971 and 1981 and another 7 points between 1981 and 1991 indicating the acceleration of the ageing process in Kerala. Our projections indicate that the ageing index for the year 2041 will be 228, 5 times higher than 2001 value of 40. This simply means that in Kerala, the rate of increase among elderly persons will be much higher. In 2061, there is likely to be 476 elderly persons for every 100 children in Kerala.

In other words, in the future, every household in Kerala has to take care of one child and an aged mother or father or both. The implications of this to the family would be quite substantial as the cost and care of an older person is different from that of a child.[1] For society, this shift in the dependency structure will mean a substantial change in the type of public sector expenditure. Furthermore, while the care of the child is the direct responsibility of the parents, the care of the extreme elderly has only a social obligation without any legal sanction.

Migration Surveys, 1999 and 2004

The Centre for Development Studies completed two migration surveys in Kerala in 1999 and 2004, covering 10,000 households throughout the State (Zachariah, Mathew and Irudaya Rajan, 2003; Zachariah and Irudaya Rajan, 2004). We have extensively tabulated raw data from this source for this paper so as to assess the various issues pertaining to the elderly.

In 1999, around 58 per cent of households in Kerala did not have any elderly persons. The number declined further to 52 per cent in 2004–a decline of six percentage points–indicating a changing household atmosphere, due to which the elderly do not stay with other members of the family. As almost half of the households in Kerala have no elderly persons to live with, they do not understand the advantages and disadvantages of elderly persons living with them. Another 33 per cent of households in Kerala accommodate just one elderly–either a widow or widower of either from the husband's or wife's side. Two elderly living in the same households have gone up from 11 per cent to 14 per cent, indicating an increase in the life expectancy among elderly males and females. Almost one in six couples in Kerala live beyond sixty as couples without losing their partners. Households with more than three elderly formed less than one per cent in 2004.

Table 6
Distribution of Households by the Number of Elderly, 1999 and 2004

No of elderly	*2004*	*1999*
Nil	51.46	58.00
One	33.47	31.00
Two	14.19	10.50
Three	0.76	0.50
Four	0.12	0.00

Note: Special Tabulations from the Kerala Migration Survey and South Asian Migration Surveys.

To understand the district profile, we have tabulated the proportion of elderly in all districts of Kerala for the years 1999 and 2004, from the migration surveys. The results are presented in Table 7. Between 1999 and 2004, the proportion of elderly to the total population in Kerala has increased from 11 to 14 in the last five years. Among the districts of Kerala, in 2004, the highest proportion of elderly is found in Pathanamthitta followed by Kottayam. Ernakulam and Alappuzha and Thiruvananthapuram districts were above the State average. The lowest proportion was found in Wayanad. However, 12 out of 14 districts in Kerala have already crossed 10 per cent mark, with Pathanamthitta district showing the maximum of 21 per cent-double than the Malappuram figure. Districts which were the forerunners in the fertility and mortality transition, have reported higher proportion of elderly. (Guilmoto and Irudaya Rajan, 2001; 2002; 2005). In 2004, almost all the districts of Kerala have reported more proportion of female elderly in the population than males, except 3 districts of Kollam, Idukki and Malappuram. Hence, any social policy measures to enhance the welfare of the elderly should take note of this phenomenon.

Table 7
District-wise Proportion of Elderly Population in Kerala, 1999 and 2004

	1999			*2004*		
Districts	*Male*	*Female*	*Total*	*Male*	*Female*	*Total*
Thiruvananthapuram	10.60	11.10	10.90	13.62	13.92	13.77
Kollam	10.70	12.00	11.40	13.21	12.27	12.73
Pathanamthitta	17.50	13.60	15.50	20.48	21.21	20.86
Alappuzha	13.90	13.10	13.40	14.29	15.60	14.97
Kottayam	12.80	12.60	12.70	17.30	19.34	18.32
Idukki	8.90	6.10	7.60	11.43	9.47	10.47
Ernakulum	12.00	13.30	12.70	15.01	16.31	15.67
Thrissur	10.50	12.00	11.30	12.25	13.89	13.11
Palakkad	11.70	11.30	11.50	12.57	14.27	13.47
Malappuram	7.90	7.70	7.70	9.64	9.58	9.61
Kozhikode	10.00	11.00	10.50	13.15	13.07	13.11
Wayanad	7.40	7.60	7.50	8.57	10.14	9.38
Kannur	8.70	10.20	9.40	12.06	13.60	12.87
Kasargode	8.00	8.60	8.30	10.51	10.53	10.52
Kerala	10.70	11.00	10.90	13.17	13.85	13.52

Note: Special Tabulations from the Kerala Migration Survey and South Asian Migration Surveys.

Among the elderly in Kerala, close to 56 per cent belong to young old (60-69 years). Another 31 per cent are old old (70-79 years) and only 13 per cent are oldest old (80 and above). Among the elderly, there are more females than males (Gulati and Irudaya Rajan, 1999). The sex ratio (males per 1000 females) of all the elderly age groups indicates the preponderance of women among elderly. In the age group 85 and above, there are 647 males for 1000 females. Most of the women lose their husbands in old age due to sex differentials in mortality and age differentials at the time of marriage. This is reflected among the sex ratios of the widowed. All these dimensions of widowhood among the aged should be considered very seriously when formulating economic and social security measures.

The majority of the men (86 per cent) were married; but among women, the majority (56 per cent) came under the 'widowed' category. Similarly, close to 5 per cent of women were reported as either single or divorced or separated as against 2.5 per cent among men. Women require more social

Table 8
Age Structure of Elderly in Kerala, 2004

Age	*Male*	*Female*	*Total*	*Sex Ratio M/F*1000*
60-64	30.44	31.02	30.75	869
65-69	25.24	25.86	25.57	865
70-74	19.45	17.67	18.50	975
75-79	12.60	12.13	12.35	921
80-84	7.86	7.29	7.56	956
85 +	4.17	5.61	4.94	647

Note: Special Tabulations from the South Asian Migration Surveys.

and economic attention in old age as most of them have no property or assets in their name. In an earlier study, around 60 per cent of rural and urban elderly females and 30 per cent of rural and urban males in India had no valuable assets in their name. Among the major States in India, Kerala ranks first in this regard, with 76 per cent of its elderly women reporting no financial assets in their name (Irudaya Rajan, 2004)

Table 9
Marital Status of the Elderly in Kerala 2004

	2004		
Marital status	*Male*	*Female*	*Total*
Single	2.0	3.1	2.6
Married	85.9	39.4	61.2
Widowed	11.5	55.9	35.1
Divorced/Separated	0.4	1.4	1.0

Note: Special Tabulations from the Kerala Migration Surveys.

We have also analysed the status of current co-residence arrangements among the Kerala elderly by sex as of 2004. Interestingly, in both Kerala and India, 2.5 per cent of elderly live alone in their respective households (Irudaya Rajan and Sanjay Kumar, 2003). 4 per cent of them are females and most likely, all of them are widows. Another 8 per cent of elderly live with their spouses. Three-fourth of elderly males live with their spouses, children and grand children compared to 50 per cent in the case of females. On the other hand, almost 40 per cent of females live in Kerala without spouses but with their children and grand children as against just 11 per cent in the case of males. Elderly living with strangers or non-relatives in a household is not common in Kerala. The number of old age homes in Kerala is 134, one-fifth of India's number. Currently, at least 5 old age homes are coming up every year. The number of inmates reported in the survey was 5076 persons, of which 60 per cent are females (Irudaya Rajan 2002).

Table 10
Living Arrangements Among Elderly in Kerala, 2004

Living arrangement	*Male*	*Female*	*Total*
Living Alone	0.95	3.94	2.54
With Spouse Alone	10.56	5.07	7.65
With spouse, children and grand children	76.11	50.51	62.54
Without spouse but with children, grand children	11.42	38.47	25.76
Without spouse, but with relatives other than children and grand children	0.79	1.87	1.36
With non relatives	0.17	0.15	0.16
Total	100	100	100

Note: Special Tabulations from the Kerala Migration Surveys.

Social Security

Kerala has made remarkable progress in its demographic transition. The State has achieved below replacement level of fertility two decades ahead of the all-India target year of 2011. The TFR (Total fertility rate denotes the average number of children that would be born to a woman during her life time, if she passes through her child bearing years confirming the current age specific fertility rates) declined from a high level of 5.6 in 1951-61 to about 1.7 in 1993, a level which is very much below the replacement level of 2.05. The population growth rate has declined to about 1 per cent per annum in 1995 from 2.3 per cent per year during 1961-71. Among all the States of India, longevity is highest in Kerala, for both men and women. (Zachariah and Irudaya Rajan 1997; Irudaya Rajan and Zachariah, 1998). While Kerala has the unique distinction of being the first State in India to complete the demographic transition, one of the immediate consequences has been population aging. In this context, let us briefly assess the social security programs in Kerala.

Successive governments in Kerala have introduced 35 social security and assistance schemes, which are currently being implemented. Among the southern states, Kerala spends close to 3 per cent of its budget for social security programs and the neighboring states of Tamil Nadu and Karnataka, the expenditure ranges between 2.3 and 2.5. Brief details about each scheme such as eligibility criteria, year of introduction, and annual expenditure incurred are given elsewhere (Irudaya Rajan, Mishra and Sarma, 1999). The schemes are classified into four categories and we shall list the programs meant for elderly.

A. *Schemes which are fully financed by the state and central governments:*

   National Old Age Pension

B. *Schemes Which Are Fully Financed By The State:*

   Kerala Destitute and Widow Pension Scheme

   Kerala Agricultural Workers Pension Scheme

   Special Pension Scheme for the physically handicapped and mentally retarded

   Old age pension to craftsmen

   Pension to sportsmen in Indigent Circumstances

   Pension to Journalists in Indigent Circumstances

   Pension to Cine Artists in indigent Circumstances

   Pension to Freedom Fighters

   Pension to Second World War Veterans

C. *Major schemes which are financed with partial state support*

   Kerala Coir Workers' Welfare Fund

   Kerala Construction Workers' Welfare Fund

   Kerala Fishermen' Welfare Fund

D. *Schemes which are financed outside the budget and operated by respective boards*

   Kerala Headload Workers' Welfare Fund

   Kerala Abkari Workers' Welfare Fund Scheme

Kerala Toddy Workers' Welfare Fund

Kerala Agricultural Workers' Welfare Fund

Among the programs, the highest number of beneficiaries is reported for agricultural worker pension (5.3 lakh), followed by widow/destitute pension (2.1 lakh), pension for persons with disabilities (1.5 lakh) and national old age pensions (1.4 lakh) (details see Table 11). In total, close to 12 lakhs elderly persons are receiving some financial assistance from the Kerala government. Do they get the money regularly? Is it enough for sustaining the livelihood? We have to do more field level research on this subject. In this paper, we would like to document the agricultural worker pension scheme in detail.

Table 10a

Social Assistance and Security Program Beneficiaries in Kerala, 2003

Schemes	*Beneficiaries*
National Old Age pension	134600
Agricultural Workers	527647
Widow/Destitute Pension Scheme	208445
Special pension for persons with disabilities	148553
Building and construction workers	37969
Second World War Veterans	5690
Handloom workers	7407
Tailoring workers	5450
Pension to Journalists	398
Pension to Toddy Workers	14929
Coir Workers	67000
Fishermen	28190
Ration Dealers	252
Abkari Workers	97
Cine artists	146
Khadi workers	17
Freedom fighters	8888
Kerala	1195678

Source: Compiled from the latest economic review published from the state planning board, Government of Kerala, Thiruvananthapuram.

The district level profiles of beneficiaries for the three major pension schemes are presented in Table 11. The highest number of agricultural pension beneficiaries is reported for Thiruvananthapuram, followed by Alappuzha and Kozhikode.

On the other hand, Malappuram leads with the highest number of widow/destitute pension beneficiaries, followed by Kollam and Kozhikode. In terms of national old age pension schemes, Palakkad leads with the highest, followed by Kollam and Malappuram. Is there any link between the number of elderly persons and the number of beneficiaries? It calls for further investigation.

Table 11
Major Pension Scheme Beneficiaries in Kerala by Districts, 2003

District	*Agricultural workers*	*Widow/ Destitute pension*	*Nationalold age pension*
Thiruvananthapuram	91024	26484	9292
Kollam	33077	28133	15971
Pathanamthitta	17933	6636	3641
Alappuzha	68500	13969	7569
Kottayam	33560	10770	8890
Idukki	7979	2792	3930
Ernakulum	33870	16426	13994
Thrissur	50650	19143	11708
Palakkad	57154	19593	18748
Malappuram	52846	29345	15175
Kozhikode	62085	27290	9454
Wayanad	11843	4475	1448
Kannur	42908	15195	9171
Kasargode	15635	10131	5609
Kerala	527647	208445	134600

Agricultural Workers Pension Scheme

One of the major social assistance schemes implemented in Kerala is the Kerala Agricultural Workers Pension Scheme which came into existence in 1980 (for more details, see Gulati, 1990; Irudaya Rajan, 1999). The pension amount was originally fixed at Rs. 45; it was raised to Rs. 60 in 1987, to Rs. 70 in 1991 and again to Rs.100 in 1996. According to the provisions of the scheme, the beneficiaries should be agricultural workers above the age of 60 and whose annual income does not exceed Rs. 11000 (State Planning Board, 2004). An agricultural worker is defined as workers, other than those covered by plantation labour Act, depending principally on agricultural wages for livelihood and residing within the state for a continuous period of at least 10 years, immediately preceding the date of application. Agricultural workers with physical infirmity are also eligible for pension. The State Labour Commissioner is the administrator of the scheme. The amount is payable once in three months, in January, April, July and October by money order.

In 1999, 3.1 lakh persons had benefited by the scheme, of which, 58 per cent were women. Kerala had 19.47 lakh agricultural labourers and the scheme covered 16 per cent of them. The expenditure on this pension scheme increased sharply from Rs. 1615 lakhs in 1986-87 to Rs. 2690 lakhs in 1991 and to Rs. 3720 lakhs in 1999 (Table 12). The increase was due to increases in the coverage of workers and the upward revision of the rates effected in 1988 and 1991.

Table 12
Agricultural Workers Pension Scheme Beneficiaries and Its Expenditure, 1980-81 to 1999-2000

Year	*Beneficiaries*	*Expenditure (in lakhs)*
1980-81	293778	1092.3
1981-82	172376	744.2
1982-83	139817	446.0
1983-84	217659	1188.0
1984-85	250116	1132.0
1985-86	277821	1801.0
1986-87	261584	1615.0
1987-88	286733	1469.5
1988-89	299758	1925.7
1989-90	308346	2197.1
1990-91	316509	3062.3
1991-92	344301	2515.8
1992-93	340776	2690.3
1993-94	345650	3551.0
1994-95	344946	2000.0
1995-96	312944	3457.3
1996-97	312944	3457.3
1997-98	300784	4301.0
1998-99	304638	3720.0
99-2000	436452	NA

Source: Various (annual) issues of Economic Review, the State Planning Board, Government of Kerala, Thiruvananthapuram.

Concluding Observations

Can Kerala afford to provide social security or assistance or financial security for the growing number of elderly? Let us assess it with facts and figures. According to the 2001 census, the number of elderly in Kerala in 2001 was 33 lakhs. Kerala has approximately 4 lakh pensioners (retired from the Kerala government services plus retired from other state governments outside Kerala and returned to Kerala after retirement plus the military, railways, post and telegraph pensioners). In other words, close to 15 per cent of the elderly in Kerala are the creamy layers of the senior citizens. They are not looking for any assistance from the Kerala government.

The work participation rates among elderly based on the NSS 1999-2000 round was around 50 per cent for elderly in Kerala. One has to view these trends in work participation rates in the context of widespread of poverty and inadequate social security system. In Kerala, even at the age of 80, 10 per cent of elderly continue to work. As long as they work, theoretically, they do not look for free money from the Government.

Two other important observations also can be made in this context. The absolute number of children has come down in Kerala and it has already led the Kerala government to close uneconomic schools. It simply means that the government can divert some money from primary education to social security.

Similarly, the fertility levels in Kerala are too low and according to our own predications, it will however around 1.5 children per woman. Recent studies indicated that more than 70 per cent of women in Kerala are protected by various family planning methods and 80 per cent of them are sterilized. What is the role of the family planning programme in Kerala in the future? If this is the ground situation in Kerala, the government can also divert some money from family planning to social security.

According to the latest economic review, around 12 lakhs elderly are beneficiaries of various social security and assistance schemes in Kerala. They account for 40 per cent of the elderly population. Not even a single systematic study exists in Kerala to assess the real beneficiaries.

If the government can implement all the schemes very seriously and provide assistance to the real needy among elderly (the senior author filed observations indicate starvation among Kerala elderly), Kerala can continue to run the social assistance schemes without much financial constraints. The budget for social welfare can be increased by diverting money from family planning and primary education. We hope that the government thorough panchayat level institutions will be able not only to identify the needy (real) beneficiaries but also enhance the financial assistance from the current level of Rs. 110 to Rs. 300 per month (Incidentally, West Bengal pays Rs. 300 as old age pension). For this, a bold step in the right direction is needed.

Note

1. In a recent discussion with a group of elderly in an institutional set up, an elderly couple remarked to the senior author: 'We want to stay with our children and grand children but they are not interested in us, hence we stay alone, and ourselves manage our day to day affairs'.

References

Christophe Z. Guilmoto and S. Irudaya Rajan (2001), Spatial Patterns of Fertility Transition in Indian Districts. *Population and Development Review*, Volume 27, No. 4, p. 713-138.

Christophe Z. Guilmoto and S. Irudaya Rajan (2005), *Fertility Transition in South India*. Sage Publications, New Delhi.

Gulati Leela (1990), Agricultural Worker's Pension in Kerala: An Experiment In Social Assistance. *Economic and Political Weekly*, Vol. XXV, No. 6, pp. 339-344.

Irudaya Rajan, S. and K. C. Zachariah (1998), Long Term Implications of Low Fertility in Kerala. *Asia-Pacific Population Journal*, Volume 13, No. 4, p. 41-66.

Irudaya Rajan, S. and Sabu Aliyar (2004), Demographic Change in Kerala in the 1990s and Beyond In B. A. Prakash (ed). Kerala's Economic Development: Performance and Problems in the Post-Liberalization Period. Sage Publications, New Delhi.

Irudaya Rajan, S. and Sabu Aliyar (2004), Gender, Ageing and Social Security. SAMYUKTA, *Journal of Women's Studies*, Volume IV, Number 2, July.

Irudaya Rajan, S. and Sabu Aliyar (2005), Fertility Change in Kerala. In Christophe Z. Guilmoto and S. Irudaya Rajan (eds). *Fertility Transition in South India*. Sage Publications, New Delhi. (forthcoming).

Irudaya Rajan, S., U. S. Mishra and P. S. Sarma (1995), An Agenda for National Policies on Aging in India. *Research and Development Journal, Journal of Helpage India*, Volume 1, No. 2, p. 38-53.

Irudaya Rajan, S., U. S. Mishra and P. S. Sarma (1999), India's *Elderly: Burden or Challenge?* Sage Publications. New Delhi/Thousand Oaks/London.

Irudaya Rajan, S. (1989), Aging in Kerala: One More Population Problem? *Asia-Pacific Population Journal*, Vol. 4, No. 2, June, p. 19 48.

Irudaya Rajan, S. (2002), Home Away from Home: A Survey of Oldage Homes and Inmates from Kerala, India. *Journal of Housing for the Elderly*, Volume 16, No. 1 and 2, Pp. 125-150.

Irudaya Rajan, S. (2002), Social Security for the Unorganized Sector in South Asia. *International Social Security Review*, Volume 55, No. 4, Pp. 143-156.

Irudaya Rajan, S. (2004), Chronic Poverty among Indian Elderly. Chronic Poverty Research Centre and Indian Institute of Public Administration Working Paper 17, Indian Institute of Public Administration, New Delhi.

Irudaya Rajan S. and Sanjay Kumar (2003), Living Arrangements among the Indian Elderly: New Evidence from the National Family Health Survey. *Economic and Political Weekly*, Volume XXXVIII, No. 1, January 4, pp. 75-80.

Irudaya Rajan, S. (2001), Social Assistance for Poor Elderly: How Effective? *Economic and Political Weekly*, Volume XXXVI, No. 8, February 24, pp. 613-617.

Jhabvala Renana and R. K. A. Subrahmanya (eds). (2000), *The Unorganized Sector: Work Security and Social Protection*. Sage Publications, New Delhi.

Leela Gulati and S Irudaya Rajan (1999), The Added Years: Elderly in India and Kerala, *Economic and Political Weekly*, Volume XXXIV, No. 44, WS-46-51.

Phoebe S. Liebig and S. Irudaya Rajan (eds) (2003), *An Aging India: Perspectives, Prospects, and Policies*. The Haworth Press Inc, New York. United States of America.

Robert J. Palacios and S. Irudaya Rajan (2004), *Safety Nets for the Elderly in Poor Countries:* The Case of Nepal. World Bank Pension Primer Working Paper No. 44.

State Planning Board, Trivandrum (1996), *Social Security Initia-tives in Kerala*. Report of the Expert Committee. Government of Kerala.

Zachariah, K. C. and S. Irudaya Rajan (eds.) (1997), *Kerala's Demographic Transition: Determinants and Consequences*. Sage Publications, New Delhi/Thousand Oaks/London.

Zachariah, K. C. and S. Irudaya Rajan (2004a), *Gulf Revisited. Economic Consequences of Emigration from Kerala–Emigration and Unemployment*. Centre for Development Studies, Thiruvananthapuram.

Zachariah, K. C. and S. Irudaya Rajan (2004b), Malayali Emigration Moving in to a Higher Orbit. *Passline*. Volume 8, No. 7.

Zachariah, K. C., E. T. Mathew and S. Irudaya Rajan (2003), *Dynamics of Migration in Kerala: Determinants, Differentials and Consequences*, Orient Longman Private Limited.

DIMENSIONS OF EMIGRATION FROM KERALA TO THE GULF COUNTRIES

P. V. Nafeesathul Misiriya

Introduction

According to the United Nations Multilingual Demographic Dictionary, migration is a form of geographical mobility between one geographical unit and another and normally involves a change of residence from the place of origin to the place of destination. Therefore, a movement of people from one place to another permanently or semi-permanently is called Migration. In other words, migration is a process of changing an individual's normal place of habitation primarily for solving his economic problems. However, migration may also be influenced by social, cultural, political and physical factors and will result in cultural transmission and demographic changes. The movement of people from one place to another may be internal or international and the impact of internal migration is limited within the country whereas international migration has its impact on the world population. Emigration is not a new phenomenon for India as large number of Indian labourers mainly Muslims, Thiyyas, Cherumas and a small number of Nairs were recruited from India as indentured labour and exported to different parts of the world like Sri Lanka, Burma, Malaysia, Mauritius, the West Indies and South Africa as plantation workers. During the Colonial period, even though such recruitment was done from almost all the regions, Kerala's contribution to this was very significant. This type of emigration of unskilled indentured labour came to an end with the outbreak of the 1st World War. Emigration continued after the end of the War, but on a much smaller scale. But this type of emigration stopped completely when India won independence.

After independence, there were large-scale emigration of skilled, semi-skilled and unskilled manpower mainly to the Gulf countries like the U.A.E, Saudi Arabia, Oman, Kuwait, Qatar and Bahrain etc. The emigration to the Gulf countries acquired massive dimensions since 1973, consequent on the ever-increasing demand for labour of all categories in the Gulf countries to meet their construction activities following the oil hike. In this emigration process from India to the Gulf countries, Kerala held a special status and accounted for 63 per cent of the total emigrants from India in 1977. Kerala's privileged position in the emigration from India is due to the experience, which Kerala already had, in international migration. Among the Kerala emigrants to the Gulf, bulk of them is Muslims. There are many factors behind the domination of Muslims in the emigration from Kerala. Muslims traditionally were a trading community and they had experience in international migration. More over, domination of gulf countries by Arab Muslims who have a definite preference for Muslims and the matrimonial contacts of Kerala Muslims with the Gulf countries all have resulted in the domination of Muslims among the emigrants from Kerala.

Emigration has made a significant change in the life of the people in Kerala especially since the end of 1970's. Economists, philosophers, sociologists and others have studied the various dimensions of foreign remittances into Kerala. Some of the earlier studies (Prakash 1978; Mathew and Gopinathan Nair 1978; Radhakrishnan and Ibrahim 1981; Economic and

Commerce Research Bureau 1982) have analysed the causes of emigration, the socio-economic background of emigrants and the impact of remittances on households apart from analysing the problems of return emigrants. A few studies have analysed the impact of male emigration on women and family and on society (Leela Gulathi 1983; 1987) while some other studies analysed the impact of emigration on the economy as a whole (Gopinathan Nair 1989; Thomas Isaac 1993; Prakash 1998; Rudy Rajan *et al* 2001). Zachariah *et al* studied the causes and problems of return emigrants such as the causes of return, socio-economic background of returnees and the problems faced by them etc. The study by Zachariah *et al* (2002) provides important information about labour market situation and employment, wages and working conditions of emigrants in the Gulf countries. A recent study (Zachaiah and Irudaya Rajan, 2004) found that emigration has been beneficial to the society in general and has resulted in reducing Kerala's high unemployment rate.

Objectives of the Study

The important objectives of the study are:

(1) To examine the causes, trends and socio-economic characteristics of the emigrants from Kerala;

(2) To evaluate the impact of emigration on the State economy and; and

(3) To examine the causes, magnitude and problems of return emigrants.

Data Sources

The study is based on secondary data collected from published and unpublished sources like reports, journals, agencies and institutions.

Concepts of Migration

There are various concepts of migration and the most important and widely used concepts are Internal Migration, In-migration and Out-migration, International migration,

Migration streams, Return emigration and Replacement migration. We may briefly explain these concepts.

Internal Migration

The term internal migration denotes the movement of persons with in a country, which involves a change of usual residence and taking up of life in a new or different place. However, the causal movements such as commuting to and from the place of work, shopping, visiting, and travelling for business or for pleasure etc. are not considered as internal migration. Similarly, movements of nomads or such population groups that have no fixed place of residence, or the seasonal movements of persons who have two or more places of residence during a year are also not considered as internal migration.

In-migration and Out-migration

Although, both of these terms are related to internal migration, in-migration is movement into a particular area whereas out-migration is movement out of a particular area. For example, migrants who come from Tamil Nadu to Kerala are in-migrants for Kerala whereas it is out-migration for Tamil Nadu.

International Migration

The term international migration is used to refer the movement of people from one country to another country.

Immigration and Emigration

Immigration and Emigration are related to international migration. However, Immigration means movement of people into a particular country, while emigration means movement of people from a particular country. Thus migrants leaving India to settle down in London are immigrants to London whereas they are emigrants to India.

Migration Streams

The term migration streams denote the total number of moves made during a given migration interval which have a common area of origin and destination.

Return Emigration

The term return emigrants denote the emigrants who are forced to return to the home country due to termination or cancellation of work contract or due to some other reasons like difficulties in working or living conditions.

Replacement Migration

The term replacement migration denotes the internal migration to compensate emigration from a particular region. For example emigration from Kerala to the Gulf have converted Kerala itself into a *Gulf* by migrating a large number of workers into Kerala from other parts of India especially from neighbouring Tamil Nadu.

Classification of Migrants

There are two broad classifications of migrants and they are by Bilsborrow and International Labour Organisation. Bilsborrow classified migrants in to the following five categories;

1. Foreigners admitted for special purposes– e.g. foreign students, foreign trainees and foreign retirees.
2. Settlers-People who are granted the right to stay indefinitely in the territory of a country other than their own and to enjoy the same social and economic rights as those of the citizens of that country.
3. Migrant Workers-People who are admitted by a country other than their own for the explicit purpose of carrying out an economic activity. It includes seasonal migrant workers, project-tied migrant workers; contract migrant workers and temporary migrant workers.
4. Economic Migrants–This category of people includes business travellers and immigrating investors.
5. Asylum Migrants–The asylum migrants covers the whole spectrum of international movements caused by persecution and conflict. Thus this category includes refugees, persons admitted for humanitarian reasons, asylum workers, persons granted temporary

protected status and persons granted stay of deportation.

International Labour Organisation has classified migrants into two categories and they are settlement migrants (brain drain) and contract migrants (block visa migration or project-tied migration). Settlement migration is migration of people from one country to another so as to secure a job and then settles there. Under contract migration a number or a group of foreign workers would be admitted to a country for the purpose of employment under a single authorization or on behalf of a single employer.

The rest of the paper is in five sections. Section I is about causes and trends of emigration from Kerala and Section II discusses the socio-economic characteristics of emigrants. Section III analyses the impact of emigration on Kerala economy while Section IV examines the return emigration followed by Conclusion (Section V).

SECTION-I

Causes and Trends of Emigration

Causes of Emigration

There are many reasons behind the massive movement of workers from Kerala to the Gulf countries especially since mid 1970's. However, theoretical literature emphasizes two types of factors viz., push factors and pull factors. Both of these factors together produced a favourable atmosphere for the out flow of workers from Kerala to the Gulf.

Push Factors

Push factors are those conditions in the home country, which encouraged people to move out of their country. There are several such factors in Kerala, which push out job seekers to the Gulf countries. High density of population, low and declining work participation rate, high rate of unemployment - both educated and uneducated, stagnant agriculture and backward Industrial sector, low percapita domestic product compared to all-India average are some of the push factors which pressed Keralites to emigrate to the Gulf countries.

Pull Factors

Pull factors are those conditions in the host country, which attract people in to those countries. The structural changes that occurred due to oil boom in Gulf region provided new opportunities for gainful employment, better income and better future prospects etc are some of the pull factors which motivated Keralites to the Gulf countries.

Apart from these push and pull factors, the historical experience of Keralites in international migration, the religious, marital and trade links of the Muslims of Kerala for several centuries with the Gulf region and the relatively high levels of literacy and education of Keralites are the other important factors in the large scale emigration of Keralites to the Gulf countries

Emigration Trends in Kerala

There were many attempts by institutional agencies and researchers to estimate the number of emigrants from Kerala to the Gulf. According to the estimate by the Department of Economics and Statistics, there were 1.86 lakhs Keralites in the Gulf in the year 1980, which has increased to 3 lakhs in 1981 (Department of Economics and Statistics 1987) in 1987. In 1999, the estimated stock of emigrants from Kerala to Gulf countries was 13.18 lakhs (Kannan and Hari 2002). (Table 1). This shows that emigrations from Kerala to the Gulf have been increasing tremendously since mid 1970's as a consequence of price hike of oil in that region. Recently, IT professionals' accounts for a significant category of emigrants from Kerala (Zachariah and Irudaya Rajan 2004).

District wise Distribution of Emigrants

During 1980s, Trichur district accounted for more than 19.3 per cent of the total emigrants from Kerala while Malappuram and Trivandrum accounted for about 17.6 and 10.9 per cent respectively (Table 2). In Trichur district, Chavakkad region accounts for the highest concentration of emigrants and was

Table 1
Estimated Stock of Kerala Emigrants in Gulf Countries (Lakhs)

Year	*India*	*Kerala*	*Kerala as % of India*
1973	1.95	0.34	17.26
1974	2.27	0.39	16.93
1975	3.05	0.44	14.50
1976	3.49	0.51	14.52
1977	3.99	0.58	14.55
1978	4.57	0.67	14.57
1979	5.23	0.76	14.59
1980	5.99	0.79	13.22
1981	5.99	0.98	16.31
1982	7.41	1.52	20.50
1983	9.17	1.83	19.96
1984	9.30	2.01	21.57
1985	9.31	2.42	26.02
1986	9.45	2.76	29.25
1987	9.58	3.05	31.85
1988	10.98	3.82	34.82
1989	12.6	4.02	31.88
1990	14.45	5.09	35.23
1991	16.57	5.40	32.58
1992	18.58	6.45	34.74
1993	20.83	7.44	35.72
1994	23.35	8.60	36.83
1995	26.18	9.63	36.78
1996	29.35	10.97	37.58
1997	32.90	12.36	37.75
1998	36.88	12.36	35.89
1999	33.74	12.11	35.89
2000	30.87	11.04	35.75

Source: Kannan and Hari (2002).

popularly known as 'Mini Gulf'. However, in 1999, Malappuram district accounts for the highest percentage of emigrants from Kerala (21 per cent) where as the share of Trichur (11.8 per cent) and Trivandrum (9.6 per cent) has gone down significantly. As per the latest studies, Malappuram accounts for about 14.8 per cent, followed by Kannur 11.0 per cent, Trichur 9.7 per cent and Palakkad 9.7 per cent. The lowest contribution of Idukki (0.40 per cent) and Wayanad (0.40 per cent) in the emigration process from Kerala may be due to the fact that these are the major plantation areas of the state and also accounts for the highest per centage of tribal population.

Table 2
District wise Distribution of Emigrants from Kerala

District	*1980 (Percentage)*	*1999-01-06 (Percentage)*	*2004 (Percentage)*
Trivandrum	10.99	9.6	9.1
Kollam	6.53	7.6	8.1
Pathanamthitta	9.26	7.2	7.3
Alappuzha	4.56	4.6	4.1
Kottayam	3.41	2.6	5.8
Idukki	0.28	0.5	0.4
Ernakulam	2.46	7.6	6.6
Thrissur	19.32	11.8	9.7
Palakkad	3.72	8.5	9.7
Malappuram	17.56	21.8	14.8
Kozhikkode	8.42	8.5	9.1
Waynad	0.14	0.3	0.4
Kannur	8.67	6.5	11.0
Kazargode	4.43	2.3	3.9
Total	100.00	100.00	100.00

Sources: 1. Department of Economics and Statistics (1980).
2. Zachariah and Irudaya Rajan (2004).

Destination of Emigrants

Distribution of emigrants according to their destination shows that more than 90 per cent of the emigrants from Kerala were to the Gulf countries like U.A.E, Saudi Arabia, Oman, Kuwait, Bahrain and Qatar. Saudi Arabia was the main destination place of emigrants from Kerala in the early phase of emigration (39.97 per cent in 1999) (Table 3). However, recent estimates

Table 3
Destination wise Distribution of Emigrants from Kerala to Gulf Region

	1999		*2004*	
Countries	*Number*	*Percentage*	*Number*	*Percentage*
U.A.E	421758	30.01	670156	41.28
Saudi Arabia	510652	39.97	489988	30.18
Oman	132443	10.37	141865	8.74
Kuwait	68130	5.33	113967	7.02
Bahrain	74619	5.84	108507	6.68
Qatar	70001	5.48	98953	6.10
Total	1277603	100	1623436	100

Source: Zachariah and Irudaya Rajan (2004).

show that the share of Saudi Arabia has gone down (30.18 per cent) while the share of U.A.E has gone up (41.28 per cent) (Table 3). However, both of these countries together constituted more than 60 per cent of the emigrants from Kerala to the Gulf region.

SECTION-II

Socio-Economic Characteristics of the Emigrants

Religious Composition of Emigrants

Many studies have confirmed that bulks of the emigrants from Kerala to the Gulf countries are the poor Muslims of coastal areas. Following the Muslims the Latin Catholic Christians, Ezhuvas, and other artisan communities send sizable number to the Gulf region in the early phase of emigration. According to the study by Prakash ((1978), about 74.74 per cent (71 out of 95 households) of the emigrants from Kerala were Muslims where as it is 78 per cent as per the study by GopinathanNair (Gopinathan Nair, 1986). A recent study shows that among the emigrants the proportion of Muslims was 43.7 per cent while Hindus and Christians constituted 31.2 per cent and 25.1per cent respectively (Zacharia and Irudaya Rajan 2004).

Education and Skill of Emigrants

There are evidences that the educational qualifications of the emigrants from Kerala to the Gulf, especially during the early phase of emigration, were very low and they were either unskilled or semi-skilled. Bulk of them does not have any work experience or technical skill (Directorate Economics and Statistics, 1980). Even during 1985-86, one-third to two-fifth of the total emigrants was unskilled workers (Gopinathan Nair, 1986). Recently, the Gulf countries have changed their immigration policies and they have stopped accepting applications for visas for unskilled workers from India, Pakistan and Bangladesh with effect from 18th July 1999 (Zacharia *et. al* 2002).

Employment and Income

There are several studies about the employment status of emigrants from Kerala to the Gulf and these studies confirmed that most of them were unemployed prior to their emigration. According to the study by the Department of Economics and Statistics, 40 per cent of the emigrants were unemployed at the time of their 1st emigration (Department of Economics and Statistics, 1987). As per the study of Gopinathan Nair, 38 per cent of the emigrants were unemployed on the eve of their 1st emigration (Gopinathan Nair, 1986). Income wise, majority of the emigrants were from poor households belonging to the coastal regions and hence were from the low-income category. According to the study by Gopinathan Nair, about 75 per cent of the emigrants borrowed money from to meet the expenses of their first emigration (Gopinathan Nair, 1986).

SECTION-III

Impact of Emigration on Kerala Economy

The massive emigration from Kerala to the Gulf countries has brought unprecedented and dynamic changes in the socio-economic characteristics of the people of Kerala. According to the study by Zachariah *et al*, there is a two-way relationship between the socio-economic changes and emigration in Kerala (Zachariah et. al, 2000). The socio-economic features of Kerala lead to emigration and emigration in turn lead to remittances, which in turn lead to socio-economic changes. Before going to analyse the socio-economic impact of emigration on Kerala Economy, we may examine the size of Kerala's foreign remittances.

Magnitude of Remittances

There are several benefits from emigration to the people and to the State economy and one of the direct benefits has been the huge volume of foreign remittances brought to Kerala by the emigrants. Remittances income data are available only for the country as whole and not for its constituent provinces and it is hence difficult to estimate the exact magnitudes (Kannan

2005. Therefore the size of annual remittances received in Kerala from its emigrant population in Gulf countries is not precisely known. According to the study by Nayyar, the inflow of remittances from Gulf countries to Kerala has reached its peak during the 1980s and the total inward remittances to Kerala (through banking channels) was estimated tc be more than Rs. 720 crores during the period 1975-76 to 1987-88 (Nayyar 1989). According to the estimate by Prakash, the remittances from the Middle East to Kerala rose from Rs. 824 crores in 1980 to Rs.1310 crores in 1990 and subsequently to Rs. 5857 crores in 1994 (Prakash 1999).

The estimate by Zacharia *et al* shows that the total remittances (cash plus goods) to Kerala are about Rs.40717 million in 1999(Zacharia et al 2000). The total annual remittances in Kerala increased from Rs.7334.64 crores in 1995-96 to Rs.14157.88 crores in 1999- 2000, which accounted for about 21.19 per cent of the net domestic product in 1995 and 22.63 per cent in 2000 (Table 4).

District wise, Malappuram accounts for the highest percentage of household remittances (18.8 per cent of the total) in 1999 although Thrissur accounts for the highest percentage of remittances in 2004 (17.1 per cent of the total) (Zhakariah and Irudaya Rajan 2004).

Economic Impact of Emigration

The economic impact of emigration on Kerala economy is analysed with reference to unemployment and poverty, consumption, saving and investment and with regard to balance of payments position.

Effect of Emigration on Unemployment and Poverty

Unemployment and poverty are the two important problems of Kerala and government has been trying to reduce the magnitudes of poverty and unemployment. One of the major beneficial effect of emigration from has been a reduction in the rate of unemployment as about 40 per cent of the emigrants from Kerala at the time of their voyage to Gulf countries were found to be unemployed (Gopinathan Nair 1986). According

Table 4
Estimated Foreign Remittances and Net State Domestic Product (NSDP) in Kerala (Rs. in crores)

Year	*Total remittance*	*NSDP*	*Remittance as % of NSDP*
1972-73	8.31	1457	0.57
1973-74	10.60	1853	0.58
1974-75	22.01	2086	1.06
1975-76	45.94	2228	2.06
1976-77	108.25	2398	4.51
1977-78	168.68	2521	6.41
1978-79	152.12	2754	5.52
1979-80	217.01	3156	6.88
1980-81	348.24	3823	9.11
1981-82	382.38	4056	9.44
1982-83	480.41	4712	10.20
1983-84	623.69	5523	11.24
1984-85	841.54	6141	13.80
1985-86	531.31	6503	8.94
1986-87	929.23	7354	12.64
1987-88	972.27	8258	11.77
1988-89	899.56	9182	9,80
1989-90	1239.93	10668	11.62
1990-91	945.84	12173	7.77
1991-92	2537.33	15102	16.80
1992-93	3124.33	17175	18.19
1993-94	4028.92	23401	17.22
1994-95	6410.34	28697	22.34
1995-96	7334.64	35087	21.19
1996-97	9999.62	40819	24.50
1997-98	11302.03	47924	23.58
1998-99	11285.62	56563	19.95
1999-00	14157.88	62557	22.63

Source: Kannan and Hari (2002).

to the study by Zachariah *et al*, emigration has resulted in a decline of unemployment by about 32 per cent and unemployment rate by about 3 per cent points (Zachariah *et al* 2000). However, there are variations among the districts with regard to the reduction of unemployment as these districts differ in the number of emigrants. Districts like Thrissur, Malappuram,

Thiruvananthapuram, Kannur etc are the main centres of exporting labourers to Gulf countries, the maximum reduction in unemployment is confined to these districts. Similar to unemployment, emigration has its beneficial effect on the incidence of poverty of the people. The proportion of people below poverty has declined by 3 per centage points annually as a result of remittances received by Kerala households from their kith and kin abroad. It is found that the decline in poverty was largest among Muslims (6 percentage points) followed by Ezhavas and Latin Christians (Zacharia *et al* 2000).

Effect of Remittances on Consumption, Savings and Investments

Emigration and consequent inflow of remittances will have its effect on the consumption, savings and investments of emigrant households. The effect of remittances on consumption would be larger as the bulk of the emigrants from Kerala were from low-income households. Studies on the utilization pattern of remittances showed that emigrant households spent a major share of their income on consumption, clothing, education, health, entertainment etc. According to the study by Directorate of Economics and Statistics, about 36 per cent of the remittances were used for construction purposes, about 22 per cent was spent for the purchase of land and about 21 per cent was used for the purchase of gold, education and repayment of loans etc. (DES, 1986). The study by Zachriah and Irudaya Rajan found significant differences in the consumption expenditure pattern between emigrants and non-emigrants. The use of consumer durables like television sets, refrigerators, washing machines, telephones, vehicles etc were higher in the emigrants households compared to non-emigrants. The study also found a positive correlation between the duration of emigration and proportion of households possessing consumer durables. Household amenities like electrified houses, flush out toilet, use of LPG for cooking etc were higher in the emigrants households compared to non-emigrants (Zachriah and Irudaya Rajan 2004). With regard to the savings of emigrants and non-emigrants, it was observed that there was a considerable increase in the asset holdings of emigrants than the non-emigrants. Assets like land, building, gold ornaments, motor vehicles, consumer durables etc were higher in the emigrant households. However, the study observed that emigrants' investment in productive sectors was comparatively lower except in the case of tertiary sectors and especially on education, health, communication, transport etc.

Social Impact of Emigration

There are studies, which establishes that emigration has its impact on the demand for education, health care etc. Emigration has exposed the emigrants to the outside world, which has brought great changes in their attitude towards the education of their children. There are studies, which found that parents of emigrant are spent liberally on education of their children. The study by Mathew and Gopinathan Nair indicated that emigration led to the emergence and growth of technical and vocational training institutions in various trades like construction related courses, motor and machine operations, welding, computer operations, catering, tailoring and paramedical courses etc (Mathew and Gopinathan Nair 1978). The study by Gopinathan Nair pointed out that emigration helped to bring a favourable change in the attitude of emigrants towards education of children, both boys and girls. Their inspirational level about the employment and social status of their children went up consequent up on their exposure to the wider world (Gopinathan Nair 1981). The propagation of English medium schools in the private sector in Kerala is definitely an out come of emigration. At the college level, emigrant households depend on private colleges to a greater extend than out-migrant and non-migrant households. The emergence of self-financing institutions in Kerala both in professional and non-professional is definitely the out come of emigration. Another study found that emigration is a promoter and leveller of education among the educationally backward Muslims of Kerala (Misiriya 1990).

There are also evidences that emigrants spend a sizable amount of their income on health care. The growth of private hospitals and other paramedical institutions in private sector in Kerala indicates the influence of emigration on health care. The vast majority of emigrants depend on the allopathic private hospitals for treatment to a greater extent than non-emigrant households. The study by Zacharia et al found that emigrants spent more on hygiene and sanitation and health care than non-emigrants' households since the emigrants' households maintain higher living standards due to the remittances (Zacharia *et al* 2000).

Demographic Impact

Demographic changes are indispensable part of migration and there are studies, which observed that emigration has brought both structural and behavioural changes in the demography of Kerala. Reduction in the growth rate of population, a unique sex ratio (favouring females), a reduction in working age of population and an increased proportion of children and the elderly, the prevalence of large number of small families etc. are some of the important behavioural changes brought about by emigration in Kerala. Emigration has resulted in a decline in the fertility and mortality rate; decline in fertility due to separation of spouses due to male migration leaving his female partner at home while decline in mortality due to the better living conditions and health care made possible with remittances (Zachriah *et al* 2000).

Some Adverse Effects of Emigration

However, it should be noted that there are some adverse effects of migration despite its various beneficial effects on the economy. Oil boom and associated increase in income of the Gulf countries created a construction boom in the Gulf countries and it took off a large number of labourers from Kerala. The emigration and foreign remittances has created another construction boom in Kerala as the major share of the remittances was spent on construction and repair of houses and buildings. As such, there are shortages of labourers in certain sectors of the economy due to emigration. This has caused an increase in the wage rate in the construction sector, which has resulted in a movement of workers from non-construction work to construction work and it led to an increase in the wage rate in both the construction and agricultural sectors. Moreover, emigration has created a lack of interest among the educated youth towards manual work and this has attracted workers from neighbouring states to Kerala and thus Kerala itself is converted in to a Gulf (Prakash 1999). The study by Harilal and Joseph argue that emigration has adversely affected the productive sectors of the Kerala economy. According to their study, emigration and consequent foreign remittances have resulted in a decline in the share of agricultural sector to the Net State Domestic Product, to stagnate the share of the manufacturing sector and to raise considerably the share of the tertiary sector to the Net State Domestic Product (Harilal and Joseph 2003). It is also argued that the higher levels of consumption on account of emigration and Kerala's weak production base have made Kerala an outlet for the neighbouring states.

Return Emigration

Emigration is a less expensive and more gainful 'industry' for Kerala, as it employs nearly 2 million persons directly and 7 million depend on it indirectly. However, return emigration is creating serious socio-economic problems in the economy; especially it increases the rate of unemployment in the state. It is estimated that there are 75,0000 return emigrants in Kerala in the year 2005 and most of them are in Malappuram district, followed by Thiruvananthapuram and Thrissur. Bulk of the returnees is from Saudi Arabia (40 per cent of the total), Dubai (11.4 per cent), Oman (9.9 per cent). Among the returnees, about 45 per cent are Muslims while Ezhava accounts for about 20 per cent. According to the Study by Zachariah *et al*, ' a typical return emigrant in Kerala is a married Muslim male in his thirties with an incomplete secondary level education and without any technical training' (Zachariah *et al* 2001). The details of return of emigrants in Kerala are presented in Table 5 and the table shows that the percentage of return emigrants was higher during the years 1996 and 1997.

Table 5
Magnitude of Return Emigrants in Kerala

Year	*No. of return Emigrants (In lakhs)*	*Percentage*
Up to 1980	34.1	4.62
1981-90	162.8	22.03
1991	20.1	2.72
1992	43.3	5.86
1993	35.3	4.79
1294	57.9	7.84
1995	93.1	9.90
1996	106.8	14.44
1997	126.9	17.16
1998	78.9	10.64
Total	739.2	100.00

Source: Zachariah *et. al* (1999).

District wise, Malappuram, Thiruvananthapuram and Thrissur accounts for the highest number of return emigrants whereas Idukki and Wayanad accounts for the lowest number of return emigrants. The differences in the number of return emigrants among the districts are due to the differences in their share in the total emigration from Kerala. Malappuram, Thiruvananthapuram and Thrissur are the major centres of emigration whereas Idukki and Wayanad accounts for the least emigration (Table 6).

Reasons for Return Emigration

There are many reasons behind the return emigration and the major reasons are the expiry of contract (30.1 per cent), resignation due to difficult living conditions (12.9 per cent), resignation due to difficult working conditions (22.9 per cent), job termination by employers (10.3 per cent), political upheavals (1.9 per cent), Illegal stay abroad due to compulsory repatriation (5.4 per cent), conditions at home requiring presence (3.77 per cent), Ill health (11.1 per cent), and injury/accident (1.2 per cent) (Table 7). It is found that unemployment rate is very high among the return emigrants households compared to the emigrants households. Similarly the work participation rate among the return emigrants and the share of the returnees engaged in economically active works are all very low.

Table 6
District wise Distribution of Return Emigrants in Kerala 1998

Districts	*Number of return emigrants*
Malappuram	123750
Thiruvananthapuram	118878
Thrissur	116788
Kollam	74106
Kozhikkode	60910
Pathanamthitta	54537
Ernakulam	45028
Palakkad	39234
Alappuzha	34572
Kannur	28263
Kottayam	18164
Kasergode	16667
Idukki	5017
Wayanad	3327
Total	739241

Source: K.C. Zachariah *et al.* (1999).

Table 7
Distribution of Return Emigrants by Reason for Return

Reasons for Return	*Percentage of Returnees*
Expiry of contract	30.3
Resigned due to difficult living condition	12.9
Resigned due to difficult working condition	22.9
Job terminated by employer	10.3
Political upheaval	1.9
Illegal stay abroad due to compulsory repatriation	5.4
Conditions at home required presence	13.7
Ill-health	11.1
Injury, accident and incapacitation	1.2

Source: Zachariah *et. al.* (2001).

SECTION-V

Conclusion

In this paper we made an attempt to examine the dimensions of emigration from Kerala to the Gulf countries along with the impact of foreign remittances on the economy of Kerala. Migration has been an important factor in the development scenario of Kerala for the last many decades and it has contributed significantly to the reduction in poverty and unemployment in Kerala. Emigration decisions are influenced by the conditions at home in comparison with the conditions prevailing in the destination places. High density of population, high rate of unemployment and the low rate of growth of the productive sectors pushed the emigrants to the Gulf countries. Rising demand for labourers was the most important pull factor behind emigration. Vast majority of the emigrants from Kerala were the poor Muslims of coastal region who do not possess high educational qualifications and technical skill and were with little work experience. A major share of remittances were utilised for the construction of houses, for the purchase of consumer durables, for acquiring gold and for meeting the marriage expenses. Emigration has helped to reduce the incidence of poverty and unemployment in Kerala although it has created labour shortages in some of the sectors of the economy. It has also increased the investments in the tertiary sector especially in education, health and communication. Although emigrants have contributed a lot to the development of Kerala, recently, the return of emigrants and their rehabilitation is creating a lot of problems in the state.

References

Bilsborrow, R. E., G. Hugo, A. S. Oberai and H. Zlotnik (1997), *International Migration Statistics,* Geneva: International Labour Office.

Department of Economics and Statistics (1987), Report of Survey on the Utilization of Gulf Remittances in Kerala, Government of Kerala.

————(1982), *Survey on Housing on Employment, 1980.* Thiruvananthapuram: Department of Economics Statistics.

Gopinathan Nair P. R. (1983), *Asian Migration to Middle East: Migration from India,* Working Paper No. 180 Centre for Development Studies, Thiruvananthapuram.

————(1989), *Incidence, Impact and Implication of Migration to the Middle East from Kerala into the Gulf and Back* in Rashid Amjad (ed.) To The Gulf and Back UNDP, New Delhi.

Gulathi, Leela (1993), *In the Absence of Their Men: Impact of Male Migration on Women,* New Delhi, Sage Publications.

Harilal K.N. and K. J. Joseph (2003), *Stagnation and Revival of Kerala Economy. An Open Economy Perspective, Economic and Political Weekly*, Vol. No. 23, pp. 2286-2294.

International Labour Organisation (ILO) (1989), World Labour Report, 1989.Geneva: International Labour Organisation.

Kannan K. P. and H. S. Hari (2000), *Kerala's Gulf Connection: Emigration, Remittances and Their Macro Economic Impact, 1972-2000* Working paper No. 328. Thiruvananthapuram: Centre for Development Studies.

Mathew E. T. & P. R. Gopinathan Nair (1978), *Socio-Economic Characteristics of Emigrants and Emigrant Households: A case study of Two Villages in Kerala, Economic and Political Weekly*, July 5.

Nayyar, Deepak (1985), *International Labour Migration from India: A Macroeconomic Analysis* in Rashid Amjad (ed) To The Gulf and Back UNDP, New Delhi

Nafeesathul Misiriya P. V. (1990), Impact of Emigration on Education. Case of Muslim Community in Kerala. An unpublished M.Phil Thesis, Kerala University Certre, Kariavattom.

Prakash B. A. (1994), *The Economic Impact of Migration to the Gulf* in B. A. Prakash (ed) Kerala's Economic Development, Issues and Problems, Sage Publications, New Delhi.

————(1998), *Indian Migration to the Middle East: Trends, Pattern and Socio-Economic Impact*, Spell Bound Publication, Rohtak.

————(2000), *Exodus Gulf Emigrants- Return Emigrants of Varkala Town in Kerala, Economic and Political Weekly*, Vol. 35, No. 51.

Pushpangadhan K. (2003), *Remittances Consumption and Economic Growth in Kerala: 1980-2000* Working paper No. 343. Thiruvananthapuram: Centre for Development Studies.

Zachariah K. C., E. T. Mathew and S. Irudaya Rajan (2000), *Socio Economic and Demographic Consequences of Migration in Kerala*: Working Paper No. 303. Thiruvananthapuram: Centre for Development Studies.

Zachariah K. C., P. R.Gopinathan Nair and S. Irudaya Rajan (2001), *Return Emigrants in Kerala: Rehabilitation Problems and Development Potential*. Working Paper No. 319. Thiruvananthapuram: Centre for Development Studies.

Zachariah.K.C.,B.A.Prakash and S.Irudaya Rajan(2002),*Gulf Migration Study: Employment Wages and Working Condition of Kerala Emigrants in the United Arab Emirates,* Working Paper No. 326. Thiruvananthapuram: Centre for Development Studies.

Zachariah K. C. and S. Irudaya Rajan (2004), *Gulf Revisited: Economic Consequences of Emigration from Kerala; Emigration and Unemployment,* Working paper No. 363. Thiruvananthapuram: Centre for Development Studies.

United Nations (1966), *Multilingual Demographic Dictionary* ST/SOA/SER. A/29, Population Studies, No. 29, New York.

HUMAN RIGHTS VIOLATION AND CHILD LABOUR: ISSUES AND EVIDENCES FROM KERALA

P. S. MOHANAKUMAR

Introduction

Values are the essence of human condition. Values are the internal guide posts of people. Universal values (life, joy, brotherhood, love, peace equal rights, compassion, service, truth, eternity etc.), cultural values (social values of the day) and individual values (private principles) must be the foundation of social life. Values and rights are the two sides of a coin for e.g. when 'protection of health' is a part of humanitarian value, 'right to health' is a part of human right. Human rights are protected with the help of national and international rules and law. The values shared by all civilizations reflect our fundamental rights. So human rights violation is the abuse of the people in a way that it abuses any fundamental human right. It is a term used when a government violates national or international law related to the protection of human rights. According to the Universal Declaration of Human rights, fundamental human rights are violated when a person is sold or used as a slave (Article 4) cruel, inhuman, or degrading punishment is used on a person (Article 5) among other provisions contained in Articles 2 to 26 of the Universal Declaration of Human rights. Values do conflict. Making value choice is the strongest test of character.

Prevalence of child labour is a clear instance of violation of human rights. The government of India through a notification on May 26, 1993, the working conditions of children have been regulated in all employment which are not prohibited under the child labour (Prohibition and Regulation) Act. The government has also prohibited employment of children in occupation processes like abattoirs/slaughter houses, printing, cashew nut descaling and processing and soldering. The Child Labour Act of 1986 of India prohibits the employment of children below the age of 14 in factories, mines and in other forms of hazardous employment and regulates the working condition of children in other employment. A child is classified as labourer if the child is in the age group, 5-14 years and economically active i.e., receives wage.

However, the goals mentioned in the Act were not attained due to a variety of reasons. The Act also is not enough to regulate the child labour in domestic or unreported labour. Children are often exploited and deprived of their rights in India. The ILO resolution also calls for the prohibition of child labour and humanizing child labour wherever prohibition is not possible. Regulating the working condition of children in occupations where they are not prohibited from working, is also absolutely necessary. The exploitation of child labour is a little known, human rights problem in India. Societies, cultures and nations have often been evaluated on the basis of how they have been treating their elderly, the children, the disabled and the deprived in course of their development.

Objectives

The major objectives of the study are the following.

(1) To portray the magnitude of child labour in Kerala and the extent of human rights violation

(2) To analyse the role of Jena Seva Sisu Bhavan in rehabilitating the children who are engaged in child labour.

Theoretical Base

The child labour theories are mainly based on poverty, family decision making and market failure. Where children had no bargaining power, parents take a decision in family decision making and determinants of child labour. Children are considered strictly in terms of value of assets. It is based on quality-quantity trade off and diversification hypothesis. The increase in fertility lowers the quality of child and they choose large number of children to earn more income. Parents who choose a large number of children are less likely to invest in quality schooling. Parents choose large number of children in order to diversify risk, formally educating some and putting the others to work. In poverty hypothesis many empirical studies report a negative correlation between GDP per capita and employment rate of 10-14 years old.

In Market Failure and Multiple Equilibria model emphasises two equilibrium in labour market. One in which children and adults work giving rise to large labour supply and low wage and the other in which only parents work giving rise to low labour supply and a high adult wage. In this circumstance a ban on child labour will have the effect of helping high-wage. Ranjan and Basu model suggest government to educate one generation to reduce child labour and the subsequent generation of family will be able to enjoy higher standard of living.

Capital market failure suggests the inability of the children to pay back education loans in future. Baland and Robinson note that the inability of the child to access the capital markets or the inability of the child to repay education loans obtained by the parents on the child's behalf may give rise to inefficiently low educational attainment. The analysis emphasizes the importance of capital market failure as a contributing factor to inefficient child labour. On the basis of these theoretical analysis, one can include the reasons of child labour in India is poverty and related socio-economic problems.

Magnitude of the Problem & Conceptual Ambiguities

India has the largest number of children under the age of 14 in the work in the world. Agencies like Oxfam estimates put the figure at 100 millions children. According to the 1991 census there are 11.28 million working children under the age of fourteen years in India. Over 85 % of this child labour is in the country's rural areas, working in agricultural activities such as fanning, livestock rearing, foresting and fisheries. This labour is outside the formal sector Moreover, nine out of ten (9/10) work with in a family setting, and outside the industry. While the Government of India reports about 20 millions child labourers, other NGOs estimate the number to be 50 million. Child labour as per 1991 census for select states are given below:

Table 1
Child labour Age group 5-14

Andhra Pradesh	21.81 lakhs (Highest)
Kerala	78,565
M.P	4.1 lakhs
Maharashtra	15.86 lakhs
U.P	15.85 lakhs
West Bengal	6.53 lakhs
Tamil Nadu	10.05 lakhs
Gujarath	5.67 lakhs
Rajasthan	7.56 lakhs
Karnataka	11.59 lakhs
India	142.17 lakhs

Working children and no where children count for 40-45% in some states, but in Kerala it is 19.2%. The proportion of child labour in Kerala is much lower than the national level. This is in addition to the "no where children." No where children are involved in unpaid work viz. in day to day household chores or looking after younger siblings in the family etc. This 'no where children' are not counted as part of workforce. The sector-wise classification of child labour is as given below.

Table 2
Classification of Child labour

Agriculture	54%
Construction	15.5%
Household work	18%
Manufacturing job	5%
Remainder	8%

Table 3
The Activities of Children in the Age Group 5-14

		No. of children (%)	
Activities	*Boys*	*Girls*	*Total*
Economic activities	4.18	3.86	4.02
Domestic activities	0.30	3.15	1.67
Domestic duties, collection of goods tailoring, weaving of HH only	0.25	1.92	1.06
Children at work	4.73	8.93	6.75
Attending schools	72.98	61.45	67.44
Children neither at work nor at school	17.26	20.42	18.80

The socio-economic factors prevailing in the country is a great hurdle to eliminate child labour in India. One can raise three different issues connected with this problem.

1. How for poverty affects child labour?
2. Is there any relationship between school drop-outs and incidence of child labour?
3. The role of human development and socio-economic well-being and its impact on child labour.

Poverty is closely related with unemployment and child labours. Increased poverty leads to increase in child labour. One can observe higher relative poverty in areas where we observe decline in schooling and increase in child labour. The school drop-outs for select states are given below (1997-98).

Table 4
School Dropout Rates in Select States

Tamil Nadu	65.74%
A.P	79.09
U.P	71.69
Rajastan	89.25
Kerala	19.78
Maharashtra	64.75
Bihar	87.68
H.P.	53.02

The drop out rates are lowest in Kerala. The drop-out rates are zero from class I to V in Kerala, and the enrolment rate in Kerala is 91% in the age 6-14. The lowest incidence of child labour in Kerala may be due to high literacy, low school drop outs and low incidence of poverty. Andhra Pradesh witnesses a high-drop out rates with a higher incidence of child labour. This is true in the case of other states having high-drop outs. The socio-economic well-being is another factor which influences poverty, drop-outs and incidence of child labour. The workforce quality and social wellbeing are the highest in Kerala and lowest in Andhra Pradesh and Bihar where the magnitude of child labour is frightening. The report of the study of the Confederation of Indian Industries is given below with respect to workforce quality and social well-being. The workforce quality is measured mainly on the basis of literacy rate and the social well being of a state in terms of 4 sets of issues such as basic education levels, genders bias, health and general awareness. The relationship between workforce quality and social well-being are given below.

Table 5
Workforce Quality and Social Well being

	Workforce quality		*Social wellbeing*	
States	*Rank*	*Rating*	*Rank*	*Rating*
Kerala	A	1.5	A	4
H.P.	A	1.5	B	3
Maharashtra	B	1	A	3
Tamil Nadu	A	1.4	B	2.7
A.P.	C	0.9	D	1.6
Bihar	E	0	E	0

Source: Report of the study of Confederation of Indian Industries.

To break the vicious circle of child labour exploitation enforcement of law alone is not necessary. It should be followed by heavy investment in education along with measures to reduce employment and incidence of poverty as proved by Kerala model of development.

The exploitation of child labour has become an accepted practice and is viewed by the people as necessary to overcome the extreme poverty prevailing in many geographical regions of the country. Many children in India work to support their families. Children perform a variety of jobs: some work in factories, making products such as carpets and matches, others work on plantations, or in the home. In addition to this many work without pay in assisting their parents or are working for employers who do not report it to the census. Children working in the unorganized sector are being highly exploited by the employers. Girls in the unorganized sector are engaged in low paid or unpaid unskilled occupations. Boys often work long-hours doing hard physical work.

Agony of Child Labour

- A 14 year-old boy who worked as a weaver's assistant in silk wearing in Varanasi, U.P, told Human Rights watch that he could not leave his loan owner because he was paying off loan, which in 2 years it only reduced from Rs. 2500/- to Rs. 475/-. The owner pays but deducts from the loan.
- A 13 years old girl working in a silk weaving factory in Kanchipuram, Tamil Nadu, told Human Right Watch "Always the owner beats me. I don't like to work. They always scold and beat me on the back and head. They are always knocking their fists on my head or hitting me with a comb (wood piece in the loan).
- Eleven years old Manjhi, a boy from Bihar, was not employed by a local land lord, and therefore, he often had to walk up to 10 kilometres each way to find work. At many of these jobs he would earn only Rs. 30/- and the jobs would only last for approximately 4 months out of the year.
- Three year old Manjumatha, found lying on the road near Angamaly (Kerala), her legs oozing pus from acid burns inflicted by her beggar father was rehabilitated by Jena Seva Sisu Bhavan, Aluva.

Kerala Experience

The percentage of child labour in Kerala as domestic workers is increasing as per the study conducted by Research Institute of Rajagiri Social Science. According to 1991 census, the total number of child labour in Kerala was estimated as 34,800; and in 2001 census as 26,156; but this does not reflect the real situation. The real number is very high since the life-style situation in Kerala forces one to employ domestic servants mainly children under the age of 14. Many of the children employed as domestic servants are Tamil migrants and the trend is visible in Tamil-Kerala border districts especially in Vandiperiyar, Andipatti, Usilampatti and also in plantation dominated districts like Wayanad, Idukki and Palakkad districts. Incidentally 90% of domestic servants are girls and many such girls work in more than one house daily. There are also instances where girls work in three to four houses daily. In brick Klein industry in Ernakulam and Trichur district male child labourers are employed for lesser wages. The paradox of child labour in Kerala is that 80 to 90 per cent are migrants from neighbouring states and especially from Tamil Nadu. Since as per the 'Child Labour Prohibition Act' the employer is liable to pay a compensation of Rs.20,000/- for every child employed, many are keeping fabricated and fake birth certificate to escape from law. The elementary right to education is denied to all such child labours in Kerala. The major cause of child labour is poverty:

As per the study conducted by Gathia (1995) Kerala records a decrease in child labour. The reason is attributed to the unique Kerala's socialist experiment in social development which emphasized elementary education and social consciousness as a primary state objective. This observation is right as far as resident population is concerned. But the high life-style acts as a reason for attracting migrant child labour. This aspect need to be investigated. The raising literacy level, decreasing poverty and enhanced social consciousness are factors which led to low incidence of child labour in Kerala.

Other instances of child labour in Kerala are children below 14 employed in restaurants, hotels and commercial establishments. The instances of children employed in hotels and restaurants are seen in temporary establishments in connection with religious festivals through out the length and breadth of Kerala. Confirmed reports show that many migrant children were being employed in the construction industry in Kerala. In Kerala there are many institutions which work for rehabilitation of child labour. Their activities helped to a great extent to bring down the impact of child labour. Increased access to education, reduced incidence of poverty, and social consciousness are other reasons which help reduction in the magnitude of child labour in Kerala.

Jena Seva Sisu Bhavan, Aluva, Kerala

The Jena Seva Sisu Bhavan working in Aluva, Kerala is actively engaged in the rehabilitation of the child labour. Jena Seva Sisu Bhavan is an assembly of like-minded people, irrespective of caste and creed, who have earnest desire to do selfless service to save and protect street children. Over 300 children are being housed at Jena Seva Sisu Bhavan. Many children at Sisu Bhavan were all castaways or kidnap victims of the "beggar mafia". The victims were put out to beg, sometimes maimed to attract sympathy. The children were given specific routes and target amounts to be collected every day. They were also given fake cards to be distributed among bus and train passengers to collect money. The gangs torture the kids if they fail to bring in enough money every day. Some of the little ones have had their nails or hair pulled out. Jena Seva Sisu Bhavan president Jose Maveli rescued and rehabilitated 300 such children. Some children were brought by destitute parents or mothers too poor or ill to care for them. There were 30 mothers to look after them, bathe and feed them. After rescuing such children they were given a reasonably good living condition and were sent to school. Survey conducted about the background information of the inmates of the children in Jena Seva Sisu Bhavan reveals some interesting facts. Poverty is the main reason for destitution of the poor children in the streets. All the 184 children housed in one of the units of the Sisu Bhavan (Near Settlement School, Aluva) were living in abject poverty. So poverty can be traced as one of the reasons for street children and consequent child labour. Of the 184 children, 34% are below 5 years old, while 31% are the age group of 10 to 15 years. The details are given the following table.

Table 6
Age wise Classification of Children

Age Group	*No. of children*
0–5	64
5–10	63
10–15	57
Total	184

Survey results.

Among 184 children 51 are females and the rest 133 are male children. All the children are school going whose details are as given below.

Table 7
Educational Level of Children

Schooling	*No. of children*
Pre Primary	44
Primary	63
Middle school	50
High School	7
Total	164

Survey results.

The authorities were keen to educate all the children. Another interesting feature is that out of 184 children, 20 are less than 1 year old. The family backgrounds of 22 children were not known, while 52 children were from neighbouring states. They were previously exploitative child labour wandering in the street for jobs. Other characteristics of family backgrounds are summarized below.

As per the study 28% of the children are migrants from neighbouring states. The parents or guardians of such children are coming from Tamil Nadu, Karnataka or Andhrapradesh for the main purpose of begging or for anti-social activities. In the case of 22 children the family backgrounds were not traceable. The family backgrounds were a clear indication of very pathetic socio-economic-psychic backgrounds of street children/child labour. Baring 22 children whose family backgrounds were not known, all the parents were illiterate and were living in abject poverty. Hence a simple ban on child labour will not be sufficient. A ban on child labour is desirable, but stress is also to be laid on rehabilitating the child labourers. The survey results conducted show that in the case of street children and child labour poverty is the main reason. Poverty forces families to send their children to streets or even sell their children for money. Thus the best way to end this problem is to remove poverty. This will help families to send their children to school instead of streets. It is the duty of the government to remove poverty and prevent violation of human rights. In many states the real poor are many times higher than the government's estimation of poverty and hence rampant is human rights violation.

Table 8
Family Background Characteristics

Family backgrounds	*No. of children*
Migrants from neighbouring states	52
Beggar mafia	30
Not known	22
Street children	40
Alcoholic parents	10
Broken families	10
Sick parents	5
Kidnap victims	5
Drug pushers	5
Domestic servants	5
Total	184

Survey results.

Conclusion

Child labour is prohibited in India under the Child Labour Prohibition and Regulation Act. A child is classified as labourer if he/she can be economically active and between the age group 5-14. It is roughly estimated that there are nearly 100 million child labourers in India. The child labour is found to be engaged mainly in informal sector. The proportion of child labour in Kerala is comparatively lower when compared to other states. The category of "no-where" children are only 19.2% in Kerala. Poverty and school dropout rates are found to be correlated with the magnitude of child labour. The low reason for child labour in Kerala can be attributed to high enrolment rate i.e. 91% in the age group 6-14 and high social well being. This is more evident in the case of Andhra Pradesh. In Andhra Pradesh the incidence of child labour is very high, so also the rate of school drop-outs. The positive relationship between workforce quality and social well being is well established in the study of Confederation of Indian Industries. Hence, heavy investment in education and measures to reduce inequality are to be positively viewed to reduce the incidence of child labour along with strict enforcement of law. Referring to Kerala situation, official reports are being contradicted by some recent studies. In Kerala the high life style situation forces people to employ more children as domestic servants, especially girls. The increased trend in child labour can be witnessed recently. Another significant feature is that majority of the child labour in Kerala are migrants from neighbouring states. The role of Jena Seva Sisu Bhavan is worth studying since it helped to rehabilitate many children engaged in unauthorised labour and those children left in the street. The family backgrounds of children based in Jena Seva also show the pathetic socio-economic conditions of the children and the extent of human rights violation.

References

Baland Jean-Marie and James A. Robinson (2000), "Is Child Labour Inefficient", *Journal of Political Economy,* Vol. 108, pp. 663-679.

Basu, Kaushik (1999), "Child Labour: Cause, Consequence and Cure with Remarks on International Standards." *Journal of Economic Literature,* 37(3), 1083-119.

Bause, Kaushik and Ranjan Ray (2002), "The Collective Model of the Household and an Unexpected Implication for Child Labour: Hypothesis and an Empirical Test", Policy Research Working Paper Series, No. 2813, The World Bank.

Gathia, Joseph (1992), "Child Labour in India", Child Labour Conference, Monash University, Melbourne, Australia.

Nielsen, Helena S. and Amaresh Dubey (2002), "Child Labour in Rural India: A Micro-economic Perspective", *Indian Journal of Labour Economics,* 45(3):479-96.

Ranjan, Priya (2001), "Credit Constraints and the Phenomenon of Child Labour" *Journal of Development Economics*, 64(1):99-105.

Ray, Ranjan (2000), "Analysis of Child Labour in Peru and Pakistan, A Comparative Study", *Journal of Population Economics*, 13(1):3-9.

Sakamoto, Shunsuke (2006), "Parental Attitudes towards Children and Child Labour: Evidence from Rural India", Discussion Paper Series No. 136 Institute of Economic Research, Tokyo, Japan.

Appendix-I
Magnitude of Child Labour

1981 census	13.6 million
1994 labour ministry	20 million
Commission on labour standards 1995	77 million
Human Rights Watch 1996	60-115 million

Appendix-II
Relationship Between Poverty and Drop-outs I to V Classes

State	*Poverty*	*Drop-outs*
A.P.	26.8	47.03
U.P.	36.6	55.98
H.P.	-	31.03
Kerala	17.3	0
Maharashtra	17.4	25.73
Bihar	47.8	62
Rajasthan	17.2	57.99
Tamil Nadu	19.7	16.18

(Head count Ratio NSS 55th Round).

Appendix-III
Percentage of Children Leaving School
(Age <12 Years) for Select Countries (1959-74)

Mexico	25.2	Brazil	80.2
India	40.5	Nigeria	4.2
Portugal	17.4	Chile	2.4
USA	0.6	Argentina	6.6

PART-IV

GROWTH, POVERTY AND REGIONAL DISPARITY

GROWTH AND SECTORAL PERFORMANCE OF KERALA ECONOMY: EVIDENCES FROM A LONG-TERM ANALYSIS

D. Shyjan

Introduction

The development literature has been loaded with discussions on Kerala economy both at the national and international levels since 1970s with the publication of a CDS-UN study on poverty, unemployment and development policy with reference to Kerala. The specificities of the development experience of the State are reviewed extensively by scholars across the border. Development of social sector sans economic progress, which received worldwide attention in the earlier decades, has now been changed to what is referred as 'turnaround' indicating the phenomenon of higher percapita income when compared to the national average (Kannan, 2005). Studies, which examine the sectoral growth pattern of the state economy, observe that services sector has been the major contributor to the NSDP right from the early 1980s (Subrahmanian and Azeez, 2000; Pushpangadan, 2003; Kannan, 2005; Chakraborty, 2005; Mohan and Shyjan, 2007; Pillai and Shanta, 2005; Pushpangadan and Parameswaran, 2007). The present study attempts to explore the growth pattern at disaggregated level for a long period of time from 1960-61 to 2005-06 with special emphasis on reform period. We try to find out which are leading and lagging sectors of Kerala economy during the reform period.

The next section deals with the theoretical background of economic growth and structural change. The third section presents the growth of NSDP and percapita income in Kerala in comparison with all India average. In section four we examine the structural change in terms of share, growth and contribution of primary, secondary and tertiary sectors. Fifth section deals with the contribution of primary, secondary and tertiary sector sub-components to growth of NSDP over the period. Summary and concerns of the study are presented in the last section.

The Theoretical Premise

According to conventional theories, economic growth proceeds in a sequential manner: from agriculture to manufacturing and then to services. As percapita income rises, the share of the agricultural sector in labour force and output declines and the share of manufacture increases, which, in turn, declines relative to the services sector (Clark, 1940; Fisher, 1933 and 1939). The reasoning behind this growth pattern is mainly based on: (a) the differentials in the income elasticity of demand for the products of the three sectors and (b) the differentials in productivity across sectors.

The sequential growth pattern associated with the increase in per capita income has also been empirically examined by Kuznets (1957). While his findings with respect to the agriculture (A) and manufacturing (M) sector corroborate with that of Clark and Fisher, the results of services (S) sector are mixed. Kuznets observes that although there is a positive relationship between growth in per capita income and the share of services sector, the association is weaker compared to the other sectors. The share of the service sector was found to be larger in the high income economies relative to the less developed regions, but, the difference between developed and developing countries in the share of service sector, both in output and labour force, is much narrower compared to the other sectors. Moreover, the time series analysis of Kuznets shows that the expansion of service sector in the low-income countries occurred before industrialisation. This, according to him, is not due to increasingly higher levels of technology and productivity in the A & M sectors, but because of population pressure on land and the limitations of employment opportunities in the M sector that drive the surplus labour into low paid service activities (Kuznets, 1959).

In the Indian context, most of the empirical studies on sectoral growth observe an excess growth and higher share of output in service sector since the early Eighties compared to agricultural and manufacturing sectors (Rao, 1987; Dholakia, 1985; Bhattacharya and Mitra, 1990). It is also observed that among the three main sectors (viz., the primary, secondary and tertiary) both in respect of income generated as well as labour absorption, the tertiary sector has almost all throughout the four decade period 1951-91 held the second position less important than that of the primary sector, but more important than the secondary sector (Kumar and Mathur, 1996). However, unlike the share of labour force, the output share of services dominates over other sectors since the mid-eighties. Therefore, it is often argued that the structural diversification has been much more progressive with respect to output than with respect to employment (Planning Commission, 1990; Hari, 2003). At the state level, it is observed that towards the end of 1990s there has been a steady decline in the share of agriculture in output, a gentle rise in the share of industry and a steady rise in the share of service for most of the states (EPWRF, 2003; Shetty, 2003).

The present study is an attempt to examine the pattern of growth and the sectoral performance in state economy of Kerala from 1960-61 to 2004-05. The study makes use of time series data on NSDP at disaggregated level from National Accounts Statistics of the Central Statistical Organisation. The data on NSDP is available at different constant prices such as 1970-71, 1980-81 and 1993-94. In order to make the long-term data comparable, we have spliced different constant prices into a single series of 1980-81.

Growth of NSDP and Percapita Income

In this section we examine the growth of Net State Domestic Product (NSDP) and percapita NSDP of Kerala from 1960-61 to 2004-05. A comparison of Kerala is also made with India's Net National Product (NNP) and percapita NNP. First we look at the growth of NSDP and NNP and then move on to a comparison of percapita NSDP and percapita NNP.

The smoothened[1] curves of annual growth rates of NSDP and NNP has been presented in Figure 1 below.

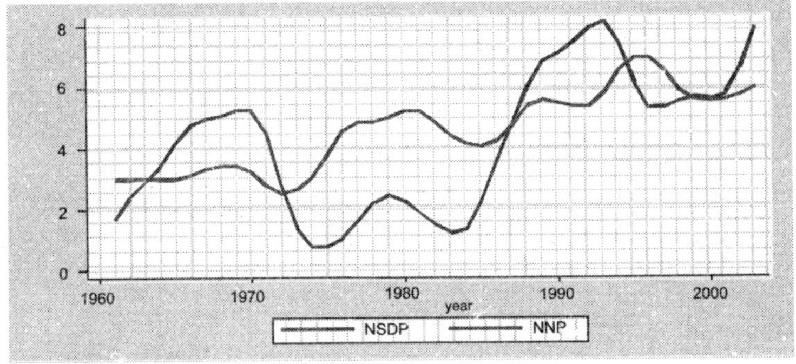

Figure 1: Growth of NSDP and NNP from 1960-61 to 2004-05

Figure 2 shows that the growth of NSDP in Kerala is highly fluctuating when compared to the growth of NNP. We may observe a sharp decline in NSDP growth from late Sixties to

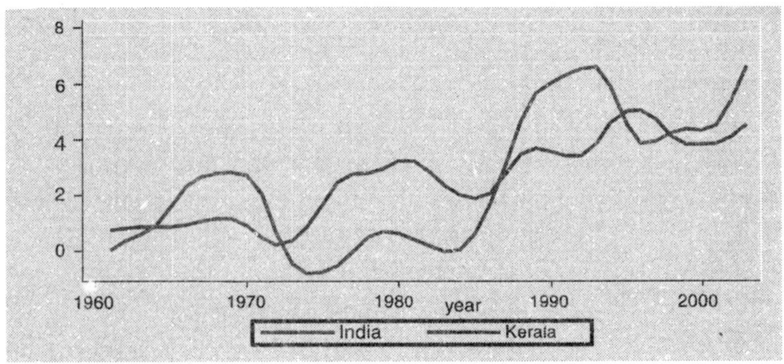

Figure 2: Annual Growth Rates of Percapita Income of Kerala and India: 1960-61 to 2004-05

Seventies and then maintains to be stagnant until mid-Eighties. After that the NSDP has been growing steadily. Except during two time periods–Sixties and Nineties–the growth of NSDP has been far below to that of NNP from 1960-61 to 2004-05. The sub-period wise rate of growth of NSDP and NNP has been reported in Table 1.

Table 1
Period-wise Average Annual Growth Rates of NSDP and NNP

Periods	*NNP*	*NSDP*
1960-61 to 1965-66	2.4	2.7
1966-67 to 1970-71	4.5	5.3
1971-72 to 1975-76	3.0	2.6
1976-77 to 1980-81	2.9	1.8
1981-82 to 1985-86	4.7	1.4
1986-87 to 1990-91	5.8	5.3
1991-92 to 1995-96	5.0	6.8
1996-97 to 2000-01	5.8	5.1
2001-02 to 2004-05*	6.2	7.0

Note: *for India the average is from 2001-02 to 2003-04.

Table 1 presents the five-yearly averages of annual growth rates of NSDP and NNP. We may note from the Table that after an increase from first period to the second, the rate of growth of NSDP has been declining continuously till mid-1980s. For the subsequent sub-periods, the rates of growth show up and down alternatively. We may also note that the rate of growth of NSDP had been higher than that of NNP during the Sixties. For the subsequent two decades-from 1970s to 1980s–NSDP growth becomes lower than the NNP. The picture of 1990s shows that the rate of growth of NSDP is higher during the first half but again become lower during the second half. During the last sub-period the NSDP growth again registers a higher rate when compared to the NNP. This implies that the state domestic product of Kerala economy tends to accelerate and becomes higher than that of national income during the reform period. The case of percapita income growth in Kerala is more or less comparable to that of NSDP except during the last fifteen years.

Similar to that of NSDP, the average annual growth rate of Kerala's per capita income is also found to be fluctuating over the period. It can be noted that for almost two decades (from mid 1970s to late 1980s), the rate of growth of Kerala's percapita income had been much lower than the all India average. But, since the late 1980s, Kerala is found to be surpassing the rate of growth of all India per capita income. The sub-period wise annual growth rate has been reported in Table 1.

Table 2
Average Annual Growth Rates of Percapita Income

Periods	*India*	*Kerala*
1960-61 to 1965-66	0.2	0.2
1966-67 to 1970-71	2.4	3.0
1971-72 to 1975-76	0.7	0.6
1976-77 to 1980-81	0.8	0.4
1981-82 to 1985-86	2.6	0.1
1986-87 to 1990-91	3.8	3.9
1991-92 to 1995-96	3.0	5.2
1996-97 to 2000-01	4.0	3.9
2001-02 to 2004-05*	4.6	5.6

Note: *for India the average is from 2001-02 to 2003-04.

Table 2 shows that after stagnation for the period from 1960-61 to 1985-86, the State's percapita income starts showing a significant positive trend and consistently been higher than that of all India. This observation formed the basis for the argument that Kerala is no longer an economically poor state, but is turning around[2]. Kannan (2005) argues that Kerala attained this turnaround in growth as a result of economic reforms and the large inflow of remittances. The outcome of economic reforms, according to him, is the discontinuation of fixed-exchange rate system in favour of a market-determined one, which have contributed to the strengthening of the role of remittances.

There was skepticism that the growth of percapita income in Kerala might be attributed to the sustained decline in the population growth rate (Chakraborty, 2005). In contrast to it we find that the movement of NSDP is almost similar to that of per capita income. It is also evident that for all the sub-periods, the average annual growth rate of NSDP is invariably higher than the average growth rate of percapita income. This may imply that the growth of percapita income might mainly be driven by the growth of NSDP rather a decline in population growth as doubted earlier.

Sectoral Performance

Conventionally NSDP has been classified into three broad sectors such as primary, secondary and tertiary sectors (see Fisher, 1939 and Clark, 1940). In some of the studies, it has been classified as Agriculture, Manufacturing and Services (see Kuznets, 1957)[3]. In the present study we follow the standard classification given by the NAS as primary sector (which includes agriculture, forestry and logging, fishing, and mining and quarrying), secondary sector (which includes registered and unregistered manufacturing, construction, electricity, gas and water supply) and tertiary sector (which includes transport, storage and communication, trade, hotels and restaurants, banking and insurance, real estate, pubic administration and other services). Here we try to examine the changing pattern of share and growth of these broad sectors in order to trace out whether the Kerala economy is registering a logistic pattern of growth predicted by the theory of growth and structural change. First we look at the percentage share of each sector to NSDP and then examine the rate of growth of these sectors over the period. Followed by this, we explore which sector has been a main contributor to the growth of NSDP over the years.

Sectoral Share

The percentage share of primary, secondary, tertiary sectors to NSDP has been plotted in the following Figure 3. It is evident from the figure that the share of primary sector had been assuming first position for about two decades from 1960-61 to 1982-83. As the share of this sector has consistently been declining over the period, the position got changes to second from 1982-83 to 1999-00 and further becomes third in position after that. The share of secondary sector is observed as almost stable and falls below to other two sectors for the entire period of analysis except during the last few years when it cuts the primary sector and assumes second position next to the tertiary sector. The decline in the share of primary sector has solely been compensated by the increase in tertiary sector, the share of which almost doubles from 1960-61 to 2004-05.

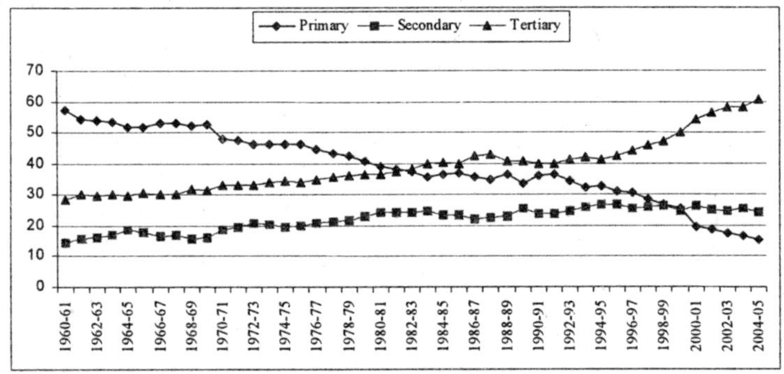

Figure 3: Percentage Share of Primary, Secondary and Tertiary Sectors to NSDP

Table 3
Sectoral Share in NSDP for Different Time Points

	Primary	*Secondary*	*Tertiary*
1960-61	57	14	28
1970-71	48	19	33
1980-81	39	24	36
1990-91	36	24	40
2000-01	19	26	54
2004-05	15	24	61

As the Table 3 shows the decline share of primary sector has been remarkable from 57 per cent in 1960-61 to just 15 per cent in 204-05. In contrast, the share of tertiary sector, which was only 28 per cent in 1960-61, has surged to 61 per cent in 2004-05. The share of secondary sector, however, has shown a 10-percentage point increase from 1960-61 to 2004-05 (see Table 3). Therefore, one can argue that in Kerala the share of tertiary sector surpassed primary much before the secondary sector's share becomes higher than the primary sector. This points to the fact that tertiarisation in the state economy of Kerala is not a pos-industrialised phenomenon but has taken its cue from the agriculture sector. The phenomenon of tertiary sector predominance before the secondary sector has been observed as a contrasting feature of the logistic pattern of growth predicted by the theory of growth and structural change.

Sectoral Growth

In Figure 4 we present the annual growth rates of three broad sectors from 196-61 to 2004-05. We may note from the figure that the line of primary sector growth rate lies below to those of other two sectors through out the whole period of analysis. After a stagnation and revival the rate of growth of primary sector registers a declining trend from the beginning of 1990s. The secondary sector, even though with frequent up down swings in the growth rates, almost moves hand in hand with tertiary sector till the later 1980s. But it shows an obvious middle position since 1990s onwards. The rate of growth of tertiary sector, which was moving above to that of primary sector over the period, becomes a dominant sector since the mid-1990s.

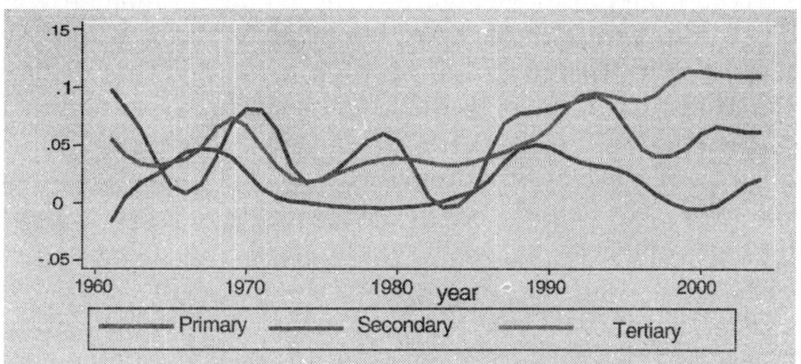

Figure 4: Annual Growth Rates of Primary, Secondary and Tertiary Sectors from 1960-61 to 200-4-05

It is interesting to note that the movement of all the three sectors shows a similar pattern observed for NSDP and percapita income from the mid 1970s to late 1980s. We may recall that during this period the growth of percapita income and NSDP has shown a sharp decline and stagnation. An 'U' shaped portion of the curve during this period is evident more with respect to primary sector, but the other two sectors also show more or less similar shape. This implies that the decline and stagnation of percapita income and NSDP in Kerala during the period could be attributed to the combined effect of all the three sectors, but more importantly due to the primary sector.

Table 4
Average Annual Growth Rates of Broad Sectors of Kerala

Periods	*Primary*	*Secondary*	*Tertiary*
1960-61 to 1965-66	0.8	7.4	4.1
1966-67 to 1970-71	3.7	6.9	7.2
1971-72 to 1975-76	1.8	3.9	3.0
1976-77 to 1980-81	-1.5	6.1	3.3
1981-82 to 1985-86	0.2	0.6	3.2
1986-87 to 1990-91	5.1	6.0	5.3
1991-92 to 1995-96	3.6	9.1	8.0
1996-97 to 2000-01	-3.9	4.9	10.4
2001-02 to 2004-05	1.0	4.7	10.0

Table 2 gives numerical evidence to the growth pattern observed from the above Figure 4. The average annual growth rates of different sub-periods give us an indication that the primary sector has not at all been promising. Except during 1966-67 to 1970-71 and 1981-82 to 1985-86, the average annual growth rates of the secondary sector have consistently been higher than those of other two sectors for all the sub-periods from 1960-61 to 1995-96. For the last two sub-periods, i.e. from mid 1990s onwards, tertiary sector dominates the other two in terms of the average annual growth rates. Moreover, the rate of growth of tertiary sector even becomes two digits during the last two sub-periods of analysis. These observations may imply that the growth of percapita income or NSDP of the state economy of Kerala owes heavily to primary sector during the initial decade and then to secondary sector, especially till the first half of 1990s since when the tertiary sector happens to be the most import sector of the growth income in Kerala. In the following section, we discuss which among these sectors contribute more to the growth of NSDP and how it varies over different sub-periods.

Sectoral Contribution

The contribution of different sectors to the growth of NSDP over the period has been examined using a simple method employed in most of the empirical studies on growth and sectoral performance (see Pillai and Santha, 2005). As per this method, the share of each sector has to be weighted with corresponding growth rates. The sum of share weighted growth rates of each sector would add up to the growth rates of total NSDP. From this, we may easily understand the relative contribution of each sector to the growth of NSDP. The sectoral contribution of each sector in terms of share weighted growth rates during different time periods are shown below in Table 5.

Table 5
Share Weighted Growth Rate

Periods	*Primary*	*Secondary*	*Tertiary*	*NSDP**
1960-61 to 1965-66	0.4	1.1	1.2	2.7
1966-67 to 1970-71	1.9	1.1	2.2	5.3
1971-72 to 1975-76	0.8	0.7	1.0	2.6
1976-77 to 1980-81	-0.7	1.3	1.2	1.8
1981-82 to 1985-86	0.0	0.1	1.3	1.4
1986-87 to 1990-91	1.7	1.4	2.2	5.3
1991-92 to 1995-96	1.2	2.3	3.3	6.8
1996-97 to 2000-01	-1.0	1.2	4.8	5.1
2001-02 to 2004-05	0.2	1.2	5.7	7.0

Note: 1. *NSDP = average of annual growth rates.
2. Primary, Secondary and Tertiary = share weighted growth.

It is interesting to note from the above table that the tertiary sector has invariably been the main contributor to the growth of NSDP in Kerala over the whole period of analysis. We may also note that the share weighted growth rate of the services sector consistently increases from 1970s onwards, whereas the rates of other two sectors are highly fluctuating. Secondary sector can be observed as a significant contributor and stands next to the tertiary sector. The primary sector seems to be an insignificant contributor to the growth of NSDP except during late 1960s and late 1980s when the contribution of this sector become higher than the secondary sector. During the second half of 1970s and 1990s, the primary sector even becomes a negative contributor to the growth of NSDP. Even though the share of primary sector had been predominant till the early 1980s, when we look at the share weighted growth rare and sectoral contribution, this sector proves to be insignificant because of its sustained decline in the rate of growth over time.

If we look at the Figure 5, it is evident that from 1991 onwards the difference between the height of the tertiary sector and secondary sector widens for all the sub-periods. In other words, we may argue that the gap between the tertiary sector and other sector in terms of their respective contribution to the growth of State Domestic Product is widening during the reform period and that the tertiary sector becomes a sole contributor at the cost of other sectors.

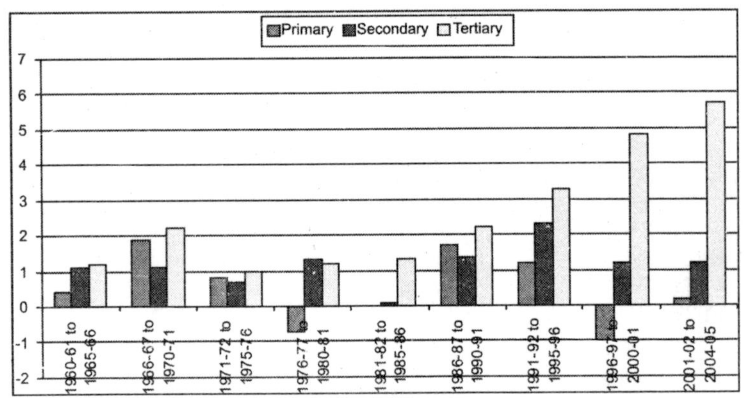

Figure 5: Sectoral Contribution to the Growth of NSDP

So far we have been discussing on the growth and structural change in the state economy of Kerala based on three broad sectors such as Agriculture, Industry and Services and observed that services sector has been major contributor to the growth of State Domestic Product for the whole period of analysis and particularly during the reform period. In the following sections we examine among these three broad sectors which sub-component is more significant in determining the overall growth of the economy. We take each of the three sectors separately and analyse its performance at disaggregated levels.

Sectoral Performance at Disaggregated Level

Share of Primary Sector Sub-components

As we mentioned earlier we include agriculture, forestry and logging, fisheries and mining and quarrying in the primary sector. The shares of sub-sectors in total primary sector for six time points–1960-61, 1970-71, 1980-81, 1990-91, 2000-01 and 2004-05–are given in the following Figure 6. The lower most area (with vertical shade) shows the share of agriculture, above to this forestry and logging, and then Fishing. The upper most area shows the share of mining and quarrying.

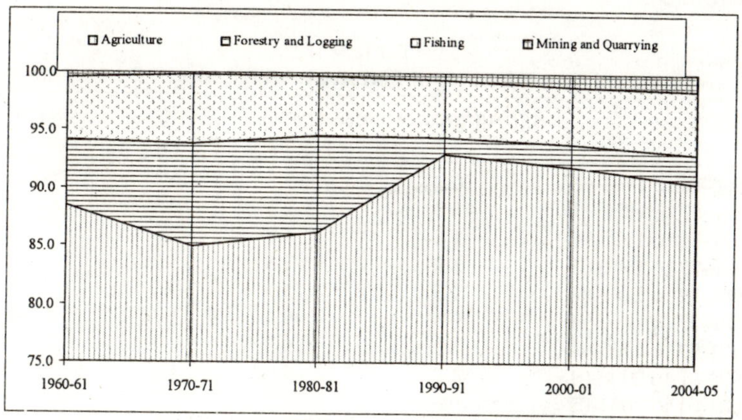

Figure 6: Sub-sectoral Shares of Primary Sector

It is evident from the above figure that for the entire period of analysis, the major sub-component of primary sector is agriculture, the share of which ranges from 88 to 90 per cent. The next important component has been forestry and logging until 1991, after that the share of fishing assumes the second position. Mining and quarrying sector has relatively very small share in primary sector, but is showing an increasing trend during reforms. It is seen that the share of agriculture in total primary sector has been increasing till 1990-91 and then it declines marginally during the reform period. The share of forestry and logging also found to be declining during the reform period. However, the decline in the shares of these two sectors has observed as mostly been compensated by mining and quarrying sub-component in the reform period. Even though the share of mining and quarrying is meager in total primary, it gets doubled during the reform period from 0.7 to 1.4 per cent pointing to the fact that this sector assumes advantage of reforms while all other sectors suffer.

Growth and Contribution of Primary Sector Sub-components

Here we analyse the annual growth rates and contribution of primary sector sub-components over the period. The average annual growth rates for different sub-periods are given below (Table 6).

Table 6

Average Annual Growth Rates of Different Sub-sectors of Primary Sector

Periods	*Agriculture*	*Forestry and Logging*	*Fishing*	*Mining and Quarrying*
1960-61 to 1965-66	0.4	13.3	-6.4	-14.3
1966-67 tc 1970-71	3.3	2.3	16.8	4.0
1971-72 to 1975-76	1.6	4.2	2.8	-4.2
1976-77 to 1980-81	-1.0	-4.3	-3.0	20.5
1981-82 to 1985-86	1.5	-15.1	-0.5	5.9
1986-87 to 1990-91	5.3	-9.3	11.8	35.7
1991-92 to 1995-96	3.8	9.5	-1.4	3.3
1996-97 to 2000-01	-4.2	-0.5	1.4	8.7
2001-02 to 2004-05	0.6	7.3	3.5	8.0

From the earlier section we found that agriculture constitutes a share of almost 88 to 90 per cent of the total primary sector. But, with respect to the rate of growth, this sector shows a dismal picture. From the mid-1980s onwards it registers a continuous decline in average annual growth rate. This would imply that the stagnant behaviour of total primary sector during the reform period is mainly due to the agriculture sub-component. Other sectors such as forestry and logging and fishing register a highly fluctuating pattern similar to that of agriculture. But, during the reform period, the sub-sector fishing is showing acceleration in the rate of growth. It is interesting to note that the rate of growth of mining and quarrying sector is more impressive than any other sub-sector. The growth of mining and quarrying has been observed to be the only reason for the tendency of total primary sector to pick up during the last period of analysis as shown earlier (see section 4.2). In sum, we may argue that during the reform period, mining and quarrying sub-component of the primary sector improves significantly both in terms of shares and rate of growth. The case of fishing is also found to be promising during this period, while the share and growth of other two sub-sectors start declining.

Table 7
Share Weighted Growth Rates of Primary Sector Sub-components

Periods	*Agriculture*	*Forestry and Logging*	*Fishing*	*Mining and Quarrying*	*Growth rate of Primary*
1960-61 to 1965-66	0.32	0.87	-0.37	-0.07	0.8
1966-67 to 1970-71	2.82	0.21	0.67	0.00	3.7
1971-72 to 1975-76	1.32	0.31	0.16	-0.01	1.8
1976-77 to 1980-81	-0.81	-0.42	-0.28	0.03	-1.5
1981-82 to 1985-86	1.36	-1.07	-0.10	0.01	0.2
1986-87 to 1990-91	5.01	-0.27	0.28	0.11	5.1
1991-92 to 1995-96	3.51	0.14	-0.06	0.00	3.6
1996-97 to 2000-01	-3.96	-0.01	0.04	0.06	-3.9
2001-02 to 2004-05	0.58	0.16	0.17	0.10	1.0

As mentioned earlier, we also attempt to analyse the share weighted growth rates of each sub-sector to understand which among these sectors contribute more to the average annual growth rate of total primary sector. We may note that since the share of agriculture sub-component is almost 90% of primary sector, its contribution to the growth of total primary has been highest for most of the sub-periods under consideration. In the other words, we may argue that the up and down of the primary sector and its contribution to the State Domestic Product of Kerala over the period is caused by the movement of the sub-component agriculture. The fluctuations in and stagnation of the agriculture sub-sector can in turn be due to the decline in the area, production and productivity of principal crops, an analysis of which is beyond the scope this study.

Share of Secondary Sector Sub-components

The sub-components included in this sector are Registered Manufacturing, Unregistered Manufacturing, Construction, and Electricity, Gas and Water Supply. The shares of each of these sectors for different time points are given below (see Figure 7). The total manufacturing sector shown in the below table is the combination of registered and unregistered manufacturing. The total manufacturing assumes highest share in sector for all the time points under consideration. However, the share of this sub-sector registers sharp decline from 63 per cent in 1960-61 to 41 per cent in 2004-05. The decline is more pronounced during the reform period–from 1990-91 to 2004-05.

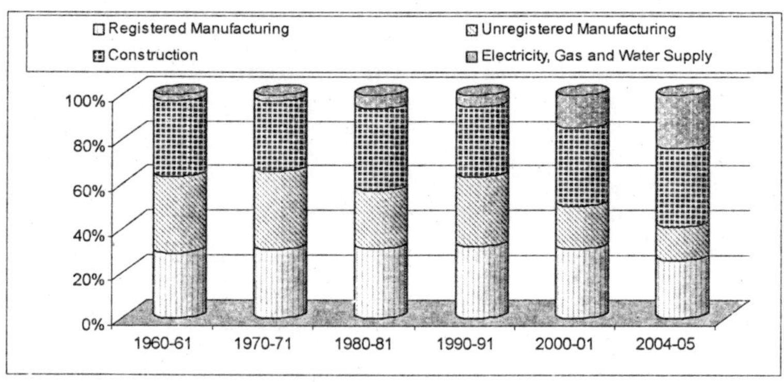

Figure 7: Share of Secondary Sector Sub-components for Different Time Points

Note: lowest portion measures Registered manufacturing, above to this Unregistered and construction respectively; and the upper most part of the cylinders gives Electricity, gas and Water supply.

If we look at the individual sub-sectors, we may find that the unregistered manufacturing had been showing highest share during the 1960s and 1970s. Since 1980s, the construction sector dominates over other sub-sectors until the recent time point. It is evident from the figure that the shares of registered and unregistered manufacturing decline over time; the decline being higher for the later compared to the former. We may observe a drastic decline in the shares of both registered and unregistered manufacturing sub-components during the reform period: from 31 per cent during 1990-91, the share of unregistered sector becomes just 15 per cent in 2004-05.

However, a considerable increase in share has been observed in the sub-sector electricity, gas and water especially during the reform period, when its share surges from 5 to 24 per cent. In the other words, decline in the share of unregistered manufacturing during the reform has been compensated mainly by the sub-components construction and electricity, gas and water supply.

Growth and Contribution of Secondary Sector Sub-components

Similar to the decline observed with respect to the shares, the registered and unregistered manufacturing sectors have been showing a diminishing trend in growth rates too. Interestingly, the decline in growth rates is found to be sharp during the reform period–from 1990-91 to 2004-05. During this period the rate of growth of total manufacturing sector declined from 8.9 (in 1990-91 to 1995-96) to –0.2 per cent (in 2004-05). The case of registered manufacturing shows a decline from 9.2 to 1.1 per cent during the same period. Unregistered manufacturing even registers negative growth rate from mid-1990s onwards. These may imply that even though the initial phase of reform has benefited the unregistered manufacturing sector of the states, it was hit heavily during the later phase–from mid-1990s to 2004-05.

Even though the rates of growth of construction and electricity, gas and water supply show a highly fluctuating behaviour, we may observe a promising positive higher growth rates for these sectors. Specifically, during the reform period the rates of growth of these two sectors are found to be much higher than that of the manufacturing sector. Among these, electricity, gas and water supply shows highest growth rates starting from 1985-86 onwards. We may recall that the share of this sector was also observed as surging during the same period.

Table 8
Average Annual Growth Rates of Secondary Sector Sub-components

Periods	*Manu-facturing total*	*Registered Manu-facturing*	*Unregistered Manu-facturing*	*Construc-tion*	*Electricity, Gas and Water Supply*
1960-61 to 1965-66	4.0	8.1	-0.1	13.2	9.7
1966-67 to 1970-71	10.7	7.3	19.0	1.7	8.4
1971-72 to 1975-76	3.4	3.6	3.6	4.5	9.4
1976-77 to 1980-81	3.8	7.6	0.3	9.9	13.3
1981-82 to 1985-86	2.1	1.5	3.0	1.1	-8.9
1986-87 to 1990-91	7.1	9.1	10.0	2.7	68.6
1991-92 to 1995-96	8.9	9.2	8.7	10.8	11.6
1996-97 to 2000-01	0.3	3.6	-3.9	6.6	36.3
2001-02 to 2004-05	-0.2	1.1	-2.0	5.7	17.4

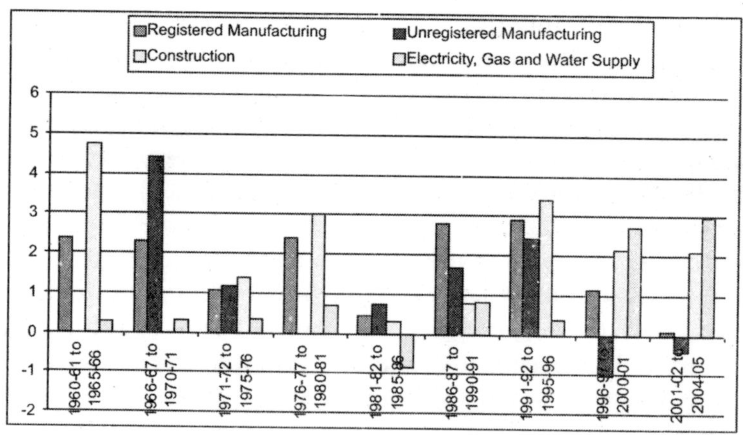

Figure 8: Relative Contribution Different Sub-sectors to the Growth of Secondary Sector

An interesting observation emerges from the above figure is that the construction sector has always been a significant contributor to the growth of secondary sector even though it has very high fluctuations through out. The contributions of registered and unregistered manufacturing to the total secondary sector had been considerable until the first half of 1990s and since then become too insignificant due to the decline in both shares and growth rates of these sector during the last two sub-period under analysis. With the rise in share and growth rate of construction and electricity sub-sectors, we could find a highest and increasing contribution of these sectors to the growth of total secondary sector in the reform period. Therefore, we may argue that within the secondary sector the important contributors of growth are construction and electricity, gas and water supply during the reform period.

The emergence of new generation banks during reforms, which provide easy and quick credit facilities for housing purposes, and increased electrification, gas connections, and drinking water facilities might be argued as important reasons for the hike in the share and growth of these sectors. Together with this, the influence of remittances from Gulf and other countries might also have contributed to the growth of these sectors in general, and construction sector in particular. The performance of construction sector during the reform period could be related to the growth performance of mining and quarrying too. The growing demand for inputs to the surging construction works in the state might have at least partly been provided by the quarrying activities within the state.

Tertiary Sector

Tertiary sector encompasses a myriad of services activities, which are broadly covered under such sub-sectors as Transport, Storage and Communication, Trade, Hotels and Restaurants, Banking and Insurance, Real Estate, Ownership of Dwellings and Business Services, Public Administration and Other Services. This section deals with the shares, growth rate and contribution of each of these sub-sectors over the period. The methodology and periodisation is similar to that discussed in earlier sections.

It is evident from the above table that the sub-sector trade, hotels and restaurants has been dominating over all other sectors in terms of percentage share to total tertiary sector for

Table 9
Shares of Tertiary Sector Sub-components

	1960-1961	*1970-1971*	*1980-1981*	*1990-1991*	*2000-2001*	*2004-2005*
Transport, Storage and Communication	6	8	10	14	24	33
Railways	0.3	0.3	0.3	0.4	0.3	0.3
Transport by other means and Storage	6	6	8	11	18	17
Communication	1	1	2	2	6	15
Trade, Hotels and Restaurants	45	50	41	34	29	24
Banking and Insurance	4	5	8	18	23	21
Real Estate, etc	13	9	9	1	0	0
Public Administration	4	6	11	15	11	12
Other Services	27	23	21	17	13	11

about four decades from 1960-61. However, the share of this sector consistently declines over time: from 45 per cent in 1960-61 to 25 per cent in 2004-05, about 20-percentage point decline. We observe a sharp decline in the share of 'other services' too during the period. The share of 'other services' declines from 27 per cent in 1960-61 to about 11 per cent in 2004-05–almost 17 per centage point decline. The sub-component real estate is also showing a decline in its share through out the whole period of analysis. The decline in the shares of these sectors has mostly been compensated by transport, storage and communication, and banking and insurance sub-components. Transport, storage and communication sector has even become a dominant sector during 2001-02 to 2004-05. Within this sector, communication is observed to be an emerging component especially since 1990s. A surge in share could be noted in the banking and insurance sector, which shows an increase from 4 per cent in 1960-61 to 21 per cent in 2004-05. Public administration registers an increasing share from 1960-61 to 1990-91, but after that it again comes down. All these imply that during the reform period, sectors such as trade, hotels and restaurants, other services and real estate are declining fast and sectors such as transport, communication and banking and insurance are emerging as important components of the total tertiary sector in Kerala economy.

Table 10
Annual Average Growth Rates of Tertiary Sector Sub-components

Periods	*1960-1961 to 1965-1966*	*1966-1967 to 1970-1971*	*1971-1972 to 1975-1976*	*1976-1977 to 1980-1981*	*1981-1982 to 1985-1986*	*1986-1987 to 1990-1991*	*1991-1992 to 1995-1996*	*1996-1997 to 2000-2001*	*2001-2002 to 2004-2005*
Transport, Storage and Communication	6	8	5	7	9	7	19	12	18
Railways	1	10	2	5	16	1	12	7	3
Transport by other means and Storage	6	8	5	6	10	8	19	10	8
Communication	14	10	7	10	6	7	19	25	40
Trade, Hotels and Restaurants	4	10	2	1	1	4	6	9	5
Banking and Insurance	10	4	11	9	11	15	10	15	8
Real Estate, etc.	3	1	3	3	-5	-19	-12	4	3
Public Administration	10	8	8	14	6	10	3	10	13
Other Services	3	5	2	2	2	2	5	7	5

The pattern of growth rates observed during the reform period is more or less similar to that of the movement of sectoral shares discussed in the earlier section. That is, the rate of growth of communication sub-component is found to be much higher than those of all other sectors over the period in general, and during the reform period in particular (see Table 10). There has been acceleration in the rate of growth of communication from 7 per cent during the late 1980s to 40 per cent during 2000-01 to 2004-05. The sub-sector public administration also registers a rise in the rate of growth in the reform period from 3 per cent during the first half of 1990s to 13 per cent during 2000s. The banking and insurance sector shows considerable growth till 2000-01, but declines thereafter. The average growth rate of transport and storage sector may also be commendable till the end of 1990s, but it fails to maintain a higher growth rate during the last sub-period. From 1980s to 1990s the growth of trade, hotels and restaurants registers acceleration and during the later period it declines. These observations point to the fact that the sub-sectors transport, communication, banking and insurance and public administration are becoming promising during the reform period with respect to the average annual growth rate. We may recall that all of these sectors, except public administration were observed as emerging sectors with respect to per centage shares also.

The above Table 11 shows the contribution of different sub-sectors to the growth of total tertiary sector during various time periods. It can be noted from table that until the first half of 1970s the highest contributor to the growth of total tertiary sector in Kerala economy had been the sub-sector trade, hotels and restaurants. Next to this comes the contribution of 'other services'. From mid-1970s to 1990-91, the sub-sectors Transport and Communication, Banking and Insurance and Public Administration become the important contributors to the growth of tertiary sector. However, since 1991 onwards the major contributor to the growth of tertiary sector has been the Transport and Communication and Banking and Insurance, among which the sub-component communication becomes the single most important contributor during 2001-02 to 2004-05.

Table 11

Contribution of Different Sub-components to the Growth of Total Tertiary Sector

Periods	*1960-1961 to 1965-1966*	*1966-1967 to 1970-1971*	*1971-1972 to 1975-1976*	*1976-1977 to 1980-1981*	*1981-1982 to 1985-1986*	*1986-1987 to 1990-1991*	*1991-1992 to 1995-1996*	*1996-1997 to 2000-2001*	*2001-2002 to 2004-2005*
Transport, Storage and Communication	9.8	8.3	13.3	18.2	31.3	17.0	41.3	26.0	51.0
Railways	0.0	0.0	0.0	0.0	3.1	0.0	0.0	0.0	0.0
Transport by other means and Storage	7.3	6.9	10.0	12.1	25.0	15.1	35.0	16.3	15.0
Communication	2.4	1.4	3.3	3.0	3.1	1.9	5.0	9.6	36.0
Trade, Hotels and Restaurants	39.0	63.9	26.7	12.1	15.6	22.6	25.0	23.1	12.0
Banking and Insurance	9.8	2.8	16.7	18.2	31.3	41.5	22.5	29.8	17.0
Real Estate, etc	9.8	1.4	6.7	9.1	-12.5	-13.2	-2.5	0.0	0.0
Public Administration	9.8	5.6	16.7	33.3	21.9	26.4	3.8	11.5	14.0
Other Services	17.1	16.7	20.0	12.1	12.5	5.7	11.3	9.6	7.0
Tertiary	100.0	100.0	100.0	100.0	100.0	100.0	100.0	100.0	100.0

Note: figures are in percentages.

The contribution of sub-sectors such as real estate and 'other services' are found to be negligible during the 1980s and 1990s. This would imply that the growth of tertiary sector during the reform period owes heavily to two sub-sectors: transport and communication and banking and insurance.

Sub-sectoral Contribution to the Growth of NSDP

So far we have been discussing the relative contribution of Primary, Secondary and Tertiary to the growth of NSDP over the period and particularly during the reform period. Then we moved on to find out the main drivers of these sectors at disaggregated level. The analysis has shown the tertiary sector as the important contributor to the growth of NSDP over the period. At disaggregate level, we observed that during the reform period, the growth of primary sector has mainly been driven by the sub-sector agriculture, but it terms of share and growth mining and quarrying was observed to the important component. The major contributor to growth of secondary sector has been found as construction and electricity, gas and water supply; whereas the growth of tertiary sector has mainly been caused by transport, communication and banking and insurance sub-sectors during the reform period.

What follows is a detailed examination to find out the leading and lagging sectors of the economy by looking at the relative contribution of all the sub-sectors to the growth NSDP for the entire period of analysis. Table 12 above gives the contribution of each sub-sector to the growth of NSDP over the period. It is very interesting to note that the sub-sector agriculture had been the single most important contributor to the growth of NSDP in Kerala from 1966-67 to 1990-91 except during 1976-77 to 1980-81, when construction overtook the predominance of agriculture[4].

The picture completely changes during the reform period in such a way that during the first half of 1990s the sub-sectors manufacturing and transport and communication drive the growth of NSDP. During the later half of the 1990s, banking and insurance sector dominates over all other sectors and during 2001-02 to 2004-05 the sub-sector transport and

Table 12
Contribution Different Sub-sectors to the Growth of NSDP

Sectors/Periods	*1960-1961 to 1965-1966*	*1966-1967 to 1970-1971*	*1971-1972 to 1975-1976*	*1976-1977 to 1980-1981*	*1981-1982 to 1985-1986*	*1986-1987 to 1990-1991*	*1991-1992 to 1995-1996*	*1996-1997 to 2000-2001*	*2001-2002 to 2004-2005*
Agriculture	6.0	28.3	24.2	-20.4	32.9	32.2	17.4	-19.9	1.3
Forestry and Logging	16.7	2.0	5.5	-10.6	-29.1	-1.7	0.7	0.0	0.4
Fishing	-7.5	6.7	3.0	-7.4	-2.7	1.6	-0.3	0.2	0.4
Mining and Quarrying	-1.3	0.1	-0.1	0.7	0.2	0.7	0.0	0.3	0.2
Primary Total	13.9	37.0	32.6	-37.6	1.3	32.8	17.8	-19.5	2.4
Manufacturing*	13.8	20.8	16.2	27.6	19.8	18.7	19.9	0.4	-1.5
Registered	13.9	7.3	7.5	27.4	7.6	10.4	10.8	5.6	0.1
Unregistered	-0.1	13.4	8.8	0.2	12.2	8.4	9.1	-5.2	-1.6
Construction	26.8	-0.7	10.2	37.2	3.9	3.5	12.3	10.4	7.4
Electricity, Gas and Water Supply	1.5	0.9	2.6	7.9	-14.5	3.5	1.3	13.5	10.7
Secondary Total	42.1	21.0	29.0	72.7	9.2	25.7	33.6	24.3	16.6
Transport and Communication@	4.8	3.7	5.0	11.5	27.6	7.2	19.9	25.4	41.1
Railways	0.0	0.1	0.1	0.3	1.5	0.0	0.2	0.2	0.1
Transport by other means	3.7	2.9	3.9	8.6	23.1	6.0	17.1	15.9	12.0
Communication	1.1	0.6	1.0	2.7	3.0	1.1	2.7	9.3	29.0
Trade, Hotels and Restaurants	17.2	26.8	10.3	7.8	13.7	9.9	11.9	22.6	10.0
Banking and Insurance	4.8	1.1	6.9	12.5	28.8	16.9	10.7	27.4	13.6
Real Estate, etc	4.3	0.6	3.0	4.8	-11.5	-5.7	-1.3	0.0	0.0

Cont...

Sectors/Periods	*1960-1961 to 1965-1966*	*1966-1967 to 1970-1971*	*1971-1972 to 1975-1976*	*1976-1977 to 1980-1981*	*1981-1982 to 1985-1986*	*1986-1987 to 1990-1991*	*1991-1992 to 1995-1996*	*1996-1997 to 2000-2001*	*2001-2002 to 2004-2005*
Public Administration	4.8	2.6	5.8	21.2	19.0	10.7	2.0	10.5	11.2
Other Services	8.1	7.2	7.4	7.1	11.9	2.5	5.4	9.3	5.2
Tertiary Total	44.0	42.0	38.4	64.9	89.5	41.5	48.6	95.2	81.1
NSDP	100	100	100	100	100	100	100	100	100

Note: 1. *Manufacturing is the sum of Registered and Unregistered Manufacturing.
2. @Transport and Communication is the sum of Railways, Transport by other means and Communication.

communication again assumes the first position in terms of relative contribution to the growth of Kerala's Net Domestic Product. These imply that until the initiation of reform in the country, the agriculture sector of the state economy had been occupying a predominant role and during the initial years of reforms the state has witnessed a highest contribution of manufacturing sector. When the reform initiatives were set motion, the role of agriculture and manufacturing gets decayed and the tertiary sector sub-components such as transport, communication, banking and insurance start driving the economy to higher growth path. These findings raise important questions as why the prominence of agriculture and manufacturing has been lost during the reforms in favorable to some service activities in the state economy of Kerala; and whether reform policy has anything to do with the pattern of growth observed in the state. Moreover, the growth of NSDP propelled by transport, communication and banking and insurance (which are conventionally classified as producer's services) during the reform period is sustainable in the long run or not can also be an important question to be researched on. There is need for a detailed enquiry into these questions, which is beyond the scope of this study.

Summary and Concerns

The present study was basically exploratory in nature. First, it tries to account for the growth of NSDP and percapita income in Kerala over a long period from 1960-61 to 2004-05. The study then proceeds with exploring the main drivers of economic growth over the years, emphasising the reforms period, both at aggregate and at disaggregated levels. At the aggregate level, the analysis indicates that tertiary sector has been the main contributor to the growth of NSDP over the whole period of analysis, and the rate of contribution is increasing specifically during the reform period. The role of secondary sector has also been considerable at the beginning of reforms in the State but remains stagnant during the later years. Primary sector maintains to be an insignificant contributor to the growth of NSDP.

The disaggregate examination shows that the share and growth of mining and quarrying sub-sector is emerging as an important component of primary sector in the reform period; while within the secondary sector, the dominant components are proved to be construction, electricity, gas and water supply. The main driver of tertiary sector has been observed as transport and communication and banking and insurance. The analysis of sources of NSDP growth at disaggregated level provides evidences that until the initiation of reforms in the country the sub-component agriculture registers higher contribution to the average annual growth of NSDP in Kerala. During initial years of economic reforms manufacturing sector contributes more to the growth of State Domestic Product and in the later years of reforms, the service sub-sectors such as transport, communication and banking and insurance found to be the dominant ones.

An important question that emerges from these findings is whether one could find out a linkage between the growth performance of the emerging sub-sectors mining and quarrying, construction, electricity, gas and water supply, transport and communication and banking and insurance over the period. First of all we may hypothesise a link between mining and quarrying sub-sector with that of the construction. It can be argued that the mining and quarrying sector can partly meet the growing input demand of the surge in construction activities in the state. Further we may link the growth of construction and banking sectors in such a way that the increasing credits facilities available at the nationalized and new generation banks are more favourable for the housing purposes. Together with this, the growth of remittances may also be causing a construction boom in the state. The remittances and reforms might also have imparted its effect on extensive use of Internet and mobile phone facilities in the state, which in turn promotes the communication sub-sector.

The decaying role of agriculture and manufacturing sectors and the emerging presence of services such as communication transport, banking and insurances in the reform period may argued to be a cause of worry. The absence of material producing sectors in the state economy may not sustain the growth of NSDP in the long run. Important questions remain to be answered are why the agriculture and manufacturing sectors have shown demise during the reform period? Can we relate the reform initiatives and the declining share and growth of agriculture and manufacturing sectors? If yes, then what are ways in which the reforms might have influenced the agriculture and manufacturing?

Notes

1. Smoothening of annual growth rates has been fitted using 4253eh formula given in the statistical software STATA.
2. See Ahluwaliah (2000), Kannan (2005), Subrahmanian (2005), and Achin (2005).
3. There is disagreement among scholars with respect to the inclusion of mining and quarrying. For some, this sector has to be included in the Primary (or Agriculture) sector, and for some others it has to be included in the Secondary (OR Manufacturing) sector. But if we follow the logic that all the extractive activities could be brought under the head of primary sector, the sub-sector, mining and quarrying would fall in the Primary sector category.
4. Our finding of the predominance of agriculture's contribution to growth of NSDP has also been observed by Pillai and Shanta (2005) during the 1980s.

References

Ahluwalia, M S (2000), 'Economic Performance of the States in the Post Reform Period', *Economic and Political Weekly*, Vol. 35, No. 17.

Bhattacharya, B. B. and Arup Mitra (1990), 'Excess Growth of Tertiary Sector in Indian Economy: Issues and Implications', *Economic and Political Weekly*, November 3, pp. 2445-50.

Chakraborty, Achin (2005), "Kerala's Changing Development Narratives" *Economic and Political Weekly*, February 5.

Clark, Colin (1940), '*The Conditions of Economic Progress*', Macmillan, London.

Fisher, A. G. B. (1935): 'Economic Implications of National Progress', *International Labour Review*.

———(1939), 'Production Primary, Secondary, Tertiary, *Economic Record,* June 24-30.

Kannan, K. P. (2005), "Kerala's Turnaround in Growth: Role of Social Development, Remittance and Reform", *Economic and Political Weekly*, February 5, pp. 548-554.

Kuznets, Simon (1958), 'Quantitative Aspects of the Economic Growth of Nations: Industrial Distribution of Income and Labour Force by States', United States 1919/21 to 1955, *Economic Development and Cultural Change.*

———(1966), '*Modern Economic Growth'*, Heinemann', London.

Mohan, R. and Shyjan, D. (2007), 'Taxing Powers and Developmental Role of the Indian States: A Study with Reference to Kerala', *Review of Development and Change,* Vol. XII, No. 1

Pillai, Mohanan and N. Shanta (2005), *Long Term Trends in the Growth and Structure of the Net State Domestic Product in Kerala,* Working Paper No. 376, Centre for Development Studies, Trivandrum, (*available from the website: www.cds.edu*).

Pushpangadan, K. (2003), *Remittances, Consumption and Economic Growth in Kerala 1980-2000,* Working Paper No. 343, Centre for Development Studies, Trivandrum, (*available from the website: www.cds.edu*).

Pushpangadan, K. (2004) Economic Growth of Kerala: A Study in Transition Dynamics, Mimeo Centre for Development Studies, Trivandrum.

Pushpangadan, K. and M. Parameswaran (2005), *Endogenous Identification of Growth Phases: An Application to Kerala Economy,* Mimeo, Centre for Development Studies, Trivandrum.

Rao, V. K. R. V. (1987), 'Growth and Structural Change in the Indian Economy' in Brahmananda, P R and Panchamukhi, V. R. (ed.) '*The Development Process of the Indian Economy*', Himalaya Pub. House, Bomaby

Subrahmanian, K. K. and Abdul Azeez (2000), *Industrial Growth in Kerala: Trends and Explanations*, Working Paper No. 310, Centre for Developments Studies, Trivandrum (*available from the website: www.cds.edu*).

EXTENT AND INTENSITY OF POVERTY IN KERALA

K. RAJAN

Introduction

Poverty is a universal phenomenon and is rampant in one form or another in almost all countries of the world. However, it is pervasive and severe in Underdeveloped Countries like India where millions of people suffer from deficiency of food due to insufficient purchasing power. One of the important objectives of government policy in these countries was to reduce the incidence of poverty by providing sufficient food at least in terms of calories. However, in spite of many decades of determined efforts to wipe out poverty, still millions of people in third world countries live in acute poverty.

There are innumerable studies about poverty in India, which provides information about various dimensions of Indian poverty. However, compared to the numerous studies about poverty at the national level, specific studies about Kerala poverty are very much limited. Nevertheless, the extent and intensity of poverty in Kerala are available from all India studies. Therefore, the present study is an attempt to examine the extent and incidence of poverty in Kerala on the basis of studies carried out at the all India level.

Objectives of the Paper

The important objectives of the paper are:

1. To highlight the major issues and debates in the measurement of poverty in India and Kerala;
2. To examine the extent and severity of poverty in Kerala, and;
3. To explain the reasons behind the changes in poverty in Kerala.

Data Sources and Methodology

The study is based on secondary information available from published and unpublished sources. The extent and intensity of poverty in Kerala is analysed on the basis of studies carried out by various institutions and individual researchers. However, there are wide differences among these studies in the methodology used, sources of data, period of study, reference period of survey, poverty line, price indices for inflating/deflating and in poverty index. Consequently, the findings of these studies are not strictly comparable. Bulk of the studies reviewed here are based on the National Sample Survey (NSS) consumer expenditure data whereas some of the studies are based on the data generated by the CSO or National Council of Applied Economic Research (NCAER). Still some studies are based on the reports of various ministries of the Central and state governments. Similarly some of the studies measured the extent of poverty in terms of the number and percentage of people below poverty line, a few others have measured the severity of poverty on the basis of severity indicators like Poverty Gap Index (PGI), and Foster, Greer, Tborbecke (FGT) and also on the basis of Human Poverty Index (HPI).

The rest of the paper is in four sections and the first section contains debates, controversies and concepts of poverty. Section 2 examines the extent and incidence of poverty in Kerala while section 3 analyses the possible reasons behind the changes in poverty. The last section is a summary of findings and conclusions.

SECTION-I

The Trickle Down-effect of Economic Growth

The developmental experts believed and propagated that poverty could be reduced after a certain level of GNP had been reached- first the cake had to be produced and made bigger before it could be equally distributed. They believed that once high-income levels were attained distribution would exert its leveling effect with greater ease through rapid percolation (Sastry 1979). For this reason, the governments and policy makers attached greater importance to rapid economic growth without considering the distributive side. In other words, the developmental experts believed in the trickle-down effect theory by which it is assumed that the benefits of economic growth would spread automatically to the lower sections of the society. Consequently, governments and policy makers in many countries considered economic growth a sure remedy for the problem of poverty. However, the development experience of most of the developing countries has been that with rapid economic growth, inequalities in income and wealth has increased without producing any "trickling-down" of benefits to the weaker sections of the society. As a result, in most of the developing countries, the number of poor has progressively increased in spite of their high rates of economic growth. The failure of economic growth to reduce poverty significantly has forced the developmental experts to recognize the failure of the Trickle–down effect theory. It is the realization of the failure of this theory that made Mahabub Ul Haq (1971) to assert "we were taught to take care of our GNP as this will take care of poverty. Let us reverse this and take care of poverty as this will take care of the GNP".

Trickle–Down Effect in India

In India too, there was a debate about the relationship between growth and poverty (trickle down mechanism). The Planners and policy makers, in the initial years believed that the benefits of growth would trickle down to the weaker sections of the society and would solve the problem of poverty. Accordingly, no significant effort was made to redistribute the gains of development to the poor. In contrast to the expectation of our planners, the benefits of growth did not percolate to the poorer segments of the society and the worst thing happened was that the poor became poorer and the number had really increased plan after plan. Thus, even with a 3.5 per cent annual growth of GNP in India during 1977-78, we could not reduce poverty annually by 3.5 per cent. Hence, it became apparent that the trickle down effect theory had failed in India too to solve the problem of poverty automatically in proportion to the growth rate of the economy. This has made Indian Planners and Policy makers to abandon the growth target for the solution of poverty and to launch specific poverty eradication programmes to redistribute income in favour of the poor during the 6th Plan period. Among the various poverty eradication programmes, till recently, the most important was the Integrated Rural Development Programme (IRDP) which was expected to make a major dent on rural poverty, which was found to be the severest in India.

Poverty Debates in India

There are a number of debates on the subject of poverty in India with reference to the superiority of data–whether the National Sample Survey data (NSS) is superior to the data generated by the National Council of Applied Economic Research (NCAER) or the data provided by the National Accounts Statistics (NAS). Similarly, there are debates about the recall period-7 day or 30 day recall period and also about the reference periods-whether 30 day Uniform Reference Period (URP) for all items is superior to a Mixed Reference Period (30 day reference period for certain frequently purchased items like food, paan, tobacco etc. and 365-day reference period for certain other infrequently purchased items like clothing and foot wear etc.), and about the comparability of poverty estimates of different rounds of NSS Consumption Expenditure Survey (CES) Data. There are also debates about poverty trends in India, about the association between rural poverty and agricultural performance, about the relationship between poverty and unemployment, and about the impact of IRDP in ameliorating poverty etc. The concept and measurement of poverty itself has resulted in a number of debates and controversies and here, we have briefly reviewed some of these controversies.

Dandekar-Sukhatme Controversy

There are many unresolved controversies in Indian poverty literature and one such controversy is about the calorie-intake required for an Indian to be above poverty line. Dandekar and Rath (1971) measured the extent of poverty in India on the basis of a poverty line of 2250 calorie percapita per day. According to Sukhatme (1981a), poor are those who cannot get a minimum of 1900 calorie percapita per day and 2250 calorie is only an average. Thus according to Sukhatme, Dandekar and Rath's poor include those individuals who obtain calories above 2250 and hence, the estimated poor include non-poor.

Minhas–Bardhan Controversy

There was a controversy between Minhas (1970) and Bardhan (1971) regarding the incidence of rural poverty in India during 1970s. According to Minhas, the incidence of poverty in rural India has declined considerably during the period 1960-61 to 1967-68 whereas the study by Bardhan found that it has increased significantly during the same period. Thus, these two studies, although based on same NSS data, have reached contradictory conclusions. The paradoxical conclusions may be due to the differences in poverty line and the methodology used for measuring the extent of poverty.

Controversy about the Price Indices

There is a controversy about the Price Indices used for inflating-deflating the poverty line. In India, poverty lines were originally calculated for two reference years 1960-61 and 1973-74. For the subsequent years, the poverty lines have been updated/down-dated by the price indices. Some researchers have used Whole Sale Price Indices (WSPI) whereas others used

Consumer Price Index for Agricultural Labourers (CPIAL) in respect of rural poor and Consumer Price Index for Industrial Workers (CPIIW) in respect of urban poor and still others used separate all-India and state-specific price indices for the rural and urban poor.

Controversy about the Comparability of Poverty Estimates

There are debates about the appropriateness of the recall period-7 day or 30 day and also about the reference periods-whether 30 day Uniform Reference Period (URP) or a Mixed Reference Period (MRP). In addition to this, there are debates about the comparability of poverty estimates of different rounds of NSS Consumption Expenditure Survey (CES) Data. Before the 50th round, National Sample Survey Organisation (NSSO) used the 30-day reference period whereas from 50th round on wards, NSSO has been using 7-day recall period. The consumption expenditure of 7-day recall period has been found to be higher than that of the 30-day recall period. As a result, there are variations in the per cent of people below poverty line as per different rounds of NSS estimates and has paused a problem about the appropriateness of comparing the trends in the extent of poverty over the years.

Poverty Debates and Controversies in Kerala

There are some debates and controversies about poverty in Kerala and these are about the poverty line and the extent of poverty. We may briefly review these controversies.

CDS Study and the findings of Dandekar and Rath

Dandekar and Rath (1971) estimated that the incidence of poverty in Kerala was very high and higher than that of the all India average. However, the study by Centre for Development Studies (CDS 1977) concluded that the high incidence of poverty as per Dandekar and Rath study is due to the omission of important items of consumption like Coconut and Tapioca, which provide substantial amount of calories to the people in Kerala. Consequently, the CDS study came to the conclusion that the incidence of poverty in Kerala would have been much lower if the omitted items are included in the consumption items of Keralites.

Controversy about the Extent of Poverty

There is a controversy about the extent of poverty in Kerala between the Planning Commission and the Government of Kerala (State Planning Board). According to the Government of Kerala, the dimensions of poverty in Kerala are unique because of its peculiar path of socio-economic development. Consequently, the extent of poverty as per the norms adopted by the Planning Commission to measure poverty has resulted in the gross underestimation of poverty in the state. According to the Planning Commission, only 25.73 per cent of the people in Kerala were below poverty line in 1993-94, which has gone down to 9.4 per cent in 1999-2000. However, according to Prabath Patnaik, Vice-Chairman of the State Planning Board, Kerala, about 84 per cent of the people (on the basis of Planning Commission's nutritional criteria of 2,400 calories), in rural Kerala were below poverty line in 1993-94, which has fallen to 82.5 per cent in 1999-2000 (Ramavarman 2007). According to him, even on the bass of lower level of 1,800 calories, the poverty level in Kerala should have been 40 per cent in 1993-94 and 38 per cent in 1999-2000. He added that there has not been any significant decline in poverty in the state as claimed by the Planning Commission and some others. Thus, according to the Planning Commission's estimate, the extent of poverty in Kerala is very low and much lower than the extent of poverty as per the estimate of Kerala government. The gross underestimate of the extent of poverty in Kerala by Planning Commission has reduced the quantum of central assistance to the state to lessen poverty in Kerala.

BPL Surveys in Kerala

In Kerala, so far, three surveys have been completed to estimate the number of households Below Poverty Line (BPL). The allocation of Central funds for poverty alleviation to states is based on the incidence of poverty in the state as per the estimate (on the basis of NSS data) of Planning Commission. However, the activities of the state and spending of funds for poverty eradication are on the basis of the state level estimate of the BPL families. The first full survey of BPL families was carried out in 1985 followed by the second in 1992 (those families who were assisted under IRDP earlier were excluded from this survey) and the third in 1997. According to the 1997 survey, 36.58 per cent of the people in Kerala were below the poverty line and the survey found that bulk of the poor were in rural areas and belongs to the category of landless agricultural labourers having only homestead. In addition, a large number of them were Women headed families and their annual income was less than Rs 10,000. Their houses were Pucca houses and they do not have sanitary latrines and most of them were illiterates (Economic Survey 2006).

Current Poverty Eradication Programmes in Kerala

In Kerala, in the past, food security, social security, land reforms and labour laws were aimed to reduce poverty apart from the implementation of specific programmes for eradication of poverty. Till recently, in rural Kerala, Integrated Rural Development Programme (IRDP) was the most important poverty eradication programme. The IRDP aimed to provide subsidized assets for self-employment at the individual or group level and also in providing wage employment with or without food security through public works programme. However, at present Swarnajayanthi Gram Swarozgar Yojana (SGSY) and Sampoorna Grameen Rozgar Yojana (SGRY) are the two most important programmes for poverty eradication in rural areas (Economic Survey 2006). In Kerala, it is the local governments, which implement the anti-poverty programmes.

The Swarna Jayanti Shahari Rozgar Yojana (SJSR), the National Slum Development Programme (NSDP), and the Valmiki Ambedkar Awas Yojana (VAMBAY) are the important programmes aimed to help the poor in urban areas. The SJSR combines elements of both self-employment and wage employment. The self-employment component has set up 16,727 micro enterprises in urban areas of Kerala out of which

1,345 are group enterprises of women. The NSDP undertakes slum development activities; particularly provision of minimum needs infrastructure and housing. The VAMBAY, although was started in 2002-03, has constructed 16,812 houses in the state, against a target of 19,454.

We will briefly review the current rural poverty eradication programmes in Kerala.

Swarnajayanti Gram Swarozgar Yojana (SGSY)

This programme was launched in April 1999 and aims to provide self-employment to the poor so as to bring them above the poverty line. The purpose of this programme is to establish a large number of micro enterprises in the rural areas by organizing the poor into Self Help Groups (SHGs) through a mix of bank credit and government subsidy. SGSY is a credit cum subsidy programme where credit forms the critical component. For group Swarozgaris, the subsidy would be 50 per cent of the project cost subject to a percapita subsidy of Rs 10,000. The programme expects at least 50 per cent of the Swarozgaris to be SC/STs, 40 per cent to be women and 3 per cent to be disabled. The total credit disbursed during 2005-07 (October) was Rs 4891.85 lakhs and the subsidy disbursed was Rs. 2519.15 lakhs.

Sampoorna Grameen Rozgar Yojana (SGRY)

SGRY, launched in 2001, aims at providing additional wage employment and to ensure food security so as to improve the nutritional levels of the poor. This programme is a Centrally Sponsored Scheme on cost sharing basis between the Center and the States in the ratio of 75:25 and is implemented through the Panchayat Raj Institutions (PRIs). Under this Scheme, per man-days, 10 Kg of Food grains (Rs. 6. 20/- per Kg for rice and Rs. 5.50 for wheat) and the balance wage is paid in cash.

Indira Awas Yojana (IAY)

The IAY, which was started in 1999-2000, is a Scheme for construction of houses for the poor. The beneficiaries of the Schemes are selected by Grama Sabhas and the selected beneficiaries are eligible for a grant-in aid of Rs. 27,500/- per house. This is a Centrally Sponsored scheme sharing cost between Centre and the State in the ratio of 75:25.

Kudumbashree Programmes

The State Poverty Eradication Mission implements this programme under the leadership of the Local Governments. The programme organizes the poor women below poverty line with a focus on self-help and demand-led convergence of available services and resources.

National Rural Employment Guarantee Act-2005

The National Rural Employment Guarantee Act, 2005 seeks to enhance the livelihood security of the households in rural areas by providing at least one hundred days of guaranteed wage employment to every household whose adult members are ready to do unskilled manual work.

After depicting the major poverty eradication programmes currently functioning in Kerala, we may briefly review the various concepts of poverty.

Concepts of Poverty

Poverty like beauty lies in the eye of the beholder. Hence, it is not easy to define poverty in precise terms. It would mean different things in different societies and to different people. Poverty is a multi-dimensional and relative concept. The dimensions of poverty are that, it is a social phenomenon, economic phenomenon and above all religious specific, caste specific, region specific, occupation specific and time specific. However, there were many attempts to define it and some defined it in terms of absolute sense while others in relative sense whereas, recently, economists talk about a human concept of poverty.

Absolute Poverty

Poverty is a condition wherein resources are insufficient to meet physical need. Absolute poverty represents a specific minimum level of income needed to satisfy the basic physical needs of food, clothing and shelter in order to have continued survival. Those who do not have this minimum of basic necessities are called absolutely poor. In developing countries like India, absolute poverty is generally reflected in inadequacy of food-intake and in other essential minimum needs such as clothing, housing, education and health. Even in absolute poverty, some times, we hear the concepts like Chronic Poverty (Permanent or for a long time) and Temporary Poverty (for a short period). The temporary poverty may be due to bad economic conditions like fall in price of one's production or rise in the price of consumption items.

Relative Poverty

According to the concept of relative poverty, poor are those whose resources (income or expenditure) are depressed from the mean and hence are deprived of the standard of living customary in that society. Thus, according to this, those whose incomes are below the mean income are called relatively poor.

Human Poverty

Human poverty is defined in terms of the denial of choices and opportunities for living a tolerable life. Thus, human poverty measures the denial (deprivations) of opportunities and choices most basic to human development for leading a long, healthy, creative life and to enjoy a decent standard of living.

Poverty Line

The extent of poverty is measured in terms of the proportion of the population living below a certain level of living called the poverty line. The important methods to arrive at a poverty line (Dandekar 1996) are :

The Proportion of Expenditure

Poverty Line is that level of consumer expenditure at which about 80 or 85 per cent of total expenditure is devoted to food or food and fuel or food, fuel and light. Here, the poverty line is not related to prices.

Physical Norms of Essential Consumption Items

Energy Intake in Terms of Calorie Value

There are various recommendations of calorie intake (Energy Requirement Approach) by individuals and institutions. Dandekar and Rath took the norm of 2250 kcal per capita per day for an Indian to be above the poverty line whereas Sukhatme recommended a minimum calorie intake of 1900 kcal for an individual whereas the Planning commission recommended a per capita calorie intake of 2400 per capita per day for rural areas and 2100 per capita per day for urban areas. The poverty line may well be the precise calorie intake or the expenditure (Consumer Expenditure Approach) or income (Income Level Approach or income poverty) required to generate the recommended calorie intake.

Normative Diets

The normative diet may be a Balanced Diet or a Minimum diet. Sukhatme (1965) has recommended a minimum and medium food baskets. His minimum basket, per person per day, consists of 0.403 kg of cereals, 0.104 kg of pulses, 0.201 kg of milk, 0.137 kg of fruits and vegetables, and certain quantities of starchy roots, sugar, oils and fats, and meat, fish and eggs. In practice, it is not possible to insist to households the prearranged diet owing to the differences in their taste and preferences. Households vary in their trend for milk and meat, etc and hence, the method usually adopted is to find the cost of the balanced or minimum diet (in terms of income or expenditure) as the poverty line.

The Cost of the Essentials of a Tolerable Human Existence

It is very difficult to define a tolerable level of human existence and identify the elements of it.

Poverty Indices

The important poverty indices widely used for measuring the intensity or severity of poverty are Head Count Ratio (HCR), Poverty Gap Ratio (PGI) or Income Gap Ratio, Sen's Index of

Poverty, Squared Poverty Gap Index, Foster, Grier, and Thorbecke (FGT) Index and finally the Human Poverty Index (HPI).

Head Count and Head Count Ratio

Head count is counting the number of people below the poverty line. The head count (*HC*) is the number of individuals '*i*' such that $yi<z$ where y is consumption or income and '*z*' poverty line. The headcount index is the proportion of the population for whom consumption (or other measures of living standard) is less than the poverty line (z). Thus, the head count ratio is the proportion of total population who are below some given poverty line. The head count ratio is expressed as

$$\text{HCR} = \frac{HC}{n},$$

where '*n*' is the total population.

Poverty Gap

The poverty gap is the average, over all people, of the gaps between poor people's living standards and the poverty line. It indicates the average extent to which individuals fall below the poverty.

Poverty Gap Index (PGI)

The poverty gap index (PGI) is defined as the ratio of the Poverty Gap (PG) to the poverty line. It is the poverty gap expressed as a percentage of the line. It is expressed as

$$\text{PGI} = \frac{1}{n} \vee \sum_{i=1}^{q} \frac{(z-yi)}{z},$$

where n is the total population, q the number of people below poverty line, z poverty line, y_i consumption or income of individual i, and $y_i<z$.

Poverty Gap Ratio (PGR)

The PGR is the ratio of the average of income (or extra consumption) needed to get all poor people to the poverty line, divided by the mean income (or consumption) of the society. The poverty gap ratio is not really a measure of poverty itself, but a measure of resources needed to eradicate it. The PGR is given by

$$\text{PGR} = \Sigma yi < z \frac{(z - yi)}{nm},$$

where n is the total population and m, is mean income.

Income Gap Ratio (IGR)

A close relative of PGR is called income gap ratio (IGR). Income gap ratio is the ratio of the average income needed to get all poor people to the poverty line divided by the total income required to bring all the poor people to the poverty line. The IGR is given by

$$\text{IGR} = \Sigma yi < z \frac{(z - yi)}{pHC},$$

where HC is just the number (head count) of the poor.

Sen Index of Poverty

Sen has arrived at a poverty index by combining the two familiar poverty indices of head count ratio and income gap ratio with income inequality amongst the poor. His index is defined as the weighted average of the individual income shortfalls, where the weights depend on the rank order of the individual in the welfare ordering of the poor. Sen index can be expressed as

$$S = H[I + (1 + \text{I})Gp\left(\frac{q}{q+1}\right)],$$

where H is the head count poverty ratio, I is the ratio of the average income shortfall to the poverty line (income gap of the poor), G_p is the Gini coefficient of income among the poor, and q is the number of people below the poverty line.

Squared Poverty Gap Index (SPGI)

The squared poverty gap index (SPGI) is defined as the average of the square relative poverty gap of the poor. This is described as a measure of the severity of poverty. While the poverty gap takes into account the distance of the poor from the poverty line, the squared poverty gap takes the square of that distance into account. When using the squared poverty gap, the poverty gap is weighted by itself, so as to give more weight to the very poor. In other words, the squared poverty gap takes into account the inequality among the poor. It is obtained as follows

$$P_2 = \frac{1}{n} \sum_{i=1}^{q} \left[\frac{z - yi}{z} \right]^2,$$

where n is the size of population, q are poor, z poverty line and yi is the income of individual i.

Foster-Greer-Thorbecke (FGT) Measure

The headcount, the poverty gap, and the squared poverty gap are the first three measures of the FGT measure. The general formula for this class of poverty measures depends on a parameter α, which takes a value of zero for the headcount, one for the poverty gap, and two for the squared poverty gap in the following expression

$$P\alpha = \frac{1}{n} \sum_{yi<z} \left[\frac{z - yi}{z} \right]^{\alpha},$$

If α = zero, the measure P_0 is just the head count ratio, if α =1, the measure P_1 is the poverty gap ratio, and if α = 2, P_2 is the squared poverty gap ratio. Thus, the FGT measure addresses the distributional problems among the poor.

Human Poverty Index (HPI)

The United Nations has constructed human poverty indices for developing countries (HPI-1). The HPI-1 uses the probability of not surviving to the age of 40, the adult illiteracy rate, an average of the percentage of the population without clean water and the percentage of babies born underweight.

International Poverty Line

For assessing the world poverty and for comparisons of poverty among countries, an International Poverty line is used which is defined in terms of a constant US $ 1 a day in PPP (Purchasing Power Parity).

SECTION-II

Rural Poverty In Kerala

There are various studies, which provide information about the incidence of poverty in Kerala. One of the earliest estimates of rural poverty in Kerala has been by Dandekar and Rath. According to their estimate, more than 90 per cent of the rural people in Kerala were living below the poverty line in 1961-62 (Table 1). The estimate by Minhas et al shows that 69 per cent of the people were living below the poverty line in the year 1970-71 which has declined to 44 per cent in the year 1988. The estimate by World Bank shows that about 72.9 per cent of the rural people in Kerala were living below the poverty line in the year 1970 which has gone down to 51.8 per cent in the year 1983 and subsequently to 49.2 per cent in the year 1988. The study by Lal et al shows that rural poverty in Kerala has declined from 29.10 per cent in 1987-88 to 23.81 per cent in 1989-90 and subsequently to 15.53 per cent in 1993-94 and finally to 9.53 per cent in 1999-2000. According to the estimate by the Planning Commission, the rural poverty in Kerala declined from 59.19 per cent in 1973-74 to 29.10 per cent in 1987-88 and then to 25.76 per cent in 1993-94 and finally to 9.38 per cent in 1999-2000. However, the incidence of rural poverty in Kerala has increased from 9.38 per cent in 1999-2000 to 13.2 per cent in 2004-05. The estimate by Deaton shows that rural poverty has declined from 25.40 per cent in 1993-94 to 9.40 per cent and 12.60 (on the basis of adjusted poverty line) in 1999-2000. The study by Datt et al shows that poverty has declined from 31.10 per cent in 1993-94 to 13.8 per cent in 1999-2000. The estimate of Sundaram and Tendulkar shows that 47.18 per cent (head count ratio) of the people in rural Kerala were living below poverty line, which has declined to 34.09 per cent (URP) and 33.53 per cent (MRP) in the year 1993-94 and subsequently to 16.47 per cent (MRP) in 1999-2000.

The number of poor declined from 98.75 lakhs in 1983 (URP) to 75.03 lakhs (URP) and to 73.79 lakhs (MRP) in 1993-94 and subsequently to 38.39 lakhs in 1999-2000 (Table 4). In terms of PGI, the incidence of rural poverty declined from 0.1301 (URP) in 1983 to 0.0830 (URP) and to 0.0771 (MRP) in 1993-94 and subsequently to 0.0280 (MRP) in 1999-2000. Similarly, in terms of FGT, rural poverty declined from 0.0491 (URP) in 1983 to 0.0291 (URP) and to 0.0264 (MRP) in 1993-94 and subsequently to 0.0076 (MRP) in 1999-2000.

From Table 1, it can be seen that incidence of poverty has been declining in rural Kerala (it has slightly increased in 2004-05 as per the Planning Commissions estimate) for the whole period from 1961-62 to 1999-2000. However, if we split the period into two from 1961-62 to 1993-94 (pre reform period), and 1993-94 to 1999-2000 (post reform period), it can be seen that the rate of decline in poverty is much faster during the period 1993-94 to 1999-2000 (post reform period). The rate of decline is very much faster if we divide the period into 1983 to 1993-94 (pre reform) and 1994 to 1999-2000 (post reform). For example, the annual average decline in the incidence of rural poverty (head count ratio) as a per centage of base year values during the pre reform period (1983 to 1993-94) is 2.65 whereas is 8.47 per cent during the post reform period which is about four times higher than that of the decline during the pre reform period (Table 4).

In terms of number of poor, the annual average decline during the post reform period (8 per cent) is nearly three times that of the annual average decline (2.29 per cent) of the pre reform period. The decline in the intensity of rural poverty in terms of PGI (Table 5) (3.45 per cent during pre reform and 10.61 per cent during the post reform period) and FGT (3.87 per cent during the pre reform period and 11.86 per cent during the post reform period) all show that the decline in rural poverty during the post reform period is more than three times that of the decline in rural poverty during the pre reform period.

Table 1
Alternative Estimates of Poverty in Kerala (Rural)

Estimate	*1961-1962*	*1970*	*1970-1971*	*1973-1974*	*1983*	*1987-1988*	*1988*	*1989-1990*	*1993-1994*	*1997-1998*	*1999-2000*	*2004-2005*
Dand. & Rath	90.75											
Minhas *et al*			69.0			44.0						
World Bank		72.9			51.8		49.2					
Lal *et al*						29.10		23.81	15.53	09.53		
Plań.Com.				59.19		29.10			25.76		09.38	13.2
Deaton									25.40		09.40 (12.60)	
Datt *et al*									31.10		13.80	
Sund. & Tend.					47.18				34.09* 33.53**		16.47**	

Sources: 1. Dandekar and Rath (1971); 2. Datt *et al* (2003); 3. Minhas *et al* (1991); 4. World Bank (1989); 5. Deepak Lal *et al* (2001); 6. Planning Commission (Various Years); the figure for 1973-74 and 2004-05 are from Economic Review (2002& 2006); 7. Angus Deaton (2003) and 7. Sundaram and Tendulkar (2003); Parenthesis denote adjusted Deaton;* on URP and** on MRP.

Urban Poverty in Kerala

According to the estimate by Dandekar and Rath, about 88.69 per cent of the people in urban Kerala were below the poverty line in 1961-62 (Table 2). The estimate by Minhas et al shows that about 62.4 per cent of the people were below the poverty line in 1970-71, which has subsequently gone down to 44.5 per cent in 1987-88. As per the estimate of World Bank, about 60 per cent of the people in urban Kerala were below the poverty line in 1970-71, which has declined to 50.9 per cent in, 1983 and then to 48.3 per cent in 1988. The estimate by Lal et al shows that about 40.33 per cent of the people were below the poverty line in 1987-88 which has subsequently declined to 34.64 per cent in 1989-90 and then to 17.65 per cent in 1993-94 and finally to 5.45 per cent in 1997-98. According to the Planning Commission's estimate, about 62.74 per cent of the urban people in Kerala were below the poverty line in 1973-74, which has declined to 40.33 per cent in 1987-88 and subsequently to 24.60 per cent in 1993-94 and to 20.27 per cent in 1999-2000. However, the incidence of urban poverty in Kerala has slightly increased from 20.27 per cent in 1999-2000 to 20.6 per cent in 2004-05. According to the estimate by Deaton, urban poverty in Kerala has declined from 24.30 per cent in 1993-94 to 19.80 per cent and 18.70 per cent (on the basis of adjusted poverty line) in 1999-2000. The estimate by Sundaram and Tendulkar shows that about 47.78 per cent (head count ratio) of the people were below the poverty line in urban Kerala in the year 1983, which has gone down to 27.09 per cent (URP) and 30.12 per cent (MRP) in 1993-94 and subsequently to 23.49 per cent (MRP) in 1999-2000.

In terms of number of poor, there were about 25.47 lakh poor (URP) in the urban Kerala in 1983 that has declined to 21.88 lakh (URP) and 23.62 lakh (MRP) in 1993-94 and finally to declined to 19.26 lakh (MRP) in 1999-2000 (table 4). In terms of PGI, urban poverty in Kerala has declined from 0.1459 (URP) in 1983 to 0.0669 (URP) and to 0.0691 (MRP) in 1993-94 and finally it 0.0493 (MRP) in 1999-2000. Again in terms of FGT, the incidence of urban poverty which was 0.0601 (URP) in 1983 has declined to 0.0235 (URP) and 0.0241 (MRP) in 1993-94 and finally to 0.0151 (MRP) in 1999-2000.

Table 2
Alternative Estimates of Poverty in Kerala (Urban)

Estimate	*1961-1962*	*1970-1971*	*1973-1974*	*1983*	*1987-1988*	*1988*	*1989-1990*	*1993-1994*	*1997-1998*	*1999-2000*	*2004-2005*
Dand. & Rath	88.69										
Minhas *et al*		62.4			44.5						
World Bank		60.0		50.9		48.3					
Lal *et al*					40.33		34.64	17.65	05.45		
Plan. Com.			62.74		40.33			24.60		20.27	20.6
Deaton								24.30		19.80 (18.70)	
Sund. & Tend.				47.78				27.90* 30.12**		23.49**	

Source: Same as Table 1.

An examination of the incidence of urban poverty in Kerala shows that, poverty has been declining for the whole period (it has slightly increased in the year 2004-05 as per the PC's estimate) from 1961-62 to 1999-2000. However, the rate of decline is faster during the period 1993-94 to 1999-2000 (Post reform period) compared to the period 1983 to 1993-94 (Pre reform period).

The annual average decline in the incidence of urban poverty as a per centage of base year values is at a faster rate during the post reform period (Table 5). The annual average decline in the number of poor (1.3 per cent annually during the pre reform period and 3.08 per cent annually during the post reform period) and the decline in terms of FGT index (5.81 annually during the pre reform period and 6.22 per cent during the post reform period) are all at a higher rate, although the rate of decline is slightly lower during the post reform period in terms of Head count ratio (3.69 during the post reform period against 3.96 during the pre reform period) and in terms of PGI (4.78 per cent during the post reform period against 5.15 per cent during the pre reform period). Altogether, it can be concluded that the decline in the incidence of urban poverty in Kerala during the post reform period is faster than the rate of decline observed during the pre reform period.

Poverty in Kerala (Rural Plus Urban)

According to the estimate by Minhas *et al*, 68 per cent of the people in Kerala were below the poverty line in the year 1970-71 which has declined to 44.1 per cent in the year 1987-88 (Table 3). In terms of Human Poverty Index (HPI), the incidence of poverty declined from 32.10 in 1981 to 19.90 in 1991. The study by Lal et al shows that 31.79 per cent of the people in Kerala were below the poverty line in 1987-88 which has declined to 26.16 per cent in 1989-90 and subsequently to 16.09 per cent in 1993-94 and finally to 8.38 per cent in 1997-98. The estimate by Planning Commission shows that about 59.79 per cent of the people were below the poverty line in Kerala in the year 1973-74 which has declined to 31.79 per cent in 1987-88 and subsequently to 25.43 per cent in 1993-94 and finally to 12.72 per cent in 1999-2000. The study by Datt et al shows that

Table 3
Alternative Estimates of Poverty in Kerala (Rural Plus Urban)

Estimate	*1970-1971*	*1973-1974*	*1981*	*1983*	*1987-1988*	*1989-1990*	*1991*	*1993-1994*	*1996*	*1997-1998*	*1999-2000*
Minhas *et al*	68.00				44.10						
HPI			32.10				19.90		15.0		
Lal *et al*					31.79	26.16		16.09		08.38	
Plan. Com.		59.79			31.79			25.43			12.72
Datt *et al*								28.80			14.40
Sund. & Tend.				47.30				32.47* 32.63**			18.30**

Source: Same as table 1. HPI – National Human Resource Development, Planning Commission, Quoted in Economic Review (2002).

about 28.80 per cent of the people in Kerala were below the poverty line in 1993-94, which has gone down to 14.40 per cent in 1999-2000. The study by Sundaram and Tendulkar shows that 47.30 per cent (head count ratio) of the people in Kerala were below the poverty line in the year 1983, which has declined to 32.47 per cent (URP) and 32.63 (MRP) in 1993-94 and to 18.30 per cent (MRP) in 1999-2000.

In Kerala, in terms of the number of poor, there were 124.22 lakh people (URP) below the poverty line in the year 1983 which has declined to 96.91 lakh (URP) and 97.41 lakh (MRP) in 1993-94 and it further declined to 57.65 lakh (MRP) in 1999-2000 (Table 4). As per PGI, the incidence of poverty in Kerala was 0.1333 (URP) in 1983 which has declined to 0.0788 (URP) and 0.0750 (MRP) in 1993-94 and finally to 0.0335 (MRP) in 1999-2000. As per FGT, the incidence of poverty was 0.0513 (URP) in 1983 which has declined to 0.0280 (URP) and 0.0258 (MRP) in 1993-94 and finally to 0.0096 (MRP) in 1999-2000.

Table 4

Head Count Ratio's (HCRs) and The Size of the Poor Population in Kerala

Year	*Rural*	*Urban*	*Combined*
Head Count Ratio %			
1983 URP	47.18	47.78	47.30
1993-94 URP	34.09	27.90	32.47
1993-94 MRP	33.53	30.12	32.63
1999-00 MRP	16.47	23.49	18.30
Number of Poor (000)			
1983 URP	9875	2547	12422
1993-94 URP	7503	2188	9691
1993-94 MRP	7379	2362	9741
1999-00 MRP	3839	1926	5765
Poverty Gap Index (PGI)			
1983 URP	0.1301	0.1459	0.1333
1993-94 URP	0.0830	0.0669	0.0788
1993-94 MRP	0.0771	0.0691	0.0750
1999-00 MRP	0.0280	0.0493	0.0335
Foster, Grier, Thorbecke (FGT)			
1983 URP	0.0491	0.0601	0.0513
1993-94 URP	0.0291	0.0235	0.0280
1993-94 MRP	0.0264	0.0241	0.0258
1999-00 MRP	0.0076	0.0151	0.0096

Source: Sundaram and Tendulkar (2003).

Our analysis of the incidence of poverty in Kerala (Rural plus Urban) clearly shows that poverty has been declining in Kerala for the whole period from 1970-71 to 1999-2000. However, the rate of decline is at a faster rate if we divide the period into two 1970-71 to 1993-94 (Pre reform period) and 1993-94 to 1999-2000 (Post reform period). The rate of decline in the incidence of poverty is very much faster if we divide the period into two from 1983 to 1993-94 (Pre reform period) and from 1993-94 to 1999-2000 (Post reform period). For example, the annual average changes in poverty in terms of head count ratio (Rural plus Urban) in Kerala (8.47 per cent) during the post reform period (1993-94 to 1999-2000) has been nearly three time that of the decline during the pre reform period (2.99 per cent) (Table 5). In terms of number of poor also, the decline during the post reform period is almost three times (6.80 per cent) that of the decline during the pre reform period (2.09 per cent). In terms of the severity indicators of PGI and FGT also, the decline during the post reform period (PGI 9.23 and FGT 10.47) is more than two times that of the pre reform period (PGI 3.89 and FGT 4.33). Hence, we can safely conclude that the incidence of poverty in Kerala has declined for the whole period and the rate of decline is much faster during the post

Table 5
Average Annual Changes in Poverty Indicators on URP and MRP as a Per centage of Base Year Values in Kerala During 1983-2000

Period 1983-1994	*Head Count Ratio 1983-94*	*No of Poor 1983-94*	*Poverty Gap Index 1983-94*	*FGT 1983-94*
Rural	-2.65	-2.29	-3.45	-3.87
Urban	-3.96	-1.34	-5.15	-5.81
Combined	-2.99	-2.09	-3.89	-4.33
Period 1994 - 2000	*Head Count Ratio 1994-2000*	*No of Poor 1994-2000*	*Poverty Gap Index 1994-2000*	*FGT 1994-2000*
Rural	-8.47	-8.00	-10.61	-11.86
Urban	-3.69	-3.08	-4.78	-6.22
Combined	-7.32	-6.80	-9.23	-10.47

Source: Sundaram and Tendulkar (2003).

reform period (1993-94 to 1999-2000) compared to the pre reform period (1983 to 1993-94).

SECTION-III

Factors in Declining Poverty in Kerala

There are many factors behind the poverty decline in Kerala. Among them, economic growth of the state economy, especially, in the late 1980s is an important factor that has helped to reduce poverty in the state. The performance of Kerala, in terms of percapita SDP has been even better than the national average during the period 1990-91 to 2001-2002 (Chakraborthy 2005). The performances of the manufacturing and the service sectors have also helped in reducing the incidence of poverty in the state. The average annual growth rates of the state income in the secondary and tertiary sectors have nearly doubled during the period 1992-93 to 2000-01. In the secondary sector, the annual growth rate has increased from 3.3 per cent for the period 1980-81 to 1990-91 to 7.6 per cent for the period 1992-93 to 2000-01 while in the tertiary sector, it has increased from 4.3 per cent for the period 1980-81 to 1990-91 to 8.3 per cent in 1992-93 to 2000-01 (Jeromi 2003). The Public Distribution System (PDS), which works efficiently in the state, has also contributed in a significant manner in helping the poor to improve their standard of living. Kerala is a state with one of the highest percapita deliveries in the country and has earned the title "model PDS state" and in spite of a rise in the issue price and targeting of PDS, distribution of essential commodities through PDS has benefited the underprivileged sections of society and has reduced the incidence of poverty (Economic Review 2002). The New Kerala Model of Development (NKMD) of redistribution of wealth with redistribution of power through Peoples Campaign which ensured 30–40 per cent of the development budget to local bodies also have helped in reducing the poverty of the people in the state. In addition, the huge volume of foreign remittances in Kerala (Remittances in 2001 were even larger than the annual budget of Kerala) and Kerala's lowest population growth rate etc., have helped much in reducing the incidence of poverty in the state. The poverty alleviation and employment generation programmes and the popular social security measures like the various pension schemes for the benefit of the weaker sections all have contributed extensively in improving the standard of living of the poor in the state. The faster reduction in the incidence of poverty in Kerala during the post reform period (1993-94 to 1999-2000) may be due to the higher growth rate of the state per capita income (largely on account of the higher growth rate of the tertiary sector), flow of foreign remittances, Kerala's lowest population growth rate and due to the implementation of the new Kerala model (Peoples Plan) of development during this period.

SECTION-IV

Summary and Conclusions

There are a lot of debates and controversies in the poverty literature. Developmental experts who believed in the trickle-down effect theory of growth expected that poverty would automatically decline along with growth. However, as elsewhere in the world, growth alone could not solve the problem of poverty in India. The failure of trickle down effect theory has made the governments in India to bring specific poverty eradication programmes to make a direct attack on poverty. Although, there are various concepts of poverty, the two important concepts are absolute and relative. However, recently economists talk about another concept of human poverty. The various poverty indices are headcount ratio, Poverty gap and Income Gap Ratio, Sen Index, Squared Poverty Gap and it's variants like Foster, Greer and Thorbecke (FGT), in addition to Human Poverty Index (HPI). The extent and intensity of poverty in Kerala has been analysed on the basis of various studies carried out at all India levels. Although, Kerala is one of the states that experienced high incidence of poverty during 1960s, the extent and intensity of poverty in Kerala has declined since then and till 1999-2000. The poverty reduction in Kerala especially since 1990s are largely due to the better performance of the state economy in general and the higher growth rate of the service sector in particular. The lowest growth rate of population in Kerala, the efficient PDS, the popular social security measures, the poverty eradication programmes and the foreign remittances into the economy and the Peoples campaign all have helped in ameliorating poverty in the state.

References

Bardhan, P. K. (1971), 'On the Incidence of Poverty in Rural India in the Sixties', in T.N. Srinivasan and P. K. Bardhan (eds), *Poverty and Income Distribution in India,* Statistical Publishing Society, Calcutta, 1974.

Centre for Development Studies (1977), *Poverty, Unemployment and Development Policy,* Orient Longman, Delhi.

Chakraborty, Achin (2005), 'Kerala's Changing Development Narratives' *Economic and Political Weekly,* Vol. XL No. 6, pp. 541-547.

Dandekar, V. M. and Rath, N. (1971), *Poverty in India,* Indian School of Politcal Economy, Pune.

Dandekar, V. M. (1996), *The Indian Economy 1947–92 Volume II: Population, Poverty and Employment,* Sage Publications, New Delhi.

Datt, Gaurav and Ravallion, Martin (1989), 'Regional Disparities, Targeting and Poverty in India', *Staff Working Paper* No. 375, World Bank, Washington DC.

Foster, J. E., J. Greer, and E. Thorbecke (1984), 'A Class of Decomposable Poverty Measures', *Econometrica,* Vol. 52, No. 3, pp. 761-766.

Frankie, R. W. and B. H. Chasin (1999), 'Is the Kerala Model Sustainable? Lessons from the Past : Prospects for the Future' in M. A. Oommen. (ed.), *Kerala's Development Experience 1: Rethinking Development,* Concept Publishing House, New Delhi.

Government of Kerala, *Economic Review,* Various Issues, State Planning Board, Thruvanathapuram.

Hagenaars, Aldi, J. M. (1986), *The Perception of Poverty, Contribution to Economic Analysis,* Elsevier Science Publishers, B.V.

http://www.ccdturkiye.gov.tr/indicators/UN$_{-MEO}$ 14.htm.

Ibrahim P. (2004), 'Liberalization and Public Distribution System, A Case Study of Kerala', *The Impact of Indian Economic Reforms,* Proceedings of the National Seminar, P.G. Department of Economics, M.D. College, Pazhanji, Kerala.

Jeromi, P. D. (2003), 'What Ails Kerala's Economy: A Sectoral Exploration', *Economic and Political Weekly,* April 19-25, Vol. XXXVIII, No. 16, pp. 1584- 1600.

Jeromi, P. D. (2005), 'Economic Reforms in Kerala', *Economic and Political Weekly,* Vol. XL, No. 30, pp. 3267-77.

Kannan, K. P. (2005), 'Kerala's Turnaround in Growth Role of Social Development, Emittances and Reform', *Economic and Political Weekly,* Vol. XL, No. 6, pp. 548- 554.

Kurian, C.T. (1999), 'Sustainability of Kerala's Development Experience' in M.A Oommen. (ed.), *Kerala's Development Experience 1: Rethinking Development,* Concept Publishing House, New Delhi.

Lal, Deepak, Rakesh Mohan and I Natarajan (2001), 'Economic Reforms and Poverty Alleviation: A Tale of Two Surveys', *Economic and Political Weekly,* March 24, pp. 1017-1028.

Mahabub ul-Haq, (1971), 'Employment and Income Distribution in the 1970s–A New Perspective', *Development Digest,* October.

Minhas, B. S. (1970), 'Rural Poverty, Land Redistribution and Development Strategy', in T.N. Srinivasan and P. K. Bardhan (eds), *Poverty and Income Distribution in India,* Statistical Publishing Society, Calcutta, 1974.

Minhas, B. S., Jain L. R., Tendulkar S. D. (1991), 'Declining Incidence of Poverty in the 1980's–Evidence Verses Artifacts', *Economic and Political Weekly,* July 6-13, p. 1681.

National Human Development Report (2002), Planning Commission, Quoted in *Economic Review,* GoK, State Planning Board, Thirivananthapuram, p. 415.

Oommen, M. A. (1999) (ed), *Kerala's Development Experience 1: Rethinking Development,* Concept Publishing House, New Delhi.

Ramavarman, T. (2007), 'Case of Poverty amidst Plenty', *The Hindu,* October 8, 2007, page 5.

Ravallion, Martin and Gaurav Datt (1996), 'How Important to India's Poor is the Sectoral Composition of Economic Growth', *The World Bank Economic Review,* Vol. 10, No. 1, January, pp. 1-25.

Sastry, S. A. R. (1979), 'Levels and Pattern of Consumption, Poverty and Inequality in Andhra Pradesh', *Ph.D. Thesis* Submitted to the Gujarath University, p. 2.

Sen, Amartya (1976), "Poverty: An Ordinal Approach to Measurement", Econometrica, Vol. 44, No. 2, pp. 219-231.

Shetty, S. L. (2003), "Growth of SDP and Structural Changes in State Economies: Interstate Comparisons", *Economic and Political Weekly*, Vol. XXXVIII, No. 49, pp. 5189-5200.

Sundaram, K. and S. D. Tendulkar (2003), 'Poverty Has Declined in the 1990 s A Resolution of Comparability Problems in NSS Consumer Expenditure Data', *Economic and Political Weekly*, Vol. XXXVIII, No. 4, January 25-31, pp. 327-337.

Sukhatme, P. V. (1965), *Feeding India's Growing Millions*, Asia Publishing House, New York.

Sukhatme, P. V. (1981a), 'Measuring the Incidence of Undernutrition–A Comment', *Economic and Political Weekly*, Vol. XVI, No. 23, June, p. 1035.

United Nations Development Programme, (1997), 'Human Poverty Index', *Human Development Report*, Oxford University Press, New York.

World Bank (1989), "India-Poverty, Employment and Social Services" Washington DC.

REGIONAL DISPARITY IN DEVELOPMENT IN KERALA: A SECTORAL DECOMPOSITION AT DISTRICT LEVEL

V. NAGARAJAN NAIDU

The spatial dimension in development is very critical for policy analysis. There are two reasons why policymakers should be concerned about spatial inequality, defined as inequality in economic and social indicators of wellbeing across geographical units within a country. First, inequality *between* a nation's regions is one component of overall national inequality across individuals (the other component being of course inequality across individuals *within* each geographical unit or region). When spatial inequality goes up then, other things being equal, so does national inequality. Second, inequality between a nation's regions may be of concern in and of itself, especially when the geographical regions align with political, ethnic, language, or religion divisions. The 'new economic geography' has emphasized that there are powerful forces of agglomeration that tend to lead to a concentration of economic activity, magnifying natural geographical advantages that a region may enjoy. Thus spatial agglomeration brings the benefits of returns to scale, and hence helps efficiency and growth. At the same time, openness to the outside world, which is well recognized as a long term source of efficiency and growth, can also lead to spatial concentration.

The regional economy of Kerala is unique in federal India. The resource endowments, manpower stock, structure of society, polity and economy of this region stand distinct from the rest of the national economy. The deep rooted mass political and social movement augmented the redistributive justice in Kerala today. The potentiality of democratic and participatory development is undeniable in the context of Kerala. Compared to other states in India, the distribution of fruits of development planning is reasonably fair. However, the natural advantage of economic geography with respect to natural resource endowment, locational advantages and the positive impacts of agglomeration could not completely be overtaken by policy imperatives of any government in Kerala. In addition to the persistence of regional imbalance at a reasonable level, the strength of relative factors or forces in creating regional inequality changes as time passes. The changes in the facets of regional inequality warrants new type of policy initiatives, which were hitherto unnoticed by planners.

In the present study, the author makes an attempt to decipher the trends in regional disparity in economic development at sub state level of district. Along with the trends is regional inequality, the sectoral contribution in creating regional disparity is also identified. The trends in regional inequality in development at district level are evaluated with respect to Net State Domestic Product (NSDP) at aggregate and sectoral level at current price level. The time period taken for the trend analysis is 1970-71 to 2003-04.

The trend in NSDP at state level reveals that the state could increase its total net SDP from Rs 1,25,464 lakhs in 1970-71 to Rs 81,11,612 lakhs in 2003-04 at current price level. In 1993-94 price level, it increased from Rs. 8,76,993.4 lakhs in 1970-71 to Rs 40,32,756 lakhs in 2003-04. The percentage increase of net SDP during this period was 6284 in current price while it was 360 times in constant price of 1993-94. The increase in net SDP across various districts is not uniform in Kerala through out the period.

The Share of Various Districts in Net SDP in Kerala

The Table 1 and Table 2 show respectively the district wise net SDP of Kerala at current price and its percentage share to state SDP.

The distribution of SDP at district level shows that the ranks of districts with respect to its share in total SDP vary at different time points. In 1970-71, Kollam districts had highest share in SDP followed by Ernankulam and Kannur. In 1980-81, Trivandrum district replaces Kannur in the third position. In 1990-91, Ernakulam could retain its first position but Trivandrum and Thrissur districts shared the second and third position. The position of Kannur has declined very drastically. The position of these districts remains same in 2003-04 also. At the same time the position of the backward districts such as Idukki, Wayanad, Kasaragod remain almost same in all time points.

The Table 3 shows the growth rate of district SDP for various time points.

The Table 3 shows the average annual growth of quinquinial period for district SDP in Kerala. The highest growth rate for the entire state was witnessed between 1985-86 and 1990-91 and lowest growth rate was recorded between 1980-81 and 1985-86. Between 1990-91 and 2000-01 the growth rate of SDP remain same at 0.26 but drastically declined after 2000-01. The growth rate of SDP is not uniform across districts in Kerala. The growth rate of district SDP reveals that there is no connection existing between the direction of growth rate and share of SDP of various districts. The growth rate of district SDP among backward districts is higher than developed districts in all time points. Despite this higher growth of district SDP among backward district, they could not catch up the developed districts with the simple reason that in absolute terms the difference in volume of income between developed and backward district are very high. After 2000-01, the growth rate of district SDP of all districts declined very drastically.

Trends in District Per capita Income

The percapita income is one important measure of economic disparity between regions. The Table 4 and Table 5 show the

Table 1

District Level Net SDP in Kerala at Current Price (Rs in lakhs) Between 1970-71 and 2003-04

District	*1970-1971*	*1975-1976*	*1980-1981*	*1985-1986*	*1990-1991*	*1995-1996*	*2000-2001*	*2003-2004**
Trivandrum	12693	22682	38268	41409	123890	277975	678445	859458
Kollam	15601	29151	43247	34476	104281	224651	518796	634059
Pathanamthitta			-	18233	52152	119316	256166	320050
Alappuzha	12498	18829	30809	28843	85112	166062	425123	542290
Kottayam	10073	17747	24633	27478	73493	185074	435358	554760
Idukki	4673	9559	19270	21145	50224	135009	294122	355732
Ernakulam	14168	24563	50997	56313	182449	414352	776888	983969
Thrissur	11813	17607	35544	38430	120632	258369	635105	792434
Palakkad	9596	15446	26581	27338	87399	200530	452237	564289
Malappuram	8385	12656	24876	24109	79943	180482	478079	607608
Kozhikode	12983	20593	41506	37487	103024	241552	572853	727859
Wayanad			-	10225	28816	81656	162810	194627
Kannur	13022	20966	46542	30160	86896	203746	455504	571902
Kasaragod			-	12990	39038	102168	230025	302575
Total	125464	209799	382273	408636	1217349	2790942	6371511	8011612

Note: figures in asterisk shows the provisional figures.

Source: (1) Economic Review (various issues), State Planning Board, Govt. of Kerala.
(2) Statistics for Planning (various issues), Dept of Economics and Statistics, Govt. of Kerala.

Table 2
Percentage Share of District SDP from State NSDP

District	*1970-1971*	*1975-1976*	*1980-1981*	*1985-1986*	*1990-1991*	*1995-1996*	*2000-2001*	*2003-2004*
Trivandrum	10.12	10.81	10.01	10.13	10.18	9.96	10.65	10.73
Kollam	12.43	13.89	11.31	8.44	8.57	8.05	8.14	7.91
Pathanamthitta				4.46	4.28	4.28	4.02	3.99
Alappuzha	9.96	8.97	8.06	7.06	6.99	5.95	6.67	6.77
Kottayam	8.03	8.46	6.44	6.72	6.04	6.63	6.83	6.92
Idukki	3.72	4.56	5.04	5.17	4.13	4.84	4.62	4.44
Ernakulam	11.29	11.71	13.34	13.78	14.99	14.85	12.19	12.28
Thrissur	9.42	8.39	9.30	9.40	9.91	9.26	9.97	9.89
Palakkad	7.65	7.36	6.95	6.69	7.18	7.19	7.10	7.04
Malappuram	6.68	6.03	6.51	5.90	6.57	6.47	7.50	7.58
Kozhikode	10.35	9.82	10.86	9.17	8.46	8.65	8.99	9.09
Wayanad				2.50	2.37	2.93	2.56	2.43
Kannur	10.38	9.99	12.18	7.38	7.14	7.30	7.15	7.14
Kasaragod				3.18	3.21	3.66	3.61	3.78
Total	100	100	100	100	100	100	100	100

Source: Estimated from Table 1.

Table 3
Growth Rate of District SDP in Kerala from 1970-71 to 2003-04

District	*1970-1971*	*1975-1976*	*1980-1981*	*1985-1986*	*1990-1991*	*1995-1996*	*2000-2001*	*2003-2004*
Trivandrum		0.16	0.14	0.02	0.40	0.25	0.29	0.09
Kollam		0.17	0.10	-0.04	0.40	0.23	0.26	0.07
Pathanamthitta					0.37	0.26	0.23	0.08
Alappuzha		0.10	0.13	-0.01	0.39	0.19	0.31	0.09
Kottayam		0.15	0.08	0.02	0.33	0.30	0.27	0.09
Idukki		0.21	0.20	0.02	0.28	0.34	0.24	0.07
Ernakulam		0.15	0.22	0.02	0.45	0.25	0.17	0.09
Thrissur		0.10	0.20	0.02	0.43	0.23	0.29	0.08
Palakkad		0.12	0.14	0.01	0.44	0.26	0.25	0.08
Malappuram		0.10	0.19	-0.01	0.46	0.25	0.33	0.09
Kozhikode		0.12	0.20	-0.02	0.35	0.27	0.27	0.09
Wayanad					0.36	0.37	0.20	0.07
Kannur		0.12	0.24	-0.07	0.38	0.27	0.25	0.09
Kasaragod					0.40	0.32	0.25	0.11
Total		0.13	0.16	0.01	0.40	0.26	0.26	0.09

Source: Estimated from Table 1.

Table 4
District Level Per capita Income at Current Price between 1970-71 and 2003-04

District	*1970-1971*	*1975-1976*	*1980-1981*	*1985-1986*	*1990-1991*	*1995-1996*	*2000-2001*	*2003-2004*
Trivandrum	583	942	1484	2389	4220	8853	20907	25856
Kollam	655	1113	1536	2441	4350	8765	20031	23882
Pathanamthitta			-	2564	4408	9432	20776	25300
Alappuzha	594	837	1311	2366	4268	7789	20158	25071
Kottayam	661	1091	1452	2507	4038	9506	22246	27655
Idukki	611	1118	1995	3376	4672	11740	26028	30667
Ernakulam	662	1030	2017	3441	6502	13812	24996	30913
Thrissur	561	732	1462	2333	4422	8857	21284	25922
Palakkad	575	847	1307	2013	3682	7898	17228	20985
Malappuram	456	604	1045	1383	2592	5472	13102	16294
Kozhikode	624	870	1588	2342	3949	8658	19836	24615
Wayanad			-	2734	4301	11389	20583	24088
Kannur	536	789	1571	2315	3872	8496	18838	23070
Kasaragod			-	2355	3659	8954	19042	24480
Total	594	893	1508	2398	4200	9004	19951	24492

Source: (1) Economic Review (various issues), State Planning Board, Govt. of Kerala.
(2) Statistics for Planning (various issues), Dept of Economics and Statistics, Govt. of Kerala.

Table 5
Ranks of District with Respect to Per Capita Income

District	*1970-1971*	*1975-1976*	*1980-1981*	*1985-1986*	*1990-1991*	*1995-1996*	*2000-2001*	*2003-2004*
Trivandrum	7	5	6	7	8	8	5	5
Kollam	3	2	5	6	5	9	9	11
Pathanamthitta	.	.	.	4	4	5	6	6
Alappuzha	6	8	9	8	7	13	8	7
Kottayam	2	3	8	5	9	4	3	3
Idukki	5	1	2	2	2	2	1	2
Ernakulam	1	4	1	1	1	1	2	1
Thrissur	9	10	7	11	3	7	4	4
Palakkad	8	7	10	13	12	12	13	13
Malappuram	11	11	11	14	14	14	14	14
Kozhikode	4	6	3	10	10	10	10	8
Wayanad	.	.	.	3	6	3	7	10
Kannur	10	9	4	12	11	11	12	12
Kasaragod	.	.	.	9	13	6	11	9
Total								

Source: Estimated from Table 4.

level of percapita income at district level and the relative ranks of various districts with respect to percapita income respectively.

In terms of percapita income, Ernakulam ranked first in 1970-71 followed by Kottayam and Kollam. In 1970-71, the lowest percapita income is reported in Malappuram and Kannur districts. Except 1975-76 and 2000-01, Ernakulam district occupies the first position with respect to per capita SDP followed by Idukki and Kottayam. These three districts are well ahead of other districts in all time points. The relatively developed district of Kollam in 1970-71 has declined to 11th position in 2003-04. The districts Palakkad, Kannur and Malappuram remain backward throughout the period. The district, Malappuram is a most backward district in Kerala.

The Table 6 shows the growth rate of district wise percapita SDP.

The average annual growth rate of percapita income in Kerala is highest during the decade 1990-91-2000-01. After 2000-01, the growth of percapita income declined very drastically in Kerala. The growth rate of percapita income is not uniform across districts in Kerala. Between 1970-71 and 1975-76, the growth rate of percapita income is highest in Idukki followed by Kollam and Kottayam. During pre 1990-91 period, the growth rate of percapita income is very high among south and central districts in Kerala. However, post 1990-91 result indicates that the northern districts in Kerala are catching up with other districts in Kerala. The growth rate of percapita income after 2000-01 is low for all districts in Kerala.

One of the measures of disparity is the percentage distance of actual value from mean value. The Table 7 shows the percentage distance of percapita income of districts from the state average. It also shows the Coefficient of variation of percapita income between districts at different points.

The result shows that up to 1995-96, the distance between district percapita and state average income has been increasing. The maximum distance in 1970-71 at higher side was 11.45, which increased to 53.40 per cent in 1990-91. At the same time, the lower side distance has declined during this period from

Table 6
Average Yearly Growth Rate of District Per Capita Income in Kerala

District	*1970-1971*	*1975-1976*	*1980-1981*	*1985-1986*	*1990-1991*	*1995-1996*	*2000-2001*	*2003-2004*
Trivandrum		0.12	0.12	0.12	0.15	0.22	0.27	0.08
Kollam		0.14	0.08	0.12	0.16	0.20	0.26	0.06
Pathanamthitta					0.14	0.23	0.24	0.07
Alappuzha		0.08	0.11	0.16	0.16	0.16	0.32	0.08
Kottayam		0.13	0.07	0.15	0.12	0.27	0.27	0.08
Idukki		0.17	0.16	0.14	0.08	0.30	0.24	0.06
Ernakulam		0.11	0.19	0.14	0.18	0.22	0.16	0.08
Thrissur		0.06	0.20	0.12	0.18	0.20	0.28	0.07
Palakkad		0.09	0.11	0.11	0.17	0.23	0.24	0.07
Malappuram		0.06	0.15	0.06	0.17	0.22	0.28	0.08
Kozhikode		0.08	0.17	0.09	0.14	0.24	0.26	0.08
Wayanad					0.11	0.33	0.16	0.06
Kannur		0.09	0.20	0.09	0.13	0.24	0.24	0.07
Kasaragod					0.11	0.29	0.23	0.10
Total		0.10	0.14	0.12	0.15	0.23	0.24	0.08

Source: Estimated from Table 4

Table 7
Percentage Distance of District Per Capita Income from State Average

District	*1970-1971*	*1975-1976*	*1980-1981*	*1985-1986*	*1990-1991*	*1995-1996*	*2000-2001*	*2003-2004*
Trivandrum	-1.85	5.49	-1.59	-0.38	0.48	-1.68	4.79	5.57
Kollam	10.27	24.64	1.86	1.79	3.57	-2.65	0.40	-2.49
Pathanamthitta				6.92	4.95	4.75	4.14	3.30
Alappuzha	0.00	-6.27	-13.06	-1.33	1.62	-13.49	1.04	2.36
Kottayam	11.28	22.17	-3.71	4.55	-3.86	5.58	11.50	12.91
Idukki	2.86	25.20	32.29	40.78	11.24	30.39	30.46	25.21
Ernakulam	11.45	15.34	33.75	43.49	54.81	53.40	25.29	26.22
Thrissur	-5.56	-18.03	-3.05	-2.71	5.29	-1.63	6.68	5.84
Palakkad	-3.20	-5.15	-13.33	-16.06	-12.33	-12.28	-13.65	-14.32
Malappuram	-23.23	-32.36	-30.70	-42.33	-38.29	-39.23	-34.33	-33.47
Kozhikode	5.05	-2.58	5.31	-2.34	-5.98	-3.84	-0.58	0.50
Wayanad	-100.00	-100.00	-100.00	14.01	2.40	26.49	3.17	-1.65
Kannur	-9.76	-11.65	4.18	-3.46	-7.81	-5.64	-5.58	-5.81
Kasaragod				-1.79	-12.88	-0.56	-4.56	-0.05
Average distance	-8.56	-6.93	-7.34	2.63	0.37	2.84	2.10	1.78
C.V	10.40	18.57	18.60	20.49	19.76	21.49	15.26	14.68
Gini coefficient	0.056	.10	0.095	0.10	0.091	0.174	0.077	0.074

Source: Estimated from Table 4.

100 to 39.23. After 1990-91, the distance between state average and district percapita income has consistently declined. The average distance reveals the skewness of income inequality. Up to 1980-81, the average distance for the entire districts is negative which implies that the income distribution is negatively skewed which means that the distance of backward (or percapita income below the state average) districts to the state average is higher than distance of developed districts to the state average. After 1980-81, the average distance for all districts is positive implies that the percapita income distributed between districts is positively skewed. This implies means that the income differences of backward districts with state average has declined and at the same time the distance of developed districts to the state average has increased.

The coefficient of variation (CV) and Gini Coefficient show the summary measures of inequality. The coefficient of variation shows that inequality in the distribution of percapita income between districts has consistently increased up 1995-96 and from 2000-01 onwards the intensity of inequality has declined. Except in the initial year of 1970-71, the C.V is lowest in 2003-04 highlight the fact that regional disparity at district level with respect to the distribution of percapita income has been narrowing down in Kerala. The Gini coefficient also reveals the same inferences as in the case of C.V. The value of Gini coefficient is lower since 2000-01 as compared to the pre 2000-01 period. The value of Gini Coefficient is highest in 1995-96. All these indicate that in recent years, the intensity of inequality with respect to percapita income at district level has been declining in Kerala. However, along with the narrowing down of the intensity of inequality in percapita income, the growth rate of percapita district SDP is also dwindling. It indicates that the decline in growth rate of percapita income is higher in developed regions compared to backward regions.

The position of districts with respect to percapita income was not uniform across different time points. The pattern of changes in ranks of districts is reflected in the Spearman's rank correlation coefficient as given in the Table 8.

Table 8
Rank Correlation of Districts with Respect to Per Capita Income in 2003-04

District	*2003-04*
1970-71	.645
1975-76	.564
1980-81	.573
1985-86	.692
1990-91	.727
1995-96	.727
2000-01	.947
2003-04	1.000

Source: Estimated from Table 4.

The rank correlation of districts with respect to percapita income reveals that though there has been some change in the ranks held by district over the time, the changes in position has not been so drastic. The rank correlation of districts with respect to 2003-04 has a very high correlation with post 1990's ranks of district compared to pre 1990's. This indicates the fact that the ranks held by districts during post 1990's could retain their ranks almost impeccably compared to pre 1990's.

Regional concentration of backwardness in Kerala

To understand the regional concentration of richness/ backwardness, clustering of districts is done based on their levels of development with respect to percapita income. The districts are categorised into backward, moderately developed and highly developed regions. The districts, which have a percapita income less than mean percapita income is considered as backward; the districts whose percapita income is greater than mean income but less than mean plus standard deviation is considered as moderately developed; and those districts whose percapita income exceed mean plus standard deviation is categorised as highly developed. The Table 9 shows that the number of backward districts in Kerala has initially increased but in recent decade the number of districts in this category has declined. At the same time, districts in the category of moderately developed has increased from three in 1970-71 to five in 2000-01. However, the number of highly developed districts has not increased to any perceptible extent in Kerala. Though the number of moderately developed districts within the present development scenario of Kerala has increased, the development is not uniform across various regions in Kerala. Historically, Kerala has three political regions such as Travancore, Cochin and Malabar regions. These regions located respectively in south, central and northern part of the State.

Table 9
Number of Districts in Various Development Clusters

Year	*Backward*	*Developed*	*Highly developed*
1970-71	5	3	3
1975-76	6	2	3
1980-81	6	3	2
1985-86	9	3	2
1990-91	6	7	1
1995-96	9	2	3
2000-01	7	5	2
2003-04	7	5	2

Source: Estimated from Table 4.

The Table 10 shows that there is a very high regional concentration of development in Kerala. Most of moderately developed and highly developed districts are located in erstwhile Travancore and Cochin regions. At the same time,

Table 10
Number of Districts in Various Clusters at Region Level

	Travancore			*Cochin*			*Malabar*		
Year	*B*	*MD*	*HD*	*B*	*MD*	*HD*	*B*	*MD*	*HD*
1970-71	1	1	1	1	1	2	3	1	
1975-76	1	1	1	1	1	2	4		
1980-81	2	1		2		2	2	2	
1985-86	3	1		1	1	2	5	1	
1990-91		4		1	2	1	5	1	
1995-96	3	1		1	1	2	5		1
2000-01	2	2			2	2	5	1	
2003-04	1	3			2	2	6		

Note: B-Backward, MD-Moderately developed and HD-Highly developed

Source: Estimated from Table 4

majority of backward district in Kerala belong to Malabar region. The districts such as Malappuram, Kasaragod and Kannur remain in the position of relative backwardness in Kerala throughout the time. Thus the historical advantages in political administration enjoyed by the regions still have their influence in tapping the development potentialities of the state.

The Table 11 shows the clustering of regions based on status of percapita income at district level.

Disparity in the Share of State Sectoral Income at District Level

The regional growth process invariably affects the relative importance of various sectors in contributing economic change. The state, Kerala is not an exception on this count. The Table 12 shows the percentage share of various districts in state's sectoral income over different time points and the Table 13 shows its ranks.

As compared to 1970-71, the districts' contribution to state primary sector income has drastically changed in 2003-04. Those districts, which could contribute a very high share of primary sector income during 70's and 80's, could not retain their position during 90's and after. Here the case of Kollam is an exception. The position of Kannur and Alleppey has declined from second and third position to eight and fourteenth positions respectively in 2003-04. At the same time the districts which contributed a low share of primary sector income in 70's and 80's could increase their contribution to a very high level in recent periods. However, for the last ten years, the relative contribution of various districts in primary sector income has not changed much. In the case of secondary and tertiary sector contribution, the relative share of various districts is almost same throughout the period particularly after 1985-86. It means that those districts, which are developed with respect to secondary and tertiary sector, could retain its position impeccably in the state. Thus the relative position of districts in terms of its sectoral contributions to the state SDP, remains almost same for all sectors for the last 20 years (Table 14). Compared to recent times, the changes in relative

Table 11
Clustering of Districts Based on Per Capita Income

District	*1970-71*	*1975-76*	*1980-81*	*1985-86*	*1990-91*	*1995-96*	*2000-01*	*2003-04*
Trivandrum	Backward	Developed	Backward	Backward	Developed	Backward	Developed	Developed
Kollam	Highly Developed	Highly Developed	Developed	Backward	Developed	Backward	Backward	Backward
Pathanamthitta	.	.	.	Developed	Developed	Developed	Developed	Developed
Alappuzha	Developed	Backward	Backward	Backward	Developed	Backward	Backward	Developed
Kottayam	Highly Developed	Highly Developed	Backward	Developed	Backward	Developed	Developed	Developed
Idukki	Developed	Highly Developed	Highly Developed	Highly Developed	Developed	Highly Developed	Highly Developed	Highly Developed
Ernakulam	Highly Developed	Developed	Highly Developed	Highly Developed	Highly Developed	Highly Developed	Highly Developed	Highly Developed
Thrissur	Backward	Backward	Backward	Backward	Developed	Backward	Developed	Developed
Palakkad	Backward	Backward	Backward	Backward	Backward	Backward	Backward	Backward
Malappuram	Backward	Backward	Backward	Backward	Backward	Backward	Backward	Backward
Kozhikode	Developed	Backward	Developed	Backward	Backward	Backward	Backward	Backward
Wayanad	.	.	.	Developed	Developed	Highly Developed	Developed	Backward
Kannur	Backward	Backward	Developed	Backward	Backward	Backward	Backward	Backward
Kasaragod	.	.	.	Backward	Backward	Backward	Backward	Backward

Source: Estimated from Table 4

Table 12(a)
Percentage Share of Various Districts in State Level Sectoral Income

	1970-1971			*1976-1977*			*1980-1981*			*1985-1986*		
District	*.P*	*S*	*T*	*P*	*S*	*T*	*P*	*S*	*T*	*P*	*S*	*T*
Trivandrum	9.07	9.58	12.39	9.09	9.06	12.30	8.36	10.04	12.33	7.77	9.84	12.93
Kollam	14.75	11.18	9.40	12.64	11.45	9.80	12.95	12.19	9.79	9.24	9.72	8.16
Pathanamthitta	0.00	0.00	0.00	0.00	0.00	0.00	0.00	0.00	0.00	4.91	4.37	4.29
Alappuzha	10.25	8.49	9.43	8.39	7.13	10.00	7.15	10.29	10.18	6.65	7.80	7.54
Kottayam	8.91	6.18	5.27	9.13	6.97	7.34	7.45	6.05	7.42	8.24	6.03	7.31
Idukki	4.66	3.31	3.98	6.24	3.57	1.98	7.02	5.68	2.55	7.63	5.33	1.87
Ernakulam	7.98	19.85	12.53	7.89	22.43	13.35	8.82	20.39	12.19	9.94	20.92	12.56
Thrissur	8.37	10.64	8.83	8.01	11.88	9.97	8.19	9.55	10.29	7.40	9.54	10.40
Palakkad	8.08	7.24	0.72	6.54	6.02	7.08	7.26	5.71	7.30	7.23	5.79	6.91
Malappuram	7.79	3.12	6.79	9.57	3.53	6.50	7.64	2.46	7.03	6.98	2.71	6.57
Kozhikode	9.60	10.84	11.29	9.97	9.21	11.12	10.42	9.79	10.46	7.03	7.62	8.82
Wayanad	0.00	0.00	0.00	0.00	0.00	0.00	0.00	0.00	0.00	4.67	4.19	1.92
Kannur	10.68	9.46	10.05	12.53	8.74	10.56	14.74	7.86	10.51	7.72	3.65	7.48
Kasaragod	0.00	0.00	0.00	0.00	0.00	0.00	0.00	0.00	0.00	4.60	2.50	3.24

Table 12(b)
Percentage Share of Various Districts in State Level Sectoral Income

	1990-1991			*1995-1996*			*2000-2001*			*2003-2004*		
District	*P*	*S*	*T*	*P*	*S*	*T*	*P*	*S*	*T*	*P*	*S*	*T*
Trivandrum	7.76	9.85	12.34	7.28	9.74	12.59	7.17	10.60	12.05	6.62	11.02	11.91
Kollam	9.35	8.98	7.87	8.70	8.04	7.44	9.51	8.62	7.41	8.97	8.46	7.39
Pathanamthitta	5.12	9.19	4.47	5.21	2.88	4.25	6.09	2.74	3.70	5.96	2.92	3.76
Alappuzha	7.48	6.38	6.99	4.72	6.22	6.93	4.00	8.67	6.95	4.42	8.38	6.94
Kottayam	7.28	2.52	7.31	8.52	2.46	7.40	6.93	5.63	7.27	7.04	5.86	7.26
Idukki	6.89	3.38	2.37	8.39	3.57	2.29	12.18	2.24	2.54	12.41	2.61	2.58
Ernakulam	10.13	24.45	12.79	9.22	24.92	13.97	8.52	15.68	12.29	8.07	15.74	12.38
Thrissur	8.23	11.32	10.36	6.75	11.44	10.26	7.07	11.57	10.49	6.30	11.31	10.52
Palakkad	7.29	7.35	6.98	7.37	7.20	7.01	7.35	6.34	7.30	7.04	6.26	7.32
Malappuram	8.41	3.63	6.98	7.52	3.69	7.17	7.46	6.14	8.06	7.67	6.13	8.07
Kozhikode	6.84	9.37	9.19	7.92	9.26	8.97	7.86	9.04	9.14	8.10	9.13	9.38
Wayanad	4.39	1.30	1.42	5.65	1.21	1.42	5.32	0.87	2.12	5.04	0.88	2.16
Kannur	5.96	6.79	8.31	7.75	6.74	7.22	6.27	0.78	7.25	6.64	7.51	7.16
Kasaragod	4.38	2.65	2.62	4.97	2.62	3.07	4.29	4.08	3.16	5.72	3.78	3.17

Note: P - Primary sector, S - Secondary and T - Tertiary.

Source: (1) Economic Review (various issues), State Planning Board, Govt. of Kerala
(2) Statistics for Planning (various issues), Dept of Economics and Statistics, Govt. of Kerala

Table 13(a)
Ranks of Various Districts in State Level Sectoral Income(Ranks)

	1970-1971			1976-1977			1980-1981			1985-1986		
District	*P*	*S*	*T*	*P*	*S*	*T*	*P*	*S*	*T*	*P*	*S*	*T*
Trivandrum	5	5	2	6	5	2	5	4	1	4	2	1
Kollam	1	2	6	1	3	7	2	2	7	2	3	5
Pathanamthitta	.	.	.	.	.	.	.	.	.	12	10	11
Alappuzha	3	7	5	7	7	5	10	3	6	11	5	6
Kottayam	6	9	9	5	8	8	8	8	8	3	7	8
Idukki	11	10	10	11	10	11	11	10	11	6	9	14
Ernakulam	9	1	1	9	1	1	4	1	2	1	1	2
Thrissur	7	4	7	8	2	6	6	6	5	7	4	3
Palakkad	8	8	11	10	9	9	9	9	9	8	8	9
Malappuram	10	11	8	4	11	10	7	11	10	10	13	10
Kozhikode	4	3	3	3	4	3	3	5	4	9	6	4
Wayanad	.	.	.	.	.	.	.	.	.	13	11	13
Kannur	2	6	4	2	6	4	1	7	3	5	12	7
Kasaragod	.	.	.	.	.	.	.	.	.	14	14	12

Source: Estimated from Table 12.

Table 13(b)
Ranks of Various Districts in State Level Sectoral Income (Ranks)

	1990-1991			1995-1996			2000-2001			2003-2004		
District	*P*	*S*	*T*	*P*	*S*	*T*	*P*	*S*	*T*	*P*	*S*	*T*
Trivandrum	5	3	2	9	3	2	7	3	2	9	3	2
Kollam	2	6	6	2	5	5	2	6	6	2	5	6
Pathanamthitta	12	5	11	12	11	11	11	11	11	11	12	11
Alappuzha	6	9	8	14	8	10	14	5	10	14	6	10
Kottayam	8	13	7	3	13	6	9	9	8	6.5	10	8
Idukki	9	11	13	4	10	13	1	12	13	1	13	13
Ernakulam	1	1	1	1	1	1	3	1	1	4	1	1
Thrissur	4	2	3	10	2	3	8	2	3	10	2	3
Palakkad	7	7	9.5	8	6	9	6	7	7	6.5	8	7
Malappuram	3	10	9.5	7	9	8	5	8	5	5	9	5
Kozhikode	10	4	4	5	4	4	4	4	4	3	4	4
Wayanad	13	14	14	11	14	14	12	13	14	13	14	14
Kannur	11	8	5	6	7	7	10	14	9	8	7	9
Kasaragod	14	12	12	13	12	12	13	10	12	12	11	12

Source: Estimated from Table 12

position of districts in sectoral contribution have been witnessed only in the 70's and that too confined mainly to the primary sector.

Table 14
Rank Correlation Coefficient of SDP Share of Various Districts As Compared to the Ranks in 2003-04

Year	*Primary*	*Secondary*	*Tertiary*
1970-71	-0.273	0.586	0.573
1975-76	0.059	0.619*	0.591
1980-81	0.114	0.627	0.6
1985-86	0.634*	0.881**	0.881**
1990-01	0.431	0.895**	0.895**
1995-96	0.889**	0.952**	0.952**
2000-01	0.95**	1.00	1.00*
2003-04	1.00	1.00	1.00

*Correlation is significant at 0.05 level.
**Correlation is significant at 0.10 level.
Source: Estimated from Table 12.

Disparity in Sectoral Contribution of District Income

District percapita net domestic product is the sum of contribution of primary, secondary and tertiary activities. The level of regional economic development is influenced by the dominance of various sectors at regional level. The Table 15 shows the district wise percapita sectoral income and the percentage contribution of various sectors in district percapita income is shown in Table 16.

The share of primary sector in district state domestic product ranges from 74% to 35% in 1970-71. The highest share was in Palakkad district followed by Kottayam district. The lowest share of primary sector in district SDP was reported for Ernakulam district. The average district share of primary sector was 54.26 per cent. This share has been declining constantly and reached to 22 per cent in 2003-04. However, the inequality of income from primary sector has been increasing in Kerala. In 1970-71, the C.V was 18.33, which increased to 20.57 in 1980-81, to 32.02 in 1990-91, to 40.36 in 2000-01 and to 52.94 in 2003-04. It implies that though there has been reduction in relative importance of primary sector in

Table 15(a)
District-wise Per Capita Sectoral Income (Rs. in Lakhs)

	1970-1971			1980-1981			1985-1986			1990-1991		
District	*P*	*S*	*T*	*P*	*S*	*T*	*P*	*S*	*T*	*P*	*S*	*T*
Trivandrum	264.37	92.35	226.27	467.85	292.55	615.21	604.30	463.59	1073.50	1059.33	1076.23	2084.13
Kollam	391.80	98.27	156.46	668.97	327.82	450.98	880.38	560.89	829.73	1562.66	1201.25	1628.29
Pathanamthitta							947.29	510.42	883.63	1732.88	2491.29	1874.89
Alappuzha	309.22	84.65	178.12	442.81	331.71	561.97	761.25	540.83	921.14	1502.66	1026.93	1738.82
Kottayam	371.11	85.09	137.45	643.01	271.80	570.67	1033.65	458.35	979.28	1601.48	444.67	1991.92
Idukki	390.43	91.51	208.64	1048.61	441.81	339.03	1619.95	685.59	423.42	2569.12	1009.12	1093.77
Ernakulam	236.35	194.45	232.42	505.29	607.90	622.46	808.38	1030.97	1090.96	1446.58	2795.65	2259.87
Thrissur	251.91	105.98	166.46	487.20	295.81	545.84	619.67	483.35	929.37	1207.85	1331.09	1883.07
Palakkad	307.53	91.12	17.08	515.52	211.12	462.24	695.35	337.29	709.75	1229.99	992.92	1458.59
Malappuram	269.26	35.69	146.83	461.56	77.26	378.59	516.80	121.63	518.78	1092.70	377.14	1122.34
Kozhikode	292.21	109.12	215.15	673.96	329.65	602.90	615.37	403.69	824.10	1049.60	1152.43	1746.76
W2ayanad							1591.34	864.50	696.98	2624.93	624.18	1051.79
Kannur	289.62	84.79	170.69	763.54	211.96	485.25	785.23	224.55	811.68	1063.64	971.03	1837.70
Kasaragod							985.15	323.69	739.81	1643.39	797.66	1217.62
Mean	306.71	97.55	168.69	607.12	309.04	512.29	890.29	500.67	816.58	1527.63	1163.69	1642.11
C.V	17.87	38.37	35.48	29.91	43.75	18.81	38.14	47.78	23.31	33.48	59.02	23.91

Note: P - Primary sector, S - Secondary and T - Tertiary.

Source: (1) Economic Review (various issues), State Planning Board, Govt. of Kerala.
(2) Statistics for Planning (various issues), Dept of Economics and Statistics, Govt. of Kerala.

Table 15(b)
District-wise Per Capita Sectoral (Rs. in Lakhs)

	1970-1971			*1980-1981*			*1990-1991*		
District	*P*	*S*	*T*	*P*	*S*	*T*	*P*	*S*	*T*
Trivandrum	2377.36	2069.46	4405.89	3137.79	4565.18	13275.54	2994.46	5600.66	17160.29
Kollam	3479.36	2093.91	3191.89	5206.62	4647.06	10223.57	5112.06	5422.68	13428.19
Pathanamthitta	4223.87	1517.31	3690.91	7004.31	3101.46	10703.82	7214.13	3974.08	14497.99
Alappuzha	2269.42	1947.56	3572.05	2697.33	5748.67	11797.95	3116.72	6635.54	15576.55
Kottayam	4486.49	841.45	4177.66	5004.03	3998.52	13209.59	5322.50	4983.22	17487.88
Idukki	7480.78	2073.39	2185.74	15239.08	2761.01	8005.39	16336.48	3867.80	10836.91
Ernakulam	3150.70	5541.93	5119.10	3891.06	7049.45	14136.57	3807.10	8350.94	18610.23
Thrissur	2372.99	2617.35	3867.02	3356.51	5408.09	12547.65	3104.18	6271.30	16529.52
Palakkad	2974.08	1891.38	3032.53	3970.11	3368.78	9922.06	3933.04	3933.26	13033.30
Malappuram	2335.90	747.24	2389.33	2908.10	2354.16	7907.96	4090.99	3672.99	13713.86
Kozhikode	2910.47	2215.02	3532.29	3860.52	4372.67	11310.31	4114.58	5214.11	15178.35
W2ayanad	8077.69	1127.20	2183.68	9574.71	1531.13	9581.58	9161.16	1806.03	12510.13
Kannur	3312.89	1875.94	3307.67	3679.39	449.30	10713.93	4055.23	5164.14	13953.32
Kasaragod	4464.42	1529.10	2960.74	5023.51	4700.00	9318.30	6893.05	5131.74	12161.87
Mean	3851.17	2006.30	3401.18	5325.22	3861.11	10903.87	5661.12	5002.03	14619.89
C.V	47.60	57.25	24.84	63.69	45.20	17.66	62.84	31.16	15.35

Source: (1) Economic Review (various issues), State Planning Board, Govt. of Kerala
(2) Statistics for Planning (various issues), Dept of Economics and Statistics, Govt. of Kerala

Table 16(a)
Percentage Share of Various Sectors in District Income

	1970-1971			1980-1981			1985-1986		
District	*P*	*S*	*T*	*P*	*S*	*T*	*P*	*S*	*T*
Trivandrum	45.35	15.84	38.81	34.01	21.27	44.72	28.22	21.65	50.13
Kollam	60.60	15.20	24.20	46.21	22.64	31.15	38.77	24.70	36.54
Pathanamthitta							40.46	21.80	37.74
Alappuzha	54.06	14.80	31.14	33.13	24.82	42.05	34.24	24.33	41.43
Kottayam	62.51	14.33	23.15	43.29	18.30	38.42	41.83	18.55	39.63
Idukki	56.54	13.25	30.21	57.32	24.15	18.53	59.36	25.12	15.52
Ernakulam	35.64	29.32	35.04	29.11	35.02	35.86	27.59	35.18	37.23
Thrissur	48.04	20.21	31.75	36.66	22.26	41.08	30.49	23.78	45.73
Palakkad	73.97	21.92	4.11	43.36	17.76	38.88	39.91	19.36	40.73
Malappuram	59.60	7.90	32.50	50.31	8.42	41.27	44.66	10.51	44.83
Kozhikode	47.40	17.70	34.90	41.95	20.52	37.53	33.39	21.90	44.71
Wayanad							50.47	27.42	22.11
Kannur	53.13	15.56	31.31	52.27	14.51	33.22	43.11	12.33	44.56
Kasaragod							48.09	15.80	36.11
Mean	54.26	16.91	28.83	42.51	20.88	36.61	40.04	21.60	38.36
C.V	18.83	32.50	32.45	20.57	31.91	19.60	22.41	28.98	24.27

Source: Estimated from Table 15

Table 16(b)
Percentage Share of Various Sector in District Income

	1990-1991			1995-1996			2000-2001			2003-2004		
District	P	S	T	P	S	T	P	S	T	P	S	T
Trivandrum	25.10	25.50	49.39	26.85	23.38	49.77	14.96	21.76	63.28	11.63	21.75	66.63
Kollam	35.58	27.35	37.07	39.70	23.89	36.42	25.93	23.15	50.92	21.33	22.63	56.04
Pathanamthitta	28.41	40.85	30.74	44.78	16.09	39.13	33.66	14.90	51.44	28.09	15.47	56.44
Alappuzha	35.20	24.06	40.74	29.14	25.00	45.86	13.32	28.40	58.28	12.31	26.20	61.50
Kottayam	39.66	11.01	49.33	47.20	8.85	43.95	22.53	18.00	59.47	19.15	17.93	62.92
Idukki	54.99	21.60	23.41	63.72	17.66	18.62	58.60	10.62	30.78	52.63	12.46	34.91
Ernakulam	22.25	43.00	34.76	22.81	40.12	37.06	15.52	28.11	56.37	12.37	27.14	60.49
Thrissur	27.31	30.10	42.58	26.79	29.55	43.66	15.75	25.38	58.88	11.98	24.21	63.81
Palakkad	33.41	26.97	39.62	37.66	23.95	38.40	23.00	19.52	57.48	18.82	18.82	62.36
Malappuram	42.15	14.55	43.30	42.68	13.65	43.66	22.08	17.87	60.04	19.05	17.10	63.85
Kozhikode	26.58	29.18	44.24	33.62	25.58	40.80	19.75	22.37	57.87	16.79	21.28	61.93
Wayanad	61.03	14.51	24.46	70.93	9.90	19.17	46.28	7.40	46.32	39.02	7.69	53.29
Kannur	27.47	25.08	47.46	38.99	22.08	38.93	24.79	3.03	72.18	17.50	22.29	60.21
Kasargode	44.92	21.80	33.28	49.86	17.08	33.07	26.38	24.68	48.94	28.50	21.22	50.28
Mean	36.01	25.40	38.60	41.05	21.20	37.75	25.90	18.94	55.16	22.08	19.73	58.19
C.V	32.02	35.61	21.83	33.72	38.69	24.00	49.16	40.36	17.26	52.94	26.94	13.86

Source: Estimated from Table 15

all districts, the inequality of income generation in this sector has been increasing at an alarming rate at district level. The average secondary sector contribution at district level was 16.91 in 1970-71, increased to 20.88 in 1980-81 to 36.01 in 1990-91 and declined to 19.73 in 2003-04. Initially the share of secondary sector increased, however, it declined in the recent periods. The coefficient of variation of secondary sector contribution was 32.50 in 1970-71, which declined to 20.57 in 1980-81, to 35.16 in 1990-91 and to 26.94 in 2003-04. In recent years the disparity in percapita income contribution from the secondary sector has declined. Compared to primary and secondary sectors, the percapita tertiary sector contribution at district has been increasing steadily. In 1970-71, the average share of tertiary sector in district income was 28.83 per cent, which become 36.61 in 1980-81, to 38.60 in 1990-91 to 58.19 in 2003-04. Though there has been increase in tertiary sector contribution, its disparity between district has a declining trend. In 1970-71, the coefficient of variation of tertiary sector was 32.45, which declined steadily to 13.86 in 2003-04. Thus among the various sectors, the growth in primary sector has a greater role in widening regional disparity in Kerala compared to other sectors.

The growth of percapita income and variation in sectoral development are interrelated. The Table 17 shows the rank correlation between the ranks in terms of percapita income and ranks of district with respect to primary, secondary and tertiary sector development.

Table 17

Rank Correlation between Aggregate Per Capita Income with Per Capita Sectoral Income at District Level in Kerala

Year	*Primary*	*secondary*	*Tertiary*
1970-71	.300	.545	.318
1980-81	.627*	.709*	.273
1985-86	.705*	.855*	.262
1990-01	.380	.701*	.292
1995-96	.719*	.160	.147
2000-01	.305	.310	.486
2003-04	-0.33	.415	.508

*Correlation is significant at 0.05 level.

Source: Estimated from Table 15.

The result indicates that upto 1985-86, the level of percapita income is influenced by the status of district in terms of primary and secondary sector development. The percapita income status and tertiary sector has less significant relation. However, the picture has changed during post 1990-91 periods. The post 1990-91 period highlight the fact that those district which are dominated by primary sector and secondary sector witnessed a decline in their status in terms of percapita income compared to other districts which could increase the share of tertiary activities. In recent periods, the role of tertiary sector in determining the district level percapita income has been increasing.

Decomposition of Regional Inequality at District Level

The relative contribution of various sectors in creating or offsetting regional inequality can be better understood only by decomposing the sectoral inequality. The methodology to decompose the inequality element is as follows. (Sabhyasachi Kar and S. Sakthivel (2004))

Let there be 'n' regions such that the output of each region is given by X_i, i=1,2,..n. Let there be 'm' sectors that contribute to each region's output Xi, such that the output of each sector in each region is given by X_{ij}, i=1,2…n, j=1,2,.m.

Then,

$$Xi = \Sigma Xij \qquad (1)$$

Let $\bar{X}$ be the arithmetic mean of Xi and $\bar{X}j$ be the arithmetic mean of Xij. Next, define Pj as the ratio between the average output of the jth sector and the average output of the economy.

Thus,

$$P_j = \bar{X}_j / \bar{X} \qquad (2)$$

Let us also assume that $\sigma(X_i)$, $Var(X_i)$, $Cov(X_{ij}, X_{ik})$ and $r_{ij,ik}$ are the symbols for the standard deviation, variance, covariance and the correlation coefficient of the corresponding variables, respectively. Then, the percentage decomposition of total inequality is given by:

$$\Sigma(P_j * r_{ij,ik} * C(X_{ij}) / C(X_j) \qquad (3)$$

Rearranging the above equation, we can write

$$C(X_i) = \Sigma(C(X_{ij})*P_j*r_{ij,ik}) \quad (4)$$

The above equation indicates that the level of aggregate inequality (measured by the coefficient of variation of aggregate output) is equal to the sum of each sectors contribution. The contribution of each sector is equal to the product of (i) the inequality in the sector, (ii) the average regional output of the sector as a proportion of the average regional output and (iii) the correlation coefficient between the sector and the whole economy. This means that the inequality for the aggregate economy is affected not only by the sectoral inequalities, but also by the relative size of the sectors and their interlinkage with the economy. The size of the sectors add a scale effect to the sectoral inequality ie, a larger sectors adds more to the economy's inequality compared to a smaller sector. The interlinkages of a sector with the whole economy, represented by the correlation coefficient between any sector and the economy implies that a region that has a relatively high output from that sector also has a relatively high aggregate output, while a region that has a relatively low output from that sector also has a relatively low aggregate output. Thus, for a given level of inequality in the sector, an increase in the correlation coefficient increases the economy's inequality.

The Table 18 shows the inequality of district percapita and its sectoral components. The time span covered is 1970-71 to 2003-04. The inequality in aggregate percapita income has increased initially and after that it has declined. Since 1995-96, there has been a steady decline in aggregate inequality in percapita income at district level in Kerala. However, the share of divergence of percapita income created by various sectors has not been uniform.

The inequality within the primary sector has been growing at a very high rate. The share of primary sector in aggregate inequality has increased over time compared to other sectors. The coefficient of variation in primary sector between districts in 1970-71 was 0.18 which increased steadily to 0.63 in 2003-04. In the case of secondary sector, though the inequality within

Table 18
Inequality of District NSDP and Its Sectoral Components

	1970-1971	1980-1981	1985-1986	1990-1991	1995-1996	2000-2001	2003-2004
Primary sector							
Coefficient of variation	0.18	0.30	0.38	0.33	0.48	0.64	0.63
Relative size	0.54	0.43	0.40	0.35	0.42	0.27	0.22
Inter Linkage	0.38	0.65	0.75	0.28	0.56	0.53	0.43
Sectoral contribution	0.04	0.08	0.12	0.03	0.11	0.09	0.06
Secondary sector							
Coefficient of variation	0.38	0.44	0.48	0.59	0.57	0.45	0.31
Relative size	0.17	0.22	0.23	0.27	0.22	0.19	0.20
Inter Linkage	0.53	0.84	0.92	0.91	0.63	0.50	0.45
Sectoral contribution	0.03	0.08	0.10	0.14	0.08	0.04	0.03
Tertiary sector							
Coefficient of variation	0.35	0.19	0.23	0.24	0.25	0.18	0.15
Relative size	0.29	0.36	0.37	0.38	0.37	0.54	0.58
Inter Linkage	0.75	0.20	0.21	0.53	0.28	0.39	0.34
Sectoral contribution	0.08	0.01	0.02	0.05	0.03	0.04	0.03
Aggregate							
Coefficient of variation	0.15	0.18	0.23	0.23	0.21	0.17	0.12

Source: Estimated from Table 15.

that sector between district has initially risen, it declined in the second half of 90's and later. In tertiary sector activities, there has been some fluctuation in sectoral inequality in the 80's and after that there has been a steady decline in inequality. Compared to primary and secondary sector, the inequality within the tertiary sector activities is very low in Kerala, especially in the recent periods.

In primary sector, the relative size and its interlinkge with the regional development has been declining in Kerala throughout the period. This decline in its relative importance has been amplified particularly from 1995-96. Had there been increase in relative importance of primary sector in Kerala, the inequality within this sector between district would have been worsened. In secondary sector also, the relative size and interlinkage with regional development has declined, which actually reduced the sectoral inequality between regions. The inequality components in tertiary sector activities are very unique in Kerala. Along with the increase in relative size and its interlinkage in regional development, there has also been a decline in inequality in this sector in Kerala. In Kerala, one of the major contributing factors in reducing regional inequality in development is the peculiar growth pattern in tertiary activities. While primary sector (and secondary sector some extend) acts as divergence inducing, the tertiary sector acts as divergence offsetting source in Kerala.

Conclusion

Spatial inequality is very critical dimension, which cannot be easily ignored in social, economic and political development. Since most of the spatial boundaries coexist with political, social, ethnic, religious and specific geographic attributes, the reduction in regional inequality is highly warranted for reduction in national inequality as well as inequality in economic development between various ethnic, linguistic, religious and other social groups. Social equity goes along with spatial equity. Compared to other states in India, the state Kerala stands unique with respect to redistributive justice in many basic human needs through mass political and social movement. However, the natural advantage of economic geography with respect to historical legacy, natural resource endowment, locational advantages and the positive impacts of agglomeration could not completely be overtaken by policy initiatives of any government in Kerala.

The growth rate of SDP is not uniform across districts in Kerala. There is no connection existing between the direction of growth rate and share of SDP of various districts. Despite higher growth of district SDP among backward district, they could not catch up the developed districts due huge absolute initial difference between these regions. However, since 1990-91, the northern districts, which are relatively backward in Kerala are catching with other districts in Kerala. The distribution of percapita income at district level in Kerala has a negative skewness upto 1980-81 and after that skewness become positive. That is the income differences of backward districts with state average has declined and at the same time the distance of developed districts to the state average has increased.

The inequality in the distribution of percapita income between districts has been consistently increasing up to 1995-96 and after that it has declined. However, along with the narrowing down of the intensity of inequality in percapita income, the growth rate of percapita district SDP is also dwindling. It indicates that the decline in growth rate of percapita income is higher in developed regions compared to backward regions. In terms of level of development, the number of moderately developed districts has increased in Kerala. However, the fruits of development are relatively more enjoyed by Central and Southern districts of Kerala. The erstwhile Malabar region consists of largest number of relatively backward districts in Kerala.

The growth of percapita income and variation in sectoral development are interrelated. The inequality of income from primary sector has been increasing in Kerala despite its declining share in district income. Compared to primary and secondary sectors, the percapita tertiary sector contribution at district has been increasing steadily. Though there has been increase in tertiary sector contribution, its disparity between district has a declining trend. Among the various sectors, the growth in primary sector has a greater role in widening regional disparity in Kerala compared to other sectors. Though there has been decline in regional divergence, the share of divergence of percapita income created by various sectors has not been uniform. The inequality components in tertiary sector activities are very unique in Kerala. Along with the increase in relative size and its interlinkage in regional development, there has also been a decline in inequality in this sector. One of the major contributing factors in reducing regional inequality in development is the peculiar growth pattern in tertiary activities. While primary sector (and secondary sector some extend) acts as divergence inducing, the tertiary sector acts as divergence offsetting source in Kerala. Thus the changes in the facets of regional inequality warrants new type of policy initiatives, which were hitherto unnoticed by planners.

References

Ahluwalia, M. S. (2000), 'Economic Performance of States in Post-Reform Period', *Economic and Political Weekly*, May 6.

Barro R. J. (1991), 'Economic Growth in a Cross Section of Countries', *Quarterly Journal of Economics*, 106, 2 (May), 407-443.

Bhattacharya, B. B. and S. Sakthivel, (2004) 'Regional Growth and Disparity in India: Comparison of Pre and Post-Reform Decades', *Economic and Political Weekly*, March 6, pp. 1071-1077.

Das, S. K. and A. Barua (1996), 'Regional Inequalities, Economic Growth and Liberalisation: A study of the Indian Economy', *The Journal of Development Studies*, Vol. 32, February.

Directorate of Economics and Statistics, Statistics for Planning (for various years), Government of Kerala, Thiruvananthapuram.

Isard, Walter and Cumberland, John H. (ed.) Regional Planning: Technique of Analysis for Less Developed Areas, Paris.

Rao, S. R. (1970), "A Note on Measuring Economic Distance between Regions in India", *Economic and Political Weekly*, January 7, Bombay.

Rao, M. Govinda, Shand R. T. and K. P. Kalirajan (1999), 'Convergence of Incomes Across Indian States', *Economic and Political Weekly*, March 27-28.

Shand, R. T. and S. Bhide (2000), 'Sources of Economic Growth: Regional Dimensions of Reforms', *Economic and Political Weekly*, Oct. 14.

Singh N. Bhandari L., Chen A. and A. Khare (2003), 'Regional Inequality in India: A Fresh Look', *Economic and Political Weekly*, March.

State Planning Board, Economic Review (for various years), Government of Kerala, Thiruvananthapuram.

PART–V

HEALTH AND NUTRITION

HEALTH CARE DEVELOPMENT IN KERALA: SOME ISSUES AND POLICY OPTIONS

A. Ashokan

Introduction

Kerala, a low income Indian state has made remarkable strides in the field of public health measured in terms of life expectancy at birth, mortality, and health transition. The progressive socio-economic policies adopted by the state governments before and after independence have substantially contributed for the transition. The preventive public health care system had been very effective in reducing the incidence and the prevalence rates of communicable and other diseases. Subsequently, the rural public health care system has become less efficient leaving a larger space to the already dominant private health care sector. The unregulated private health care sector, on the one hand, and the inefficient rural public health care system, on the other, have increased the out-of pocket medical care expenditure for both outpatient and inpatient care, which, in particular, deteriorated the health status of the poor and other vulnerable sections. Maintaining health is expensive and health care has become a commodity just like any other commodity exchanged in the market. The nature of transition to the life style and modern neo-plastic diseases has been in tune with the morbidity profile in Western societies. A number of factors such as the socio-cultural and religious reform movements, redistribution of land through progressive land reforms, effective public distribution system and, above all, the typical geography of the region have been significant in the educational, demographic and health transition (CDS,1975; Panikar and Soman, 1984; Kannan et.al, 1991; Kabir and Krishnan, 1992; Ashokan, 2005).Specific steps have been taken by the government of Kerala in the post-independence period to improve the preventive and curative health care policies and programmes through comprehensive and diversified primary, secondary and tertiary level health care institutions. The birth and death rates had always been much lower and the literacy levels much higher in Kerala compared to the national average even from the early years of the last century. Similarly, expectation of life at birth has been consistently higher in Kerala since 1960 and the latest figure puts it at 72 for males and 75 for females as against 64 and 65 in India, respectively. In a multi-cultural society, morbidity prevalence rates would be dissimilar. Kerala is increasingly exposed to life style related and other long standing diseases. A recent study has estimated an acute morbidity rate of 218 and chronic morbidity rate of 155 per thousand population and a higher acute and chronic morbidity rates among the females (23.8% and 17.5%) compared to the males (19.9% and 13.4%). Similarly, wide variations have been reported across caste, religion, and socio-economic status (Ashokan, 2007a; 2007c). Even though Kerala has achieved remarkable progress in health indicators, infrastructural constraints and other problems restrict service delivery and its utilisation. The rural public health care sector in Kerala has been overburdened with allocative, financial, organisational and managerial inefficiencies. The policy option, *interalia*, has accelerated the choice of privatisation of health care services. The basic issue addressed in this paper is the morbidity-cost-society linkage and the need for redefining the health care needs through a policy shift.

The Issues

Public provisioning of health care facilities has been marginal and as low as less than 20 per cent in India and in many developing countries. The private health care sector controls more than three-fourths of the health care services in Kerala. In this backdrop, the paper examines the growth of the health care sector and the relevant policy options for sustainable health care development. In particular, the study aims at:

(i) Examining the health care infrastructure across sectors and systems of medicine

(ii) Analysing the nature and problems of health care service delivery and its utilisation

(iii) Identifying options for a policy shift.

Health Care Infrastructure

The remarkable progress made by the state of Kerala particularly in the fields of education, health and social transition is not exclusively a post 1956 phenomenon. Even during the pre-independence period Kerala had been contributing substantially to the overall development. However, these positive changes were mostly confined to the erstwhile princely states of Travancore and Cochin ruled by the local Maharajas and not to British Malabar. The indigenous medical systems particularly ayurveda has been dominant and contributed 2 significantly to the regional health care development. Unani and ayurveda, two indigenous medical systems similar in several respects, have contributed and enriched the materia medica and pharmacopoeia as well as to the improvement in diagnostic and therapeutic skills. The Kerala society accepts medical pluralism as a holistic health care practice for reducing the incidence of both short duration and long standing morbidity and maintaining the health status.

Public Health Infrastructure

Public health care system in Kerala consists of allopathy, ayurveda, homeopathy and unani. The distribution of these systems of medicine and the spatial spread of the health care institutions has been highly unequal. Of the total allopathic institutions 941 (71.8 per cent) are primary health centres, 107 (8.27 per cent) community health centres and 143 (10.9 per cent) hospitals. The proportion of medical institutions has undergone substantial changes during the past two decades. For instance, the proportion of allopathic medical institutions declined from 52 per cent in 1980-81 to 47 per cent in 1999-2000 whereas the proportion of ayurvedic medical institutions declined from 39 per cent to less than 33 per cent and the percentage of homeo medical institutions increased substantially from 9 per cent to 20 per cent during the same period. The proportion of the allopathic doctors declined from 70 per cent in 1991-92 to 67 per cent in 1999-2000.The proportion of ayurvedic doctors has marginally increased from 20 to 21 per cent and homeopathy doctors from 10 to 12 per cent during the same period. Nevertheless, the proportion of beds across the systems of medicine retains more or less the same pattern during the last two decades. Considerable changes have been noticed in the strength of public health care personnel. For instance, the staff strength in the state grew at an annual average rate of 0.9 per cent between 1992 and 2001. However, the proportion of nurses grew at an annual rate of 3.1 per cent as against 1.8 per cent, 0.3 per cent and 0.4 per cent respectively for doctors, pharmacists and field staff during the same period. The spread of health care institutions, medical and paramedical personnel has been more unequal across both urban and rural Kerala. For instance, 86 per cent of the government and 66 per cent of the private medical institutions are 3 concentrated in rural areas whereas the corresponding shares of doctors and beds are 33 per cent, 49 per cent, 25 per cent and 53 per cent respectively. The spread of modern private medical institutions has reduced the spatial health inequality on the one hand and encouraged the utilization of private (allopathic) medical care services on the other. Since the 1980s the number of both medical institutions and beds in the government sector has been consistently coming down and the proportion of private sector has been progressively moving up.

Private Health Sector

The private sector is the largest health care provider in India. For instance, 85 per cent of the doctors, 93 per cent of the hospitals and 37 per cent of the beds are in the private sector (Muralidharan, 2001). The role of the private health care sector in Kerala has been very decisive and significant. There were 12618 private medical institutions in the state of which 34 per cent are allopathic institutions, 39 per cent ayurvedic institutions, 25 per cent homeopathic institutions and 2.3 per cent other medical institutions. At the same time 45 per cent allopathic institutions had inpatient facilities and less than 5 per cent ayurvedic institutions and 1.4 per cent of the homeopathic institutions had inpatient facilities. Thirteen per cent of the private allopathic medical institutions have just one physician and above 42 per cent have not more than 4 physicians. More than three-fourths of the medical institutions across different systems of medicine (allopathy, ayurveda and homeopathy) are in the private sector. In terms of the proportion of hospital beds, the share of allopathy in the private sector is 58 per cent as against 40 per cent in the public sector. In ayurveda, the share of both the sectors is identical and in homeopathy the share of public sector beds is as high as 66 per cent as against 27 per cent in the private sector (Ashokan, 2005).

Studies on the private health care sector both in India and Kerala are very limited. However, three specific surveys on the private health care institutions have been carried out in Kerala (GoK, 1985; 1995; 2004). The number of private medical institutions has increased by 31 per cent, 11 per cent in the case of private medical institutions with beds and 36 per cent private institutions without beds during 1986 and 1995. Similarly, the growth in 4private medical institutions has also been observed across systems of medicine. At the same time, the proportion of allopathic institutions with beds has declined from 91 per cent in 1986 to 86 per cent in 1995 whereas private ayurvedic institutions have increased from 6.5 per cent to more than 10 per cent during the same period. Homeopathic institutions have marginally increased from 1.7 per cent to 2 per cent whereas other systems of medicine like Unani and Sidha have shown substantial increase. The private medical institutions without beds retain more or less the same pattern across the different systems of medicine. The proportion of allopathic doctors has increased marginally from 50 to 52 per cent where as ayurvedic doctors declined from 32 per cent to less than 29 per cent and the share of homeopathy doctors remains unchanged. As far as the number of para-medical staff is concerned 88 per cent is the share of allopathy, 9 per cent ayurveda and a little more than 2 per cent homeopathy. System wise details of the private health care sector reveal that 34 per cent, 39 per cent and 25 per cent are the respective shares of allopathy, ayurveda and homeopathy. Medical institutions with IP facility differ much across systems of medicine. For instance, 86 per cent, 10 per cent, 2 per cent are the respective shares of these three systems of medicines as far as IP is concerned. The same pattern is observed with respect to the number of outpatients, inpatients, doctors and para-medical staff. The percentage share of the different systems of medicine for OP and IP care provides a dissimilar picture. More than 97 per cent of the inpatients and 63 per cent of the outpatients revealed their preferences for allopathy (modern) health care services. The inequality in health care infrastructure across regions is more disturbing in Kerala. The share of allopathy institutions with IP facility in Kasaragod district is as low as 2.5 per cent where as it is as high as around 10.5 per cent for Kollam and Trivandrum districts. The same is the case with respect to ayurvedic and homeopathic health care system. With regard to the number of (allopathy) beds the share of Kasaragod district is as low as 1.8 per cent as against 16 per cent in Ernakulam and between 10 and 12 per cent in Thrissur, Kottayam and Kollam districts. (Ashokan, 2005) Most districts in the Malabar area (particularly North Malabar) are experiencing regional inequality in the distribution of health care institutions and other health infrastructural 5 problems both in the private and public sectors and across systems of medicine compared to South Kerala. Inter-regional differences in health infrastructure and medical and para-medical personnel encourage the North-South dichotomy in health care development. Nevertheless, in terms of both medical and para-medical staff the private health care sector is much ahead of the public health care sector across social geography in Kerala.

Utilisation of OP and IP Health Care Services

A recent study has revealed that 66 per cent of the sample households utilized outpatient (OP) health care services in rural Kerala. It is estimated that 41 per cent of the sample households reported one OP, 19 per cent two OPs, and 6 per cent three or more OPs. On the other hand, hospitalization or inpatient (IP) care during the last one year before the date of survey revealed that 41 per cent of the sample households utilized IP care services, and 31 per cent households reported one IP, 8 per cent reported two IPs and a little more than 2 per cent reported three IPs. On an average, one person per household reported to have utilized medical care as an outpatient and at least one hospitalization (IP) per two households (Ashokan, 2005). The private health care sector is the dominant provider of both outpatient and inpatient health care services and it accounts for 78 per cent of the OP and 88 per cent for IP health care services. Allopathy is the dominant system of medicine for both OP and IP care services.

Health Care Expenditure

Health care expenditure indicates considerable differences across socio-economic groups (SEG). The average OP expenditure is Rs. 244 and it is Rs. 131 for the SEG1 (poorest) and it is Rs. 538 for the (richest) SEG4 (Ashokan, 2007). Health expenditure inequality is more striking across SEGs in rural Kerala. This is consistently observed across different items of medical expenditure, such as doctor's fee, medicine, diagnostics, travel and others. The average medical expenditure for inpatient care is estimated at Rs. 4999, Rs. 4054 for the SEG1 and Rs. 6850 for the SEG4 (see Tables 1 & 2). Medical expenditure has become a significant component of household monthly consumption expenditure. The increased morbidity prevalence rates and health care expenditure have deeper societal implications. Increased medical expenditure has deteriorated the health status of the rural poor and other vulnerable groups. Specifically, 19 per cent of the households reported deterioration in their health status due to high health care expenditure and more than 24 per cent of the inpatients either borrowed or indebted and a little more than 3.4 per cent either sold or mortgaged their property to finance the health care expenditure(Ashokan,2005). Most of the patterns of medical treatment are physician induced and they are liberal in prescribing larger number of drugs and medicines even for short duration morbidity. The public health care system constrained by lower capacity utilisation particularly in the context of privatization of health care services has accentuated the household burden of health care. In Kerala, convenience and quality act as important determinants of increased utilisation of private health care services. Better provision and quality of the public health care system in urban areas has increased their utilisation in districts like Trivandrum. For instance, the share of the public sector is as high as 50 per cent for OP services in Trivandrum district as against less than 15 per cent in Kollam district. In a poor district like Palakkad IP health care services utilisation is as high as more than 52 per cent as against less than 10 per cent in Idukki (Table 3). Nevertheless, the private sector is the significant provider of both OP and IP health care services across different systems of medicine in Kerala. For instance, 63 per cent is the share of modern medicine for OP services followed by ayurveda and homeopathy. More than 97 per cent revealed their preferences for allopathy (see table:4). Quality provisioning of services followed by the location specific factors (defined in terms of the availability of multi and super speciality hospitals at a single sight) have contributed for the increased utilisation of private health care services. On the other hand, bypassing of public health care services is basically attributed to poor quality and provisioning of health care services. More than three-fourths (78 per cent) and more than four-fifths (88 per cent) of the OPs and IPs utilised private health care services, respectively in rural Kerala (Ashokan, 2005). However, the

Table 1
Average Medical Expenditure per Ailment for OP and IP

		OP			*IP*		
State	*Year*	*Government*	*Private*	*Total*	*Government*	*Private*	*Total*
Rural							
Kerala	1998	103	163	136	1616	2805	2293
Kerala*	2004	68	293	244	1443	5523	4999
India	1998	129	186	176	2080	4300	3202
Urban							
Kerala	1998	90	140	120	1527	2254	1927
India	1998	166	200	194	2195	5344	3921

Sources: 1. NSSO, 1998 2.* Ashokan, 2005.

Table 2
Outpatients and Inpatient Health Care Expenditure by SEG (Rs.)

Socio-Economic Group	*Outpatient*	*Inpatient*
SEG_1	131.34	4054.75
SEG_2	220.50	4978.10
SEG_3	182.47	5316.82
SEG_4	537.56	6850.14
All Groups	243.61	4999.12

Source: Ashokan, 2005.

Table 3
Sectoral Distribution OP and IP in Kerala by Districts (%)

	OP			*IP*			
Districts	*Public*	*Private*	*Total*	*Public*	*Private*	*Total*	*OP/IP*
Trivandrum	49.82	50.18	7797016	39.58	60.42	442197	17.63
Kollam	14.37	85.63	7550801	20.23	79.77	505436	14.94
Pattanamthitta	28.92	71.08	4070673	15.01	84.99	193202	21.07
Alappuzha	45.10	54.90	6574080	32.18	67.82	183870	35.75
Kottayam	28.51	71.49	8022762	16.57	83.43	480770	16.69
Idukki	31.82	68.18	4175035	9.88	90.12	249552	16.73
Ernakulam	25.41	74.59	11994712	18.83	81.17	733023	16.37
Trichur	31.43	68.57	6224469	13.29	86.71	509042	12.23
Palakkad	48.29	51.71	4057585	52.47	47.53	204894	19.80
Malappuaram	42.77	57.23	6457589	30.33	69.67	339133	19.04
Kozhikkode	40.79	59.21	8536852	48.55	51.45	394361	21.65
Wayanad	24.09	75.91	2339918	32.79	67.21	132588	17.65
Kannur	37.78	62.22	5314996	27.03	72.97	323950	16.41
Kasaragod	38.48	61.52	2278715	27.90	72.10	114338	19.93
State	34.41	65.59	85394509	25.83	74.20	4807056	17.76

Source: Ashokan, 2005.

utilisation of public (tertiary and specialised) health care services in districts like Trivandrum has been quite remarkable implying that people's choices are a reflection of the quality of health care services. It is also estimated that in Kerala there are 18 outpatients per inpatient. It is as high as 36 OPs per IP in Alappuzha district as against 12 in Trichur.

Lower proportion of OPs per IP reveals higher rate of hospitalisation which, of course, increases the socio-economic burden at the household level (Table 3). Modern medicine (63 per cent) is the dominant system utilised for OP health care services, followed by ayurveda (21 per cent) and homeopathy (15 per cent).On the other hand, more than 97 per cent of the IPs utilised modern medicine.

Public Spending on Health and Education

Public spending on health and education has been consistently coming down since the initiation of the economic reforms. Public spending on health as a percentage of gross state domestic products has been coming down since 1980-81. For instance, it was 2 per cent in 1980-81 which declined to 0.95 per cent in 1998-99. It has important policy implications when majority of the primary health care centres, community health centres, rural and taluk hospitals are being starved of medical and para-medical personnel and other essential medical and surgical equipments. The percentage share of different expenditure categories in Kerala's health care budgets has undergone major transition particularly after the 1960s. For instance, pays and allowances have increased substantially from 36.6 per cent in 1960 to 62.8 per cent in 1995 (Sadanandan, 2001). What is more revealing is the decline in the share of the state health budget and the proportion allocated to drugs and medicine which was as high as 39 per cent in 1960 and which declined sharply to 18 per cent in 1995. The plan expenditure on medical and public health excluding family welfare declined from 13.8 per cent in 1995-96 to the lowest 7.8 per cent in 2001-02 and slightly revived to 9.5 per cent during 2002-03. Similarly, the non-plan expenditure increased from 71.5 per cent to more than 80 per cent during the same period and declined to around

Table 4
System wise Details of OP and IP Private Healthcare Facilities in Kerala: 1995

	OP					IP				
Districts	*Allopathy*	*Ayurveda*	*Homeopathy*	*Other*	*Total*	*AllopAthy*	*Ayurveda*	*Homeopathy*	*Other*	*Total*
Trivandrum	70.37	15.44	12.57	1.61	3912384	92.92	5.64	0.52	0.92	267182
Kollam	63.71	24.90	11.17	0.22	6465820	97.40	1.81	0.54	0.25	403173
P.thitta	74.36	13.78	11.35	0.51	2893633	99.22	0.11	0.39	0.28	164194
Allappuzha	57.66	19.71	22.35	0.28	3608913	98.43	1.11	0.22	0.24	124693
Kottayam	61.05	19.12	19.52	0.31	5735670	99.17	0.74	–	0.09	401090
Idukki	74.78	13.78	10.67	0.77	2846500	99.29	0.47	0.24	–	224883
Ernakulam	67.28	15.36	16.98	0.38	8945671	99.38	0.35	0.22	0.05	594986
Thrissur	62.16	26.32	10.93	0.59	4268215	97.44	2.28	0.22	0.06	441389
Palakkad	50.14	35.97	12.79	1.09	2098147	98.27	1.28	0.45	–	97387
Malappuram	54.52	32.97	11.57	0.93	3695313	89.65	9.97	0.28	0.09	236269
Kozhikode	53.11	24.57	20.70	1.62	5054007	95.03	4.15	0.46	0.36	202880
Wayanad	74.98	10.89	11.94	2.18	1776188	97.83	2.17	–	–	89107
Kannur	60.66	18.09	20.19	1.05	3306616	98.12	1.55	0.33	–	236362
Kasaragod	56.29	36.04	7.35	0.32	1401859	99.69	0.01	–	0.38	82429
State	63.00	21.11	15.15	0.75	56008936	97.30	2.22	0.28	0.18	3566724

Source: Computed from GoK, 1995.

78 per cent during 2002-03. The expenditure on family welfare declined from 44.7 per cent during 1995-96 to less than 13 per cent during 2002-03 (GoK, 2004).

Need for a Policy Shift

In the context of epidemiological transition to life style and long standing diseases and health inequality across spatial and social groups, the public health care system, it is argued, should be revamped to cater to the changing health care needs of the people. Unethical clinical and medical practices and increased out of pocket health care expenditure call for regulating the private health care sector through appropriate regulation on the one hand and improving the quality of the public health care system and service delivery on the other. There should be a basic shift in the health care strategy addressing at least the health care needs of the poor and the marginalized. That is, the health policy should provide adequate space to address the changing disease profiles across spatial and social groups. As a guideline to health policy, the present study recommends appropriate legislation to regulate the private health care sector by ensuring social accountability and, as a viable policy option, improve the operational efficiency of the public health care system through proper health care management reforms. The men-morbidity-medicine linkage is very crucial in understanding the real health care burden within the overall institutional framework.

Conclusion

In Kerala, where the private sector is dominant, the doctor-patient relationship is taking precisely a consumerist shade adding unethical dimensions to it (Ashokan, 2005). In such a system, the doctors are increasingly becoming mere health care providers and patients just service receivers. Health management and systematic medical auditing shall improve the quality of health care and ensure better performance and accountability on the part of the physicians. In general, the physician-technology-hospital network system has significantly increased the out of pocket health care expenditure and those relating to child birth through C-section delivery, in particular (Ashokan, 2006; 2007b). The sector wise distribution reveals that one-third of the OPs and more than one-fourth of the IPs have utilised public health care services and more than 97 per cent of the IPs and 63 per cent of the OPs accepted modern medicine as their health care choice. The low utilisation of public health care services has been attributed to its poor quality and the weak links in its chain act as the basic constraint on the functional efficiency of the system. Thus, health policy requires a radical shift aimed at translating values and visions into actual policies and programmes through committed public action.

References

Ashokan, A. (2005), Self reported Morbidity, Inpatient and Outpatient Care and Utilization of Health Care Services in Rural Kerala, Unpublished Ph.D. Thesis. Pondicherry Central University, Pondicherry, India.

Ashokan, A. (2006a), Health Care System and its Utilization in India: Implications for Maternal and Child Health, *Manpower Journal*, Vol. XXXXI, Number 1, January-March.

Ashokan, A. (2006b), Expenditure on Child Birth in Rural Kerala: An Inter-community Analysis in K. Rajan (ed) *Indian Economy: The Post Reform Scenario*, New Delhi, Serial Publications.

Ashokan, A. and Ibrahim P. (2007a), Kerala Under Morbidity Trap? *Kerala Calling*, Vol. 27, No. 5, March.

Ashokan, A. (2007b), Nature and Pattern of Outpatient Health Care Expenditure in Rural Kerala, *Journal of Rural Development*, July-September.

Ashokan, A. (2007c), Patterns and Determinants of Acute Morbidity: Lessons from Rural Kerala, *Indian Journal of Economics*, October.

Caldwell, J. C. (1986), Routes to Low Mortality in Poor Countries, *Population and Development Review*, Vol. 12, No. 2, pp. 171-220.

CDS/UN (1975), Poverty, Unemployment and Development Policy: A Case Study of Selected Issues with Reference to Kerala, New York: Centre for Development Studies/United Nations.

Eastaugh, Steven R. (1981), Medical Economics and Health Finance, Auburn House Publishing Co. Boston, Massachusetts.

Fuchs, V. (1972), Essays in the Economics of Health and Medical Care, NBER, New York.

GoI (2002b), Bulletin on Rural Health Statistics in India, Rural Health Division, Directorate General of health Services, Ministry of Health and Family Welfare, Government of India, New Delhi.

GoI (2006), Economic Review, State Planning Board, Government of Kerala.

Kabir, M. and Krishnan, T. N. (1992), Social Intermediation and Health Change: Lessons from Kerala, *Working Paper* No. 251,Centre for Development Studies, Thiruvananthapuram.

Kannan *et. al.* (1991), Health and Development in Rural Kerala, Kerala Sastra Sahitya Parishad, Thiruvananthapuram.

Mehrothra, S. and Jarret, S. W. (2002), Improving Basic Health Service Delivery in Low Income Countries: Voice to the Poor, *Social Science and Medicine* Vol. 54, No. 11 June, pp. 1685-1690.

Muralidharan, V. R. (2001), Private-public Sector Partnership in Health Care Sector in India: A Review of Policy Options and Challenges, IIT, Madras.

NSSO (1998), Morbidity and Treatment of Ailment, NSS 52nd Round, Report 441, *National Sample Survey Organisation*, Government of India, New Delhi.

Sadanandan, R. (2001), Government Health Care Services in Kerala: Who Benefits, *Economic and Political Weekly*, August 11, pp. 3071-3077.

NUTRITION AND HEALTH TRANSITION: LESSONS FROM KERALA

K. GANGADHARAN

Introduction

Conventional emphasis in public policy for economic growth and development has generally been on physical capital accumulation and technological progress for productivity improvements. There was little by way of recognition of the importance and role of human capital in promoting growth and poverty reduction. This is not to state that governments had little concern for these dual dimensions of human capital. In fact, the emphasis on health was largely based on welfare considerations rather than the perspective of human capital as a factor of production. Good health would enhance growth by:

(i) Reducing productivity losses due to illness

(ii) Permitting utilization of resources which otherwise would have remained in accessible or unutilized.

(iii) Promoting school enrollment of children and enabling them to learn.

(iv) Saving on resources required for treatment of illness (World Bank 1993).

Nutritional deficiencies and poor health of children are major public health concerns in developing countries, where they present both a cause and a reflection of poverty. After the Independence the elected Governments in India has undertaken a lot of steps for the improvement of the health and well being of the population especially the health of the children. But still malnutrition is a severe problem in India, according to NRHS-3, 46 per cent of the India's children under the age of three are suffering from underweight and 79% of them are categorized anaemic. This malnutrition is a severe hurdle in the way of proper health care development at the global level and the developing countries are the greatest victims of this nutritional deprivation.

Table 1 provides the nutritional status of children at the global level and it indicates the pathetic condition of India with 47% of underweight children. Similarly in the case of stunting and wasting also India dominates over all other developing countries.

Table 1
Nutrition Status of Under Five–A Global View

	% of under five suffering from		
Region	*Under Weight*	*Stunting*	*Wasting*
Latin America & Caribbean	6	14	2
Africa	24	35	8
Asia	28	30	9
India	47	45	16
Bangladesh	48	45	10
Bhutan	19	40	3
Maldives	45	36	20
Nepal	48	51	10
Pakistan	40	36	14
Srilanka	33	20	13
All Developing Countries	22-27	28-32	7-9

The present paper takes up the issues pertaining to health sector in Kerala in a larger comparative perspective in the Indian Context. It would focus on the changes that occurred in the nutritional status over the time period and also on the incidence of morbidity across socio economic dimensions and their implications for economic policy.

Nutrition and Its Determinants

Nutrition is an integral part of the health and well being of all individuals. Good nutrition is determined by the consumption of an adequate diet and also a person's ability to resist disease and infections that interface with digestive and absorption process of the biological system. On the one hand, good nutrition enables us to lead a socially and economically active life whereas malnutrition has an adverse impact on morbidity. It hinders physical growth and lead to functional impairment disability and diminishes productivity and reduces resistance to diseases.

The important determinants of Nutritional status are educational facilities for all the members of the society and also facilities for continuing informal education. Similarly the living environment like good sanitation, safe drinking water, proper facility for travel and communication, electrification, proper health care facilities, family income, members in the family, proper spacing among children, housing set up, occupation of the household members etc influence a lot in the nutritional enrichment of the society. Chart 1 provides how poverty and education are connected with nutritional deprivation:

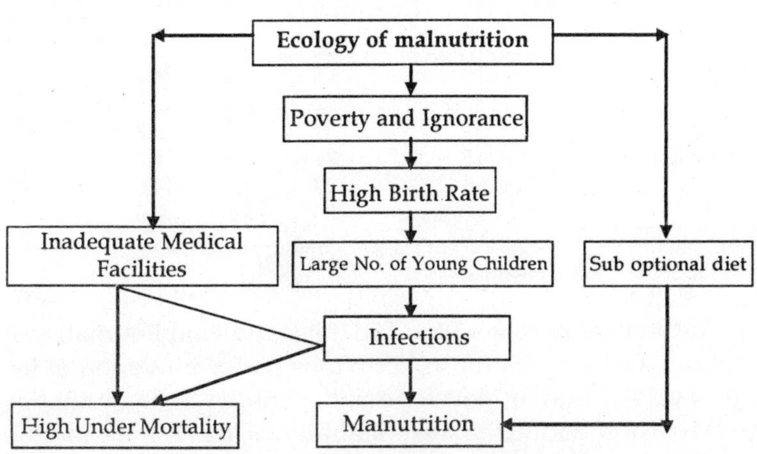

Chart 1: Ecology of Malnutrition

Why Study Kerala?

The state of Kerala is located in the Southern tip of India. It is a narrow strip of land flanked by Arabian Sea on the west, and Western Ghats mountain ranges on the East. With over 30 million living in an area of 38,863 Km^2, Kerala's, density of population stands at 950/Km^2.

Kerala has been recognized as a state with better health care indices, which is even comparable with most advanced nations of the world. This achievement has been stated as the culmination of great stress on social development (Nag, 1983), better social justice (Ratcliff 1978) or a combination of greater stress on education and improved health delivery system (Nair, 1974). Table 2 provides a summary of key health indices of Kerala in comparison with India and some other countries. These figures indicate the advancement the state has gained in many spheres of health. The gains are all the more impressive since the income of the state falls below the national average.

Table 2
Kerala's Health Indicators in
Comparison to India and to Some Other Countries

					Healthe xpenditure (as % of GDP)	
Countries/ State	*IMR*	*Under 5 Mortality rate*	*Life Expectancy*	*TFR*	*Total*	*Govt. (%)*
Kerala	14	19	73.5	1.8	6.2	1.4 (22)*
India	60	87	62	3.0	6.1	1.3(21)
China	27	37	71	1.8	5.8	2.0(34)
Sri Lanka	11	15	71	2.0	3.7	1.8(49)
US	7	8	77	2.1	14.6	6.6(45)
Canada	5	6	80	1.5	9.6	6.7(70)

World Health Report 2005 except for Kerala which was taken from SRS for the year 2005* Indirect estimates.

The state of Kerala within India has received international attention and acclaim for its conscious policy intervention for high levels of human development. Contrary to the previous apprehension about the sustainability of the Kerala model, recent evidence seems to show that high levels of human development have also been instrumental in registering sustained economic growth. However the recent trends related to morbidity, nutrition etc. reveals that Kerala is passing through a stage of health care transition in which the advancement gained in health care in the initial stages of development in 1960's and 1970's and 1980's as now eroding fastly due to the hike in the morbidity load on the one side and gaining momentum of the nutritional deprivation among the under five children. The Human Development Report 2005 for Kerala and NFHS 3 shows trends in this direction.

Nutritional Deficiency and Calorie consumption

Clearly India is eating less. People are increasingly becoming poor and marginalized, which directly tells upon their food intake and so the nutrition their bodies receive. Moreover what the Indians and eating is also bad. Its nutritional deficiency adversely affects the health and working potential of all.

Table 3
State wise Population with Calorie Intake Less than 90% of Recommended Norms (in percentage)

	Urban		*Rural*	
State	*1983*	*1999-2000*	*1983*	*1999-2000*
Andhra Pradesh	53.8	50.8	39.3	51.0
Assam	49.9	46.6	48.8	61.5
Bihar	44.4	43.5	39.6	45.9
Gujarat	52.1	51.3	46.7	53.6
Haryana	43.5	46.2	27.5	30.2
Karnataka	48.8	51.2	42.3	54
Kerala	55.9	52.5	61.2	61.6
Madhya Pradesh	44.6	49.1	33.7	50.7
Maharashtra	57.1	52.7	44.4	52.4
Orissa	35.7	31	46.2	42.1
Punjab	48.1	44.6	24.1	31
Rajasthan	42.6	34.5	28.8	24.3
Tamil Nadu	65.6	55	62.9	65.2
Uttar Pradesh	52.1	46.5	31	32.9
West Bengal	53.1	49	53.6	47.8

Source: C.P.Chandra Shekhar & Jayanthi Gosh, 2003, The calorie consumption puzzle in Business line, February 11.

What is shocking is that, the state like Kerala also witnessed a slight improvement in increasing the population of people with caloric intake less than 90% of the recommended norms. Still in Kerala around 52% of the people are getting less than 90% of the recommended calories intake which reveals the extent of nutritional deprivation and vagaries of malnutrition in Kerala. The class wise calorie consumption (Table 4) also reveals that the BPL Categories and poverty line categories in Kerala have respectively obtained only 1100 and 1389 calories per day (rural) instead of the basic minimum of 2738.6 calories recommended by the ICMR[1]. In this case it is pitiable to note that Kerala records the rock per day for the rural poor

Table 4
Class wise Calorie Consumption 1999-2000 (in kilo-calories/day)

		Rural	
States	*B.P.L. Below Poverty Line*	*Poverty Line*	*A.P.L Above Poverty Line*
Andhra Pradesh	1406	1662	2095
Assam	1585	1767	2136
Bihar	1769	1977	2401
Gujarat	1468	1684	2065
Haryana	1523	1745	2539
Himachal Pradesh	1982	1942	2495
Karnataka	1442	1646	2151
Kerala	1100	1389	2073
Madhya Pradesh	1649	1888	2305
Maharashtra	1584	1780	2145
Orissa	1792	2117	2421
Punjab	1506	1712	2440
Rajasthan	1755	2003	2532
Tamil Nadu	1307	1543	1960
Uttar Pradesh	1839	1990	2548
West Bengal	1664	1935	2296

Source: Computed from Govt. of India (2007).

Maternal and Child health

Though the state of Kerala has witnessed rapid strides in the health sector, the recent NFHS data related to child health, nutritional standards among women and children reveals that

Table 5

Child Immunization, Vitamin Supplementation and Treatment of Childhood Diseases, Child Feeding Practices and Nutritional Status of Children-Variation Over Time Period in Kerala

	NFHS I	*NFHS II*	*NFH III 2005-06*		
Particulars	*All*	*1998-99*	*All*	*Urban*	*Rural*
Fully immunized children in percentage (in the age group 12-23 months)	54.7	79.7	75.3	87.5	69.4
Children who have received BCG (%) in the age group of 12-23 months	86.1	96.2	69.3	100	94.6
Children who have received 3 doses of polio vaccine in %	75.2	88.4	83.1	91.7	78.9
Children who have received 3 doses of DPT vaccine in %	73.2	88	84	93.1	79.6
Children who have received Measles vaccine in %	60.5	84.6	82.1	-	76.9
Children with diarrhoea In the last two weeks who received ORS in %	16.6	47.9	34.6	-	34.4
Children within the last two weeks taken to a health facility in %	71.4	82.1	67.4	-	75
Children with acute respiratory infection of fever in the last two weeks taken to health facility	NA	NA	81.4	85.7	79.8

Full dose means BCG, Measles and 3 doses each of polio and DPT

Kerala is now in the reverse trend in the health care advancement or in other words Kerala now finds it very difficult to sustain the tempo of advancement that gained in the health sector for the last three decades and it is passing through a health transition in all its spheres. The data related to overweight of women steadily increased over 14 % during the short span of 1998-99 to 2005-06. Similarly though infant mortality reduced to considerable extent in Kerala compared to all India level (see Table 1), they are celebrating their each birthday with acute health problems. The proportion of children in the age group of 6 to 35 months with anaemia actually increased from 43.9 in 1998-99 (NFHS I) to 55.7% in 2005-.2006 (See Table 6). Similarly anaemia among the women also increased from 22.7% to 32.3% over the same period (see Table 6). The problem of anameia has been also severe among the pregnant women and the same has increased from 20.3% in 1998-99 to 33.1% in 2005-06. The children's nutritional status at the Inter State level (Table 7) reveals that though the states of Kerala is for better compared to other Indian states, the reduction in nutritional problem like underweight, wasting and stunting over the time period is far speeder and better in other Indian states compared to Kerala.

The population of children who are having under weight and wasted also recorded a hike in the last two NFHS reports (Table 6) indicating that over the time period the health status of the children in Kerala deteriorated heavily. This transition in the child health may be due to the change in the dietary habit of mothers and the involvement of mothers in the active labour force. Even during pregnancy period the employed women are not able to eat properly due to the stress and strain of the work in which they are indulged and the nature of food consumption also changed a lot. A sort of fast food culture has emerged in urban Kerala which culminated in breeding diseases like diabetics, blood pressure and hike in cholesterol even among youngsters. The urbanization and migration to urban centres in Kerala is also accounts for the change in dietary style and health transition of the people.

Table 6

Nutritional Status and Anemia among Children and Adults Variation Over Time Period in Kerala

	NFHS I	NFHS II	NFH III 2005-06		
Particulars	*All*	*1998-99*	*All*	*Urban*	*Rural*
Women whose Body Mass Index is below normal in %	NA	18.7	12.5	9.1	14.3
Women whose Body Mass Index is below normal in %	NA	-	11.9	11.2	12.3
Women who are over weight or obese n %	NA	20.6	34	40.1	30.9
Men who are over weight or obese in %	NA	-	24.3	28	21.9
Children in the age of 6 to 35 months who are anemic in %	NA	43.9	55.7	51.3	57.9
Married women in the age of 15 to 49 who are anaemic in %	-	22.7	32.3	32.3	32.4
Pregnant women in the age of 15 to 49 who are anemic in %	-	20.3	33.1	27.7	35.8
Children under 3 years who are stunted in %	25.2	21.9	21.1	21.3	21.1
Children under 3 years who are wasted in %	12.8	11.1	16.1	10.1	19.1
Children under 3 years who are underweight in %	27	26.9	28.8	22.5	31.9

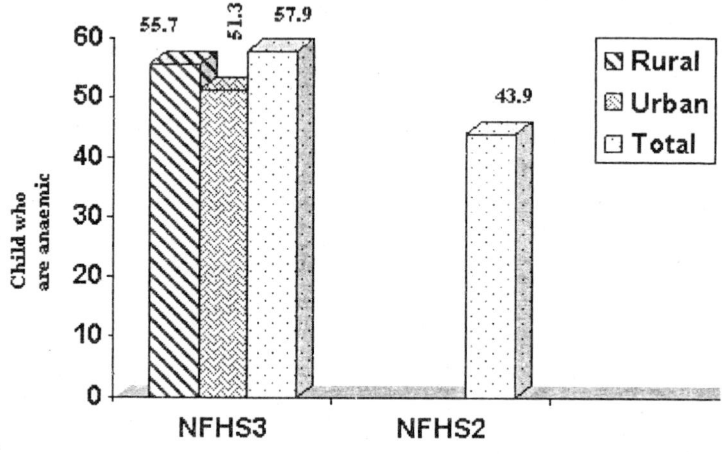

Child who are anaemic
60
50
40
30
20
10
0
55.7
51.3
57.9
43.9
NFHS3
NFHS2
Rural
Urban
Total

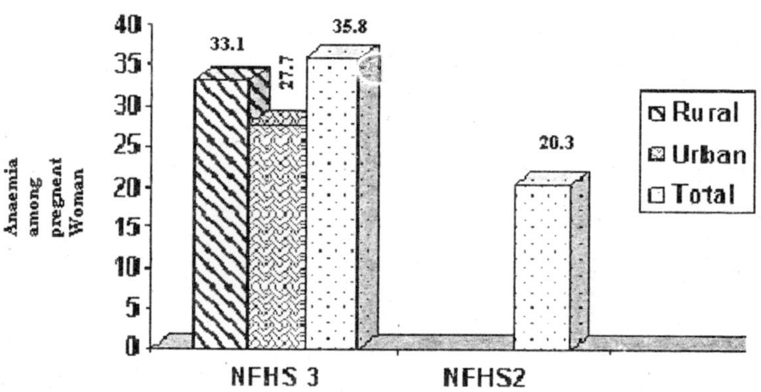

Anaemia among pregnent Woman
40
35
30
25
20
15
10
5
0
33.1
27.7
35.8
20.3
NFHS 3
NFHS2
Rural
Urban
Total

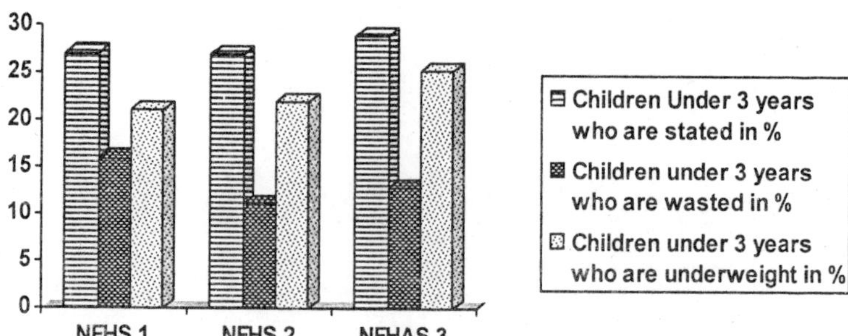

30
25
20
15
10
5
0
NFHS 1
NFHS 2
NFHAS 3
Children Under 3 years who are stated in %
Children under 3 years who are wasted in %
Children under 3 years who are underweight in %

Table 7
Children's Nutritional Status: Interstate Trends

	Percentage of children							
	Stunting		*Wasting*		*Underweight*		*Children age 6-35 months who are Anaemic*	
States	*NFHS-2 1998-99*	*NFHS-3 2005-06*	*NFHS-2 1998-99*	*NFHS-3 2005-06*	*NFHS-2 1998-99*	*NFHS-3 2005-06*	*NFHS-2 1998-99*	*NFHS-3 2005-06*
Andhra Pradesh	39	34	9	13	38	37	72.3	79
Assam	50	35	13	13	36	40	63.2	76.7
Bihar	55	42	20	28	54	58	81.1	87.6
Chattisgarh	58	45	19	18	61	52	87.7	81
Delhi	37	35	13	16	35	33	69	63.2
Goa	18	21	13	12	29	29	53.4	49.3
Gujarat	44	42	16	17	45	47	74.5	80.1
Haryana	50	36	5	17	35	42	83.9	82.5
Himachal Pradesh	41	27	17	19	44	36	69.9	58.8
Jharkhand	49	41	25	31	54	59	82.4	77.7
Jammu & Kashmir	39	28	12	15	35	29	71.1	68.1
Karnataka	37	38	20	18	44	41	70.6	82.7
Kerala	22	21	11	16	27	29	43.9	55.7
Madhya Pradesh	49	40	20	33	54	60	71.3	82.6
Manipur	31	25	8	8	28	24	45.2	52.8
Meghalaya	45	42	13	28	38	46	67.6	68.7

Contd...

	Percentage of children							
	Stunting		Wasting		Underweight		Children age 6-35 months who are Anaemic	
States	NFHS-2 1998-99	NFHS-3 2005-06	NFHS-2 1998-99	NFHS-3 2005-06	NFHS-2 1998-99	NFHS-3 2005-06	NFHS-2 1998-99	NFHS-3 2005-06
Mizoram	35	30	10	9	28	22	57.2	51.7
Maharashtra	40	38	21	15	50	40	76	71.9
Nagaland	33	30	10	15	24	30	43.7	na
Orissa	44	38	24	19	54	44	72.3	74.2
Punjab	39	28	7	9	29	27	80	80.2
Rajasthan	52	34	12	20	51	44	82.3	79.6
Sikkim	32	29	5	13	21	23	76.5	56.9
Tamilnadu	29	25	20	22	37	33	69	72.5
Tripura	40	30	13	20	43	39	61.8	67.9
Uttaranchal	47	32	8	16	42	38	77.4	61.5
West Bengal	42	33	14	19	49	44	78.3	69.4
India	46	38	16	19	47	46	74.2	79.2

Morbidity Profile and Health Transition

The urban community as a whole including the kids going to K.G. School is experiencing a hectic life cycle from to morning to evening. Faty foods and lack of any sort of exercise or body movement on the part of urban dwellers and overall negligence of environmental hygiene caused for the morbidity hike in Kerala. (Table 7). Incidence of morbidity is higher in Kerala than India as a whole. (Table 12 and 13) for the population as a whole. It is 25.11% for Kerala as against 9.11% for All India. For both men and women. It is higher, though marginally in the rural sector than in the urban in Kerala and the reverse at the all India level. Similarly though life expectancy has improved a lot in Kerala (Table 8) compared to other Indian States the 60+ categories are experiencing a bitter life due to hike in morbidity among them.(Table 9). Arthrities, blood pressure, asthma, pain in joints, mental illness, Hypertension, Urinary complaints, Cardiological, paralysis etc. are the important ailments faced by the 60 + categories. The better and advanced health care facilities provided by the high-tech private hospitals in Kerala is one important factor responsible for hike in life expectancy in Kerala. Though they are morbid due to chronic illness, the advancement of modern medical care facility and regular and continuous treatment enabled , majority of them to succeed better in extending their life and this can be noticed as an important health care transition that occurred recently in Kerala.

In the case of treatment also majority of the aged prefers allopathic care from private (409/1000) followed by Govt.(288/ 1000). Moreover 32 out of 1000 prefers self treatment and on the other extreme 38 out of 1000 prefers no treatment at all (Table 10). The ranking of states in terms of life expectancy at birth has always put Kerala on the top. However in terms of absolute improvement in life expectancy at birth between 1970 and the 1990's Kerala ranked in the 9th position among the states in India indicating the deteriorating quality of life of the people.

Fertility, Mortality and Morbidity

With regard to total fertility rate in Kerala, it can be seen that it is declining from the 1960s. Total Fertility Rate (TFR) which

Table 8
Life Expectancy and Birth by Sex in India (1996-2002)
(Average for Four Years)

	Life Expectancy			
	1996-2000		*1998-2002*	
States in India	*Male*	*Female*	*Male*	*Female*
India	61	62.7	61.6	63.3
Andhra Pradesh	61.7	64.3	62	64.6
Arunachal Pradesh	-	-	-	-
Assam	57.4	57.7	57.7	58.1
Bihar	60.9	59.1	61.4	59.5
Goa	-	-	-	-
Gujarat	62.1	64	62.4	64.4
Haryana	64.4	65.1	64.7	65.4
Himachal Pradesh	65.4	66	65.7	66.3
Jammu & Kashmir	-	-	-	-
Karnataka	62.5	65.8	62.8	66.2
Kerala	70.7	76.7	70.8	75.9
Madhya Pradesh	56.6	56.3	57	56.7
Maharashtra	64.7	67.2	65	67.4
Manipur	-	-	-	-
Meghalaya	-	-	-	-
Mizoram	-	-	-	-
Nagaland	-	-	-	-
Orissa	57.8	58	58.4	58.5
Punjab	67.1	69.2	67.4	69.5
Rajasthan	60.1	61.1	60.5	61.6
Sikkim	-	-	-	-
Tamil Nadu	63.9	65.9	64.2	66.3
Uttar Pradesh	59.1	57.9	59.4	58.5
West Bengal	63	64.5	63.3	64.8

was 5.6 per woman in the 1950s declined to 3.7 in the 1970s and reached to 1.8, which is below the replacement level in the 1990s. The fertility rate declined in both rural and urban areas and there is virtually no difference between the two. By contrast in India, the TFR was 6.3 in the 1950s and declined to 3.3 in the 1990s. Though Kerala and India had a difference of 0.7 children during 1950s, the difference has widened to 1.5 children 1990s indicating a faster decline in Kerala than in India as a whole.

Table 9
Morbidity Prevalence among the 60 + Categories in Kerala

	Age Group					
Type of Ailment	*60-70*	*70-80*	*80-90*	*Above 90*	*Total*	*Per 1000*
Diabetics	566	331	92	11	1000	155
Hypertension	537	346	104	13	1000	214
Arthritis	512	347	122	19	1000	273
Asthma	520	347	117	16	1000	88
Abdominal problems	555	320	108	17	1000	39
Urinary Complaints	525	334	123	18	1000	14
Liver Problems	556	315	112	17	1000	5
Skin diseases	577	303	105	15	1000	11
T.B	589	313	91	7	1000	5
Brain Disease	531	335	119	15	1000	6
Cardio logical	558	337	95	10	1000	38
Cancer	559	338	95	8	1000	4
Psychological Problem	553	330	104	13	1000	5
Paralysis	273	343	277	107	1000	4
Others	561	311	109	19	1000	139

Source: Report on Survey of Aged in Kerala 2003-04.

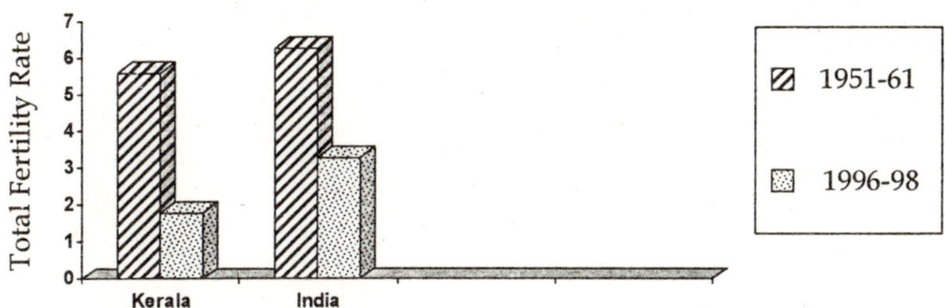

Among the numerous indicators available to measure health status of a population, the most dominant among them one are mortality, fertility and morbidity. It can be seen that (Table 11) IMR in Kerala declined steadily for the last 6 decades and now records the lowest rate of 14 per thousand live births.

At the beginning of the century the IMR of the state was very high and did not differ much from the all India average. While in Kerala the IMR declined steadily throughout this century to the present level of 14 per thousand live birth. It can be seen that (Table 11) IMR also began to increase recently

Table 10
Age and Method of Treatment (in per 1000)

Age Group	*Self Treatment*	*No Treatment*	*Allopathy (Govt.)*	*Allopathy (Pvt.)*	*Ayurveda (Govt.)*	*Ayurveda (Pvt.)*	*Homeo (Govt)*	*Homeo (Pvt.)*	*Others (Govt)*	*Others Pvt.*	*All*
60-70	34	39	294	409	93	83	10	9	14	15	1000
70-80	28	36	285	413	98	94	10	8	13	15	1000
80-90	28	38	273	404	108	104	8	8	14	15	1000
Above 90	30	45	262	401	105	116	7	6	12	16	1000
Total	32	38	288	409	97	89	10	9	13	15	1000

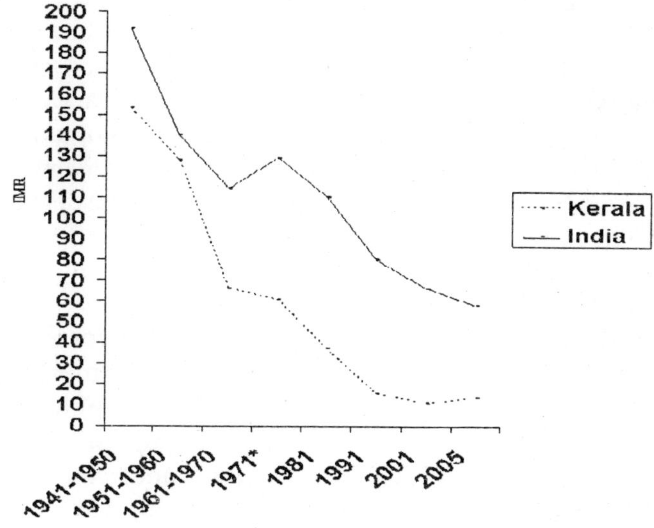

and it was 11 for the year 2001 now in 2005. This has reached to 15 indicating a sort of transition, which is a...signal to the health status of Kerala.

The Crude Birth Rate (CBR), which remained at 17.7/1000 in 1992, has declined to the present level of 15.3 per thousand populations and the Crude Death Rate remained the same at the rate of 6.4 for the same period. A unique feature of Kerala's

Table 11
Infant Mortality Rate of Kerala and India

Year	*Kerala (K)*	*India (I)*	*K as % of I*
1941-1950	153	192	80
1951-1960	128	140	91
1961-1970	66	114	58
1971*	61	129	47
1981	37	110	34
1991	16	80	20
2001	11	66	17
2005	14	58	24

Kannan K. P. Thankappan K. R. *et. al.* 1991. Health and Development in Rural Kerala KSSP P 06 For years 1991 and 2001 SRS Registrar General of India From 1971 onwards SRS started providing vitals statistics data.

population profile is that, unlike in the rest of India, the gender ratio favours women (1058:1000). The Projection of birth rate and death for Kerala for the next 10 years revealed that constant birth rate will reduce to 13.47 per thousand population and death rate will come down to 7.04 per thousand Population. This indicates that the demographic transition in Kerala is moving in such a way that natural growth rate will be declined from 9.75 in 1996-2001 to 6.42 in 2011-2016.

Morbidity Indicators

Though mortality and fertility has declined sharply for the last few decades in Kerala, the available data related to morbidity is surprising in nature. The morbidity data available from different studies reveals that Kerala surpasses all other Indian states with regard to the prevalence of chronic and acute illness (Sharief 1995, Gangadharan 2005, 2006, 2006a, 2007, KSSP 2006). Among the chronic illness diabetes, heart diseases, mental, asthma, blood pressure, cancer etc. are having highest prevalence. The Table 8 reveals pattern of morbidity prevalence among the 60 + categories and Table 6 shows the nature and pattern different acute and chronic illness reported in the public health centres in Kerala (Govt. of Kerala 2005) and Table 12 gives incidence of morbidity by gender and Table 13 provides incidence of morbidity by sectors.

Table 12
Incidence of Morbidity by Gender and Sex Kerala and All India (2004)

	All Kerala			*All India*		
Gender	*Rural*	*Urban*	*Combined*	*Rural*	*Urban*	*Combined*
Male	24.28	23.56	24.06	8.36	9.11	8.56
Female	26.66	24.51	26.10	9.30	10.86	9.69
Total	25.53	24.06	25.15	8.82	9.95	9.11

The data reveals that infectious and parasitic diseases contribute a significant share of total illness in the population and incidence of morbidity is higher in Kerala than India as a whole.

Table 13
Incidence of Morbidity by Sector: Kerala and All India (2004)

Per cent

		Kerala			*India*	
MPCE Decile Group	*Rural*	*Urban*	*Combined*	*Rural*	*Urban*	*Combined*
1	22.4	17.10	20.60	6.10	7.80	6.20
2	19.7	19.40	20.00	6.30	8.50	6.50
3	22.6	18.80	23.10	6.60	8.20	7.30
4	27.10	23.20	24.90	7.7	8.5	8.00
5	21.30	21.50	21.90	8.0	9.5	8.7
6	23.80	21.50	24.80	8.8	9.9	9.10

Discussion

In spite of many short falls in the nutritional intake and health care spending, the state has been successful in managing the mortality, and fertility and Gender equality to a great extent compared to other Indian States. The secret behind this management lies in the Cost Rican development path followed by the successive Governments in Kerala.

The domination of adult literacy and universalisation of primary education acted as the lubricant force in creating better health awareness among the people. The enrollment of children in the age group of 6-11 in the lowest annual income groups (less than 20,000 per annum) household is 96.9% (HDR, 2007) whereas at the all India level this was only 60.6%. A unique feature of the educational system in Kerala is the high enrollment of girls in schools and college education. The gross enrollment ratio for females in Kerala is 96.7% and literacy rate among the female is 94.2% compared to 87.9% among men.

Female literacy has been treated as a very important determinant for affecting decline in mortality (Cald Well, 1986) This indomitant linkage is responsible for fall in Infant mortality Rate (IMR) and rise in female literacy in Kerala.

An examination of the growth of health services in Kerala reveals, the rapid expansion and spread of health care facilities. The number of PHCs functioning in the state at the end of the 6th plan was only 199 and this has reached to 944 by the middle of the Tenth Plan. (Govt. of India, 2007). Similarly the number of sub centres also increased from 2270, in 1981 to 5094 in 2004. The availability of number of beds, doctors etc. also increased abundantly during this period. The number of rural and urban hospitals identified in 2004 was 189 with a bed capacity of 25839. It is often suggested that improved health status of Kerala is also the result of Kerala's egalitarian policies dating back to last century. This is particularly true of the Travancore -Cochin region where the former rulers pursued progressive health policies which were continued by the democratically elected Governments after Independence (Soman 1992).

The most dominant factor related to health transition in Kerala is the low nutritional status due to low in take of food, cereals, proteins etc. The calorie consumption of Below Poverty Line categories in rural Kerala v.as 1100 and for poverty line group, it was 1389 (Table 15). The percapita cereal consumption of poverty line classes in rural Kerala was 9.2 kgms per month in 1993-94 (Table 15) which has declined to 8.18kgm in 1999-2000. Similarly for urban areas also, it declined from 9.24kgm to 8.67kgms for the same period.

This sharp decline in cereal consumption by the poor classes is due to the fact that cereals no longer occupy the same space in the consumption choice of the poor that they had in earlier times and they considered cereals as inferior goods (Pranab Sen, 2005). Though this is the case of nutrient intake in Kerala, but the growth performance is better to that of high intake states.

The positive interaction of health care and nutrition is responsible for better health care status of the people. The utilization of health care services and maternal and child health services is far better in Kerala compared to other Indian States, though slight reduction in utilization began to observe recently. The reduction in M.C.H Services is mainly due to domination of private health centres in Kerala and also due to the increase in the proportion-working woman in Kerala. For the workingwomen timely utilization of health care services will be a problem since they loss income of the day in which they have to go for the checkup. The predominant form of malnutrition in Kerala is growth retardation, stunting and wasting and under weight problem among children is also severe in Kerala. Compared to NFHSI the data released by NFHS III is really a shock for Kerala in the sense that Kerala represents 28.8% of underweight children, 16.1 wasted children and 21.1% stunted children. By considering the sound human development trends that existed in Kerala for the last few decades the present the nutritional picture of Kerala is not attractive compared to the rest of the country (Table 3,14,15) except for a slight decrease in the severely malnourished children.

Table 14
Consumption of Pattern of Poverty Line Class 1999-2000
(Percentage Adjusted Norms)

	Rural			*Urban*		
State	*Calories*	*Proteins*	*Fats*	*Calories*	*Proteins*	*Fats*
Arunachal Pradesh	69.3	109.8	48.3	85.3	100.4	62.4
Assam	73.6	100.9	46.6	70.4	99.8	40.2
Bihar	82.4	111.6	46.8	93.0	115.0	48.9
Gujarat	70.2	116.2	89.0	77	713.6	107.1
Hariyana	72.7	124.1	73.9	69.4	123.0	76.1
H.P	80.9	126.3	73.8	-	-	-
Karnataka	68.6	110.6	65.7	87.7	106.3	69.6
Kerala	57.9	100.9	63.4	76.3	109	72.6
Madhyapradesh	78.7	114.7	52.3	93.4	119.7	74.7
Maharashtra	74.2	116.4	65.6	84.4	115.9	88.7
Orisa	88.2	94.9	29.2	116.7	100.0	34.9
Punjab	71.3	126.0	80.1	75.7	124.3	82.6
Rajasthan	83.5	135.2	76.9	94.6	123.7	95.2
Tamil Nadu	64.3	97.7	55.7	77.3	100.5	69.3
Uttarpradesh	82.9	123.9	52.1	85.5	124.2	66.6
West Bengal	80.6	101.7	59.4	84.3	104.0	54.6
All India	77.8	111.3	53.1	91.0	111.6	77.9

Source: (Computed from Government of India (2001)).

In the consumption basket the proportion of protein is comparatively higher than the ICMR norms of balanced diet (i.e. 66.6 gram of proteins per day is the minimum requirement for balanced diet) and in the case of fats it is very close to 66.6 gms.

Table 15
Per Capita Cereal Consumption of Poverty Line Class (Kgs Per Month)

	Kerala		*Urban*	
State	*1993-94*	*1999-2000*	*1993-94*	*1999-2000*
A.p.	11.40	10.95	11.25	10.62
Assam	12.98	12.11	10.96	10.33
Bihar	15.11	13.32	12.74	12.79
Gujarat	9.87	9.88	8.97	8.07
Hariyana	11.33	9.79	9.98	7.91
Himachal Pradesh	12.37	11.48	11 89	9.80
Karnataka	11.84	10.18	10.69	9.71
Kerala	9.21	8.18	9.24	8.67
M.P	14.11	12.48	12.08	11.28
Maharashtra	11.25	20.89	9.80	9.46
Orissa	16.96	15.44	14.20	17.18
Punjab	9.09	9.24	8.10	8.37
Rajasthan	13.71	12.84	11.80	11.61
Tamil Nadu	10.86	9.79	10.32	9.14
Uttarpradesh	13.82	12.89	11.4	20.34
West Bengal	14.57	13.03	11.92	10.97
All India	13.19	12.27	20.89	10.75

Source: Govt. of India (1995) and (2001).

What the Kerala health demonstrates is that though the calorie intake is comparatively less compared to other Indian states especially among the BPL and poverty line categories, higher rate of education among females and the cent per cent educational enrollment etc. influenced considerably for the improved health status. Along with this the massive spread of private health care centres in different parts of the state augmented the health expenditure of even the lowest socio-economic classes in Kerala (KSSP 2006). What actually needed for the state is more income generating outlets and activities supported by proper infrastructural facilities including good drinking water, sanitation, drainage and proper solid waste management system for the urban and rural folks.

A proper nutrient package with good living environment and proper supportive infrastructure along with a change in the life style of the people will certainly bring a hike in the nutritional status, improvement in health status and accelerate the process of positive health care transition and health care development.

Note

1. According to ICMR a balanced diet should yield 2738.6 kcals per day and it should include 66.6 grams of proteins and 66.9 grams of fats).

References

Caldwell J. C. (1986), Routes to Low Mortality in Poor Countries, *Population and Development Review*, Vol. 12.

Census of India (2001), Preliminary Tables–Kerala, New Delhi.

Gangadharan K. (2005), Life After Sixty. Problems of Ageing and Ill Health, *Kerala Calling*, Vol. 25.

Gangadharan K. (2006), Deteriorating Health of Mothers and Children. A Study on Urban Kerala, *Asian Economic Review*, Vol. 48, No. 2.

Gangadharan K. (2006), Emerging Issues in Urban Health Care with Special Reference to Kerala, *India Journal of Social Development*, Vol. 6, No. 1.

Gangadharan K. (2007), Changing Health Profile of Kerala, *Economic Affairs*, April-June.

Gangadharan K. (2007), Health for all in Kerala, Kerala Calling, June.

Govt. of India (1995), Nutritional Intake in India 1994-95. National Sample Survey Organization, Ministry of Statistics and Programme Implementation, New Delhi.

Govt. of India (2001), Nutritional Intake in India. 1999-2000. National Sample Survey Organization, Ministry of Statistics and Programme Implementation.

Govt. of India (2004), Health Information of India, Ministry of Health and Family Welfare, New Delhi.

Govt. of India (2005), Economic Review, State Planning Board, Thiruvananthapuram.

Govt. of India (2006), National Family Health Survey, NRHS-3, Fact Sheet, India, International Institute for Population Science, Mumbai.

Govt. of Kerala (2005), Report on Survey of Aged in Kerala, Dept. of Economic and Statistics, Thiruvananthapuram.

Govt. of Kerala (2006) Human Development Report 2005, Centre for Development Studies, State Planning Board, Thiruvananthapuram.

Kerala Sastra Sahithya Parishath (2006), How Kerala Thinks and Acts in Sastra Sahitya Parishath, TVM.

Nair, P. R. G. (1974), Decline in Birth Rate in Kerala. An Explanatory Hypothesis About the Relationship between Demographic Variables, Health Service and Education, *Economic ad Political Weekly*, Vol. 9.

Panicker P. K. and Soman C. R. (1984), Health Status of Kerala Economic Backwardness and Health Development, Centre for Development Studies, Thiruvananthapuram.

Pranab Sen (2005), Of Calories and Things, Reflections on Nutritional Norms, Poverty Lines and Consumption Behaviour in India, *Economic and Political Weekly*, October, 22.

Ratcliffe, J. (1978), Social Justice and Demographic Transition. Lessons from India's Kerala State, *International Journal of Health Services*, Vol. 8.

Sharief (1995), Health Transition in India. Differentials and Determinates of Morbidity in India by Disaggregated Analysis Working Paper No. 57, NCAER, New Delhi.

Soman C. R. (1992), Nutrition and Health Development Lessons from Kerala, *Proceedings of the Nutrition Society*, Vol. 51.

World Bank (1993), World Development Report 1993. Investing in Health, Oxford University Press, New York.

PART–VI

KNOWLEDGE ECONOMY AND E-GOVERNANCE

KNOWLEDGE ECONOMY: STUDY OF KERALA

S. Harikumar

Awareness of knowledge is a critical element of economic growth and increased welfare is not new. What is new is the speed of changes in the production and dissemination of knowledge made possible by the increase in scientific understanding and very rapid advances in information and communication technologies. The economics of information and knowledge analyses the process by which information is produced, diffused stored and used. In 1962, Machlup estimated that production and distribution, in an industrial economy account for 29 per cent of GDP. Trends in R & D expenditure, the employment structure, educational activity and consumer expenditure pattern suggest that the share of information and knowledge may well be increasing. The importance of knowledge management is not only because these processes absorb such a large share of resources, but also government finances a large part of theses activities. They give rise to important externalities; inelastic supply of labour exist in the information and knowledge industry; the lack of markets for the industry's products create difficult problem of valuation for social accounting; one; product technology, results in continuing changes; the employment structure may be responding to a shift from physical to the rare of economic growth; and some of the component activities and their associated institutions may be operating inefficiently.

Investment in ICTs has expanded and the direct linkages between producers and customers imply a reduced role of intermediaries in many markets, including consumer goods, food, manufactured components and primary products. Entirely new markets are being created through networking delivering services such as health and education, and with major effects on governance through the re-organisation of administrative and political institutions. The pervasiveness of these changes and their impact even at the macro economic level has given rise to the concept of the new economy. The ICT revolution involves significant reallocation of jobs across industries, and changes in the skill and occupational composition of the workforce. In the OECD countries, low technology manufacturing jobs have declined, while the effects on the jobs in high technology manufacturing have been mixed. Overall employment in the OECD countries has been shifting away from manufacturing into services. Within services, there has been strong growth in high-value-added service sectors such as finance, insurance, real estate and business services which tend to be the most skill and information intensive. As demand for low skilled workers declines, the overall occupational structure of the workforce in the OECD countries is moving toward higher skills in both industry and services. High-skilled, white collar workers makeup an increasing proportion of the workforce, account for between 25 and 35 per cent of total employment.

Significant investments have taken place in training; these are aimed at helping workers make use of the new technologies and perform new functions. There are also important investments in other intangibles: expenditures on R&D investment and makes up more than 10 per cent of gross domestic investment. When other investments in intangibles , such as in patents and licensing, design, marketing, education, training and software are added, investment in intangibles may represent as much as gross domestic investment. The rapid development of knowledge facilitated by technological progress and the ICT revolution is creating a more competitive and interdependent world.

The effective use of knowledge is becoming the most important factor for international competitiveness and for creating wealth and improving social welfare. It means that a country must encourage its organisations and people to acquire, create, disseminate, and use knowledge more effectively for greater economics and social development. There are four pillars of a knowledge based economy viz., an economic and institutional regime that provides incentives for the efficient use of existing knowledge and the creation of new knowledge and entrepreneurship; an educated and skilled population that can create and use knowledge; a dynamic information infrastructure that can facilitate the effective communication, dissemination and possessing of information and an effective innovation system comprising a net work of firms, research centers, universities, consultants and other organisations that can tap into the growing stock of global knowledge, assimilate and adapt it to local needs and create new knowledge and technology.

World Bank mentions a number of strengths of India for transforming itself into a knowledge based economy–skilled human capital in sciences democratic institution, widespread use of English, macro economic stability, dynamic private sector , free market economy large local market, well developed financial sector abroad and diversified Science and Technology infrastructure and booming IT sector. India is also a sought after venue for services in global production chains. India is thus well placed to embrace knowledge economy and enhance its position on the global stage. In terms of the four interrelated pillars of knowledge economy, India occupies the top of the bottom third of the distribution on the global knowledge economy map among a group 128 countries, India's ranking in the Growth Competitiveness Index is 55 and Business Competitive Index, India's rank is 30 in 2004 mainly because of strong growth impetus and also due to company's operation and national business environment although scope for improvement exists. With this macro picture let us trace the progress made in Kerala, which is said to be one of the educationally advanced and socially developed state in India.

The modern face of India, shows all the features of a transforming society where knowledge and information have made significant inroads. Information and communication technologies are emerging as major earners of foreign exchange. An appropriate policy response would be to expand manpower production for a knowledge-driven society through the institutions of higher learning since the knowledge base of the future economy, though unpredictable, can only be expected to expand. The requirement of modern industry is for more trainable and trained manpower. It is well accepted that technological changes sweeping the world today are not even in all sectors. But its impact on education is tremendous and observable.

In the past, educational processes were not confronted with the challenges that have to be faced today. Now technologies are changing much more rapidly than ever before. These technological changes are resulting in changes not only in the tools, the infrastructure and work related activities but also in the organizational structures. The idea of a 'once trained and further enriched by experience work force is increasingly replaced by a 'well educated and constantly skill upgraded 'one. Then the process and content of education too will have to be significantly different from what these are today. Obviously the educational system will have to train people not just for the present; it has to prepare them essentially to meet the challenges of future. Higher education leading to the development of mind and the power of brain as a crucial input for developing newer knowledge which empower the people to dominate the global scenario. So there is need for a sustained effort by the state to formulate an educational policy adjusted to the broad spectrum of a global policy package embracing the labour market and the socio economic policies along with economic, technological and cultural rejuvenation. In a global environment that is increasingly information- based, the role of knowledge and the acquisition of skills are critical elements that determine a nation's competitive advantage.

Emergence of the Knowledge Economy

The waves of globalisation have initiated the evolution and development of Kerala as a knowledge society. Knowledge society is a society where creating, sharing and using knowledge are key factors in the prosperity and well being of its people. It is a work in progress requiring significant investment in harnessing skills, technology and learning. In a knowledge-driven economy the generation and exploitation of knowledge play a predominant part in the creation of wealth. The idea of the knowledge society which has been spreading rapidly around the world is described as 'Knowledge Revolution'. Knowledge Revolution is leading to knowledge-cantered trade and industry. Half of the GDP of the OECD countries is knowledge-based. The research, science and technology investment of the state have to be effectively exploited in order to make Kerala a knowledge society. Knowledge has become an international public good and with the development of IT the transmission of knowledge has become easier and cheaper. Once knowledge is discovered and made public there is zero marginal cost to sharing it with more users. Ideas can be sold without exhausting their source, they do not depreciate in value through their use and their resale value may continue to be high while their reproductive cost remains next to nothing. The knowledge economy represents a shift from raw materials and capital to information and knowledge as inputs for production. Liberalisation has opened up the gate way of Indian economy to foreign investment particularly in the IT sector and it has given a chance to our technocrats to prove their capabilities in the knowledge based industry. Interdependence in international trade and economy, cyber networking, technology sharing and globalisation of Research and Development will bring the nation more prosperity and uniquely identify its position in global scenario. This new technology greatly facilitates the acquisition and absorption of knowledge offering the state unprecedented opportunities to enhance educational system, improve policy formation and execution and widen the range of opportunities for business and the poor. One challenge for the government, therefore, is to recognize the persistence and universality of knowledge gaps and information problems. For countries in the vanguard of the world economy the balance between the knowledge and resources has shifted so far towards the former that knowledge has become perhaps the most important factor determining the standards of living-more than land, than tools, than labour (World Development Report, 1999). Today's most technologically advanced economies are truly knowledge based. They are creating millions of knowledge-related jobs in an array of disciplines that have emerged overnight–knowledge engineers, knowledge managers, knowledge-coordinators etc.

Influence of Globalisation, Knowledge Revolution and Information Technology on Education

The competitive edges of countries especially in the context of globalisation are built around the quality of human resources as measured in terms of health condition and level of education. The need for higher education is based on the requirement of the third level manpower which depends essentially on the service activities in research, education and government administration. In the field of education the current trend emphasizes on technical and professional education and newer varieties of lucrative employment opportunities. Wider prospects for the development of skills, efficiency and productivity and possibilities for greater social and economic contacts have come to stay as some of the major dimensions of economic life. Because of this opening of broad social and economic contacts the role of education has been extremely important in the global network. Superior technology is invariably linked up with promotion of higher labour productivity provided they are operated by a highly specialised group of technically skilled persons. This calls for increasingly greater proliferation of training and education especially in the technical and vocational field. Higher education leading to the development of the faculty of mind is visualized as an input for developing superior technologies of production and management which empower the educated persons to dominate the global trade and investment scenario. A growing economy like Kerala needs people with up to date technical skills to participate in the global economy.

The globalisation of the economy has led to a globalisation of higher education. The higher education institutions everywhere are subject to global trends-massification and all of its implication, the impact of the new communication technologies, accountability of academic institutions to government, an increasingly international and mobile academic profession, global research network and other phenomena. There is a virtual invasion of foreign universities into India either hunting for students or indirectly enrolling through associate institutions. The students, without any hesitation, pay the unduly high fees charged by these institutions as the course content and exposure offered by the foreign universities are of a high order. There is no need to feel shy of such association if they serve to enhance academic standards and provide scope for diversifying and exchanging the standards and contents of current programmes. (Kerala Education Commission, 1999). The migration of students to other states is also important. Many students either migrate to other states or opt for an area of study or specialization such as computer education, travel and tourism, hotel management etc. that are offered by private providers because government institutions do not provide these courses.

The Influence of IT on Education

Now the world is at the frontiers of a new era where the new technology can be put to use to disseminate information and be used as a tool for education. Increasingly economic integration and growing interdependence among nations have led to a considerable reduction of cost, time and space in communication among the economic agents of production. Information has become not only the most crucial factor of production but also a major resource that seeks to determine our culture. With the huge demand for IT professionals in India and abroad the Government of India has initiated several useful steps to create an atmosphere of war for Indian latent in next ten years and to make it a reality by changing the earlier concept of products which had 90% material and only 10% of knowledge component to products which have 95% knowledge component and 5% material component which is a revolution by itself. As IT is transforming products of materials into products of knowledge, definitely it has impact on the country's political and economic sectors. India has a sound democratic system of governance and successfully entered the second phase of economic liberalization, the talented Indian intellectual information technology human capital will definitely take the global economic slow down as an opportunity to create a suitable climate for growth of world class IT at regional, national and international level. The process of globalization of technologies has been addressed as 'technoglobalism'.

Consequent on liberalisation some structural changes are observed in the Kerala economy. There is a shift away from agriculture to industry and services. Therefore the quality of education required in the future would be a different one with an emphasis on scientific and technical education. To take advantage of a fast moving global economy the countries cannot afford to limit them to accumulating physical capital. It is necessary to capture the benefits of technological progress (World Development Report 1999). In Kerala the system of education fails to meet the global challenges. Technology, particularly substantially knowledge based technologies such as IT, will thrive only in the ambiance of excellence in higher learning, and scientific research. Kerala educational system does not appear to be adequate in this regard. The failure to diversify and modernise our system of education, comes at a time when the state's economy is getting integrated with the global economy which is becoming increasingly knowledge-driven. Kerala's educational system seems to be oblivious of both the emerging threats and opportunities provided by a globalising society driven by science, technology and management. The social sector development, the legacy of the Kerala Model, has created a necessary condition for growth in the present day world. The knowledge base of the economy has been strengthened in the past and it is the efficiency of the system which can translate this into a sufficient condition for the future growth of the economy. A major opportunity for growth in the Kerala economy lies in orienting production towards more knowledge based products. In the situation of globalisation a diversification of programmes for revamping the higher education system will link the economy with the global challenges and will not only help build upon what has already been achieved but also to sustain a high rate of growth of the economy. Globalisation has brought about a shift from manufacturing economies to knowledge economies as a result of which the knowledge content of production has grown. In knowledge based production the sale of ideas has a higher premium than goods. Education, no doubt, enhances human capacity and choices to improve the knowledge content of production. Educational systems within many countries are adapting themselves to these changes. The examples of Korea, Indonesia, Japan indicate a move towards expanding higher education (George, 2000).

One of the key factors driving 'Knowledge Revolution' is the role of research, science and technology in creating knowledge to solve business, social and environmental problems. The Industrial Research and Development Expenditure indicate the speed at which the economy moves towards the knowledge society. Some of the selected statistics relating education in Kerala is given in the following tables.

Table 1
Enrolment of Students in Educational Institutions in Kerala

Category	*Total Number*
Lower Primary	18.25
Upper primary	14.75
High School	14.94
Higher Secondary	3.67
Vocational Higher secondary	25382
BA	24512
BSc	23722
BCom	8567
MA	4557
MSc	5395
MCom	3625
BTech	24452
Diplomas	9660
Technical High School	2295

Note: Serial No 1to 4 in lakhs and 5 to 14 in thousands Serial Number 6to 12 Admission for the first year.

Source: Economic Survey 2006.

Table 2
Grant in Aid to Various Universities

Year	*Amount in Lakhs*
2004-05	12601.43
2005-06	11642.58
2006-07	14732.86

Note: 2005-06 Revised estimate 2006-07 Budget estimate.
Source: Economic Review.

Table 3
Expenditure on Education Stagewise

Stage	*2004-05*	*2005-6*	*2006-07*
Primary	1331.28	1532.50	1527.75
Secondary	1141.75	1399.85	1486.09
University	515.36	570.05	562.28
Adult Education	0.19	0.50	0.50
Language Development	22.40	15.34	15.18
General	31.39	36.68	32.69
Subtotal	3047.65	3590.01	3624.48
Technical education	159.91	213.00	202.77
Total	3207.56	3803.01	3827.25

Source: Economic Review 2006.

Table 4 indicates the growth rate of Research and Development Expenditure across the states.

Table 4
Research and Development Expenditure Across the States

State	*1976-96*	*1981-90*	*1991-96*
Andhra Pradesh	10.11	2.87	10.10
Bihar	7.04	2.28	-16.94
Gujarat	8.44	5.35	14.66
Haryana	10.91	10.15	3.51
Kerala	7.96	8.65	6.86
Karnataka	9.71	11.39	-9.26
Madhya Pradesh	9.58	3.80	13.26
Maharashtra	14.65	9.23	11.55
Orissa	7.42	0.87	-20.76
Punjab	10.31	17.92	26.86
Rajasthan	16.33	7.11	.11
Tamil Nadu	9.36	9.03	8.53
U P	11.64	5.39	-0.90
West Bengal	5.82	7.56	-4.16

Sources: Research and Development in Industry (Various issues) Department of science and Technology, Government of India.

The growth rate of expenditure on Research and Development in the post reform period shows dynamism in some states and retardation in others. In Kerala the rate of growth registered a slight decline during the post reform period. It declined from 8.65 in 1981-90 to 6.86 in 1991-96. But in states like Gujarat, Madhya Pradesh, Punjab etc. there has been significant boosting up of Industrial Research and Development expenditure consequent on the process of globalisation. So it is time for Kerala to recognize the fact that any sophisticated technology will require a highly skilled workforce that may not be readily available. The state has to restructure the educational system to suit the needs of the economy.

Therefore the quality of education required for Kerala would be a different one with an emphasis on scientific and technical education. The type of education to meet the needs of liberalization, globalisation and a rapidly industrializing economy requires some consideration. Accumulation of knowledge in specific areas which impart technical and vocational skills, knowledge of markets and knowledge to deal with people, accountancy, financial and banking skills and exposure to computer and their application etc are essential.

Realising the impact of globalisation on higher education the Government of Kerala felt that computer industry which is growing at exponential rates in India need to be supported. Since a serious mismatch is observed between the type of qualified personnel already available in the state it is imperative that a massive planning exercise is undertaken to identify new areas of higher education that will match the needs of the industry and the markets on the one hand and enable the people to reap the benefits of industrialisation and globalisation. Higher education and technical training are needed to build a labour force that can keep up with a constant stream of technological advances.

As Information Technology industry is one of the emerging industry segments in the country the Govt. of India has drawn up an ambitious programme to make India a software power by 2010. The Department of Electronics has formulated vision document- software industry vision-2010 to achieve this goal.

The Government of Kerala announced its IT policy in 1998 and a separate government department was formed for effective coordination and implementation of the programme. The measures taken so far have been based on the recommendation of the Taskforce on IT.

The IT Revolution is making a tremendous impact on industry and trade by relentless technology innovation, massive growth in computer power, world wide networks and ever growing electronic factories. It works like a lubricating oil to make the system work better. Now the role of higher education is much more than that of orienting people towards skill and specialization. These changing trends in education levels of the labour force offer positive opportunities for Kerala.

In the early 1990's there were two major institutional interventions to promote the growth of software industry in the state. The first was the setting up of a software technology park in Trivandrum. Further in accordance with the recommendations of the Eighth Five Year Plan Taskforce on Software Development a Techno park was set up by the Government of Kerala. It aims at providing infra structural support to electronics research, design development and manufacturing as well as for software development units. With the setting up of software technology parks and the techno park Kerala experienced substantial improvement in software development activity in the state.

Demand for Manpower in the Current Situation of Knowledge Economy

There is a general perception that technological change would lead to unemployment. This is unfounded in the case of knowledge-based production catering to global markets. The unemployment rate in all countries that established a lead in knowledge-based production has declined. Many future jobs will be based on technology which is today in its infancy and these jobs call for undreamed of skills. Nations, enterprises and individual workers who are able to acquire, transform and use Information Technology productively and imaginatively will benefit from the technological advances now set in motion.

The knowledge-based economy is reshaping the job market. Some IT related jobs did not even exist prior to 1994-95. The history of the developed countries indicate a growth path wherein at first there was a shift in the share of GDP and total employment from agricultural to manufacturing sector. When the supremacy of the manufacturing sector gets established and per capital income increases considerably there will be a shift of the major share of incomes and employment to the service sector. But now the situation has changed. Information Technology allows leap frogging, which can help countries skip generation of technology and stages of growth and place them directly in the service-dominated economy. It integrates the world into a closer community of interdependent producers and consumers of goods and services. It creates new jobs, destroys a whole lot of traditional middle management jobs and has the potential to reallocate jobs globally.

In the post liberalization period since 1991 the productivity norms and work culture have changed in the industry. But the rate of unemployment is mounting up and this is clearly due to the mismatch of the quality produced by educational institutions and the industry expectations. The demand for IT professionals is bound to grow in geometric proportions and India still produces operators and programmers while upper end jobs like systems design go to non Indians. Globalization has forced us to change our own game rules in economic sector. Job pattern is changing internally also and for a uniform development through out India there is need for creation of trained human power in specialised areas and in basic fields with sound knowledge base in core disciplines with abilities to adopt new demands.

The possibility of generating employment through trans-national networking depends on education and training to create requisite skills. The capabilities developed through schooling are the ability to absorb and understand and the ability to apply these skills to daily life and work. Some of the new IT based services may provide opportunities for creation of better jobs especially for the educated work force and provide opportunities for expanding the base for entrepreneurship because of their relatively low capital intensive and highly skill intensive nature. The structure of labour demand shifts as industrial structure and technology change and then the so far successful educational regime may not be adequate to cope with the future demand structure. The major input for the software industry is skilled labour. But in Kerala the colleges and universities are producing conventional science and social science graduates who cannot find adequate job opportunities. On the other hand there is a grave scarcity of computer trained manpower. Among measures to increase competitiveness, growth and employment in a globalising world economy, the critical role of a high quality educated and skilled workforce must gain more prominence (World Employment Report, 1998-99).

The major institutions in the state imparting software training are the Lal Bahadur Shastri Centre for Science and Technology (LBS) and the institute of Human Resource Development for Electronics (IHRDE). The total intake in various computer courses offered in the state is 18,923. Out of this government institutions account for about 15,393. Apart from this there are some private institutions also which impart training to students in software training. It is estimated that about 60,000 to 70,000 students are being trained each year (Govt. of Kerala, 1997). The structure of the out turn of software manpower in India during 1999 shows that it is only a small share of the world out turn and is highly insufficient to meet global demands.

Table 5
Structure of the Out Turn of Software Manpower in India during 1999

Course	*Numbers*	*Per cent*
PhD	95	0.4
M.Tech	2130	3.14
B.Tech	16160	23.84
M.Sc	2800	4.13
B.Sc	3200	4.72
B.C.A/M.C.A	7700	11.36
P.G. Degree	6000	7.38
P.G. Diploma	16700	25.64
ITI	14000	20.65
Total	69463	20.65

Source: Companies (NASSCOM, 1999).

The data explain that the contribution of India in the matter of software manpower, especially those holding post graduate qualifications and research degrees is meagre.

Global Demands

Our graduates fail to find a job at a time when educated and professionally qualified people are becoming an imperative for further growth in the more developed world. Some estimates indicate that Europe and the USA alone will need an additional 20 million IT professionals by 2002 and Korea requires 50,000 IT professionals. The corresponding estimates for other countries are 17,000 for Hong Kong and 0.8 million for Thailand in the next 15 years. India requires 2.2 million by 2008 and Singapore needs 10,000 IT professionals annually. Further it is estimated that nearly 0.24 million Indian IT professionals will be migrating to the USA within a period of three years starting from 2001. Nearly half of the foreign IT workers in Malaysia are from India. The battle is now for the 'best brains'. All these support the view that Indian experts are the backbone of the 'Knowledge Revolution' in the world over. According to the NASSCOM- Mc Kinsey Study Indian IT sector will require 2.2 million globally.

The National Taskforce on Information Technology and Software Development (NTITSD) has also projected that the software industry will employ 2.2 million workers by 2008. The industry is creating job opportunities for highly qualified engineering graduates. According to the NASSCOM surveys the software industry employed some 3,40,000 professionals as on march 31, 2000 including software professionals working in software organizations compared with 1,60,000 professionals in 1996. Yet another survey showed that 900,000 IT jobs were available this year, about half of which will remain vacant due to a lack of skilled workers.

To fulfill the target and an edge in global competitive environment the Indian IT professionals will be in great demand. It has been found that there is a deficit of about 10,000 teachers in software training. The Task force on Human Resources Development in IT recommended that the intake of students in IT related programmes needs to be doubled in 2001-2002 and tripled by 2003-04 for doubling info Tech student intake next year While the cost of software manpower in India is much less than that in the developed economies

The Trend in the Demand for Technically Qualified Persons in Kerala in the Present Situation

The current world situation is characterized by a powerful shift from manufacturing economics to knowledge economies. The idea conveyed in the development theories of the 1950's was that capital was the missing link in development and that industrialization was the route to economic growth. During the 90's the development concerns have shifted to human development. Also the conventional wisdom that capital is the prime mover of economic development has now yielded to Sen's thesis that building capabilities is the key to opening opportunities especially in a knowledge based society. Therefore a major challenge for the policy makers is to increase the supply of trained manpower quickly enough to satisfy the growing demand for domestic industry as well as that of other countries. Increasing competition for knowledge workers means that management of human resources is becoming a key to corporate success in the industry. Info power has become an inescapable phenomenon in every day life.

Education becomes meaningful when the products of education succeed in finding chances of productive employment. If the labour market can adjust itself to changes in demand for different types of manpower and if the educational system could adjust by producing workers with the necessary knowledge there may not be a question of utilisation or underutilization of manpower. In Kerala in the light of the wide spread unemployment and underemployment there is no doubt that neither the labour market not the educational system satisfies this condition. A balance between manpower of various grades and types produced by the educational system and the demand that the economy generates for different levels and types of manpower is significant in educational planning. No country can afford to set up its target for enrolments on the basis of manpower requirements for economic growth alone. But since the level of employment is the single crucial variable determining the efficacy of the educational system the authorities will have to keep an eye on the employment trends in the changing economic scenario. So decisions regarding the courses to be started and the maximum available seats for different courses have to be guided by the fact that expansion of education for high level manpower should be based on realistic demand and not on wishful anticipations.

In this situation it is imperative to have an idea of the changing trends in the demand for technically qualified persons in Kerala. To some extent, the placement of engineering graduates by campus interviews throws light on the emerging trends in the demand for manpower. It follows from the fact that so long as an inevitable link exists between production sector and education, such placements represent a portion of the society's demand for the type and quality of manpower. The data regarding the campus placements from the four leading engineering institutions in the state, viz, the Government Engineering College, Thiruvananthapuram. T.K.M. College of Engineering, Kollam, Regional Engineering College, Kozhikode and Govt. Engineering College, Kannur for a period of five years from are used to analyse the trend in the demand for engineering graduates in Kerala in the situation of globalisation and the emergence of the knowledge economy. The courses available in common in these four institutions are considered and comparison is made between the placements from those courses. The comparison, in essence, is between the traditional courses such as Civil Engineering (C.E), Mechanical Engineering (M.E) and Electrical and Electronics and the emerging courses such as Electronics and Communication Engineering (ECE) and Computer Science and Engineering (CSE) which seems to be a sinequanon of the knowledge society.

The comparisons between placements show a relatively higher and consistent percentage for Electronics and Communication Engineering and Computer Science and

Engineering. The trend in the demand for different B.Tech courses, as is done in the foregoing analysis has some significant implications. The trend is positive for all the five branches. But for conventional branches such as civil and mechanical there is no remarkable variation in the demand which in itself is an explanation to the changing trend. Regarding Electrical and electronics also the trend is not decisive. But as the regards Electronics and Communication Engineering (ECE) and Computer Science and Engineering (CSE) the positive trend is remarkable. This proves the fact that the emerging perspective for the state is in favour of computers and communication. In the case of computer science and Engineering (CSE) course the demand shows a trend to outstrip the total supply in the coming years which indicates that an increase in the number of seats for the course is called for. A perusal of the list of candidates placed through campus recruitment reveals that the leading companies like WIPRO, Infosys, IBM, TCS, SIEMENS etc considered persons with good academic performance. The minimum percentage for recruitment by these companies stood at 74% in 1999. This also brings to light the fact that the new technology requires only the best brains.

The impact of globalisation, knowledge economy and IT Revolution on education and employment lead to the conclusion that the state cannot afford to set up its target for enrolments on the basis of manpower requirement within the state. The products of our educational system are for the global market. There is in essence an internationalization of human capital. In a growth led employment approach the prospects for generating employment depends on the growth rate and composition of the GNP. The experience of Kerala in general, has shown that the output growth in different sectors has not been able to absorb the backlog of the unemployed because of lower and more declining employment output elasticities .So the state has to find economically feasible alternatives for the productive employment of the products of education. Education that helps to make workers more flexible and adaptable to new technologies is now considered a valuable way of contributing to manpower development just as much as education that prepares them for specific jobs. The Information Age records one of the master narratives of our times and the market prefers only those graduates who have practical application of knowledge. In that sense the reorientation of the educational system towards the emerging demands of the economy is the need of the hour.

Suggestions

1. The emphasis is given on quantity than on quality. The educated students must be competent enough to meet any international competition. For this training imparted by institutions of higher learning must overhauled and tuned to match the international level. The application level must be emphasised.
2. The method of training imparted to students needs change. Still spoon feeding is the rule.
3. The method of evaluation and the scales used for measuring has to be more realistic and must reflect the quality of the students. The present system of assigning has served as a method to implement discipline; quality reflection is not reflected in this.
4. It is high time to diversify higher education. The present system of diversification is mere replication. To achieve these universities and various academic bodies involved in it and its composition has to be rearranged. In the academic bodies of the universities representation must be given to qualified persons from industries, who can highlight the requirements of the industry. The course content and the syllabus framed etc must be properly vetted by experts from industries. Then the industry university linkage gets more strengthened.
5. The level of political interference, in the name of democratization, in the management of higher education must be reconsidered. It is high time to think in these lines.
6. Universities must have list of new courses/programmes that could be offered. The list and other related details must

be formulated in advance and on the basis of this, affiliations could be considered.

7. Too much emphasis given to languages for degree programmes needs change. Instead of this specialisations could be introduced. Inter-disciplinary studies need more encouragement.

References

Altback, Philp G. (1993), 'Dilemma of Change in Indian Higher Education' in Altbach, P.G. (ed.), *Higher Education in International Perspection*, cited in Rema Devi. T, (2003), The Higher Education System and Structural Disequilibrium in the Job Market for the Educated in Kerala, Unpublished Ph.D Thesis, Department of Economics, Pondicherry University.

Anthony, Giddens (1990), 'Consequences of Modernity Cambridge Polity, cited in Rema Devi. T, (2003), *The Higher Education System and Structural Disequilibrium in the Job Market for the Educated in Kerala*, Unpublished Ph.D Thesis, Department of Economics, Pondicherry University.

Arora, Ashish, Arunachalam V. S. (2002), 'The Indian Software Services Industries' Carnegie-Mellon University, Pitsberg.

Carl, Dahlman and Thomas Anderson (2000), ' Korea and the Knowledge-based Economy, Making the Transition', World Bank Institute.

Chanda, Nayan (2000), 'The Tug of War for Asia's Best Brains', *Far Eastern Economic Review*, Vol. 163, No. 45.

Chandrashekhar, C. P. (2005), 'Who Needs a Knowledge Economy? Information, Knowledge and Flexible Labour', *Indian Journal of Labour Economics*, December.

Debdas, Banerjee (2005), 'Knowledge Workers and Information Technology Reliving Early English industrial Revolution', *Indian Journal of Labour Economics*, December.

Deshpande H. V. (2000), 'Information Technology and Higher Education', University News, June 4–10.

Economic Review (1999), State Planning Board. Government, Press, Thriruvanathapuram.

Freeman, C. and Hagedoorn (1992), Globalisation of Technology Brussels , FACT, DECP.

Human Development Report (1999), UNDP, ILO, Geneva.

Joseph K. J. (1998), Software Development in Kerala in B. A. Prakash (ed), *Kerala's Economic Development-Issues and Problems*, Sage Publications, New Delhi.

Kerala Education Commission (1999), 'KSSP', Kochi.

Knowledge Commission Report, 2006.

Kumar (2001), Developing Countries in the International Division of Labour in Software and Service Industry–A Background Paper for the World Employment Report, New Delhi.

Lamberton, D. M. (1971), 'Economics of Information and Knowledge', Penguin Modern Economics Readings.

Low L. (2000), 'Economics of Information Technology and the Media', Singapore University Press, Singapore.

Machlup F. (1962), 'The Production and Distribution of Knowledge', Princeton University press.

Manoj P. K. (2007), 'ICT for Governance: The Kerala Experience', *Proceedings of the Third National Conference on Innovations in Information and Communication Technology*, Department of IT, PSG college of Technology, Coimbatore, Tamil Nadu, September.

Mashelkar R. A. (2000), 'Address to the 87th Indian Science Conference', New Delhi.

NASSCOM-Me Kinsey Study, cited in Rema Devi T., (2003), The Higher Education System and Structural Disequilibrium in the Job Market for the Educated in Kerala, Unpublished Ph. D Thesis, Department of Economics, Pondicherry University.

Nigavekar, Arun (2001). Convocation Address, Amaravati University, March.

Oommen M. A. (2000), National Conference on Education December, Thiruvanathapuram.

Pattnaik, Satyanarayana and Pattnaik, Suchismita (2001), 'Economic Slowdown–An Opportunity for Indian IT sector', *Yojana,* Vol. 45, November.

Pissarides, Christopher (1997), Learning by Trading–World Bank, *Economic Review,* January.

Prakash B. A. (1999), 'Kerala's Economic Development Issues and Problems', Sage Publications, New Delhi.

Psacharapaulos G. and Wood hall M. (1995), Education for Development, World Bank.

Rath, Shashibhushan (1998), Human Resource Strategy for the Next Millennium, *Indian Management,* Vol. 37, No. 1, July.

Rema Devi T. (2003), 'The Higher Education System and Structural Disequilibrium in the Job Market for the Educated in Kerala', Unpublished Ph.D thesis, Department of Economics, Pondicherry University.

Sanyal, Kishore C. (1999), 'Privatisation of Higher Education', Man and Development, Vol. XXI, No. 3, September.

Surjit Singh (2005), 'India and the Knowledge Economy: Overview and Global Context', *Indian Journal of Labour Economics,* December.

Tapiola, Kari (1999), Symposium on Multimedia Convergence; World of Work ILO.

Varghese N. V. (2000), 'National Conference on Education', December, Thiruvanathapuram.

Venkata Subramaniam (2000), 'National Conference on Education', December, Thiruvanathapuram.

Vinod Abraham and R. K. Sharma, (2005), 'New Technology and the Emerging Labour Market: A Study of Indian IT Industry', *Indian Journal of labour Economics,* December.

World Development Report (various years), ILO Geneva.

ROLE OF INFORMATION TECHNOLOGY IN KERALA

V. R. Sathish

Introduction

Today Information is becoming a commodity like income and wealth and countries are classified as rich and poor on the basis of information. Investment in infrastructure, physical capital, and in education is the key to economic development. Hence, Information Technology (IT) today is the world's fastest growing economic activity and the use of IT is so widely spread throughout the world economy that no single country can avoid investing in this technology if it wants to improve the standard of living of its citizens. The flow of information has changed our life style and at present Information is the backbone of every system. Nowadays Information is very vital for running our day-to-day activities smoothly and if we do not have information for one minute it may result into a big disaster. The recent advances in information technology (IT) are becoming central to the process of socio-economic development and it offers new ways of exchanging information, transacting business, the nature of the financial and other service sectors and provides efficient means of using the human and institutional capabilities of countries. IT has made our lives more and more simple and people can work on the Internet without really having to go outside to their workplace.

In an increasingly globalized economy, information technology is one of the key determinants of competitiveness and growth of firms and countries. Firms are becoming more competitive on the basis of their knowledge, rather than on the basis of natural endowments or low labour costs. It is maintained that the adoption of high-technology manufacturing methods is no longer optional, but forms part of a critical strategy for the survival of any country. The basis for this claim is that technology has now become universally available and whoever uses it wins. The world is rapidly moving towards knowledge-based economic structures and information societies, which comprise networks of individuals, firms and countries that are linked electronically and in interdependent relationships.

The competitive and comparative advantages of countries are gradually being determined by access to information technology and knowledge. The comparative advantage that now counts is man-made, engineered by knowledge through the application of information. Since man-made comparative advantage can only be acquired by knowledge and brainpower, the newly emerging knowledge-based economic structures have far reaching implications with regard to labour markets and the roles of technical education, human capital formation and research and development in the process of economic growth. The evolution of the knowledge-based economy is expected to result in an increase in the demand for skilled labour and reducing the employment prospects of unskilled labour. Countries that invest in and adopt information technology quickly will move ahead and those that fail to rapidly adopt information technology will be left behind.

The role of IT is significant in underdeveloped countries like India and it is all the more important in a state like Kerala in the context of backward industrial sector along with high educated unemployment and highest number of emigration to the gulf countries. Hence, in this paper we have made an attempt to examine the role of IT in the economic development of Kerala.

Objectives of the Study

The specific objectives of the study are:

1. To examine the role of Information Technology in the Economic Development of Kerala;
2. To evaluate the IT policy of the Government of Kerala and;
3. To examine the necessity and benefits of setting up of IT parks in Kerala along with the profile of key players.

Data Sources

The necessary data for this study has been collected from published sources like Government reports, Journals, and websites.

Meaning of Information Technology

Information Technology means the use of hardware, software, services, and supporting infrastructure to manage and deliver information using voice, data, and video. Information Technology includes all computers with a human interface and all computer peripherals. Thus IT is that branch of technology, which is devoted to the study, and application of data and the processing thereof and the development and use of the hardware, software, firmware and procedures associated with this processing. As such IT refers to the digital processing, storage and communication of information of all kinds. In the broadest sense, information technology refers to both the hardware and software that are used to store, retrieve, and manipulate information.

Information Technology industry is one of the fastest growing segments in India and it is integrated with every sphere of life and is an essential ingredient of modern education. All our Railways, Air and even sea networks are connected with the help of IT. Information Technology has changed the whole scenario. Companies can share technologies online. Even the doctors can guide the other doctors while operating on a patient with the help of Information Technology. A whole new world is coming in our way. In Kerala, Information

Technology has abundant scope in the context of large scale educated unemployment and scarcity of capital. Kerala is lagging behind many other south Indian states in Information Technology. In this context, the present paper examines the role of IT in the economic development of Kerala.

The Development Experience of Kerala

Kerala is known for its development paradox of high PQLI with low percapita income. The achievements of the social sectors in the State are unique among the Indian states although production base of the state is very weak. Thus, the development experience of Kerala shows that it is lagging behind in productive sectors. However, educational achievements of Kerala show that the state is far ahead of other Indian states. Another notable feature of Kerala is that the state accounts for about 60 per cent of the total emigrants from India to the gulf countries. Hence in the present context of high achievements in the educational sector especially in the technical education (Computer Science, MCA and B Tech Information Technology), and higher percentage of emigrants from Kerala to the Indian emigrants, there is a lot of scope for using IT for the economic development of Kerala. Thus, in Kerala IT can generate massive employment especially in the context of large-scale educated unemployment in the state and it can also earn valuable foreign exchange by way of software exports. It can also reduce the cost of production and services, especially the cost of telecom services, which may help to accelerate economic development of Kerala. The following section summarises the role of IT in economic development followed by a review of IT policy of the Government of Kerala. Next section examines the benefits and problems of IT parks in Kerala along with a review of the soft ware exports from Kerala.

Role of IT in the Economic Development of Kerala

Recently, experts advocated that information technology revolution would change the world, as investments in IT will have a visible impact on productivity and economic growth of a country. The use of IT in the production of goods and services has had a strong influence on productivity and economic growth in industrial and in newly industrialized countries. The role of IT is very important in the context of Kerala where there exists a highest rate of educated unemployment and deficiency of capital. More over, among the Indian emigrants, bulk of them is from Kerala and they bring substantial amount of foreign remittances into the state. IT can substantially increase the number of emigrants, can improve the quality of emigrants, and increase the amount of foreign remittances by imparting training in computer science and IT.

There may exist a two-way causation between economic development and IT as economic development may lead to the development of IT and IT may lead to the economic development. Thus, IT can influence the economic development of Kerala by raising efficiency of all sectors and activities especially in industries and manufacturing and services industries. IT can raise productivity and create high value additions to production. More over, IT can reduce the cost of production and increase revenues, which may be used for reinvestment by firms. Productivity can also be increased with the help of Information Technology as Internet can change the market by search for efficient markets.

The development of IT requires investments for the creation of infrastructure, which may increase the demand for IT related goods and services, which in turn will also increase the demand for output. Economic development may also lead to the development of IT. Investment in the creation of infrastructure in IT can increase the employment opportunities, which will result in a faster growth of the State Domestic Product. Increased employment in the IT sector in Kerala can generate increased purchasing power, which finally increases the demand for other products. Altogether investment in IT will boost production and employment in other related sectors finally resulting in a multiple increase in income and employment. Hence, we can conclude that investment in IT can generate favourable impact on the SDP of Kerala and so IT can be used as a tool of economic development of Kerala.

Role of IT in Kerala's Industrialisation

As the information technology evolves, the world is now in paradigm shift from the industrial age to the information age. As a result, there is a growing demand in the service fields that require expert knowledge and information. Information technology has contributed a lot to the existing service industries such as banking and insurance and IT has enhanced efficiency and expansion of business. New industries on the basis of information technology such as software industry and information processing services are rapidly growing.

Kerala is backward industrially and there are many explanations for this industrial backwardness. In Kerala, the share of industry to GDP is very low and this can be increased by development of Information Technology. Thus, Kerala is a fertile ground for the growth of the IT industry and it is found to be ideal for Kerala in terms of its potential to generate opportunities and employment with little pressure on land, environment and other resources. This is one of the most people-friendly and environment-friendly industries of modern times.

As a whole IT can boost the industrial sector and can increase its contribution to Kerala's State Domestic Product (SDP). As information technology changes the aspects of competition, investment is made more in the area of information and communications that promotes productivity and expedites decision-making process than in the facilities increasing the production capability. For economic growth, we are prepared to take a positive action to introduce advanced information and communication services and to provide an environment where various information technologies can be used.

Role of IT in Employment in Kerala

Kerala is known for its highest unemployment rates in India and it is a labour surplus economy. Shrinking share of its production drastically reduces the number of workers in manufacturing sector. On the other hand, employment in information and knowledge-intensive service sector is increasing with investment in information technology. In the occupational categories, there are more demands for experts with creativity and information technology. Strengthening information infrastructure is a prerequisite for the creation of knowledge and information based society. Among IT, telecommunication networks, education, software exports are all very important in economic growth. Internet industries can create new jobs. An information education plan targeting the entire population will help to meet the needs of each group of citizens, ensuring a society without "information-have-nots" and will result in the creation of massive employment in the state. The Government understands the enormous potential of Information Technology not only as a tool for improving governance and creating more jobs, but more significantly, as a means to greatly enhance the standard of living of the people. Use of IT in enhancing the delivery of Government services leads to a very responsive and transparent administration facilitating the empowerment of the people and satisfying their right of information.

Software Exports from Kerala

The IT industry is currently a very small segment of Kerala economy although the market for its products and services is relatively large and growing. Kerala is the most favourable location in India for Information and Communication Technology (ICT) and Information Technology Enabled Services (ITES) industries to flourish. However, the performance of Kerala in IT is not spectacular compared to that of other southern states. The contribution of Kerala to the software export of India is only nominal and this shows the low level IT activity in the state. The software export of Kerala was only Rs. 885.47 crores against the software exports of Rs. 37000 crores by Karnataka (Table 1). Hence, there should be determined efforts by the government of Kerala to increase the software exports from Kerala.

There are certain advantages to Kerala to exploit the possibilities offered by IT and software exports. Kerala has abundance of educated and technically qualified personnel, highest telephone density, 100 per cent digital connectivity, high P.C penetration, better human resource development, availability of low-cost IT professionals at the bottom/entry level, presence of International gateway at Kochi and significantly lower operational costs compared to other cities.

Table 1
Software Exports from Kerala and Neighboring States (2005-06)

State	*Export (Rs. crore)*
Kerala	885.47
Karnataka	37000.00
Tamil Nadu	13960.00
Andra Pradesh	12521.00

Source: Economic Review (2006).

Major Problems of Kerala with Regard to the Software Exports

The major problems of Kerala with regard to the software exports are the absence of major Indian and multi national firms, shortage of highly skilled and adequately trained manpower in the middle level and top level, inadequate language and communication skills and other soft skills essential for the ITES industry. In addition, lack of interaction between industry, academia and the state, non–availability of metropolitan social infrastructure to retain its human resources, lack of associated infrastructure including convenient and frequent national air, connectivity to centres of technical and management excellence, poor perception of the investors to accept the state as an investment destination due to false image creation are the other problems faced by Kerala.

Internet and E-commerce

Digitalization of administrative work will boost the government productivity and transparency. Internet and electronic commerce can accelerate the speed of economic development of Kerala. It can improve the fiscal affairs of the government including revenue, expenditure and management of government properties. Information technology can make public administration more transparent and efficient. Government can promote new business by utilizing information technology and infrastructure. Besides providing citizens with access to IT and to IT education and training, governments should promote participation in the information society, thus generating a sufficiently strong demand base for information products. By developing advanced applications of IT, and by becoming a model for the private sector, governments can alter worker, firm, and consumer attitudes, and lower their costs of adopting IT. This paper discusses the possibilities for broad-based IT-led economic growth in India, including increasing value-added, using better telecom links to capture more benefits domestically through offshore development for developed country firms, greater spillovers to the local economy, broadening the IT industry with production of telecom access devices, improving the functioning of the economy through a more extensive and denser communications network, and improving governance. We also examine the policy environment, arguing that government policy is better focused on removing labour market distortions and infrastructure constraints, rather than providing output or export subsidies to the software industry. In banking, Information Technology (IT) enables us to transact any amount of money from part of the world to other.

Today e commerce helps us to buy and sell things through internet. If we want to buy something and are not getting it nearby store then we can purchase it online with the help of debit and credit cards. We can order goods on the Internet and we will get it delivered at our doorstep with just few clicks of mouse. Similarly if we want to travel around the world we can book airline tickets online and even book rooms for our hotels.

Kerala Government's IT Policy

The features of Kerala economy are best suited for the development of Information Technology. To mention a few, Kerala is a 100 per cent literate society and therefore, is a preferred base for a knowledge society. Kerala is emerging as a powerful destination with many cost advantages. Kerala is a state where we can build a strong communication backbone-both telecom and datacom. Kerala has a pro-active government with an investor-friendly approach with well-structured policies, initiatives and incentives supported by world-class infrastructure. Kerala's IT policy accords the highest importance to creating opportunities for citizens and IT ventures. Kerala is a place where everyone is for IT and IT for everyone.

Kerala government has announced its IT policy to make Information and Communication Technology (ICT) a tool for improving governance and promote economic development through investment in the sector. The IT policy provides various incentives to the IT, ITES units in the state. The government is trying to make Kerala as an ideal investment destination. Kerala has always been giving highest priority to IT sector and has been doing everything possible to facilitate investment in the IT sector. The IT policy aims to generate employment opportunities and to make the government more accessible to the citizens.

The IT Policy Statement of Kerala emphasizes the need for increased application of Information Technology in all walks of life. It also aims to enhance the IT industry base so as to make Kerala a very fertile location for ventures in Information Technology and also aims to create a robust State Information Infrastructure. The policy also aims to develop human resources for IT. The policy also aims to promote the use of IT for the PC penetration of 10 per 1000 of the population. The policy aims to extent the benefits of IT to all Colleges and Schools and to Panchayat wards for the modernisation and integration of Government functions using IT. A High Power Committee has been proposed, chaired by the Chief Minister, to co-ordinate and direct strategies to achieve rapid penetration and use of IT in all sectors.

Government realises the significance and potential of this sector in the economic development of the State and will facilitate the creation of a sound IT production base through conscious efforts and policy initiatives. The government aims to create IT-specific infrastructure in different parts of the State and incentives and concessions for IT ventures. Government likes to promote Kerala as a location for IT investments and specific proposals include strengthening of Techno park and setting up of Software Technology Parks and Software Complexes in major cities in the State. A venture capital fund is also proposed to cater to the financing requirements of the IT industry.

The establishment of a sound Information Infrastructure with a communication backbone, switches, nodes, access networks and data warehouses has been identified a high priority area. The existing infrastructure will be harnessed, developed and integrated to create an Information Infrastructure that can effectively handle the traffic for several years to come. Human Resource Development is a very critical aspect in the development of Information Technology. The Government is seized of the urgency for consolidating and strengthening the core competence of the state on the human resources front to propel the development of IT industry. The proposals in this regard include establishment of an Institute of Information Technology, introducing Information Technology as a specialised branch of study, development of Centres of Excellence in Information Technology, creating a fund for up gradation of training/educational infrastructure and introduction of a system for accreditation.

The ICT industry, either hardware or software production, is currently a very small segment of Kerala economy although the market for its products and services are relatively large and growing. The State Government has an IT policy and a number of related programmes like setting up of IT parks for attracting ICT-based companies, e-governance projects for the introduction of ICT-based public services and educational programmes.

Details on investment, employment, turnover, export etc. in IT sector in Kerala is given in the Table 2.

Table 2
Important Information on IT Industry in Kerala as on March 2006

Institution	*Total Investment (Rs. Crore)*	*No. of Units*	*Total Employment (Nos.)*	*Total Turnover (Rs. Crore)*	*Total Export (Rs. Crore)*
Techno park	850	104	12500	650	600
Info park	94	32	3514	67.23	66.67
Cochin SEZ	17	20	1388	219	219
e-pay centres	0.30	100	200	-	-
Training Institutes	113.12	4545	22725	-	-

Source: IT Mission.

Development of ICT Sector in Kerala

The Government of Kerala has already taken many steps to exploit the emerging opportunities of ICT applications. As a result of concerted efforts to promote Kerala as a premier investment destination, blue chip companies like Infosys, Wipro, TCS, Ernst and Young etc now have their presence in Kerala. The existing Techno park, Info park, Software Technology Parks of 507 India-Thiruvananthapuram (STPI - T), KINFRA IT Parks, IIITM-K, CSEZ etc. have to be strengthened and an integrated IT complex is to be established as part of a growth strategy for the ICT industry in Kerala. The investment Promotion & Management Cell set up by the State Government through Kerala State IT Mission granted subsidies to the tune of Rs. 25 crore to eligible IT units in the State to enhance the contribution of medium and small investors in IT and to generate employment opportunities.

Human Resource Development for IT/ITES

In order to sustain the growth of ICT industry, regular supply of fresh stock of human resources with varied skills, experience and exposure is needed. Improving the quality of training in both the formal and informal sectors is a priority requirement for this. A beginning has already been made in the incorporation of ICT in the school curriculum. With a view to provide skilled manpower in the growing IT and ITES industries, the ITES Habitat in Kochi and world class training facilities in IIITM-K offer variety of quality training programmes to the students. Currently, there are 4545 ICT training institutes in the State. The Indian Institute of Information Technology and Management-Kerala (IIITM -K) is an institute of excellence in education, research, development and training in basic and applied information technology and management. The Institute supports HRD for industry, teachers training for colleges, IT ventures incubation, multimedia authoring for faculty and experts and development of IT and IT enabled services for the region. The Institute was established in March 2001 at Techno park. Four batches of students have successfully completed the PGDIT Course from

IIITM-K. Students have been placed in the companies like MindTree, IBM, Oracle, TCS, Vimoksha, Kanbay etc. A project wing at Nila building was established in 2003. The Institute hosts a unique library which includes Digital Library, lending services, online search and other services and has been extending the services to other units in and outside Techno park.

In Kerala around 15,000 IT graduates/postgraduates are coming out from Govt./Private institutions. Universities have their own IT training centers with courses like MCA (Master of Computer Applications), M.Sc (Commuter Science/IT), B.Tech, etc. The admission to these courses is done on the basis of entrance examination conducted by the Government.

Profile of Major Multi National IT Companies in Kerala

The important multinational IT companies operating at present in Kerala are IBS Software Services, IVL India Ltd, Softex Computer Consultants, Seaview Support Systems Pvt. Ltd, Sun Tec Business Solutions, Tata Consultancy Services (TCS), Toonz Animations India Pvt. Ltd and Kerala Industrial Infrastructure Development Corporation (KINFRA).

IBS Software Services was set up in 1997 as a joint venture between the International Business Services Group and Atraxis AG, the IT arm of the erstwhile Swiss Air Group. The company is a provider of software services for global travel, transportation and logistics businesses with operations in USA, Europe, the Middle East and Asia Pacific. The company provides superior software solutions in areas such as airlines, airport operations, mail tracking and cargo handling. It has a large offshore software production and competence development centre in Thiruvanathapuram and has announced plans to commence operations at its second development centre at the Info park in Kochi.

IVL India Ltd, a wholly owned subsidiary of IVL GmbH, is a business technology consulting company specializing in SAP implementation, optimization, integration and development of knowledge services. It develops software for its parent company's global clients in Germany, Italy, United States, Japan,

Taiwan, Finland, France and Singapore. It is also a major player in the domestic ERP market with 85 mega projects under its belt. The company is based in Thiruvananthapuram.

Softex is a global leader in developing games for mobile phones and software solutions. Its product and project portfolio includes wireless applications, Internet, Intranet and client server applications for industries such as healthcare, ITES, business and entertainment. The company 's clients include international telecom giants such as Nokia, Ericsson and Siemens.

Seaview is one of the country 's largest IT Enabled Services companies offering medical transcription, legal transcription, business transcription undertaking of Kerala located at Athani, near Trichur. SIFL's diverse product mix includes complex and high precision forgings for defence, specialised forgings for aero and space research, heavy forgings for commercial vehicles and spares for light automobiles.

SunTec, a US$20 million company, provides transaction management solutions for the financial services and telecommunications industries. The company has developed billing systems for domestic clients such as the Department of Telecommunications, HFCL, Escotel 's ISP project, server and international clients such as KPN (Finnish), Essnet Cabletron and Tritone. The company currently offers solutions in the wireless, cable & broadband, wire line and Internet space. The company is based in Thiruvananthapuram.

Tata Consultancy Services, a US$2 billion IT services company, was one of the first IT companies to invest in the state. TCS has a state-of-the-art facility at the Techno park in Thiruvananthapuram. Today, this facility operates as a training college for new global recruits. TCS plans to operate another facility at Kochi. This centre will house about 600 software professionals and will serve as a base for software development and IT services to meet the requirements of both domestic and overseas customers.

Toonz Animation India Pvt. Ltd. is a world-class animation studio delivering content for Film, Television, DVD, Internet and other interactive platforms. Based in Trivandrum, Toonz is among the most advanced studios in the country and Kerala.

US Software, a wholly owned subsidiary of US Technologies, is one of the leading IT solution providers in the country and the company was established in 1999 at the Infotech Park in Thiruvananthapuram. The facility at Thiruvanathapuram is built on 180 acres and employs over 1,800 developmental resources. The facilities are connected by high bandwidth dedicated leased lines as well as Internet leased lines. It has emerged as a potential player in the international animation industry promoted by the Canada-based Comcraft Group.

Toonz Animations is a 100 per cent subsidiary of Multitech Investment, Mauritius. The company has successfully completed commercial films for clients such as Pepsi, Nestle, Bharat Gas, Coca-Cola, among others. Kerala Industrial Infrastructure Development Corporation (KINFRA) aims at bringing together all the suitable resources available in the state and developing infrastructure for industrial growth. KINFRA has identified over 20 core areas of competency. It has 12 well-defined industrial parks, each offering comprehensive infrastructure and support services to its clients.

Conclusion

Information is the backbone of every system and information technology is one of the key determinants of competitiveness and growth of firms and nations. Countries that invest in and adopt information technology quickly moves ahead and those who fail will be left behind. The role of IT is significant in underdeveloped countries like India and it is all the more important in a state like Kerala where there exists a backward industrial sector, high educated unemployment and maximum number of emigrants to the gulf countries. In this paper, we have made an attempt to examine the role of IT in Kerala. The specific objectives of the study were: to examine the role of IT in the Economic Development of Kerala; to evaluate the IT policy of the Government of Kerala and; to review the major problems with regard to software exports from Kerala along with the profile of key players. The study was on the basis of secondary data available from published sources. Our analysis shows that there are many ways that IT can contribute for the economic development of Kerala state. IT can accelerate industrialization of Kerala, can generate more and more employment opportunities, can increase export of software from Kerala, which in turn can raise the State Domestic Product and ultimately would result in the rapid economic development of the state. The government's IT policy can help to attract more and more investments in the IT sector of the state and it can also provide infrastructural facilities for IT companies which in turn will increase production and productivity, employment and income, demand for products and finally will boost the development of the state. The policy would attract more and more foreign investment in the IT sector in the state. The government should also provide a conducive and competitive climate for more and more investment in the IT sector in the state so as to create and build a strong IT infrastructure in the state. There is no doubt that Kerala can go a long way in economic development by promoting IT and ICT infrastructure, which will accelerate economic development. However, the benefits of IT will not automatically trickle down to the lower segments of the society. For this, the State should adopt special programmes like provision of training to the poor, which will spread the benefits of IT to the public in general, and to the poorer segments in particular in the State. Kerala state can overcome the current crisis and cope effectively with paradigm shift in the development strategy by utilizing information technology.

References

Arora, Ashish and Suma Athreye (2002), The Software Industry and India's Economic Development, *Information Economics and Policy*, 14, 253-273.

Arora, Ashish and V. S. Arunachalam, Jai Asundi and Ronald Fernandes (2000), 'The Globalization of Software: The Case of the Indian Software Industry', A Report Submitted to the Sloan Foundation, Carnegie Mellon University, Pittsburgh PA.

Arora, Ashish, V. S. Arunachalam, Jai Asundi and Ronald Fernandes (2001a), 'The Indian Software Service Industry', *Research Policy*, 30, 1267-1287.

Banerjee, Abhijit V. and Esther Duflo (2000), Reputation Effects and the Limits of Contracting: A Study of the Indian Software Industry, *Quarterly Journal of Economics*, 115, 3, 989-1017.

Basu, S. and Weil, D. N. (1998), Appropriate Technology and Growth, *Quarterly Journal of Economics*, 113, 4, 1025-1054.

Biswas, Soutik (2001), "Digital Empowerment-Seeds of E-volution", *Outlook* , April 9, New Delhi, *www.kerala.gov.in*

Chuang, Y. C. (1998), 'Learning by Doing, the Technology Gap, and Growth', *International Economic Review*, 39, 3, 697-721.

Dataquest (2001), 'SW INDUSTRY: Working Around the Slowdown', February 14.

Dossani, Rafiq and S. Manikutty (2000), 'Reforms in the Telecommunications Sector in India: An Institutional View', Paper Presented at Conference on Telecommunications Reform in India, Asia/Pacific Research Center, Stanford University, November 9 & 10.

Dudley, Leonard (1999), 'Communications and Economic Growth', *European Economic Review*, 43, 595-619.

Economic Review (Various Issues), 'State Planning Board', Government of Kerala, *www.it_taskforce.nic.in*

Economist, The (2001a), Another Kind of Net Work: Mobile Phones in India, March 3, 59.

Economist, The (2001b), Outsourcing to India: Back Office to the World, May 5, 59.

Eggleston, Karen, Robert Jensen and Richard Zeckhauser (2002), 'Information and Government of India', Ministry of Information Technology, *Annual Report 2000*, New Delhi.

Government of Kerala (2006), 'Economic Review', Thiruvanathapuram, State Planning Board.

Government of Kerala, IT Policy–Kerala. *www.akshaya.net*

Grossman, Gene and Elhanan Helpman (1991), '*Innovation and Growth in the Global Economy*', Cambridge, MA: MIT Press.

Hanna, Nagy (1994), 'Exploiting Information Technology for Development: A Case Study of India', World Bank Discussion Paper 246.

Harilal, K. N. and K. J. Joseph (2003), 'Stagnation and Revival of Kerala Economy An Open Economy Perspective', *Economic and Political Weekly*, Vol. XXXVIII, No. 23, June 7-13, pp. 2286-2294.

http://dqweek.ciol.com/content/search/showarticle.asp?artid=21244.

http://www. heinz.cmu.edu/project/india/publications.html.

Khoo, Ernest (2002), 'The Simputer: A Handheld for the Masses?', *CNET News.com,* January 11, *http://news.com.com/2100-1040-808321.html.*

Kremer, Michael (1993), 'The O-Ring Theory of Economic Development', *Quarterly Journal of Economics,* 108, 3, 551-575.

Miller, Robert R. (2001), 'Leapfrogging? India's Information Technology Industry and the Internet', IFC Discussion Paper No. 42, May, The World Bank, Washington, DC.

National Association of Software and Service Companies (2002a), 'Domestic IT Market', New Delhi, *http://www.nasscom.org/it_industry/domestic_it_market.asp.*

National Association of Software and Service Companies (2002b), Domestic software. New Delhi. *http://www.nasscom.org/it_industry/domestic_sw_services.asp.*

Pohjola, Matti (1998), 'Information Technology and Economic Development: An Introduction to the Research Issues', *WIDER Working Paper* No. 153, November, United Nations University.

Rao, M. Govinda, and Nirvikar Singh (2000), 'How to Think about Local Government Reform in India: Incentives and Institutions', Paper presented at International Conference on Second Generation Reforms in India, Madras School of Economics, Chennai.

Saxenian, AnnaLee (2000), 'The Bangalore Boom: From Brain Drain to Brain Circulation?', forthcoming in Kenneth Keniston and Deepak Kumar, eds., *Bridging the Digital Divide: Lessons from India,* Bangalore: National Institute of Advanced Study.

Singh, Nirvikar (2002), 'Information Technology as an Engine of Broad-Based Growth in India', in P. Banerjee and F. J. Richter (ed), *'The Future of India and Indian Busines'*, Macmillan, London.

Singh, Nirvikar and T. N. Srinivasan (2002), 'Indian Federalism, Economic Reform and Globalization', Paper for Comparative Federalism Project, CREDPR, Stanford.

Tschang, Ted (2001), 'The Basic Characteristics of Skills and Organizational Capabilities in the Indian Software Industry', *Working Paper* No. 13, ADSB Institute, Tokyo.

INFORMATION COMMUNICATION TECHNOLOGY AND GOVERNANCE IN KERALA

C. Krishnan

Introduction

Information Technology (IT) of today is what the steam engine was during the era of industrialization in Great Britain. So much has been said about the IT sector and its great growth potential in today's world economy. India, the home to the world's second largest population with poverty and illiteracy still remaining unabated, is regarded as one of the forerunners in the field of IT, and its migrated manpower has been recognized as the main force behind the IT growth of the USA. Thanks to its highly skilled manpower and English speaking population, India has been able to make a breakthrough in the field of IT. As a result, IT Products have become one of the major items in the export basket of India. The software sector witnessed unprecedented growth, with exports growing at annual growth rate of around 45 per cent. Seventy-five per cent of our software industry is exports, unlike China, where the domestic market consumes 75 per cent of the business. Barring a recent deceleration in IT exports owing to the appreciation of Indian currency against the US dollar; Indian

IT exports have shown tremendous improvement over the last years. It is argued that the main sector, which has reaped the benefits of liberalized economic environment, is the IT and IT Enabled Services (ITES).

A detailed analysis of the Indian IT industry conducted recently by the securities firm CLSA revealed that India's IT exports will cross the country's oil imports from 2007-08 onwards. It also exposed that 20-25 per cent of India's GDP expansion over the next three to four years will come from IT. Along with the competitive and productivity gains of IT, it is said that IT is an instrument of the country's strategic and economic diplomacy (Jairam Ramesh, 2007).

IT, undoubtedly, has fueled the growth of Indian economy over the recent years. However, IT and allied sectors have some negative impact on the overall growth process of the economy. It has less employment effect in terms of the employment of the unskilled workers, and it has resulted in the widening of the gulf between rural and urban areas. Since the sector has been awarded undue advantage of tax holidays, it has, in effect, eaten into the revenue sources of government. The irony here is that a sector, which is said to have been contributing immensely to the growth of economy, is not being properly taxed. Notwithstanding these negatives, one cannot downplay the impact that its products have made on the various spheres of economic activities. Sectors like finance, manufacturing, communication etc., have immensely been benefited by the boom of the IT sector as it has made their functions cost effective, efficient, time saving and transparent.

One important area where IT has proved itself to be useful is in the field of governance. With the implementation of IT in governance at various levels, we have now what is rightly called e-governance. E-governance has made the functioning of the government timely, cost-effective, accessible and transparent. Having given this bird's eye view of the IT sector, this paper attempts to:

- Trace out the evolution IT policy in Kerala and its relevance on governance;
- Review the major e-governance initiatives of Kerala, and

- To examine the impact that the IT has made in the field of e-governance with special reference to the most celebrated initiatives in Kerala viz., 'Friends'.

Methodology

This study mainly makes use of secondary data for the analysis. Articles, reports, seminar papers and authenticated books, newspaper reports, magazines, websites etc., have been used at appropriate places to get full grasp of the study. Informal talks held with experts pertaining to the field have been helpful in arriving some general comments on the subject.

Role of Technology in Development

The role of technology in the development process of an economy has been a subject matter of great debate. The Neo-classical growth model of Solow (1957) had recognized that technology is an important source of economic growth. Similarly, Griliches (1957), Arrow(1962) and Mansfield(1968) study the ways in which technology could lead to economic growth. Though there are various applications of IT in the society, this study focuses its attention on the role of ICT in governance. Since the late 1980s, good governance has been on the international development agenda. Good governance served as an orientation for state reforms and development since the requirements of transparency and efficient public service delivery would initiate market oriented growth(World Bank, 1992).

The potential of ICT in governance has been studied by many. It ranges from narrating country experiences to anecdotal accounts on specific projects. Much of the focus on e-governance has been on e-administration and e-services which would finally pave way for e-democracy (Heeks, 1999). In another occasion the same author (2001) provides an overview of the potential of ICT to promote good governance in developing countries by outlining three main contributions, namely, in the area of improving government process, connecting citizens and building external interactions. He also highlights the challenges posed by e-governance in terms of a country's e-readiness levels and e-governance models. Ndou (2004) suggests that e-government initiatives should be integrated with other development strategies and policies to ensure a broad based diffusion.

In the Indian context also, attempts have been made by some scholars to study the role and impact of e-governance. An overall view of the requirements of e-governance in various spheres is analysed by Bajaj (2000). Haque (2002) contends that beyond the issues of public access and participation, e-governance in India has not shown promising results even in terms of service delivery. Sreekumar (2002) found that many of the e-governance projects arise out of the relationships of community-led development and Civil Society Organisations (CSOs).

Aravindan's (2005) study tries to investigate the larger argument that ICT led e-governance strategies could lead to better outcomes, meet desired objectives and facilitate the empowerment of citizens when the pre-conditions in the form of 'development fundamental' are in place. The study serves as a detailed description of strategies and implementation of e-governance in the states of India. Rajagopalan (2007) argues that e-government can be a more productive version of government in general, if it is well implemented and managed. What stands in the way of good e-government and e-governance is the establishment resistance from many who do not wish to change the status quo, and public cynicism, the latter being a much larger issue above and beyond e-government and e-democracy

Another study (Rony Thomas Rajan, 2007) tries to evaluate as to how far the FRIENDS initiative could attain its objectives from a survey conducted among the customers and also tries to evaluate the long term sustainability of the project. Vittal (2007) has examined the role of IT and administration in government. He concluded that the IT in government would increasingly play a major role in keeping India a well governed country. The study by Rajeev Chawla and Anirban Mukerji (2007) describe some of the landmark e-governance projects implemented in Karnataka and their impact. An in-depth analysis of the projects like Bhoomi, Nemmadii, Bangalore One, Khajane and Kavery are done in this paper. The study by Kuriakose (2005) analyses the 'e-seva' e-governance experience of Andhra Pradesh.

IT and Governance

Information and Communication Technology (ICT) provides the basic tools required to eliminate some of the deficiencies in the present system of governance, to improve quality of service to the people and make it more responsive. ICT is a very useful means to ensure that the government reaches out to the people and that the people are able to reach the government with ease. The extensive use of Information and Communication Technology in every walk of life has redefined the fundamental principles of delivery of services and operation of service sectors, resulting in faster and easier delivery of much better services than before. Governments around the world have started realizing that the advancements in IT can as well be utilized to provide better services to citizens and business. As a result, a wide range of IT applications are being developed in various Government departments. Electronic Governance (popularly referred to as e-Governance) has emerged as a keyword for all such IT applications, that take advantage of IT to redefine the way the Government works. Its goal is to create a more responsive, productive and effective administration. E-Governance is also referred to as SMART Governance because it aims at using IT to the processes of Government functioning to bring about Simple, Moral, Accountable, Responsive and Transparent Governance.

The e-governance is much more than mere computerization of the activities of the departments or operations having public or citizen interface. This extended scope demands change in the mindsets of the legislature, executive and citizens. E-governance makes use of the Internet as a driving tool for providing essential services to the users. The Internet offers huge advantages for governance to turn around and create a special relationship with the people. With the wide acceptance of Internet, government and local bodies across the world have started initiating steps to modernize their operations using various IT tools. Like many corporate bodies, they are also facing key challenges of high quality service, transparent mechanisms, faster and quicker response. To meet the expectations of the citizens, the government/local bodies have started assuring people as well as foreign investors to provide single window processing of their requests offering 24-hour service, seven days a week. It is transforming the way public services are delivered. The Internet has enabled many governments to ensure transparency by providing information to citizens through websites and helping them to interact with the government effectively. The Government of Kerala took some initiatives in this direction and has already framed the Information Technology Policy.

There are two broad based uses of IT for improved government functioning. First, back office procedures can be made more efficient, so that internal record keeping flows of information, and tracking of decisions and performance can be improved.

Second, when some basic information is stored in digital form, it provides the opportunity of easier access to that information by citizens. The simplest examples are e-mailing requests or complaints, checking regulations on Web page, or print out forms from the Web so that a trip to pick up the forms from a physical office can be avoided.

Over a period of last few years, while referring e-governance, certain projects have kept coming up again and again as examples of successful experiments. Some of them are:

- Computer-aided registration of land deeds and stamp duties in Andhra Pradesh, reducing reliance on brokers and possibilities for corruption.
- Computerization of rural local government offices in Andhra Pradesh for delivery of statutory certificates of identity and landholdings substantially reducing delays.
- Computerized checkpoints for local entry taxes in Gujarat, with data automatically sent to a central database, reducing opportunities for local corruption.

- E-mail request for repairs to basic rural infrastructure such as hand pump, reducing reliance on erratic visits for government functionaries.
- FRIENDS, a consolidated bill payment sites in Kerala, allowing citizens to pay bills under seventeen different categories in one place, from electricity to university fees.
- Another area of governance where the IT has been effectively used is elections through electronic voting machines.
- The National Stock Exchange has been using IT extensively.
- The Railways have become an excellent role model in the use of IT.
- Uttaranchal's computer-aided education programme called 'Aarohi',
- E-Seva, an initiative of the government of Andhra Pradesh which involves offering different services to the citizens at one counter.

E-Governance Initiatives of Kerala

The Government of Kerala has a comprehensive view of ICT as a vehicle for transforming Kerala into a knowledge-based, economically vibrant, democratic State where the benefits of the transformation should reach every single citizen of the State. In order to materialize these objectives the State Government has initiated a number of measures. Kerala has been selected as the Second Best State in India in the implementation of e-governance. The award instituted by India-tech Foundation was declared at the Telecom India 2005 Seminar in Mumbai.

The Department of Information Technology was established in the year 1998 and a separate Kerala State IT Mission (KSITM) was constituted as an executive wing under the department that was entrusted with the implementation of various IT initiatives and the promotion of the State as a preferred destination of IT investments. In 1998, the State announced its first IT Policy which included aspects related to the development of a vibrant industry, infrastructure, human resources, IT applications in government and social informatics. Following a change of Government in the State, a 'New IT Policy 2001-05' on IT and ITES industry was announced in 2001. The policy supplemented the initiatives of computerization and automation of government departments which were prioritized on the basis of two parameters namely revenue earning capacity and the degree of citizen interface. The momentum for the promotion of IT in various spheres of the State economy came up seriously with the implementation of the Modernizing Government Programme (MGP) in 2002. MGP seeks to address the two core problems faced by the State, viz., decline in performance of public service system and the breakdown of the State finances. As a consequence, a series of 14 e-governance initiatives were identified that are believed to complement the implementation of MGP.

The most recent development in the State is the announcement of the IT Policy in 2007. We shall make a detailed discussion of this IT Policy for the benefit of the reader. The IT policy document "Information Technology Policy: Towards an inclusive knowledge society, 2007" (Government of Kerala) defines the Government's vision, mission and strategy for achieving the same. From the mission document, it is understood that the government is also committed to turn Kerala into a knowledge society with sustainable economic growth, social harmony and high quality of life for all. The Government considers its mission to achieve this vision through proactive measures meant to accelerate the process of transforming the State into a knowledge society. The government also realizes the importance of Free and Open Source Software(FOSS) and its usage. Considering the growing economic opportunities happening around FOSS, the Government also wishes to develop the State as the FOSS destination in the country.

To keep the traditions of the world's largest democratic country, the Government will ensure that all sections of the society are included in this process of transformation and will adopt conscious, positive steps to confirm the inclusion of the disadvantaged sections of society in the transformation process. The Government will also adopt such measures as are necessary to encourage the willful participation of the digitally privileged sections in the efforts to prevent the less privileged sections from getting marginalized in the transformation process.

The Government realizes that Free Software presents a truly unique opportunity in building a truly egalitarian knowledge society. Also The Government is of the view that knowledge generated through public funding should be freely available to the public. Since the basic philosophy of Free Software is nothing but sharing of knowledge, the Government will take all efforts to develop Free Software culture in the society and shall encourage and mandate the appropriate use of Free Software in all ICT initiatives. As a positive step, the government already started using GNU/Linux Operating System and software on these platforms in their departments.

Kerala's distinctive edge in ICT lies in the quality and adaptability of its human resources base. The high quality of manpower available can be leveraged not only for attracting IT investments into the major IT hubs of the State, but also to small towns spanning the entire length and breadth of the State. Kerala has the highest density of science and technology personnel in the country, with its engineering colleges producing more than 23,000 qualified engineers each year.

The Government feels that the ability to use ICT is just the basic requirement and not the fully sufficient condition to empower the society through ICT. The Government envisages making each citizen a creative participant and contributor of the Knowledge Society through the use of ICT. The Government will make use of ICT to ensure transparency, efficiency and quality of services to the citizens. Every village in Kerala will have presence in the Internet by 2010. This will contribute towards creation of local content and in the evolution of Kerala as a Knowledge Society. The State will also try to make maximum use of ICT in governance, to provide the best possible services to the citizen. The State will structure its e-governance projects based on the National e- Governance Plan and suggestions given by the National Knowledge Commission, in addition to locally relevant factors. Digital signature will be introduced in all departmental computerization processes, so as to ensure authenticity and integrity of electronic data interchange.

E-Governance Projects in Kerala

In line with the increasing role of IT in governance, the State Government has seriously involved in introducing several e-governance projects. At attempt is made here to briefly document them.

Friends

FRIENDS is an attempt by the Government of Kerala for citizen-government interface through ICT. This project cannot be highlighted as a successful solution for ICT diffusion but plausibly as an appropriate technology solution for citizen needs. FRIENDS (Fast, Reliable, Instant, Effective, Network for Disbursement of Services), a "Single Window Mechanism" is based on the concept of using ICT for better citizen-government interface. The idea of Friends has its origin from the e-seva project of Andhra Pradesh. "Friends" was introduced on an experimental basis in Trivandrum in June 2000. Now it provides services in all the fourteen districts of Kerala.

The salient feature of the project is the effective integration of IT and logistics for citizen services. Payments to departments/organizations under the Government of Kerala and Government of India like KSEB/KWA/Local Bodies/Civil Supplies/Revenue/Motor vehicles/Universities/BSNL can be made in the FRIENDS centres. . The Centres work from 9.00 AM to 7.00 PM on all days including Sundays, except national holidays. The counters are equipped to handle around 1000 types of bills (in various combinations) originating from various departments. The overall investment in FRIENDS Centres amounts to Rs. 4.50 Crores. Each FRIENDS centre has multiple counters and the citizens can remit any payment at any counter. Citizens who walk into a FRIENDS center are issued tokens, and queue management is also computerized, minimizing waiting time. FRIENDS Janasevana Kendram, Thiruvananthapuram has been awarded **ISO 9001:2000** Certification for its citizen friendly services and quality standards. FRIENDS collection and transaction is increasing day–by day as the public acceptance to the project is found to be growing, as shown in Table 1.

Table 1
Collection and Transaction of FRIENDS (Rs. Crores)

Year	*2000-01*	*2001-02*	*2002-03*	*2003-04*	*2004-05*
Collection	5.30	106.20	52.30	158.80	202.00
Transaction	1237.09	10269.19	20238.11	26680.71	34001.81

E-payment Facility (E-pay)

E-pay is an on-line bill payment facility introduced by Government of Kerala through Akshaya e-kendras as an extension of FRIENDS project in Malappuram district during August 2004. Presently, facility for remitting KSEB and BSNL (mobile and landline) bills are available in e-pay facility. Internet banking facility of State Bank of India is being used for transferring funds. The details of the bills remitted by Akshaya entrepreneurs are communicated to KSEB/BSNL through the Malappuram FRIENDS Centre. At present 162 e-payment centres are functioning in Malappuram district.

Akshaya

Akshaya e-literacy programme is one of the champion pilot projects of the State commenced operation in December 2002 in Malappuram district. The State facilitated the entry of entrepreneurs using a Public-Private Partnership(PPP) model and sought to address the problem of digital divide. The aim of the project initially was to train at least one person in every household in the district in basic computer skills. It is one of the world's largest e-literacy drives, to reach over 6 lakh households, representing more than 3.6 million people, in less than 6 months. The project has now evolved into an e-governance platform for various Government-Citizen interactions. The focus of Akshaya will be for 'making technology and e-government services accessible to common man'. The Akshaya e-centres also intend to deliver several value added services to the people. E-payment, e-learning, e-business etc., are the priority objectives of the Akshaya e-centres. The Akshaya will tailor its services on locally relevant themes and in Malayalam language, so that it will be directly relevant to the ordinary people. Akshaya is now operational in all the districts of the State.

Other Major E-governance Projects

Citizen Call Centre

The Citizen Call Centre, first of its kind in the country, set–up in the State capital, provides information on transactions pertaining to various Government Departments which are required by common citizens, over telephone. The information, which can be ascertained, includes details of Government schemes/programmes/entitlements/welfare benefits etc., modalities of accessing such entitlements/benefits etc., procedures for availing such benefits and receiving various kinds of certificates (Eg.: - nativity, caste, transfer of residence etc.) can be had from the Citizen Call Centre by dialing the telephone No. 155300. The Call Centre is equipped with full-fledged data base having details of more than 200 Government processes and with key search facilities incorporated in the software for speed access.

Information Kerala Mission (IKM)

IKM seeks to computerize and establish a statewide network connecting State Planning Board and its 14 District Offices, Directorate of Panchayath and its 14 District Offices, Directorate of Urban Affairs and its 3 Regional Offices, 1219 local bodies and to develop a mechanism for the regular monitoring of the plan implementation and targets achieved by the local bodies over the network. The project is the single largest computerization programme for local bodies involving deployment of software developed in an Indian language in the country. IKM which has successfully implemented Jansevana Kendras in all Municipalities, has piloted the Panchayath Computerisation projects in two Panchayaths, Vellanad and Talikkulam, by making them the first 'Computerized Panchayaths in the country. IKM is also implementing another project called the 'Hospital Kiosks' connecting all hospitals of the five cities of the State with the respective Corporation offices for on-line registration of birth and death.

Secretariat WAN

Government has decided to set up a Secretariat Wide Area Network (Sec. WAN) connecting the Secretariat, Secretariat Annex, Vikas Bhavan and Public Office Complex located in Thiruvananthapuram. At present, there are 1400 computers (approx) installed in the Secretariat, out of which about 500 numbers works in the networked environment. It is planned to enhance this facility up to 3000 numbers in the final phase. The tele-printer system for connectivity of the Secretariat to all the District Headquarters, Advocates General's Office and the office of the Special Representative in New Delhi has already been replaced by a network of computers at all these locations, called 'Internet Based Messaging System'.

Knowledge Archive System for Secretariat (K-BASE)

Effective knowledge management solution is also planned by the implementation of Knowledge Archive System (K-BASE) in the Government Secretariat. Main objectives of K-BASE include the creation of knowledge repositories for effective decision support system, improve the speed/transparency/ objectivity/consistency in decision making and to provide public access to important Acts, Rules and Orders of the Government.

D.C. Suite

The pilot phase of DC Suite was launched in District Collectorate, Palakkad on 26th October 2004. It is an integrated suite of applications for the Collectorate.

Smart Move

The Motor Vehicles Department has implemented a software, viz., 'Smart Move' that enables them to offer test on any working day, issue of license immediately on passing the test and selection of the test date by the applicant.

TRIMS

In order to streamline the working of all treasuries, the e-governance project TRIMS is implemented in the State. All activities from bill submission to payment can be done through this programme.

Thozhil

This project of Employment Exchanges provides for online renewal of registration, addition of experience certificate, search for vacancies etc.

Pearl

This is a package implemented in the Registration Department that provide for the automation of Sub Registrar Offices, registration of documents within 15 minutes, computerized encumbrance certificate, stamp duty and fee worked out automatically, prevention of loss and damage of document.

Swift

This is a system of a common application form designed for all the certificates issued from Taluk Offices.

Other notable IT initiatives of the State include, IT @ School, KISSAN, e-Krishi, Education Grid, Treasury Network, Tele-medicine, Police portal and so on.

E-governance in Kerala: A Case Study of Friends

As mentioned elsewhere in this paper, FRIENDS brought in the concept of 'Single Window' for the citizen to pay various taxes and utility bills to the government. A citizen of the state of Kerala is expected to pay utility bills or taxes to at least seven departments. For this he will have to pay it at the department counters. It creates many problems to the citizens. In fact, this has led to the creation of a one stop ICT enabled payment counter project, FRIENDS where the payments to all these seven plus departments could be made. The counters are equipped to handle around 1000 types of bills originating out of the various departments as listed below:

- KSEB (power) Bill
- KWA (Water) Bill
- BSNL (Telephone) Bill
- Local Body
  - Property Tax
  - Professional Tax
  - Traders License Fee
- Revenue Department
  - Building Tax
  - Basic Tax
  - Revenue Recovery
- Civil Supplies
  - Fee for new ration card and various certificates
  - Fee for trade licenses-11 types
- Motor Vehicles
  - One time vehicle tax
  - Motor vehicle tax-105 types
  - Fee for Licenses from Motor vehicles Department-20 types
  - Fee for permits from Motor Vehicles Department-142 types
  - Registration fee for Motor vehicles-37 types
  - Fee for Fitness Certificate of Motor Vehicles
- University
  - University exam fee-352 types
  - Fees (General)-96 types.

A study conducted on the customers of FRIENDS by Rony Thomas Rajan (2007) gives encouraging results, which is an eye opener to the fact that people greatly appreciate this type of IT enabled services. We repeat the major finding of this study for the reference of readers. This study has been considered for reproduction because it covers sample from the three geographical regions of the State namely, Thiruvananthapuram, Ernakulam and Kozhikode. It was revealed that out of the 375 respondents of the study 76.26 per cent were households and only 23.73 per cent were shops, which is evident to the fact that households in Kerala find "FRIENDS" as more useful. Similar findings were also brought out by Aravindan (2005).

Table 2
Profile of the Customers of Friends

District	*Households*	*Shops*	*Total*
Trivandrum	68 (54)	57 (46)	125 (100)
Ernakulam	106 (85)	19 (15)	125 (100)
Kozhikode	112 (89.6)	13 (10.4)	125 (100)
Total	286 (76.27)	89 (23.73)	375 (100)

Source: Rony Thomas Rajan, Proceedings of the UGC sponsored national Seminar, Government College, Kodanchery.

The study also brings to light the fact that officials dealing with customers at the FRIENDS have shown more friendliness towards the customers compared to the officials at the department counter. Customer friendliness was done on a five-point scale and the average was taken. In this point 5 was assigned for the officials being friendly and 1 assigned for officials being not at all friendly. The results are encouraging as evident from the following table.

Table 3
Customer Friendliness of official of the FRIENDS and the Department Counter

District	*FRIENDS*	*Department Counter*
Trivandrum	3.61	2.53
Ernakulam	4.72	3.38
Kozhikode	4.70	2.21

Source: Ibid.

Another encouraging results of the study is that the number of customers who faced problems while dealing with the officials of the FRIENDS was also very marginal. This is apparent from the table given below.

Table 4
Distribution of Customer who Faced Problems after Using Friends Counter

District	*Payment not Accounted*	*Warning notice issued*	*No problems Encountered*	*Total*
Trivandrum	6	1	118	125
	(4.8)	(0.8)	(94.4)	(100.0)
Ernakulam	3	0	122	125
	(2.4)		(97.6)	(100.0)
Kozhikode	17	3	105	125
	(13.6)	(2.4)	(84)	(100.0)
Total	20	3	352	375
	(5.3)	(0.8)	(93.9)	(100.0)

Source: Ibid.

People living in an environment of fast life prefer services, which are speedy, transparent, efficient, and time saving. The coming up of ICT and its vast use in the governmental functions has surely helped people in getting their works done in a stipulated time and in an effective manner. Therefore, it is not surprising that more that 90 per cent of the customers surveyed have shown preference to FRIENDS than that of the corresponding departmental counters. Similar observation was found in the study by Madon and Kiran (2002) where it was pointed out that 97 per cent of the users surveyed preferred FRIENDS to departmental counters. Table 5 is a testimony to it.

Table 5
Preference of FRIENDS to Department Counter

District	*Yes*	*No*	*Total*
Trivandrum	123	2	125
	(98.4)	(1.6)	(100)
Ernakulam	123	2	125
	(98.4)	(1.6)	(100)
Kozhikode	99	26	125
	(79.2)	(20.8)	(100)
Total	345	30	375
	(92)	(8)	(100)

Source: Ibid.

Regarding the question of whether information technology should be used for improving the efficiency of the government machinery, a significant percentage(86) customers of FRIENDS is of the view that IT can enhance the quality of services being delivered by the government to its citizens, and therefore IT should be used in all possible areas of government functioning.

Conclusion and Suggestions

As mentioned at the very outset, this paper intends to depict the growth of ICT sector and its impact on governance in Kerala. A study on "FRIENDS" is mainly intended to bring out the extent to which IT has become useful to the citizens. The study, taking evidences from various sources, has arrived at the conclusion that, notwithstanding its enclave nature, IT sector has become an engine of growth in India nowadays. It has, beyond doubt, become a major item in the export basket of India. What the mushrooming growth of this sector requires is sustained improvement in basic infrastructure like road, rail, air connectivity and electricity. It is also a matter of concern that although India has been a forerunner in the IT services, it has not become a major IT producer. Many of the IT products are still imported in India. Hence, it is imperative that in the coming years India should give more thrust to the IT production sector from where it is possible to tap more foreign exchange for Indian economy. Our discussion on the study of FRIENDS has proved that common men respond positively to the use of IT, and hence it calls for the widespread application in various spheres of human activities including the functions of the government.

Another area of concern in the progress of IT sector is the growing gulf between the rural and urban areas in India primarily due to the flourishing of IT industries in urban areas. Although Kerala has a literacy level of 90.92 per cent, the population connected to Internet remains shockingly below 1 per cent, the issues relating to lack of connectivity remain a big problem. Though several e-governance initiatives have been launched simultaneously, most of the projects have not been able to make substantial headway and many of them continue to lag without any time-frame for implementation (Indian Express, 2004). Hence, e-governance projects are no longer just a fancy for those who want to show off, nor are they merely a source of big orders for hardware/software vendors, they are now an integral part of any serious governance efforts. Though several e-governance projects have been evolved and implemented over the years both at the Centre and States, the success rate of them in terms of their impact need careful consideration. In the Kerala context, FRIENDS and AKSHAYA have become more popular and rated high, while other initiatives are yet to catch up.

References

Aravindan S. (2005), *Exploring E-governance for Development: A Comparative Analysis of Two Southern States of India,* M. Phil Dissertation submitted to Jawaharlal Nehru University, Centre for Development Studies, Thiruvananthapuram.

Arrow, K. J. (1962), "The Economic Implications of Learning by Doing", *Review of Economic Studies,* Vol. 29, pp. 155-173.

Bajaj, K. K. (2000), "Citizen-IT Interface", *Electronic Information and Planning,* March-April.

Chawla, Rajeev and Anirban Mukerji (2007), "E-governance Initiatives of Karnataka", *Yojana,* Vol. 51, pp. 26-29.

Editorial, (2004), "Many Projects Fail to Make Head Way", *Indian Express,* Thiruvananthapuram, October, 19.

Griliches, Z. (1957), "Hybrid Cone: An Exploration in the Economics of Technological Change", *Econometrica,* Vol. 48, pp. 501-522.

Haque, Shamsul, M. (2002), "E-governance in India: Its Impacts on Relations among Citizens, Politicians and Public Servants", *International Review of Administrative Services,* Vol. 68, pp. 231-250.

Heeks, R. (1999), *Reinventing Government in the Information Age,* London: Routledge.

Heeks, R. (2001), *Understanding E-governance for Development,* IDPM Working Paper, No. 11, University of Manchester.

Kuriakose, P. M. (2005), "Citizen's Right to Convenience and Comfort", *Yojana,* Vol. 49, pp. 70-71.

Madon, Shirin and Kiran, G. R. (2002), *Information Technology for 'Citizen-Government' Interface: A Study of FRIENDS Project in Kerala*, World Bank Study.

Mansfield, E. (1968), *Industrial Research and Technological Innovation*, New York: W.W. Norton.

Nambiar, A. C. K. (2005), Decentralised Planning and E-governance, in A.C.K. Nambiar and C. R. Pathak (ed), *Decentralised Planning and E-Governance in India: Problems and Prospects*, Department of Economics, University of Calicut.

Ndou, V. (2004), "E-government for Developing Countries: Opportunities and Challenges", *Electronic Journal on Information Systems in Developing Countries (EJISDC)*, Vol. 8, No. 1, pp. 1-24.

Rajagopalan, A. (2007), "E-governance—ICT Policy and Strategy of Kerala" in Krishnan C. (ed.), *E-Governance in Kerala*, Proceedings of the UGC Sponsored National Seminar, Department of Economics, Government College, Kodanchery, Kerala, March.

Rajan, Rony Thomas (2007), "E-governance in Kerala: A Study of FRIENDS", in Krishnan C. (ed.), *E-Governance in Kerala*, Proceedings of the UGC Sponsored National Seminar, Department of Economics, Government College, Kodanchery, Kerala, March.

Ramesh, Jairam (2007), "Big Successes, Large Gaps", *Yojana*, Vol. 51, pp. 1-2.

Seshagiri, N. (2007), "IT: Ambience for Growth", *Yojana*, Vol. 51, pp. 12-16.

Solow, R. (1957), "Technical Change and the Aggregate Production Function", *Review of Economics and Statistics*, Vol. 39, pp. 312-320.

Sreekumar, T. T. (2002), Civil Society and ICT-based Models of Rural Change: History Rhetoric and Practice, Paper prepared for International Seminar on "*ICTs and Indian Development: Processes, Prognosis and Policies*", Bangalore, 9-11, December.

Vijaybhaskar, M. and Gayathri, V. (2003), "ICT and Indian Development: Processes, Prognoses, Policies", *Economic and Political Weekly*, Vol. 38, No. 24, pp. 2360-2364.

Vittal, N. (2007), "IT and Administration in Government", *Yojana*, Vol. 51, pp. 23-25.

World Bank (1992), *Governance and Development*, Washington: World Bank.

PART–VII

DEMOCRATIC DECENTRALISATION IN KERALA

DEMOCRATIC DECENTRALISATON IN KERALA

M. N. Sudhakaran

Participatory development is accepted as a strategy of development and democratic decentralisation is being increasingly experimented all over the world to enhance the quality of governance (Fung and Wright 2003). Participation, it is argued, would strengthen democracy and thus promote good governance (Blair 2000). The proximity between the state and the people facilitates better understanding of the needs of the people. Moreover, bringing people closer to the administration will facilitate tapping of the creativity and resources of local communities by providing opportunity to participate in development (Crook and Manor 1998). The involvement of the people and utilisation of their knowledge and expertise will make development sustainable. This requires regular involvement of the people not only in identifying development needs but also in seeking solutions. The most important aspect of participation is effective devolution of power to the people so that they have a decisive role in making decisions concerning them. Moreover, participation also creates opportunities for the marginalised sections to influence decisions (Eversole 2003). The interest in decentralisation as an engine of economic growth is not limited to the developing and transitional countries, but has emerged as an agenda of the developed countries too (World Bank 2004).

The rationale for decentralisation can be broadly classified into efficiency arguments and democratisation arguments. Economists justify decentralisation on the ground of allocative efficiency. In the case of stabilisation function it will be better performed by central government than by local government. Because of the small size of the local government, expenditure multiplier will be low and fiscal policy will have less impact. Similarly, local bodies may not be effective in the operation of redistributive policy (Musgrave 1959). Decentralisation enhances both static and dynamic efficiency in the production of public goods. Oates (1972) argues that welfare maximisation takes place only when services are provided considering the spatially differentiated taste and preference of the people. The allocative efficiency may be high due to the decentralised provision of public goods and services in accordance with local preferences. In addition, the technical efficiency also may be high due to the utilisation of local resources and technology. Tiebout (1956) argues that welfare gains are increased with decentralisation, since allocation of public services can be done by governments taking into account the preferences of those most directly affected which facilitates the avoidance of the dead weight losses. The closeness of points of decision-making and action reduces the cost of information (Marschac 1959). Efficiency, accountability, manageability and autonomy are the acclaimed advantages of decentralisation (Shah 1991). Democratic decentralisation improves the efficiency of implementation, particularly when the development process is made participatory and transparent. Effective monitoring during implementation prevents misuse of resources. Moreover, community participation can mobilise human resources to create community assets.

Democratisation argument focuses mainly on deepening and widening of democracy. Decentralistion facilitates direct democracy in which everybody participates in decision-making. Participation as an end envisages transferring of power in which the excluded groups are able to influence the decision-making in favour of them. It is a way of empowering people by enabling them to make their own analysis, take their own decisions, open out their perspective and act on their own. This will reverse the power relations. The broad aim of participatory development is to increase the involvement of socially and economically marginalised people in decision making over their own lives (Shaw 1991). Participation as a means aims at improved delivery system. It may be used to harness resources, to share information, to reduce resistance to projects or programmes by receiving their consent. The means approach is called 'instrumental' participation, wherein, the approach is often 'top down' in which participants are treated as tools. The 'end' perspective is called 'transformational' in which there is empowered participation. It is participation, which affirms faith in the capability of the people, hence, it is presumed that people know their problems and means to redress it (Chambers 1997) and are capable of alternating their conditions.

This paper examines the democratic decentralistion in Kerala. It has V parts. Part I examines the evolution of local governments in Kerala. Part II examines the architecture of decentralisation in Kerala and part III examines the decentralised planning experience. Part IV analyses the participation in planning and part V examines the impact on outcome.

PART–I

Decentralisation in Kerala

Public activism can influence governmental policies particularly in promoting positive functions of the government. These positive functions include the provision of public services such as health care, child immunisation, primary education, social security, environmental protection and rural infrastructure. The vigilance and involvement of the public can be quite crucial not only in ensuring adequate expansion of these services, but also in monitoring their services (Dreze and Sen 1995). Kerala's higher level of Physical Quality of Life index (PQLI) has been primarily due to the tradition of having a high level of political participation and activism. Quality of life benefits are relatively fairly distributed among men and women, urban and rural, low and high castes (Franke and Chasin 1992). The mass movements played an important role in this change and this tradition is an asset for launching developmental programmes with people's participation.

Prior to the formation of Kerala state in 1956, local bodies existed, but were different in the three regions of Travancore, Cochin and Malabar. In Travancore, the earliest legislation relating to local self government was passed in 1894, when Town Improvement Committees were set up in Thiruvananthapuram, Nagarcoil, Quilon, Alappey and Kottayam. Later in 1925, it was extended to rural areas by a regulation called Village Panchayat Regulation VII of 1100 ME (GoK 1985). The duties were classified as obligatory and discretionary. The village panchayats were vested with the power of taxation. Only seven village panchayats were constituted. Subsequently, to foster and encourage rural development, the Travancore Village Union Act was enacted in 1940. Village unions had almost the same functions and fiscal powers as those of the earlier panchayats. Thus, there were two categories of panchayats in Travancore.

In 1871, the Local Funds Act of Madras was passed, following Mayo's resolution. Thus, a Local Fund Circle with a Local Board was constituted in the erstwhile Malabar district. In 1884, Madras Local Board Act was passed. The Madras District Municipalities Act and Madras Village Panchayat Act were passed in 1920. The entire Malabar area was not covered by these panchayats. The areas, which were not covered by the panchayats, were under the administrative jurisdiction of District Board. District Boards derived income from professional tax, education cess, surcharge on stamp duty, license fees and grants-in-aid by government (GoK 1958). In 1930, the Village Panchayat Act was abolished and panchayats were included with in the scope of Madras Local Boards Act. Another step was taken when the Local Boards were filled by election.

In Cochin State, civic administration was first introduced in the form of Sanitary Boards in towns in 1902. They were reconstituted as town councils in 1909. Village panchayats were established in 1913. Initially there were five panchayats, which increased to eighty-seven by 1934. The important activities of panchayats were construction and maintenance of minor irrigation, village roads, canals, supply of drinking water, sanitation, supervision of elementary education etc. (GoK 1958).

There were 100 panchayats in the Cochin area at the time of integration of Travancore and Cochin in 1949. The total number of panchayats at the time of formation of Kerala state was 852, governed by two panchayat laws- the Madras Village Panchayat Act of 1950, applicable to the Malabar and Kasaragod area and the Travancore-Cochin Panchayats Act of 1950, applicable to the Travancore-Cochin region. The Kerala Panchayat Act of 1960, which came into force in 1962, superseded these two acts. The three-tier system of panchayati raj administration, as suggested by Balwant Ray Mehta was not introduced. Village panchayats were only constituted at the lowest level.

The first Administrative Reforms Committee (1958) chaired by Chief Minister E M Sankaran Nampoothirippad (EMS) argued for a two-tier set up of panchayats and municipalities at the grassroots and district council. The committee went much beyond the Balwant Ray Mehta[1] committee, which looked at the panchayat raj institutions as popular development agencies. Participation was emphasised. Panchayats should have functional committees for different subjects like sanitation, communications, public health, education, etc consisting of both panchayat members and representatives of local inhabitants. The work of these committees should be complementary to that of panchayats (GoK 1958). The District Council Bill introduced in the assembly in 1958 was a comprehensive one which could co-ordinate functions of both panchayats and municipalities. The bills could not be passed since the ministry was dismissed by the central government in 1959. The legislation passed in 1960 was a diluted version of the draft bill proposed by the EMS ministry. The role of panchayats was limited to civic duties and the district council was not a part of it (Isaac and Franke 2000). For urban areas, Municipalities Act 1960 and Kerala Municipal Corporation Act 1961 were passed.

The second ministry of EMS again proposed a two-tier system- village panchayat at the lower level and zilla parishad (district council) at the district level. The bill also lapsed since the ministry fell in 1969. The Kerala District Administration Bill was introduced in 1971, re-introduced again in 1978 and finally passed in 1979, when Mr. A. K. Antony was the chief minister. But, District Council election was conducted only in February 1990 by the Left Democratic Front (LDF) and District Councils were constituted in March 1990. This aroused much enthusiasm for making the district governments. But, the hope was short-lived since the first decision of the new government, which came to power in Kerala in 1991, was to amend the District Administration Act and to limit the powers of the District Councils. The offices and institutions transferred to District Councils were taken back.

In Kerala too, there were no periodic elections to the local bodies. Withdrawal of powers also had taken place with the change in rule of the state, which influenced the functioning of the local bodies. Constitutional support was a welcome step in Kerala as well. The 73rd and 74th constitutional amendments came into force in 1993. A three-tier panchayati raj structure became inevitable. The Kerala Panchayat Raj Act (1994) and Kerala Municipalities Act (1994) were passed in conformity with the 73rd and 74th Constitutional Amendments. Election to local bodies was held in 1995 and the local bodies were constituted on 2nd October 1995.

Decentralisation of Planning in Kerala

Indian constitution assigns an important role for state-level planning. The subject of "Social and Economic Planning" has been included in the concurrent list of the constitution. But planning at sub-state level was not significant. It was only in the early 1970s the District Planning Offices were started. A significant step in the direction of decentralised planning was taken in mid-1980s with decentralisation of Special Component

Plan (SCP) and Tribal Sub Plan (TSP). Decentralisation of SCP and TSP had a positive impact on the functioning of the schemes. But, these plans were bureaucratic and departmental without any participation of the people.

The government took serious efforts towards setting up district councils in the state. The draft approach paper for the VII plan proposed by the State Planning Board emphasised decentralisation of planning. The District Development Council (DDC) was given the duty of preparing the district plan in consultation with the Block Planning Committee (BPC) and Grama Panchayat Committees. The DDC was to set apart a portion of the district allocation for district level schemes and apportion the rest on a clearly set out formula to various development blocks. The district level department officers prepared schemes for district level allocation while the BPC in consultation with grama panchayats prepared schemes for block level allocation. The sub-committees were to integrate the district and block level proposals into sectoral plan and into a comprehensive plan for the district to be placed for the DDC. The district collector was in charge of the overall programme in each district. The plans approved by the DDC were to be forwarded to the Sate Planning Board for inclusion in the state plan.

The formation of district councils aroused hope for decentralised planners. The annual plan of 1991-92 had earmarked Rs. 250 crores to be implemented by the newly formed District Councils. In addition, the plan also provided Rs. 18 crores to grama panchayats. As mentioned earlier, the change in government at the state level resulted in withdrawal of powers and finances earmarked for District Councils.

Election to the panchayats and municipalities was held in 1995. For the financial year 1996-97, the last year of eighth plan–the plan allocation to the grama panchayat was significantly increased to Rs. 212 crores (Isaac1999). There was a change in guard at the state level in 1996. One of the major decisions of the new LDF government was to earmark 35-40 per cent of the state plan outlay to local bodies and to launch the 'People's Campaign for Ninth Plan'. In order to make recommendations as regards strengthening of democratic decentralisation the Government appointed the Committee on Decentralisation of Powers (popularly known as Sen Committee) under the chairmanship of Subrato Sen[2], which submitted report in 1997, with valuable suggestions that paved the way for major amendments of the Kerala Panchayat Raj Act 1994 and Kerala Municipality Act 1994 in 1999.

PART–II

The Architecture of Decentralisation

The architecture of decentralisation is important since the outcome depends primarily on this. Political decentralisation–the devolution of power to the lower tiers-is the crucial aspect in this. The architecture of democratic decentralisation in Kerala has four dimensions-Functional, financial, administrative and planning.

The Functional Architecture of Decentralisation

Planning by the local bodies is possible only if necessary power has been devolved to them. Thus, political decentralisation is a pre-condition for successful decentralisation of planning. Defining the functional domain of each local body is the crucial aspect of democratic decentralisation, in which the demarcation of functions of each layer of government is specified. If the local bodies are to function as genuine local self-government institutions, functional autonomy is essential, which also requires precise definition of functions assigned. Functional co-ordination among different tiers of government is needed to avoid duplication and gaps.

The Kerala Panchayat Raj Act 1994 is far ahead of other states in the matter of devolution of functions. (World Bank 2004, 2005, Narayana 2005). However, the amendment in 1999 (Act 13 of 1999) made it more comprehensive in terms of functional devolution, following the recommendation of Sen Committee. The amendments enhanced the role of local bodies and brought more clarity in the functions of different tiers. The range of functions of local bodies can be classified as:

regulatory functions like regulation of buildings, mandatory functions, which are to be performed by the panchayats concerned, general functions, which are more of directive principles, promotional functions, which deal more with motivating groups of people, agency functions where the panchayat is an agent of the government as in the execution of certain works, managerial functions where the panchayat manages institutions and agencies transferred to it, shared developmental functions where for a particular development area both the state and the panchayat have different roles to be played together or separately, supportive development functions where the panchayat complements or fills up gaps in the development plans for the two tiers, autonomous development functions when the panchayat is solely responsible for performing such functions (GoK 1997).

Grama Panchayat Functions

The Grama Panchayat (GP) has been given prime importance in functional devolution. Mandatory functions are for GP only and many regulatory functions have been given. Many functions are civic functions or provision of local public goods such as roads, waterways, street lights, drainage, solid waste management, public markets, burial grounds, bathing places, ferries, parking places, waiting sheds etc. The regulatory functions assigned to the GP are regulating building construction, slaughtering of animals, sales of meat, fish and perishable articles, regulating eating places, prevention of adulteration, regulation of fairs and festivals, licensing of destructive and offensive trades. Environmental protection, registration of birth and death, immunisation, vector control, and management of stray dogs are also the mandatory functions. Interestingly, the allocation of functions appears to be in conformity with the subsidiarity principle. These activities do not have much cross-boarder spill over effects.

The general functions of the GP are mainly promotional in nature. They include collection of data, organising voluntary work, campaigning for thrift, neighbourhood groups and self help groups, ensure people's participation, generation of communal harmony and awareness building on civic duties. The sectoral functions are mainly developmental, managerial and welfare oriented. Nineteen sectors have been listed in the Act. Cultivation of wasteland, optimum utilisation of land, soil protection, production of organic manure, establishment of nurseries etc are some of the developmental functions in the agriculture. Similar list has been given for each sector. Management of the institutions transferred to the local bodies such as *Krishi Bhavan*, veterinary hospitals, primary health centres, primary schools, and nursery schools for Scheduled Castes (SCs) and Scheduled Tribes (STs) is the function of GP. Obviously, sectoral and managerial functions mentioned here are unlikely to be watertight compartments. They will dependent on activities taken up by other tiers of government as well as the non-governmental sectors. As such overlaps, duplication etc, cannot be overlooked.

Many welfare functions have been assigned to the GP. Identification of the homeless and provision of dwellings, implementation of family welfare programmes, running of *Anganwadies*, sanctioning and distribution of various pension schemes for the poor, implementation of poverty alleviation programmes, protection of relief works are some of the welfare functions assigned. The promotional functions are the development of co-operatives, self help groups among farmers, planting of trees, promotion of cottage industries, handicrafts, traditional industries, encouragement of use of biogas etc. The implementation of various schemes of central and state governments is also the function of the local bodies so that it performs the agency function.

Functions of Block and District Panchayats

Only limited functions have been envisaged for Block Panchayat (BP). The general functions mainly consist of providing technical advice to the GPs, utilisation of technical expertise at Block level and preparation of complementary schemes to that of GP. The District Panchayat (DP) is the apex of local bodies, but each layer is autonomous. The general functions of the DP are similar to the BP such as mobilisation of technical expertise and provision of technical advice to BPs and GPs and Municipalities and preparing complementary schemes for the programmes at lower levels. The sectoral functions for BP as well as DP have been specified in the Act.

The functional distribution appears to be relatively well-defined and clear in the case of mandatory functions. There is a fair degree of role clarity, which reduces probability of overlaps, conflicts, and confusion. General functions, which are promotional in nature, need not also give rise to confusion and conflicts. However, this is not true of sectoral functions. The constitution and the Act leave many open-ended questions regarding division of responsibilities and powers across different tiers of government. In Kerala, the government issued rules and orders to settle issues that arose on account of lack of role clarity. In spite of such timely intervention grey areas continue to exist creating problems such as overlaps, duplication etc.

In devolving functions, the GP is considered as the vital institution. Provision of local public goods and regulatory functions are with them. In the developmental role also GP is given primacy. The DP has an important role in managing important institutions and co-ordinating various activities. Complementary activities to the lower tiers of government are assigned to the DP. The BP has a relatively insignificant role. Promotional and agency role have been given to it. The DP is not endowed with powers to function as district government. Lack of clarity of functions among the three tiers of local government is a major lacunae in the functional devolution. Lack of co-ordination and consequent operational difficulties among the tiers may lead to inefficiency. But, precise assigning of function is not easy at the outset, since, much can be learned only from experience.

The GP is the lowest tier, which is closer to the people, hence, activities related to everyday life of the people need to be assigned to it. Many welfare functions have been given to the GP, such as, provision of houses, house sites, shelter up-gradation, running of *Anganwadies,* distribution of various pensions, employment schemes for poor and women.

Assigning functions without providing sufficient finance will drain the credibility of these institutions. The State and Central governments have the responsibility to finance these programmes. Withdrawal of governments from the welfare functions placing the responsibility on the local bodies is not justifiable. A mechanism for flow of funds to the local bodies along with functions shall be ensured. Allocation of welfare functions, without ensuring finance either through assigned taxation rights or through guaranteed grants-in-aid can lead to major developmental crisis in the future.

The Architecture of Fiscal Decentralisation

Strengthening local governance requires substantial fiscal devolution to local bodies. When the authority of a specific activity is transferred from the state to local government, the latter should have the prerogative of taking decisions in respect of planning and implementation of such activity. In fact, functions, funds and functionaries are complementary to one another in the process of devolution of responsibilities and powers up on panchayats (GoI 2001). Therefore, fiscal devolution is sine-qua-non of effective functional devolution.

The revenue sources of the local body can be broadly classified into (a) tax revenue (b) non-tax revenue (c) grants and (d) loans. Tax revenue can again be classified into (1) own taxes, (2) assigned taxes and (3) shared taxes. Own taxes are assigned by state and levied and collected by the local body. Assigned taxes are those statutorily assigned to local bodies, but collected by state government and made over to local bodies. Shared taxes are assigned to the states and collected by them but a share of the proceeds is distributed among the local bodies. Non-tax revenue consists of income from property, markets, license fees, contributions etc. Grants-in-aid may be broadly divided into (a) plan grant (b) specific purpose grant, (c) general purpose grant and (d) central Finance Commission grant. Loans mainly consist of loans from government and other financial institutions (GoK 1996). The Kerala Panchayat Raj Act empowers the panchayats to raise loans (Section 197).

Figure 1 depicts the sources of revenue of panchayats- Part A shows the sources of GP and Part B that of block and district panchayats. Of the own tax sources of GPs, property tax/ building tax is the major source. Professional and entertainment taxes are the other important sources. Other taxes are not important sources of revenue. Land tax is an optional tax hence no local body is collecting it. GP can impose a five per cent surcharge on any tax with the approval of the Government (Section 199, Kerala Panchayat Raj Act 1994). The urban local bodies in Kerala are allowed to collect two more taxes in addition to those assigned to GPs. They are: (1) Tax on animals, vessels and vehicles (2) Tax on timber. The assigned taxes are surcharges on duty on transfer of property and basic tax. Motor vehicle tax is shared between the state government and the GP/ Municipality. *The assigned and shared taxes are now given as General Purpose Grant following the recommendations of Second State Finance Commission. Grants-in-aid, especially plan grant, have become a major source of revenue of the local bodies with the launching of the People's Plan Campaign (PPC). Government also provide tied and untied grants. The Eleventh Finance Commission provides grants to the local bodies. The local bodies receive fund (grants-in-aid) from the Centrally Sponsored Schemes (CSS) and State Sponsored Schemes (SSS) as well.

The panchayats can raise loans from government financial institutions. Local bodies are given power to raise loans from other sources. The DP can issue bonds for raising revenue (Section 197 KPA 1994). Panchayats are allowed to collect fees from beneficiaries of the institutions run or financed by it (Section 198 KPA 1994).

Only the GP (also for urban local bodies) has got the power to tax. The newly created BP and DP have no tax source. Only assigned tax is part of basic tax to these bodies, which is provided in the form of a grant. Hence, these bodies are almost fully relying on grants of the state government for it's functioning. Reliance on external sources is against the principle of fiscal autonomy. Strengthening fiscal autonomy of these tiers of 'government' is an urgent matter to be taken

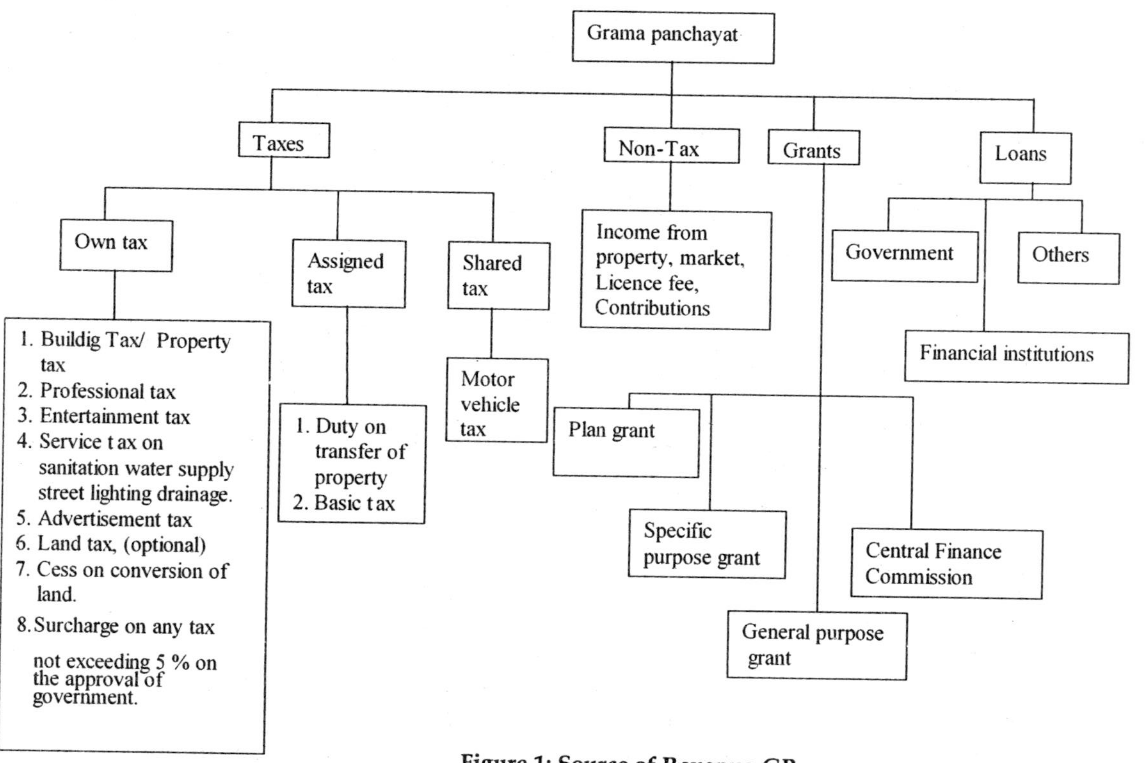

Figure 1: Source of Revenue-GP

B Source revenue BP and DP

- BLOCK / DISTRICT PANCHAYAT
  - Non-Tax
    - Income from property /contributions
  - Grants
    - Plan grant
    - Specific purpose grant
    - General purpose grant
    - Rural Infrastructure Development Fund
  - Loans
    - Government
    - Financial institutions
    - Others

into account. The observation of the first State Finance Commission of Kerala is very relevant and valid today. The tax domain of the local bodies remains almost exactly the same as were available in the pre-1994 period and those resources were insufficient even for meeting their pre-1994 responsibilities. This sharply increases the already existing adverse mismatch between functional responsibility and financial resources, which need to be corrected by allocation of additional resources.

The financial condition of the local bodies in Kerala is very fragile. The World Bank study (2004) revealed that, in 1993-94, 88 per cent of the GPs in Kerala did not have enough revenue from own source, to meet salary, office expenses and routine maintenance expenditures. If the assigned taxes were also included with the own sources of revenue, percentage of 'deficit panchayats' was 48. In 1998-99, the percentage of panchayats with deficit was 56. Thus, more than half of the GPs failed to meet their revenue expenditure even after accounting for assigned taxes.

The Plan Grant-in-Aid

With the launching of people's campaign, the plan grant[3] became the major component of financial resources of the local bodies accounting for more than three times the sum of all other receipts put together (Isaac 1999; Harilal 2004). In 1997-98 Rs. 749 crores was given as plan funds to local bodies, in addition to Rs. 246 crores as state sponsored schemes. This needs to be compared with the un-tied grant given of Rs. 213 crores in the previous year, ie, 1996-97. The un-tied grant given to the local bodies in 1995-96 was only Rs. 30 crores.

There was a quantum jump in the devolution of grants-in-aid (plan grant) to the local bodies. Table 1 shows the plan grant specified in the budget. In 1997-98, Rs. 749 crores was earmarked for the local bodies. (Appendix 4, Budget, Kerala State 1997-98). During the IXth plan period, Rs. 4130.25 crores were devolved to the local bodies and the total expenditure was Rs 3454.92 crore (83.65 per cent of the release) and during X plan Rs.6703 crores were devolved (Economic Review 2006, SPB, Kerala).

Table 1
Budgeted Plan Grant to Local Bodies

Year	*Budgeted Plan grant (Rs in Crores)*
1997-98	749
1998-99	950
1999-2000	1020
2000-01	1045
2001-02	890
2002-03	1342
2003-04	1317
2004-05	1350
2005-06	1375
2006-07	1400
2007-08	1540

Source: Budget Appendix IV–various years.

The plan grant-in- aid made a big difference in the financial position of the local bodies, not only because of the size but also for the important reason that it was earmarked entirely for development/plan expenditure (Harilal 2004). The plan grant-in-aid devolved was almost twice the size of own resource sources of the GP (see Table 2).

Table 2
Comparison Between Own Revenue and Plan Grant-in-aid: Grama Panchayats (Rs.Crores)

Item	*1993-94*	*1996-97*	*1997-98*	*1998-99*
Total own revenue	118.0	209.9	241.4	259.8
Plan grant-in-aid	–	100.0	420.5	549.5

Note: (1) In1996-97 plan grant-in-aid was given as untied funds. (2) total own revenue includes own tax, assigned tax, shared tax, non-tax revenue and grant-in-aid (excluding plan-grant-in-aid) from government.

Source: Second State Finance Commission, 2001.

The percentage of GP expenditure to State Domestic Product rose from 0.8 per cent in 1993-94 to 1.44 per cent in 1998-99.The ratio of GP expenditure to state expenditure increased from 3.5 per cent in 1993-94 to 7.3 per cent in 1998-99 (World Bank 2004).

The financial devolution is not commensurate with the functions delegated. The own resource base of the local bodies has not been expanded. No new taxes have been assigned so far. Local bodies have no power to impose new taxes. The rates of tax, fee, cess, fine etc. are determined by the government. There is no autonomy for the local bodies in raising revenue. Lack of financial autonomy limits the power of the local governments in planning. The overwhelming power enjoyed by the state government in devolving financial resources is a major weakness in our decentralisation effort. The state government takes unilateral decisions on the tax base of the local bodies. Grants are the legal rights of the local bodies. Unfair practices of government such as, withholding of a part of the grant, cut in the grant allotted in the budget etc hamper the financial autonomy of local bodies. A disquieting feature we observe is the fall in per capita plan expenditure, which is primarily due to the cut imposed by the state government on plan grant. The local bodies are constrained to make expenditure due to treasury restrictions on plan fund utilisation. The state government apply the 'rule of lapse' and take away the unspent balance of the local bodies at the end of the financial year. There are serious limitations in raising the tax base of the local bodies. Vertical transfer is therefore an important method of correcting the mismatch between functions and finance. One major source is the plan grant-in-aid. The budgeted plan grant shall be made available to the local bodies. There shall be no restriction in availing the fund. Penalising the local bodies for non-utilisation of fund due to delay in sanctioning the amount and treasury restrictions is against the spirit of decentralisation The grant shall be available to the local bodies on a monthly basis. Making available the amount at the end of the financial year is not helpful. In addition to this, local bodies shall be given freedom to raise loans from different sources according to their financial capability.

Administrative Decentralisation in Kerala

Decentralisation requires flow of power from political executives and administrative executives to local bodies and through local bodies to the people. Administering different matters and resources delegated by law is the crucial aspect of decentralisation. This requires dispersal of the administrative authority in matters of service delivery, support for developmental activities and tax collection. Administrative decentralisation requires the deployment of staff with necessary expertise and authority at appropriate levels to discharge the functions devolved by law. Administrative decentralisation implies the autonomy enjoyed by sub-national governments.

Lesser number of personnel is now required at the state level due to decentralisation, since functions and finances were transferred. Hence, the surplus staff need to be deployed. Theoretical sequence of decentralisation requires the devolution of function and finance after creating the capacity at the local level. Adequate staff need to be deployed and trained. Rules, orders, procedures, circulars and guidelines for effective functioning should be made. Then, gradual transfer of functions and resources should be made in accordance with the development of the absorption capacity at the lower level. This kind of step-by-step approach towards decentralisation has been suggested by many as the ideal one towards decentralisation. The main feature of Kerala's decentralisation process was the 'reversal sequencing' (Isaac and Franke 2000) in which power and resources were transferred at one go without creating capacity at the lower level. The logic behind this approach was that decentralisation after creating conditions will not be easy to realise and power and finance will never be devolved. Those wielding power are reluctant to devolve powers. But, once finance and functions are transferred, it becomes the duty of the government to ensure that the system works. Hence, necessary rules, orders, procedures, deployment of staff will follow.

Deployment alone will not be enough, since; their capability to undertake the new tasks is to be enhanced. Administrative decentralisation also necessitates an attitudinal change in the bureaucracy (GoK 1997). Awareness regarding the new role and responsibility of the bureaucracy and working under the political leadership of the local bodies necessitate training and orientation. Deployment to lower level is not easy, since, the staff are concerned with the promotional prospects. Moreover, the officials do not prefer a control close to them in the local body. In addition to this, there can be possibility of 'ego clash' between the officials and the political executive on the one hand and officials transferred to the local bodies and those existing in the local body on the other hand.

Transfer of Institutions and Staff

In accordance with the functional devolution as per the Kerala Panchayat Raj Act 1994 and Kerala Municipalities Act 1994, institutions and staff were transferred as per Government Order (G.O. (P) No. 189195 LAD, Sept. 18-1995) effective from October 2nd 1995, when the local bodies were first constituted after the Constitutional Amendments. The staff were also transferred along with institutions.

In agriculture, the *Krishibhavan* (Village Agricultural Office) has been transferred to the GP/municipality/corporation. Agriculture officers and the staff there were transferred to these local bodies. In the health sector all institutions other than medical colleges and big regional specialty hospitals have been transferred. In the education sector all schools have been transferred. The entire responsibility of poverty alleviation has gone to the local bodies; all the centrally sponsored anti-poverty programmes are planned and implemented by them. As regards social welfare, barring statutory functions relating to juvenile justice, all the responsibilities have gone to local bodies. ICDS is fully implemented by the GPs and the urban local bodies. Barring highways and major district roads, connectivity has become a local government responsibility. The whole of sanitation is with the local bodies. All the welfare functions are with them (GoK 2001).

The local self-government department issued detailed orders delegating full control over the staff including transferred and authority to take disciplinary action. Administrative decentralisation will be effective only if the political executive of the local bodies have control over the officials. The officers should be answerable to the executive and the power to impose punishment in the event of indiscipline also should be with executive. Full managerial power of the institution has been transferred to the local bodies but salary will be given by the government. The government has got undue control over the administrative system of the local body. The transferred staff remain under the control of the department and the vertical relation is very strong. There is the absence of active involvement of the staff in planning process. The transferred staff have not yet become a part of the local body. Figure 2 illustrates the architecture of decentralised administratiion.

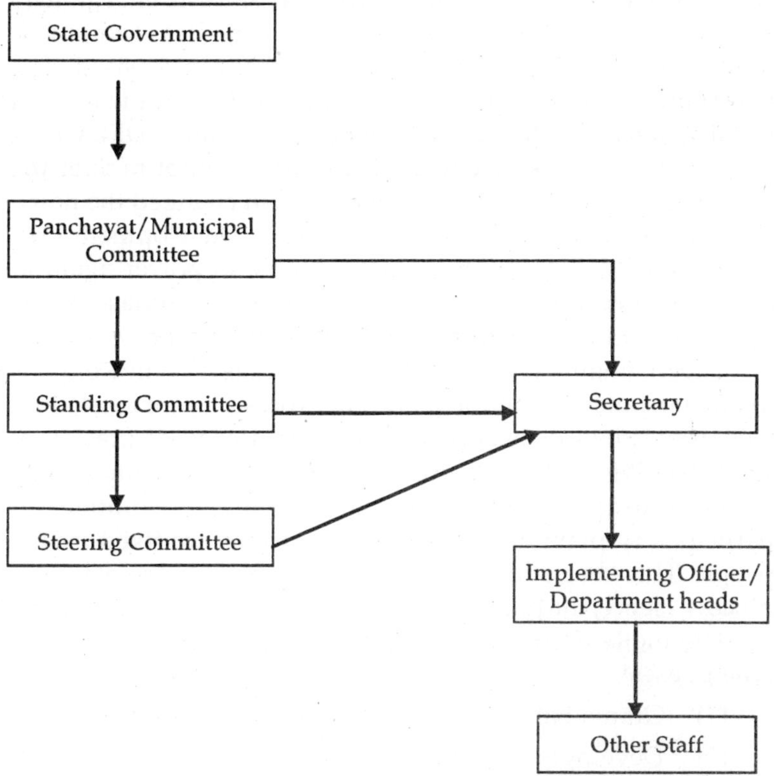

Figure 2: Administrative Decentralisation State Government

PART–III

The Architecture of Planning

The 73rd and 74th constitutional amendments of 1992 provided the necessary statutory support for the emergence of the third layer of government of the Indian federation. Following this, The Kerala Panchayat Raj Act and Kerala Municipalities Act were passed in 1994 and the first elected local bodies with constitutional backing took charge on October 2nd 1995. The new state government led by the Left coalition, which assumed power in 1996, made a historic decision to allocate 35-40 per cent of the Ninth plan outlay to the local bodies and to launch a People's Plan Campaign (PPC) (GO. No. 10/96/plg dated 30-7-96). This was a landmark decision since it enormously enhanced the resource base of the local bodies. Moreover, participation of the people in planning was emphasised. The launching of the PPC gave 'big push' for decentralization in Kerala (GoK2001). The United Democratic Front (UDF), which came to power in Kerala in 2001, did not attempt to alter the methodology of planning substantially; but changed the name of People's Plan Campaign (PPC) to Kerala Development Plan (KDP). The LDF government which came to power again in 2006 launched the Eleventh Plan as the second phase of the PPC. Thus, PPC has become irreversible in Kerala.

The distinguishing feature of decentralisation in Kerala is the democratisation of the planning process. There existed no well-established or experimented methodology of grass root level planning for the state to emulate. Therefore, a methodology for bottom-up participatory planning was developed. In participatory planning, choice and priorities are fixed by the people. This necessitates drawing the people into the planning process. Hence, the planning process was launched as campaign.

The methodology for the planning evolved for this had nine phases[4]

(1) Grama Sabha

(2) Development seminar

(3) Task forces

(4) Preparation of local plan
(5) Preparation of higher level plan
(6) Plan appraisal and sanction
(7) Implementation
(8) Monitoring
(9) Evaluation

All the voters in a ward are the members of the Grama Sabha (GS). Kerala Panchayat Raj Act 1994 empowers the GS to make decisions regarding the developmental issues in the locality. Special GSs were called for the purpose of prioritising local needs and elicit their opinion to solve the problems. (In urban areas Ward Sabhas (WS) were called). There were subject-wise group discussions and at the end reports were presented in the plenary session. Trained resource persons participated in the GS as facilitators.

The objective of the development seminar was to discuss on what could be done to solve the issues raised in various GSs of the local body. An objective assessment of the resources was made in relation to the requirements. A printed development report was prepared consisting of fifteen chapters. Discussions at the GS were a major input to the development report. Secondary data were collected from various offices. The problems in each development sector were discussed in detail. The participatory planning cycle is illustrated in Figure 3.

Preparation of the project was the next step for which task forces were constituted. The development seminar had listed the important issues to be taken up in the plan. The task forces for each development sector were constituted by the local body. It consisted of officers, retired officers and other experts drawn by the local body. Preparation of the project is a technical work, which necessitates expertise and hence training. The task forces prepared a shelf of projects. The task force was a major innovation of the PPC, which could mobilise the expertise of the retired officers as well as others ready to work voluntarily for the development of the locality.

The local body concerned was responsible for selecting the projects and programmes prepared by the taskforces to be

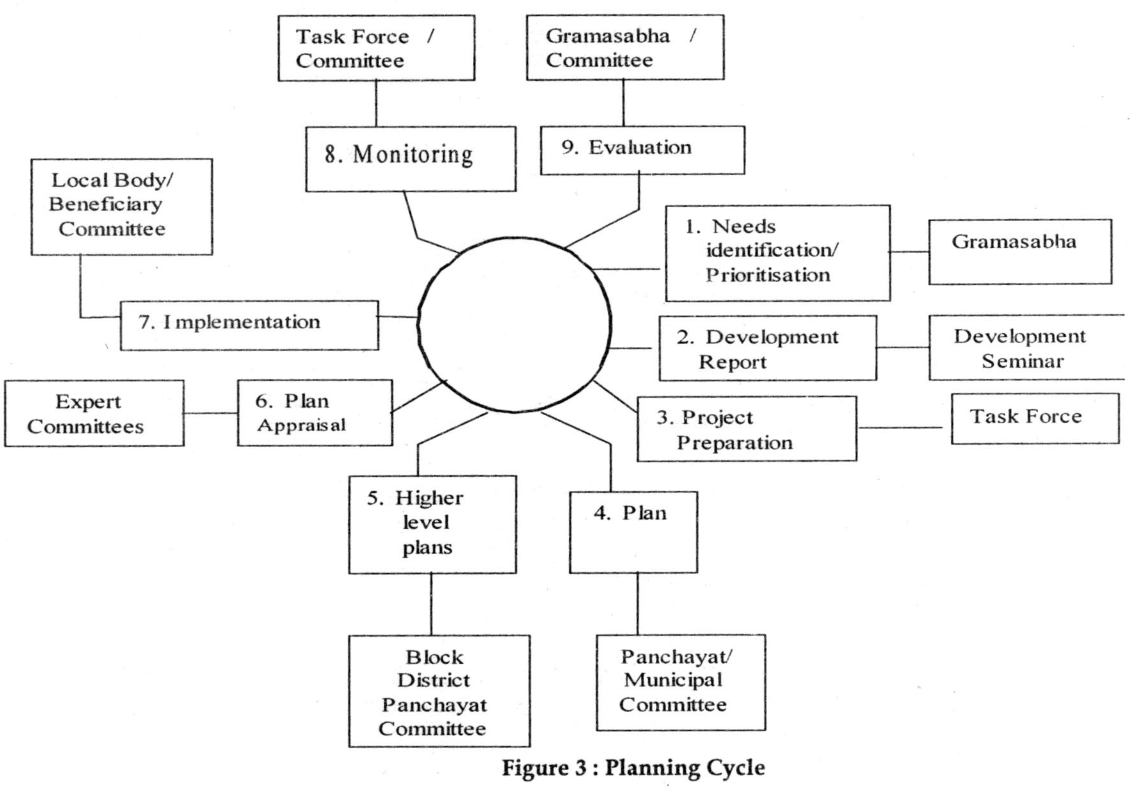

Figure 3 : Planning Cycle

included in the plan. The Planning Board gives broad directions as regards sectoral allocation. Thus, the preparation of local plan, taking into account the deliberations in the GS and the development seminar was done by the elected committee of the local body.

BPs and DPs were to prepare their plans taking into account the plans prepared at the lower level. Integrating the lower level plans was expected from the higher level plans. Thus, the BP plans can be prepared only after preparation of the GP plans and the DP plan can be made only after preparation of the BP plans. The methodology for planning for the higher level plans was similar to that of GP plans except that of the GS. A meeting of all the elected members within the BP was held, in the place of GS, to elicit their views regarding the issues to be taken up in the plan. Similar was the methodology of planning of DP. Development report, development seminar, taskforces and preparation of projects were to be followed as done at the lower level panchayats.

The plans of the local bodies shall be approved by District Planning Committee (DPC) for implementation. Each project has to be appraised for technical and financial viability. On the average, Grama Panchayats had 45 projects in Thrissur district in 1997-98 (Sudhakaran 2004). The official machinery was unable to do this function within a short period. This necessitated the creation of Expert Committees (ECs) at block, district and state level. It consisted of serving officers, retired officers, and other experts in field. The block level expert committees (BLECs) verified the projects of GPs within its purview and recommended to the DPC. At the Municipal level there were municipal level expert committees (MLECs). The district level expert committees (DLECs) verified the plans and projects of BPs. The state level expert committee (SLEC) verified the plans and projects of the DPs and Municipal Corporations prior to the approval of (DPC). The expert committees could attract the expertise of retired officers in a big way.

Implementation is the crucial stage, since the fruits of the developmental activities flow only after implementation.

Implementation is the responsibility of the local body. PPC encouraged the implementation of the projects by the people by forming 'beneficiary committees' so as to enhance the quality of work. The Government also issued orders for monitoring the projects by the task forces and people's monitoring committees. Evaluation of the project is done at GS. Thus, the PPC developed a methodology for planning from below with people's participation in all phases of planning process. But, from the second year onwards there was a change in methodology in which the task forces prepared a draft development plan to be discussed in the GS.

In every phase of the planning cycle, there is space for people's involvement, of course, except in selecting the projects to be included in the plan, which is a prerogative of the elected members. But, this can be done only considering the priority set by the people. The planning process does not deny the due role of the elected members. The whole process goes under the leadership of the elected panchayat/ municipal committee. The ECs constituted for appraising the projects and plans do not have the right to alter the preferences of the people or reject a project. The ECs are expected to help the local bodies by correcting the projects, if necessary, if it is not technically feasible or financially viable.

The Special Component Plans

Another feature of the decentralised planning in Kerala is the empowerment of women, for that, a mandatory allocation of 10 per cent of the plan grant to Women Component Plan (WCP) was made. This amount has to be spent exclusively for the projects/programmes for the development of women. Programmes/projects for income generation, skill development, awareness making etc can be undertaken.

The allocation of plan grant for Scheduled Castes is given as Special Component Plan (SCP) and for Scheduled Tribes as Tribal Sub- Plan (TSP), which is given separately for each local body in appendix IV of the state budget document. A project benefiting a group of people such as roads or water supply can be considered under SCP or TSP only if more than 50 per cent of the beneficiaries belong to the category concerned. In the 10th Plan (KDP) it was insisted that 5 per cent of the plan assistance shall be devoted to the aged, infants and handicapped. Moreover, a poverty sub-plan also should be prepared.

PART-IV

Participation in Planning

The democratisation of planning is reflected in the participation of people in different stages of planning. Democratic decision-making requires equal control over the decisions, in which all sections of the society participate and the decisions shall reflect the views of all. The number or rate of participation is important; but more relevant is the quality of participation-whether participation is active or passive. The number of participants, their occupation, age, level of education, sex etc are important in influencing decisions. Equally important is to know whether participation is inclusive or not. Therefore, the participation of the marginalised sections of the society, especially that of the Scheduled Castes and Scheduled Tribes population and women is important.

Participation rate is an indicator of the democratic involvement of people in local development. Crook and Manor (1998) concluded that participation had positive effect on performances of local government. But, some of the studies reveal a dismal picture of GS participation (Bandyopadhyay and Mukherji 2004, Besley *et. al.* (2007). The World Bank (2005) study on four South Indian states revealed that only 20 per cent of the household respondents ever attended the GS. The GSs functioned just as a formality in Haryana and Rajastan and often the attendance was below quorum. No important issues were discussed and the participation of women and Scheduled Castes was very low (Nambiar 2001). Ghatak and Ghatak 2002) pointed out that the participation rate of the well-off sections in the society in GS, in West Bengal, was higher than that of their population share. In Kerala, the participation in GS is falling. (Chaudhari *et. al.* 2004; Narayana 2004).

The details of participation of people in GS were collected from eleven GPs in Thrissur district. The period of analysis of participation in GS is divided into two sub-periods–first and second (I &II). The first sub-period is between October 1995 and September 2000, the period of the local bodies after the first election and second sub-period is from October 2000 to September 2005. The period does not correspond exactly to the Ninth and Tenth plan.

Participation Rate

Average number of participation across panchayats is not meaningful because of variation in the number of voters. The average participation for all the panchayats in the first-sub period was 116 members. Thus, generally the highest average participation in numbers was attained in 1997-98 period and there after participation shows a declining trend. But, higher averages were recorded in the second sub-period for all panchayats,. Some of the increase in average may be due to increase in population, but the increase creates doubts regarding the veracity of GS documents. The increase in average in the second sub-period was sharp in comparison to the trend in the first period, which was showing a decline. This result is contrary to the observations and opinions of people that generally, there was a fall in participation in sub-period two compared to the first period. In 1999, with the amendment of the KPA (1994), the quorum of the GS was raised to 10 per cent of the voters. If the quorum is below 10 per cent, a fresh GS has to be called again, for which, the quorum is only 50 members. This stipulation might have prompted some to show a higher participation in records to avoid calling the GS again. Hence, in our analysis; primary focus is given to the first sub-period for which the data is more reliable.

Participation rate is the proportion of voters that participated in the GSs, which is a more reliable yardstick of participation. The average participation rate for all the panchayats for the first sub-period was 7.5 per cent. The participation rate was only 5.1 per cent in 1996, which increased to 9 per cent in 1997, and declined thereafter. The participation rate was falling in the first sub-period, on the average, after 1997, although there was variation among the panchayats. This pattern is in agreement with the findings of the study by Chaudhari *et al.* (2004) that there was a secular decline in participation after the initial years of the campaign.

Participation of Women and Scheduled Castes

One of the acclaimed advantages of the people's campaign was the mobilisation of women into this process and hence to the public sphere. It is to be examined whether this has been reflected in participation in the GS. In order to examine this, the proportion of women participation in total participation is examined. The proportion of women participation in the first sub-period was 37.1 per cent. The proportion was only 26.2 per cent in 1996, which increased to 40.8 per cent in 1997, which declined to 38.5 per cent in 1998, and then increased to 40.6 per cent in 2000. The women participation hovers around 40 per cent of total participation in the first sub-period. But, there was an improvement after that. The overall decline in participation and increase in the share of women implies that there is a big decline in the participation of men. This is something that needs to be underlined and probed into.

There is no doubt that the PPC had helped in mobilising women into this process as reflected in a relatively higher participation of women in GSs. The participation of women is relatively better than in other states.

In the PPC special attention was given to address the issues of the Scheduled Castes and the Scheduled Tribes. The average participation of SCs in the total participation was 17.2 per cent, higher than the over all share of SCs in the total population (13.5 per cent) in the first sub-period. The participation share was high in 1997 (18.7 per cent) when the overall participation was high. The range of participation for all the Panchayats taken together was between 15.9 per cent and 18.7 per cent.

Occupation and Purpose of Participants

The participants are broadly classified into five groups– farmers, casual labourers, government employees, other employees and the unemployed. The occupational classification recorded in the GS minutes is not in conformity with the census classification; hence, a meaningful comparison with population in general is not possible. Of the participants, the largest share is unemployed- 38.4 per cent followed by casual labourers with 29.7 per cent. Traders and other self-employed categories comprise the third position with 15.6 per cent. Farmers constitute 15.5 per cent. Government employees constitute less than one per cent. The data reveal the fact that the majority of the participants are the poor, the unemployed and casual labourers, who constitute 68 per cent of the participants.

Grama sabhas may be broadly classified into three, based on purpose- (a) planning (b) beneficiary selection (c) others. It is in the planning GS that the local priorities are determined. The beneficiary selection GS is part of the implementation stage of planning, which is usually called after the plan is approved by the DPC. The average participation in GS for beneficiary selection was higher than GS for planning. Higher participation for beneficiary selection was observed in the case of all panchayats. Purpose is an important determinant of participation. Many participate in GS due to the expectation of getting some personal benefits. In some panchayats, participation for other purposes is higher than planning. Hence, more interest is shown in participation for other purposes, than for planning.

The Reasons of Low Participation

The respondents were asked to report the reasons for low participation according to their perceptions. All categories of respondents opined that the GS is seen as a forum for beneficiary selection. As a corollary to this, most participants expect some benefit from participation. The reasons cited by the respondents are given here according to the importance attached by them: (1) Grama sabha is seen as a forum of beneficiary selection (2) Once a benefit is got, less likely to get the next; hence participation falls (3) Fall in the number of projects with individual benefits (4) Benefits are limited to particular sections only (5) People are busy with their own personal affairs/opportunity cost of participation (6) GS is dominated by political activists (7) Dissatisfaction with the functioning since the issues raised are not done (8) Political bias in decision-making (9) Lack of information regarding convening of GS (10) Inconvenient timings of GS (11) Lack of initiative of the elected member in mobilising people.

There is an opportunity cost for participation. The opportunity cost of employed persons is high. Therefore, their participation is low. Another reason is the feeling of the people that the scene is dominated by the political activists and that the opinions of others are not counted. Dissatisfaction with the GS, since many of the issues raised there are not addressed, makes people disinterested in participation.

The Development Seminar

In the development seminar, an in-depth and informed dialogue on developmental issues in each locality is made. A comprehensive development report was made for the discussion highlighting the issues in each sector. An objective assessment of the natural, human and financial resources was also attempted. There was a decline in the number of participants over the years. The participation in 2004-05 was only 43 per cent of that of 1997-98. In all the panchayats a fall in participation was observed. In sharp contrast to the general picture, women participation was showing an upward trend and in which the total participation increased from 571 in 1997-98 to 589 in 2004-05. The trend is significant in the context of the observed fall in total participation in development seminars, which points towards a decline in male participation both in absolute and relative terms.

There was a steady increase in the proportion of women participation till 2003-04 and a fall in the next year. In 1997-98, the share of women participation was only 22.3 per cent, which rose to 58.2 per cent in 2003-04. In the tenth plan period, the participation of women was over 50 per cent. There was an increase in women participation in the GS as well as in the development seminar over the years. One major reason for increased participation was the growth of the Kudumbasree/ women self-help groups. In all the panchayats the Kudumbasree project was implemented. The development of the self-help groups has an empowering effect on women. The mandatory women component plan also had a positive effect on women's participation, since there was a discussion group for women.

PART–V

Impact on Outcome

Participatory approach is expected to reorient development in favour of the vulnerable sections of the society (Mathur 1995). For example, the participatory budgeting in Porto Alegre, in Brazil has improved the quality of governance. The investment in poorer residential districts in the city exceeded that of investment in wealthier sections. Higher tax collection was made possible. It dampened corruption and encouraged accountability. The methodology of budgeting was copied in 100 other municipalities in Brazil as well as in Peru, Uruguay, and Venezuela (UNDP 2002, Biocchi 2003). The impact on outcome of participatory planning shall be assessed, ideally, by analysing the effectiveness of participation on the individual and collective well-being of the people as well as on the control over decisions by the people. But, limitations of data do not permit to look in to the details. Here, some of the outcomes are examined mainly analysing the physical achievements as well as the opinions of the people on the impact on various aspects.

Planning Commission (2006) in their evaluation report on decentralised experience of Kerala concluded that GSs have emerged as a prominent body of need articulation in the villages. Most of the projects emanated from the needs articulated in the GS. The projects in PPC are more appropriate prior to the launching of the Campaign.

Physical Achievements

The physical achievements of the PPC are impressive and the Economic Review published by the State Planning Board gives details of this. The study by Choudhary *et al* (2004) revealed that during Ninth plan more than 2,50,000 houses were constructed by the panchayats. In 2005-06, 38166 houses were constructed. House plots were distributed to 4088 families. The number of toilets constructed was 86563 in 2005-06. Computer training was given to 160923 in 2005-06.The removal of deceased coconut trees was 164126. Beneficiaries of drinking water was 112446. Road constructed was 12054 Kms (Economic Review 2006).

But, performance in the productive sectors was not impressive. In agriculture there was a decline in the share of plan expenditure in the IX plan compared to the VIII plan and in the X plan there was further decline (Planning Commission 2006). In employment and income generating activities the ratings of the local bodies was not impressive (Choudhary et al 2004). One serious limitation of PPC was the limitation in preparing integrated projects (Planning Commission 2006, Sudhakaran 2006). There was serious drawback in making vertically integrated plans. Sectoral as well as spatial integration was lacking. There was a tendency to spread resources thinly among different wards and projects. The District Planning Committee (DPC) is the body to make an integrated plan for the district as a whole. But, such a district plan was attempted only once.

Service Delivery and Implementation

There were marked improvements in the quality of services provided by the local governments. The study by Choudhary *et al* (2004) revealed that there was remarkable progress in the service delivery in health care, childcare and child development, education, drinking water etc. The facilities in schools, health centres anganwadies improved considerably. Major share of the expenditure of the local bodies was on the service sector.

In the implementation stage marked improvement was noticed in the case of beneficiary selection. Beneficiary selection through the GS could reduce nepotism and corruption considerably. In the case of beneficiary committees, there were many success stories; but there were many fake committees too.

Conclusions

The architecture of dcentalisation in Kerala has four dimensions-functional, financial, administrative and planning. In the devolution of functions as well as finance Kerala is ahead of other states in India. Substantial advancement in administrative decentralisation has taken place but the existence of dual control among the transferred staff is a major issue. The PPC gave impetus to the decentralisation process in Kerala. The fiscal devolution was substantial which in turn necessitated changes in devolution of functions and functionaries. One of the major contributions of PPC was the methodology of bottom-up planning which provides space for people's involvement in all phases.

The participation of people in GS is low and it is falling. But, the participation is relatively more inclusive. The women participation is relatively high and it is showing an increasing trend. The participation rate of the SCs is higher in proportion to their population. In the higher stages of planning also the participation is showing a declining trend. The participation of the young, educated and the rich is very low. GS is seen mainly as a forum for beneficiary selection. Lack of publicity, inconvenient timing etc. also contribute to low participation.

PPC has brought substantial improvements in service delivery. The facilities in health institutions, schools and *anganwadies* improved substantially. In drinking water projects as well as in road connectivity there were marked improvements. But, the impact of the decentralised planning on productive sector and income generating activities was not impressive. There was serious limitation in integration of plans both horizontally and vertically. Although beneficiary committees were successful in many cases, there were many bogus committees. The primacy of the GS in deciding the projects as well as in beneficiary selection has been noticed as major achievement. Studies have shown that most projects originate from the GS. In beneficiary selection, nepotism and corruption has been considerably reduced. The waning enthusiasm of the people in the planning process is a major concern. The participation of the people in the GS shall improve and efforts shall be made in this direction.

Notes

1. *Report of the team for the Study of Community Projects and National Extension Service,* New Delhi, Popularly known as Balwant Ray Mehta Committee. Balwant Ray Mehta was the chairman who was an MP, recommended three tier panchayati raj system.
2. Committee on decentralization power was appointed in 1997.The chairman was Subrato Sen. The committee made valuable suggestions and the Kerala Panchayat Raj Act 1994 and Kerala Municipality Act 1994 were amended in 1999,following the recommendations.
3. The third state finance commission named the plan fund as development fund and now this term is used.
4. From the second year of the Ninth plan onwards the task force prepared a draft list of projects to be discussed in the Gramasabha. When the UDF came to power in 2001, during the tenth plan period, the name of the Task Force was changed to Working Group and the name of the Expert Committees was changed to Technical Committees. In the Eleventh plan, Technical Committees are called Technical Advisory Groups. A stakeholder consultation has been insisted prior to the GSs in the Eleventh plan.

References

Bandyopadhya, D. and Mukherjee, Amitava (2004), *New Issues in Panchayati Raj*. Concept Publishing Company, New Delhi.

Bandyopadyay, D. (1997), 'People's Participation in Planning-Kerala Experiment', *Economic and Political Weekly,* September 27.

Behar, Amitabh (2003), 'Experiment with Direct Democracy', *Economic and Political Weekly,* May 17.

Besley, Timothy, Pande, Rohini, Rao, Vijayendra (2007), 'Political Economy of Panchayats in South India', *Economic and Political Weekly,* February 24.

Baiocchi, Gianpaolo (2003), 'Participation, Activism and Politics-The Porto Alegre Experiment', in *Deepening Democracy Institutional Innovations in Empowered Participatory Democracy* edited by Fung, Archon and Wright, Erik Ohlin 2003, Verso.

Blair, H. (2000), 'Participation and Accountability at the Periphery: Democratic Local Governance in Six Countries', *World Development,* 28 (4).

Chambers, Roberts (1997), *Whose Reality Counts? Putting the Last First,* Intermediate Technology Publications, U.K.

Chaudhari, Shubham, K. N. Harilal and Heller, Patric (2004), *Decentralisation Make a Difference? A Study of the People Campaign for Decentralised Planning in the Indian State of Kerala.* Centre for Development Studies, Thiruvananthapuram.

Chathukulam, Jose and John, M. S. (2002), 'Five Years of Participatory Planning in Kerala: Rhetoric and Reality', *Economic and Political Weekly,* December 7, 2002.

Crook, Richard C. and Manor, James (1998), *Democracy and Decentralisation in South Asia and West Africa,* Cambridge University Press.

De Mellow, Luiz (2000), *Can Decentralisation Strengthen Social Capital?,* International Monetary Fund, Working Paper No. 00/20 IMT, Washington.

De Mellow, Luiz and Barenstein Matias (2002), 'Fiscal Decentralisation and Governance: A Cross Country Analysis' in George T. Abed and Sanjeev Gupta (eds) *Governance corruption and Economic performance* International Monetary Fund, Washington D.C.

Debroy, Bibek and Koushik, P. D. (ed.) (2005), *Energising Rural Development Through Panchayats,* Academic Foundation, New Delhi.

Dreze, Jean and Sen, Amartya (1995), *India Economic Development and Social Opportunity,* Oxford University Press.

Eversole, Robyn (2003), 'Managing Pitfalls of Participatory Development: Some Insights from Australia', *World Development,* Vol. 3, No. 5.

Fung, Archon and Wright, Eric Ohlin (ed) (2003), *Deepening Democracy: Institutional Innovations in Empowered Participatory Democracy,* Verso Press, London.

Franke, W. Richard and Chasin, H. Barabara (1992), *Kerala: Development Through Radical Reforms,* Promila Publishers, New Delhi.

Ghatak, Maitreesh and Ghatak, Maitreya (2002), 'Recent Reforms in the Panchayat System in West Bengal Toward Greater Participatory Governance', *Economic and Political Weekly,* Vol. XXXVII, No. 1.

Government of India (2001), *Report of the Committee on Panchayati Raj Institutions,* Ministry of Agricultural and Irrigation, New Delhi.

Government of India (2006), *Evaluation Report on Decentralised Experience of Kerala,* Planning Commission Evaluation Division.

Government of Kerala (1958), *Report of the Administrative Reform Committee,* (Chairman EMS Nampoothiripad).

Government of Kerala (1985), *Report of the Panchayat Finance Commission,* Chairman, Avukkadarkutty Naha.

Government of Kerala (1994), *Kerala Municipalities Act.*

Government of Kerala (1994), *Kerala Panchayat Raj Act.*

Government of Kerala (1996), *Report of the First State Finance Commission.*

Government of Kerala (1997), *Report of the committee on Decentralisation of Powers* (Sen Committee).

Government of Kerala (2001), *Report of the Second State Finance Commission.*

Harilal, K. N. (2004), Reforming Local Governance Structures in India: Lessons from Kerala Experiment. Paper presented in the International symposium on '*Citizen's participation in Local Public Policy Making. European Experiences in Global Perspectives*' 8-9, November 2004 VNG International, The Hague Holland.

Harris, John (2002), *Depoliticizing Development. The World Bank and Social Capital,* Leftword, New Delhi.

Isaac, Thomas, T. M. and Franke, Richard, W. (2000), *Local Democracy and Local Development People's Campaign for Decentralised Planning in Kerala,* Left word, New Delhi.

Isaac, Thomas, T. M. and Heller Patric (2003), 'Democracy and Development: Decentralised Planning in Kerala' in *Deepening Democracy. Institutional innovations in Empowered participator governance* Fung and Wright 2003, Verso.

Isaac, Thomas, T. M., Harilal, K. N. (1997), Planning for Empowerment: People's Campaign for Decentralised Planning in Kerala', *Economic and Political Weekly,* Vol. XXXII, No. 39.

Isaac, Thomas T. M. (1999). *Peoples' Planning-Towards a Handbook,* Kerala State Planning Board, Thiruvannathapuram.

Jain, L. C. (Ed.) (2005), *Decentralisation and Local Governance,* Orient Longman.

Koushik, P. D. (2005), Panchayati Raj Movement in India. Retrospective and Present Status in Debroy Bibek and P.D. Koushik (Eds) *Energising Rural Development Through Panchayats,* Academic Foundation, New-Delhi.

Martinez, Vazqez Jorge and McNab, Robert M. (2003), 'Fiscal Decentralisation and Economic Growth', *World Development,* Vol. 31, No. 9.

Mohan Kumar, S. (2002), 'From Peoples' Campaign to Plan Sans People', *Economic and Political Weekly,* Vol. XXXVII, No. 16.

Mukharji, Nirmal (1989), 'Decentralisation Below State Level: Need for New Systems of Governance', *Economic and Political Weekly,* March 4.

Musgrave, R. A. (1959), *The Theory of Public Finance,* McGraw Hill New York.

Mathur, Harimohan (1995), 'Role of Social Actors in Promoting Participatory Development at Local Level: A View from India' in *Participatory Development from Advocacy to Action* Edited H. Schneider H. OECD, OCDE Paris.

Marchac, H. Thomas (1959), 'Centralisation and Decentralisation in Economic Organisation', *Econometrica,* Vol. 27 (3) July.

Nagaraj, K. (1999), *Decentralisation in Kerala: A Note, Discussion Paper* No. 2, Kerala Research Programme on Local Level Development Centre for Development Studies Thiruvananthapuram.

Nambiar, Malini (2001), 'Making the Gramasabha Work', *Economic and Political Weekly,* Aug 18.

Narayana, D. (2005), 'Local Governance Without Capacity Building: Ten Years of Panchayati Raj', *Economic and Political Weekly,* June 25.

Oates, Wallace, E. (1972), *Fiscal Federalism,* Harcourt Brace Jovanovich Inc. New York.

Prudhomme, Remy (1995). 'On the Dangers of Decentralisation'. *The World Bank Research Observer,* Vol. 10 , No. 2.

Puri, Ellora (2004), 'Understanding Participation Theoretical Foundations and Practical Implications', *Economic and Political Weekly,* No. 24, Vol. XXXIX.

Putnam, Robert, D. (1993), *Making Democracy Work, Civic Traditions in Modern Italy,* Princeton University Press, New Jersey.

Robinson, Mark (2005), 'A Decade of Panchayati Raj Reforms: The Challenge of Democratic Decentralisation in India', in *Decentralization and Local Governance* edited by L.C. Jain, Orient Long man.

.Schneider, Hartmut with Libercier, Marie-Helene (ed.) (1995), *Participatory Democracy from Advocacy to Action,* OECD, Paris.

Schroeder, Larry (ed.) (1989), *Financing Governmental Decentralisation. The Case of Bangaldesh,* Westview Press Colarado.

Shaheena, P. (2003), *Fiscal Devolution and Revenue Mobilisation–A study of Gramapanchayat finances in Kerala,* Unpublished Ph.D. Thesis, Centre for Development Studies Thiruvananthapuram.

Sharma, Rasmi (2003), 'Kerala's Decentralisation Idea and Practice', *Economic and Political Weekly,* September 6-12.

Shaw, Anwar (1991), *Perspectives on the Design of Inter-governmental Fiscal Relations, Policy, Research and External Affairs,* Working paper 726, World Bank.

State Planning Board, Kerala (1997), *Ninth Five Year Plan 1997-2002 and Annual Plan 1997-98, Volume 1.*

State Planning Board, Kerala (1998), *Report of the Working Group on Evolving Formula for Interse Distribution of Plan Grants to Local Bodies'.*

Subramanian, Madhu (2004), 'Decentralisation Without Social Mobilisation in Kerala in Wignaraja Ponna and Sirivardan, Susil (ed) *'Pro-poor Growth and governance in South Asia'* Sage Publications, New Delhi.

Sudhakaran, M. N. (2004), *Plan Integration in the Context of Multi-level Planning–A Study Based on Thrissur District,* Discussion Paper Series. No. 102, KRPLLD, Centre for Development Studies Thiruvananthapuram, Kerala.

Sudhakaran, M. N. (2006), *'People's Campaign for Planning in Kerala-A Study of the Methodology of Planning and Implementation'* Unpublished Ph.D. Thesis submitted to the Mahatma Gandhi University, Kottayam.

Sunder, Nandini (2001), 'Is Devolution Democratisation?', *World Development,* Vol. 29, No. 12.

Tiebout, C. M. (1956), 'Pure Theory of Local Expenditures', *Journal of Political Economy* 64 (5).

United Nations (1975), *Integration of Economic and Physical Planning*, UN, New York.

UNDP (1993), *Human Development Report 1993*, Oxford University Press.

UNDP (2002), *Human Development Report 2002*, Oxford University Press.

World Bank (2004), *Fiscal Decentralisation to Rural Governments in India*, Oxford.

World Bank (2005), *The Political Economy of Gram Panchayats in South India: Results and Policy Conclusions from a Research Report.*

---

1. *Report of the team for the Study of Community Projects and National Extension Service*, New Delhi, Popularly known as Balwant Ray Mehta Committee. Balwant Ray Mehta was the chairman who was an MP, recommended three tier panchayati raj system.
2. Committee on decentralization power was appointed in 1997.The chairman was Subrato Sen. The committee made valuable suggestions and the Kerala Panchayat Raj Act 1994 and Kerala Munincipality Act 1994 were amended in 1999,following the recommendations.
3. The third state finance commission named the plan fund as development fund and now this term is used
4. From the second year of the Ninth plan onwards the task force prepared a draft list of projects to be discussed in the Gramasabha. When the UDF came to power in 2001, during the tenth plan period, the name of the Task Force was changed to Working Group and the name of the Expert Committees was changed to Technical Committees. In the Eleventh plan, Technical Committees are called Technical Advisory Groups. A stakeholder consultation has been insisted prior to the GSa in the Eleventh plan.

TRENDS IN URBANISATION AND URBAN GOVERNANCE IN KERALA

SUNNY GEORGE

Introduction

Kerala has made significant progress in establishing a good local governance system. Following the 73rd and 74th constitutional amendments, legislations were made for developing the governance system. The hallmarks of the local governance in Kerala are people's participation, transparency and accountability. Powers, functions and responsibilities have been transferred to them to function as institutions of self governments. One-third of the plan-grant-in-aid of the State has been earmarked for the local bodies for the Tenth Five Year Plan. The Plan Grant-in-Aid is distributed among the local bodies based on pre-determined criteria.

Land, People, and the Regional Economy

Kerala is the Southern-most State in India having geographical area of about 39,000 sq. km. with population of 3,18,38,619 as recorded by the 2001 Census. It is one of the densely populated states with population of 819 per sq.km. There are four major geographical zones in the State: the Highlands, the Middle zone, the Lowland plain, and the Coastal plain. Kerala is a region of relatively heavy monsoon rain. There are 44 streams/ rivers in Kerala.[1] The even availability of water rendered possible an even settlement pattern, as distinct from the cluster villages in the rest of the sub-continent.

Kerala's achievements in development are legendary, particularly in quality of life measured in terms of human development index. The index of human development of Kerala is found to be comparable to that of the middle-income countries in the world whereas its per capita income is lower than that of the average per capita income of the low-income countries. Thus, the Kerala model[2] shows how an economy can achieve high quality of life with low per capita income. Many of the development trends/features in Kerala have been tending towards the capacity building of local level planning, and recently, these centrifugal forces have gained momentum and resulted in sustained improvement in the quality of life, despite very low per capita income.

Urbanisation in Kerala

An idiosyncratic feature of the development trends in Kerala is the absence of rural-urban polarisation. The public policy has been so targeted that the disparity between the rural and urban area is reduced to the minimum. These developments in Kerala–'rural-urban continuum'–have resulted in the coinage of a new term 'rurban'. Woodcock, during the late Sixties, described the situation very beautifully in the following way.

Kerala villages bear little resemblance to the tight, squalid settlements of North India which huddle along a single street or in a knot of houses for mutual protection. In spite of their unorganised appearance, the Malayali villages have quite elaborate social structures. Each will have at least one school and a public library; it will have a public health service, trade union branches and political party groups, places of worship (often a temple, a church and a mosque) and always a few tea shops which serve as meeting places for the various communities. Many Malayali intellectuals and officials return to their native villages in middle age and take an active part in local activities, so that there is a cultural sophistication about rural life in Kerala. In many respects, it is urban (Woodcock, 1967, pp. 44-45).

About twenty five per cent of the population in Kerala live in urban areas. This is a little less than the National average. However unlike the other parts of the country the Urbanisation in Kerala is not limited to the designated cities and towns. Barring a few Panchayats in the hilly tracts and a few isolated areas here and there, the entire state depicts the picture of a rural-urban continuum. The Kerala Society by and large can be termed as urbanised (Govt. of Kerala, 2002).

Trends in Urbanisation

The urbanization process in Kerala acquired a faster pace during the latter half of the last century. Now about 25.97 per cent of the population in Kerala live in urban areas covered by five Municipal Corporations and 53 Municipalities. This is a little less than the national average. Barring a few Panchayats in the hilly tracts and a few isolated areas, the entire state depicts the picture of an urban rural continuum.

In 1981 there were 106 census towns which accommodated 4,771,275 population which worked out to 18.7 per cent of the total population; and in 1991 there were 197 census towns with a population of 7680294 which was 26.44 per cent of total population. The census of India 2001 recorded an urban population of 8267135 in the state which is 25.97 per cent of the total population of 31838619 and is spread over 159 census towns. It is interesting to note that when the urban content of the total population increased from 18.74 per cent in 1981 to 26.44 per cent in 1991, it showed a declining trend during the decade 1991 to 2001, with an urban population of 25.97 per cent in 2001. The percentage decennial growth of urban population in the state was 60.89 during 1981 to 1991; but during 1991 to 2001 it was only 7.64 per cent. The number of census towns reduced to 159. This may partially be due to changes in the definition of urban area. The Table 1 and Figure 1 give trends in urbanisation of urban population during 1971 to 2001, and the district-wise population and its decadal growth rate is given in Table 2. There are 17 urban agglomerations and its number of households and population are reported in Table 3.

Table 1
Trends in Urbanisation in Kerala, 1901 and 2001

		Kerala	
Year	*Total Population*	*Urban Population*	*Level of Urban Population*
1901	6396262	454499	7.11
1911	7147673	524661	7.34
1921	7802127	680900	8.73
1931	9507050	916330	9.64
1941	11031541	1195550	10.84
1951	13549118	1825832	13.48
1961	16903715	2554141	15.11
1971	21347375	3466449	16.24
1981	25453680	4771275	18.74
1991	29098518	7680294	26.39
2001	31838619	8267135	25.97

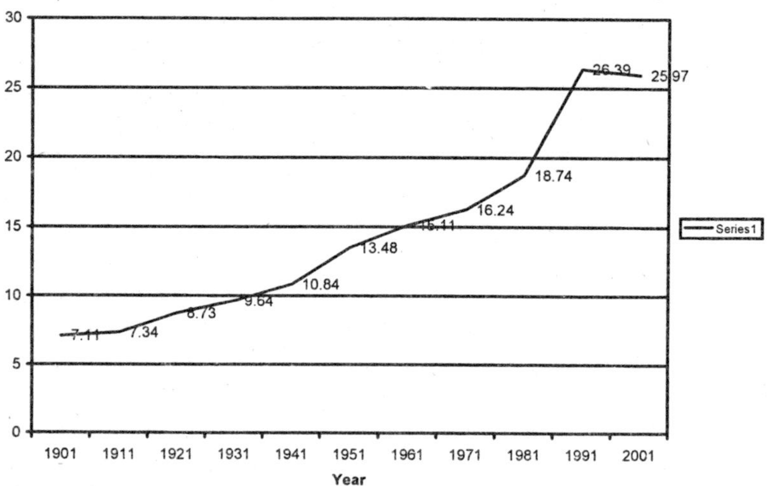

Figure 1: Trends in Urbanisation

Table 2
District-wise Distribution of Urban Population in, 1971 to 2001

Districts	*Urban Population in Persons*				*Decadal Growth Rate (%)*		
	1971	*1981*	*1991*	*2001*	*1981-91*	*91-2001*	*Difference*
Ernakulam	636010	1002892	1373177	1476488	36.92	7.52	29.40
Kannur	210975	612659	1145476	1217163	86.97	6.26	80.71
Kozhikode	561570	610232	1004497	1100946	64.61	9.60	55.01
Thiruvananthapuram	571566	655761	998243	1092685	52.23	9.46	42.77
Thrissur	249845	514783	720216	839507	39.91	16.56	23.34
Alappuzha	321129	344287	609610	618113	77.06	1.39	75.67
Kollam	189903	337153	446036	465850	32.29	4.44	27.85
Palakkad	214079	206669	374577	356461	81.24	-4.84	86.08
Malappuram	124852	177774	282454	355983	58.88	26.03	32.85
Kottayam	208762	159107	320918	299779	101.70	-6.59	108.29
Kasaragod	113929	43137	176226	233745	308.53	32.64	275.89
Pathanamthitta	38567	62192	155034	123573	149.28	-20.29	169.58
Idukki	25262	44629	50881	57240	14.01	12.50	1.51
Wayanad	-	–	22949	29602	–	28.99	–
All Kerala	3466449	4771275	7680294	8267135	60.97	7.64	53.33

Census of India 2001. Series-33.

Table 3
Urban Agglomerations with Households and Population

		Total Population (including institutional and houseless population)		
Name of District/ Taluk/Village/ City/Town	*No of House-holds*	*Population*	*Males*	*Females*
Kochi	301079	1355972	670340	685632
Thiruvananthapuram	207460	889635	437407	452228
Kozhikode	150906	816915	398250	418665
Kannur	87592	498207	237108	261099
Kollam	82341	380091	186924	193167
Thrissur	71891	330122	160443	169679
Alappuzha	61299	282675	137244	145431
Palakkad	41349	197369	96928	100441
Kottayam	39115	172878	84960	87918
Malappuram	30050	170409	83709	86700
Guruvayoor	31877	159867	74417	85450
Kanhangad	25275	129367	62002	67365
Vadakara	22692	124083	59803	64280
Cherthala	26727	117040	56926	60114
Kodungallur	20504	94883	45317	49566
Kasaragod	13676	75968	37197	38771
Chittur-Thathamangalam	13973	67935	33346	34589

Source: Census of India.

Approaches to Decentralisation

In the process of decentralisation, Kerala has followed certain fundamental principles. The following are the important principles, among others, that guided the transfer of power to local self-governments in Kerala.

Autonomy

Among the LSGIs, autonomy is guaranteed by limiting the supervision of the State Government to the obligatory and regulatory functions. It has got three dimensions: (1) Financial autonomy; (2) Functional autonomy; and (3) Administrative autonomy. Autonomy implies that various levels of LSGIs should not be seen as hierarchically organised, with unit one controlling the others below it. However, there exists active 'cooperation, coordination, complementation, and integration'. Nevertheless, the State Government has a very pro-active role in formulating the state priorities within the framework of the national perspective. Thus a multi-level exercise of developmental functions implies, "the existence of a sphere of independent action, at each level, a sphere of cooperative and coordinated action, a sphere of delegated agency function, and a sphere of agency from above, in the descending order of magnitude" (Committee on Decentralisation, 1996).

Subsidiarity

This principle governs the division of functions among different tiers of LSGIs. Subsidiarity implies what can be done best at a particular level shall be done at that level and only residual functions are given to the higher level. The process starts from below, transferring functions and powers from the level of Grama Sabhas/Ward Committees and go up to the Union Government.

Complementarity

Integration is perhaps the most important task in decentralised planning. The entire system has to work with unity of vision and diversity of means. While integrating the functions, there must not be any chance for overlapping and repetition. This means that the activities of higher levels should complement those of the lower levels and the programmes implemented by all agencies in a given local body will be consistent with local needs and priorities and will in turn, converge into an integrated local plan.

Uniformity

The principle of uniformity stipulates that norms and criteria for selection of beneficiaries, identification of sites, prioritisation of activities and pattern of assistance within a given local body shall be the same for a particular programme irrespective of the agency sponsoring such programmes. This helps in formulating criteria for decision making, which may be made open to the people so that transparency can easily be ensured.

Participation of People

In decentralised governance, participation of the people is envisaged by empowering them to take their own decisions after they analyse their problems themselves. In fact, the local self- government provides an institutional framework for participatory democracy. People's participation is expected in all stages of a development programme including identification of needs, formation of scheme, its implementation, monitoring and evaluation. The reservation of seats for women, Scheduled Castes and for Scheduled Tribes is one of the ways of ensuring participation of the vulnerable sections in the mainstream development activities. The institutions like Grama Sabhas/ Ward Committees are meant for facilitating people's participation in terms of mobilisation of resources in cash, kind and of decision making. Participation also helps in ensuring transparency by examining the activities at various stages. Furthermore, the citizen's pro-active role is expected in augmenting harmony among various sections of the people, promotion of literacy, improvement of public health, etc.

Transparency and Accountability

Local Self-Government Institutions are primarily accountable to the people and this is guaranteed by ensuring transparency in its function. This calls for a social audit system for examining the performance of the local bodies. The social auditing is performed by the Grama Sabhas and Ward Committees by examining the activities of development programme in the respective area. Every decision taken has to be based on certain predetermined norms and criteria, which are evolved on the basis of social consensus and the rationale behind each decision has to be made public. For this purpose, the procedures and the language of administration have to be made people-friendly by simplifying it. In such a system the people have the right to know details of project documents, procedure of its execution, estimates, its monitoring, financial expenditures and evaluation. The people are also expected to play a facilitative role for smooth functioning of the developmental activities.

Urban Governance

The Kerala Municipality Act, 1994

The Kerala Municipality Act, 1994 which came into force on the 30th day of May 1994 replaces the Kerala Municipality Act, 1960[3]. The new Municipality Act, 1994 has incorporated several provisions in tune with the Constitution (Seventy Fourth) Amendment Act. The Kerala Municipalities Act, 1994 was amended by Act 8 of 1995, Act 8 of 1996, Act 14 of 1999 and by Act 14 of 2000 for strengthening the urban governance in the State.

There are 58 urban local bodies in Kerala with 53 Municipalities and 5 Corporations. There is no Town Panchayat since there is no area under transition from rural to urban. The urban local bodies in Kerala are smaller than the urban local bodies in other states, particularly regarding the size of population. It is interesting to note that Kerala does not have any metropolitan area.

Municipal Councils

Out of the total population in Kerala 8.58 per cent are living in area under Municipal Councils. There are 53 Municipal Councils in Kerala. The average population of a Municipal Council is 51530. Table 4 shows the distribution of Municipalities according to the size of population. It may be noted that there are only three Municipalities having population above one lakh, and six Municipalities are having population less than 25000 population. Majority of them are within the range of 25000 to 75000 population.

Municipal Council comprises of 20 to 50 wards. There will be 20 wards where the population in the area of Council does not exceed twenty thousand; and where the population of the Council exceeds twenty thousand, twenty, for the population for first twenty thousand, and one each for every two thousand and five hundred of the population exceeding twenty thousand. A Councillor who is elected directly by the people represents each ward. The Chairperson of a Council is elected from among the elected members. MLAs and MPs are not given

Table 4
Distribution of Municipalities According to Population

Range of population	*Municipalities (No.)*
(1)	*(2)*
Below 25,000	6
Below 25,000 and 40,000	18
Below 40,000 and 50,000	9
Below 50,000 and 60,000	7
Below 60,000 and 75,000	8
Below 75,00 and 100,000	2
Above 100,000	3
Total	53

Source: Economic Review 2004, Govt. of Kerala.

any representation in the Council. The Chairperson is a fulltime functionary and he is the Executive Head of the Council. Policy decisions of the Council are taken on the basis of majority support.

Municipal Corporations

There are five Municipal Corporations in Kerala. The average population of a Corporation in is 491330. Table 5 gives total population in the five Corporations. It is interesting to note that the most populous Corporation in Kerala (Thiruvananthapuram) has only about seven lakhs population. The smallest Corporation is Thrissur which is having around three lakhs population.

Table 5
Population of Corporations

Corporation	*Population (No)*
(1)	*(2)*
Thiruvananthapuram	704375
Kollam	346013
Kochi	564589
Thrissur	296788
Kozhikode	419831

Source: Economic Review 2004, Govt. of Kerala.

There are 50 to 100 elected members in a Municipal Corporation. There will be 50 wards where the population in the area of the Corporation does not exceed four lakhs; and where the population exceeds four lakhs, fifty, for the population of first four lakhs and one each for every ten thousand exceeding four lakhs, subject to a maximum of one hundred Councillors. The Councillors are elected directly by the people from the wards. A ward is represented by a single Councillor. The Chairperson (the Mayor) is elected from among the elected members. MLAs and MPs are not represented in the Corporation. The Mayor's job is fulltime and he is the Executive Head of the Corporation. Policy decisions of the Corporation are taken on the basis of majority support. It may be noted that elections to the local bodies in Kerala are conducted on the basis of party politics.

Reservation of Seats

Scheduled Castes and Scheduled Tribes are given reservation of seats in proportion to their population to total population and such seats are allotted by rotation to different wards in a Municipality. One-third (including the number of seats reserved for women belonging to the Scheduled Castes and Scheduled Tribes) of the total number of seats in Municipalities are reserved for women and such seats are allotted by rotation to different wards. As in the case of reservation of seats for Councillors, reservation for Scheduled Castes and Scheduled Tribes and for Women is given to Chairmanship in proportion to their population. And the seats are given by rotation.

Powers, Functions and Responsibilities of Municipalities

Apart from the administration of the municipal area, planning for economic development and social justice has become the prime responsibility of local bodies in Kerala. Functions, functionaries and finance have been devolved to local bodies to function as institutions of self government. At present, the local bodies are also managing the institutions transferred to them, subject to the guidelines and technical directions from the Government and in accordance with the State and National policies.

Table 6 lists the institutions transferred to the Municipalities/ Corporations.

Table 6
Institutions and Posts Transferred to Municipal Councils/Municipal Corporations

Department	Institutions/Posts
1. Agriculture Dept.	(i) Krishi Bhavans of respective places; (ii) One Post of Dy.Director of Agriculture (this post should be under the Municipality of District headquarters but his services should be extended to all Municipalities of the District)
2. Animal Husbandry Dept.	The Veterinary Polyclinic, Sub Centre, Dispensary of the respective places.
3. Fisheries Dept.	One post of Fisheries Sub Inspector (to the Municipalities wherever necessary)
4. Industries Dept.	One post of Industries Extension Officer
5. Health Services Dept. (Allopathy)	Community Health Centres, Govt. Hospitals, Taluk Hospitals of the respective places.
6. Health Dept. (I.S.M.)	Taluk Hospitals of respective places.
7. Health Dept. (Homeo)	Taluk Hospitals of respective places.
8. General Education Dept.	Govt. Primary Schools and High Schools of the respective places.
9. Co-operative Dept.	One post of Senior Co-operative Inspector (this post should be under the Municipal Council of District Head Quarters and the concerned officer will attend to the works in all the Municipalities of the District.

Powers and Functions of Chairperson

The Chairperson convenes the meetings of the Council and exercises the powers and discharges the duties of the urban local body listed in the Act. He supervises the working of the Municipality and coordinates the various functions and functionaries. The Chairperson is the Executive Head and he controls the administration, prepares the confidential report of the Secretary and authorises the payments.

Committee System and Decentralisation within Local Bodies

One of the salient features of local governance is the decentralisation within local bodies by means of committee system. The following are the important committees within urban local bodies.

Standing Committees

There are five Standing Committees in Municipal Council and seven Standing Committees in Municipal Corporation as listed in Table 7.

Table 7
Standing Committees

Municipal Council	1. Standing Committee for Finance
	2. Standing Committee for Development
	3. Standing Committee for Welfare
	4. Standing Committee for Health and Education
	5. Standing Committee for Works
Municipal Corporation	1. Standing Committee for Finance
	2. Standing Committee for Development
	3. Standing Committee for Welfare
	4. Standing Committee for Health and Education
	5. Standing Committee for Works
	6. Standing Committee for Town Planning
	7. Standing Committee for Appeal Relating to Tax

All the functions of a local body have been divided among the Standing Committees.

Steering Committee

There is a Steering Committee consisting of the Chairperson, Deputy Chairperson and Chairpersons of Standing Committees for coordinating and monitoring the Standing Committees.

Joint Committee

The Council of Municipality may join with any other Local Self Government Institution and constitute a Joint Committee for matters of common interest.

Managing Committee

There is a Managing Committee consisting of not more than fifteen members including its chairman for public health institutions transferred to the Municipality.

Ward Committees and Ward Sabhas

In every Municipality where the population exceeds one lakh Ward Committees are constituted in each ward (constituency of a Councillor). In the case where population does not exceed one lakh, Ward Sabhas are constituted and all persons included in the electoral roll of that ward are members of the Ward Sabha. The Councillor who represents the Ward is the Convenor of the Ward Sabha. The Ward Sabha has to meet at least once in three months and the meeting will be presided over by the Chairperson of the Municipality.

District Planning Committee (DPC)

District Planning Committee has been constituted with 15 members. The District Panchayat President of the concerned district is the Chairperson and the District Collector is the Secretary to it. The plan documents of local bodies have to be approved by DPC.

State Development Council

There is a State Development Council for formulating policy for local level development and regional level development and for co-ordinating the District Plans and the State Plans. The Chief Minister is the Chairman and the Leader of Opposition is the Vice Chairman. The other members of the Development Council are Chairpersons of District Planning Committees, Mayors of Municipal Corporations, Vice Chairman of State Planning Board and nominated persons from Panchayats and Municipalities. The Chief Secretary is the Member Secretary. The State Development Council also handles the common issues concerning development, among the districts.

Financing of Urban Local Bodies

The revenue sources of Municipalities comprise of own tax, assigned tax, shared tax and grants from government. The details are given in Table 8 and Table 9.

Table 8
Sources of Revenue of Urban Local Bodies

A. Own Taxes	i.	Property Tax
	ii.	Profession Tax
	iii.	Tax on Animals, Vessels and Vehicles
	iv.	Entertainment Tax & Additional Entertainment Tax
	v.	Service Tax
	vi.	Advertisement Tax
	vii.	Cess on Conversion of Land Use
	viii.	Show Tax and Surcharge on Show Tax
	ix.	Tax on Timber
	x.	Surcharge not exceeding 10% of the Taxes
B. Assigned Tax		Surcharge on duty on transfer of property
C. Shared Tax		Motor Vehicles Tax
D. Non-Tax Revenue	i.	Income from properties, markets, licence fees, contributions, miscellaneous items, etc.
	ii.	Contributions, Endowments, etc.
E. Grants from Govt.		Specific Purpose Grants
		Specific Purpose Grant for Development Purposes
		General Purpose Grant
		Loans from Govt. and Financing Institutions

Table 9
Non-Plan Grants to Urban Local Bodies

1. General Purpose Grant
2. Surcharge on Duty on transfer of property
3. Vehicle Tax compensation grant
4. Grant for Maintenance of Isolation Hospitals
5. Maintenance of maternity and child welfare centres
6. Maintenance of Family Planning Centres
7. Anti-Mosquito and Anti-filaria operations
8. Maintenance of Nursery Schools
9. Maintenance of poor homes, begger homes and relief centres
10. Maintenance of Town Planning and Town Survey Operations
11. Maintenance of the Public ferry Service
12. Grant for constructions and equipments for the furtherance of any of the above services.

The urban local bodies are supposed to generate their own financial resources. However, these bodies do not often muster the courage to levy taxes under their powers. Inadequate taxation and inefficient management both render the municipal services far from satisfactory. The infrastructure development is not in a position to keep pace with the population growth of such cities resulting in serious inadequacies in service. Since public funds for urban infrastructure projects are inadequate urban organizations have to look for alternative source of funding from financial institutions. Participation and availability of private sector funds for development of infrastructure therefore becomes not only desirable but also absolutely essential (Govt. of Kerala, 2002).

Plan Grant-in Aid and Kerala Development Plan

Kerala introduced a novel approach in decentralised planning in 1996 which is popularly known as Kerala Development Plan (earlier it was known as 'People's Campaign'). The primary objective of this process is to ensure that the local bodies prepare and prioritise a shelf of integrated projects in a scientific manner. The State Government has earmarked one-third of the plan grant-in-aid to the local bodies during the five year period of the Tenth Plan. The Plan Grant-in Aid may be classified into three categories: (1) General (2) Special Component Plan (SCP) and (3) grant-in-aid based on the recommendations of the Eleventh Finance Commission (EFC). The general and EFC grant is divided into, at first, to rural local bodies and urban local bodies in the ratio of rural-urban population. *The share of each local body is published in the Appendix IV of the Budget Document of the Government of Kerala.*

New Institutions

Appellate Tribunals and Ombudsman are the two new important institutions. The Tribunal is meant for dispensing appeals very quickly while the Ombudsman looks into defective administration by the local bodies by employing an investigative approach.

Appellate Tribunals

In the context of the emerging scenario of decentralisation in the State, conflicts may arise and dependence on the existing Judiciary for appeals would cause much delay in getting verdict. An Appellate Tribunal consists of one Judicial Officer, having the rank of District Judge, will be appointed by the Government in consultation with the High Court. The Tribunal will have the same powers as that of a civil court. The Tribunals are expected to be citizen-friendly by means of adopting simple procedures.

Ombudsman

Ombudsman investigates independently complaints from individuals, groups, and from Government relating to defective administration by local bodies. It is envisaged as a cost-free mechanism for complaint redressal and is essentially investigative in character. The Ombudsman goes beyond the judicial process, as after redressal of a grievance it can choose to monitor the behaviour of the local authority concerned and it can point out systemic deficiencies and suggest improvements. To be more specific, the Ombudsman will conduct investigations and inquiries on any complaint with regard to any action involving corruption, misadministration or irregularities in the administration by the LSGIs and disposal of such complaints.

Performance Audit

In view of the increased delegation of powers and devolution of funds to LSGIs, a new set of financial procedures has been evolved. The LSGIs are require to be guided properly in maintaining records and following principles of financial procedures and propriety. In this context, a new audit system namely Performance Audit, has been introduced. It is a running audit system, which is more friendly, helpful and acts as on-line corrective system, which would detect irregularities and deviations, almost simultaneously, allowing for easy rectification.

At the state level the Secretary, Local Administration Department is the Performance Audit Authority. The Authority will be supported by a State Performance Audit Officer, at the state level, and by the Performance Audit Officers at the regional level. Under the Performance Audit Officers, Performance Audit Teams will visit each Panchayat once in three months for conducting the audit.

Summary and Conclusion

The State of Kerala has made considerable progress in developing a system of urban governance following the 74th Amendments to the Constitution of India. The urban local bodies have been made institutions of self governments by devolving powers, functions and finance and by transferring institutions according to the fundamental principle of subsidiarity. The basic tenet of the system is massive participation of the people. The decentralisation is ensured within the local body itself by introducing committee system in its administration. Total activities of a local body are divided among the Standing Committees and every Councillor is a member of one (and only one) Standing Committee. The local bodies have been made responsible for planning for economic development and social justice. One-third of the plan grant-in-aid of the Government of Kerala has been earmarked for the local bodies for its development activities. At present the local bodies are in a position to prepare and implement their own Five Year Plans and Annual Plans.

The regional economy of Kerala has certain unique features with low per capita income and high quality of life index. It is an industrially backward state with high level of literacy. The nature of urbanisation in Kerala is significantly different from that of the other states in India. Kerala is considered to be an urban village having spatially distributed settlement pattern. Interestingly, there is no metropolitan area. In this context the urban problems of Kerala are very different from those of other states in India. The urban spread demands thin investments in large area, which is uneconomic in many situations. The urban policy of the State focuses on public-private participation for urban infrastructure development.

Notes

1. For basic data on Kerala, see Gazetteer of India (1986, 1989), and for socio-economic details see Govt. of Kerala (1999).
2. There is disagreement among scholars regarding calling 'Kerala Model', because a model is meant to have possibility of replication/adoption. Some are of the opinion that the Kerala experience may not be replicable because of its unique features. Therefore, according to them, it is not appropriate to call the experience as a model.
3. Prior to the enactment of the 1960 Act, the laws regarding Municipalities in force were the Travancore District Municipalities Act, 1116 in Travancore area and Cochin Municipal Act, 1113 in the Cochin region. Similarly the Mdras District Municipalities Act, 1920 was in force in the Malabar area of the State. The reason for the enactment of the 1960 Act was to enforce a uniform law on the subject applicable to all the Municipalities in the State of Kerala and the Act came into force on 1-9-1961.

References

Centre for Development Studies (CDS) (1980), *Some Notes on Possibilities of Decentralised Development in Kerala,* Working Paper No. 106, Thiruvananthapuram.

Committee on Decentralisation (1996), *Interim Report,* Government of Kerala, Thiruvanathapuram.

Committee on Decentralisation (1997), *Final Report,* Volume 1, Part A & B, Government of Kerala, Thiruvanathapuram.

Government of India (1978), *Report of the Working Group on Block Level Planning,* Planning Commission, New Delhi.

Govt. of Kerala (nod.), *The People's Campaign for Ninth Plan in Kerala: An Introduction,* Kerala State Planning Board, Thiruvananthapuram.

Govt. of Kerala (nod.), *Power to the People's Plan-Ninth Plan,* State Planning Board, Thiruvananthapuram.

Govt. of Kerala (1996), *People's Campaign for 9th Plan in Kerala: An Approach Paper,* Kerala State Planning Board, Thiruvananthapuram.

Isaac and Harilal (1997), "Planning for Empowerment: People's Campaign for Decentralised Planning in Kerala, *Economic and Political Weekly,* Jan. 4-11, p. 53.

George, Sunny and P. P. Balan (2005), "Urban Governance in Kerala", *Shelter,* Vol.VIII, No. 1.

Government of Kerala (1994), *The Kerala Municipality Act, 1994,* Government of Kerala.

Govt. of Kerala (1999), *Economic Review 1998,* State Planning Board, Thiruvananthapuram.

Government of Kerala (2002), *Urban Policy and Action Plan for Kerala, Department of Publications,* Government of Kerala.

Govt. of Kerala (2003), *Economic Review 2004,* State Planning Board, Thiruvananthapuram.

Isaac, Thomas T.M. (1996), *People's Campaign for 9th Plan: An Approach Paper,* Kerala State Planning Board, Thiruvananthapuram.

Isaac, Thomas T. M. (1997), *Janakiyasoothranam: Sidhanthavum Prayogavum (in Malayalam),* Kerala State Planning Board, Thiruvananthapuram.

Isaac, Thomas T. M. (1999), *People's Planning: Towards a Handbook,* Kerala State Planning Board, Thiruvananthapuram.

Lelithabhai, K.N., K. Rajasekharan and Sunny George (1998) (Ed.) *Handbook on Transfer of Functions, Institutions and Schemes to Local Self Government Institutions,* Kerala Institute of Local Administration, Thrissur, Kerala.

Oommen, M. A. (n.d.), *'Development Experience, Development Priorities and Fiscal Resources of Kerala',* in *People & Development,* Centre of Science and Technology for Rural Development, Thrissur.

Ramachandran, V. (1995), *"Kerala", Status of Panchayats in the State of India,* Institute of Social Sciences, Concept, New Delhi.

Woodcock, George (1967), *Kerala–A Portrait of the Malabar Coast,* Faber and Faber, London.

INDEX

D

E

F

G